THE COMPLETE ILLUSTRATED
ENCYCLOPEDIA OF
Alternative Healing Therapies

THE COMPLETE ILLUSTRATED
ENCYCLOPEDIA OF
Alternative Healing Therapies

CONSULTANT EDITOR

C. Norman Shealy M.D., Ph.D.

BARNES
&NOBLE
BOOKS
NEW YORK

Designed and created with
THE BRIDGEWATER BOOK COMPANY LIMITED

ELEMENT BOOKS LIMITED
Editorial Director Sue Hook
Group Production Director Clare Armstrong
Production Manager Stephanie Raggett

THE BRIDGEWATER BOOK COMPANY LIMITED
Art Director Terry Jeavons
Designer Kevin Knight
Editorial Director Fiona Biggs
Managing Editor Anne Townley
Project Editor Sarah Bragginton
Editor Sara Harper
Picture Research Liz Moore
Studio Photography Guy Ryecart, Ian Parsons
Illustrators Amanda Cameron, Michael Courtney, Jerry Fowler,
Gill Bridgewater, Kim Glass
3D-Model Maker Mark Jamieson

Printed and bound in Great Britain by Butler & Tanner Limited,
Frome and London

British Library Cataloguing in Publication data available

Library of Congress Cataloging in Publication data available

ISBN 0-7607-1961-6

Acknowledgments

The publishers wish to thank the following for the use of pictures:

AKG: 61 top right, 74 bottom left, 186 top left, 200 top left, 246 center left

Association for Applied Psychophysiology and Biofeedback: 213 bottom center and top right

Bridgeman: 78 top left, 194 center left, 204 bottom right, 230 center left, 231 top right, 334 top right

British Chiropractic Association: 118 bottom left

Camera Press: 63 center, 86 top right

Center for Reiki Training 74 top center

Colour Library Images: 243 bottom right

CRCS Publications: 64

Fortean: 188 center left, 194 top center, 205 center left, 247 top right

General Osteopathic Council: 106 bottom right

Sally and Richard Greenhill Photo Library: 116 top right

Hulton Getty Picture Library: 106 center left, 190 top left, 154 bottom left, 172 top right, 192 top right, 196 center left, 214 top left, 218 center left, 218 bottom left, 224 center left

The Hutchison Library: 42 center left

Images Colour Library: 76 top right, 95 center right, 175 bottom right, 257 top right, 260 bottom left: above and below, 331 top center, 337 bottom right, 338 center right (third from top)

Imperial War Museum: 236 center left

Ingham Publishing, Inc.: 66

London Floatation Center: 94/95

Leila Malcolm, Feldenkrais Practitioner: 142 bottom right

Marion Chace Foundation: 226 bottom left

Science Photo Library: 72 top right, 108 top left, 121 bottom right, 132 center left, 172 bottom left, 212 center, 234 top right, 272 top center, 321 top left, 328 top center, 338 center right (bottom), 340 center right, 346 center, 347 top right, 349 center right, 353 top right

Still National Osteopathic Museum, Kirksville, MO:106 bottom left

Stock Market: 208 bottom left, 261 bottom right, 325 bottom left, 332 center, 357 bottom left

The Theosophical Society in America: 88 center left

Tony Stone Images: 44, 46, 47 bottom, 85 bottom right, 88 right, 93 top right, 95 top right, 143 bottom right, 158 top center, 160 center left, 164 top right, 166 bottom left, 171 top left, 173 bottom right, 176 bottom left, 179 bottom left, 187 top left, 200 bottom right, 210 bottom left, 214 bottom left, 215 bottom left, 216 bottom left, 224 bottom left, 237 top left, 240 center, 241 center left, 244 bottom right, 258 bottom right, 281 top right, 286 top right, 295 bottom left, 307 bottom left, 322 bottom right, 323 center right, 339 top right

Tony Stone Worldwide: 52 top right

Trager Institute: 154 top center

Trip: 48 top, 78 top right, 226 bottom right, 257 top left, 264 top right

Special thanks go to:
Paul Bailey – Bowen Technique
Roberta Blyton – Cranio-Sacral Therapy
Ron Cavedaschi – Kinesiology
Amanda Clarke – Osteopathy
Paul Cohen – Zero Balancing
Deborah and Simon Fielding
Wendy Griffith – Metamorphic Technique
Helle Henriksen – Chiropractic
Elaine Liechti – Shiatsu
Stewart Mitchell – Massage
Annie Morrison – Sound Therapy
Pru Rankin-Smith – Rolfing
Tracy Silver – Reiki
William Wheen – McTimoney Chiropractic
Tom Williams – T'ai Chi
for help and advice with text and the photography of the therapies

and to:
Maria Anderson, Mary Armstrong, Gavin Bates, Clare Bayes, Sarah Bragginton, Adam Carne, Yana Casquero, Rob Chappell, Guy Corber, Ben Davis, Gemma Davis, Maggie de Freitas, Linda Fleischmann, Anette Gerlin, Louise Gorst, Sally Hardy, Sam Hollingdale, Justin Huckle, Pat Infanti, John Lane, Linda Langton, Mette Lauritzen, Lisa McRory, Carol Passmore, Sharon Rashand, Emma Richardson, Isaac Richardson, Caron Riley, Michelle Sawyer, Jacob Scott, Francesca Selkirk, Flo Snook, Wendy Stevens, Phillippa Vaughan
for help with photography

and to:
Wilbury Clinic
for help with properties

CONTENTS

PART ONE

ENERGY THERAPIES

PART TWO

PHYSICAL THERAPIES

PART THREE

MIND AND SPIRIT THERAPIES

PART FOUR

COMMON AILMENTS

FOREWORD

How very welcome it is to see a fully comprehensive and beautifully illustrated encyclopedia of alternative healing therapies. It comes as no surprise to one who has worked in this field for so many years that public enthusiasm for the natural therapies has steadily increased. The life forces around us – which cannot always be simply explained – are rich, mysterious, and complex. Many of us are instinctively receptive to these forces and are inclined to reject the increasingly alarming developments in medical science. We all know that our body has the ability to heal itself and that increasingly invasive and complex medical procedures can do more harm than good.

When one considers physical therapies such as chiropractic and osteopathy, both of which have enjoyed considerable and sustained successes over many decades, it is very clear that medical science has no viable alternatives to offer us. Disorders that may, in an orthodox context, demand surgery with its attendant risks of anesthesia and infection can frequently be easily, cleanly, and effectively treated on the chiropractor's bench with a return to a full life within a few days. We all know, too, that the mind plays an inestimably significant part in healing. Cognitive therapy, for example, one of the great success stories of the twentieth century, can do much to alleviate disorders and eliminate stress-related conditions.

We have seen an explosion of interest in the alternative healing therapies in the last twenty years and this is a trend that is clearly set to continue into the twenty-first century. And, with it, there is a receptiveness to using the life forces around us in a positive way in order to heal our mind, body, and spirit.

ABOVE Many therapies have their roots in Greek or Roman culture.

The Complete Illustrated Encyclopedia of Alternative Healing Therapies is the comprehensive, weighty reference book that we need for the dawn of the third millennium. It examines in considerable depth what can be described as the physical therapies, from acupuncture to do-in and from chiropractic to Trager work. In keeping with the mind, body, spirit ethic of alternative therapies, this book deals, in equally substantive fashion, with healing, with psychotherapy, with cognitive therapy, with dreamwork (including how to interpret your own) and with all of those therapies that refresh the mind as well as the body – dance movement therapy and music therapy, for example.

If you would like to learn about the complementary therapies in depth, this is the book for you. You will find out about the history and principles of each of the therapies (listed on the Contents page), the different types of the therapy, how to find a practitioner, what happens during a consultation, and excellent, detailed guidelines for following the therapy at home.

LEFT Less well-known therapies, such as reiki, are steadily becoming more popular.

The secrets of our vital life force are complex, joyful, colorful, rich, and elusive. This marvelous book opens the door for us.

C. NORMAN SHEALY, M.D., Ph.D.

May 1999

INTRODUCTION

I nterest in alternative therapies has been growing at a phenomenal rate over recent years and continues to do so. There are many reasons for this, but prominent among them is the realization that conventional medicine has limitations and is not infallible, together with an increasing desire on the part of individuals to take a more active role in improving and maintaining their own health and well-being. In the last years of the twentieth century, many people have come to accept that ideas and principles of healing once considered unscientific or eccentric can yield valuable insights into the causes of ill health.

ABOVE *A family may be treated as a complete unit in, for example, family therapy.*

Not only that, but therapies based on traditional medicine or, in many instances, developed from them, open up a whole different approach to illness and its prevention and treatment. Increasingly, people are no longer content to accept "a pill for every ill," partly because this approach sometimes doesn't work in practice, but also because they want to take more responsibility for their own health, rather than simply accepting the role of passive recipients of orthodox medicine. What's more, alternative therapies offer you not just the opportunity to fight the symptoms of illness, but also to look beneath the surface to its possible origins. So, as well as being helpful when you are actually unwell, such therapies can be a way to prevent problems arising in the first place, or make them less likely to recur.

It is reasonable to compare this approach with modern theories about weight control. Most people now realize that short-term "slimming" diets are doomed to failure in the long-term if you just go back to your old eating habits once you have shed the pounds. The only way to maintain your weight at the right level is to change to a healthy eating program and stick with it for ever. Similarly, alternative therapies do not offer a "quick fix" but a different way of looking at the roots of good health, which often involves adopting new principles and making them a regular part of your life. A course of therapy can be helpful in dealing with a particular illness or symptom, but there is more to it than that. Alternative therapists aim to help you achieve and maintain optimum health, which is not purely an absence of symptoms but rather encompasses a positive state of physical, psychological, and spiritual well-being.

When you consult an alternative therapist for the first time, you may well be surprised by the course the encounter follows. Like conventional doctors, alternative practitioners will want to know about any

ABOVE *Natural oils and homeopathic remedies are used in tandem with some alternative treatments.*

symptoms, but they will also ask many more questions relating to your lifestyle, personality, and history and, if they examine you physically, they are likely to use methods which you have not encountered in an orthodox consulting room. The way in which they define the source of your lack of well-being may also be unfamiliar – those using approaches based on oriental medicine, for example, may talk about the life force and restoring natural balance and harmony.

Aspects of your lifestyle such as diet, psychological and emotional responses, dreams, physical and mental tension, and stress may be explored in depth before any decision is made about appropriate treatment. This leads on to another important principle of alternative therapy, which is that it tends to focus primarily on the individual, rather than on the symptoms or the underlying disease. Thus you may be recommended to follow a different course of therapy from someone else whose symptoms are apparently similar. This approach is often referred to as "holistic": in other words, it looks at illness and its prevention and treatment in terms of you as a unique individual rather than in terms of a specific disease or collection of symptoms.

That is not to imply, however, that all alternative therapies are alike. They differ not only in their underlying beliefs and philosophy, but also in their methods and approach and in terms of what they set out to achieve. These differences are in part historical. Some therapies have their basis in traditional medicine, often derived from Chinese or Indian practices in use for thousands of years. Others have adapted and changed long-established approaches, introducing modern elements. Some are of relatively recent origin and make use of ideas that were not available to practitioners of earlier centuries.

Also, the way in which the

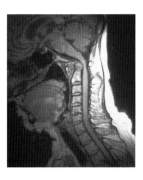

ABOVE *Chiropractors may use more orthodox practices, such as an X-ray.*

BELOW *Herbs are used in many therapies, from Ayurveda to aromatherapy massage.*

ABOVE *An aura healer will try to heal by repairing your aura, which is said to be a glow that surrounds all life forms.*

ABOVE *Eating fresh fruit is important, whether you are being treated for an illness or not.*

ABOVE *Bodywork therapies, such as the Alexander Technique, can even improve the way you hold your pen.*

different therapies are categorized in the following three chapters reflects other important distinctions, although there is inevitably some overlap between what are defined here as energy therapies, physical therapies, and mind and spirit therapies. Furthermore, some therapies in each category are aimed primarily at treating illness and existing symptoms, and some are more educative in intent, with prevention rather than cure as the aim. Western scientific medicine has recently begun to unravel the links between mind and body, links which have long been taken for granted by practitioners of alternative medicine. It isn't just the mind and spirit therapies that recognize the importance of psychological and emotional factors in achieving freedom from ill health; many are based on the assumption that the various elements cannot be disentangled. Treating physical symptoms with physical or energy therapies will frequently involve techniques designed to relieve stress and tension, anxiety, depression, and emotional troubles. Often, the ultimate goal is to restore an inner balance or harmony, although different therapies will define and work towards this in different ways. You will be encouraged to follow the precepts and practices underlying your chosen therapy during treatment and after it is complete.

Some therapies make more demands on you than others. You can enjoy and benefit from massage and aromatherapy, for example, without making much effort other than turning up for a session, but many others require your active participation and some degree of commitment. At one extreme is psychoanalysis, which often involves at least twice-weekly sessions over a number of years, but even shorter courses of therapy, such as learning the Alexander Technique, require regular attendance and practice. With some therapy, such as meditation, Heller work or visualization, you may be given exercises to do at home, while a system such as ayurveda may be less effective if you are not prepared to adapt your lifestyle according to its principles. If you choose, you can continue to attend sessions of yoga or t'ai chi indefinitely, and the longer you continue, the greater the benefits that will accrue. With many of the psychotherapy and counseling approaches, you will have to be prepared to put in considerable emotional effort, and working with this kind of therapist can be difficult and demanding at times. Whatever therapy you are considering, you need to weigh up the demands it will make on you with the benefits on offer. It may help to discuss this in detail with the therapist at an initial consultation before deciding to go ahead.

For most people, the other important consideration before embarking on a course of therapy is the cost. Again, you need to talk to the individual therapist about this before committing yourself. It isn't always possible to say exactly how many treatment sessions a person will need, but you should be able to get enough of an idea to help you decide whether you are willing and able to bear the cost. There may, of course, be situations where this issue doesn't arise – you may not have to pay directly, for example, for the cost of a course of psychotherapy or some kinds of physical therapy if you are referred for treatment by your doctor.

Finally, when choosing a therapy, you need to be comfortable with both the underlying approach and principles and with the personality of the therapist. If you are by nature a practical, down-to-earth person, you may be more in tune with physical therapies such as osteopathy, chiropractic or hydrotherapy, or with biofeedback or autogenic training for example, rather than with those based on oriental philosophies and concepts. On the other hand, you may be looking for something with a more spiritual element, such as meditation, ayurveda or yoga. You don't necessarily have to accept all the underlying

ABOVE *Mind and spirit therapies can help marriage problems.*

ABOVE *Keeping your vitamin intake consistant is always vital.*

tenets of a particular therapy to benefit from it, but you are likely to gain more from it if you are in sympathy with its overall aims and philosophy.

By the end of your first consultation, you will probably know whether you would be happy to work with the therapist. There's no need to be embarrassed if you feel that he or she simply isn't the right person for you; this is especially important if you are contemplating some form of psychotherapy or counseling. A personality clash is no one's fault if it occurs, but it is not conducive to healing. It is better to find someone with whom you feel more at ease than to press on regardless.

When you have decided which therapies appeal to you most and have most to offer you, the next step is to find a practitioner in your area. This will be easier if you have opted for one of those that are widely available but you may have to compromise if the one you favor isn't available locally. Unless you have been referred by your doctor or by someone who has had good experiences with a particular therapist, it is worth checking out the individual's training and credentials for yourself. A great

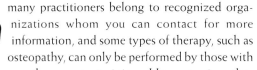

ABOVE *Sigmund Freud founded psychoanalytic treatment, a very influential therapy.*

many practitioners belong to recognized organizations whom you can contact for more information, and some types of therapy, such as osteopathy, can only be performed by those with the proper training. However, in other spheres there are no restrictions – anyone can set themselves up as a counselor, for example – so it's up to you to make sure your potential practitioner is properly qualified and experienced before committing yourself.

One of the major attractions of alternative therapy is that it invites you to take back from the medical profession some of the power to manage your own health. While it is important that you don't take this to the extreme of refusing or stopping effective conventional treatment, you will find that it opens up whole new horizons. Whatever your health problem, it is virtually certain that there is a range of alternative therapies which may help and, in some cases, make you less prone to recurrence. In the chapters on specific therapies, you will find suggestions as to the types of problem for which each is likely to be most beneficial. In some cases, treatment can only be given by a professional, but in the chapter on Common Ailments, you will also find suggestions as to how you can adapt aspects of some therapies to treat yourself at home. Often you will be able to use these methods even if you have never before tried the therapy

ABOVE *A.T. Still revolutionized the way bones are treated with his osteopathic therapy.*

concerned because they don't require any deep knowledge of the principles involved. If you find they are effective, you may then want to follow up with a full course of treatment – especially if you have a recurrent problem which is not controlled by conventional medicine, such as migraine or pre-menstrual syndrome, for example. In this chapter you will also find many simple and practical tips which may alleviate your symptoms without requiring any special effort or complicated equipment.

One of the beauties of alternative medicine in all its forms is that if focuses on you as a unique individual and empowers you to take from it whatever you personally need.

BELOW *T'ai Chi Chu'an exercises can regulate breathing and ease stress and tension.*

HOW TO USE THIS BOOK

This comprehensive and fully color-illustrated reference book describes the whole range of alternative healing therapies – from the most well-known to those that are more obscure. Aimed at the general reader who is curious about the alternative side of medicine, this exhaustive volume covers Energy Therapies, Physical Therapies, Mind and Spirit Therapies, and includes a useful section on the most common ailments, and how these alternative methods can help.

Part One: Energy Therapies. Seventeen chapters detail all the known energy therapies, from those that are more mainstream to the more obscure practices. For each therapy, its history and background are described, as are precautions and watchpoints that can be carried out at home are also included. **Part Two: Physical Therapies.** Nineteen chapters describe the physical therapies and, again, detail the background of each therapy. There are clear illustrations of what to expect when you visit a practitioner and possible self-help exercises. **Part Three: Mind and Spirit Therapies.** Eighteen chapters introduce each therapy, its history, background and theories. There are also step-by step descriptions of meditative

and visualization processes, and what to expect when you visit a therapist – whether you are in a one-to-one session or a group. **Part Four: Common Ailments.** All the most well-known common ailments are detailed here, including those that can affect any group, to diseases of childhood, the elderly, and specific reproductive complaints. Each ailment's symptoms are described, the development of these symptoms and how each relevant alternative therapy can help. There are also caution boxes (when a therapy is not suitable) and boxes that describe more orthodox treatment. **Reference Section.** This consists of a full glossary, a list of useful addresses, and books for further reading.

Part 1 describes the Energy Therapies.

the "Origins" box tells you the history of that theory

the "Orthodox" view box tells you the doctor's view of the therapy the "founder" of each therapy and their specific theory is introduced

Part 2 lists all the Physical Therapies.

"pathfinder" boxes help you locate other possible therapies for a condition

specially commissioned photographs show self-help therapies, and therapists at work

CRANIO-SACRAL THERAPY

ORTHODOX VIEW

In the 1970s, Dr. John E. Upledger, an American osteopathic surgeon and doctor, developed a variation of cranial osteopathy that he called Cranio-Sacral Therapy. Upledger had become fascinated by the "Cranio-Sacral system" – the cranium and spinal cord, which runs down to the sacrum in the lower back, and their contents – while working as a clinical researcher at Michigan State University. His work was based on the theories of cranial osteopathy developed by Sutherland, but Upledger placed more emphasis on the importance of the soft tissues encased by the cranium and spinal cord than on the actual bones themselves.

THE THEORY

Inflexible Meninges

CONSULTING A PRACTITIONER

PRECAUTIONS

PATHFINDER

116   117

"Conventional treatment" boxes tell what a doctor would prescribe for this ailment

the "Datafile" sets out relevant statistics about each ailment

Part 4 details many common ailments and how therapies can help.

each ailment, its incubation period, and symptoms are described in the main text

the therapies appropriate to the ailment are listed fully

Eyestrain

SYMPTOMS
- feeling of tightness around the eyes • difficulty in focusing • recurrent headaches, particularly across the forehead and behind the eyes

CAUTION

CONVENTIONAL TREATMENT

THERAPIES

BATES METHOD

ACUPRESSURE

AROMATHERAPY

Tinnitus

SYMPTOMS
- tinkling, buzzing or ringing in the ears

CONVENTIONAL TREATMENT

DATAFILE

THERAPIES

ACUPUNCTURE

RELAXATION AND BREATHING

PSYCHOTHERAPY AND COUNSELING

CRANIAL OSTEOPATHY

BIOFEEDBACK

280   281

many therapies may recommend
a lifestyle change

the "Precaution"
boxes warn that all
therapies must be
followed with care

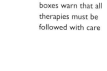

specially commissioned photographs
illustrate, especially with physical
therapies, step-by-step treatment by
a therapist

in many cases you
can do self-help
exercises

the history and background of each therapy is explored

Part 3 presents Mind and Spirit Therapies.

LIGHT THERAPY

information about what happens when you visit a practitioner is given

the "Watchpoint" warns you of any contraindications associated with each therapy and any special requirements

the "Caution" box indicates when a symptom may suggest a more serious disorder

Headache

the symptoms of each ailment are described in detail

Migraine

photographs clearly illustrate the therapy in practice

there are often many therapies worth looking into for a particular ailment

1

ENERGY THERAPIES

INTRODUCTION

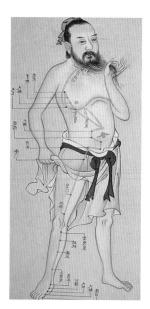

ABOVE *The system of meridians is central to most energy therapies.*

For anyone brought up in Western cultures, the concept of energy as it is employed by complementary therapists is often difficult to grasp. It cannot as yet be measured scientifically and the way it is defined and manipulated varies subtly, not only from one type of therapy to another, but also sometimes between practitioners of different forms of the same therapy. Despite the variations, however, those therapies which have their origin in ancient Eastern medicine all work on something which may be best termed the "life force," although there are several different words used to describe it.

It is only when this force is able to flow freely and is in the right balance that we can be said to be in optimum health, physically, psychologically, and spiritually. The aim of most so-called energy therapies is to restore and maintain this harmony and balance, so as to improve overall well-being and, in some cases, to treat symptoms resulting from a serious disruption to the life force from a variety of causes.

Despite the variations, however, those therapies that have their origin in ancient Eastern medicine all work on something which may be best termed the "life force," although there are several different words used to describe it.

Therapies that have their origin in Chinese medicine, such as acupuncture, refer to the life force as "qi" (or "chi"), and describe a system of "meridians" (or channels) through which it flows to all parts of the body. Shiatsuists, and others working with therapies originating in Japan, use the term "ki," while practitioners and teachers of yoga, for example, which comes from India, mean something similar when they refer to "prana." Other therapies which draw on some principles of traditional Eastern medicine and philosophies have adapted and applied the idea of this fundamental energy as part of their approach to treatment.

As well as the basic concept of life force, some therapies take into account additional aspects of energy, that must also be brought into harmony, such as yin and yang. These were defined by Chinese physicians as constituting the dual nature of energy, each having its own distinctive qualities that exist in a constant state of flux within every individual. The balance between them may be adjusted in a wide variety of ways, including yoga and qigong breathing and postures, t'ai chi ch'uan movement, or do-in exercises, among others.

The philosophies which underlie traditional therapies or systems of medicine such

BELOW *The practice of yoga aims to maintain good health and a balanced lifestyle.*

as Ayurveda are complex and subtle, and require many years of study before they can be thoroughly understood and practiced. Because of this, practitioners are not often easy to find in Western countries. In some cases, the forms of ancient Eastern therapies widely used today have been developed and modified while still retaining many of the original principles. In fact, such modifications have gone on over many centuries and still continue, from the ancient Greeks to medieval physicians to practitioners of the present day, resulting in the existence of different "schools" of therapists as well as in newer therapies derived in part from older ideas. For example, acupuncture exists in both traditional and modern forms, while a therapy such as reiki is relatively new, although its roots are partly in the past.

How Energy Therapies work

As a general rule, energy therapies seek to restore a proper balance and harmony, using a variety of approaches and techniques. There are differences, however, in what precisely their practitioners aim to achieve in terms of actual results for the person concerned. Although there is considerable overlap, some types of therapy focus more on what modern medicine would call the preventive approach: aiming to avoid ill health rather than treating existing symptoms or conditions. Examples of this type of therapy include yoga, t'ai chi ch'uan, do-in, and metamorphic technique. For instance, the aim of yoga is to achieve and maintain a state of peace and happiness so that any health problems can be avoided. Although yoga can be successfully used to treat more specific problems – for example people who suffer from backache, arthritis or rheumatism can benefit from yoga, and the postures can help just about every physical ailment known to date – in a more general sense, yoga can encourage relaxation, normalize high blood pressure, help stave off anxiety and deal with stress, all emements that may harm our general health and well-being. On the other hand, acupuncture and acupressure, reflexology and

ABOVE Energy therapies are strongly based on the principles of yin and yang.

LEFT Qigong postures help strengthen the body and regulate breathing.

therapeutic touch, for example, may be given in order to treat specific ailments or symptoms. It is important to understand that the way illness is diagnosed and treated will often differ markedly from the way similar problems would be tackled by orthodox medicine. Concepts such as the Five Elements, used in Ayurveda, shiatsu, and polarity therapy, or the need to adjust the flow of qi in particular organs, are likely to seem strange to someone accustomed to the ways of Western-trained doctors and many people may begin their treatment with some scepticism. Before treatment begins, you are likely to be asked a range of questions about your lifestyle, eating habits – even your person-ality traits – and the precise way in which the therapy is tailored will be influenced by your answers. Although the ideas behind holistic treatment – regarding the patient as a unique individual rather than simply as one with a recognized disease or set of symptoms – are grad-ually permeating orthodox medicine, they are by no means universally accepted as yet. The need to indi-vidualize treatment in this way is one of the main reasons why it is usually advisable to consult a trained and expe-rienced therapist before considering self-treatment. Nevertheless, some therapies can be adapted to be used by the person concerned, though often in a modified or limited form. Examples include acupressure, shiatsu, and meditation. You will also be encouraged to practice techniques such as yoga, t'ai chi, and meditation on your own once you have been taught how to breathe correctly and do the exercises properly.

ABOVE Acupuncture has become much more popular and treats a wide range of complaints.

ABOVE The endlessly repeating circle of the five elements is important to these therapies.

SUMMARY

When you are choosing an energy therapy, the best approach is the one that is the softest and the gentlest, that avoids dangerous and traumatic procedures, that treats the client as the "whole" individual, that encourages the body's natural healing processes to do their job, and in which the client takes a positive and active part in his or her own recovery and health maintenance. It is this emphasis on the client's willing and active participation that is the main core to any energy therapy, indeed any alternative therapy. Most practitioners will treat you for the precise way that you are feeling at the time that you see them. If, for example, you are suffering from a cold or influenza at the time of your appointment, your practitioner will want to treat that as well as the back pain you made the appointment for in the first place. The principle here is that there is a reason for the infection and it should be cleared first since it may be linked to the basic problem. Your practitioner will adjust your treatment for that visit, to encourage your body to heal itself in the best way possible. Most therapists will encourage you to "take control" of the problem; actively participating in your own healing has been proven to be an important factor in the success of most alternative therapies. so to make the most of your chosen energy therapy, it is very important to make your own decisions about how the treatment can work best for you.

How Energy Therapies can help you

In the following chapter, you will find details not only of the history and principles of each type of therapy, but also of what you can and can't expect it to do. It is important to spend some time considering your options before embarking on any specific therapy; to decide firstly whether it can offer what you need, and secondly whether it appeals to you personally. Some require more time and commitment than others; some require considerable effort on your part, while in others the main burden falls on the therapist. In virtually all cases, you will be given important advice about lifestyle, especially on the question of diet, and it is unreasonable to expect optimum results if you do not choose to follow it.

To some extent, your choices may be limited by what is available locally and you may need to do some research to find a well-trained and sympa-thetic therapist in your chosen field. Even if you cannot find precisely what you want, there are likely to be other options which may suit you just as well.

ABOVE Acupressure is one of the more accessible self-help therapies.

ACUPUNCTURE

BELOW Healing with acupuncture has its roots in ancient Chinese tradition.

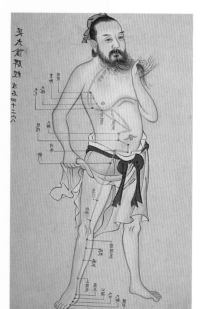

P robably the most widely known of the complementary healing therapies, acupuncture has been practiced in China for thousands of years and is becoming increasingly popular in the West. Part of the Traditional Chinese Medicine health system, acupuncture is a means of regulating the "life force" that is thought to flow through the body by the insertion of fine needles into carefully selected points. As well as to promote general good health and well-being, acupuncture is used to treat a number of specific conditions. Many Western doctors now practice a form of it.

The basic principles of acupuncture were laid down in a series of Chinese texts written between about 300–100 B.C.E. But much of the theory behind the therapy practiced today is to a large extent medieval or later in origin – simply because the ancient texts would have been all but incomprehensible to later physicians without explanation. As a result, each generation of practitioners added its own notes to what had come before.

As trade routes between China and the rest of the world started to open up, knowledge about acupuncture began to spread, and it first reached the West in the late 17th century. Even so, the technique was little known and only rarely practiced for nearly 300 years. Everything changed, though, when U.S. President Richard Nixon visited China in 1972. His hosts laid on numerous demonstrations of acupuncture that greatly impressed the media representatives who accompanied him. Their reporting led to a wave of interest in all things Chinese, and in acupuncture in particular.

Two Versions

This interest has grown exponentially over the last few decades, to the extent that a number of Western doctors have included acupuncture in their repertoire of therapies. However, they have tended to develop a different framework to explain how acupuncture works, and one that is rooted in modern science. As a result, there are now two versions of acupuncture: traditional and modern.

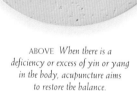

ABOVE When there is a deficiency or excess of yin or yang in the body, acupuncture aims to restore the balance.

Traditional Acupuncture

The traditional form of acupuncture is part of the wider system of Traditional Chinese Medicine (TCM), in which the use of herbs is more prominent than the use of needles. The fundamental principle underpinning traditional acupuncture is that there are two interactive qualities in nature called yin and yang, which interweave with each other both in the universe as a whole and within each individual. Good health depends on the maintenance of a balance between the two, and if this balance is disturbed the result is disease. In China, a whole regimen of diet, exercise, and other therapies is geared to balancing yin and yang.

The Life Force

One of these therapies is traditional acupuncture. It works, practitioners believe, by influencing "qi" (also "chi"), a "life force" that flows through the body in the blood vessels and also in a set of energetic pathways known as meridians (also yin and yang), which link the various organs of the body.

Traditionally, the Chinese recognize 12 internal organs, which generally have the same names as their Western counterparts (heart, liver, spleen, and so on) although the functions that are ascribed to them are different to those that we would recognize.

Numerous meridians are described in the traditional texts, but only 14 of them are important in practice – 12 are paired and two are in the midline of the body. Situated mainly along the meridians are about 500 recognized acupuncture points, of which about 100 are commonly used. Generally, these are sites at which a meridian runs close to the surface of the body, which means that needles can be inserted in order to rebalance the flow of qi when it is disturbed.

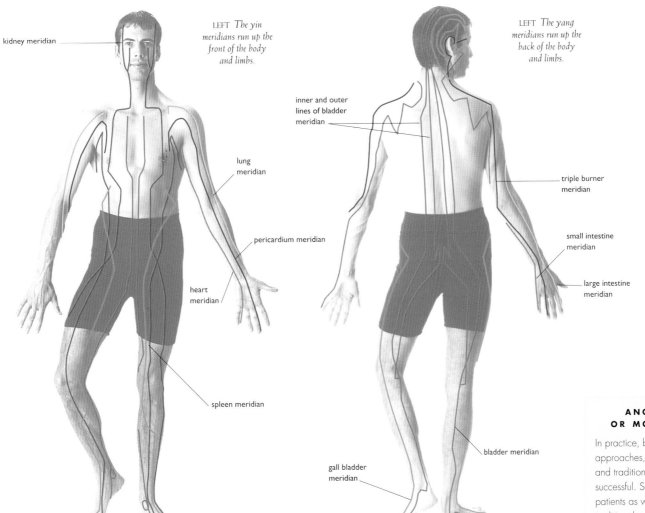

kidney meridian

LEFT *The yin meridians run up the front of the body and limbs.*

lung meridian

pericardium meridian

heart meridian

spleen meridian

inner and outer lines of bladder meridian

LEFT *The yang meridians run up the back of the body and limbs.*

triple burner meridian

small intestine meridian

large intestine meridian

bladder meridian

gall bladder meridian

Engineering Qi

In order to decide what alterations to make to the flow of qi, a traditional practitioner first takes a history, both of the patient and the problem, paying particular attention to the causes of disease that are considered important in this system – examples include medical history, diet, emotions, way of life, the weather, and so on. Next come the two main diagnostic examinations: the appearance of the tongue and the character of the pulse at the wrist. On the basis of what the history and these examinations reveal, a decision is made about whether some of the points need stimulation or sedation, and this determines the course of treatment, which may either be by means of herbal medicine or acupuncture. If the latter, a number of needles are inserted into the appropriate acupuncture point or points and left in place for about 20 minutes (sometimes longer), often being stimulated by hand. The number of points used and the length of time needles are left in place depend upon the desired effect.

One common misconception about the theory of traditional acupuncture is that it is somehow mysterious, or even mystical. In fact, the concept is a rather mechanical one. An acupuncturist is thought of as a type of engineer, who regulates the flow of qi through the body by stimulating and reducing acupuncture points on the meridians. Nevertheless, the traditional system is holistic, in the sense that it takes into account a range of factors involving lifestyle, personality, and environmental influences that are not considered to be of such importance in modern medicine.

Modern Acupuncture

While not accepting much of the rationale of the traditional system, many Western doctors and physiotherapists acknowledge that the ancient Chinese were astute observers who found successful methods of treatment, and, above all, that the use of needles is effective. They think that acupuncture achieves its effects through the nervous system and, probably, the immune

ANCIENT OR MODERN?

In practice, both approaches, modern and traditional, can be successful. Some people, patients as well as traditional practitioners, feel a psychological affinity with the traditional system and may prefer it for that reason; others, including many doctors, feel more at ease with the modern version.

In any case, acupuncture is still a developing art. Some of today's acupuncturists have introduced new techniques, including electrical or laser stimulation of the acupuncture points. Electronic devices have also been developed for home use to treat minor ailments, but you must always consult a qualified practitioner before trying home treatment.

a reading is taken for 12 different pulses

the color, coating, and texture of the tongue are assessed

RIGHT *Diagnosis involves pulse readings and an examination of the tongue.*

ACUPUNCTURE TODAY

After the 1970s, following the opening up of China to the West, acupuncture has become widely available in most countries, but it is particularly common in France, Canada, and New Zealand. Its legal position is variable, though: in some European countries only doctors may practice acupuncture, but in Britain anyone can claim to be an acupuncturist, with or without any form of training. In the U.S.A., the position varies from state to state: in many, only physicians may perform acupuncture (sometimes only after receiving training or a licence); in others acupuncture can be practiced by anyone who has received training and a licence.

There is an obvious danger in accepting treatment from an acupuncturist who has not had any systematic, recognized course of training and been registered as having done so successfully. Most such courses are part-time and last for two to three years. Shorter course are available for physiotherapists and doctors, but this does not mean that they are less effective therapists or inadequately trained since the non-traditional form of acupuncture that they generally learn makes use of all their existing anatomical and clinical knowledge.

and endocrine systems (in the latter case, perhaps as a result of a side-action of the release of endorphins – themselves natural painkillers – that acupuncture triggers). Pulse and tongue diagnosis are not used in modern acupuncture, and the traditional apparatus of "meridians" and points is either ignored or reinterpreted, as are theories about yin-yang polarity and qi.

A doctor using modern acupuncture will conduct a normal medical consultation – in this form of acupuncture, the disease categories used are the same as in modern Western medicine – but may well carry out a

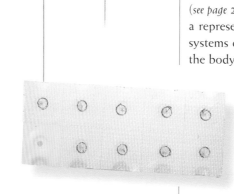

ABOVE *The needles are usually made of stainless steel, and vary in size and thickness.*

more detailed physical examination than usual, paying particular attention to the presence of trigger points in the muscles (*see box, page 23*). The precise method of treatment varies from practitioner to practitioner, but generally only a few needles are used – sometimes just one – and they are left in place for very short periods, on occasions for just a few seconds.

Types of Acupuncture

There are many different acupuncture techniques, but there is little evidence to show that any one is significantly better than any other.

In "mainstream" acupuncture, needles are inserted in various sites in the body, the ones chosen being dictated by the approach that the practitioner is using, be it traditional, modern, or based on trigger points. Once the needles are in place, they may be stimulated by hand (by "twiddling," pumping, or flicking) or electrically. How long the needles are kept in place varies from practitioner to practitioner. Many "modern" acupuncturists, for example, leave them in for a very short time. This may seem strange, but there is considerable evidence to show that the nervous system adapts quickly to a new stimulus and ceases to register it after a very short time (this is why you are not normally conscious of feeling your clothes). As a result, modern acupuncturists tend to believe that most of the effect of acupuncture is produced within the first few seconds after the needle is inserted.

Acupuncture Variants

In addition to whole-body acupuncture, there are some so-called "micro-systems" of acupuncture. Probably the best known of these is ear acupuncture (auricular therapy (*see page 28*)), which depends on the belief that there is a representation of the whole body in the ear. Other systems claim that there are similar representations of the body elsewhere – on the scalp, for example.

There are also forms of electroacupuncture that use electrical apparatus of various kinds. One such is the German Voll system, and another is the Japanese system called Ryodoraku. Both involve the electrical stimulation of acupoints. Laser acupuncture is another variation that is becoming increasingly popular. In this therapy a fine laser beam is directed onto the acupoint. The benefits of this for pain relief are uncertain.

Pain Relief

"Acupuncture analgesia," or the use of acupuncture for pain relief, is well established – in fact, the technique is sometimes used to control pain during childbirth, although more often transcutaneous electrical nerve stimulation (TENS) is used for this purpose. It can be taken a stage further, however, to allow surgery to be conducted without pain, while the patient is fully conscious. When American doctors visited China in the early 1970s they were amazed to see major operations being carried out under acupuncture analgesia. But the success rate of the technique turned out not to be as high as was first claimed, and it became clear that it is only suitable for a small proportion of people. As a result, acupuncture analgesia during surgery has not been taken up widely in the West.

Related Forms of Treatment

Two forms of treatment closely related to traditional acupuncture are moxibustion and cupping. Both treatments adhere to the theory of the meridians and treat specific acupoints along them. Acupuncture is often carried out with moxibustion or cupping.

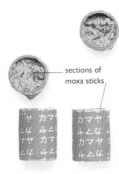

BELOW *Moxa is prepared from the leaves of* Artemesia vulgaris latiflora, *otherwise known as mugwort.*

sections of moxa sticks

moxa preparation

TRIGGER POINTS

One possible explanation of the efficacy of acupuncture, so adherents of modern acupuncture believe, comes from the phenomenon of "trigger points." These are tender areas found in muscles, where they are often hard, knotted spots, and elsewhere that can cause pain and other effects to radiate to a distant area. Like the medically accepted concept of referred pain (in which, for example, a pain originating in the gall bladder is felt in the shoulder), trigger points can also be caused by a muscular problem elsewhere in the body.

TRIGGER POINTS AND ACUPUNCTURE

It is not possible to say exactly what trigger points are, though there are many theories about them. However, it seems certain that they are a real phenomenon – for one reason, it can be demonstrated that they are unusually active electrically. But trigger points seem to have a lot in common with acupuncture points: nearly all the trigger points listed in Western medical literature are situated close to a traditional acupuncture point. Simply needling trigger points can inactivate them and some people say that the whole of acupuncture can be explained in terms of trigger points.

Moxibustion

The treatment called moxibustion concerns the application of heat to specific acupoints in order to regulate the body's flow of qi and to treat specific ailments such as a stiff neck, back problems, and fatigue. The heat is usually obtained by burning moxa – dried mugwort leaves (*Artemesia vulgaris latiflora*) – either directly or indirectly on the skin. The skin itself is never burned. In the direct method, the moxa is formed into a cone which is placed on the skin, lit and left to smolder. It is removed when the skin becomes warm. Alternatively, pieces of moxa may be placed on the end of acupuncture needles so that the heat not only warms the skin but is also drawn down into the meridian through the needle.

In the indirect method, which is more commonly used, smouldering sticks of moxa are held near the skin. Moxa cones can also be used indirectly by being burned on a slice of ginger or garlic.

FAR LEFT *The heat from a moxa stick can move stagnant qi and blood from an injured shoulder and relieve the pain.*

BOTTOM LEFT *Moxa can also be burned under a box that is placed on the skin.*

When moxa burns it gives off a rather pungent odor and copious amounts of smoke, which some patients may find unpleasant.

Cupping

Cupping is an ancient technique whereby small rounded "cups" (made of glass or bamboo) are placed over acupoints in order to draw blood and qi towards them. A lighted taper is placed in a cup, then quickly removed. This is applied to the skin (generally the back), where it sticks tightly because the flame has consumed the oxygen and created a vacuum.

Several cups may be applied, and they are placed over specific acupoints and left there for 10 to 15 minutes. As the cup cools, the skin and underlying tissues are drawn up into it, increasing the blood flow and circulation, and hence the body's flow of qi. To release the cup, the skin next to the edge of the cup is pressed to break the vacuum.

BELOW *Cupping can be a useful treatment for acute or chronic back pain.*

ABOVE *A lit alcohol swab held inside the cup creates suction which can be used to move blocked energy.*

DOES IT WORK?

So can acupuncture cure diseases? To a large extent, the answer depends on what condition is being treated. Acupuncture cannot be expected to reverse structural damage that has already occurred; for example, it cannot restore an arthritic joint to normal by reversing arthritic damage, although it may well relieve the pain for long periods. On the other hand, if the problem is one from which the body can, in principle, recover, acupuncture may produce a cure. For example, a painful scar may become pain-free after a few acupuncture treatments – and this is a permanent cure; there may be visible changes as well, for sometimes such scars are red and angry at first, but become pale after acupuncture. Again, a pain that is due to an active trigger point, caused perhaps by a sudden strain or an accident, may be permanently relieved by acupuncture.

Apart from its pain-relieving qualities, acupuncture is particularly successful when it comes to relieving symptoms of disorders that recur at intervals, as, for example, in the case of migraine. Sufferers from such problems can often be helped considerably, and it may be possible to keep the symptoms at bay for long periods, but most will need "top-up" treatments at intervals; however, these can often be several months apart. Acupuncture can treat a wide range of conditions – from disorders of the mind to infertility, insomnia, and ulcers, for example.

WATCHPOINT

Before you embark on a course of treatment, ask how many treatments will be required. It may not be possible for the practitioner to say this with certainty, but it should be possible to give a rough estimate. In general, you should see at least some degree of improvement after an average of five treatments. If there has been no effect at all by this stage, it is seldom worth continuing. There is no point returning time after time if there is no response – you may be one of those people for whom acupuncture is not an effective treatment.

PATHFINDER

Disorders that respond well:
ADDICTIONS SEE P. *258*
ALLERGIES SEE PP. *338–9*
ANGINA SEE P. *304*
ARTHRITIS SEE PP. *346–7*
ASTHMA SEE PP. *294–5*
BEDWETTING SEE P. *352*
BRONCHITIS SEE P. *299*
BURSITIS SEE P. *349*
CATARACT SEE P. *279*
CATARRH SEE P. *285*
COLD SORES SEE P. *275*
CONSTIPATION SEE P. *313*
DENTAL DISCOMFORT (FOLLOWING TREATMENT) SEE P. *287*
DEPRESSION SEE P. *261*
DIARRHEA SEE P. *312*
DIZZINESS SEE P. *271*
EATING DISORDERS SEE P. *265*
FLU SEE P. *298*
GOUT SEE P. *337*
GUM DISEASE SEE P. *289*
HEADACHE SEE PP. *268–9*
HIGH BLOOD PRESSURE SEE P. *302*
HIV AND AIDS SEE PP. *340–1*
HYPERACTIVITY SEE P. *351*
INDIGESTION SEE P. *310*
INFERTILITY SEE P. *324*
INSOMNIA SEE P. *264*
KIDNEY COMPLAINTS SEE PP. *318–9*
LABOR PAINS SEE P. *328*
MIGRAINE SEE P. *269*
MISCARRIAGE SEE P. *325*
NEURALGIA SEE P. *267*
OBESITY SEE PP. *334–5*
OSTEOPOROSIS SEE P. *358*
PEPTIC ULCER SEE P. *311*
SCIATICA SEE P. *348*
SINUSITIS SEE P. *284*
STROKE SEE P. *359*
TINNITUS SEE P. *281*

Consulting a Therapist

The first thing you must decide is whether you want to see a traditional acupuncturist or prefer a modern approach, in which case you will almost certainly see a practitioner who also has conventional qualifications, probably as a doctor or a physiotherapist. But if you decide on a traditionalist, you need to make sure that he or she has adequate training, especially if you live in a country or state that has little or no regulation. Make sure that the acupuncturist has been trained at a recognized college. The best way to find a practitioner of any kind is to ask your doctor or contact the professional body.

What the consultation will be like and how long it lasts depends both on the type of practitioner and the nature of the problem for which you want treatment. In Traditional Chinese Medicine a diagnosis is made based on four examinations: observing, hearing and smelling, questioning and touching. A traditionalist will probably ask you a lot of questions about your medical history, digestion, sleeping patterns, diet, your emotions, and your way of life, and will then look at your tongue and take your pulses at both wrists. The treatment will probably take about 20 minutes and a considerable number of needles will be inserted; moxa (*see page 23*) and electrical stimulation may also be used. The whole appointment will last about an hour.

A doctor who practices modern acupuncture will start with a normal medical consultation, but is likely to carry out a more detailed physical examination than usual, paying particular attention to the presence of trigger points in the muscles and elsewhere. Only a few needles may then be used, and often they are only left in place for a short time.

What Will I Feel?

The amount of pain felt when the needles are inserted varies from person to person: most people feel a small amount of pain – similar, or perhaps less in degree to that experienced during a blood test, say – though some people feel no pain at all. But acupuncture often gives rise to curious local sensations peculiar to the technique, often described as a tingling sensation or dull ache. Limbs often feel heavy and the patient generally feels relaxed. These sensations are often considered to be confirmation that the treatment is working, though their absence does not mean that it is not working.

Sometimes you will feel an immediate reduction in any symptoms, but more often it takes from several hours to several days for the effects of treatment to be felt. And sometimes the condition worsens temporarily before improvement starts. How long the improvement lasts varies, too. Quite often the improvement

BELOW *Acupuncture has helped people of all ages with a broad range of complaints.*

IS IT RIGHT FOR ME?

People vary considerably in their sensitivity to acupuncture. A small number of people show an exceptionally strong response: known as "strong reactors", they may feel very relaxed and happy, even "high", after acupuncture – for example, some people have been known to laugh or cry for some time after treatment: one-third of people don't respond at all. The only way of knowing which category you fit into is to try acupuncture and see – assuming that your condition is one that is suitable for this treatment.

Perhaps surprisingly, in view of the known phenomenon of the "placebo effect" in which any procedure that is believed to be a treatment has some positive results, it does not seem to matter at all whether a patient believes in acupuncture; the result is not dependent on faith in the technique. People who are frightened of needles can be treated by other techniques such as laser acupuncture. Age is no barrier to treatment, with both children and the elderly responding well, nor is the presence of obvious disease, such as osteoarthritis, a handicap to acupuncture treatment.

PRECAUTIONS

■ The risks of acupuncture are small when treatment is carried out by a qualified practitioner – much lower, for example, than those of taking the pain-killing drugs prescribed to treat arthritis.

■ The main risk is of damage to an internal organ, such as the heart or lungs (especially when the practitioner has not been properly trained), but the transmission of infections, especially hepatitis and also HIV, is also possible if rigorous standards of hygiene and sterilization are not followed.

■ There is also a risk in that acupuncture's ability to relieve pain may temporarily mask the symptoms of a serious disorder – such as a brain tumor. Because of this, it is vital that a doctor's examination rules out any such problems before treatment is started.

■ Patients should not drive or use heavy machinery after acupuncture treatment, especially after the first session. There is a risk that judgment may be impaired.

■ Acupuncture is probably best avoided during pregnancy, especially in the first three months, because of reports that it may cause a miscarriage. It does seem to help early morning sickness and some doctors and traditional acupuncturists use it for this purpose, avoiding needling certain areas of the body.

brought about by the first treatment lasts for only a short time, but persists for longer after the second treatment, and for longer still after the third, until a plateau of improvement is reached. In an ideal case this represents complete freedom from symptoms, but the plateau may be reached at a partial freedom – which is nevertheless worthwhile. And it is quite common, especially in the case of problems of long standing, for patients to remain well for some time but to need follow-up treatments.

The success rate of acupuncture varies according to the kind of problem being treated. About 70 percent of those with conditions that respond well to acupuncture show good results; with other ailments the success rate may be lower, but treatment may still be worthwhile if little conventional treatment has been effective. And a condition that does not usually respond well to acupuncture may do so if the patient reacts exceptionally well to the treatment.

1 *Acupuncture needles, available in varying lengths and thicknesses, are made of silver, gold, or stainless steel and are either disposable or thoroughly sterilized after use. Finer, shorter needles are used in areas where the skin is thinner and closer to the bone; longer, slightly thicker ones in padded areas such as the buttocks.*

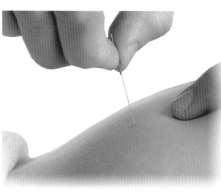

BELOW *A sensation of tugging or a dull ache may be felt as the needle reaches its target.*

2 *Insertion is quick and usually painless and bloodless. Depending on the position of the acupoint, the practitioner usually inserts the acupuncture needles to a depth of 4–25mm (⅙–1 in).*

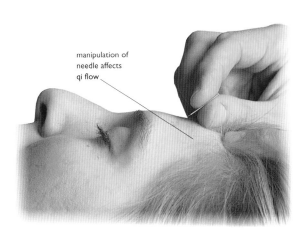

manipulation of
needle affects
qi flow

5   Acupoints on the hands, feet, face, abdomen,
   shoulders, and back are widely used. At
the end of a session the needles are withdrawn,
usually painlessly. Because their rounded
ends divide the flesh rather than pierce
it, acupuncture needles rarely draw
blood, although a small bruise may
develop at the site.

LEFT Needles
are disposable
and are packaged
in sterile containers.

3   Once in position, the practitioner will manipulate the
   needles, usually by twirling them between his thumb and
forefinger or by using a gentle pumping action to stimulate the
flow of qi. This procedure may cause a slight feeling of numbness
or tugging, but it should not last. The needles are sometimes
simply left in place.

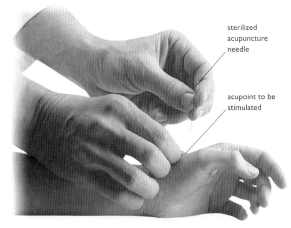

sterilized
acupuncture
needle

acupoint to be
stimulated

LEFT The
practitioner may
pinch the skin to aid
painless insertion.

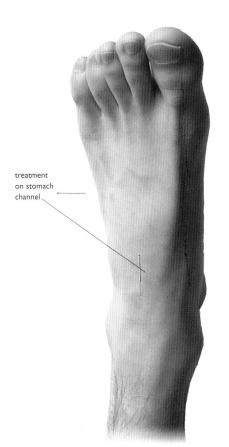

treatment
on stomach
channel

6   After treatment, a patient
   may feel tired or that the
symptoms have worsened, but
this usually passes quickly. On
the other hand, a patient may
feel invigorated. It often takes
several hours or even days
before the effects of treatment are
felt. A patient should see some
improvement in their condition
after about five sessions of
acupuncture.

4   The site of the acupoint and the condition being treated will
   determine the length of time the needles remain in the body.
Needles may be left in position for as little as a few seconds or as
long as an hour. The number of needles used during a treatment
will vary according to the condition being treated.

treatment on
bladder channel

Scientific research has confirmed that massage of the acupoint Pericardium 6 on the wrist is effective in relieving nausea and vomiting in early pregnancy. However, many Western doctors are skeptical of the meridian theory and would find it hard to believe that what is basically a form of massage could affect the internal organs in such a specific way.

AURICULAR THERAPY

The ear has long been considered of great importance in Traditional Chinese Medicine as an indicator of health because all the major meridians are thought to cross it. Practitioners believe there are more than 120 acupoints on each ear, related to different parts of the body, which can be used for pain relief, to treat ailments, and promote anesthesia. The color of the ear and condition of its skin are also taken into consideration.

Modern auricular (ear) acupuncture, or auricular therapy, was developed in the 1950s by Paul Nogier, a French doctor who identified 30 points on the ear that appeared to have a reflex response in an associated area of the body. He claimed that when one of these points is stimulated a surge can occur in the wrist pulse, indicating a disharmony in the related body part.

In auricular acupuncture, treatment is designed to stim-ulate the acupoints on the ear to affect the corresponding body part. The points may be stimulated by laser, a mild electrical current, acupuncture needles, or even by hand. Needles may be held in place with small pieces of tape for several days, but there is a risk of a small local infection if the needles are left in for more than a week.

Auricular acupuncture may be used in conjunction with body acupuncture, but it tends to be used on its own. During treatment a tingling sensation or slight dull ache may be felt, as well as a sensation in the related part of the body. Ear acupuncture is based on the idea that each part of the ear is a mirror of the body as a whole. There are, for example, kidney meridian points on the ear. As a result almost any ailment can be treated with ear acupuncture. Sometimes it is used together with body acupuncture, but some practitioners use ear acupuncture on its own for diagnosis and treatment.

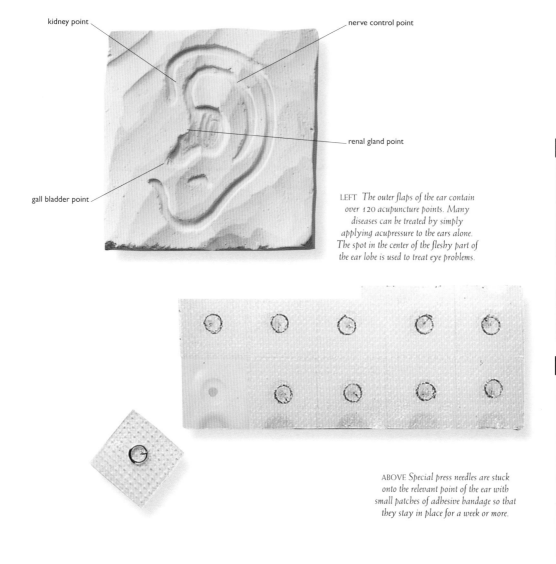

kidney point

nerve control point

renal gland point

gall bladder point

LEFT *The outer flaps of the ear contain over 120 acupuncture points. Many diseases can be treated by simply applying acupressure to the ears alone. The spot in the center of the fleshy part of the ear lobe is used to treat eye problems.*

ABOVE *Special press needles are stuck onto the relevant point of the ear with small patches of adhesive bandage so that they stay in place for a week or more.*

Auricular acupuncture has traditionally been used to treat addictions and for pain relief (during labor, for example). Today it is also used to treat sports injuries, musculoskeletal problems, headaches, skin disorders, and digestive problems.

Because this therapy can be adapted to suit the age and health of the sufferer, it is safe for most people. It is still, however, considered to be unproved in the West, and it is advised that you consult your physician before undergoing treatment.

ACUPRESSURE

The principles that underpin acupressure are the same as those that lie behind acupuncture. In fact, acupuncture developed out of acupressure, which is sometimes known as "the mother of acupuncture" and predates it. Today acupressure is widely practiced in China, where an individual's responsibility for his or her own health is emphasized more than it is in the West, as a form of self-help treatment. It is also recommended and taught by many traditional acupuncturists as a useful adjunct to acupuncture itself; therapists often use the technique alongside acupuncture as part of a consultation. Mainstream medical practitioners also recognize the value of acupressure as a self-help measure, though once more they explain its efficacy in terms of trigger points (see page 23). However, they take the view that it is far less effective than acupuncture: the effects are seldom long-lasting, but the technique can relieve symptoms fairly well, although only for short periods.

Finding an Acupoint

The diagrams will give you the approximate location of the acupoint you need (remembering that distances are measured in the breadth of your fingers), but you will have to identify it precisely yourself. Explore the area, probing until you feel a slight twinge of discomfort. This may be followed in a few minutes by a feeling of numbness, and in some cases you may experience a tingling sensation in the area around the point, but you will soon become less sensitive to it.

Acupressure Techniques

The amount of pressure that it is recommended you apply to acupoints depends on which system you prefer (see Combination Systems, page 31). Generally, however, a moderate probing pressure is the most effective for self-help treatments. Use the point of your finger or thumb, a knuckle, or a blunt, smooth object such as the eraser end of a pencil, and apply for one to two minutes. You may find it helpful to make small rotational movements over the acupoint. Repeat the treatment several times each day, working on the relevant acupoint on each side of the body.

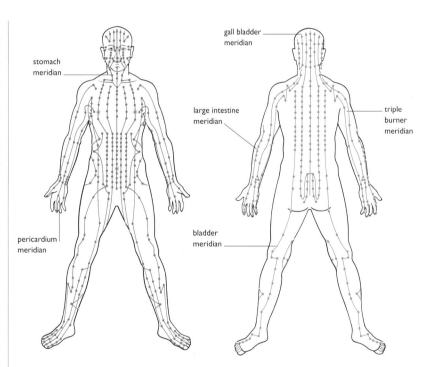

stomach meridian

gall bladder meridian

large intestine meridian

triple burner meridian

pericardium meridian

bladder meridian

ABOVE *Acupressure involves the stimulation of points along the 12 meridians.*

ABOVE *Your hand (or a blunt, smooth object) may be used in acupressure.*

ABOVE *Use the point of your finger or thumb.*

ABOVE *Make small rotational movements over the acupoint.*

Acupoints to Try

Applying pressure to certain acupoints seems to be especially effective, so try working on these in particular if you have a problem that relates to them:

＊ Acupoints in the head and neck – many people have tender areas at the top of their shoulders, in the neck muscles, and at the base of the skull, often caused by bad posture and resulting in stiffness and headaches;

＊ Acupoints in the lower back – stimulation here is an effective way of relieving back pain;

＊ Acupoints in the buttocks – look for tender points deep in the muscles while lying on your side with your hip tilted forward;

＊ An acupoint on the front of the wrist called "Pericardium 6" – stimulation here can be effective in relieving nausea, vomiting during early pregnancy, and travel sickness;

＊ An acupoint called "Large intestine 4," found on the web between the thumb and forefinger. Do not massage this point if pregnant. Stimulation here can be effective in relieving toothache (rubbing with a piece of ice can be helpful, too);

＊ Acupoints on the inside of the lower leg, about a hand's breadth above the ankle – stimulating these can be a useful way of relieving menstrual pains, but they must not be massaged if pregnant.

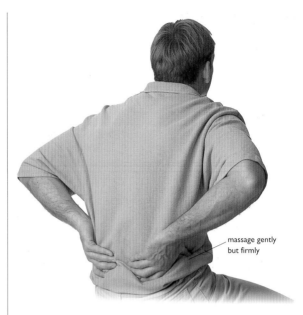

massage gently
but firmly

2 *Stimulation of the acupoints in the lower back, particularly Bladder 25, found to the lower side of the fourth lumbar vertebra (around the waist), is recommended for treating constipation, diarrhea, and acute lower back pain.*

this can be a
tender point

use the pads of
the fingers

1 *Massaging the acupoints in the back of the head and neck is a particularly effective way of relieving some types of headache, stiff neck, and dizziness. However, be very careful not to massage Gall Bladder 21 on the shoulder if pregnant.*

3 *To relieve sciatica, lie on your side and apply pressure to Gall Bladder 30, found two-thirds of the way down from the bottom of the spine to the top of the thigh bone. However, note that this point can be quite sensitive.*

PRECAUTIONS

■ Consult your doctor before starting to use acupressure, to rule out the possibility that any pain you are experiencing is being caused by a serious disorder; also consult your doctor if any pain becomes worse or spreads after treatment.

■ Unless to control vomiting during the early months (by applying pressure to the inside of the leg a hand's breadth above the ankle), do not use acupressure if you are pregnant; certain acupoints should not be stimulated during pregnancy.

COMBINATION SYSTEMS

Over the centuries, numerous different types of acupressure have developed, and many therapeutic systems utilize one or other of them alongside a variety of techniques and spiritual approaches.

In shen tao, for example, a Chinese system that is thought to be the oldest of them all, light pressure from the fingertips over acupressure points is combined with the application of Taoist principles of diet and energy balance. Jin shen and do jin shen use prolonged massage together with other techniques such as meditation.

Acupressure is also an important component of do-in (*see pp. 38–41*), and some forms of qigong (*see pp. 44–5*). In Japan, acupressure plays a major part in shiatsu (*see pp. 32–7*), but in China the most common form of acupressure is tuina, in which it is combined with massage (*see pp. 96–103*) and manipulation techniques.

HOT AND COLD

Applying manual pressure is not always the most effective way of stimulating acupoints: sometimes the application of heat or coldness can be more successful. Try stimulating the acupoints in your neck and shoulders with a strong, warm shower while lying in a warm bath; or rub an acupoint with an ice cube – strapping on a packet of frozen peas will do just as well, but take care to place a thin damp cloth between the skin and the ice pack or the skin may be burned.

this is a useful point to settle the stomach

4 To ease nausea, morning sickness, or travel sickness, press Pericardium 6, found below the wrist crease in line with the ring finger.

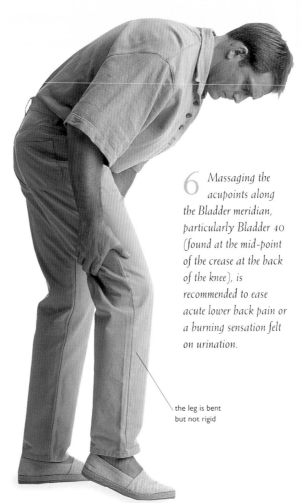

6 Massaging the acupoints along the Bladder meridian, particularly Bladder 40 (found at the mid-point of the crease at the back of the knee), is recommended to ease acute lower back pain or a burning sensation felt on urination.

the leg is bent but not rigid

acupressure can ease sinusitis

5 Manipulation of the acupoint known as Large Intestine 20, level to the midpoint of the nostril, is thought to ease nasal congestion, nose bleeds, hayfever, and loss of sense of smell.

SHIATSU

*S*hiatsu is a Japanese therapy that uses touch and pressure in a combination of techniques to stimulate energy flow in the meridians and promote self-healing, vitality, and well-being. The term "shiatsu" literally means "finger pressure" and the roots of the therapy, like those of acupressure, are found in Traditional Chinese Medicine, but it was only officially recognized in Japan in 1955. Shiatsu is increasingly popular in the West, where it is not only performed by qualified practitioners, but is also sometimes employed as a self-help therapy for minor ailments. The many distinctive styles of shiatsu developed throughout the 20th century.

Knowledge of the principles and practices of Traditional Chinese Medicine – including the therapeutic massage system known as "tuina" ("anma" in Japan) – spread to Japan during the 6th century C.E., along with Buddhism and Chinese philosophy. Before long, they had become established and started to evolve independently of their origins, especially during the Edo period – Japan's cultural and artistic renaissance – between the early 1600s and the late 19th century.

It was decreed that anma could be performed by the blind. This ruling was sensible in that blind people have a very highly developed sense of touch (many of today's physiotherapists are blind), but unfortunate for the reputation of anma at the same time. In those days blind people were, inevitably, less able to acquire an all-round education in the sciences: as a result, while other forms of medicine leapt ahead in Japan, overlaying traditional theory with new techniques that owed more to contemporary science than spirituality, anma came to lose its medical aspects and was therefore less highly regarded – except, that is, as a treatment, known as "ampuku," for problems associated with pregnancy and childbirth.

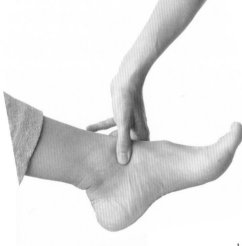

Anma Revived

At the turn of the 20th century, the practice of anma was in serious decline. But its savior was Tamai Tempaku, who wrote a book called *Shiatsu Ho* in 1919. In it, he combined anma, ampuku, and do-in (*see pages* 38–41) with elements of anatomy, physiology, and traditional spirituality. The publication of Tempaku's book was the trigger for a significant revival of interest in anma and its uses, and three of his students – Tokujiro Namikoshi, Katsusuke Serizawa, and Shizuto Masunaga – developed individual systems of shiatsu: Zen shiatsu; Namikoshi shiatsu; and tsubo therapy. Each system has significant differences, and so will be treated separately here. In practice though, the distinctions between the various types of shiatsu are often blurred, since in many countries practitioners (shiatsuists) are encouraged by their regulatory bodies to study more than one system.

Zen Shiatsu

Though Shizuto's Masunaga's system – Zen shiatsu – was developed after Namikoshi shiatsu (*see below*), it is now probably the most popular form of the therapy. Zen shiatsu blends anma with the traditional Chinese concepts of yin and yang, qi ("ki" in Japanese), and meridians (*see pages* 20–21), as well as the idea of manipulating the flow of ki to restore balance between yin and yang.

However, Masunaga took these concepts a stage further: he described "supplementary" meridians, so extending the traditional network of acupuncture meridians; he made use of the Five Elements theory (*see page* 35), a classification of yin and yang into various forms of ki; he used a theory of energy balance known as kyo-jitsu (*see page* 35) to diagnose imbalances by means of palpation, then interpret them and treat them; and he devised a system of diagnosis by palpation of the abdomen (*see Diagnosis by Touch, page* 36). In Zen shiatsu the concept of yin and yang is also extended to all aspects of life, including diet, exercise, and general psychological health.

Namikoshi Shiatsu

Also known as "shiatsu massage," shiatsu in the Namikoshi style is a therapy that utilizes anma pressing and rubbing techniques, but downplays – often to the point of ignoring them – the significance of yin and yang, ki, and meridians. Instead it concentrates on healing through massage of specific areas of the body, many of which are trigger points (*see page* 23), and draws on Western knowledge of anatomy, physiology, and neurology; advice on diet, exercise, and lifestyle is also given.

FOUNDERS OF MODERN SHIATSU

Shizuto Masunaga developed Zen shiatsu, a system based on modified TCM theories of ki and meridians, which is probably the most popular form of the therapy in the West. In contrast to other forms of shiatsu, a Zen shiatsuist always uses both hands on the body and works the whole length of the imbalanced meridian as opposed to specific points.

Namikoshi shiatsu, named for its originator, concentrates on healing through massage of specific areas of the body and downplays the aspects of ki and meridians. Tokujiro Namikoshi's major contribution was the gaining of official recognition for shiatsu in Japan. He also established a training school and spread information about shiatsu to America.

Katsusuke Serizawa devised tsubo therapy, a form of shiatsu that is based on TCM theories but looks for a scientific explanation of the meridian system. Tsubo therapy is specifically concerned with the stimulation of individual points (tsubos) and, depending upon the ailment, the techniques that can be applied to them.

Masunaga

Serizawa

Tokujiro Namikoshi was the first of Tempaku's students to formulate a shiatsu system, and it was the first one to spread to the West; his son, Toru, continued to popularize the Namikoshi system in America, and promoted it in a comprehensive guide called *The Complete Book of Shiatsu Therapy*. However, because of its emphasis on the physical techniques, Namikoshi shiatsu would not be the system of choice for someone who was interested in the more spiritual aspects of the therapy.

Tsubo Therapy

The approach adopted by Katsusuke Serizawa, the third of Tempuka's students, was halfway between that of Namikoshi and that of Masunaga. He reverted to the traditional theory of meridians, but concentrated on research into the nature of the acupoints, known in Japanese as tsubo: one important part of this research was his use of sophisticated measuring devices to demonstrate that the electrical resistance of the skin changes over a tsubo.

Serizawa devised tsubo therapy, in which treatment concentrates on the stimulation of tsubo by means of massage, needles, electrical devices, and moxa (*see page* 23). The therapy is not in widespread use in the West, but acupressure shiatsu, which is derived from it, is practiced in the U.S.A.

SHIATSU MERIDIANS

LEFT *The stomach channel runs from beneath the eye down to the middle toe.*

SHIATSU VARIANTS

There is a considerable amount of cross-fertilization in the world of shiatsu, and a large number of different techniques exist, apart from the main ones described here. However, there are several distinctive styles, named according to their theoretical approach or originator.

❧ Macrobiotic shiatsu, taught at the Kushi Institute in Massachusetts, U.S.A., blends traditional theories with dietary and lifestyle teachings.

❧ Barefoot shiatsu, devised by Viola M. Timbers, of New York City, U.S.A., involves massaging meridians with hands, elbows, knees and feet.

❧ Nippon shiatsu, generally confined to the U.S.A., combines Namikoshi shiatsu with traditional meridian theory.

❧ Ohashiatsu®, developed by Watura Ohashi, of the Ohashi Institute, New York City, U.S.A., combines shiatsu with exercises and meditation.

❧ Bodywork Tantra, devised by school teacher Harold Dull, combines meditation, chakra healing, and Zen shiatsu. It incorporates:

❧ Tantsu, short for tantric shiatsu, in which meridians are stretched by pulling and squeezing;

❧ Watsu, in which shiatsu is performed in chest-high, warmed water to release meridian blockages;

❧ New Age Shiatsu®, developed by Reuho Yamada, a Zen priest.

How Shiatsu Works

To a large extent, Namikoshi shiatsu works in the same way as therapeutic massage (*see pages 96–103*), by triggering the release of endorphins – the body's natural painkillers – thus lowering blood pressure, breaking down muscle spasms, increasing blood flow, and mobilizing the lymphatic drainage system. Zen shiatsuists, however, who follow a system that was developed from the principles of Traditional Chinese Medicine (*see pages 20–21*), believe that their form of shiatsu has a considerable number of extra benefits. They maintain that a therapist does not need to work only on tsubo – as tsubo therapists and acupuncturists (*see pages 20–28*) do – but can manipulate the flow of ki along a meridian by massaging its whole length: this is one of the important differences between Zen shiatsu and acupuncture.

Temporal and Spiritual

Another difference between the therapies lies in their approaches to treatment. In acupuncture and acupressure, a problem is identified and the practitioner stimulates specific acupoints in order to treat the problem and alleviate pain. Zen shiatsu, however, is more holistic; the shiatsuist endeavors to treat the whole person, in both physical and spiritual senses, in the course of a session. While the way a traditional acupuncturist manipulates is essentially mechanical (*see page 21*), the concept of balancing ki in Zen shiatsu involves a considerable element of spirituality and an understanding of what this involves.

Diagnosis and treatment are almost indivisible in shiatsu and both continue throughout a shiatsu session. A practitioner will constantly reassess what he is feeling and modify the treatment accordingly. It is, however, very rare for an acupuncturist to change treatment once the principle and points have been selected and the treatment has begun.

ABOVE *The process of hara breathing is fundamental to shiatsu.*

RIGHT *The kidneys and heart correspond to yin and yang, or water and fire, energies in the body.*

Ki, Yin, and Yang

It is difficult to give a coherent account of the spiritual basis of Zen shiatsu in the space available in this book – look to Further Reading (*see pages 372–5*) if you wish to investigate the subject in more detail. As far as definitions go, ki is said to be the energy that provides the substance of all things in the universe and also drives all change to them. When time began, all the ki in the universe, the theory maintains, took one of two forms: yin, said to be "the shady side of the hill" – meaning Earth, lunar, dark, cold, damp, water, passive, soft, and feminine qualities; and yang, originally "the sunny side of a hill" – meaning qualities of Heaven, light, heat, fire, dryness, activity, hardness, and masculinity. It is important to note that these qualities are not absolute but dynamic and flexible, and there is a constant flow of ki from yin to yang and vice versa.

Since ki is all-embracing and all-encompassing, the various different areas of the body, and attributes of personality, too, can be described in terms of yin and yang. But, by their very nature, these qualities are not absolute, which makes it difficult to use them to assess the state of ki in order to decide on treatment. This is where various different interpretative systems come into play, the most commonly used being the TCM theory of the Five Elements (sometimes known as the Five Transformations or the Five Phases) and Masunaga's kyo-jitsu theory – the latter is favored in Zen shiatsu, though many shiatsuists use both. Good health depends upon a free and harmonious flow of ki throughout the body and it is the shiatsuist's function to realign the imbalanced ki.

The Five Elements and Kyo-Jitsu

The Five Elements theory, which shiatsuists use to assess the state of ki in the body, essentially provides a more specific set of subdivisions of yin and yang qualities that describe ki as it changes. The Elements – Wood, Fire, Earth, Metal, and Water – have properties that call to mind, by association, certain general qualities such as season, climate, and color; and what are known as "correspondences" with the human body and mind. Each element has a yin and a yang organ, plus specific senses and emotions. Qualities belonging to the same element are thought to support each other.

Kyo-jitsu, as an interpretive tool to explain yin and yang imbalances, depends on the theory that kyo is the yin quality and jitsu is the yang quality. Since yang is active, and yin passive, jitsu might be thought to drive kyo. However, another way of looking at the relationship between the two – and one in which Masunaga (*see pages 32–3*) believed – is that something that is passive cannot drive anything: kyo, the active quality, responds to a fluctuation in jitsu, the passive one, and tries to correct it. In practice, this means, for example, that someone who is depressed or exhausted, and so feels a general sense of emptiness – kyo – may develop symptoms as a result of an increase in jitsu in other areas of the body. A Zen shiatsuist will try to reach a conclusion about the precise relationship between kyo and jitsu before deciding on initial treatment.

ABOVE *The Five Elements create and destroy each other in an endless cycle.*

THE FIVE ELEMENTS

The Five Elements theory considers that Wood, Fire, Earth, Metal, and Water reflect not only a number of general qualities, but also have specific correspondences to areas of the human body, emotional states, and mental qualities.

GENERAL QUALITIES

ELEMENT	WOOD	FIRE	EARTH	METAL	WATER
SEASON	SPRING	SUMMER	LATE SUMMER	AUTUMN	WINTER
PROCESS	BIRTH	GROWTH	CHANGE	HARVEST	STORAGE
CLIMATE	WIND	HEAT	HUMIDITY	DRYNESS	COLD
COLOR	GREEN	RED	YELLOW	WHITE	BLACK/BLUE

CORRESPONDENCES WITH THE HUMAN BODY AND MIND

ELEMENT	WOOD	FIRE	EARTH	METAL	WATER
YIN ORGAN	LIVER	HEART	SPLEEN	LUNGS	KIDNEYS
YANG ORGAN	GALL BLADDER	SMALL INTESTINE	STOMACH	LARGE INTESTINE	BLADDER
TISSUE	MUSCLES	BLOOD VESSELS	FLESH	SKIN	BONES
SENSE	SIGHT	SPEECH	TASTE	SMELL	HEARING
TASTE	SOUR	BITTER	SWEET	SPICY	SALTY
SOUND	SHOUTING	LAUGHING	SINGING	CRYING	GROANING
POSITIVE EMOTION	HUMOR	JOY	SYMPATHY	POSITIVITY	COURAGE
NEGATIVE EMOTION	ANGER	HYSTERIA	SELF-PITY	GRIEF/MELANCHOLY	FEAR/FRIGHT
CAPACITY	PLANNING	SPIRITUAL AWARENESS	IDEAS/OPINIONS	ELIMINATION	AMBITION/WILLPOWER

Meridians and Manipulating Ki

Adherents of the principles of Traditional Chinese Medicine believe that though ki – as a result of its very nature – moves throughout the whole body, it is to be found in a concentrated form in channels called meridians. Shiatsu uses the same traditional Chinese model of meridians as acupuncture (see pages 20–21). Each of the 12 meridians is named after the organ with whose function it is concerned – Lung, Large Intestine, Heart, and so on – and there is a specific function relating to the yin and the yang aspect of each one. In addition, there are two central channels, the "Governing Vessel" and the "Conception

WATCHPOINT

Shiatsu is not a self-help technique – though some elements of it can be learnt and performed at home (see Do-in, pages 38–41) – so it is essential that you consult a shiatsuist if you want to make use of the therapy. Before you choose one, enquire about which technique he favors, so that you are treated in the way that you prefer; make sure, too, that the shiatsuist has trained at and is recognized by a reputable shiatsu school.

energy ascends to head

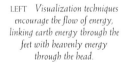
energy descends to feet

Vessel": the former influences yang functions and qualities; and the latter influences those relating to yin. Each of the meridians is associated with a particular two-hour period during the day when Ki reaches a peak. This clock cycle is used as a diagnostic tool to assess a patient's strengths and weaknesses.

It is at this point that one major difference between acupuncture and shiatsu, apart from the obvious one concerning the use or non-use of needles, becomes apparent. In acupuncture, attention is generally only paid to acupoints. But shiatsuists believe that the flow of ki can be manipulated by using a variety of massage techniques all along the relevant meridian, as well as by stimulation of tsubo. Depending on the shiatsu system being followed, a practitioner will also use healing techniques, visualizing the transmission of healing energy into the patient's body, techniques derived from Western physiotherapy, such as passive rotations and stretches, and general body massage (see pages 96–103).

LEFT *Visualization techniques encourage the flow of energy, linking earth energy through the feet with heavenly energy through the head.*

DIAGNOSIS BY TOUCH

Shiatsuists believe that some areas of the body form a whole body map, and that information about the state of ki in a particular organ can be gained by palpating the part of the map that relates to it. There are three main maps: the hara diagnosis map on the abdomen; the map of yu points alongside the spine on the back; and a map of bo points on the front of the body. The hara diagnosis map, which is the most used, divides the abdomen into areas that relate to the 12 meridians, and the individual bo and yu points also relate to specific meridians.

The relative tenderness, softness, or hardness of the hara areas and the yu and bo points when palpated gives the shiatsuist information about the balance of yin and yang in a particular organ. Additional information comes from assessing the condition of ki in the meridians and from taking the radial pulse at the wrist, where there is a pulse position for each of the meridians.

Once the shiatsuist has assessed the overall state of ki in the body, he or she can interpret the information – either in terms of Five Elements theory or kyo-jitsu theory (see page 35).

THE FUNCTIONS OF KI

Ki has five basic functions in the body:

🍃 movement (any form of physical or mental activity)

🍃 protection (against the environment)

🍃 warmth (overall body temperature and peripheral circulation)

🍃 transformation (of food into life-sustaining units)

🍃 retention (keeping everything in place in the body)

Consulting a Therapist

One of the fascinations of shiatsu is that no two sessions are the same. However, this means that it is only possible to give you an idea of what to expect when you visit a shiatsuist; what follows refers primarily to Zen shiatsu, since it is probably the most common form of the therapy. Clothes are worn throughout a session, partly because shiatsuists prefer not to be distracted by looking at the meridians and to rely on touch alone, and partly because they claim that treatment can slow the body's metabolic rate and so make patients feel cold. However, it is advisable to wear light clothing so as not to impede the therapist's sense of touch too much. Treatment normally takes place on the floor, with the patient lying on a futon or mattress, though if necessary it can be given in a chair.

First the shiatsuist makes a diagnosis, not of any specific condition, but of the overall state of your ki and whether it shows imbalances. There are four stages to this process: taking a history; general observation; hearing and smelling; and touch. In the first stage, the shiatsuist will not just take down a full medical case history, but also ask questions designed to reveal your personality, because this gives information about your yin and yang balance. Observation is more of an ongoing process than a stage: it is not only concerned with general physical appearance and manner, but with the intuitive feelings of the therapist about the patient's state. Hearing and smelling, the third part of diagnosis, investigate the Five Elements categories of sound and taste (see page 35). Then – and most important of all – comes touch (see box, page 36).

Once the shiatsuist has come to an understanding of the state of your ki, treatment will begin – but diagnosis does not stop, because your condition, and your response to treatment, is assessed continually, partly through touch and the other diagnostic processes, but also through the therapist's intuition, so that treatment and diagnosis blend seamlessly into each other throughout the session. Meridians are massaged, using a variety of techniques – including deep thumb pressure and the use of elbows, knees, and feet – but that is not all a shiatsu session involves. There are also more general muscle and joint mobilizations and stretches involving the whole body, which are not dissimilar to those used in Western physiotherapy, as well as deep pressure and long, slow holding – these are emphasized in Namikoshi shiatsu. The shiatsuist will endeavor both to transmit healing energy to the patient and to stimulate the patient's own capacities for self-healing.

A session usually ends with a short period for recovery, because shiatsu can be both physically and emotionally demanding for the recipient. A patient may experience after-effects, such as flu-like symptoms, which are a sign that the body is trying to expel toxins. Then the therapist may give advice about diet and lifestyle, and suggest a range of self-help exercises (see *Do-in*, pages 38–41).

RIGHT *The hara diagnosis map divides the abdomen into 12 areas, each relating to a major organ.*

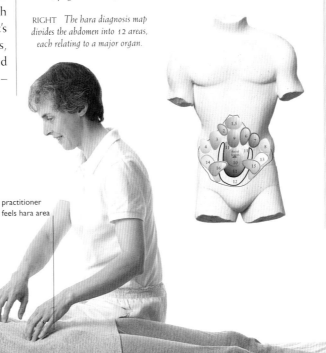

practitioner feels hara area

BELOW *Observation and touch are essential parts of shiatsu diagnosis.*

patient wears light clothing

PATHFINDER

Shiatsu should not be seen as a curative treatment for any medical disorder. Its primary function is to promote good emotional and physical health. However, it can be a useful adjunct to treatment of chronic disorders and emotional problems.

ANEMIA SEE P. *303*
ANGINA SEE P. *304*
ARTHRITIS SEE PP. *346–7*
ASTHMA SEE PP. *294–5*
BACK PROBLEMS SEE PP. *344–5*
COMMON COLD SEE P. *300*
DIZZINESS SEE P. *271*
FAINTING SEE P. *270*
HEADACHE SEE PP. *268–9*
HIV AND AIDS SEE PP. *340–41*
INSOMNIA SEE P. *264*
MENSTRUAL PROBLEMS SEE PP. *322–3*
MIGRAINE SEE P. *269*
OBSESSIONS AND COMPULSIONS SEE P. *259*
PEPTIC ULCER SEE P. *311*
SCIATICA SEE P. *348*
SINUSITIS SEE P. *284*
SORE THROAT SEE P. *291*
STRESS SEE PP. *262–3*

DO-IN

ORIGINS

Do-in is a form of self-shiatsu that incorporates acupressure with breathing exercises, stretches, and meditation techniques to improve physical and spiritual well-being. During the 20th century, do-in developed as a therapy alongside shiatsu (*see pages 32–7*) and it is very popular in Japan and China. Do-in is becoming more well known in the West in its own right.

ABOVE *Michio Kushi introduced do-in to the U.S.A. and is seen as the father of the macrobiotic food movement.*

W hile shiatsu must be administered by a trained practitioner, do-in (also known as daoyin, dao-in and Tao-in) is a self-help therapy that combines some of the principles of shiatsu with ancient Japanese and Chinese stretches, exercises, breathing techniques, and meditation; in its more extreme forms, it also encompasses a macrobiotic diet. Though do-in is primarily a preventive therapy that promotes health by balancing spiritual energy – its ultimate aim is to achieve spiritual harmony with the universe – it can also be used to a limited degree, and in conjunction with other treatments, for self-healing. Do-in exercises are often taught by shiatsuists as part of a treatment session.

Originally, do-in – the Japanese term for self-stimulation – was purely a self-help version of traditional anma massage (*see page 32*) that had also borrowed from ancient Japanese stretching and body toning techniques. However, as shiatsu developed during the 20th century, do-in started to take on board many of the precepts of Shizuto Masunaga's Zen shiatsu (*see page 32*). Today it includes hara breathing, makko-ho exercises, meridian massage (the original do-in), meditation and, only for the therapy's closest adherents, a macrobiotic diet – this is a diet in which individual foods are said to have yin and yang qualities (*see pages 34–5*) and a balance is kept between their intake to help maintain a healthy state of ki (*see page 20*) in the body. In fact it was Michio Kushi, the guru of macrobiotics, who introduced do-in to America in 1968. Today the therapy flourishes in Japan and America, and is becoming more and more popular in Europe.

A DO-IN SESSION

The exercises that comprise today's do-in are best performed first thing in the morning, in order to establish and strengthen ki in the body, expel harmful toxins, known as jaki, center ki in the hara – the abdomen (*see page 36*) – increase the flow of ki along the meridians (*see pages 20–21*), increase spirituality, and promote self-development; 15 minutes is all you need. However, some people prefer to have a do-in session last thing at night – the important thing is to practice when it feels right for you. Ideally, start with hara breathing, progress to self-shiatsu, continue with Makko-ho stretches, and finish with meditation (*see pages 60–63*).

Hara Breathing

1 If possible, sit in the Japanese seizu position. Your hands should be in your lap, your back should be straight and your heels underneath your buttocks. Breathe deeply and try to relax completely.

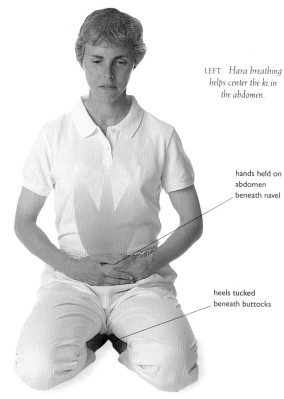

LEFT *Hara breathing helps center the ki in the abdomen.*

hands held on abdomen beneath navel

heels tucked beneath buttocks

2 When you are relaxed take a slow, deep breath, but use your abdominal muscles instead of those of your chest – put one hand on your chest and the other on your lower abdomen so that you can check that the former does not move. Continue breathing in this way for two to three minutes. You may find this technique difficult, but it can be mastered with practice; do not move on to the next stage of hara breathing until you have done so. (Take care that you do not overdo things or you may hyperventilate – stop if you feel dizzy.)

3 Close your eyes, put both hands on your abdomen below your navel and take a long, slow breath in through your nose. Imagine the air traveling down through your body and the ki concentrating in your hara. Hold the breath for a few seconds, then allow the air to escape gradually from your mouth. Imagine old ki and jaki leaving your body as you do so. Repeat the sequence for two or three minutes.

ABOVE *A macrobiotic diet is part of do-in therapy.*

SELF-SHIATSU MASSAGE

As with received shiatsu (*see pages 32–7*), the aim of a self-shiatsu massage is to restore the flow of ki along the meridians. Obviously, there is a limit to how much of your body you can massage, but the face, neck and shoulders, chest and arms, and legs and areas of the back are all within reach for most people. Make this sequence of massages – with acknowledgements to Elaine Liechti, author of *Shiatsu* (*see Further Reading, pages 372–5*) – part of your daily do-in session.

1 *Tap all over the top of your head with your fingertips. Then smooth your forehead before circling round your temples and squeezing along your eyebrows. Use your fingertips to stimulate the points around your eyes, then rub your cheeks and the end of your nose, before attending to the points around your nostrils. Pull your ears in all directions and rub them, then pinch along the line of your jaw.*

2 *Next, turn your attention to your head and neck. Rotate your head to the sides and the front – make sure that you do not strain – and use the pressure of your hands on your head to stretch the neck to relieve any tension. Then massage the area in front of each collar bone, moving along to the shoulders, hitting them lightly with a fist to relieve tension.*

rotate head to release tension

tap chest with fingertips

3 *Tap gently all over your chest with your fingertips, then move to the meridians on the inner arm, tapping up and down them. Turn your arm over and work on the meridians of the outer arm, before finishing off by squeezing and pulling your fingers – but not so hard that you cause a knuckle joint to "pop," as this can cause joint damage.*

ORTHODOX VIEW

Most Western doctors view the principles of yin, yang, and ki with skepticism, especially in the absence of any compelling scientific research to support these ideas.

However, they take the view that do-in is unlikely to do any harm, unless it is used as a substitute for conventional treatment of a disorder. In fact, they believe that many of the stretches and exercises, while having no effect on "energy balance," may improve posture, increase suppleness and fitness, and reduce stress levels.

Generally, however, most doctors would not approve of any form of do-in that involved a macrobiotic diet. Macrobiotics depends on grading foods according the their perceived yin and yang qualities and achieving a balance between them; this gradation does not necessarily take account of a food's nutritional value, and so does not guarantee a balanced diet, which is essential for good health.

PRECAUTIONS

■ It is best to consult a shiatsuist in order to learn the techniques of do-in and the spiritual principles that lie behind them.

■ Do not attempt to complete a do-in session as soon as you take up the therapy, especially if you are elderly or unused to exercise. Take the exercises slowly. Stop exercising if you begin to hyperventilate while deep breathing.

MEDITATION

Contemplation and meditation is an important part of a do-in session, as it is of shiatsu itself, with its emphasis on spiritual harmony and understanding. So try to set aside part of your do-in session for ten minutes or so of quiet meditation.

massage areas either side of the spine

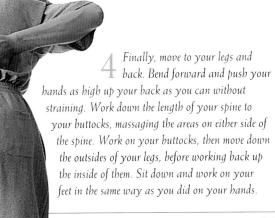

4 *Finally, move to your legs and back. Bend forward and push your hands as high up your back as you can without straining. Work down the length of your spine to your buttocks, massaging the areas on either side of the spine. Work on your buttocks, then move down the outsides of your legs, before working back up the inside of them. Sit down and work on your feet in the same way as you did on your hands.*

MAKKO-HO STRETCHES

There is some similarity between Makko-ho stretches (named after their originator) and Hatha yoga (*see pages 52–9*). However, each of the six Makko-ho stretches is designed to stimulate and rebalance the flow of ki along a particular meridian; shiatsuists also use them as a diagnostic technique to assess the state of their own ki. Makko-ho stretching exercises are also very good for suppleness and flexibility, and can be performed at any time. Each stretch is named for the meridians it stimulates – these are illustrated on page 21.

It is important that your ki is centered in your hara and that you are fully relaxed before you start these stretches, so it may be necessary to do some hara breathing for a few minutes beforehand. Breathe in before each stretch, and then breathe out as you start the movement, but breathe steadily while holding the position. Make sure that you do not force a stretch so that it feels uncomfortable and hold each one no longer than a couple of minutes. After you have done each stretch, lie quietly and relax for a few minutes before getting on with your day.

1 *Lung and Large Intestine Stretch. Place your feet a shoulder's width apart and hook your thumbs behind your back.*

hold hands behind back with thumbs linked

stand with feet shoulder width apart

hold fingers straight and thumbs linked

drop arms gently forward

allow head to relax

2 *Bend your head and shoulders forward and down, without moving your legs, but moving your arms forward over your head as you do so, making sure that you keep your arms straight. Hold, then straighten up, breathing in as you come up.*

3 *Spleen and Stomach Stretch. Kneel on the floor with your ankles tight in to your buttocks, and your elbows on the ground. Then, keeping your knees on the ground, lean your torso back, moving your hands back beneath your head until your head is resting on your hands, which are resting on the floor. Hold, then grasp your ankles, put your chin down onto your chest, and push off with your elbows to come back up.*

4 *Heart and Small Intestine Stretch. Sit down and pull the soles of your feet together, then pull your feet into your body. Next, with your elbows outside your legs, lean forward and move your head over your feet and down onto them. Hold, then straighten up.*

5 *Kidney and Bladder Stretch. Sit on the floor with your legs straight out in front of you. Then bend forward at the hip, with your head lowered toward your knees, and push your hands as far down your legs toward your feet as you can. Hold, then sit back up.*

bring hands as close to feet as possible

6 *Heart Governor and Triple Heater Stretch. (These organs are not recognized in orthodox medicine.) Sit on the floor with your legs crossed and each hand holding the opposite knee. Bend your head and chest forward, while pushing your knees down, so pulling your hands away from each other. Hold, then sit back up.*

bend forward at the hip

7 *Liver and Gall Bladder Stretch. Sit on the floor with your back straight and your legs spread as wide apart as possible. Keeping your back straight and facing forward all the time, move your right arm as far down your right leg as it will go without straining; then move your left arm over the top of your head in line with the same foot. Hold, then relax before repeating on the other side of the body.*

hold right side of waist with left hand

ld each hand on e opposite knee

cross legs

pull down with raised arm

PATHFINDER

Do-in should not been seen as a curative self-help therapy, but primarily as a preventive one that promotes good health. However, it may be helpful as an adjunct to the conventional treatment of a variety of chronic disorders and emotional problems.

ANEMIA SEE P. 303
ANGINA SEE P. 304
ARTHRITIS SEE PP. 346–7
ASTHMA SEE PP. 294–5
BACK PROBLEMS SEE PP. 344–5
COMMON COLD SEE P. 300
DIZZINESS SEE P. 271
FAINTING SEE P. 270
HEADACHE SEE PP. 268–9
HIV AND AIDS SEE PP. 340–1
INSOMNIA SEE P. 264
MENSTRUAL PROBLEMS SEE PP. 322–3
MIGRAINE SEE P. 269
OBSESSIONS AND COMPULSIONS SEE P. 259
PEPTIC ULCER SEE P. 311
SCIATICA SEE P. 348
SINUSITIS SEE P. 284
SORE THROAT SEE P. 291
STRESS SEE PP. 262–3

SHAOLIN

ABOVE *Shaolin kung fu takes its name from the Chinese monastery where the system of exercise was developed.*

While thought of by many as just a martial art, shaolin is, in fact, a unified system of ancient origin, that aims not just to make the human body an effective fighting machine, but also to increase the levels and balance of the "life force" within the body and to promote emotional and psychological development and health. As such, it is practiced by millions in China and by increasing numbers in the West.

Shaolin – its full name is "shaolin kung fu" – is both a martial art and a path to enlightenment, and it is one of the oldest such systems in existence. It has three aims: to develop the physical body into an effective fighting machine; to increase the levels of qi – the life force – in the body (*see page 20*); and to promote emotional and mental development in order to achieve spiritual harmony and cosmic enlightenment through Zen meditation.

Shaolin was first developed at Shaolin Monastery, an imperial temple inthe Henan province of central China founded in 495 C.E. by Batuo, a Buddhist monk from India. In about 527 C.E., Batuo was succeeded by an Indian prince called Bodhidharma, who is regarded as the founding father of Zen Buddhism. His original intention was to teach the monks how to meditate. However, finding that they were physically too weak to meditate for any length of time, he developed a series of exercises designed to increase their strength and stamina – these were the first kung fu techniques. Over the centuries, Bodhidharma's simple exercises were developed by successive generations of Shaolin monks, who also used techniques to harness qi and focus the power of meditation. Shaolin Monastery gained a considerable reputation within China, and numerous scholars, scientists, and military leaders visited it to study and learn under its kung fu masters.

Later, shaolin kung fu was adapted by various Chinese masters into a vast range of other types of martial art. These are normally classified as predominantly either "hard" (external) or "soft" (internal), though most employ a mixture of each type of component. For example, t'ai chi chu'uan (*see pages 46–51*) is usually considered a soft martial art because it employs soft, flowing movements, while kung fu is classified as hard, because its physical side emphasizes developing controlled power and stamina. Today, martial arts are extremely popular, both in China and throughout the Western world.

ABOVE *Qigong and meditation are also components of shaolin.*

A Combined System

Some people concentrate on the purely physical side of shaolin, confining themselves to its practice as a martial art. And the increased physical control, fitness, and strength achieved by means of practicing this component of shaolin certainly increases well-being and maintains health. However, shaolin teachers maintain that the system is a combined one, and that its full benefits cannot be experienced without the complete study of all its components.

The other components of shaolin are Zen meditation and qigong – a blanket term that covers a number of different methods of developing qi (one form of qigong that is popular in the West is discussed overleaf). Shaolin qigong has four basic components: exercises to generate an internal flow of qi throughout the body; particular positions that move the internal qi from one area to another area of the body; breathing exercises performed while standing or sitting to induce a harmonious flow of qi into the body and within it; and a form of meditation, where the mind is used to increase the flow of energy or qi from the outside world into the mind and body to deepen and strengthen the connection between the mind, body and universe. Two examples of shaolin qigong exercises are given here.

Lifting the Sky

This is a typical shaolin qi exercise that draws qi into the body and stimulates its flow within it to improve health and well-being. Do five repetitions of the exercise at first, but build up slowly when it becomes more familiar – up to 20 for full effectiveness.

When you can repeat the exercise without conscious effort, add an element of meditation (*see pages 60–63*) or visualization to it (*see pages 214–17*). As you breathe in, imagine positive qi flowing into your body and mind – in particular bathing any problem areas or emotions. As you breathe out, imagine any harmful substances or negative emotions being exhaled.

1 *Make sure that you will not be disturbed for about 20 minutes. Stand straight with your feet a shoulder's width apart and your arms hanging loosely by your sides.*

2 *Keeping your elbows straight and your fingers together, move your hands in front of you and turn them toward each other so that your fingertips are touching and your palms are facing the ground.*

3 *Keeping the rest of your body still, lower your head to look down at your hands.*

4 *Raise your hands up in front of you until your palms are facing the sky, breathing in through your nose at the same time. Follow the movement with your head and eyes.*

5 *Maintain this position for a count of three, while holding your breath, and then push your hands farther above you three times.*

6 *Gently lower your arms down by your side, keeping your elbows straight while you breathe out through your mouth.*

7 *Maintain the position without breathing for a further count of three.*

8 *After the exercise has been repeated for the last time, remain standing in the last, neutral position for up to 10 minutes to meditate or visualize.*

9 *When the time is up, give yourself a shake and move around briskly for a few minutes to awaken yourself fully.*

Dancing Fairies

This exercise moves qi round the body and focuses it in your head.

The head contains several important meridians – Bladder, Gall Bladder, Triple Heater, and Governing Vessel – which govern functions in the body ranging from protection to warmth, movement, and excretion. If qi is blocked in the head, headaches, migraine or dizziness may result. Perform this exercise about 20 times, becoming slower and slower until you stop.

1 *Stand with your feet slightly more than a shoulder's width apart. Let your knees relax and bend slightly. The exercise should be performed in a very controlled, slow way with your mind as empty as possible. Breathe slowly and naturally.*

2 *Move your right hand above your head, with your palm facing up and the fingers pointing toward the left. Move your left hand down by your side, with the palm facing the ground and the fingers facing left.*

3 *Shift your weight onto your right leg at the same time as looking down at your left hand.*

4 *Lower your right hand down to your right side as you raise your left hand up toward the sky, and shift your weight over to your left leg. Your eyes should follow the movement so that you end up looking at your right hand.*

5 *Repeat the whole exercise 20 times, making the last few repetitions slower and slower until you eventually stop.*

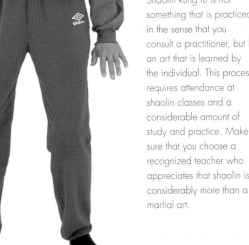

PATHFINDER

Shaolin kung fu is a whole body therapy that aims to incorporate the mind, body, and spirit, so enabling the whole to function perfectly at peak efficiency. It can also be used to maintain well-being and alleviate stress-related disorders.

ANXIETY *SEE PP.* **256–7**
INSOMNIA *SEE P.* **264**
REPETITIVE STRAIN INJURY
(RSI) *SEE PP.* **342–3**
STRESS *SEE PP.* **262–3**

CONSULTING A PRACTITIONER

Shaolin kung fu is not something that is practiced, in the sense that you consult a practitioner, but is an art that is learned by the individual. This process requires attendance at shaolin classes and a considerable amount of study and practice. Make sure that you choose a recognized teacher who appreciates that shaolin is considerably more than a martial art.

QIGONG

ABOVE *Qigong – or "energy practice" – expressed in Chinese characters.*

*O*nce a secret art known to only one person in each generation of a few select families, today the ancient Chinese system of qigong is practiced by millions in China and is becoming more and more popular in the West. Qigong is a gentle therapy that combines undemanding exercises with breathing techniques, meditation, and visualization to develop and improve the circulation of qi, or "life force," throughout the body. Suitable for people of all ages, qigong is thought to increase vitality and promote self-healing.

Qigong, sometimes called chi kung, is an integral part of Traditional Chinese Medicine that is thought to derive from a mixture of Taoist yoga, Buddhist meditation, and traditional Chinese breathing exercises developed around 5,000 years ago. During China's Ming Dynasty (1368–1644), this system of healing exercises was refined into the therapy known as qigong. The term literally means "energy practice": it is the art of cultivating and balancing the qi (*see page* 20) within the body in order to heal and maintain health.

For many centuries, the art of qigong was a closely guarded secret taught only to one person in each generation of élite Chinese families. In fact, it was not until the mid-20th century that qigong became practiced openly – and then only for a short time, because Mao Tse-Tung banned qigong during the Chinese Cultural Revolution (1966–9). However, Mao changed his mind when he fell ill and Western medicine failed to cure him, while qigong, he believed, proved successful. Today, qigong is widely practiced by all age groups throughout China and is rapidly gaining in popularity in the West.

The Theory

Qigong is based on similar principles to those that underlie other traditional Eastern health systems and stresses the need for harmony between yin and yang (*see Shiatsu, pages* 32–7) and the free flow of qi – the life force – in the meridians (*see Acupuncture, pages* 20–8). Qi is said to be the energy of the universe, of which all matter is made. This energy is split into two types – yin and yang – and, though both have discernible qualities and are represented by different parts of the body and mind, they are in a state of flux from one to the other.

Practitioners of qigong postulate that illness, be it physical, mental, or emotional, is caused by an inadequate flow of qi between the yin and yang principles and between the qi in nature and the qi within each person – but that this depletion or imbalance can be regulated and harmonized by treatment.

The essence of qigong is that its system of simple exercises, breathing techniques, and meditation with

ABOVE *Qigong is a widely practiced group exercise in modern-day China.*

visualization improves the circulation of qi, thereby maintaining or restoring physical and mental health to optimum levels. Qigong exercises are slow, gentle, and rhythmical. They are not meant to strengthen the body in any way, but to stimulate the flow of energy from one area to another. Breathing is controlled during the exercises to help focus the mind inside the body rather than externally. Visualization techniques (*see pages* 214–17) are often taught so that one can "feel" and "see" the qi as it flows freely from place to place. Meditation (*see pages* 60–63) is also practiced in order to achieve a deeper state of relaxation and inner harmony as qigong practitioners place great importance on the connection between mental and physical health.

The basic qigong exercises are easy to learn and are suitable for everyone, including the elderly and the infirm. The exercises can be performed in any order; clothing should be loose and comfortable.

CONSULTING A PRACTITIONER

Qigong is normally taught and practiced in a class, though once you have learned the exercise routines and other techniques you can perform them anywhere, at any time, as a self-help measure. It is important that you choose a practitioner who has been trained adequately, though you may find it difficult to do so.

You will be shown certain flowing exercise movements – they often have exotic names, such as "Soaring Crane," "Rainbow Dance," "The Tiger," and "Golden Dragon Wags Tail," and often represent the movement of animals – so wear flat, flexible shoes and loose clothing. It is important that all your movements are easy and slow – you must not strain or stretch your joints or muscles – and that you should not allow your attention to wander, but stay aware of what your body is doing and how it feels.

You will be taught various breathing techniques (see pages 166–71) that will help you to gain more control over your breathing and increase the oxygen supply in the blood and tissues – if you start to feel dizzy or faint return to breathing normally for a while. You will also be taught how to meditate, to clear your mind and let your body and mind achieve a state of deep relaxation, and how to visualize the qi flowing freely throughout your body. As you become more adept at doing this, you may be able to feel the qi as a warm or tingling sensation.

Qigong teachers who reach the highest levels of attainment and control can, reportedly, pass on their qi to a patient or pupil as required to assist healing. However, it is rare to find master practitioners such as these outside China.

LEFT The posture "Golden Cockerel Stands on One Leg" develops balance.

upper body relaxed

knee gently flexed

BELOW "Snake Creeps Down" is a demanding posture requiring strong thighs and knees.

knees positioned over foot

ABOVE The "Horse" stance develops strength in the legs for better "rooting."

PRECAUTIONS

■ Qigong is not a diagnostic tool, nor is it a treatment for any specific disease, so it is vital to consult your family doctor if you are at all concerned about your physical or mental health.

■ Do not stop taking any medication or treatment while practicing qigong.

■ Qigong is not recommended for those suffering from severe psychological problems.

PATHFINDER

Qigong, a gentle form of self-healing that can be practiced by all age groups, is an ancient form of Traditional Chinese Medicine that aims to encourage the free flow of qi around the body in order to maintain or improve health. The technique engenders a deep state of relaxation and improved self-awareness, and can relieve stress and stress-related disorders, improve breathing control, and increase self-esteem. Because it is such a gentle technique, qigong can be used to maintain agility and fitness in elderly people:

ANGINA SEE P. 304
ANXIETY SEE PP. 256–7
ARTHRITIS SEE PP. 346–7
DEPRESSION SEE P. 261
HIGH BLOOD PRESSURE SEE P. 302
INFERTILITY SEE P. 324
INSOMNIA SEE P. 264
KIDNEY COMPLAINTS SEE PP. 318–19
MALE REPRODUCTIVE SYSTEM PROBLEMS SEE PP. 332–3
MENOPAUSE SYMPTOMS SEE PP. 330–1
OSTEOPOROSIS SEE P. 358
STRESS SEE PP. 262–3
STROKE SEE P. 359

T'AI CHI CH'UAN

YANG THE EVER-VICTORIOUS

In 19th-century China, it was a capital offense to steal the secrets of a martial art, as t'ai chi ch'uan then was. So when Yang Lu Chan wanted to learn t'ai chi ch'uan, he became a servant to the family of a descendant of Cheng Wang Ting, who had developed the art into its form at that time. Over the months and years, Yang became a master of the art in secret.

One day a visiting kung fu expert challenged the Chen family to combat. The head of the family was away, so his son and a disciple accepted the challenge – and both were defeated. The expert returned week in, week out, to issue his challenge and win, until the matter became an embarrassment for the family. Eventually Yang stepped forward, took up the challenge – and won. Yang threw himself at his master's feet and begged forgiveness. After much debate, this was granted.

Armed with his knowledge, Yang traveled around China issuing challenges to all its kung fu masters and was never beaten – thus "Yang the Ever-Victorious." Eventually, he settled in Beijing and taught t'ai chi ch'uan to the Imperial Army.

At one time, t'ai chi ch'uan was primarily a martial art, whose secrets were acquired by guile by "Yang the Ever-Victorious," and taught to the Chinese Imperial Army. Today it is much more a preventive health therapy than a fighting system, using exercises that incorporate Taoist philosophy to harmonize yin and yang and, at the same time, maintain health and vigor. As such, it is used on a daily basis by an estimated ten million Chinese and by an increasing number of Westerners.

For centuries, China's Taoist monks performed exercises based on Shaolin kung fu (*see pages 42–3*) to maintain health and vigor, since their religion did not differentiate between the physical and spiritual worlds. Then, in the 13th century, according to tradition, a Shaolin Taoist monk called Chang San-Feng decided to modify Shaolin to develop a type of martial art that enhanced internal power and flexibility rather than external strength. According to legend, his inspiration came when he saw a crane – a magpie or a sparrow, in some versions – fight with a snake. The graceful, elusive movements of the snake and the swooping movements of the bird reminded him of the interplay of yin and yang (*see pages 34–5*) in all things. San-Feng decided to develop a martial art that was based on this interplay, using the internal forces of yin and yang – and the basis for t'ai chi ch'uan was laid down.

Until the 17th century, t'ai chi ch'uan was only practiced in monasteries, but then a retired general, Chen Wang Ting, learned the art and taught it to his family. He refined it into a series of continuous exercises – each exercise being called a "form" and each series of exercises a "set." T'ai chi ch'uan remained a secret art, known only to selected initiates, until the 19th century. Then one Yang Lu Chan (1799–1872) acquired its secrets from one of Chen Wang Ting's descendants. Having become a famous martial arts expert, Yang further developed the t'ai chi ch'uan and taught it to the Imperial Army in Beijing, from where it spread through all China. In 1949, China's new communist regime promoted the art as a preventive health regime, rather than as a martial art – today over ten million Chinese practice the art daily.

Different Styles

Today there are various forms of t'ai chi ch'uan, taking their names from the masters who developed and taught them – the most famous styles are: Chen, Yang, Sun Wu, and Woo. The Yang style, developed from the Chen style by Yang Lu Chan in the 19th century, is the one that is known best in China and the rest

ABOVE *T'ai chi ch'uan is widely practiced in China, with people exercising before work and during their lunch hour.*

of the world. This style has almost most of the original, being primarily a martial art, and is used to promote and maintain physical and mental health, and increase vigor and longevity.

THE PHILOSOPHY

There are three main philosophical principles behind the practice of t'ai chi ch'uan: the existence of qi, the universal life force; Taoism; and the yin-yang principle. Different schools of t'ai chi ch'uan place more importance on one or other of the last two, but all stress the importance of qi (*see page 20*) as the internal power within a flexible body and calm mind.

Taoism is one of several Eastern philosophies – Buddhism is another – that holds, among other things, that the "Tao" is what enables things to "be" or to exist, and that when anything reaches an extreme state, it reverses back into what it was. The standard analogy is that when water boils, it forms steam and water vapor – which cools and then reverts to water. In t'ai chi ch'uan, this principle is interpreted as meaning that you should be aware of your physical and mental behavior, because things taken to extremes are non-productive and possibly self-defeating. A specific exercise, known as Push Hands, is often taught to t'ai chi ch'uan students to illustrate this. Two students stand still opposite each other, with the palms of their hands in contact; one student pushes his or her opponent, while the other maintains contact, but yields. If the first student continues to push, he will lose balance and fall over – to yield to aggression can be more effective than meeting force with force.

The Supreme Ultimate

One of the best-known Chinese symbols in the West is that of The Supreme Ultimate, or the yin and yang sign. This symbol was drawn by a Taoist monk, Chou Tun-yi, in the 11th century in order to demonstrate pictorially how eternity of harmony can be achieved. Yin is shown by the black side, while yang is the white side: the two dots of opposing color portray that nothing is either completely yin or completely yang – where there is yang, there will be yin and vice versa. Therefore yin and yang are two opposing yet complementary aspects of all things in the universe.

Traditionally, and at its simplest, yin is seen as feminine, dark, and passive, while yang is male, light, and active. A t'ai chi ch'uan set – a continuous series of exercises, or forms – represents an interplay between yin and yang, and its aim is to harmonize the flow of yin to yang and vice versa so that the flow of qi is unimpeded.

ORTHODOX VIEW

Western doctors accept that t'ai chi ch'uan is an effective form of physical exercise that helps relaxation and improves breathing control, and that it is suitable for people of all ages and levels of fitness. However, the philosophy of t'ai chi ch'uan with its reliance on the principles of qi, yin, and yang continues to be viewed with skepticism by the majority of them.

However, research in Atlanta, Georgia, U.S.A., between 1989 and 1996 has shown that elderly people who practice t'ai chi ch'uan enjoy a high level of fitness and well-being. The technique appeared to improve the functioning of the musculoskeletal system, lessen the incidence of osteoporosis, and improve the functioning of the cardiovascular and nervous system. Two research projects in 1984 and 1989, in Toronto, Canada, and Illinois, U.S.A., both showed that t'ai chi ch'uan improves respiratory function by slowing the rate and increasing the depth of breathing. A study in Britain in 1992 reported that t'ai chi ch'uan reduces the symptoms of stress.

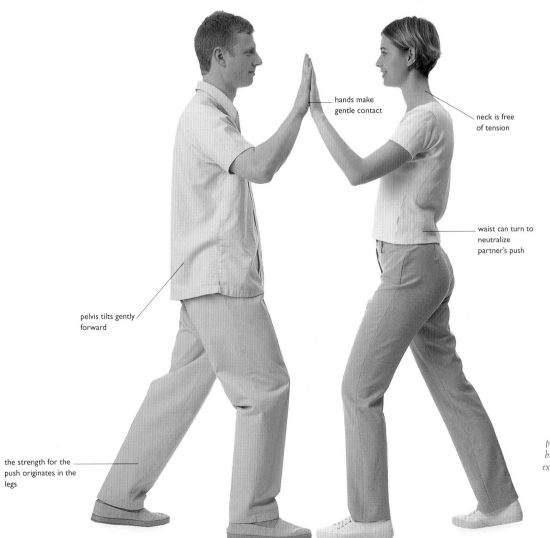

hands make gentle contact

neck is free of tension

waist can turn to neutralize partner's push

pelvis tilts gently forward

the strength for the push originates in the legs

LEFT *In t'ai chi ch'uan the principles of yin and yang are brought into harmony through exercises such as "Push Hands".*

How to perform a set of forms in t'ai chi ch'uan

T'ai chi ch'uan masters generally give advice as to how exercises should be practiced in such a way that health, vitality, and longevity can be achieved. This advice can be simplified as follows:

❧ Stand in a relaxed, upright posture with relaxed shoulders and arms, feel the weight of your body pass down through your body, legs, and feet to the ground, so that you feel balanced and stable.

❧ Start each movement at your waist, keeping it flexible, and not by using your arms or legs, though every movement, no matter how small it may be, must eventually incorporate the whole body.

❧ Become aware of which leg is bearing your body weight – many t'ai chi ch'uan exercises depend on the ability to bear the body weight on the correct leg, otherwise they feel clumsy and unbalanced. Teachers term the weight-bearing leg "solid" and the non-weight-bearing leg "apparent."

❧ The slower any movement is performed the better, since the breathing is slowed, which, in turn, allows the unimpeded flow of qi and makes it easier for the mind to be centered.

❧ One of the main aims of t'ai chi ch'uan is to store extra qi in the abdominal energy field called the dantien – a point just below the navel – until it may be needed. Abdominal breathing (*see Breathing Techniques, pages 166–71*), meditation (*see pages 60-62*) and t'ai chi ch'uan exercises produce this qi (*see Qigong, pages 44–5*), but it will be forced upward and outward if the shoulders are held high, the chest is puffed out, or if you allow your mind to wander or think negatively.

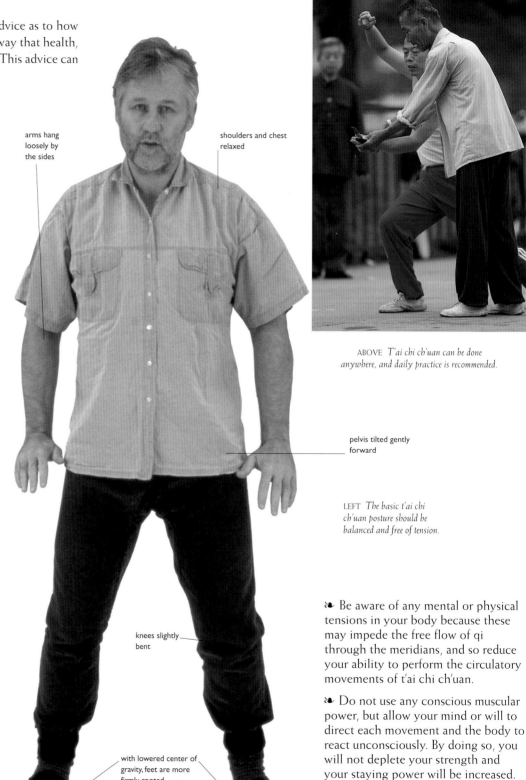

arms hang loosely by the sides

shoulders and chest relaxed

ABOVE *T'ai chi ch'uan can be done anywhere, and daily practice is recommended.*

pelvis tilted gently forward

LEFT *The basic t'ai chi ch'uan posture should be balanced and free of tension.*

knees slightly bent

with lowered center of gravity, feet are more firmly rooted

❧ Be aware of any mental or physical tensions in your body because these may impede the free flow of qi through the meridians, and so reduce your ability to perform the circulatory movements of t'ai chi ch'uan.

❧ Do not use any conscious muscular power, but allow your mind or will to direct each movement and the body to react unconsciously. By doing so, you will not deplete your strength and your staying power will be increased.

CONSULTING A PRACTITIONER

T'ai chi ch'uan associations exist in most countries, and it is sensible to consult one to ensure that you enroll with a reputable teacher. There are many different standards of teacher. Some have practiced the art for years and others have taken a few weekend courses. A good teacher will practice the art himself rather than having learned the sets in order to teach others – if your teacher does not appear fit and serene, you may not get the most out of the lessons or achieve more than a certain level of fitness. Courses are also available at numerous martial arts centers, but it is sensible to check that the one you choose does not over-emphasize the art's martial, fighting aspect if you are interested in its more philosophical, healing side.

The majority of students learn t'ai chi ch'uan in group classes and you will be advised to attend one each week until you have mastered some of the set forms and feel confident that you can practice on your own. Thereafter, practicing t'ai chi ch'uan is usually regarded as an important part of everyday life, not just something reserved for the odd occasions – in fact, t'ai chi ch'uan should be seen as a life-long commitment if you wish to reap its full benefits.

It is usual when practicing t'ai chi ch'uan to wear loose clothes and flat, thin-soled shoes – no trainers or socks. The teacher will not take any form of medical or lifestyle history, but it is important to tell him of any relevant medical problem, such as a bad back, recent operation, or high blood pressure, or if you are pregnant.

The teacher will start by explaining some of the theory behind t'ai chi ch'uan and remind the class of how to practice the art successfully to promote health and vitality. Then the class will be taken through various warm-up exercises before starting to learn a sequence of forms that makes up a set. (Beginners are usually given simple positions and movements to practice so that they become used to the feel of being centered – balanced and mentally and physically relaxed – before they start to learn a set.) The number of forms in a set varies: the Yang-style set has 48 forms, but there are shortened versions containing 24 forms. At a higher level of the art, the sequence may contain more than 100 forms. It can take up to a year to learn a short set correctly, but once learned it should take about ten minutes to perform; longer ones can last for up to 45 minutes.

At the end of a session, you will be asked to rub your hands together, shake yourself – rather in the way that a dog shakes off water – and move around energetically so that you reconnect with the outside world.

PRECAUTIONS

■ T'ai chi ch'uan is safe for people of all ages and with all levels of fitness. It is not however, a cure for any disease or disorder, but rather a method of maintaining and improving general health.

■ Consult your doctor before attending t'ai chi ch'uan classes if you suffer from any medical condition, and inform your teacher of any such condition if you attend.

■ Reports from America indicate that there can be damage to the knee joints if t'ai chi ch'uan is performed incorrectly. It is important, therefore, that you are taught by a well-qualified teacher and that you inform him or her if you have any knee problems.

■ Consult your doctor if you have any concerns about your health.

■ Your balance could be affected if you are pregnant.

PATHFINDER

T'ai chi ch'uan is a form of Traditional Chinese Medicine that is much practiced in the East and has gained in popularity in the West over the last 20 years. In the East it is practiced as a way of maintaining health and vigor and increasing the flow of healing qi throughout the body. In the West, t'ai chi ch'uan is mainly considered to be a form of exercise that improves overall fitness, reduces the symptoms of aging, reduces stress, and promotes well-being.

ANGINA SEE P. 304

ANXIETY SEE PP. 256–7

ARTHRITIS SEE PP. 346–7

ATHEROSCLEROSIS
SEE P. 305

BACK PROBLEMS
SEE PP. 344–5

BREAST PROBLEMS
SEE P. 320

DEPRESSION
SEE P. 261

HIGH BLOOD PRESSURE
SEE P. 302

HIV AND AIDS
SEE PP. 340–41

INFERTILITY SEE P. 324

INSOMNIA SEE P. 264

IRRITABLE BOWEL
SYNDROME (IBS)
SEE P. 314

KIDNEY COMPLAINTS
SEE PP. 318–19

MALE REPRODUCTIVE
SYSTEM PROBLEMS
SEE PP. 322–3

MENOPAUSE SYMPTOMS
SEE PP. 330–31

OSTEOPOROSIS
SEE P. 358

STRESS SEE PP. 262–3

STROKE SEE P. 359

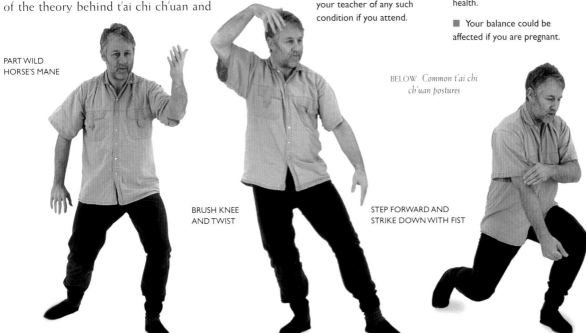

PART WILD
HORSE'S MANE

BRUSH KNEE
AND TWIST

BELOW *Common t'ai chi ch'uan postures*

STEP FORWARD AND
STRIKE DOWN WITH FIST

T'ai Chi Ch'uan at Home

It is vital that you attend classes run by a reputable, experienced teacher if you wish to learn t'ai chi ch'uan. However, the basic exercises below will give you an idea of what the art is like, and may help you get a little more out of your first few sessions. You will need to try to master each one in turn.

YIN EXERCISES: BASIC MOVEMENTS

These stances work on yin, making you rooted, calm, relaxed, earthbound, and still.

The Infinite Ultimate Stance

1 Stand with your feet a hand's length apart and pointing straight forward. Do not lock your knees back, but let them bend slightly.

2 Let your hands and arms hang by your side.

3 Relax your face and shut your eyes (keep your eyes open if you suffer from vertigo or dizziness). Empty your mind completely and focus on breathing slowly and evenly.

4 Feel the weight of your body passing equally through each foot into the ground until you feel rooted to the spot.

5 Remain in this position for three minutes to start with, building up to ten minutes with practice.

It sounds easy to master this stance, but it is not easy when done correctly: you should not be using any muscles to maintain your balance. With practice you can use it to achieve a profound sense of peace and calmness.

T'ai Chi Ch'uan Stance

1 To move from the Infinite Ultimate Stance to the T'ai Chi Ch'uan Stance, open your eyes and, without moving, transfer the whole weight of your body to your left leg.

2 Move your right leg out to the right so that the feet are nearly a shoulder's width apart. Transfer your weight from your left to your right leg.

3 Now, move your left leg into your right leg, hold for a few seconds and then take your left leg further out to the left side, so that your feet end up in a broad, comfortable stance.

4 Distribute your body weight evenly over both feet.

5 To take up the T'ai Chi Ch'uan stance, bend and turn your knees slightly in – as though you are gripping a balloon between them.

6 Raise your arms and elbows in front of you to just below elbow height and position your hands and fingers with your palms facing your chest. Position your thumbs so that the fingers and thumbs describe an incomplete circle.

7 Hold the position and relax completely, gradually shutting your eyes and emptying your mind. Maintain the stance for a few minutes (gradually build up the time you remain still, balanced, and centered over time – months rather than days – until you can retain the position for 30 minutes).

8 Reverse the order of the movements and return to the Infinite Ultimate Stance. Again, remain still for a few minutes. Open your eyes and finish the stance with the general warm-down routine as before.

With practice and tuition, some people are able to feel their internal qi as a strong force that seems to make the body shake or vibrate; this is quite a powerful feeling but only comes with time and patience. When this can be done, divert the qi to the dantien center, just below and behind the navel, where it can be stored for later use, and accessed when you are feeling low or drained and need some extra energy.

YANG EXERCISES: BASIC MOVEMENTS
Green Dragon Shoots Out Pearl

This dynamic exercise works on yang, increasing energy flow. To begin the posture, take up the T'ai Chi Ch'uan Stance, as shown left, with knees bent and turned slightly in, and arms and elbows held in front of you.

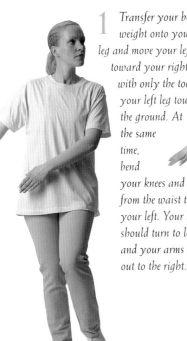

1 Transfer your body weight onto your right leg and move your left leg in toward your right leg, with only the toes of your left leg touching the ground. At the same time, bend your knees and turn from the waist toward your left. Your head should turn to look left and your arms move out to the right.

2 Maintain your body weight over your right foot and move your left foot a step forward. Bend your left leg and straighten your right leg. Transfer your body weight equally through both legs.

3 Bring your right arm forward in an anti-clockwise circle to shoulder height and thrust it forward with the palm of your hand facing forward – do not straighten your elbow completely. Move your left hand in a clockwise circle, ending near the left knee with the palm of your hand facing the ground.

Hand Movements

Various hand movements are used in t'ai chi ch'uan. When they follow on fluently, one from another, they produce circular movements. Start by standing upright with your hands resting down by your side and your body relaxed. Cup your hands slightly, then place your right hand opposite the dantien with your palm facing upward.

1 Hold your left hand at chest level with the palm facing down toward your right palm. Imagine that you are holding qi between your two palms.

2 Now move your right arm and hand forward and up with its palm turning in until it is opposite your face, while your left hand moves across to face your right elbow.

4 Bring your hands together in front of you at chest level with the palms facing, then press your left wrist with your right palm in order to gather qi within your hands.

3 Continue by moving both hands down to your left side at waist level, with your right hand above the left and facing up while the left palm faces down.

5 Turn both palms out and up and push the fingers forward as though moving an invisible object – do not allow the elbows to straighten. Return to the starting position.

YOGA

YOGA

Yoga means to "yoke together or to join," and is understood by many people as union with the Divine. Yogis have refined yogic practice through many centuries of devoted effort, their aim being nothing less than a return to the state of grace which most Eastern religions imply that we once enjoyed with God or some kind of heaven world.

Westerners think of yoga as being something only for the body, which is by far the most popular form practiced by them, although actually it is also a more general term comprising a number of different methods involving the mind, emotions, and body which can contribute to the health of a human being. They include various spiritual and intellectual practices which are as analytical as the system primarily for the body called "hatha" yoga. In its most complete form, yoga is a fully integrated system comprising these many different methods and governing all aspects of life.

*A*s it is practiced in the West, yoga is usually thought of as a system of exercises and breathing techniques, sometimes allied to meditation. For Westerners, it is not so much a form of therapy as a means of achieving a sense of physical and mental well-being. Nevertheless, there is a mass of evidence to show that yoga can have a beneficial effect on a variety of conditions – for example, high blood pressure – and specific exercises are becoming increasingly popular in the treatment of a number of different diseases.

Yoga originated in India 5,000 or more years ago, and played an integral part in the growth of Hinduism, Buddhism, and Indian civilization as a whole. Yogic practices are described in the sacred Hindu texts, from the *Vedas* of 1500 B.C.E. to the *Bhaghavadgita* or "Lord's Song" – the most famous work of Hindu literature.

The form of yoga most widely practiced in the West is based on the principles of "hatha" yoga, which were first elaborated by the Hindu sage Patanjali in the *Yoga Sutras* around 2000 years ago. It is from this work that the familiar yogic postures ("asana") and breathing exercises ("pranayama") are derived.

Yoga was introduced to the West in the 19th century, when translations of Hindu texts began to appear, but it excited little interest. It was not until the second half of the 20th century, when interest in Eastern philosophy and alternative methods of healing began its explosive growth, that yoga began to attract attention. Today, its popularity in the West is assured – there are thought to be more teachers of yoga in the U.S.A. and the U.K. than there are in the whole of India, and millions of people have practiced yoga at one level or another.

THE TEACHINGS OF YOGA

Yoga is both a philosophy and a methodology of life. It is not a religion, although its close association with Hinduism and Buddhism has led some to believe that it is. The word "yoga" is derived from the Sanskrit for "union" or "oneness", and all forms of yoga have as their aim the realization of "oneness" with the universe as a whole. "Oneness" can only be achieved through meditation and by following certain moral codes that govern the ways in which people act and lead their lives.

An important aspect of yoga is the belief in "prana". This is the universal energy that gives structure and form to matter, life, and spirit. We participate in the flow of "prana" when we breathe – which is why correct breathing is an important part of yoga – and the flow of "prana" within the body is fundamental to inner harmony and health. The exercises of yoga are all designed to direct the flow of "prana" and to release the body's internal energy to create spiritual awareness.

ABOVE *Yoga is a complete discipline for mind, body, and spirit, and has its roots in an ancient, sacred Hindu past.*

Yoga is thus a form of preparation of the mind, body, and spirit, which must be unified through conduct, right-thinking, and meditation, before the ultimate merging of the self with the universe, or the totality of all that is – the equivalent of God or the Hindu goal of "nirvana." In this wider context, the postural and breathing exercises of "hatha" yoga are simply a means of promoting meditation and internal balance, through which the final goal of "oneness" can be achieved. "Hatha" yoga is a yogic system in its own right, although in the West emphasis is generally placed on its exercises (*see overleaf*).

History of Yoga

The first treatise on "hatha" yoga – "The Eight Limbs of Yoga" – was written by Patanjali, who described the spiritual stages yogis pass through on the way to "enlightenment" or "nirvana." It outlines a system of guidelines comprising healthy eating habits and high standards of internal hygiene, and progresses through physical postures, breathing techniques, and meditation until one comes to what is considered the supreme level of pure consciousness. The serious yogi strives for the highest ethical, mental and physical standards possible. By this, he calms and masters both body and mind.

It is said that the main goal of yoga is to achieve a state in which one is the best, most sane, and most mature human being that it is possible to be.

THE PATHS OF YOGA

There are many different forms of yoga, known as "paths" – each with its own methodology and emphasis. However, in practice, the different forms merge together, one leading to or complementing another, and it is rare for serious students of yoga to find themselves restricted to a single path. The main traditional paths of yoga, besides "hatha" yoga, are: "ashtanga" yoga, "raja" yoga, "jnana" yoga, "karma" yoga, "bhakti" yoga, "tantra" yoga, "kundalini" yoga, and "mantra" yoga.

"**Ashtanga**" **yoga** is the system set out in the *Yoga Sutras* by Patanjali, and can be regarded as the wellspring from which all other forms of yoga have drawn over the centuries. "Ashtanga" means "eight limbs", and Patanjali describes an eightfold path which leads to transcendence, freedom, and "oneness".

The first two limbs prepare the trainee mentally and emotionally for the rigors that lie ahead. They are "yama," demanding honesty, compassion, non-violence, moderation, and cleanliness in everyday life, and "niyama," requiring purity, contentment, self-knowledge, and surrender and commitment to the path of yoga.

The next three limbs are primarily devoted to the physical aspects of yoga: "asana," or postural exercise; "pranayama," or the use of breathing to control the flow of the life force or "prana", through the body; and "praty hara," the internalization of awareness by deep relaxation and the reduction of sensory awareness.

The final three limbs are concerned with different levels of meditation, which culminates in the merging of the self with the universe as a whole, and the attainment of the "oneness" that is the ultimate goal of all yogic practice.

"**Raja**" **yoga,** or the Royal yoga, is based on meditation. It is the yoga of the mind, employing the energy of consciousness and thought to allow the mind to achieve mastery over concerns, fears and desires. "Raja" yoga derives from the final stage of "ashtanga" yoga, and "hatha" yoga is an essential preliminary to it.

"**Jnana**" **yoga**, or the yoga of wisdom, is meditative and contemplative. It harnesses

ABOVE Yogic exercise emphasizes the holding of postures, known as asanas.

the power of the mind to probe the most profound questions of existence – what is reality? what is life? what is truth? – leading to a deep intuitive understanding of what is real and what unreal, and what is permanent and what transient.

"**Karma**" **yoga** is the yoga of everyday life. Karma is often thought of as destiny, but in fact it concerns our actions and reactions as we go through life. Any action taken for selfish reasons creates karma and binds us to the "wheel of life" or "samsara" – the eternal cycle of birth, life, and death. "Karma" yoga, through "asana" and "pranayama," and meditation, teaches us to act selflessly and with concern only for the merits of the act itself in the service of others or of God. We are then freed from karma and have broken the bonds of "samsara" to attain "nirvana."

"**Bhakti**" **yoga** is the yoga of devotion and love, in which emotion is channeled into the worship of the divine. As in other forms of yoga, the object is "oneness," but meditation is essentially religious.

"**Tantra**" **yoga** is a means of transforming the energy of physical action and the energy of desire into a state of spiritual ecstasy. One often misunderstood aspect of "tantric" yoga involves ritualized sexual activity as a means of heightening awareness. More important are "asanas" and "pranayama," particularly when used to arouse the powerful force known as "kundalini" (*see below*).

"**Kundalini**" **yoga** is a form of "hatha" yoga in which the "kundalini," or "coiled serpent," at the base of the spine is awakened. This is a powerful force, associated with sexual desire, which moves up the spine, stimulating the various energy centers, or "chakras" (*see pages 78–85*), until it reaches the crown "chakra," leading to the experience of transcendence and bliss.

"**Mantra**" **yoga** involves the use of repeated phrases, or "mantras," as an aid to concentration and meditation. "Mantras" have always been part of yogic practice, but they have become prominent because of the popularity of Transcendental Meditation (*see pages 60–63*).

ABOVE Yogic meditation can be deeply empowering and transformational.

PRECAUTIONS

Almost anyone can benefit from yoga, including the elderly, children, pregnant women, and those with chronic health problems. However, you should not attempt yoga postures without consulting your doctor and without instruction from a trained teacher if you have any of the following conditions:

■ Heart or circulatory problems

■ Neck or spinal problems

■ Ear or eye problems

■ Multiple sclerosis

■ Chronic Fatigue Syndrome (or ME)

■ Broken or fractured bones

■ Recent injury or surgery

■ Pregnancy

■ Be wary of following a practice that does not seem to agree with your mind or body. Signs of this include mental and material instability or obsessional conditions. Find a good teacher who helps you to overcome such states or at least to understand them.

■ After you eat a meal, allow three hours to pass before you practice yoga.

■ Certain movements should not be performed by people with health problems. Ask for the advice of a qualified yoga instructor if you have heart disease; high blood pressure; an injury involving your neck or back; or problems with your brain, circulation, ears, or eyes. Headstands and some other "asanas" are generally not advised for people with such problems.

■ Do not practice the Headstand if you are pregnant or menstruating.

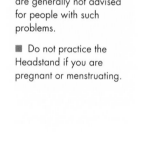

ABOVE *The correct breathing technique is fundamental to yogic practice.*

YOGA POSTURES

The popularity of yoga in the West is undoubtedly due to the fact that it works. When practiced regularly, it tones muscles and improves posture, movement, and balance. It can help to reduce blood pressure and improve the efficiency of the lungs. Many of the postures also affect the internal organs so that the digestive system, liver, and pancreas may function better.

Advanced practitioners of yoga are able to perform astonishing feats. Some have demonstrated the ability to reduce their heart rates to very low levels, or even to stop the heart altogether; they are able to control the temperature of different parts of the body independently of each other; and they are capable of extraordinary muscular strength. However, this degree of control takes many years of practice for several hours a day, and few Western devotees of yoga have either the time or the patience for it. Most are content to enjoy the general improvement in fitness and well-being yoga brings.

Meditation is seldom an explicit part of Western yoga teaching, but it has considerable benefits. Concentration and mental clarity are enhanced and stress and anxiety reduced. People feel calmer and more relaxed, but at the same time more mentally alert and alive. Physical and emotional well-being go hand-in-hand.

SELF-HELP

Yoga is an excellent form of self-help therapy, although you would be well-advised to begin by attending a course of classes run by a qualified teacher. It is important that you learn the basic principles of both "asana" and "pranayama" – posture and breathing – if you are to derive full benefit from the exercise; generally, these are based on the principles of "hatha" yoga. A good teacher can also detect imbalances of posture of which you may be unaware, and recommend the best postures for you to practice.

THE ASANAS

There are hundreds of different postures in yoga. Here are some illustrated examples, including a sequence called "Surya Namatura," "Salutation to the Sun" (*see opposite*).

YOGA AT HOME

Little or nothing is needed by way of equipment, and yoga can be effective whether a session lasts for as little as 10 or 15 minutes – although the benefits are correspondingly greater the longer you can manage. Daily

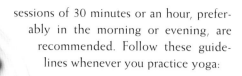

ABOVE *Pure, fresh, and natural foods help maintain energy and clarity of thought.*

sessions of 30 minutes or an hour, preferably in the morning or evening, are recommended. Follow these guidelines whenever you practice yoga:

✳ If you are at home, choose a quiet, warm, and uncluttered room – the fewer distractions there are, the better. Avoid thick pile carpets, because they make it difficult to balance, but thin pile carpets and bare wooden floors are both suitable. Special, thin non-slip mats can be bought and are ideal. The room should have a long mirror, so that you can check that you are correctly balanced. You will also need a blanket, sweater, and socks for relaxation, and some postures require a chair, a scarf, or a small cushion.

✳ Do not take a bath or shower for at least a half hour before or after practice.

✳ Wear comfortable clothing that gives you maximum freedom of movement (for example a leotard). Always perform yoga in bare feet.

✳ You may find it useful to do some simple stretching exercises to warm up before a session, particularly if you are new to yoga.

✳ Always remember that yoga is not a series of challenges. Habitual imbalances take time to overcome, and some postures may prove very difficult. Do not strain to achieve them or you may damage your muscles or joints and thus miss the point of yoga.

✳ You should be aware of your whole body while practicing. Yoga concerns harmony and balance, so note what a particular posture is doing to the different parts of the body, and how each part contributes to the holding of the pose.

✳ Balance should also be evident in the sequence of postures you adopt. Always follow a posture that stretches a particular group of muscles with one that relaxes them, and one that stretches one side of the body with one that stretches the other side.

✳ Breathing, or "pranayama," is an important aspect of "asana." Learn to breathe deeply and evenly throughout the practice session.

✳ You may experience some aches and pains after a session, as unfamiliar muscles are utilized, but these should not be severe, and should reduce in intensity. Always end a practice session with the Relaxation Pose.

SALUTATION TO THE SUN

Ritual salutations to the rising Sun, the source of all energy for life, are found in many religious and pagan societies. However, there is nothing mystical about this particular sequence of postures. While it does not approach the rigor of normal yoga, in which the individual postures are held for much longer, it does provide a refreshing way to start the day. But be careful not to overstretch. The practitioner here is young, flexible, and experienced at yoga. You should not try this if you have lower back problems. And you should stop immediately if you experience pain or discomfort.

12 Exhale as you return to an upright stance with your hands at your chest in the Prayer Position and feet together. Inhale and relax before you repeat the exercise – with the left leg from Step 4. It is important to exercise both sides of the body in order to improve its balance.

1 Start with the back straight and hands in the Prayer Position in front of the chest. Stand squarely upon the soles of the feet, which are placed together so that you feel relaxed and upright.

11 Inhale as you stretch forward and up, stretching your arms up over your head as you straighten your body and bend backward.

2 Inhale as you stretch your arms above your head and lean backward as far as you comfortably can.

3 Exhale as you return to an upright stance and bend forward, keeping your knees as straight as you can until you can place your hands flat on the floor beside your feet.

10 Exhaling, bring the left foot to rest beside the right, with palms still flat upon the floor. Straighten your legs as much as possible.

4 Inhale, without moving your palms from their position, and stretch the right leg behind you, resting upon the floor the right knee and the top of the right foot. Look upward as you relax into the pose.

9 Inhale as you place your right foot between your hands and drop your left knee to the floor.

5 Hold your breath as you bring your left leg back beside your right leg - feet together and on your toes - raising your right knee from the floor so that both legs and arms are straight and in a "push-up" position.

8 Exhale as you lift your hips as high as you can without moving your hands as you form a triangle shape with your body and place your heels upon the floor. Keep your head facing the floor between straight arms. Keep your back and legs straight.

7 Drop your hips to the floor, placing your palms flat on the ground and beneath your shoulders, bringing together straight legs and feet whose tops rest upon the floor. As you breathe in, stretch backwards, arching your back and opening your chest.

6 As you exhale, place your knees upon the floor and slide your body backward so that you almost sit upon your toes, then slide forward until your chest and forehead touch the floor.

THE STANDING POSTURES

The standing postures are an essential foundation for the practice of yoga. They create balance, suppleness, and strength from the feet to the neck and shoulders. The more complex twisting and bending postures will put unwarranted strain on the muscles and joints, so do these first, coordinating your breathing with the movements.

Mountain Pose (Tadasana)

This is the first posture you should learn, and it is far from being as easy as it looks. It involves some of the most basic aspects of asanas.

- *Stand with your legs together, with ankles and feet touching. Your weight should be evenly distributed between your feet, and also across the sole of each foot.*
- *The legs should be straight. This means raising the kneecaps with the front thigh muscles. In this position, the weight of your body is transmitted directly from the pelvis to the feet.*
- *The pelvis and shoulders should be level, not tilted to one side (use a mirror to check). The eyes should be kept level, with head and neck forming a natural extension of the spine.*
- *The chest should be opened by gently raising the ribcage and abdomen. Shoulders should be drawn back and relaxed so that they do not slump, but are not held in an unnatural "military" position.*
- *Stand like this for a while, with your eyes closed if it helps, and sense what is happening in each part of your body. This is also a good time to practice correct breathing (see pages 58–9).*

Side Warrior Pose (preparation for Virabhadrasana)

Stand in the Triangle Pose with arms outstretched at shoulder level. Feet and toes face forward. Turn your left foot sideways so that the toes point left, but keep your body facing forward. Exhale as you bend your left knee so that it is above your left heel. Turn your head to look toward the fingers of your left hand. Notice your breathing while holding the position for ten seconds. Return to your original starting position upon an inhalation. Then repeat, turning your right foot toward the right.

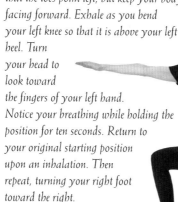

Head to Knee Pose (Uttanasana)

While breathing out, bend from the waist, keeping your legs straight, until your fingers touch the floor. Move your hands back to hold your ankles, straightening the arms, and look straight ahead. Finally, still holding your ankles, bring your elbows behind your knees and continue to bend from the waist until your chest and stomach touch your thighs. Hold for ten seconds. Avoid this pose if you suffer from lower back problems.

Triangle Pose (Trikonasana)

Stand upright with your feet one leg-length apart. Turn your right leg, foot, and toes to the right. Make sure that your weight is evenly distributed upon the center of the soles of your feet. Stretch the muscles running through your ankles and knees. Lift your torso up from your hips. Inhale and extend your arms sideways at shoulder level. Exhale as you lower your right hand down your right leg and stretch your left arm upward. Turn your head to look at your left hand. Continue lengthening the spine and arms as you stretch, and opening the hips which face forward. Breathe as you hold this position for ten seconds, then repeat on your left side.

Folded Triangle Pose (Padottanasana)

Stand as in the Triangle Pose with your feet facing forward and parallel, hands on hips. Lengthen your legs and torso. Inhale and lift your body from your hips. Exhale, bend forward from the hips, keeping them centered between your feet, and stretch your hands forward and down to the ground below the shoulders, keeping your back straight and opening your chest. Inhale.

Upon exhaling, align your hands with your feet and move your head down toward the ground as you continue extending the spine. Breathe while holding this position for ten seconds. Inhale and return to the starting position. Avoid this pose if you suffer from lower back problems.

FLOOR POSTURES

The floor postures are especially effective for toning the abdominal muscles, and for improving the efficiency of the digestive system, liver, and kidneys. They can be practiced on their own, or used to provide relaxation from the more strenuous standing poses, but the standing poses must be practiced regularly as well.

Forward Bend (Paschimottanasana)

Sit on the floor in the Staff Pose, legs straight in front of you, feet together, back straight. Inhale as you lean back slightly, raising your arms perpendicular to the legs. Then lean forward and reach toward your toes, touching your feet if possible. Breathing in and out, gently lower your head and chest until they rest comfortably near or upon your legs. Relax your head, neck and shoulders. Hold the pose for ten seconds, then return to a sitting (or lying) position.

[Beginning] Staff Pose (Dandasana)

Sit on the floor with your legs extended in front of you, hands by the hips, your fingers pointing forward. Lengthen your torso, keeping it at a 90° angle to your legs. Relax your shoulders, lengthen your spine, press your heels outward and your hips downward. Stretch upward, opening your chest, as you imagine lengthening your spine through the crown of your head. Breathe while holding the position for ten seconds.

Spinal Twist (Bharadvajasana)

Sit straight with your legs apart. Bend the left leg and place the foot close to the groin. Lift the right leg and place the right foot outside the left knee. Place the left arm along the outside of the right leg and hold the foot. Move the right arm toward the back, easing the right shoulder backward as you do so. Inhale as you lengthen the spine. Exhale and turn the head and trunk toward the right. Hold the position for ten seconds while breathing slowly and effortlessly. Release the foot and relax into a normal sitting position upon an inhalation. Repeat on the opposite side.

[Beginning] Cat Pose (Adho Mukha Svanasana)

Get down on all fours with knees a shoulder-width apart and hands positioned beneath shoulders. Breathe out. Breathing in, lower your back and raise your head. Hold the position for a few seconds. Breathing out, arch your back as high as you can while dropping your head between your arms. Hold the position for a few seconds. Repeat 10 to 20 times, then sit back on your heels, arms by your side. Lower your head until your forehead touches the mat. Relax, breathing gently, for two or three minutes, before getting up slowly.

[Deep] Relaxation Pose (Savasana)

Lie on your back in a straight line with your neck straight, legs slightly apart and arms resting a little way from your body, palms facing upwards. Imagine that you are sinking through the floor, starting with the toes and working your way up the body until every part of it is relaxed, particularly the legs, arms, torso, hips, lower back, ribs, shoulders and face. When comfortable, become aware of your breath. Slow your breathing, relaxing more with each exhalation. After you reach total relaxation, imagine air moving into your extremities and then into the rest of the body, gradually speeding your breathing rhythm. Wriggle your toes, yawn and begin to stretch your limbs and torso. Turn to your side and slowly lift yourself up with your arm, then sit for a while breathing normally before slowly rising.

RELAXATION

Always end a session of asanas with a short period of relaxation. This is both an essential preliminary to "pranayama" and meditation and a valuable way of releasing tension in both body and mind. Relaxation can be practiced on its own as a way of reducing stress.

It is important to keep warm while relaxing, so put on socks and a sweatshirt, or cover yourself with a light blanket.

Lie in the relaxation pose (Savasana), and follow the instructions given on pages 58–9. Concentrate on tensing and then relaxing the muscles in each part of the body in turn. You should be aware of a feeling of lightness as the tension drains gently away. Examine your body for any areas where tension still remains and concentrate on the area until you can feel the tension seeping away.

When you are completely relaxed, continue to lie in the relaxation pose, for 5–10 minutes, or until your breathing and heartbeat are calm, smooth and regular. You should feel physically and mentally refreshed and your mind should be clear and alert.

SITTING POSTURES

The sitting poses are intended to harmonize and stabilize body and mind, allowing the mind to concentrate on "pranayama" (breathing) and meditation. For the true student of yoga, these represent the true essence of yogic practice, for which the "asanas" are only a preparation. Even those for whom yoga is primarily an exercise regime have reported great benefits from periods of "pranayama" and meditation, including greater clarity of thought and understanding, feelings of calm self-confidence, and freedom from negative or confusing thoughts and emotions.

There are many sitting poses, of which the best known is the Lotus position "Padmasana." However, this can cause excessive strain to untrained limbs, and it may take some time before the beginner is able to achieve it with comfort. If you find the Lotus position difficult to begin with, you should try a less strenuous pose, such as the Easy Pose "Sukashana," or you can even simply sit on a firm chair with your back straight and chest open with your hands on your knees or in your lap.

LOTUS POSITION *"PADMASANA"*

This is the classic position for "pranayama" posture and meditation in yoga. If you can't manage the full Lotus Position, don't worry. Above all, do not force your legs into position if it causes pain and discomfort.

1 *Sit on the floor as for the Easy Posture (see above right), with your legs stretched out in front of you. Gently lift your left foot, and place it on top of your right thigh, with the sole pointing upward.*

2 *Bend your right knee and bring your right foot to the left knee.*

3 *Finally, lift your right foot onto your left thigh, as high up and close to the groin as possible. Straighten the spine and place your hands, palms up, on each knee. Join the index fingers with the thumbs. Relax and breathe. You may wish to close your eyes.*

Two other techniques are also often used while in the sitting positions. One is "mula bandha," which involves simultaneously contracting the muscles that control the pelvic floor and lower abdomen. This retains the energy of "prana" within the body and helps the conversion of physical and sexual energy into spiritual energy. It also stabilizes and protects the muscles and organs in the abdomen, and is often recommended for use with "asanas" as well. The other technique involves "mudras," or gestures, such as the joining together of thumb-tip and the tip of the forefinger. These have specific purposes and have traditionally been given to students by their gurus after they have gained control of their breath and purified their systems.

EASY POSTURE (*"SUKHASANA"*)

Sit on the floor with your legs extended forward. Tuck your left foot under your right thigh, and place your right foot under your left shin. Keep your spine straight, your chest open, and your shoulders and pelvis level.

rest hands on knees

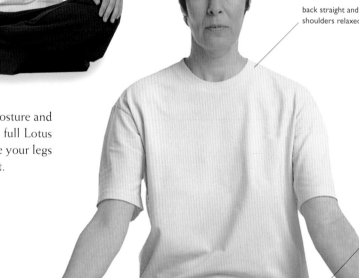

back straight and shoulders relaxed

foot rests on thigh

BREATHING

Just as anyone can benefit from the suppleness, balance, and control that "asanas" give, so too can they benefit from improvement of breathing through "pranayama." Although it is a "limb" of "hatha" yoga in its own right, "pranayama" is also an integral part of "asana," relaxation and meditation.

Each time we inhale, we breathe in "prana." The more deeply we inhale, the more "prana" we can absorb. We also take in more oxygen, and expel more carbon dioxide when we exhale. When we breathe shallowly or irregularly, we use only the upper part of the lungs and severely limit the amount of "prana" and oxygen we take in. The purpose of yogic breathing is, therefore, to use the lungs as near as possible to their full capacity, employing all respiratory muscles – abdominal, diaphragmatic, upper and lower ribcage – to best effect. This is achieved through conscious awareness and control of every phase of breathing.

"Pranayama" should, ideally, be practiced in one of the sitting positions, although the techniques can be practiced lying flat on your back on the floor; however,

ABOVE *Breathing exercises, or pranayama, harmonize the flow of prana within the body.*

in some medical conditions, including late-stage pregnancy, this is ill-advised. Read and follow the instructions for inhaling and exhaling given elsewhere in this book (*see Breathing Techniques, pages 166–71*). Concentrate your mind on the way that the parts of the respiratory system are working together. It may help to visualize the air entering your lungs – filling them from bottom to top – and emptying from top to bottom.

Keep the muscles of the abdomen taut and feel the movement of the diaphragm against them. Examine the movements of the ribcage, starting at the top and working down to the lowest, floating, ribs.

Do these breathing exercises at the end of any yoga session, for 10 to 15 minutes or until your breathing is deep, measured, regular, and smooth.

Once you have mastered the basic breathing techniques, you can count breaths rather than seconds whenever you do "asanas". You can also move on to more advanced techniques, such as alternative nostril breathing (*see pages 170–71*), or retention, in which the breath is held, to allow greater absorption of "prana".

MEDITATION

Meditation is the culmination of the practice of yoga. The final three "limbs" of the "eightfold path" of "ashtanga" yoga are devoted to it.

The first of these is "dharana," in which the mind is focused deeply on a single thought or object, leading to the control and elimination of extraneous thoughts. This leads directly into "dhayana," or absorption, in which the object of concentration becomes a conduit through which the energy of the body can merge with the energy of the mind. Perception of one's surroundings – of the here and now – is acute, and personal concerns for the past and future fade away. "Dhayana" is accompanied by a feeling of peace and well-being.

In the final stage of meditation, "samadhi", the distinction between the self and the object of attention, and between the object of attention and the surroundings, disappears, and is replaced by a sense of true reality and an awareness of the essence of all things. The self is not deposed but transcended, so that one feels one with "all that is".

The basic techniques of meditation are the same as those used in other forms of meditation (*see pages 60-63*). However, the combination of meditation with "asanas" and "pranayama" makes yogic meditation a uniquely powerful and rewarding experience. Even if your main interest is in the physical aspects of yoga, it is well worth devoting some time to meditation in order to appreciate the value of a very ancient tradition.

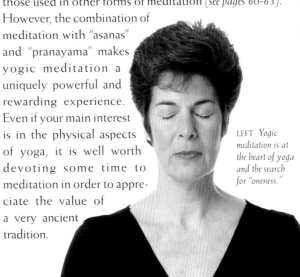

LEFT *Yogic meditation is at the heart of yoga and the search for "oneness."*

PATHFINDER

In addition to its benefits for general physical and mental well-being, yoga may help in the treatment of a variety of emotional and physical disorders. These include:

ADDICTIONS SEE P. 258

ANEMIA SEE P. 303

ANGINA SEE P. 304

ANXIETY SEE PP. 256-7

ARTHRITIS SEE PP. 346-7

ASTHMA SEE PP. 294-5

ATHEROSCLEROSIS SEE P. 305

BACK PROBLEMS SEE PP. 344-5

COMMON COLD SEE P. 300

CYSTITIS SEE P. 316

DEPRESSION SEE P. 261

DIABETES SEE PP. 336-7

DIARRHEA SEE P. 312

FAINTING SEE P. 270

FIBROSITIS SEE P. 348

GASTROENTERITIS SEE P. 309

HEADACHE SEE PP. 268-9

HIGH BLOOD PRESSURE SEE P. 302

INDIGESTION SEE P. 310

INFERTILITY SEE P. 324

INSOMNIA SEE P. 264

IRRITABLE BOWEL SYNDROME (IBS) SEE P. 314

MALE REPRODUCTIVE PROBLEMS SEE PP. 332-3

MENSTRUAL PROBLEMS SEE PP. 322-3

NEURALGIA SEE P. 267

OBESITY SEE PP. 334-5

OBSESSIONS SEE P. 259

OSTEOPOROSIS SEE P. 358

PALPITATIONS SEE P. 307

PREGNANCY PROBLEMS SEE P. 326-7

STRESS SEE PP. 262-3

VARICOSE VEINS SEE P. 306

MEDITATION

ORTHODOX VIEW

Doctors generally agree that meditation is an effective way of reducing stress and stress-related illnesses. It has been shown that people who meditate regularly make fewer visits to the doctor and require hospital treatment less often. Some doctors now recommend meditation and relaxation to their patients as part of a general lifestyle approach to health.

Few doctors would dispute the physiological effects of meditation, and the sometimes astonishing physiological self-control of which advanced practitioners are capable. There has been some interest in the use of meditation, combined with biofeedback or autogenic training, in the control of high blood pressure and the management of other forms of heart disease. Practitioners sometimes claim that meditation helps to reverse and even eliminate diseases, but mainstream medical doctors in the West have yet to accept this as possible. However, traditional medical practitioners in the East often require it as part of a patient's therapy or healing treatment.

Widely used in the West in a non-religious context in order to treat stress-related conditions, meditation is considered a form of mental therapy by many people and a means of calming the mind by others. The idea is to reverse our everyday habit of allowing ourselves to be controlled by our thoughts and emotions. Long used by religious and spiritual practitioners in the East as the method by which they achieve "enlightenment" or "nirvana," interest in meditation has grown with the spread of Eastern religions. However, it has also been identified in Western religions as a form of contemplation.

There are good reasons, both spiritual and physical, for the almost universal practice of meditation throughout history and in all the world's main cultures and religions. It is through meditation that we can experience the "wholeness" that the Swiss psychologist, Carl Jung, claimed was the driving force behind human needs and desires (*see pages 192–5*).

The effects of meditation on such physiological processes as heartrate, blood pressure, hormone secretion, brain waves, and breathing have been extensively studied and demonstrated. For instance, more alpha waves are produced by the brain during meditation. Alpha waves encourage the parasympathetic section of the autonomic nervous system to predominate and are associated with quiet, receptive states. They switch off the "fight-or-flight" response produced in times of perceived or actual stress.

Meditation appears simple. It requires no special equipment and can be practiced at any time and in almost any circumstances. However, it is not easy. Most of us are unused to deliberately clearing the mind of thought and sensation. Because of this, as with most healing therapies, there is no real substitute for initial training with an experienced teacher.

WHAT IS MEDITATION?

There are many different forms. In the hands of an experienced practitioner of yoga (*see pages 52–9*), ayurveda (*see pages 78–85*) or t'ai chi (*see pages 44–9*), for example, it is a rigorous discipline aimed at the achievement of "oneness" with the universal energy that underlies creation. It allows us to release our own physical and sexual drives as spiritual energy. The altered state of consciousness that meditation brings – neither dreaming nor waking – is an end in itself and is the source of a greater awareness that permeates all other aspects of life.

In other, more therapeutically oriented, traditions, meditation is used in a directed and purposeful way. In hypnotherapy (*see pages 218–22*), for example, meditation techniques are used to induce a trance-like condition – basically identical to a state of deep meditation – so that the mind becomes receptive to suggestions and affirmations that will have a beneficial effect on attitudes and behavior. Visualization (*see pages 214–17*) has similar aims, using the mind's power of imagery. In color therapy (*see pages 248–51*), meditation is harnessed to the therapeutic power of color and its effects on the body's aura. Autogenic training (*see pages 210–11*) and biofeedback (*see pages 212–13*) both use the techniques of meditation to gain awareness of, and control over, the body's physiological processes. Meditation is also an important aspect of flotation therapy (*see pages 180–81*) and other forms of deep relaxation (*see pages 158–65*). There are also walking meditative practices and other activities involving rhythmic movement that can help to focus the mind.

Although different techniques are taught in different schools, they all have in common the intense focusing of the mind on a single thought until heightened awareness, clearer perception, and a sense of being "open" are experienced.

It is difficult to define the difference between meditation, concentration, and contemplation, because the term "meditation" is often used for all three. In general, it may be defined as an activity that removes the mind from external stimuli so that it reaches a state of quiet, relaxed alertness or awareness. If thinking exists in meditation, it is non-conjectural. Thoughts which arise "dissolve" without conceptual elaboration – that is, one simply sees a carrot without considering what it is, how it tastes, or what it does or does not do.

Some people consider the true meditative state to be a place where a kind of intuition exists that is inextricable from a universal awareness of which everyone and everything is a part. It has been described as being "perception" itself, or beyond personal desire where a kind of maturity and selfless love is possible that may or may not be experienced. However it is described, it is generally thought to be a condition from which actions arise that are in harmony with the universe.

Whole systems of spiritual training within complex and diverse religions like Hinduism and Buddhism have been built upon techniques of meditation. In fact, meditation covers a multitude of different practices.

CONSULTING A PRACTITIONER

There are many books, videos, and tapes that will help you learn to meditate. However, initial training with an experienced teacher remains the best way to begin. Classes are widely available and tuition may be on a group basis or one-to-one. Techniques vary widely, according to the tradition from which they are drawn, so choose a type of meditation that you feel comfortable with. If you do not like simply sitting passively on the floor, you might prefer to try meditation through t'ai chi, or some kinds of yoga. If you find that sound is more helpful than objects or images, then you would probably prefer mantra meditation. Your teacher will help you to choose an appropriate mantra to repeat.

Sessions usually last for 15 to 20 minutes, and should continue until you feel comfortable and confident about meditating alone. Ideally, you should practice on your own for at least 15 to 20 minutes every day as well as in group classes.

The best meditation teachers stress that if your mind is agitated or disturbed, then you are not meditating properly. You are meant to "drop thoughts" and allow the mind to return to its natural state of calm. Although there are many different methods used to reach or create this condition, good teachers do not encourage obsessional states and sometimes actively discourage them.

ABOVE *Meditation can give you "time off" from the pressures and stresses of everyday life.*

FOCUSING THE MIND

All techniques of meditation involve directing the mind to some single focus of attention. The nature of the focus – or "seed" – varies from one school of meditation to another. The following are common practices.

Breathing

Steady, calm, and regular breathing is not only important as a way of relaxing before and during meditation (*see pp. 166–71*), but is often recommended as an ideal focus of attention. The basic technique is described on the next page. Those who have good visual imaginations may find that color breathing (*see p. 250*) works well.

ABOVE *Focus on simple shapes such as the sacred mandala, symbol of the universe.*

Sound

Many Eastern forms of meditation rely on the use of a mantra – a sound or phrase repeated over and over again, either out loud or silently to oneself. Mantras are usually derived from Sanskrit or Tibetan. The most famous, the word *om*, is said to be the sound of the universe, and the phrase *om mani padme hum*, known as the mani or great mantra, is translated as "*om* to the thought in the lotus." Both the sound of the mantra and its meaning matter. It is best to have the help of a teacher when selecting a mantra, and once you have chosen one, you should stick with it. Sometimes accompanied by a mala, a string of 108 beads that are counted with each repetition, in much the same way as a Catholic rosary, mantras are central to the practice of Transcendental Meditation (*see overleaf*).

Objects

Traditionally, objects like a flower, a bowl of water, or a candle flame are used to focus the attention. However, almost anything will do – for example – a pebble, a patch on the wall, or an item of religious significance such as a crucifix.

Pictures and patterns

Simple geometric shapes and patterns can assume great symbolic significance during meditation. Mandalas and "yantras," derived from Buddhist and other Eastern tradition, are examples, and they are often used to focus the mind. The most famous of the "yantras" is the "sri yantra," or "wheel of sri," whose components are rich in symbolic meaning. Again, the important thing is to experience the picture yourself, rather than dwelling on the interpretation to be placed on it.

Images

People with a good visual imagination often find that an internal image works better than an external object. You simply visualize a scene in your mind and allow yourself to experience it in all its aspects. Visualization is, in fact, recognized as a valuable therapeutic technique in its own right (*see pp. 214–15*).

Koans

These are puzzles set by masters of Zen Buddhism for their pupils. They are not puzzles in any ordinary sense; rather they are questions that are not susceptible to logical thought and must be resolved through feeling and intuition. Examples include: "what is the sound of one hand clapping?", and "what is nothing?".

Movement

Repetitive or formalized movements may also be used as "seeds," as in t'ai chi and some types of yoga. In Sufi-style meditation people clasp hands in a circle and chant while alternately raising and lowering their arms in imitation of the opening and closing of a flower.

LEFT *Flowers and buds also make a good focal point for meditation.*

MEDITATION TECHNIQUES

Whichever technique you use to focus the mind, there are certain preliminaries that should be observed:

1 Choose a place and time of day when you are sure of being uninterrupted for 15 to 20 minutes. Disconnect the telephone if necessary. Keep warm and wear comfortable clothing. Remove belts, watches, and jewelry from your person and any distracting machines from the room, e.g. loudly ticking clocks.

2 Take up your chosen position for meditation. The classic pose is sitting on the floor, cross-legged or in the "Lotus position" favored by yoga practitioners. However, a firm stool or chair can serve equally well. The important thing is that you should not feel strain or discomfort. Shoes are usually removed although this is not necessary.

3 Check that you are sitting upright, with your back straight and weight centered on what you imagine to be the central line of your body. You should be relaxed but not slumped, and your head should be erect. Rest your hands in your lap or on your knees.

4 Breathe deeply and evenly, sensing the rise and fall of your chest, the movement of your abdomen, and the flow of air through the nostrils down to the lungs. Check your body for any feelings of tension, and concentrate on relaxing taut muscles until the tension drains away.

5 Focus on your chosen "seed" – your breathing, an object, a mantra, or an image – and feel the mind dissociating itself from the outside world and extraneous thought. Do not move or fidget or you will dissipate the energy you have built up through concentration. If you develop an itch, ignore it.

6 After 15 to 20 minutes, return slowly to normal consciousness. Breathe deeply and more quickly as you look at your surroundings . Rise slowly and stretch. You should feel alert, calm, confident, mentally refreshed and lively.

7 You should meditate at least once a day, and preferably twice a day. Many busy people even find time to take a short break for meditation as a way of combating stress during the course of the working day.

sit with your back straight so that you may breathe easily

remain erect but relaxed with your hands upon your lap or knees

when sitting in a chair your feet should be flat on the floor

BREATHING MEDITATION

Breathing gives us life. It is a rhythmical and symmetrical activity, utilizing air, lightness, and freedom. Even if you decide on some other "seed" on which to focus your attention, some experience of breathing meditation is a good way to start.

❖ Concentrate on breathing smoothly and regularly. Breaths should be deep, exercising the diaphragm fully without overextending it or straining.

❖ Choose a point of concentration – usually the abdomen or the nose is chosen – and focus your attention on the physical sensations that accompany the inflow and outflow of air.

❖ You can meditate either in silent contemplation of your breathing, or you can count at the same time.

❖ The simplest way of counting is to count both the inhalations and exhalations. Start by exhaling to the count of one. Then inhale to the count of two. Continue like this up to a count of ten, and then return to one.

❖ A more complicated method is to count only inhalations, or only exhalations.

❖ If your mind wanders and you lose count, simply acknowledge the fact and return to a count of one.

ABOVE *Breathing meditation is both relaxing and energizing.*

PRECAUTIONS

■ If you feel light-headed or dizzy, you should cease the breathing technique.

BUBBLE MEDITATION

This is a form of visualization, in which extraneous thoughts and feelings are imagined to be encapsulated in bubbles, and carried away.

✳ When you are comfortable and relaxed, imagine that you are sitting at the bottom of a warm, clear lake. It is peaceful and quiet and you are breathing normally.
✳ Clear you mind of thoughts and feelings, and keep it completely blank for as long as possible
✳ When an unwanted thought arises in your mind, imagine a large bubble forming at the bottom of a lake. As it rises slowly to the surface – for six or seven seconds – contemplate the thought or feeling in your mind until the bubble reaches the surface of the lake and disappears, carrying the thought with it.
✳ If the same, or any other, thought enters your mind again, repeat the process and watch calmly as it is carried to the surface and away from you.
✳ Try this for ten minutes initially, lengthening the time gradually as your technique improves.

ABOVE *Visualize bubbles carrying away and dispersing negative emotions.*

TRANSCENDENTAL MEDITATION

Transcendental Meditation (TM) was originally conceived by an Indian religious leader, Swami Brahmananda Saraswati of Jyotir Math, as a simple and practical form of meditation for the poor of India. It was brought to the West in the 1960s by Swami Brahmananda Saraswati's disciple, the Maharishi Mahesh Yogi, and achieved instant fame through its adoption by the Beatles. However, the Beatles later disavowed TM on the grounds that it had become too materialistic, and it is somewhat ironic that a system devised for the Indian poor should have ended up as a pastime for the affluent citizens of the West.

TM is essentially a form of mantra meditation, with the twist that your mantra is to be kept secret and is told to you in confidence by your guru. Everybody is said to have different rhythms and vibrational frequencies in the organs of their bodies, and so the mantra is individually "tuned."

The TM induction process consists of two introductory, inspirational, lectures, followed by an initiation ceremony at which you are given your secret mantra. You are also asked to

ABOVE *Transcendental Meditation gained a high profile in the West in the 1960s through the figure of the Maharishi Mahesh Yogi.*

bring flowers, some fruit, and a white handkerchief. After some ritual chanting and incantation, you are asked to contemplate the objects on the table, while repeating your mantra over and over until you fall into a meditative trance. Most people approach the induction ceremony with high expectations. Since expectation and belief are crucial to the success of meditative and hypnotherapeutic techniques, the process is often perceived as highly effective.

Although it is not cheap to learn, TM claims to have as many as four million adherents worldwide, and many claim that it has changed their lives. The attention attracted by TM led to an investigation of its effects in the late 1960s by Herbert Benson and Robert K. Wallace of Harvard Medical School. They concluded that, while TM undoubtedly produced all the physical manifestations typical of deep meditation – changes in blood pressure, heart rate, brain-waves, and reduction of stress hormones – it was no more effective than ordinary mantra meditation, or even the repetition of simple Christian prayers or the counting of rosaries.

PATHFINDER

For most people, the benefits of meditation are concerned with general emotional and mental well-being. Most meditators experience greater calmness and clarity of thought, and improved self-confidence and self-esteem. Their quality of life may change considerably for the better after they begin meditating.

There are also certain specific conditions in which meditation has been proven to have therapeutic value. These include:
ADDICTIONS SEE P. 258
ANGINA SEE P. 304
ANXIETY SEE PP. 256–7
ASTHMA SEE PP. 294–5
ATHEROSCLEROSIS SEE P. 305
BREAST PROBLEMS SEE P. 320
DEPRESSION SEE P. 261
GASTROENTERITIS SEE P. 309
HEADACHE SEE PP. 268–9
HIGH BLOOD PRESSURE SEE P. 302
HIV AND AIDS SEE PP. 340–41
HYPERVENTILATION SEE P. 301
INFERTILITY SEE P. 324
INSOMNIA SEE P. 264
IRRITABLE BOWEL SYNDROME (IBS) SEE P. 314
MENOPAUSE SYMPTOMS SEE PP. 330–31
MIGRAINE SEE P. 269
OBESITY SEE PP. 334–5
PREMENSTRUAL SYNDROME (PMS) SEE P. 323
REPETITIVE STRAIN INJURY (RSI) SEE PP. 342–3
STRESS SEE PP. 262–3
STROKE SEE P. 359

POLARITY THERAPY

ABOVE *Randolf Stone was the founder of polarity therapy.*

*S*ince the establishment of the American Polarity Therapy Association in 1984, polarity therapy has become increasingly popular, although it is still little known outside America. This therapy was the brainchild of Randolf Stone, an osteopath, chiropractor, and naturopath, who combined the knowledge he acquired through these Western therapies with traditional Eastern philosophies. It promotes energy circulation and treats energy blockages to maintain well-being.

Randolf Stone (1890–1981), the founder of polarity therapy, was born in Austria as Rudolf Bautsch. He moved to America as a child and qualified there in the 1920s as an osteopath, chiropractor, and naturopath. Bautsch changed his name to Stone when he married later that decade, but the marriage was short-lived, and after his divorce he became fascinated by spiritualism, mysticism, and Eastern medicine. He was particularly interested in Ayurveda (*see pages 78–83*), yoga (*see pages 54–61*) and acupuncture (*see pages 20–25*) and traveled widely in the East to learn about them, while maintaining a conventional practice in Chicago.

ABOVE *The principles of yin and yang inform polarity therapy.*

Combining the Eastern theories of the life force – of qi and prana – with the knowledge gained through his conventional training, Stone came to the conclusion that good health depends on the uninterrupted flow of energy through and around the body. Stone likened this energy to that of the electromagnetic field that flows between two opposing electrical poles – hence the term "polarity therapy." Stone publicized his beliefs in a book called *Energy*, published in 1947, and went on to write six more books and numerous articles in an attempt to gain medical acceptance for his ideas – generally with little success. However, the upsurge in interest in Eastern holistic therapies in the 1960s brought renewed interest in polarity therapy and it started to rise in popularity. Stone started to teach his theories and methods to others, continuing to do so until he retired from his Chicago practice in 1974 at the age of 84, after which he spent the rest of his life in India.

Stone's followers continued to promote his ideas about life energy patterns. In 1984, some of them launched The American Polarity Therapy Association, which monitors standards of practice both in certified schools and practitioners; students must study for between 18 months and two years before they are certified to practice as polarity therapy practitioners. The therapy had spread to Britain and the rest of Europe by the late 1970s, although it is still not widely known.

THE THEORY

Polarity therapy is based on a mixture of Eastern and Western treatments. Practitioners see the body as a vibrational electromagnetic energy field, in which the head and the right side of the body represent the positive electrical pole, and the feet and the left side of the body represent the negative pole. The spine, the central core of the body, represents the neutral, but it carries the most potent of all the energy flows in the body within its cerebrospinal fluid. Energy flows around and through the body from one pole to the other. These poles correspond closely to the *yang* – positive – and *yin* – negative – of Traditional Chinese Medicine (*see also shiatsu, pages 32–7*) and not only enable the continuous flowing of energy but also represent the positive and negative states of the mind.

Stone believed that five different types of energy circles, or elements, surround the central core and govern both the production of energy and its flow around the body. These correspond to the "chakras" of Ayurveda (*see pages 78–85*), but they are also similar to the elements of traditional Chinese medicine (*see shiatsu, pages 32–7*). They are known as ether, air, fire, water, and earth, and each one corresponds to different parts of the physical body, as follows: ether – the throat chakra; air – the heart chakra; fire – the solar plexus chakra; water – the sacral chakra; and earth – the pelvic chakra.

Maintaining the Equilibrium

Polarity therapists believe that in order for a person to maintain physical, mental, and emotional health and well-being, all the energy fields must be in balance and that energy must flow freely between them all. Any blockage or depletion of energy within an energy field may result in physical or emotional problems within the areas governed by that field. As a result the whole body will be put out of balance and be less able to cope with and adapt to both everyday stresses and strains and more serious life events.

CONSULTING A PRACTITIONER

At your first session, your polarity therapist will take a detailed case history from you, asking about your medical history, lifestyle, diet, exercise regime, work, and present physical, emotional, and mental health. A session lasts from 40 minutes to an hour, so treatment may not begin until the second session. Therapists recommend that clients have one session per week for around eight weeks, followed by occasional sessions to maintain health. For a treatment session you will be asked to lie on a therapy couch, either in your underwear or lightly dressed.

THE CHAKRAS

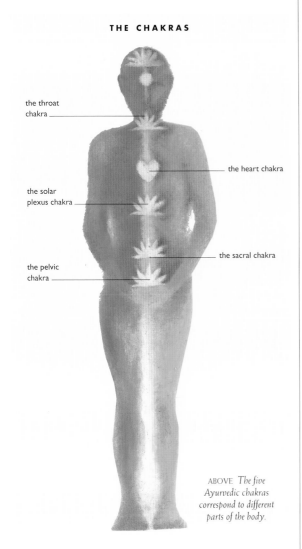

the throat chakra

the heart chakra

the solar plexus chakra

the sacral chakra

the pelvic chakra

ABOVE *The five Ayurvedic chakras correspond to different parts of the body.*

Bodywork

The therapist will work on specific points of your body using one of three levels of touch: a light touch is given to restore the correct balance in the neutral fields; medium pressure is used to stimulate the positive fields; and deep pressure is given to remove blockages in the

negative fields. The therapist also uses his or her own energy fields, so the therapist's right hand will stimulate positive energy, while the left hand works on the negative field.

Many polarity therapists also during the session incorporate a form of Cranio-Sacral therapy (*see pages 116–17*) to stimulate and release the energy found in the cerebrospinal fluid, while others use gentle bodywork techniques similar to those of Zero Balancing (*see pages 156–7*) to improve vitality and restore the body to balance. Any suspected blockage or depletion in the Five Elements may be treated by a form of acupressure (*see pages 26–31*).

ABOVE *Cranio-Sacral techniques will be incorporated into the therapy.*

Polarity Yoga

Your therapist is likely to teach you a series of simple stretching exercises aimed to release any stagnant energy at the body's chakra points. These simple stretches can be performed between treatment sessions to maintain and improve energy levels.

Diet

If the therapist feels that any of your problems have been caused by an inadequate or unhealthy diet, a detoxification diet may be suggested. This is likely to be followed by a diet rich in fresh fruit and vegetables. Some practitioners advise a strict vegan diet.

Counseling

Polarity therapists believe that an emotional shock or negative thoughts can deplete the body's energy and, if the problem is not resolved, a blockage can be the result. So you may be encouraged to talk through any emotional problems, to enhance a positive attitude and increase your own self-awareness and self-esteem. However, note that only polarity therapists with appropriate counseling qualifications, registration, and insurance may do so.

PATHFINDER

Polarity therapy is a holistic energy therapy that aims to release and stimulate the body's energy fields in order to return the body to a state of balance. The polarity therapist so not try tp alleviate specific problems, as these are seen as a symptom of imbalance, but aim to stimulate the body's own energy so that healing can occur.

ALLERGIES SEE PP. *338–9*

ANXIETY SEE PP. *256–7*

ARTHRITIS SEE PP. *346–7*

BACK PROBLEMS SEE PP. *344–5*

HEADACHE SEE PP. *268–9*

INSOMNIA SEE P. *264*

MIGRAINE SEE P. *269*

STRESS SEE PP. *262–3*

PRECAUTIONS

■ Polarity therapy is not suitable for those suffering from severe mental disorders – any counseling should be done by a qualified psychotherapist (*see pages 188–209*).

■ Check with your doctor before starting any detoxification diet. Consult a nutritionist as well if you intend to follow a vegan diet strictly and you have not done so before.

■ If you are in any doubt about your health, consult your doctor. Polarity therapy is not a diagnostic treatment. It claims to boost energy levels to stimulate the body's own self-healing abilities, rather than to treat any specific disorder.

REFLEXOLOGY

Today, reflexology is one of the most popular of all the complementary therapies, and reflexologists practice in most countries in the West. Although foot massage was a staple of many ancient healing systems, the rudiments of reflexology were only noted in America in 1913, and not properly formulated into a therapeutic practice until the 1940s. It has taken its place alongside Traditional Chinese Medicine treatments in many clinics and hospitals in China.

As with many complementary healing therapies, the roots of reflexology lie deeply buried in the past: in the therapeutic use of foot massage as practiced in the ancient civilizations of Africa, China, India, Egypt, and the Native Americans. But for centuries foot massage was overlooked by the West, as science-based medicine held sway – until its use as a therapy was rediscovered in 1915 by an American ear, nose, and throat (ENT) surgeon called Dr. William H. Fitzgerald (1872–1942), who trained in America, in London, England, and in Vienna, Austria, before settling in Hartford, Connecticut, U.S.A.

While working in Hartford, Fitzgerald discovered that he could perform minor ENT operations without giving the patient any painkillers if he applied pressure to certain bones or joints in the feet or hands – it seemed that the patient's appreciation of pain was diminished by the pressure. Fitzgerald called his technique "zone therapy," having come to the conclusion that the body is divided into ten equal parts that run vertically down the body, with five zones on each side of a line drawn down the middle of the body. Fitzgerald believed that each zone contained its own "bioelectrical energy," and that this energy traveled from the toes to the brain and out to the fingers, or vice versa. Pain relief, or lack of appreciation of pain in a particular area, could be achieved by pressing the joints of the finger and/or the toe in the same zone. The energy in the whole zone was stimulated by the pressure, he believed, so it did not matter where that pain relief was required.

Fitzgerald then theorized that his technique was not only anesthetic, but that it also treated the cause of the pain. His theory bears an obvious resemblance to that underlying acupressure (see pages 28–31) although his book, Zone Therapy, or Relieving Pain at Home (1917) contains no hint that he was influenced by Eastern medicine – indeed, very little was known about it in the West at that time.

ABOVE Eunice D. Ingham helped spread reflexology in the West.

Reflex "Compression Massage"

Fitzgerald's idea of "zone therapy" found numerous converts among chiropractors (see pages 118–25) and osteopaths (see pages 106–13), who favored forms of treatment that did not include the use of drugs. One such interested student was Eunice D. Ingham (1889–1974), who had previously qualified as a nurse. Ingham developed Fitzgerald's concept further and published two books on the subject – called The Stories The Feet Can Tell in 1938 and The Stories The Feet Have Told in 1945. She theorized that the application of pressure to a specific point on the feet would not only stimulate the energy in the zone containing that point but that any organ in the same zone would also benefit from it.

Ingham called her technique the "Ingham Reflex Method of Compression Massage"; a series of lecture tours and training courses for students quickly spread news of it through America. It was only later that the term "reflexology" came into use. It had been coined by a Russian, Dr. V. M. Bechterev, a colleague of Dr. Ivan Pavlov, physiologist and winner of the Nobel Prize for Medicine, to refer to the study of reflexes, particularly behavioral, rather than to the feet and health.

Spreading the Word

One of Eunice Ingham's students was Doreen Bayly, who took the technique back to Britain on her return there in 1960. Her mission was startlingly successful, because reflexology was at the forefront of Britain's extraordinary growth of interest in complementary medicine during the 1970s and 1980s; more than 80 books were published on the subject. Meanwhile, some of Ingham's other students were spreading the technique to the rest of Europe and to Australia and New Zealand, with the result that reflexologists who follow Ingham's method can now be found in most countries in the Western world. Reflexology is even popular in China, having arrived there in the 1960s. It is now practiced by tradi-

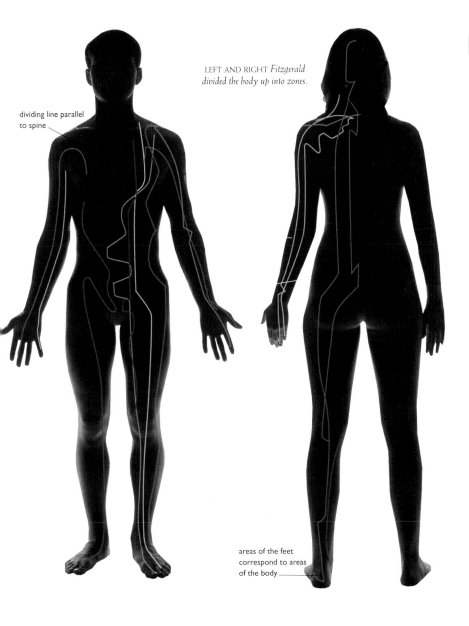

LEFT AND RIGHT *Fitzgerald divided the body up into zones.*

dividing line parallel to spine

areas of the feet correspond to areas of the body

PRECAUTIONS

■ Ensure that you go to a qualified practitioner (*see Useful Addresses pp. 368–71*). Inform your practitioner if you are on any medication (medical, homoeopathic or herbal) as reflexologists feel that treatment may interfere with the effect of other medication.

■ Avoid reflexology if you have any heart problems or circulatory disorders such as thrombosis, phlebitis and distended varicose veins. Care is required from reflexologists if you have diabetes, thyroid or other hormonal problems. Do not have treatment in the first three months of pregnancy or if you have a history of miscarriages.

■ Do not visit a reflexologist if you have a severe fungal or viral infection, especially on the feet, or any systemic infection disease. In any case, a reflexologist won't treat you if you have an acute infectious disease. If you have a foot infection, your hands will be treated.

ORTHODOX VIEW

The majority of orthodox practitioners find it difficult to accept that pressing a specific point on a foot or hand can have an effect on another area or organ of the body. This view is reinforced by the lack of scientific evidence to support the theory behind reflexology.

However, one 1993 clinical trial by orthodox gynecologists showed that women with premenstrual syndrome (PMS) had fewer psychological and physical symptoms during and after reflexology than women with PMS who received reflexology but at incorrect reflexology points. In 1996, Chinese reflexologist Dr. Wang Liang reported that reflexology was effective in treating 63 disorders after studying 8,096 clinical cases. And a Dutch study between 1990 and 1993 found that a combination of reflexology treatment and teaching correct lifting techniques decreased the number of days that postmen took off as a result of musculoskeletal problems, headaches, and gastrointestinal problems.

While this evidence is considered interesting, orthodox doctors feel that far more clinical research is needed before reflexology is considered anything more than a soothing and relaxing foot massage that reduces stress and benefits the circulation. Meanwhile, it is seen as harmless, so long as it is an adjunct to conventional medicine rather than a replacement for it.

tional doctors along with Traditional Chinese Medicine treatments in many hospitals and clinics.

Reflexology today

While reflexology is undoubtedly extremely popular, and continues to become more so as its benefits are more widely realized, there are some unfortunate difficulties about its regulation. In most American states, reflexologists must have a massage license to practice. The American Reflexology Association is attempting to change this situation, claiming that reflexologists have to do up to a thousand hours of irrelevant training to obtain a license, and that, as there is no specific license for reflexologists, anyone with a massage license can claim to practice reflexology. (People who have orthodox medical training in, for instance, nursing or physical therapy, do not require a massage license to practice reflexology.) In America, therefore, it is extremely important to ensure that your practitioner has trained at a school accredited by the American Reflexology Association. Even so, there is considerable disparity between the courses and accreditations offered by different colleges. Some require as little as 60 hours of training before offering a qualification, while others demand a minimum of one year.

In Britain, the situation is different again. The British School of Reflexology only accepts previously qualified nurses, physiotherapists, or medical practitioners for training. However, on the other hand, anyone can practice without a license and there is no requirement that a practitioner must have indemnity insurance cover.

THE THEORY

All reflexologists share common ground about the basic principles of reflexology, but there are differences when it comes to how and why it works. Broadly speaking, these differences can be expressed in terms of the "Eastern theory" and the "Western theory."

Common ground is the belief that reflexes for all body parts – physical and emotional – can be found at specific points on the feet, with the result that a stylized "map" of the body can be drawn on the feet. The left foot contains reflexes for the left side of the body and the right foot those for the right side. The body is split into ten vertical zones: five on each side of a line drawn straight down the center of the body, so that any reflex stimulated in a particular zone will have an effect on other body parts in that zone. The zones go from the toes

to the brain and down to the fingers, so that zones connect the limbs on each side; this means that it is possible to apply pressure to the thumb in order to treat a sore big toe, or vice versa. The hands and ears also contain a reflex map of the body in the same way, but, as the points are smaller there, the feet are usually preferred for treatment (see also hand reflexology box page 71). The midline of the body, the spine, is represented by the longitudinal inner arch of the foot, with the neck at the big toe, the sacrum and coccyx at the heel, and the spinal processes pointing down toward the sole of the foot. Because of these connections, reflexologists believe that pressure in the area can affect the spinal nerves where they pass out from the spinal column between the vertebrae. This means that the pressure applied can affect the body parts supplied by each spinal nerve.

ABOVE *Hand reflexology is often combined with foot reflexology and provides a good way for patients to continue their treatment independently.*

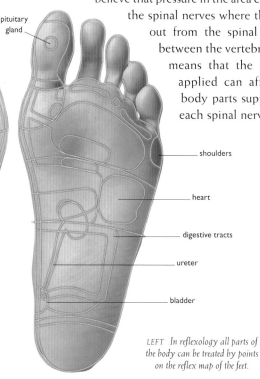

pituitary gland

lungs

shoulder

liver

kidney

appendix

genitals

shoulders

heart

digestive tracts

ureter

bladder

LEFT *In reflexology all parts of the body can be treated by points on the reflex map of the feet.*

ABOVE *The ear is harder than the hands and feet to manipulate. However, it also contains the reflex map of the body.*

EASTERN THEORY

The majority of reflexologists believe that reflexology is similar to acupuncture and acupressure (see pp. 20–31) in that a life force is said to flow through the body – and through what they call zones. If this force is blocked or depleted in any way, the body parts in the affected zone will suffer.

Reflexologists believe that massaging a reflex point on the foot or hand stimulates the flow of energy through the zone, clearing any blockages and replenishing the supply of energy to it, thus stimulating the body's own healing mechanism; while acupuncturists and acupressurists believe

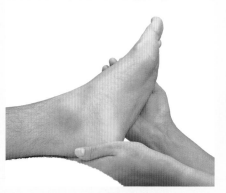

ABOVE *Reflexologists use small pressure movements to stimulate energy flow.*

that energy flow can be stimulated by pressure at numerous meridian points throughout the body, rather than just at the hands and feet. Another difference between reflexology and both acupuncture and acupressure is that reflexologists claim that tiny deposits, the size of sugar grains, can accumulate at a reflex point if there is a disturbance in the zone on which it sits, even before there is any outward symptom of a problem in the body. They believe that massaging the reflex point can break down these grains and eliminate them, thus allowing the free flow of energy along the zones.

WESTERN THEORY

Some reflexologists believe that the effects of reflexology can be partially explained through the conventional Western understanding of anatomy and physiology.

They point out that the feet and hands contain thousands of sensory nerve endings that relay information to the sensory cortex of the brain. Many of these sensory endings can be stimulated by pressure, especially in the foot. These are known as proprioceptors – they inform the brain of the position and movement of the body in relation to its other parts and its surroundings. It is the sense of proprioception that enables you to put a finger accurately on your nose, even in the dark, and tells you where your legs are, even when they are covered in bed. The brain reviews information from the proprioceptors and responds by sending commands to the appropriate body areas through the voluntary and involuntary (autonomic) nervous systems. The voluntary system is under your conscious control – you use it when you pick up a pencil, for example; the involuntary system operates as a subconscious control – it acts to maintain vital organs and a balance between their various functions.

Such reflexologists believe that the body's involuntary response to information relayed to the brain as a result of stimulating the sensory nerves via a reflex point on the foot improves the blood circulation to the area affected by that reflex point and reduces muscular tensions. As too much muscle tension can impede blood flow and therefore the removal of waste products, the cumulative effect of this is to allow more nutrients to reach the area through the circulatory system and to encourage the elimination of waste products. In addition, deep pressure on a point stimulates the production of endorphins – the body's own natural painkillers – which might explain the analgesic affect of the treatment.

All this explains why reflexology treatment is so relaxing. However, it does not conform to conventional anatomy, since reflexology zones are confined to one side of the body or the other. However, nerve pathways, along which sensory information travels, have been demonstrated to cross sides at the bottom of the brain. This means that the left side of the brain controls the right side of the body, and vice versa.

spinal cord

LEFT *Western medicine explains reflexology as information being relayed to the brain through stimulation of the reflex points on the feet.*

the complex network of the nervous system

PRECAUTIONS

■ Reflexology should be used only as an adjunct to orthodox medical treatment and not as a replacement for it. Consult your doctor if you have any concerns about your health.

■ Ensure that you go to a qualified practitioner. Inform your reflexologist if you are on any medication (medical, homeopathic, or herbal), as reflexologists believe that their treatment can interfere with the effects of other medication.

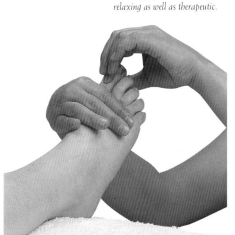

BELOW *Most people find foot massage pleasurable and relaxing as well as therapeutic.*

PATHFINDER

Reflexology is a form of hand and foot massage that concentrates on particular reflex points that represent other body parts within the same zone. Reflexologists claim that treatment eliminates any distortion or depletion in the flow of energy in a zone, which in turn stimulates the body's own self-healing mechanism. They do not claim that reflexology is suitable for every disorder, but that it is useful in a great number of them – and, in particular, in the ones listed below. Many people find the treatment deeply relaxing.

ABSCESSES AND BOILS *SEE P.* 277

ANGINA *SEE P.* 304

ANXIETY *SEE PP.* 256–7

ARTHRITIS *SEE PP.* 346–7

ASTHMA *SEE PP.* 294–5

CATARRH *SEE P.* 285

CONSTIPATION *SEE P.* 313

DIZZINESS *SEE P.* 271

ECZEMA AND DERMATITIS *SEE P.* 273

HEADACHE *SEE PP.* 268–9

HIGH BLOOD PRESSURE *SEE P.* 302

INSOMNIA *SEE P.* 264

KIDNEY COMPLAINTS *SEE PP.* 318–19

MENOPAUSE SYMPTOMS *SEE PP.* 330–31

MIGRAINE *SEE P.* 269

NEURALGIA *SEE P.* 267

PEPTIC ULCER *SEE P.* 311

PREMENSTRUAL SYNDROME (PMS) *SEE P.* 323

PSORIASIS *SEE P.* 272

SCIATICA *SEE P.* 348

SHINGLES *SEE P.* 266

SINUSITIS *SEE P.* 284

STRESS *SEE PP.* 262–3

STROKE *SEE P.* 359

CONSULTING A PRACTITIONER

Because of the relative lack of regulation of reflexologists, it is important that you check thoroughly the credentials of any therapist you choose. You need to ask whether he or she has had specialist reflexology training, is licensed by a national body, and is covered by indemnity insurance.

On your first session, you in turn will be asked about your medical history, your lifestyle, and the specific reason for your visit. Most reflexologists prefer to work on the feet (wash your feet before treatment to avoid embarrassment), so you will either sit in a comfortable chair or rest on a couch in a semi-reclining position. Each session will take up to an hour and you may be recommended to have a few weekly visits – six to eight is about average. Some people visit monthly as a preventive measure.

Your reflexologist may teach you a few exercises to practice at home between visits and advise you on posture, correct footwear, and diet. And don't worry if you experience what is called a "healing crisis" – sometimes triggered by an initial treatment – in which you develop a rash or a cough.

1 *The practitioner will look at your feet to see if there any areas of scaliness, puffiness, corns or calluses, to check the state of your nails, and to see whether you have high arches or flat feet.*

patient is relaxed

practitioner assesses the feet

patient sits on a comfortable bench

2 *Many reflexologists start treatment with a general foot massage to aid general relaxation and to feel whether there are any tense areas on the foot.*

3 *The practitioner will then massage all the reflex points on each foot in turn, usually starting with the right foot, and make a mental note of any problem areas or any painful or tender spots. These indicate an imbalance or blockage in the corresponding zone – the greater the tenderness, the greater the congestion.*

acupoint to be stimulated

firm, precise movements

4 *After the initial treatment, the practitioner will return to these tender spots and massage them further in order to break down the crystalline deposits – caused by the sluggish flow of energy – so that the energy can flow freely throughout the zone and stimulate healing.*

TECHNIQUES

The reflex points on the foot are very small so a reflexologist must use precise and controlled movements in order to "work" all the different points and not miss a congested or tender area. The pressure can vary, but it is firm rather than painful. Reflexologists use the pad and side of the thumb to press into a reflex point for about 30 seconds; the pressure is then eased and the thumb rotated and slid slightly over onto the next point. The pad of the thumb is kept in contact with the skin throughout (the pads of the fingers may be used over small bony areas).

Various techniques are used to "work" patients' reflex points. One is known as "creeping" or "walking." The "caterpillar walk" is a movement in which the practitioner pushes down on a reflex point, maintaining pressure upon it while his thumb "walks" or creeps forward as he moves the patient's foot up and down. Another, known as the "webbing pinch" requires the reflexologist to gently pinch the web between each toe and then pull individual toes slightly.

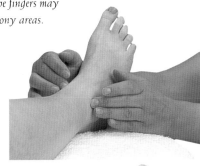

1 *The pads of the fingers may be used over bony areas.*

2 *The side of the thumb is used on a pressure point.*

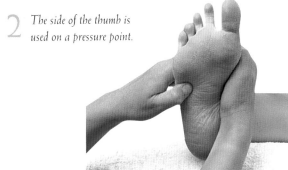

3 *Stretching out your own feet is encouraged.*

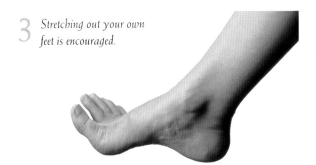

SELF-HELP

Reflexology adapts well as a self-help treatment. Use the charts on these pages to find the relevant reflex points and use the techniques given to decongest any problem areas. If you wish to take things further, buy one of the many self-help books that are available.

Depending on how flexible you are, it may be easier to massage your hands rather than your feet in a self-help reflexology treatment. If so, walk around on your bare feet as much as possible, because doing so stimulates the sensory output from the feet to the brain.

Many specialist foot massage aids are also available, including contoured wooden shoes and sandals. You could also try rolling a golf ball or a rolling pin around the sole of your foot against the floor or between the palms of your hands.

Exercise your feet and hands by stretching out your toes and fingers as widely as possible, curling them in and out, twisting ankles and wrists, and finishing with an overall shake.

If, however, you have any concerns about your health, contact your doctor. Self-help reflexology is neither diagnostic nor a specific cure, but should be used as part of a "wellness" regime.

HAND REFLEXOLOGY

Hand reflexology is as old or even older than foot reflexology. Traditional Chinese medicine holds that using pressure techniques on the hands has great health benefit. Dr. Fitzgerald, the father of reflexology, worked more on the hands than the feet while developing "zone therapy."

The hands represent the physical body in a similar way to the feet, though on a much reduced scale. Because Eunice Ingham concentrated on the feet when she was developing reflexology as we know it today, and since the reflex points are much larger on the feet, hand reflexology is now used more as an adjunct to foot reflexology. But it comes into its own if the feet cannot be treated for some reason, like a fungal infection, or if the reflex point on the foot is too painful to be touched. Hand reflexology also lends itself to self-help (*see above*) and as an immediate form of emergency treatment.

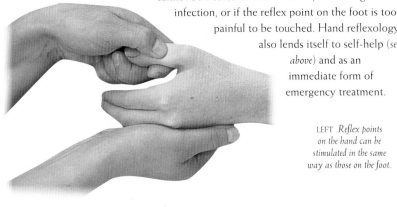

LEFT *Reflex points on the hand can be stimulated in the same way as those on the foot.*

METAMORPHIC TECHNIQUE

The Metamorphic Technique was originally termed "Prenatal Therapy," but its founder Robert St. John did not regard it as a therapy because it was not a cure or a treatment for specific ailments; rather it provided the conditions for positive changes to occur internally in the body. It focuses on reflexology's spinal zones in the foot, which are said to contain blockages from the body's gestation period in the womb. These can affect the rest of a person's life because most of our emotional, mental, and physical patterns and the illnesses we suffer are created during this time. St. John believed that we can rid our bodies of these blockages through his gentle technique.

Robert St. John, a British naturopath and reflexologist, developed the Metamorphic Technique in the 1960s, after he became disappointed with the results of his reflexology treatments on children with learning disabilities. He found that he had equal if not better results when he concentrated his therapy on the spinal reflex points on the soles of the feet – and that this treatment seemed to affect the children psychologically as well as physically. St. John believed that these points represented the prenatal period (the gestation period in the uterus). He thought that, although normal reflexology could unblock channels and ease the stresses and strains of life, only work along the spinal reflex zone of the foot could release energies blocked during gestation. For this reason, St. John at first named his new technique Prenatal Therapy. St. John was unhappy about the word "therapy," however, as he did not believe that his method was a treatment for specific problems. In addition, he soon found that clients believed that his kind of therapy applied purely to pregnant women.

The new name of Metamorphic Technique was coined by Gaston St. Pierre, a student of St. John's, to reflect the fact that St. John believed his method was not a cure or a treatment, but that it enabled beneficial psychological and physical changes to occur. In 1979, Gaston St. Pierre set up the Metamorphic Association in London, England.

THE THEORY

St. John was a reflexologist who believed in the zone theory and reflex points of reflexology (*see pages 66–71*). As in reflexology, St. John thought that the inner edge of the foot corresponded to the spine and the spinal reflexes.

However, he further postulated that this zone corresponds with the time that is spent in the uterus from conception to birth. St. John believed that most of our emotional, physical, and mental patterns and responses are formed during gestation, so any block in the energy

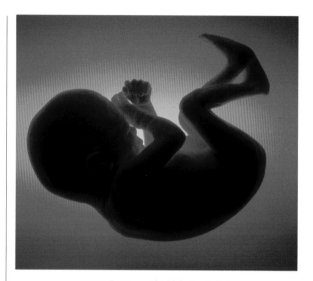

ABOVE *In Metamorphic Technique the foot represents the gestation period during which our physical, emotional, and mental patterns are set.*

zones during this period could have a lasting effect on the rest of a person's life. By massaging this area, St. John felt that he could not only unblock any recently created obstructions, but also older, deep-seated blockages from a person's gestation period.

From there, he would move on to other parts of the body. The hands and the center of the back of the head, he believed, had spinal reflex points which helped effect change. The left foot – representing the past, internal, and spiritual life – and the right foot – representing the present – have the greatest potential to effect change in a person. The hands allowed the changes to be accepted. And the head understood what changes had occurred.

St. John did not believe that his technique could treat any specific disease, but, as he said in the booklet he wrote in the early 1970s, "I always say that this method is a handling of the subject and not of the complaint. If the subject changes, if they become whole and able to manage life, they have no need of their complaints, and so they disappear."

CONSULTING A PRACTITIONER

The Metamorphic Technique is similar in many ways to reflexology and some practitioners also practice other alternative therapy techniques. To find a qualified practitioner in your area, see the useful address section (*see pages 368–71*).

Practitioners recommend that you have two or three sessions of an hour each, about a week apart. They believe that the feet should not be treated for more than an hour in any one week, as the Technique could produce too many changes to handle at once.

Metamorphic Technique practitioners prefer to be called "catalysts" rather than therapists, as their aim is to stimulate your own life energies to effect changes in yourself. They do not attempt to treat anything specific, nor do they concentrate on any nodules or painful areas found during the session. The practitioner will start by taking your medical history. You should wear loose, comfortable clothes and ensure that you are sitting comfortably. The practitioner will sit slightly to one side of you, avoiding involvement in any changes stimulated by the massage.

Your right foot will be massaged first, with particular attention paid to the line from the big toe, down the inner foot to the heel, then your left foot. This will take between 20 and 40 minutes.

The practitioner massages each hand, starting from the tip of the thumb and then moving down the side of the hand and then over the back of the wrist.

The session is completed by the practitioner massaging your head from the crown down to the nape of the neck and then up behind the ears to the tip of each ear. You will then be left quietly for a few minutes to relax and come round from the treatment.

PATHFINDER

The Metamorphic Technique does not claim to treat anything specific, but rather acts to allow and stimulate change within a person and to boost their own self-healing abilities by removing any blockages in the flow of energy in their bodies that could be inhibiting change. Orthodox medicine would probably not recommend this technique for any medical condition, but would note that it could help with stress-related problems, as many people feel relaxed and at ease following a session.

ANXIETY *SEE PP.* **256–7**
HEADACHE
SEE PP. **268–9**
MIGRAINE *SEE P.* **269**
STRESS *SEE PP.* **262–3**

PRECAUTIONS

■ Always visit your orthodox doctor if you have any concerns about your health. This technique is not a treatment for any specific disorder. It is not recommended for highly suggestible people or those suffering from severe mental disorders.

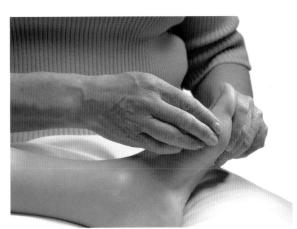

1 *The experience of the Metamorphic Technique is much like reflexology.*

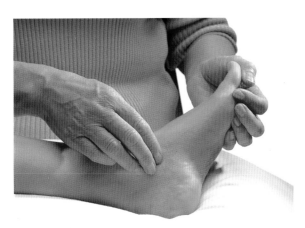

2 *The therapist will pay particular attention to the line from the big toe to the heel.*

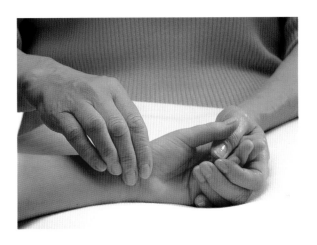

3 *The practitioner massages each hand.*

4 *The session is completed with a head massage.*

REIKI

Reiki is a spiritual healing discipline which its founder, Japanese theologian Dr. Mikao Usui, thought was once part of Tibetan Buddhism. In the 19th century, he spent fourteen years seeking the secrets of healing, and finally found information about reiki in Sanskrit texts. After he fasted and meditated for 21 days on top of a Japanese mountain, a vision showed him their meaning.

"Reiki" is a Japanese word that comes from "rei," meaning "universal," and "ki," meaning the "life force" – the same as "qi" in Chinese and "prana" in Sanskrit – that permeates and surrounds every living thing. The term was coined in the late 19th century by Dr. Mikao Usui to describe the new method of healing that he had devised.

Both the history of reiki and that of Usui himself are somewhat vague and lacking in documentation. Some people say that Usui was a Christian teacher at a school in Japan, others that he was a Buddhist monk. However, Mrs. Hawayo Takata, a Hawaiian reiki practitioner who introduced the technique to the West, maintained that Usui was originally a Christian and that he spent many years trying to understand how Jesus Christ performed miracles. Failing to find an answer, he turned his attention to Sanskrit texts describing how Buddha performed healing, but this took him no further. He fasted and meditated on the top of a sacred mountain for 21 days. On his very last night there, the meaning of the symbols Dr. Usui found in the Sanskrit texts came to him in a vision, along with an ability to heal others.

Those with a cynical outlook take the view that Mrs. Takata may have said that Dr. Usui was a Christian to make reiki slightly more acceptable to the Christian Americans in Hawaii. Certainly, the reiki adherents in Japan maintain that Usui was a Buddhist monk who rediscovered the ancient "sutras" (chants) that invoked the Medicine Buddha of Tibet.

Before he died, Usui passed on his theories to Dr. Chujiro Hayashi, who passed them on to Mrs. Takata in turn. She moved from Hawaii to California, U.S.A., in the 1970s and introduced the practice of reiki there – from where it gradually spread to other Western countries and became more popular.

ABOVE Dr. Mikao Usui devised the Reiki system.

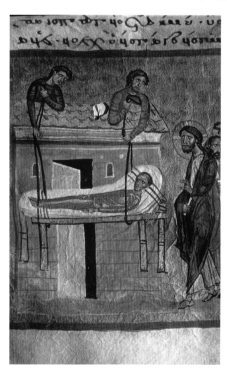

ABOVE It is claimed that Usui spent many years trying to find out how Jesus performed his miracles.

THE THEORY

The practice of reiki is based on the belief that it has the power to heal and can be passed on by each of us once we are connected with the "universal life force energy" which is used for healing. A reiki practitioner identifies his or her healing ki and uses it to strengthen the ki of others. But as reiki is omnipotent, neither the practitioner nor the client need know where or what the problem is; it may be physical, emotional, or spiritual.

The theory is that when ki is strong and free, it maintains the body and mind in a positive state of health and well-being, affecting it physically, emotionally, and spiritually. If ki is weak or blocked, either consciously or subconsciously, then the body may succumb to a physical disorder, become emotionally unbalanced and spiritually barren. Reiki practitioners channel "universal life force energy," which is drawn through them by the recipient. The strong healing energy clears any blockages in the recipient.

Channeling Ki

Before reiki practitioners can treat others, a reiki master must open their healing channels. They follow guidelines set down by Dr. Usui known as reiki ideals. These are concerned with ethics and behavior, and include: living in harmony with others; doing good; being positive about all things; taking responsibility for one's own health and happiness; and using one's powers to help others. Practitioners also learn certain ancient symbols and how to use them to progress in knowledge of the technique. A "First Degree" student might be a practitioner of reiki, but it is more usual for him to have attained "Second Degree" status before he offers treatments. Each level is achieved through an "initiation" (sometimes referred to as an "attunement"). Once Second Degree attunement is reached, a student may train as a reiki master who can pass on the ability to channel reiki.

CONSULTING A PRACTITIONER

Contact the International Reiki Association to find the nearest practitioner to you (*See Useful Addresses pages 368–71*). Practitioners with Second Degree reiki claim to be able to "send" healing reiki so that a distant client is able to receive it.

Wear loose comfortable clothes for a session, which lasts about an hour. As you lie fully clothed on a treatment table, the practitioner will place his or her hands either on or just above your body. Twelve basic positions are used by reiki practitioners, roughly coinciding with the major organs and glands of the body: four are on the head; four

ABOVE *The "universal life force" of yin and yang energy is important to reiki healing.*

on the back; and four on the abdomen. The belief is that ki passes out of the practitioner through his or her hands and enters your body, rejuvenating and balancing your own ki.

One important aspect of the reiki approach is that you play a positive part in your own treatment. Your desire to be healed and being open to the possibility that reiki may help you ensures that you will always receive some kind of benefit, although it may not be in the way that you anticipated. Most important is that you have enough treatments to heal the real cause of your problem, which usually resides at the level of mind, emotion, or spirit.

PATHFINDER

"Reiki" is an Eastern therapy that does not claim to cure any specific disease. It helps the body-mind-spirit to heal itself using the "universal life force" (called "reiki" in this form of healing) that is in and around all things. It is not obtained by developing your own personal life force or ki, nor from another person, but rather is a method through which a practitioner acts as a channel to connect another person with the universal healing or life force.

Reiki can help to promote a more positive approach to life and may help treat stress-related problems and:

ANXIETY *SEE PP.* 256–7

DEPRESSION *SEE P.* 261

HEADACHE
SEE PP. 268–9

MIGRAINE *SEE P.* 269

STRESS *SEE PP.* 262–3

patient is thinking positively

practitioner places hands over head

ABOVE *The reiki practitioner uses twelve basic positions during the treatment.*

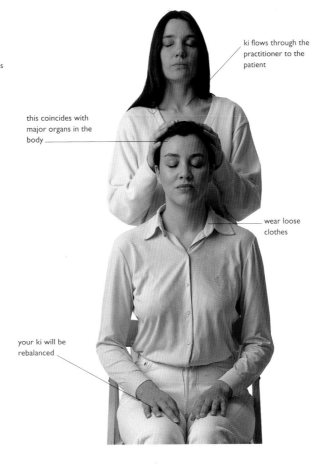

ki flows through the practitioner to the patient

this coincides with major organs in the body

wear loose clothes

your ki will be rebalanced

ABOVE *As the practitioner opens the energy channels, the patient's ki is refreshed and cleansed.*

PRECAUTIONS

■ Just as you cannot learn t'ai chi from a book, neither can you learn to heal through reading books. So be sure that your reiki practitioner is a qualified one, with, preferably, Second Degree initiation at least.

■ Reiki is a form of natural healing, its aim being to put individuals in touch with the "universal life force" which can heal them. As such, it is not a form of treatment *per se*. If you have any real concerns about your health, consult your doctor.

THE BOWEN TECHNIQUE

A recent addition to the arsenal of complementary healing therapies in America and Europe, the Bowen Technique has long been popular in Australia and New Zealand. It was developed by Thomas Bowen, who refused to say why or how it worked, but nevertheless attracted to his practice some 13,000 patients a year by word-of-mouth alone. The Bowen Technique is gentle and non-invasive, and therefore suitable for people of all ages. It aims to restore structural harmony to body and mind.

Thomas A. Bowen (1916–1982) left his school in Geelong, Victoria, Australia, at the age of 15, and supported himself by means of laboring jobs. However, at the same time, he began to develop a form of body-work, and soon started to practice it with such effect that he gained something of a reputation locally as a healer. Eventually, Bowen's success was such that he was able to give up his full-time job and set himself up as an osteopath – even though he had neither the qualifications nor a license to do so. He continued to thrive, attracting patients by word-of-mouth and treating them with what he called "the Bowen technique," and by 1974, when he gave evidence to the Australian Government Investigation on Complementary Therapies, Bowen claimed to be treating 13,000 people a year.

Bowen never wrote about his technique – in fact, he never tried to explain it. He seemed to diagnose problems and formulate a treatment for them by instinct. However, he allowed six apprentices, who were mainly either chiropractors (*see pages 118–25*) or osteopaths (*see pages 106–13*), to watch him at work and study his methods. Unfortunately, they all studied with him at different times, and since Bowen continued to alter his ideas and develop new methods right up to the time of his death, each student completed the apprenticeship with slightly different ideas about his technique. The result was a degree of controversy about the precise nature of this healing practice after Bowen's death.

One of Bowen's students was a massage therapist called Oswald Rentsch, who studied under him for two-and-a-half years. After Bowen's death, Rentsch incorporated the Bowen Technique into his own treatments and also started to teach it to others. By 1990, it had spread from Australia to America and it reached Britain in 1993.

THE THEORY

As Bowen never expounded the theory behind his technique it was left to his followers to come up with a theoretical justification. Consequently, several different

ABOVE *Like switching on a light bulb, vibrational energy can be harmonized by small movements.*

theories exist. The most widely held view among Bowen technique practitioners is that the Technique depends on harmonizing "vibrational energy." All the cells of the body vibrate at a certain frequency at all times, the theory suggests, and the vibrational energy on which this phenomenon is based can become blocked or depleted – with the result that the body's self-healing mechanism cannot function and a disease or a malfunction may develop. But, Bowen therapists believe, the body's vibrational energy can be harmonized, and only a small movement is required to achieve this. They use the analogy of switching on a light bulb to explain this – the bulb does not glow any brighter the harder you push the light switch, nor does more electricity pass down the cable.

An alternative theory put forward by some Bowen therapists is that the small, simple movements of the technique connect the part of the body being treated to the brain by means of the sensory nerves. As the movements are so gentle, the brain does not fire off a specific motor response, but examines how the area is functioning and then works to restore its structural integrity and its well-being.

CONSULTING A PRACTITIONER

Although the Bowen Technique is becoming increasingly popular, it is still relatively new outside Australia and New Zealand, so it may be difficult to find a practitioner near you in other countries (*see Useful Addresses, pages 368–71*). Other bodywork techniques that are similar to this in concept are Zero Balancing (*see pages 156–7*), Trager Work (*see pages 154–5*) and McTimoney Chiropractic (*see pages 124–5*).

At your first session, you will be asked to give a short medical history of yourself and the specific reason for your visit. However, Bowen practitioners do not want too much detail, since much of their training is directed at learning how to treat each person and problem intuitively. Because the theory is that patients heal themselves, it is unnecessary for the practitioner to make an exact diagnosis. Each session lasts about 40 minutes and the majority of people need only about three sessions to complete their course of treatment.

The treatment starts with the patient lying lightly clothed on a soft massage table – so wear loose, comfortable clothes. The technique can be applied through light clothing or directly onto bare skin. The practitioner uses his fingers and thumbs to roll your muscles and other connective tissues with a light pressure at specific points – these correspond to a marked extent to trigger points (*see Massage pages 96–103*) and acupuncture points (*see pages 20–31*). There will be gaps between the movements during the session where the therapist leaves the room to allow your brain to assimilate the information it has received and to "reset" the body. You will also be asked to rest quietly for a few minutes at the end of the session for the same reason. Bowen practitioners believe that "less is more," so their primary aim is to make as few movements as possible to achieve the desired result of structural integrity.

Method and Results

This gentle, non-invasive form of bodywork focuses on the fascia, the connective tissue that covers the muscles. It involves firmly taking up the slack across the muscle and moving over it, but it is not painful.

The light, rolling movements made on your muscles and tendons by the practitioner's fingers and thumbs are believed to encourage circulation in your body, improve its mobility, and promote lymphatic drainage of waste products. Muscle spasm is reduced while blood supply is increased by this treatment, so that tension and debris are cleared and the body is freed to heal itself.

The technique benefits any condition, practitioners claim, but is especially useful for asthma, back and joint pain, bedwetting, bronchitis, chronic tension headaches, menstrual problems, and sports injuries. It can also relieve stress problems.

Because the Bowen Technique is meant to simply stimulate "energy flow," releasing energy which may be trapped temporarily in one area of the body, few sessions are normally given to patients. It is a non-manipulative, down-to-earth, hands-on technique said to enable the body to use its own healing abilities to restore harmony.

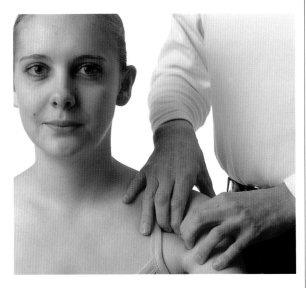

ABOVE *The practitioner makes light, rolling movements on the muscles and connective tissue.*

PATHFINDER

The aim of a Bowen Technique practitioner is to restore and harmonize the innate energy in the human body so that its own healing mechanisms can restore health and balance. Conditions that seem to respond well to treatment are musculo-skeletal disorders, sports injuries, stress-related disorders, circulatory disorders, and emotional disturbances.

ANXIETY *SEE PP.* 256–7
ARTHRITIS *SEE PP.* 346–7
FIBROSITIS *SEE P.* 348
REPETITIVE STRAIN INJURY (RSI) *SEE PP.* 342–3
STRESS *SEE PP.* 262–3

HOME REMEDIES

Tom Bowen had many ideas for home cures, including that cancer patients take regular baths of washing soda and Epsom salts to raise the body temperature. His proponents are loath to make claims regarding their success, but they note that some people respond well to them. A few remedies for specific ailments follow:

For arthritis: Put Epsom salts in your bath water.

For bedwetting: Bowen said that while this problem is often psychological, children who wet their beds should be put on an 80 per cent alkaline/20 per cent acid diet and avoid apples and apple juice (which he believed weakens the bladder), and dairy products.

For bladder problems and dizziness: Drink the juice of two slices (no more than 50g/2oz) of raw beetroot daily.

For bruises: Apply apple cider vinegar to bruises or sprained wrists to take away pain and tenderness.

For bunions: Every night for at least three weeks, soak your feet in warm water containing three tablespoons of Epsom salts to break down calcification.

For rheumatism: Take regular doses of honey mixed with cider vinegar.

AYURVEDA

AYURVEDA

Ayurveda is the oldest holistic system of medicine now being practiced. Its adherents believe that it is the "mother" of the concept of medicine and healing, and that its influence spread over the earth to form the basis for all other medical systems, from that of Tibet to Western herbalism and modern medicine.

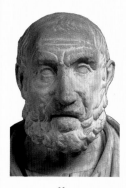

ABOVE *Hippocrates, commonly regarded as the father of Western medicine, was deeply influenced by Ayurveda.*

For instance, the predominant medieval notion of "humors" probably came from Ayurveda's "panchamahabhuta" (five basic eternal substances) and "tridosha" (basic elements of the body) concepts. Even earlier, Hippocrates, the so-called "father" of Western medicine, probably based his entire medical system on Ayurveda.

A few Ayurvedic practitioners today also hold Western medical qualifications and hope for a fruitful exchange of ideas with Western medicine practitioners.

Almost certainly the most ancient of all medical systems, Ayurveda had its origins in India more than 3,000 years ago. It is still the most important form of medicine in the Indian subcontinent, and, like other Eastern therapeutic systems, is attracting increasing interest in the West. Ayurveda is holistic – in the sense that the physician treats the whole person, both mind and body, and not just the disorder or disease – and all-embracing in that it offers prescriptions for all elements of an individual's lifestyle – from diet and personal relationships to meditation and astrological influences. Its aim is to maintain good physical and emotional health through the balancing of physical and spiritual energies. It is only when this balance is disturbed that the traditional healing techniques of purification, herbal remedies, massage, and exercise are brought into play.

Tradition states that the basic principles of Ayurveda were laid down by a gathering of Indian holy sages, or "rishis," building on the available wisdom of the time. The basic texts – shared with Hinduism and yoga – were the "vedas," the ancient Sanskrit sacred writings dating from around 1500 B.C.E.

The first writings to deal specifically with Ayurvedic medicine were the *Charaka Samhita*, composed about 2,500 years ago, and the later *Sushruta Samhita*. Together, these represent an astonishingly prescient body of medical knowledge, declaring that the body is made of cells and identifying more than 20 different disease-causing microbes. In them, there are also explanations of such surgical techniques as suturing, Cesarian sections, and the importance of hygiene.

It is generally thought that most Western medicine is derived from the ancient Greeks. However, it has been shown that Greek medicine relied heavily on knowledge imported from India. Indeed, it is probable that Pythagoras, who was a major influence on Hippocrates, now considered the father of Western medicine, based his entire medical system on Ayurveda.

Ayurveda Today

In India itself, Ayurveda was discouraged by the British Raj and fell into disrepair, leaving a prevalence of poorly trained teachers and a vanishing oral tradition. However, after India gained independence in 1947, the Government set out to reverse this decline. This was partly out of recognition of the impossibility of bringing sophisticated and expensive Westernized health care to the huge population of the subcontinent, but also in deference to the intrinsic value of a medical system that had been honed by use and experience over thousands of years. For much the same reasons, and at around the same time, China deliberately returned to the practice of Traditional Chinese Medicine (TCM), which itself

ABOVE *In India, Ayurveda is the principal system of healthcare for many people.*

owes much to Ayurveda, as a way of providing health care to a vast and expanding population.

Today, the statistics are impressive. Around 85 percent of India's population of more than 850 million are served by more than 400,000 practitioners of Ayurveda. In Sri Lanka, the related system of Siddha medicine serves a similar proportion of the population, and in north-west India and Pakistan, Unani-tibbi – a mixture of Ayurveda and Arabian medicine – does likewise.

Ayurveda in the West

Ayurveda is becoming more widely available in the West. In the UK, practitioners are found most easily in areas with substantial British-Asian populations. The situation has been complicated, particularly in the U.S., however, by "Maharishi Ayur-Veda," an offshoot of Transcendental Meditation (*see pages 60–63*). This is not considered to be true Ayurvedic medicine, since it depends on proprietary (and expensive) preparations, rather than the individually prescribed remedies offered by the genuine practitioner. However, properly qualified practitioners, albeit with a limited repertoire of herbs, are slowly becoming established.

THE PHILOSOPHY OF AYURVEDA

The word "Ayurveda" comes from Sanskrit and can be roughly translated as "the science of life". While Ayurveda mainly teaches ways of achieving health and self-fulfillment, it is, in fact, a complete philosophical and spiritual system. Over thousands of years, Ayurvedic philosophy has become subtle, sophisticated, and highly complex. It would take a lifetime of study to become conversant with it in all its aspects, but the basic tenets are reasonably easy to understand, and have changed little through the centuries.

The Five Elements and the Creation

In the beginning, everything was "one," and took the form of undifferentiated pure consciousness. Then, in this cosmic state of awareness, the first sound, "om" or "aum," the noiseless sound of the universe, was heard. The vibrations of om created the first of the Five Elements, or "panchamahabhutas," of Ayurveda: ether or space. Movements in the ether gave birth to the element air, and movements of the air in turn gave rise to heat and to thus: the third element: fire. The fourth of the five elements, water, was formed by the action of fire on the ether, which then solidified to create the final element: earth.

ABOVE Ayurveda in Sanskrit translates as "the science of life".

The five great elements – ether, air, fire, water, and earth – are the foundations on which the Ayurvedic interpretation of all matter and life is based. But the elements should not be interpreted literally. Each represents qualities and different types of force and energy, as well as some kind of physical manifestation. Water, for example, represents not just the liquid state, but also the cohesive forces that bind things together and the qualities of softness and coolness.

The Five Elements and the Human Body

Although each of the Five Elements has its own characteristics and corresponds to specific senses and functions within the human body, they do not act in isolation. Three different combinations of the elements, the "tridoshas," are defined and it is these rather than the individual elements that form the basis for diagnosis, treatment, cure and health maintenance in Ayurvedic medicine. It is the balance of the "doshas" and the relative predominance of one over the others that determines what type of person each of us is, both in terms of our anatomy and physiology and in terms of our personalities and susceptibility to ill-health. The interplay of the three "doshas," and their effects, are described more fully overleaf.

Air
vayu

Ether or space
akasha

Fire
tejas

Water
jala

Earth
prthvi

THE FIVE ELEMENTS (PANCHAMAHABHUTAS)

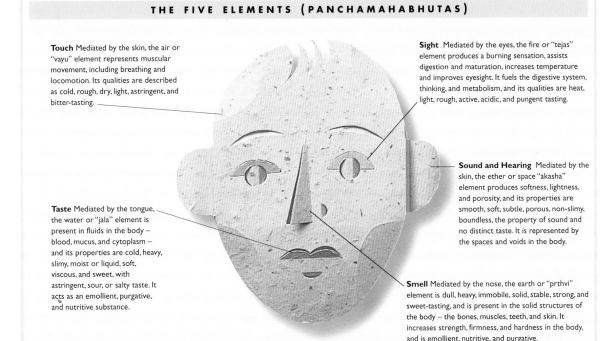

Touch Mediated by the skin, the air or "vayu" element represents muscular movement, including breathing and locomotion. Its qualities are described as cold, rough, dry, light, astringent, and bitter-tasting.

Taste Mediated by the tongue, the water or "jala" element is present in fluids in the body – blood, mucus, and cytoplasm – and its properties are cold, heavy, slimy, moist or liquid, soft, viscous, and sweet, with astringent, sour, or salty taste. It acts as an emollient, purgative, and nutritive substance.

Sight Mediated by the eyes, the fire or "tejas" element produces a burning sensation, assists digestion and maturation, increases temperature and improves eyesight. It fuels the digestive system, thinking, and metabolism, and its qualities are heat, light, rough, active, acidic, and pungent tasting.

Sound and Hearing Mediated by the skin, the ether or space "akasha" element produces softness, lightness, and porosity, and its properties are smooth, soft, subtle, porous, non-slimy, boundless, the property of sound and no distinct taste. It is represented by the spaces and voids in the body.

Smell Mediated by the nose, the earth or "prthvi" element is dull, heavy, immobile, solid, stable, strong, and sweet-tasting, and is present in the solid structures of the body – the bones, muscles, teeth, and skin. It increases strength, firmness, and hardness in the body, and is emollient, nutritive, and purgative.

AYURVEDA

THE TRIDOSHAS

Each of us is determined by the balance of the "doshas" in our make-up, and each "dosha" is a combination of two of the Five Elements. "Doshas" are life forces and are found only in living things, not in inanimate matter. The term "dosha" means the force that darkens or causes things to decay. The three "doshas" are named "vata," "pitta," and "kapha."

"**Vata**" is formed from the combination of "akasha" (space) and "vayu" (air). "Vata" is the force that moves things. Without it, the other two "doshas" would lack the driving force that enables them to operate. "Vata" represents all movement in the body. It controls the movement of air during breathing, the circulation of blood and the movement of ideas, thoughts and sensations through the mind. It is also responsible for speech and for the elimination of waste from the body.

"**Pitta**" is formed by the combination of "tejas" (fire) and "jala" (water). It is the force that burns, producing heat, and driving digestion and assimilation. "Pitta" is responsible for all metabolic activity in the body, for normal vision, for body temperature and skin condition, for the sensations of hunger and thirst, and for the functioning of the intellect.

"**Kapha**," formed by the combination of "jala" (water) and "prthivi" (earth), is the force for stability and cohesiveness. It is responsible for form and structure within the body, from the individual cell to the joints, bones, and muscles. It moistens and lubricates body processes. "Kapha" is largely passive, and counteracts any excess activity of "vata" and "pitta." It confers mental and emotional, as well as physical, strength, and promotes such qualities as generosity, tolerance, virility, and courage.

Every human individual is made up of different proportions of the three "doshas." Our essential character and constitution – our "**prakriti**" – is determined by the relative dominance of each over the others. "Prakriti" is the result of inheritance and depends on the exact state of our parents' "doshas" at the time of conception. Once formed, it is unchangeable and is the foundation of what we are, from our appearance and physical strengths and weaknesses, to our behavioral traits, our likes and dislikes, and our mental and emotional characteristics. For each of us, there is a right balance of "doshas": disturbance of this balance is the cause of ill-health.

"**Prakriti**" are usually described in terms that assume the total dominance of only a single "dosha." However, very few people exhibit this degree of dominance. The other two always exert some influence, and these descriptions represent tendencies rather than absolutes.

RIGHT *In the West, Ayurveda is becoming increasingly popular for both healing and lifestyle guidance.*

vatas have poor long-term memory

vatas speak quickly and have a restless mind

vata people often have dry skin

Air

LEFT *The vata person tends to be thin, highly active, and mentally restless. Emotionally, they are often frightened and insecure.*

Vata Prakriti

The following point to a predominantly "vata" constitution:

❖ tall or short stature with thin, poor physique;
❖ dry, cool, and rough skin;
❖ large, crooked teeth;
❖ small and dark-colored eyes;
❖ irregular and erratic appetite;
❖ high (or absent) sexual desire;
❖ restless, rapid movements;
❖ intolerance of cold and dry;
❖ mentally restless, creative and alert;
❖ irregular sleeping patterns;
❖ difficulty in sustaining relationships;
❖ active and often interested in sport.

Unbalanced "Vata"

A lack of balance in "vata" shows itself as poor digestion and excretion, mental confusion, poor memory, general lethargy, and loss of joie de vivre. Anxieties and worries may surface along with a tendency to procrastinate, possible weight loss, constipation, insomnia, and headaches.

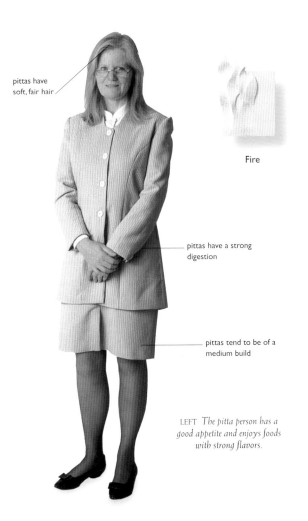

pittas have
soft, fair hair

pittas have a strong
digestion

pittas tend to be of a
medium build

Fire

LEFT *The pitta person has a
good appetite and enjoys foods
with strong flavors.*

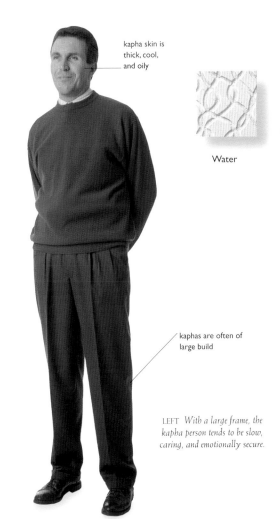

kapha skin is
thick, cool,
and oily

Water

kaphas are often of
large build

LEFT *With a large frame, the
kapha person tends to be slow,
caring, and emotionally secure.*

ORTHODOX VIEW

It is unlikely that any doctor would view Ayurvedic medicine as an acceptable alternative to orthodox Western medicine. Many, however, acknowledge the efficacy of Ayurvedic herbal remedies, some of which have aroused considerable interest. Ayurveda is completely different from Western medicine, not only in its techniques but also in its philosophical and ideological foundation. It is such a well-developed and respected system that Western general medicine practitioners may find it competitive or too much a part of Hindu culture to be accommodated.

Pitta Prakriti

The pure "pitta" constitution would have the following characteristics:

❖ medium stature with moderate physique;
❖ reddish or yellowish skin, with a tendency to freckles and moles;
❖ sharp green, brown, or gray eyes;
❖ fine hair that goes gray and falls out easily;
❖ intolerance of heat or sun;
❖ a tendency to perspire freely;
❖ a good appetite;
❖ moderate sexual desire;
❖ high intelligence and ability to make decisions;
❖ a tendency to irritability, impatience, jealousy.

Unbalanced "Pitta"

A lack of balance in "pitta" may result in poor digestion, with heartburn, irritable bowel, and diarrhea. The skin becomes hot and dry, often with inflammation, and vision is impaired. Anger and anxiety may lead to foolish behavior.

Kapha Prakriti

The following are the main characteristics of the kapha constitution:

❖ heavy build with strong, well-muscled physique;
❖ a tendency towards plumpness;
❖ large, clear, attractive eyes;
❖ thick, dark, sometimes oily, wavy hair;
❖ attractive appearance with smooth, soft skin;
❖ graceful, balanced, sometimes heavy movement;
❖ intolerance of cold and damp;
❖ sensual with strong sexual desire;
❖ mental stability, tending to laziness;
❖ slow learning, but good retention;
❖ reliable and honest, slow to anger.

Unbalanced "Kapha"

A lack of balance in "kapha" may lead to obesity, flabbiness, weak or soft muscles, poor digestion, excessive sleep, and oily skin. Disturbance in the respiratory passages may occur with allergies and sinus congestion. Generosity may turn to intolerance, suspicion, and greed.

AYURVEDA AND HEALTH

While the balancing of the "tridoshas" is the most important aspect of Ayurvedic health and healing, there are several other fundamental concepts that underlie Ayurvedic diagnosis and treatment. In the classic Ayurvedic texts, health is said to be experienced when the following conditions are met:

* all three "doshas" are in balance;

* all the "dahtus," or tissues, of the body are working normally;

* the "srotas," or channels, of the body are flowing normally;

* the "agni," the fire that drives digestion and metabolism, is burning well;

* the three "malas" – sweat, urine, and feces – are being produced and eliminated normally;

* the five senses are all functioning normally;

* mind and body are in harmony, creating a sense of physical and emotional well-being.

Dahtus

Seven fundamental types of tissue are defined in Ayurveda: plasma; blood constituents; muscle; fat; bone and nerves; bone marrow; and reproductive tissues. Each of these is formed from the one before, through the action of "agni," or fire. Each "dhatu" is made up of all five of the fundamental elements ("mahabhutas"), with one, or at most two, predominating in each case. The fundamental element of plasma is water, for example, and that of bone and nerves is a combination of air and earth.

Srotas

Traditionally, there are 13 "srotas," or networks of distribution channels, in the body. Three connect the human body with the outside world, bringing in food, water, and "prana," the life force contained within the air we breathe. Seven "srotas" are concerned with the distribution of food and energy to the tissues; and three are devoted to the elimination of "malas," or waste. In the yogic aspects of Ayurveda, "prana" assumes particular importance, and has its own network of "nadis," or energy channels, which interconnect at the seven "chakras" in the spine as they distribute the life force throughout the body. The postures ("asanas") and breathing exercises ("pranayama") of yoga (*see pages 52–59*), which are designed to control and adjust the flow of "prana" in preparation for meditation (*see pages 60–63*) are an important part of advanced Ayurvedic practice.

ABOVE *Ayurvedic principles of diet emphasize fresh, light, and natural ingredients.*

ABOVE *Ayurvedic treatment may include an herbal enema to cleanse the body of accumulated toxins.*

BELOW *Physical and emotional well-being are promoted through the practice of yoga.*

Agni and Ama

"Agni" is the fire that provides energy for digestion, metabolic processes, the immune system, and the processes of thought and feeling. It is the driving force behind the pitta dosha.

The correct functioning of "agni" is vital to health. Without it, food is imperfectly digested, and the tissues are poorly nourished. Malfunction of "agni" manifests itself as an accumulation of "ama," a sticky, white toxic substance that accumulates in the digestive system before spreading to other "srotas," or channels. Wherever "ama" exerts its malign influence, there will be weakness, malfunction and disease.

Many things, from the environment to diet and lifestyle, can affect the functioning of "agni," and an important part of the Ayurvedic physician's task is to identify the cause of the problem and then cure or alleviate it.

Malas

The three "malas" are "purisha," or feces, "mutra," or urine, and "sveda", or sweat. If these are not formed properly in the body and eliminated regularly and correctly, symptoms and disease will result. Unhealthy elimination is a sign of imbalance in the "tridoshas."

Great importance is attached to the proper elimination of wastes. A course of Ayurvedic treatment often begins with a purging of the body to cleanse it of the residues and consequences of accumulated waste.

Gunas

We describe things, whether tangible or intangible, in terms of their "gunas" – properties or qualities. These qualities are important in Ayurveda, since the effect that such things as herbs, diet, and emotions have on the "doshas" depends on the degree to which they possess, or don't possess, them. Ayurveda recognizes 20 qualities, each quality being paired with its opposite. For example, hot is paired with cold, soft with hard, and heavy with light. Each quality has a particular effect on each of the "doshas," either increasing or decreasing it, while its pair has the opposite effect. As with the yin and yang of Chinese medicine, the "gunas" represent the essential polarity of the universe, and the constant interplay of forces of death and renewal, and growth and decay.

"Gunas" play an important part in Ayurvedic remedies, since each has its own distinctive combination of opposites. Finding the remedy with the correct combination of "gunas" to balance the "tridoshas" is one of the secrets of successful treatment.

CONSULTING A PRACTITIONER

If you do not have recommendations from a friend or relative, you would probably be best advised to ask the advice of your doctor. Many doctors and hospitals now maintain lists of approved practitioners for a range of complementary therapies. You should, in any case, consult your doctor before undergoing any form of Ayurvedic treatment if you are on medication or are suffering from any acute or chronic illness. Also, professional Ayurvedic associations in most countries will assist you.

What the Practitioner Will Do

The first session, lasting about an hour, will be devoted mainly to diagnosis and assessment. Practitioners vary in the diagnostic techniques they use, but most will conduct a thorough examination – not just of your current physical condition and appearance, but also of your lifestyle, relationships, family history, health history, and possibly such things as your astrological influences.

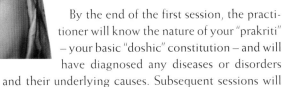
the eyes are examined

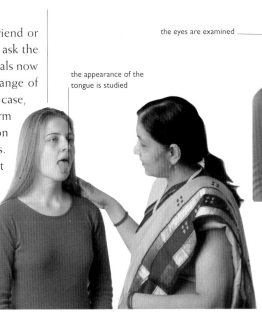
the appearance of the tongue is studied

ABOVE *The condition of the skin and eyes are also examined.*

ABOVE *The color and texture of the tongue provide important information on the patient's general state of health.*

Diagnosis

The basic "three-point" diagnosis consists of evaluation through questioning, observation of appearance, and examination by touch. Some practitioners use a more detailed eight-point diagnosis. This involves close examination of your pulse ("nadi"), your tongue ("jihva"), your voice ("sabda"), your skin ("sparsa"), the eyes ("drika"), general appearance ("akriti"), urine ("mutra") and stools ("purisha").

Pulse diagnosis in Ayurveda, as in Traditional Chinese Medicine, is an exact science. Three deep and three superficial pulse points are checked on each wrist. These correspond to the three "doshas"; the relative strength of each pulse and its particular characteristics reveal any imbalances. The "vata" pulse is irregular and "snake-like"; the "pitta" pulse is jumpy, like a frog; and the "kapha" pulse is slow and "swan-like." The pulse reveals the state of particular organs of the body and the vitality of the life force, or "prana," and the channels, or "nadis," through which the life force flows.

BELOW *The strength and character of three pulses are read to reveal any imbalances in the doshas.*

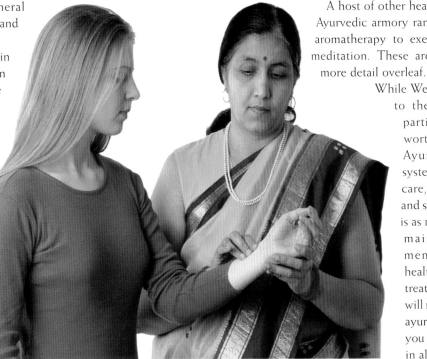

By the end of the first session, the practitioner will know the nature of your "prakriti" – your basic "doshic" constitution – and will have diagnosed any diseases or disorders and their underlying causes. Subsequent sessions will be devoted to a careful explanation of the nature, cause, and prognosis of any disease, and to the implementation of an appropriate course of treatment.

Treatment

You will be given advice on diet and how to change to a healthier lifestyle. You may be prescribed a course of purification to eliminate toxins from the body and to energize the body's elimination mechanisms. Herbal preparations may be prescribed.

A host of other healing techniques in the Ayurvedic armory range from massage and aromatherapy to exercise, breathing, and meditation. These are described in much more detail overleaf.

While Western minds are tuned to the concept of curing particular diseases, it is worth remembering that Ayurveda is a holistic system of mind and body care, with both physical and spiritual aspects. There is as much emphasis on the maintenance of good mental and emotional health as there is on the treatment of disease. You will reap the full benefits of ayurvedic medicine only if you attend to its precepts in all respects.

AYURVEDIC TREATMENT

The scope of therapies available in Ayurvedic medicine is vast, ranging from treatments that restore balance to the individual as a whole, to localized ones for particular complaints, such as the pouring of warm oils into the eyes. Most courses of treatment will involve a combination of several different types of therapy.

Purification (shodana)

This is often the first step in treatment, since it is essential that the body is cleared of accumulated toxins. It consists of two stages, "purwakarma" and "panchakarma."

• "Purwakarma" is a form of preparatory treatment prior to more rigorous forms of detoxification. It involves massage with herbal oils, and sweating induced by steam baths.

• "Panchakarma" is considerably more demanding. It involves any or all of five different purgative treatments: oil or herbal enemas; herbal laxatives; emesis (vomiting); nasal drops or snuff; and bloodletting (rarely used).

Diet

Ayurveda places considerable emphasis on diet as a way of achieving and maintaining health. Your diet should reflect three things: your constitution, or "prakriti"; the season; and any imbalances in the "doshas."

All foods are classified according to taste. There are six tastes – sweet, sour, saline, bitter, astringent, and pungent, and any meal should contain small amounts of all six. They are also classified according to their qualities. For example, light foods include vegetables, fruits, nuts, dairy produce, wheat, rice, and honey. These promote balance and harmony, and should predominate in the diet. Heavy foods, which include processed and junk foods, strong alcoholic drinks and meat, promote selfishness and lethargy and should always be eaten sparingly.

In general, food should always be fresh. It should be lightly cooked, so as not to destroy the life force present in natural ingredients, contain oils and appropriate spices to promote digestion, and be presented in a way that looks appetizing. The heaviest meal of the day should be eaten around midday, and supper should be early and light. Food should never be eaten until the previous meal has been digested.

BELOW *Herbal remedies are often used as part of Ayurvedic treatment.*

Herbal Remedies

Ayurvedic medicine has a vast natural pharmacopoeia, comprising more than 8,000 tried and tested herbal remedies and other preparations. Only about 1,000 of these are likely to be available in the West. A full description of Ayurvedic herbal medicine is outside the scope of this book, but the subject is fully covered in a companion volume, *The Illustrated Encylopedia of Healing Remedies* (Element Books, 1998) and also in *The Complete Illustrated Guide to Ayurveda* (Element Books, 1997).

Massage and Marma Puncture

Just as much of Traditional Chinese Medicine is based on the manipulation of the flow of "qi," or "chi," throughout the body, so Ayurveda massage and puncture techniques are based on the flow of "prana" through the 107 "marma" points on or near the surface of the body. These therapies should be applied by an experienced practitioner and are basically the same as those used for acupuncture and acupressure (*see pages 20–31*).

There are many forms of therapeutic massage in Ayurveda, including self-massage. Oil plays an important part in all of these, and different oils are recommended according to the predominant "dosha": for "vata" types, sesame, almond, olive, wheatgerm, and castor oils are recommended; for "pitta" types, coconut, sandalwood, almond, and sunflower oils are considered appropriate; while "kapha" requires sesame, safflower, mustard, and corn oils.

The techniques generally recommended for massage should be followed (*see pages 96–103*), including, particularly, those for self-massage (*see page 100*). Similarly, aromatherapy (*see pages 104–5*) with the appropriate oils is recommended.

Meditation and Yoga

The yoga postures ("asanas") breathing exercise ("pranayama") and yogic meditation are an integral part of Ayurvedic medicine (*see Yoga, pages 52–9, and Meditation, pages 60–63*). It is important that you consult your practitioner before embarking on any aspect of yoga, since the appropriate techniques and "asanas" (postures) differ from one constitutional type and form of "doshic" imbalance to another.

LEFT *Ayurveda is a complete system, and patients are also advised on meditation and breathing techniques.*

PRINCIPLES OF HEALTHY LIVING

Ayurveda places great importance on the need to follow a healthy daily routine.
Ideally, your day should follow the routine set by the following instructions:

❦ get up before dawn;

❦ evacuate bladder and bowels;

❦ examine and clean your teeth, tongue, hands, and face; shave, if appropriate, and trim your nails;

❦ perform self-massage using herbal oil, for up to 20 minutes if you have the time; massage your whole body, from the head and neck down, paying particular attention to the hands and feet, then relax briefly;

❦ take some exercise, for example, a brisk walk or yoga;

❦ bathe or shower, and dress in clean, comfortable clothing;

❦ spend some time in meditation;

❦ eat a light breakfast;

❦ work or study for at least three hours;

There can be few people who would be able to follow this daily routine in its full rigor. However, the principles upon which it is based are sound. Early to bed and early to rise, regular, healthy meals, and adequate exercise are advised by many people besides Ayurvedic practitioners.

ABOVE *The day should begin with a thorough cleansing routine.*

ABOVE *A structured routine will enable you to find time for relaxation and meditation.*

ABOVE *Work or study should be finished before sunset.*

❦ have lunch – this should be the largest meal of the day and should be taken around midday;

❦ resume work or study;

❦ stop work before sunset and meditate for 20 minutes;

❦ have a light supper;

❦ take a short walk;

❦ spend the evening in non-strenuous, enjoyable activity;

❦ have sex if appropriate –
Ayurveda recommends unrestricted sex in winter, with the frequency dropping to about three times a week in spring and autumn, and only two or three times a month in summer;

❦ go to sleep before 10 o'clock.

ABOVE *Common-sense principles, such as getting sufficient sleep, underpin much of the lifestyle plan.*

PATHFINDER

Ayurveda is a total health-care system, as well as a way of life. As such, it has remedies and different types of therapy for virtually all common conditions and many rarer ones as well, ranging from influenza and migraines to infertility, neurosis, and cancer.

It is also important to note that Ayurveda is as much concerned with the maintenance of overall good health as it is with the treatment of specific diseases.

Most people in the West, therefore, are most likely to have encountered Ayurveda in the form of one of the many therapies that are related to or are derived from it. As well as such exotic practices as astrology, gem and crystal therapy, and radiesthesia, these include:

ANEMIA
SEE P. *303*

ARTHRITIS
SEE PP. *346–7*

ASTHMA SEE PP. *294–5*

BRONCHITIS
SEE P. *299*

CONSTIPATION
SEE P. *313*

COUGHS SEE P. *297*

FEAR OF DENTAL
TREATMENT SEE P. *286*

FIBROSITIS SEE P. *348*

FLU SEE P. *298*

GRINDING OF TEETH
SEE P. *287*

GUM DISEASE SEE P. *289*

IRRITABLE BOWEL
SYNDROME (IBS)
SEE P. *314*

RAYNAUD'S DISEASE
SEE P. *306*

TONSILITIS SEE P. *290*

HEALING

An age-old technique sometimes called the "the laying on of hands," the practice of healing was viewed as witchcraft by the Christian Church during the Middle Ages. In the 20th century, however, healing has undergone a renaissance. Today, healing is commonplace in evangelical and born-again Christianity, and "new age" healers flourish, too. The former work by asking for the intercession of God, and the latter by transmitting healing energy. Other healers work as they have always done, using an instinctive gift of unknown origin.

Since time immemorial, a selection of people have claimed to have healing powers – and have confirmed the existence of such powers. However, the source of these powers seems to vary according to the tradition and belief system of the healer. Differences are great in healers' terminology, understanding, and approach to healing, yet there is a considerable degree of similarity between them all, and still, in this age of technological medicine, healing is as popular a form of treatment as ever.

There are essentially two different types: "faith healing" and "spiritual healing." Faith healers believe that the patient's belief – "faith" – either in the powers of the healer, or of the deity that the healer represents, is vital to success. Spiritual healers, on the other hand, believe that they are merely channels by which the power, or energy, of some outside force is transmitted to the patient. As a therapy, spiritual healing can be subdivided according to healers' claims about the nature of this force.

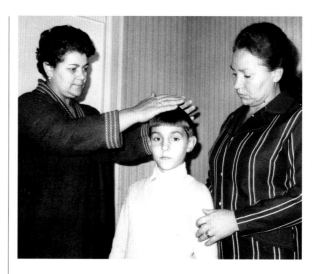

ABOVE *Faith healers are very popular and often have a large following.*

FAITH HEALING

The term "faith healing" is generally used to describe healing in a religious context and requires a patient to have faith in the healer's or deity's powers. Typically, an evangelist, whether on television or at a meeting large or small, proclaims that people in the audience will be cured if they have faith in the deity – which may or may not be the Judeo-Christian God – and truly believe that they will be healed. (There is another type of healing that involves orthodox religion – *see Prayer Healing, below*.)

Other faith healers reject large-scale religious settings, and work privately with patients on a one-to-one basis. Many of them regard themselves as possessing healing powers, but have no specific ideas about their nature or origin. Such healers often use techniques other than the application of healing energy, such as auto-suggestion – the implanting of an idea in the subconscious mind while the patient is in a state similar to that of a light trance (*see Hypnotherapy, pages 218–23*) – and the projection of their own personality as

authoritative. The motive behind these techniques is to mobilize and strengthen the patient's energy, will, and abilities for self-healing.

SPIRITUAL HEALING

The essence of spiritual healing is that practitioners, individually or in groups, either act as channels for a spiritual or supernatural healing force, or ask for divine intercession to bring about healing. The main types of spiritual healing now practiced are listed below, but the list is far from complete (*see also Therapeutic Touch, pages 88–9 and Reiki, pages 74–5*). Many of them involve "absent healing," also known as "distant healing" and "remote healing." This term covers healing practices, including all of those listed below except aura healing, that do not require the presence – or, necessarily, the knowledge – of the patient to be effective.

Aura Healing

Practitioners of aura healing maintain that everyone has an aura – a field of energy that surrounds the body – which manifests as different colors, and that they can see or sense it. When a person is ill, this aura changes, but it can be repaired by the practitioner "laying on" his hands or visualizing the appropriate colors. Aura healers may also use some Ayurvedic techniques (*see pages 78–85*) as well as color therapy (*see pages 248–53*).

ABOVE *Aura healers work on the energy field known as the aura, which emanates from the human body.*

Prayer Healing

Prayer healing is essentially different from faith healing in that its success does not depend on the faith of the recipient. Prayer healing has always been a cornerstone of the religion known as Christian Science, but in the last 20 years it has also been taken up enthusiastically by born-again Christians and evangelical Christian churches. It is also a feature of many other leading world religions. The aim is to ask for intercession from a deity to effect a cure.

A number of studies have been carried out to test the efficacy of prayer healing. The majority have failed to prove that it works, although a study, by Dr. Randolph C. Baird of 393 patients at the San Francisco General Hospital Coronary Care Unit between 1982 and 1984, appeared to indicate that a group for whom prayers were said suffered fewer complications than a group for whom no prayers were said. However, the methodology used for this study has been severely criticized by Western practitioners.

Psychic Healing

Though some psychic healers believe that their healing power derives from a deity, many think that they are just channeling "psychic" or spiritual energy that they possess as a gift. Psychic healing is also known as "psi healing" – "psi" being an instinctive awareness of events both natural and supernatural, outside the body and any parameters of time. Psychic healers use a variety of techniques, according to their own preferences.

Shamanistic Healing

Revered by tribal cultures all over the world – from South America to Ireland – shamans are said to perform an intercessionary function for the inhabitants of this and other realms. They believe different things according to their experiences as "travelers in spirit worlds" and may utilize various rituals, sounds, or edible substances to gain access to them for the purposes of healing and curing.

Spiritualist Healing

Spiritualists believe that they can contact the spirits of those who are dead, sometimes with the help of a "medium" who passes on messages. Spiritualist healers may contact the spirits of great healers and doctors and channel their healing energies to their clients. Healers have different ways of working, but often patients are told to relax before undergoing treatment. You may be asked to wear comfortable clothes, remove jewelry or shoes, close your eyes, or even to ask a question, but generally healing does not require anything but, perhaps, receptivity from your subconscious mind. It is said that the best healers do not require anything from you and merely act as vessels or conductors for beneficent, positive, or balancing forms of energy. It is best to rise slowly after a spiritual healing session and to avoid stressful situations for as long as possible both before and after treatment.

LEFT *A healer may interact with the patient's energy by moving his hands across the patient's body.*

PATHFINDER

By its nature, healing – whether faith healing or spiritual healing – claims to be able to cure each and every disease. Doctors think this unlikely, but accept that healing may well comfort some people, and may be of some use in conditions that are chronic, especially when they are linked to anxiety and stress.

ANXIETY *SEE PP.* 256–7
ARTHRITIS *SEE PP.* 346–7
HEADACHE *SEE PP.* 268–9
HIGH BLOOD PRESSURE *SEE P.* 302
MIGRAINE *SEE P.* 269
SCIATICA *SEE P.* 348
STRESS *SEE PP.* 262–3

PRECAUTIONS

■ Healing is not a substitute for medical treatment. Consult your doctor if you suffer from any condition, or think that you may do so, before visiting a healer, particularly if you suffer from any emotional or psychiatric disorder.

■ Continue any medical treatment you are undergoing during and after spiritual healing. Do not stop a course of treatment because you think that you have been cured – you may be mistaken.

■ Do not commit yourself to any healer who charges excessive fees – he or she may be a charlatan.

■ Avoid healers who irritate or disturb you, or who claim that their treatment fails only when the subjects do not have sufficient belief in a healing system or agency, or subconsciously want to remain ill.

THERAPEUTIC TOUCH

Therapeutic touch (TT) has become orthodox in many nursing institutions, especially in America. However, orthodox medicine and science are deeply skeptical of it. Skeptics point to the fact that TT is based on a blend of mysticism and a scientific theory that precludes measurement. Skeptical concerns were increased by a 1996/7 investigation that led to the 1998 publication of a paper (Rosa, Sarner, and others) in the *Journal of the American Medical Association*. Since the whole basis of TT is that practitioners can detect a human energy field (HEF), this proposition was tested. Skeptics say that if TT works, its practitioners should have had a 100 percent success rate; in fact, they were successful in only 44 percent of cases. However, studies of TT recipients prove that it has a positive, measurable effect. Patients showed an increase in hemoglobin levels in studies conducted by Prof. Krieger in the 1960s. Then, in the 1980s, TT was shown to be more helpful than ordinary touch in relieving tension headaches and anxiety. Finally, a study in the U.S. in 1997 offered proof that TT can reduce the effects of stress on the immune system.

A blend of the ancient technique of "laying on of hands," spirituality, and an alternative form of science, the technique of therapeutic touch has become extremely popular since it was developed in the early 1970s. Today, it is used to increase the body's self-healing abilities by nurses in around 80 hospitals in North America, and the practice is becoming increasingly common around the world. In recent years, however, the level of controversy surrounding therapeutic touch has also increased.

While "laying on of hands" has been a feature of medical practice in most civilizations over the centuries, it gained a new rationale in the late 18th century when Franz Mesmer, a doctor, set up a "Magnetic Institute" in Paris, France. Mesmer's idea was that the hands could transmit "animal magnetism," the healing force of the cosmos, to reawaken the body's own healing powers. His theories were debunked by France's *Académie des Sciences* in 1784, but some of them were taken up later by The Theosophical Society. Founded in 1875, this society concerned itself with the mystical and spiritual nature of the cosmos, a variety of Eastern and other philosophies, and the divine nature of human beings, the combination of which is called "theosophy." Dora van Gelder Kunz, President of the Theosophical Society of America between 1975 and 1987, co-founded the therapeutic touch system with her colleague Professor Dolores Krieger. Known as a "sensitive" and a gifted healer, Kunz taught the art of "laying on of hands" to Krieger, PhD RN, of New York University's Division of Nursing.

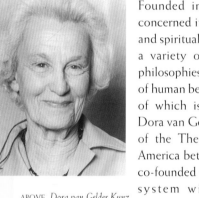

ABOVE *Dora van Gelder Kunz pioneered the technique of therapeutic touch in the 1970s, attempting to bring it into mainstream nursing.*

Krieger became determined to bring this therapeutic power into nursing's armory. Kunz went on to devise a system for what they called therapeutic touch (TT), and she and Krieger started teaching it in 1972.

Recognition

As Krieger continued to teach TT, her theories about why it appeared to work changed (*see below*), while the technique steadily gained in popularity. She published the first of several books, *Living the Therapeutic Touch: Healing as a Lifestyle*, in 1978. TT was recognized as a legitimate nursing skill by the Order of Nurses of Quebec in the same year; and, in 1990, it was incorporated into the Ontario College of Nurses' *Implementation Standards of Practice*. Today, the technique is practiced by

ABOVE *Hospital nurses often perform TT as part of the program of care.*

nurses in around 80 hospitals in North America; workshops in TT are held under the auspices of the American Association of Nursing; TT is taught at a number of American nursing schools and universities; and it is estimated that around 100,000 people have been taught TT worldwide, of whom some 43,000 are health professionals. In short, TT has achieved considerable recognition from the world of nursing in a remarkably short time.

THE THEORY

There are several strands to the theory behind TT, though in practice the distinctions between them become blurred. Originally, Kunz and Krieger theorized that TT's power involved currents of "prana," the "life energy" of Ayurvedic Medicine (*see pages 78–85*). But Krieger changed her ideas in the early 1970s, after being influenced by the late Martha Rogers, Dean of Nursing at New York University, who was developing an alternative view of the cosmos known as "The Science of Unitary Human Beings," or "Rogerian Science." And, in 1982, Krieger decided that it was not necessary actually to touch: TT works just as well if the practitioner's hands are held a short distance from the body.

Human Energy Fields

Krieger adopted Rogers' view that human beings not only have energy fields but are themselves energy fields and that these constantly interact with energy fields outside the body.

TT practitioners maintain that they can detect "human energy fields" (HEFs) by means of "laying on of hands," and any disturbances in an HEF – the result of injury, illness, pain, or stress. Then, as appropriate, they can transfer energy to the recipient to bolster his or her own defences, "flick off" any "excess energy" or modify patterns of energy flow; as a result, the recipient's natural powers of self-healing are boosted. Most importantly, the recipient of TT does not have to have any belief in its efficacy or theory; this appears to rule out any placebo effect.

Today, many TT practitioners still talk of "prana" and "chakras"; others say that they can feel HEFs. A third, smaller, group, which has studied Rogerian Science in more depth, maintains that HEFs are not felt but "perceived." However, many in fact find it difficult to explain this.

CONSULTING A PRACTITIONER

In many hospitals, especially in the U.S., TT is performed by nurses as part of routine care, often without the patient requesting it, or, as many doctors complain, without physicians and surgeons being consulted. However, many trained nurses administer TT in private practice and there are also a large number of lay practitioners. The technique is harmless if used correctly, so it is important to choose a practitioner who has been accredited by a recognized organization (accreditation can be obtained by a lay person from some institutions after a course lasting just 12 hours in total).

A TT treatment lasts between 15 and 30 minutes and generally consists of five phases: centering, assessing, "unruffling" or clearing, treatment or "modulation," and evaluation (there are numerous variations on this method). You will be asked to sit in a chair, fully clothed or to lie horizontal on a bed; it is not necessary for the practitioner to have any physical contact with you.

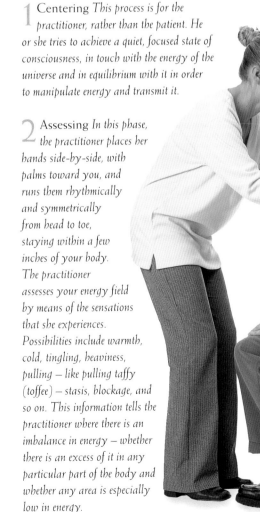

1 Centering *This process is for the practitioner, rather than the patient. He or she tries to achieve a quiet, focused state of consciousness, in touch with the energy of the universe and in equilibrium with it in order to manipulate energy and transmit it.*

2 Assessing *In this phase, the practitioner places her hands side-by-side, with palms toward you, and runs them rhythmically and symmetrically from head to toe, staying within a few inches of your body. The practitioner assesses your energy field by means of the sensations that she experiences. Possibilities include warmth, cold, tingling, heaviness, pulling – like pulling taffy (toffee) – stasis, blockage, and so on. This information tells the practitioner where there is an imbalance in energy – whether there is an excess of it in any particular part of the body and whether any area is especially low in energy.*

3 Unruffling (or clearing) *The same movements used in the assessment phase are interspersed with circular, sweeping hand movements. This moves excess energy to areas with low energy and achieves a consistent, symmetrical balance of energy across the body; any excess energy in the body overall may be "flicked away" from the practitioner's fingers.*

4 Treatment (or modulation) *The practitioner concentrates on any areas in which there is still an energy imbalance, and holds her hands over them, while visualizing the transmission of energy to them and making delicate adjustments in energy balance.*

5 Evaluation *The practitioner will reassess your energy balance throughout the session and may ask for feedback from you in order to determine when to conclude treatment.*

PATHFINDER

Practitioners of therapeutic touch believe that they can increase, reduce, or modify a person's "human energy field" to increase that person's self-healing ability, whether or not the recipient has any faith in the technique. TT is not in itself a curative technique, but its adherents claim that, in general, it is useful in speeding cure or recovery from injuries and illnesses, and can relieve pain, reduce stress, and boost the immune system. In particular, it has been used to aid recovery in the following conditions:

ALLERGIES *SEE PP.* 338–9

ARTHRITIS *SEE PP.* 346–7

BACK PROBLEMS *SEE PP.* 344–5

HEADACHE *SEE PP.* 268–9

HIGH BLOOD PRESSURE *SEE P.* 302

HIV AND AIDS *SEE PP.* 340–41

MENSTRUAL PROBLEMS *SEE PP.* 322–3

MIGRAINE *SEE P.* 269

PREMENSTRUAL SYNDROME (PMS) *SEE P.* 323

STRESS *SEE PP.* 262–3

WATCHPOINT

While therapeutic touch is harmless, it is an adjunct to, rather than a substitute for, any form of medical treatment for a pre-existing condition and extra care should be taken with patients who are elderly, emaciated, pregnant, or suffering from a head injury or psychosis. If you suspect that you suffer from some medical problem, consult your doctor before a TT practitioner.

2

PHYSICAL THERAPIES

INTRODUCTION

As their name implies, physical therapies focus primarily on the structures and systems of the body, including the circulation and lymphatic system as well as soft tissues, bones, and joints. However, while some are purely physical, involving various types of manipulation, massage, and movement, others incorporate psychological and emotional factors, and some include elements derived from Eastern "energy" therapies, such as the "life force" (chi or prana). Nevertheless, you can expect even those therapies in which practitioners work directly on bodily structures — massage, osteopathy and chiropractic, for example — to have an overall effect on your sense of personal well-being as well as to relieve physical symptoms.

With therapies of this kind, it is particularly important to make sure that the therapy you choose is appropriate for your condition. Used in the right way for the right person, they can sometimes be effective, but there are also pitfalls for the unwary. It makes sense to consult your doctor about any new symptoms so that you can be sure that either you are given any necessary conventional treatment, or that the therapy you propose to try does not hold any potential risks. The same applies if you are already being treated by your doctor for an existing illness; it is always wise to ask his or her advice before embarking on a course of physical therapy. While many practitioners are well informed about conditions, such as certain cancers or rheumatoid arthritis, for example, which are not amenable to some forms of physical therapy (and may actually be made worse by the wrong treatment), others are less knowledgeable.

As always, you should be particularly cautious if you are or could be pregnant: some types of massage and certain essential oils used in aromatherapy are not appropriate at this time. Similarly, those therapies that work at least in part on bringing to the surface underlying emotional or psychological difficulties may not be a good choice for anyone with severe problems in this area. Some may even reveal unrecognized factors – for example, you may only discover you suffer from a degree of claustrophobia when you are immersed for the first time in a flotation tank!

Responsible alternative therapists will take a careful history before starting treatment and should tell you if they do not feel qualified to diagnose or help with your particular problem, but it is possible that they may still miss some serious underlying condition. However, provided there is no risk attached, you may well find that your medical practitioner will encourage you in your chosen course, especially if you have a chronic condition for which he or she can offer no effective means of treatment.

Relief for Back Pain

One of the most widespread and intractable health problems in western society is what is known as "non-specific back pain." Not only it is responsible for a great deal of actual pain and immobility experienced by those affected, it also keeps thousands of people away from work and other productive activities for lengthy and repeated periods of time. One of the reasons for this is that orthodox medicine is not good at diagnosing the origin of such pain or at treating it. Our upright stance places enormous strains on the spine and associated soft and nervous tissues, and combined with lifestyle factors such as stress and poor posture, it is hardly surprising that back problems are so common. However, some alternative therapists have had enormous success with this type of complaint, and even conventional doctors may now refer patients for certain types of therapy.

The Range of Therapies

In general, physical therapies tend to be of relatively recent origin, having been developed since the last century. Some, like zero balancing and some breathing techniques, combine new approaches with traditional elements derived from Chinese or Indian medicine in a specific way, and many have developed from long-held beliefs about the importance of touch and the sense of smell, which have always played a part in healing. However, it is also the case that some therapists have a good understanding of modern knowledge about human anatomy and physiology and some may use orthodox techniques, such as X-rays, in their work. In fact, in the U.S., all osteopaths, for example, are trained in conventional medicine, while physical therapists (physiotherapists in Britain) undertake a lengthy "orthodox" paramedical training. Nevertheless, there is considerable variation in the approaches and training of therapists even within a specific field. Cranial osteopaths and those doing Cranio-Sacral therapy do not use the same techniques as "ordinary" osteopaths. Similarly, there are distinct differences in method between "ordinary" chiropractors and those using the McTimoney variation, which is gentler and slower. Kinesiology is particularly confusing in this respect in that the term is used to include a wide range of therapies, and practitioners may have widely different training and approaches. It is important that you establish the background and type of treatment offered by a specific therapist before deciding whether to go ahead.

Some types of treatment have been shown in studies to have clear benefits for certain conditions: as mentioned above, many conventional doctors now accept that a trained and experienced osteopath or chiropractor may be able to do more to relieve chronic low back pain, for example, than they themselves are able to do. There is also wide acceptance of the potential benefits of some kinds of relaxation techniques in easing psychological tension and its consequences, while educative approaches such as the Alexander Technique can often prevent such problems occurring or recurring.

All the therapies in this group are holistic to a greater or lesser extent in that their practitioners will tailor their recommendations and/or treatment to you as an individual and not purely toward treating your symptoms or condition. However, the spectrum ranges from those that are closer in approach to conventional medicine (such as osteopathy, chiropractic, and some types of hydrotherapy), to those that are more obviously

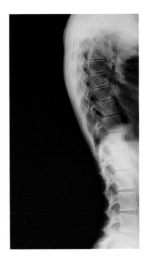

ABOVE *Chiropractors often take X-rays of back problems.*

LEFT *Severe back pain can be eased by alternative bodywork therapies.*

LEFT *Muscle energy and release techniques are widely used in osteopathy.*

patient attempts to resist

osteopath stops the movement

"alternative" (for example, Rolfing, with its concept of "body memories," and Trager work, in which energy is "transferred" from therapist to client during therapy).

Alternative therapists will take different approaches to dealing with symptoms that have their origin in structures such as the skeleton and soft tissues, and most accept that stress and tension may often lie behind such problems or, at the very least, exacerbate them. For this reason, many therapists will work with the individual on dealing with underlying issues of a psychological or emotional nature at the same time as tackling the physical aspects.

Your choice of therapy will depend to some extent on whether you are looking to alleviate existing symptoms and, if so, on their nature and origin, or whether you are more concerned to prevent problems developing or recurring. Hellerwork, the Alexander Technique, and the Feldenkrais Method may well be effective at relieving symptoms, but they are predominantly educative and preventive in intention. Some, like kinesiology, require commitment on the part of the person being treated if they are to be effective; massage and aromatherapy, on the other hand, are effective even though the recipient is passive while the treatment takes place.

Although their theoretical principles vary, many physical therapies are of particular benefit in relieving pain originating in the musculoskeletal system. Massage, for instance, is particularly effective for soft tissue damage, including sports injuries, while osteopathy and chiropractic help to correct bone and joint misalignments which may be the root cause of pain. Physical tension caused by emotional or psychological stress is often behind many common aches and pains, even when there is no direct damage, and here therapies which address nonphysical problems may be the most effective.

This means that if you are looking to relieve existing symptoms (as well as to prevent them recurring) you may need to spend some time considering what would be the right type of therapy for you. It may be that you will need more than one sort. For example, if you are suffering pain and stiffness that you feel is related to some aspect of your lifestyle — such as sitting for long hours at a computer or tension caused by chronic stress

— you may do best with an approach that combines easing tense and knotted muscles with relaxation or posture therapy. This could mean massage, plus the Alexander Technique, or breathing or relaxation therapy, for instance. On the other hand, if you have specific joint problems, hydrotherapy and/or flotation might suit you best. If your problem seems to have a psychological as well as physical origin, Hellerwork or Trager Work might be a better option.

It is likely to be a question of trial and error to some extent, although if you have back pain which has come on suddenly or recurred, early treatment from an osteopath or chiropractor is very likely to be effective, provided your doctor has ruled out any condition that could be exacerbated by these approaches.

Initially, you will need to consult a professional practitioner, and most forms of physical therapy cannot be done on a "self-help" basis. However, once the sessions are under way, you may be taught some aspects of the technique, as with relaxation and breathing therapies, that you can practice on your own. You may be encouraged to complete exercises at home between treatment sessions — special structured movements performed between and after the completion of treatment are important features of Rolfing and Hellerwork, for example. In therapies that are primarily educative, you will need to maintain indefinitely the new postures and

ABOVE Most physical therapies need to be performed by a practitioner — at least to begin with. You will be taught aspects of the technique you can practice alone.

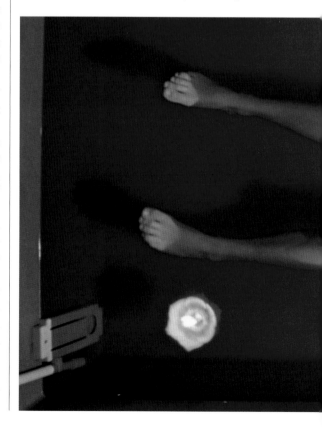

SUMMARY

A reputable therapist will want to be sure that you have come to the right person, and will be happy to explain in as much detail as you want. You should also make sure that the therapist has received a specialized training in their particular field and has experience of dealing with the sort of problems for which you personally need help.

Although the better known forms of physical therapy are widely available, some of the newer or more unusual ones may be harder to track down. You should have no trouble finding a good masseur, aromatherapist, osteopath, or chiropractor for example, and forms of hydrotherapy are available in health farms as well as hospitals. You may even find that your doctor is happy to recommend a good local practitioner. Zero Balancing, Trager Work, and Hellerwork practitioners may be harder to track down, however, especially outside the U.S.

ways of moving that you have been taught, as with the Alexander Technique.

During your first consultation with a therapist, you will probably know instinctively whether you feel comfortable with his or her particular approach and feel it is right for you. Don't be shy about asking exactly what is involved; what, if anything, will be expected of you; and how long the course is likely to last. It's best to bring up any concerns you may have at this stage so that you know whether they are really important or merely based on a lack of understanding. For example, some people are put off osteopathy or chiropractic because they have heard it involves sharp or even painful manipulation, but this is largely a myth. However, if you are still concerned, you may be more comfortable with gentler forms, such as cranial osteopathy or McTimoney chiropractic. Sometimes, though, it may be necessary to suffer a little to get the benefit of treatment: deep massage or Rolfing can sometimes be painful although not unbearably so. Hellerwork and Trager Work, while not physically painful, may be more difficult from an emotional perspective for some individuals. Alternative therapies rarely offer a "quick fix," but if you are concerned that the level of commitment or the amount of time required for a particular course of therapy may be too great for you, ask the therapist for more details of what's likely to be involved.

There's nothing wrong with opting for a treatment that is enjoyable, even a positive pleasure. Many people have an aromatherapy massage on a regular basis, even if they have no current symptoms, simply because it boosts their morale and well-being. The same can be said of other kinds of massage, of flotation therapy, and of some types of relaxation therapy – successful treatment doesn't have to involve hard work or discomfort!

ABOVE *Because the Feldenkrais Method also brings greater flexibility and extends the range of movement in the joints, it can be of great benefit to athletes.*

ABOVE *Massage oils and essential oils are often used in physical therapies.*

LEFT *Flotation therapy can ease anxiety and stress.*

THERAPEUTIC MASSAGE

ORIGINS
OF MASSAGE

Massage is an art which was practiced long before written historical records. In China, a system called "anma" existed, which later became today's "tuina." "Shiatsu" was created in Japan by combining "anma" with other techniques. India's Ayurveda medical system uses massage to enhance its therapies. Arabs called massage "masah" and it was considered part of standard medical practice throughout Greece, the Roman Empire, and Egypt for centuries after the famous Persian doctor Avicenna deemed it important in 1000 C.E. in his Canon of Medicine.

Some forms of massage focus only upon physical movements which will affect the body – not upon the flow of "spiritual energy" within it. Therapeutic massage – sometimes known as "Swedish massage" – involves only the manipulation of the soft tissues of the body, like the skin, muscles, tendons, and ligaments. It has a healing and preventive effect that has been known and demonstrated for thousands of years. For this purpose, therapeutic massage is used by physical therapists, physiotherapists, and trained masseurs in hospitals and clinics throughout the world. Some basic massage techniques can be learned easily and used at home for self-help, both to promote general well-being and to relieve certain specific medical conditions.

"Therapeutic massage" is a relatively new name for an ancient art that must have been practiced long before records began – after all, it is instinctive to hold and rub a part of the body that has been injured or is causing pain. Certainly most great civilizations have had a tradition of massage, although its effects have been explained in different ways. For example, long ago, the Chinese formulated the system of "anma" (*see page 32*), which evolved into the "tuina" of today, while the Japanese combined "anma" with other techniques to develop "shiatsu" (*see pages 32–7*); all of these therapies are underpinned by the concept of "spiritual energy" known as qi or ki. In India, Ayurvedic practitioners (*see pages 78–85*) have long encouraged the use of massage to rub various oils, spices, and herbs into the skin – and the art of massage is taught in the majority of Indian families to this day.

Ancient Arabic, Egyptian, Greek, and Roman doctors all promoted the benefits of massage, too. The Greeks knew massage as "anatripsis," and the Arabs knew it as "masah." Hippocrates, often called "the father of medicine," wrote in 380 B.C.E.: "The physician must be experienced in many things, but assuredly in rubbing." Celsus and Galen, two renowned Roman doctors wrote numerous books on the efficacy of rubbing, and massage was a part of the daily routine of many Romans. Julius Caesar, who suffered from neuralgia, was massaged daily. And around 1000 C.E., Avicenna, a famous Persian doctor, devoted a large section of his Canon of Medicine to the benefits of massage – it was to be Europe's standard medical textbook for centuries.

The Swedish Connection

Massage continued to thrive as a therapy over the centuries. (Interestingly, it was at one time known as "friction and shampooing": this was before the lotions we use to wash our hair were invented; the "shampoo" we buy today takes its name from a

head massage.) However, therapeutic massage as we understand it today was first developed by a Swedish gymnast called Per Henrik Ling (1776–1839) in the late 18th century. Ling utilized some of the massage techniques of "anma," although not its underlying spiritual principles, having visited China. His form of massage spread rapidly, and the "Swedish Institutes" in which it was practiced were set up in many European cities. This is why therapeutic massage is sometimes known as "Swedish massage." Two other Swedes took Ling's ideas to America and opened the first massage clinics there in the second half of the 19th century; partly as a result of presidential patronage, they became extremely popular.

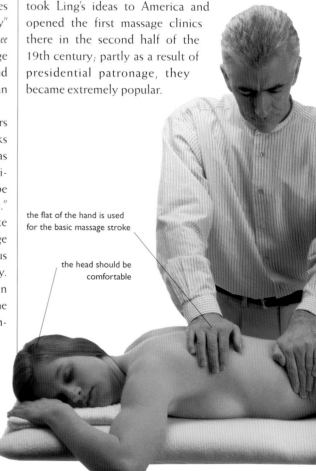

the flat of the hand is used for the basic massage stroke

the head should be comfortable

HOW THERAPEUTIC MASSAGE WORKS

A massage has both a physiological and psychological effect. The various movements employed (*see pages 98–9*) affect the skin, muscles, blood vessels, lymphatic drainage channels (lymph has roughly the same constituents as serum (blood, less the blood cells and blood proteins)), nerves, and some of the internal organs. Deep pressure stimulates the body's systems – such as the immune, circulatory, lymph, and digestive systems – while slow, gentle, more superficial movement slows them down, and relaxes them.

Sensory nerve endings in the inner layer – the dermis – of the skin respond to touch and pressure. When these receptors

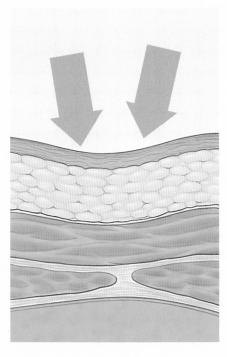

ABOVE *Pressure on the skin penetrates deep within the body's systems, affecting messages sent to and from the brain.*

are stimulated, they send nerve impulses up a sensory nerve to the spinal cord and these are transmitted along it up to the brain. Signals from touch nerve fibers take precedence over those from chronic pain fibers while traveling to the brain, so that some of the sensations of chronic pain do not reach the brain – so less pain, or no pain, is felt.

The sensation of touch also stimulates the release in the brain of chemicals known as endorphins, which act as the body's own painkillers. These not only dampen down the perception of pain, but also induce a feeling of well-being and relaxation, so lightening your mood and increasing your self-esteem.

Achieving Respectability

By the end of the 19th century, therapeutic massage had become so respectable and well-established that it was common for doctors to prescribe a course of massage for a variety of ailments. Generally, a specially trained masseur gave the treatments, and in 1894 some British masseurs banded together to form The Society of Trained Masseuses (the intention was to differentiate medical therapeutic massage from less reputable forms of massage offered at the time at houses of ill-repute). In time, this society developed into the state-regulated Chartered Society of Physiotherapy, and similar ones were organized in Europe and America – where physiotherapists are known today as "physical therapists."

Therapeutic massage continued to thrive until the first World War – during which it was used as a treatment for "shell shock," which we would today call "post-traumatic stress disorder."

LEFT *Most people think of massage as relaxing, but its effects can also be energizing and rejuvenating.*

Afterward, western medicine started to look more to technology than to traditional practices, and medical massage went into a decline. It was not to regain its standing until the 1960s, when there was a revival of interest in complementary medicine and a surge of public enthusiasm for preventive methods and relaxation techniques, to combat stress.

Nowadays, therapeutic massage is recognized as being beneficial in the treatment of many medical disorders – from asthma and circulatory problems to musculoskeletal disorders. It also increases weight gain in premature babies. Massage aids relaxation and reduces stress – and since stress is known to be one of the main predisposing factors in many conditions, massage is an extremely good preventive therapy.

It is surprising that massage is only now being recognized by official medical bodies in the West, as the habit of mothers massaging babies, and of children massaging their grandfathers' feet, etc., has been practiced for centuries in places like India. There, it is considered a normal part of everyday life and its good effects may be observed in the well-formed bodies of Indian country people, who still maintain these old traditions.

BABY MASSAGE

Babies and children – and even teenagers if they will allow it – benefit considerably from being massaged. Babies who receive a regular massage put on weight more rapidly after birth than those who do not. Massage also helps a baby or child to develop a positive body image – a mental picture of the body, its components, and boundaries – and helps teenagers to come to terms with their changing shape and to accept their body. Recently it has also been suggested that babies lay down myelin (a substance that coats certain nerve fibers and speeds up the transmission of nerve impulses) more rapidly if they are massaged regularly. Certainly babies who are massaged seem to be more content and to suffer from less irritability and episodes of colic. Also, bonding between a baby and its siblings and parents is strengthened by the physical contact between them.

ABOVE *Baby massage is becoming more popular as its benefits are known.*

MASSAGE TECHNIQUES

Four basic types of movement – physical therapists call them "strokes" – are used in therapeutic massage. Generally, either plain talcum powder or a massage oil, such as baby oil, is used as a medium to allow the hands to glide easily over the skin. An essential oil (*see Aromatherapy, pages 104–5*) can also be used.

Effleurage

This is the basic stroke of massage and is used both to start and finish a session, because it relaxes the superficial muscles and enables the subject to become used to the feel of the masseur's hands on his or her skin. Effleurage is also used as a connecting movement when moving between one part of the body to another, since a masseur's hands should stay in contact with the skin as much as possible.

The stroke is performed with the flat of the hand, with the fingers held together but relaxed; however, the masseur must conform his hands to the natural contours of the body. The movement is slow and rhythmical, and is usually made toward the heart, with the return stroke being slightly lighter. Firmer, more rapid effleurage can be used to stimulate blood flow, increase flexibility, and warm up muscles – for example, as part of a warm-up routine before taking part in sport.

Pettrisage

This stroke is performed with the pads of the thumbs and fingers and the palms of the hands. The soft tissues are kneaded deeply and squeezed and rolled in a rhythmical movement – as if you are kneading dough or plasticine. Pettrisage is used to release tension from both superficial and deep muscles that are taut, and also to increase blood flow to the area.

Pettrisage strokes are especially effective on deep muscles like those of the shoulders, buttocks, hips, and legs. When working on fleshy areas of the body, the knuckles are held in a loose fist and moved in circles to knead and pummel any underlying muscles that are taut, to help them relax and lengthen.

Friction

This stroke breaks down adhesions between tissues and relaxes any muscle fibers that have gone into spasm – as such, friction is often used in trigger point therapy (*see pages 22–3*); trigger points are often found around the shoulders and neck. Friction is performed with the pads of the thumbs, never the tips. A small, deep, circular movement, in which the pad of the thumb stays in contact with the same area of skin, is used to grind the tissue in spasm against the underlying tissues or bone.

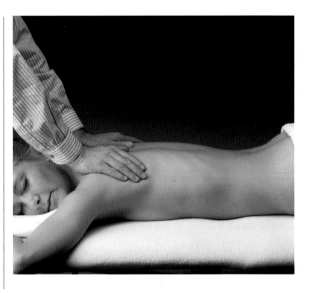

ABOVE *Effleurage: these slow, relaxing strokes are the simplest form of massage and can easily be practiced at home, on yourself or on your partner.*

ABOVE *Pettrisage or kneading: this "deeper" stroke, alternately grasping and squeezing the flesh, is especially effective for relieving muscular tension and stimulating the circulation.*

This is the only massage stroke that can cause pain, but it is the type of pain often described as "sweet agony"; if friction causes too much pain, it will be counterproductive, since the muscles will tense up even further. In a variant of this technique, known as "pressuring," the pads of the thumbs and fingers simply press down rather than describe small circles.

Friction is performed only after effleurage and pettrisage, after muscles are generally relaxed and blood flow has been increased. Usually, the technique is used little and often in order to break down any spasm or adhesion gradually.

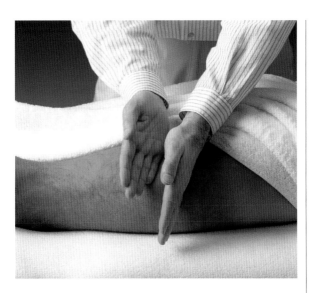

ABOVE *"Hacking" requires more expertise, as it can be painful if done too vigorously. But it is useful for toning the skin and breaking down cellulite.*

ABOVE *Applying gentle pressure to the dents on either side of the temples for about ten seconds creates a pleasant tingling sensation and helps to ease headaches.*

Tapotement

This term covers a variety of percussive strokes that stimulate the skin and the soft tissues and increase blood flow to the area being worked on: they include "hacking," "cupping," "flicking," and "pummelling," of which "cupping" and "hacking" are the most often used. However, both are confined to the fleshy areas of the body, and are not used over bony regions, broken veins, tender areas, or lumps. If the massage is for relaxation, tapotement is always followed by effleurage.

Hacking is performed with the little-finger edge of the hand with the fingers relaxed. If the fingers are tense,

the stroke can resemble a karate chop and be painful. The movement should be rhythmical and fast, and each hand should strike the skin directly after the other and just beside it – practice is needed to do this properly.

Cupping

Cupping is performed with the finger joints straight but bent at the knuckles and the thumb pressed close to the forefinger to make the shape of a cup – as if you were to drink water out of your hands, but with your hand held so that the cup faces the skin. Like hacking, this, too, is a rapid rhythmical movement, with each hand in turn drumming on the skin – it should make a sound like a horse trotting. Because of the shape of the hand, the "cup" forms a slight vacuum, and, as the hand is taken off the skin, the blood is pulled toward the surface, giving the skin a rosy hue. Cupping is very good for improving the texture of the skin, the peripheral nerve endings, and the subcutaneous tissues.

Techniques like cupping, hacking, flicking, and pummelling are good for stimulating the skin and for awakening the muscles and organs beneath them. Very tense, physically weak, or sick people, however, must be treated with great care when using them. They may find painful and stressful massage techniques which are enervating to normal healthy bodies. Also, pain thresholds in individuals differ.

CONSULTING A PRACTITIONER

If you suffer from a medical condition that may benefit from massage, you are likely to be referred to a physical therapist or physiotherapist by your family doctor. Otherwise, you may be able to find a massage therapist at a local health club. On your first visit, you will be asked about your general health and lifestyle, and whether you are taking any medication or are having treatment for any problem. You will be asked whether you would like a massage for any particular reason – in order to relax, for example, to relieve tense, sore muscles, or to prepare for a sporting event. The massage room should be warm and softly lit. You will be asked to undress to your underwear and lie on a special massage table. Warm blankets or towels will be draped over the areas that are not to be massaged immediately. A reputable masseur will have short nails and no jewelry. Most massage sessions will last an hour and include a full body massage, though the masseur may concentrate on certain tense muscles, such as the trapezii at the neck and shoulders. At the end of the session, you will be covered with a warm blanket and left to relax for a while.

PRECAUTIONS

Check that a massage therapist you consult has received adequate training, is registered with the authorities, and has the appropriate professional indemnity insurance. Physical therapists and physiotherapists, to whom a doctor is likely to refer you, have had such training, are state-registered, and have this kind of insurance. Certain conditions are contraindications to massage. These include:

■ Cancer – unless by a trained specialist, or self-massage, having been instructed by a specialist about what to do and what to avoid

■ Contagious diseases

■ Fever

■ Infectious skin conditions

■ Lumps or bumps, or over a fractured bone or ruptured tendon

■ Severe osteoporosis

■ Phlebitis and thrombosis (a blood clot may be disturbed)

■ Pregnancy, when performed on the abdomen

■ Varicose veins (across the affected area)

WATCHPOINT

Check the precautions box above to make sure that you do not have any contraindications for massage.
Make sure that you do not have long nails, otherwise you may cut your or others' skin.
Certain essential oils should not be used with certain conditions (*see Aromatherapy, pp. 104–5*).

SELF-HELP

As you will see below, a certain degree of self-massage is possible. Although massaging oneself is not nearly so relaxing and enjoyable as being massaged by someone else (see over), it still has many of the same effects as a received massage, in that it eases pain and stimulates the production of endorphins. Self-massage can also relieve tension headaches, tight, sore muscles, and swollen ankles, and improve skin tone and blood flow. Even shampooing your hair can give your scalp a good massage, and rubbing moisturizer into your face can help relax tense facial muscles. What follows is a full self-massage, but you can always choose a particular area and treat it alone when time is short or there is a partic-ular problem.

Preparations

Choose a warm, quiet room, in which you will not be disturbed by anyone – not even by the telephone. Wear loose clothes. Keep your feet bare. Remove any jewelry and if you have long hair, pin it up off your neck. It is a good idea to take a warm bath before a massage, because the heat of the water helps to relax the muscles, eases away tensions, and increases bloodflow to the skin.

Sit in a chair or a sofa that is firm but comfortable, or propped up with pillows on a firm bed. Whatever you choose, it may be wise to cover it with a towel if you intend to use massage oil (most health shops stock this, but you can use baby oil at a pinch).

---

1 *Start with your feet. Place the ankle or foot (which one depends on how supple your hip joints are) of one leg across the thigh of your other leg. Using your thumb and forefinger, move each toe through its full range of movements and then squeeze them all (see Reflexology, pp. 66–71, for other foot massage movements). Repeat with your other leg.*

2 *Move your thumb in circles over the ball of each foot, pressing in quite deeply, and then over the rest of the foot to the heel.*

3 *Using your whole hand, squeeze and stroke each whole foot in turn up to its ankle.*

sit in a comfortable position on the floor to massage your feet

---

SELF-HELP

* Set up a warm, quiet room.

* Prepare yourself and the space for massage.

* Sit to massage your feet, toes, and ankles.

* Stand to massage your legs and hips.

* Sit to massage your lower back in circular movements.

* Massage your face and neck.

* Rest quietly and breathe deeply for a few minutes.

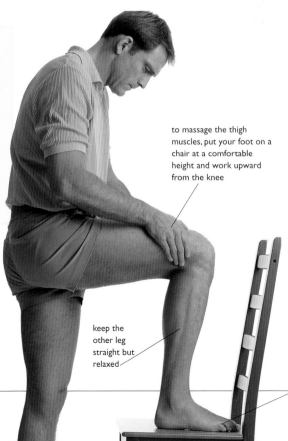

to massage the thigh muscles, put your foot on a chair at a comfortable height and work upward from the knee

keep the other leg straight but relaxed

keep your foot flat on the chair to avoid tensing the thigh muscles

4 *Put your foot on a high stool or the arm of a chair – anything will do, so long as it is much higher than the hip. Place both hands just above your ankle, encircling it. Stroke firmly down across the ankle and up to the knee. Repeat at least five times, and more times if your ankles are swollen. Repeat with other leg.*

5 *Knead your calf muscle firmly with both hands and finish by repeating firm downward strokes. Repeat with the other leg – if one ankle tends to swell more than the other, massage that ankle last.*

6 Knead each thigh in turn (still with your foot up), back and front, starting from the knee and working up to the groin. Finish with firm upward strokes from the knee to the hip and groin. These will loosen the large muscles and improve the circulation of blood and lymph.

7 Sitting straight, work the balls of the fingers of both hands in small circular movements over the muscles on each side of the spine at the lower back. Knead the back muscles between your thumbs and fingers. Move as far up the back as possible, but finish with the circular movements at the lower back.

8 Turn to your shoulders. This area often becomes painful because the shoulder muscles react to any tension, whether physical or emotional, by tightening up, and some of the muscle fibers will go into spasm as a result. Place your finger pads on the muscles on either side of your neck, being careful not to press down on the spine itself. Knead the muscles up to the skull, using small, circular movements.

9 Massage your face using the strokes for a facial massage (see over).

10 Knead and manipulate each hand in the same way as your feet (see above), then continue up your forearm and upper arm to your shoulder.

to massage your back, sit with spine straight and shoulders well back

bend your elbows as far as possible to reach the muscles at chest height

gradually work down to the lower back

11 Tilt your head slightly toward the side to be massaged, because doing so shortens the muscle slightly and reduces the tension held in it. Press down with the balls of your fingers, using small circular movements, on the thick muscle that runs from each shoulder to the base of the neck.

12 Knead the muscles between your thumb and fingers. If any point is particularly tender, push down with either the ball of your thumb or a finger.

hold your head in a relaxed position, at a slight angle

knead the muscles across your shoulders, then run your fingers up your neck to stretch it

keep your elbows as high as possible so that you can move your hands comfortably from the base of your neck up to your skull

GIVING MASSAGE

In this busy world, it is important to deal with stress. It is widely acknowledged that stroking a pet lowers your blood pressure, slows your heart rate, and reduces tension and feelings of anger and anxiety. But research has shown that a person who gives a massage also becomes more relaxed, and so benefits in many of the same ways as the recipient. Use this argument to persuade a partner or friend to learn the simple techniques of massage (see pages 98–9) and apply them to you.

Back Massage

A back massage is the normal starting point to a whole body massage, but it is also used alone to induce a state of relaxation. This is because much of the stress of our fast-moving modern lifestyle is felt in the upper back, shoulders, and neck. However, the spinal column, down the center of the back, should never be massaged unless by a qualified medical therapist, such as an osteopath, physical therapist, or physiotherapist. First, ask the recipient to lay face down on a firm bed. Rub some massage oil into your hands, then begin with Step 1.

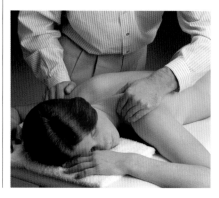

1 *Start the massage with effleurage strokes, moving from the small of the back up either side of the spinal column to the neck, continuing over the top of the shoulders to their tips and then down the side of the back to the small of the back again. Start each upward stroke slightly farther out than its predecessor, so that the whole back is covered by five upward strokes. Repeat until the recipient is relaxed.*

2 *Knead the shoulders to release any tension, working on each one in turn. At the same time, feel for any tight nodules or areas of tenderness – they are normally found in the trapezius muscles at the base of the neck.*

3 *Start breaking down any nodules by friction or pressuring. You may need to work a little and often on them, returning to them many times during the course of the massage to avoid causing any undue pain.*

4 *Apply pressuring upon the long muscles that run down the back on either side of the spine, starting from the shoulders and working down little by little so that no area is overlooked.*

5 *If the muscles of the back seem particularly taut and the skin appears dull, the area can be hacked, cupped, and knuckled. Remember not to work over the spinal column itself.*

6 *Complete the massage by repeating step one, although you can alter the movements so that you move across the body in a figure eight as well as straight up and down. The last movements should be gentle, feathery strokes from the neck down to the bottom of the back which grow progressively slower and slower.*

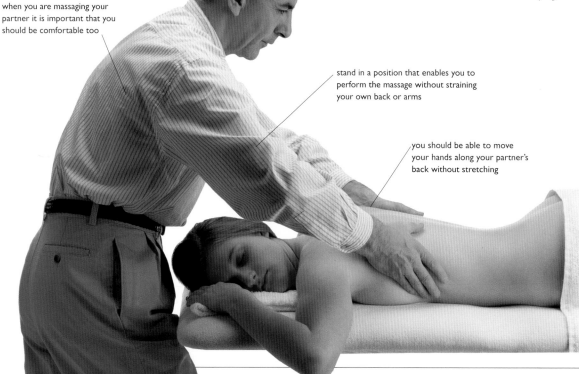

when you are massaging your partner it is important that you should be comfortable too

stand in a position that enables you to perform the massage without straining your own back or arms

you should be able to move your hands along your partner's back without stretching

WATCHPOINT

Do not allow anyone but a therapist with medical or paramedical qualifications to massage your spine directly.
Check the precautions box on page 99 to make sure that you do not have any contraindications for massage.
Make sure that anyone giving you a massage has short nails and takes off any jewelry; otherwise, your skin may be cut. Certain essential oils should not be used with certain conditions (see Aromatherapy, pp.104–5).

FACIAL MASSAGE

A facial massage can improve a poor and dull complexion, and release tensions held in the facial muscles. It is wonderfully soothing and relaxing. Ask the recipient to lie face-up on a bed without any pillow and with the shoulders bare. Hair should be pinned back or put into a turban or cap. You should stand behind the head. Rub some massage oil into your hands, then:

2 *Massage the temples in a circular movement, using the balls of your fingers. Concentrate on the dip above the outside of each eye.*

3 *Rub the scalp all over with the pads of your thumbs and fingers, as though giving a thorough shampoo.*

1 *Using your thumbs, stroke gently outward from between the eyebrows to the hairline, moving slightly up the forehead with each outward stroke.*

4 *Stroke gently under the eyes and across the cheeks from the nose to the ears.*

5 *Cup the chin with your hands and stroke outward along the jawline to the bottom of the ears.*

6 *Using the balls of your thumbs, make small circular movements where the jaw meets the skull and then down the upper rim of the jaw to the chin.*

7 *Gently pinch the nose and the ears between your thumb and forefinger.*

8 *Lay your hands over the whole face and lightly stroke up from the chin to the forehead. As you finish, leave your hands resting lightly over the face for a few seconds, retaining as much skin contact as possible.*

cover the whole face with your hands to let your partner relax in the darkness

use the gentlest of pressure on the face, so as not to drag at the skin

PATHFINDER

Massage promotes good health and is a general preventive treatment and therapy for many ailments, including:

ADDICTIONS *SEE P.* 258
ANXIETY *SEE PP.* 256–7
ARTHRITIS *SEE PP.* 346–7
ASTHMA *SEE PP.* 294–5
ATHEROSCLEROSIS *SEE P.* 305
BACK PROBLEMS *SEE PP.* 344–5
BRONCHITIS *SEE P.* 299
CATARRH *SEE P.* 285
CHILBLAINS *SEE P.* 277
COLIC *SEE P.* 350
COMMON COLD *SEE P.* 300
CONSTIPATION *SEE P.* 313
CRAMP *SEE P.* 349
DANDRUFF *SEE P.* 274
DEPRESSION *SEE P.* 261
DIZZINESS *SEE P* 271
EARACHE *SEE P.* 282
EATING DISORDERS *SEE P.* 265
FAINTING *SEE P.* 270
FIBROSITIS *SEE P.* 348
FLU *SEE P.* 298
HEADACHE *SEE PP.* 268–9
HICCUPS *SEE P.* 301
HIV AND AIDS *SEE PP.* 340–41
HYPERACTIVITY *SEE P.* 351
INSOMNIA *SEE P.* 264
LABOR PAINS *SEE P.* 328
MIGRAINE *SEE P.* 269
MISCARRIAGE *SEE P.* 325
NEURALGIA *SEE P.* 267
PALPITATIONS *SEE P.* 307
PREGNANCY PROBLEMS *SEE PP.* 326–7
STRESS *SEE PP.* 262–3
STROKE *SEE P.* 359

AROMATHERAPY MASSAGE

I f a therapeutic massage confers undoubted physical and psychological benefits, an aromatherapy massage certainly enhances and maximizes these benefits, and is also very pleasurable for the recipient. For this reason, essential oils are used during therapeutic massages at many hospitals and hospices. Many aromatherapists claim that the essential oils used can be chosen according to an individual's specific needs, and play their part in the treatment of a variety of disorders; some say that the recipient responds positively to the scent which is correct for his or her needs.

From the ancient Chinese to the Native Americans, most cultures have a history of using essential oils – aromatic essences extracted from plants – to alter moods and to heal. The ancient Egyptians were perhaps the most sophisticated in this respect, using essential oils as perfumes, healing tools, and embalming agents for mummification. Their main method of extracting essential oil was to infuse a herb in castor or olive oil for a few days. Later, the Arab philosopher and doctor Avicenna (980–1037) developed a method of distillation that is very similar to the one used in modern practices today.

The word "aromatherapy" was not coined until early in the 20th century, when René-Maurice Gattefossé, a French chemist who worked in his family's perfumery business, burned his hand. On impulse, he thrust it into a pot of lavender oil that was standing nearby – and to his surprise the burn healed rapidly. Gattefossé decided to use his knowledge of perfumes to experiment with essential oils to discover their effects and properties. He wrote a book on the subject in 1928; unfortunately, his work went largely unregarded at the time. However, in the 1960s, Jean Valnet, a French doctor, revived and developed Gattefossé's work, and started to study the effects and medicinal uses of many types of essential oils.

Aromatherapy Today

Valnet concentrated on the medical uses of essential oils. He treated shell shock and burns in Second World War patients – and gave essential oils to them internally. Valnet's methods became well-established in France, and are still used there today.

However, aromatherapy as we know it, and the use of aromatherapy with massage, was popularized by an Austrian-born biochemist and beautician called Marguerite Maury, who worked in France. She started to use essential oils when massaging her clients, and

found that not only did they find the massage more pleasurable and effective, but that the oils conveyed benefits other than those deriving from the massage itself. Maury continued to research the use of aromatherapy oils, choosing specific oils to suit each individual's needs; unlike Valnet, though, she did not recommend their internal use. Maury's work triggered a rapid rise in the popularity of aromatherapy massage in both Europe and America as a kind of beauty treatment that also had beneficial effects. Maury herself found that a massage with essential oils was useful in promoting relaxation, treating skin conditions, and relieving certain types of pain, but since then many aromatherapists have claimed that aromatherapy is a curative treatment in a large number of disorders. The medical profession treats these claims with considerable skepticism.

WHAT AROMATHERAPY OILS DO

In this book, we are concerned only with the effects of aromatherapy oils massaged into the skin, but numerous books discuss the other uses and effects of essential oils (*see Further Reading, pages 374–5*).

It has been shown that essential oils are absorbed into the body through the skin, but in such small quantities that any internal effect is likely to be minimal. The main

ABOVE Massaging with aromatherapy oils can be very relaxing.

BELOW AND RIGHT *Buy essential oils in small quantities so that they are always fresh.*

COMMON ESSENTIAL OILS AND THEIR EFFECTS

Lavender – is a sedative, antidepressant, and antiseptic: for stress, digestive disorders, headaches, migraine, burns, bites, acne, and chilblains.

Rosemary – is a stimulant, decongestive, and analgesic: for sinus congestion, catarrh, circulatory disorders, stress, and musculoskeletal aches and pains.

Tea Tree – is an antiseptic, anti-fungal, and antibacterial agent: for acne, bites, wounds, cold sores, athlete's foot, headlice, scabies, dandruff, and coughs and colds.

Neroli – is a sedative, antidepressant, and anti-inflammatory: for depression, poor self-esteem, insomnia, stress, and premenstrual tension.

Camomile – is a sedative, anti-spasmodic, anti-inflammatory, and antidepressant: for allergies, stress, insomnia, headaches, eczema, acne, colic, flatulence, and indigestion.

Peppermint – is an anti-spasmodic, decongestant, and stimulant: for colic, flatulence, indigestion, nausea, vomiting, sinus congestion, catarrh, and mental fatigue.

Sandalwood – is a sedative, antiseptic, decongestant, and antidepressant: for eczema, psoriasis, stress, insomnia, depression, and premenstrual tension.

Eucalyptus – is an antiseptic, anti-allergy, antidepressant: for eczema, acne, allergies, stress, headaches, premenstrual tension, depression, sprains, aches and pains, and influenza.

Rose – is an antiseptic, sedative, and antidepressant: for sinus congestion, stress, depression, anorexia nervosa, broken capillaries, poor circulation, insomnia, menstrual problems, and menopausal difficulties.

effect of aromatherapy oils – apart from the purely tactile pleasure that their use gives during a massage – is upon the sense of smell. This can be significant because, while odors can evoke a strong emotional reaction, they can also have further effects. They are picked up by smell receptors in the nostrils, which pass the information to the areas of the brain that control emotional responses and memory. But the information is also sent to the hypothalamus, a small gland at the base of the brain that controls the internal body systems – and especially those involved with digestion, body temperature, sexuality, and the stress reaction.

USING AROMATHERAPY MASSAGE OILS

1 *Mix two to three drops of essential oil – use the chart above to choose an appropriate oil, but make sure that you like its smell, too – to one teaspoon (5ml) of carrier oil. Common carrier oils include almond, avocado, soy, and grape seed oil.*

2 *Follow the instructions for a therapeutic massage (see pp. 96–103).*

CONSULTING A PRACTITIONER

When choosing a practitioner, make sure that she has been properly trained, since anyone can claim to be an aromatherapist. A trained aromatherapist will also be a practicing masseur and will only use high-quality oils. She will take a short medical history and ask about any problems you have before choosing the appropriate oils and giving you a massage (see pages 96–103) that takes about 30 minutes.

PATHFINDER

The use of aromatherapy oils with a massage can increase its relaxing and other beneficial effects (see pages 96–103). Although the oils are absorbed into the body through the skin, little reaches the internal body systems, so their physiological effects, which are not known for certain, are mild. However, the psychological effects of their aromas include altering mood and emotion and creating a feeling of well-being. Use them for:

ADDICTION SEE P. 258

ALLERGIES SEE PP. 338–9

ANXIETY SEE PP. 256–7

DEPRESSION SEE P. 261

EATING DISORDERS SEE P. 265

ECZEMA SEE P. 273

HEADACHE SEE PP. 268–9

INSOMNIA SEE P. 264

MENSTRUAL PROBLEMS SEE PP. 322–3

STRESS SEE PP. 262–3

PRECAUTIONS

■ Never take essential oils internally unless prescribed by a medically qualified aromatherapist, since they can be toxic.

■ Do not use clary sage, camomile, pennyroyal, or rosemary during pregnancy.

■ Avoid fennel oil, which stimulates the production of estrogen, the female hormone, if you have – or have a family history of – breast cancer.

■ Do not use an oil if your skin has an allergic reaction.

■ Basil oil can be carcinogenic if used in large quantities.

OSTEOPATHY

*A*ndrew Taylor Still, an American doctor, developed osteopathy as a new way of treating disease – one that did not rely on the gruesome surgical techniques and dangerous drugs of the time – after working among the Shawnee tribe of Native Americans and as an army surgeon in the American Civil War. At first his ideas were derided by doctors and preachers alike, but gradually they gained in popularity until, in 1972, osteopaths were recognized in America as medical doctors. A different tradition of osteopathy developed in Europe, but in recent years the therapy has become recognized and accepted there, too.

The term "osteopathy" – from the Greek words "osteo," meaning "bone," and "pathos," meaning "disease" – was coined by Andrew Taylor Still (1828–1918) and given to a new system of health care that he developed. Still was born near Jonesboro, in Lee County, Virginia, U.S.A., the son of a Methodist preacher, doctor, and millwright who moved his family first to Tennessee and then, in 1837, to a remote area of Missouri. He enjoyed the frugal lifestyle of the frontier, and was especially interested in local wildlife – he hunted animals for the pot and started to collect their bones, which led to a recurrent interest in anatomy. As this developed, Still started to help his father with his medical practice and eventually became his apprentice. Later, he was awarded a license to practice as a doctor in the state of Missouri and, during the 1860s, he completed his medical education at the College of Physicians and Surgeons in Kansas City, Missouri.

Dr. Still was a fervent advocate of the abolition of slavery, and he and his new wife decided to leave Missouri, which was in favor of slavery. He moved to the state of Kansas, where he ministered to the Native Americans of the Shawnee tribe. There, Still became disillusioned with how little he could do to cure disease, and his feelings were reinforced by service as an army surgeon during the American Civil War. He was repelled by the war's gruesome realities and its rough-and-ready 19th-century surgical methods. At the war's end, he determined to extend his studies of the human body and to devise a different way of treating disease.

The Body's Healing System
Still's strict upbringing and strong religious beliefs – he had helped with his father's spiritual work as well as his medical activities – drew him to the conclusion that God would never have made human beings so imperfect that they succumbed so easily to so many diseases. The answer to the conundrum, he decided, was that within each person there must be a system for the body to heal itself, and this meant that a physician's job was to stimulate the body so that it could do so. His determination to find a new method of medical care that achieved this without reliance on the drugs of the day, which were often dangerous and frequently useless, was reinforced when his three children died from meningitis despite having the best available care of the time.

The River of Life
Still's first step was to return to his study of human anatomy, examining bones that he dug up from old Native American graves. Having worked as a millwright with his father, he was aware of the laws of mechanics and he decided that the musculoskeletal system was similar to a piece of machinery; as such, it was subject to similar laws and stresses. Still also came to the conclusion that blood was "the river of life" and carried the necessary ingredients for healing around the body. This meant that if any stress upon the musculoskeletal system impeded the flow of blood in the body, the tissues could not heal themselves and disease followed. He believed that it was possible to mend any damage to the musculoskeletal system by manipulations

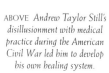
ABOVE *Andrew Taylor Still's disillusionment with medical practice during the American Civil War led him to develop his own healing system.*

ABOVE *Still was one of the first Western doctors to consider the effect of physical structure on the functioning of the body.*

and pressure and – as all the systems in the body are interrelated – normal function could be restored without the need for drugs.

Still wanted to announce his theories at Baker University in Kansas in 1874, but the local medical and religious communities thought his ideas so outrageous that he was forced to return to Missouri. He became so successful and popular with his patients – although still derided by his more orthodox colleagues – that in 1892 he founded a school of osteopathy at Kirksville, Missouri.

John Martin Littlejohn, a British forensic scientist and physiologist, came to the school. Littlejohn developed the holistic side of osteopathy – the idea that humans are affected by the world around them and that, to maintain health, the body must to be able to adjust to these outside influences. After a spell as Dean of Kirksville, Littlejohn opened a school of osteopathy in Chicago before returning to Britain in 1913.

Osteopathy Today

There has been a significant difference between the way osteopathy has developed in America and in Europe. In the early part of this century, the British government was unwilling to make legal a profession whose practitioners were largely trained overseas. In America, however, osteopathy was put on a proper legal footing from the start, with graduates obtaining a diploma in osteopathy. Dr. John Martin Littlejohn established Europe's first osteopathic school, the British School of Osteopathy, in London in 1917, and in 1925 led a deputation to the Minister of Health to explore the possibility of statutory recognition for osteopathy. However, it was made clear that no official recognition could be granted to a profession whose members were graduates of schools outside British jurisdiction. After several failed Osteopathic Bills, it was suggested that those practicing osteopathy would either qualify themselves for admission to the medical register or constitute a voluntary register of osteopaths: the latter is what happened and the General Council and Register of Osteopaths was formed. In 1993 the Osteopaths Act was passed, which made sure that all practitioners wishing to call themselves osteopaths would have to register under it, and by May 2000 all currently practicing osteopathy must be registered (by a rigorous process of demonstrating safety and competence) with the General Osteopathic Council. After May 2000, the only route into osteopathy will be by means of a recognized qualification.

Another split between America and Britain is that in 1972 American osteopaths were recognized as medical doctors who practice osteopathy – they can treat all medical problems and prescribe drugs. British osteopaths are not allowed to prescribe drugs (even though a medical doctor may refer a patient to an osteopath). However, British osteopaths, in keeping with Still's original thinking, see osteopathy as an alternative to drugs. They practice physical therapy and they do not want to be medical doctors.

STILL'S VIEW OF THE BODY

the musculoskeletal system is similar to a piece of machinery

LEFT *Still developed his own way of looking at the body.*

Still saw blood as carrying the necessary ingredients for healing

if bloodflow is impeded, disease may follow

ABOVE *Some osteopaths believe that the whole body is affected by its environment and emotions; the "fight or flight" instinct is an example.*

RIGHT *Osteopaths believe that our musculoskeletal system has a profound effect on the workings of our internal organs, and therefore on our general health.*

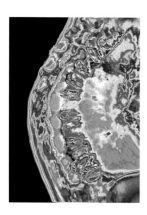

ABOVE *The pain of osteoarthritis can be eased by osteopathy.*

THE THEORY

Osteopaths take a holistic view of the human body, believing that each part is interdependent with the other parts and that the whole is affected by its environment and emotions. They also believe that the human body is self-regulating and has the ability to heal itself, and that it strives to adapt itself to and maintain itself in balance with its internal and external environment right up to the point of death. This state of balance is termed "homeostasis." When the homeostasis of the body is impaired by stress, injury, poor diet, pollution, inadequate rest, or drugs, then illness and disease can result.

The musculoskeletal system is the framework of the body. It supports and protects the internal organs, interacts with the nervous system, and enhances the circulatory and digestive systems. If the musculoskeletal system is not kept in the correct alignment – because of an injury, for example, or poor posture – the performance of the other systems suffers. The nervous system will send incorrect and damaging messages to the brain, and the circulatory and digestive systems may become lazy and sluggish.

RIGHT *A body that is badly aligned cannot be functioning with optimum efficiency – in other words, it cannot be truly healthy.*

This is significant, because blood transports oxygen and other nutrients to every cell in the body and, with the help of the lymphatic system, removes all waste products. If its function is impaired, the cells or organs affected will not be able to maintain homeostasis.

The nervous system also connects each part of the body with the whole, with the result that every part can be affected by the action of another individual part.

For example, if your body perceives a threat, your nervous system slows digestion, increases your breathing and heartrate and the flow of blood to your muscles in preparation for either fight or flight (*see Relaxation Techniques, pp. 158–65*). If the threat demands no physical response, such as running away, it takes time for your body to dissipate the stress reaction – leaving you physically tense and emotionally irritable.

The Vicious Circle of Pain

Pain, too, has a general, rather than purely local, effect. This is observed when an injury or disorder affects the musculoskeletal system.

If a vertebral joint is damaged, for example, the surrounding muscles go into spasm to reinforce and protect the joint from excessive movement. Pain signals from the taut muscles and the

---

PRECAUTIONS

■ Osteopathic manipulation is not recommended as part of the treatment of some disorders. These include: active infections; cancer; bone diseases, such as osteoporosis and osteomyelitis; fracture; vascular diseases, such as thrombosis, aneurysm, and high blood pressure; nerve or spinal cord damage. Osteopaths are trained to spot contraindications to treatment and will refer you to your doctor if a condition is indicated that is not appropriate for osteopathic treatment.

VISCERAL OSTEOPATHY

The majority of osteopaths confine themselves to the treatment of problems of the musculoskeletal system, but some also manipulate the soft tissues to treat internal problems like digestive or gynecological disorders. The theory is that, since reflex nerve pathways link muscles to internal organs, it is possible to affect an organ by stimulating the reflex pathway. This is done by massaging and palpating the appropriate muscles and by stimulating nerves at the point where they leave the spinal column. Treatment is also applied by gentle, direct manipulation to the organs through the chest, abdomen, and pelvis. There is, however, little scientific evidence for its efficacy.

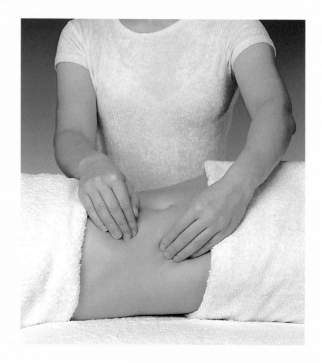

RIGHT *Treatment by visceral osteopathy feels more like a gentle massage than manipulation.*

injured joint pass up through the spinal segment whose nerves supply them to the brain. This, in turn, sends messages down to the whole area supplied by that spinal segment. As a result, the muscles surrounding the injured joint become even more tense, as do all the muscles supplied by that spinal segment, and the area will feel stiff and sore. The damaged joint grows inflamed and constricted and the nerves more excitable – they will react to less stimulation so that progressively less pain needs to be felt before the nerves fire off pain signals to the brain.

Then a vicious circle develops. The initial, acute injury causes pain signals to be sent to the brain, the muscles tense, the tense muscles then send off more pain signals – and so on. Even after the initial injury has healed, this vicious cycle can still lead to chronic pain. This explains why pain can often still be felt even though there is no sign of any injury. In order to break this pain–tension cycle, the muscles must be encouraged to relax and lengthen. Then, in time, the nerves will become less irritable and the perception of pain will fade.

Dysfunctions

Osteopaths believe that, for the reasons given above, the musculoskeletal system plays an important role in maintaining homeostasis. Unfortunately, many external stresses – whether physical or emotional – can upset this balance and put the body out of alignment, leading, for example, to poor posture, tense muscles, and inhibited movements.

The musculoskeletal system can be affected by internal illness or injury because it tries to adapt to accommodate the problem. If you hurt your foot, for example, you may limp to avoid putting weight on it and thus producing pain, but even after the injury to your foot has healed completely, you may still limp, especially when you are over-tired or stressed.

Osteopaths use the word "dysfunction" to denote problems that occur in the body but have no pathology – that is, they do not seem to be directly caused by any disease or injury. One such dysfunction is a joint that is not used to the limits of its full range of movement (osteopaths used to call this problem a "lesion," though now it is more usual to refer to it as a "somatic dysfunction"). The problem can occur, for example, if the spinal joints have adapted to a habitual curvature of the spine, the result being wear and tear – osteoarthritis – in the joint and consequent muscular stiffness and pain.

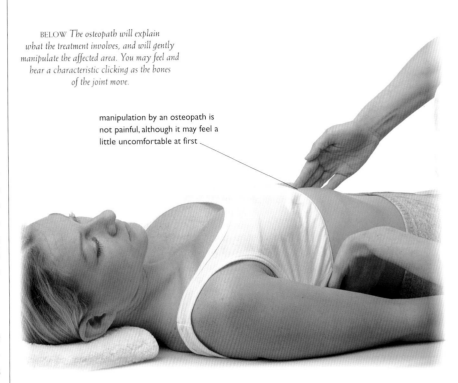

BELOW *The osteopath will explain what the treatment involves, and will gently manipulate the affected area. You may feel and hear a characteristic clicking as the bones of the joint move.*

manipulation by an osteopath is not painful, although it may feel a little uncomfortable at first

BELOW *The body needs healthy food to fight disease.*

NATUROPATHIC OSTEOPATHY

Some osteopaths combine the orthodox techniques of their profession with naturopathy. In fact, it is possible to take a course in naturopathic osteopathy. Successful graduates receive a diploma in both subjects; the emphasis of the course is on naturopathy. This qualification on its own is insufficient to practice as an osteopath in either Britain or America, although some properly qualified osteopaths, confusingly, also claim to be naturopaths – it is wise to check the precise qualifications of anyone claiming to be a "naturopathic osteopath."

Naturopaths believe that three main factors must be in in place if health and well-being are to be maintained and the body armored with the necessary biochemical attributes to fight disease: a good, wholesome diet including large quantities of fresh, preferably raw, fruit and vegetables; plenty of pure water; and clean air. They also believe that a person's emotional and mental state affects other body systems.

CONSULTING A PRACTITIONER

If you decide to visit an osteopath yourself, without a referral from your family doctor, make sure that he or she is properly qualified and a licensed member of the appropriate osteopathic organization (see *Useful Addresses*, pp. 368–73). Doing so is important, because in the past some so-called "colleges" awarded qualifications in osteopathy to people who had received little or no training; this is not the case today. Do not allow someone unqualified to manipulate your spine.

In America, osteopathy is a medical specialty, while in Europe it is generally a form of physical therapy. American osteopathic doctors are fully trained doctors of medicine who have specialized in osteopathic techniques. They are, therefore, legally qualified to prescribe drugs and, depending on their further qualifications, they can treat a wide range of medical problems. Some orthodox European doctors – usually family or orthopedic surgeons – also take a year's course in osteopathy in order to broaden the range of treatment techniques at their disposal. Usually, however, European osteopaths are physical therapists, who are concerned primarily with musculoskeletal problems.

Your first appointment will last about an hour. You will be asked for a full medical history and details of any past injuries or diseases. The osteopath will also ask about your lifestyle, work, exercise routine, dietary habits, and whether you take any drugs – medical, herbal, or homeopathic. You will be asked when and how your problem developed and how it affects your life: for example, the osteopath will want to know how much pain you are in, what it feels like, whether it is

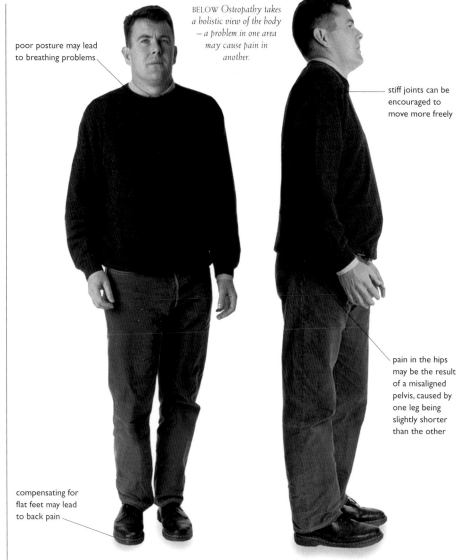

poor posture may lead to breathing problems

BELOW *Osteopathy takes a holistic view of the body – a problem in one area may cause pain in another.*

stiff joints can be encouraged to move more freely

pain in the hips may be the result of a misaligned pelvis, caused by one leg being slightly shorter than the other

compensating for flat feet may lead to back pain

continual or variable, how you cope with it, whether you have any limitation of movement or whether movement increases or decreases the scale of the problem.

After the discussion, you will be asked to undress to your underwear so that the osteopath can assess the structure of your body. You will be observed while standing, while performing various actions, and while sitting, as a check is made on your posture, muscle tone, the way you breathe, and the way you hold and move your body. The osteopath will be looking for possible problem areas in the musculoskeletal system, such as tense muscles, stiff joints, flat feet, unequal leg lengths, a twisted pelvis, and an incorrect curvature of the spine. Your body will then be examined more thoroughly by means of manual palpation and passive movements. You will be asked to lie on a treatment mat, and then the

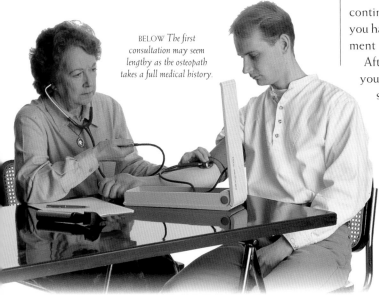

BELOW *The first consultation may seem lengthy as the osteopath takes a full medical history.*

be asked to lie on a treatment mat, and then the osteopath will palpate each vertebral joint in turn before turning to the peripheral joints – he or she will be testing for ease of movement and joint function, as well as your muscle tension, skin suppleness, and tone. An osteopathic examination may also include some standard medical tests, such as a blood-pressure reading, reflex testing, blood tests, and X-rays. After the examination, the osteopath will either decide on a course of treatment or refer you to your family doctor for further examination and treatment.

A session of treatment takes about a half-hour and most people require between three and six sessions. The precise nature of osteopathic treatment varies from problem to problem and from one individual to another, and may incorporate any of various different techniques (see below). Many people think that osteopathy treatment consists solely of manipulation and are nervous about the notorious "crack" (caused by bubbles of gas bursting inside the joints) that is often heard. In fact, manipulations or thrust techniques are only part of an osteopath's arsenal and they may not be appropriate in every case. Some people may have a slight increase in discomfort after the first treatment session – or feel a new pain – but this should pass after a couple of sessions.

As well as giving you specific treatments, your osteopath is likely to give you general advice on your posture, both at home and at work, and on relaxation techniques, nutrition, exercise routines, and general lifestyle. You may also be taught a few simple exercises to perform between sessions, and advised to consult another practitioner, such as a naturopath or a medical specialist, for further, more detailed advice on how to improve your overall well-being and diet.

Soft Tissue Manipulation

The soft tissues of the body include the skin, muscles, fascia (connective tissue), tendons, and ligaments. Soft tissue manipulation is a form of massage that can be superficial or deep, and fast or slow, depending on what the practitioner feels under his or her hands. The technique is used by most osteopaths, either as a treatment in itself when a problem is of muscular origin or as a precursor for other treatments. The osteopath will

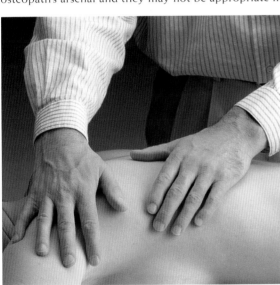

ABOVE *Pregnant women find osteopathy helpful in preventing backache.*

LEFT *Soft tissue manipulation is a form of massage used by most osteopaths.*

the osteopath will apply gentle pressure to the affected area

tense muscles will relax and pain should ease

you will be asked to lie down and be made as comfortable as possible

massage, knead, and pummel the problem area to ease stiffness, release tension, relax muscles, and stimulate circulation. Specific tender areas, such as taut bands of tight muscle fibers, areas of scar tissue in the muscles, or "trigger points" (*see Acupuncture, pages 20–27*), may also be kneaded with the ball of the thumb to break down the muscle spasm or scar tissue to enable the whole muscle to relax; osteopaths call this procedure the "neuromuscular technique."

Articulatory Techniques

Designed to increase the flexibility of the muscles and other soft tissues and to promote free movement, articulatory techniques used by osteopaths involve the passive movement of joints through their range of movement to stretch shortened muscles, ligaments, and adhesions. The technique used may be a gentle, passive stretch of the soft tissues, or traction, or a springing motion, but the movements are always rhythmical and can be deeply relaxing and soothing.

A gentle, passive stretch encourages any tense muscle fibers to relax and any taut ligaments to elongate gradually. Traction – when two joint surfaces are passively pulled slightly apart – is used to loosen joint capsules, ligaments, and the muscles and tendons surrounding the joint. Osteopaths normally use their hands, rather than the mechanical methods employed on a traction table, so that the practitioner can feel

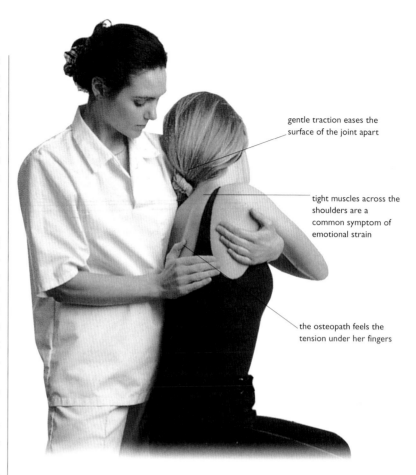

gentle traction eases the surface of the joint apart

tight muscles across the shoulders are a common symptom of emotional strain

the osteopath feels the tension under her fingers

ABOVE *Articulatory techniques may be used to lengthen contracted muscles and ligaments.*

the effect of the traction on the tissues during treatment. A small, springing movement or bounce may be used on certain joints that have little inherent movement, such as the spinal joints or sacroiliac joint, in order to increase the range of movement there.

High Velocity Techniques

Fast, abrupt thrust manipulations, known as "high velocity techniques," are perhaps the osteopathic techniques that are best known by lay people. However, though they are often used by osteopaths, they are not synonymous with the osteopathic art. High velocity thrust techniques are mainly used on the spinal column, but they may also be used on the peripheral joints. The osteopath gently pushes the joint to be treated to the limit of its range of movement and then gives a fast, downward thrust that lasts a few seconds. The thrust moves the joint outside its normal range for a short time and it can, although not always, cause the gas bubbles in the synovial fluid – the fluid inside the joint – to burst, making an audible "pop." This noise is what most people are nervous about, but it is not painful or uncomfortable. You may be asked to cooperate in the movement by either breathing in or out at a particular moment. Manipulations may be uncomfortable for a moment or two, but they are very rarely painful.

RIGHT *High velocity techniques can be used on peripheral joints as well as the spinal column.*

manipulations such as these are rarely painful

the osteopath will gently push the joint before the sharp thrust

SELF-HELP

The majority of osteopathic techniques are unsuitable for self-help use. In fact, many of them – manipulations in particular – can be dangerous in untutored hands, which is why it is so important that you make sure that you only consult an osteopath who is properly qualified and accredited. However, you can always observe these four basic tenets of osteopathy:

✳ maintain a good posture;

✳ take adequate exercise;

✳ learn how to relax fully and completely;

✳ ensure a healthy diet

BELOW *Learning to relax is vital.*

PATHFINDER

Osteopathy is mainly used to treat problems of the musculoskeletal system, although treatment may have a knock-on effect to other body systems – the ciruclatory system in particular.

ANGINA *SEE P.* 304

ARTHRITIS *SEE PP.* 346–7

ASTHMA *SEE PP.* 294–5

BACK PROBLEMS *SEE PP.* 344–5

BEDWETTING *SEE P.* 352

BRONCHITIS *SEE P.* 299

COUGHS *SEE P.* 297

DIZZINESS *SEE P.* 271

EARACHE *SEE P.* 282

FAINTING *SEE P.* 270

HEADACHE *SEE PP.* 268–9

HYPERACTIVITY *SEE P.* 351

INDIGESTION *SEE P.* 310

INFERTILITY *SEE P.* 324

MENSTRUAL PROBLEMS *SEE PP.* 322–3

MIGRAINE *SEE P.* 269

OSTEOPOROSIS *SEE P.* 358

PNEUMONIA *SEE P.* 296

PREGNANCY PROBLEMS *SEE PP.* 326–7

REPETITIVE STRAIN INJURY (RSI) *SEE PP.* 342–3

SCIATICA *SEE P.* 348

Muscle Energy Techniques

Osteopaths in the U.S.A. developed muscle energy techniques around 20 years ago. They are similar to techniques used by other physical therapists and are used to increase the range of movement at a joint. The patient moves a joint in a given direction with the assistance of the osteopath, and when the osteopath senses a barrier to a continued, smooth motion, he or she stops the movement. When this happens, the patient attempts to pull away from the barrier – in other words, tries to return to the movement's starting point – while the osteopath resists this attempt. This technique encourages the muscles involved in the movement – both those that make the initial movement and those that lengthen to allow the movement – to relax and lengthen.

Release Techniques

There are similarities between release techniques and muscle energy techniques, except that in the former the patient remains passive and attempts to relax completely. The osteopath moves a joint through its range of movement until a barrier is felt and then holds the joint in this position before gently moving it a little farther. The joint is then held in this new position while the patient stays relaxed. Often the osteopath can sense that the barrier has shifted to the new position by sensing a slight lengthening of the muscles and soft tissues.

osteopath stops the movement

patient attempts to resist

patient is relaxed

LEFT *Muscle energy and release techniques are widely used in osteopathy.*

CRANIAL OSTEOPATHY

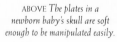

ABOVE *The plates in a newborn baby's skull are soft enough to be manipulated easily.*

Cranial osteopathy is an extension of traditional osteopathy. Osteopaths using cranial techniques maintain that the bones of the skull do not fuse completely during a child's early growth and that rhythmic impulses can be detected in the cerebrospinal fluid that bathes the brain and spinal cord. These impulses are produced at different rates from normal as a result of ill-health, but they can be returned to their normal state – which, in turn, stimulates the body's healing powers – by small-scale, gentle manipulations of the skull.

William Garner Sutherland, an osteopath, was working as a teacher at Kirksville Osteopathic College, Missouri (*see page 107*) when he developed a form of osteopathy known as "cranial osteopathy." While he was still a student, Sutherland had become intrigued by the bones of the skull – the cranium. He had been taught that the seven bones it comprises fuse together tightly soon after birth, but he believed that even in adulthood there remains some "give," or ability to move, between the bones. Sutherland then reasoned that if there was even a slight ability for movement, then there was also a possibility of dysfunction.

When he became a teacher, Sutherland experimented with the skulls in the museum at Kirksville College and later worked out some of his techniques by practicing on his own head. He found that by compressing parts of his skull he could not only alter his personality and moods, but effect physical changes in other parts of his body. Sutherland gradually crystallized his ideas and formulated his therapy during the 1930s, and cranial osteopathy was born.

THE THEORY

At birth, the seven bones that form the cranium – two frontal bones, two parietal, two temporal, and an occipital bone – have the ability to slide over each other, and this makes it possible for the baby's head to pass down the birth canal; every parent knows the "soft spots," called fontanels, on a baby's head at which the membranes that line the cranium can be seen pulsating. During infancy, the bones gradually knit together to form one structure. However, cranial osteopaths believe that this fusion is not rigid, but allows a little flexibility.

The cranium and spinal cord interiors are lined by three membranes called the meninges. Within them is a clear fluid known as cerebrospinal fluid. Secreted in the brain, it bathes the tissues of the brain, spinal cord, and spinal nerves as they leave the spinal cord. Cerebrospinal fluid supports and buffers the brain, supplies various nutrients, and assists in the disposal of waste products. Sutherland detected certain rhythms in

the cerebrospinal fluid and, echoing Andrew Taylor Still's "river of life" (*see Osteopathy, pages 106–13*), he called them "the breath of life," since they seemed to be influenced by the breathing rate.

Sutherland concluded that the cranial rhythms were connected to the body's own healing system. He believed that they pulsate at a rate of between six and fifteen times a minute in a healthy person, and that any abnormality in them reflects disturbances in the brain, head, or body. He taught that normal pulsations may be corrected by manipulating the cranial bones, which will stimulate the body's own healing powers.

Gentle Manipulations

Cranial osteopaths aim to restore the normal rate of cranial rhythmic impulses in the cerebrospinal fluid by means of small-scale, gentle manipulative techniques. Treatment is principally to the head, spinal column, and the sacral area, at the bottom of the spine, though other areas of the body may be treated as well.

Because the technique is such a gentle one, it is very suitable for use on babies (although not newborn), young children, and the frail and elderly. Adults who are nervous about the use of high velocity thrust techniques (*see Osteopathy, pages 106–13*) may also prefer this more gentle and soothing alternative.

Cranial osteopathy can treat all the same conditions as conventional osteopathy, but osteopaths recommend it in particular as a treatment for distortions of the skull caused by difficult births and for fretful, crying babies who suffer from colic. Young children who seem to be perpetually under the weather and catch infections repeatedly are also said to benefit from treatment, and the therapy is also believed to be useful in conditions such as otitis (glue ear), hyperactivity, and lack of concentration. And as cranial osteopathy is claimed to improve the circulation in the brain and head and increase the efficient of lymph and sinus drainage, it is also recommended for head and neck problems, sinusitis, migraines, dizziness, tinnitus, and many dental-related problems.

CONSULTING A PRACTITIONER

Cranial osteopathy is a branch of osteopathy, so a practitioner will be a fully qualified osteopath. The first session will take around an hour and will follow the same lines as an osteopathic examination (*see pp. 110–11*).

After taking a detailed history from you and examining your physique, the cranial osteopath will ask you to lie on your back on a treatment table. The practitioner will then cradle your head with his or her hands to feel for the cranial rhythm. The osteopath may then ask various questions about your physical or emotional well-being based on the rate of the rhythms.

Each subsequent treatment session lasts around a half-hour, and four to six sessions are usually enough to resolve the problem. The practitioner will hold your head and use small manipulative techniques to exert slight pressures on certain areas of your skull to change the cranial rhythmic impulses. The pressure is so light that the procedure can be extremely soothing and relaxing. A cranial osteopath does not treat only your head, and so soft manipulation techniques (*see Osteopathy, pp. 106–13*) may be used on other areas of your body, upon the spine in particular, to release tensions and to encourage the cranial rhythmic impulses to change and stimulate the body's own healing system. It is not uncommon for patients to feel that their symptoms have become worse after the first treatment session. This, cranial osteopaths believe, is the result of an improvement in the way the body's healing system functions – in the same way that a high temperature makes you feel ill, even though it is a sign that the body is trying to fight infection.

BELOW Although the soft bones of a newborn soon knit together to form a harder skull, the treatment can work for adults too.

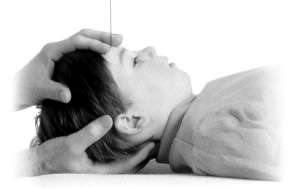

the practitioner feels the impulses inside the skull

BELOW According to cranial osteopaths, a difficult birth or subsequent accident can cause an imbalance in the rhythms of the cranium, possibly leading to colic, severe headaches, or even behavioral problems. Manipulation of the movable bones that make up the skull can help to restore balance and relieve the problem.

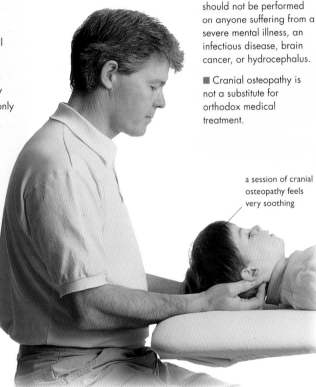

a session of cranial osteopathy feels very soothing

the practitioner makes tiny adjustments to redress the balance

PRECAUTIONS

■ When performed by a qualified osteopath who has taken an additional course in cranial osteopathy, this therapy is a safe treatment for people of any age. However, it is important that it is not confused with Cranio-Sacral therapy (see over), as therapists of this technique may not be qualified osteopaths.

■ Cranial osteopathy should not be performed on anyone suffering from a severe mental illness, an infectious disease, brain cancer, or hydrocephalus.

■ Cranial osteopathy is not a substitute for orthodox medical treatment.

PATHFINDER

Cranial osteopathy can treat the same disorders as osteopathy, so it is inclined to concentrate on musculoskeletal problems. Cranial osteopathy, however, is said to be useful in helping to realign the skull bones when they have been malformed following a difficult birth. Fretful, colicky babies and certain childhood problems benefit from treatment. In adults, the gentle manipulations are used for frail elderly patients and those who suffer from disorders of the head, face, and neck.

ARTHRITIS *SEE PP. 346–7*

BEDWETTING *SEE P. 352*

COLIC *SEE P. 350*

DIZZINESS *SEE P. 271*

EARACHE *SEE P. 282*

GLAUCOMA *SEE P. 279*

HEADACHE *SEE PP. 268–9*

HYPERACTIVITY *SEE P. 351*

MIGRAINE *SEE P. 269*

SINUSITIS *SEE P. 284*

TINNITUS *SEE P. 281*

TOOTHACHE *SEE P. 288*

CRANIO-SACRAL THERAPY

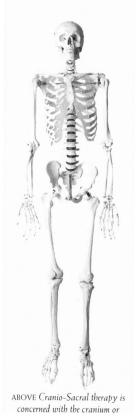

ABOVE *Cranio-Sacral therapy is concerned with the cranium or skull, the sacrum, a bone in the pelvis, and all the complex spinal cord in between.*

I n the 1970s, Dr. John E. Upledger, an American osteopathic surgeon and doctor, developed a variation of cranial osteopathy that he called Cranio-Sacral Therapy. Upledger had become fascinated by the "Cranio-Sacral system" – the cranium and spinal cord, which runs down to the sacrum in the lower back, and their contents – while working as a clinical researcher at Michigan State University. His work was based on the theories of cranial osteopathy developed by Sutherland, but Upledger placed more emphasis on the importance of the soft tissues encased by the cranium and spinal cord than on the actual bones themselves.

THE THEORY

Like Sutherland, Upledger believes that the bones of the cranium do not fuse completely in childhood, but still retain some "give" where one bone joins the next, and that the tiny joints or sutures between them contain elastic fibers, nerve endings, and blood vessels. Unlike Sutherland, however, Upledger insists that the Cranio-Sacral rhythm is separate from the heartbeat or respiration rate. He maintains that the cerebrospinal fluid, surrounded by the meninges, circulates within the cranium and spinal column in a type of hydraulic system, and that the efficient working of this system is vital to overall well-being.

Inflexible Meninges

It is thought that the meninges control the circulation of the cerebrospinal fluid and so the cranial rhythmic impulse. If the pulse is too fast, too slow, or erratic, not only will the Cranio-Sacral region be affected, but the repercussions will be felt in the connective tissue that links every part of the body to every other part. Over-taut meninges are thought to be one common cause of autism – Upledger found that the majority of autistic children that he examined had taut, inflexible meninges. Why the meninges stiffen is not known, although the phenomenon might well be a response to a problem to be found elsewhere in the connective tissue system.

Cranio-Sacral therapists believe that there is a flow of energy from the therapist to the patient during treatment. This boost of energy allows the cranial rhythm to readjust itself to its normal state and stimulates the patient's own inherent healing system. The difference between each therapist's natural healing ability explains why different Cranio-Sacral therapists feel different rates of cranial rhythmic impulses in the same patient.

Good Cranio-Sacral therapists are said to be able

ABOVE *Cranio-Sacral therapy can help loosen over-taut meninges in many autistic children.*

to feel a hair beneath a telephone book. This very gentle therapy is somewhat more esoteric than cranial osteopathy, and focuses on psychological as well as physical release, which its founder Dr. Upledger believed was necessary for true healing to occur. Few people will find it uncomfortable, and it is often used in tandem with other forms of bodywork, such as shiatsu or massage, or psychological treatment which involves counseling, regression, or guided imagery.

CONSULTING A PRACTITIONER

Although there are similarities between Cranio-Sacral therapy and cranial osteopathy, the therapist will not take a full medical history as a cranial osteopath would. The therapist's main aim is to rectify any disturbance in the rate of cranial rhythmic impulse (felt anywhere in the body) and then to ensure that the rate stays within its normal ranges.

You will be asked to lie down on a treatment table while the practitioner palpates your head or sacral area – the bones at the base of the spine. The touch is so slight – less than 5 grams of pressure – that you will hardly feel anything. A session generally lasts from 30 to 60 minutes, and you may be advised to return for a few further sessions.

Many people claim to feel deeply relaxed during and after treatment, and often experience a spontaneous release of physical or emotional trauma. This may manifest itself as pain or tears, and sharp images may flash through the patient's mind. At the end of the session, people usually feel relaxed, calm, and very clear-headed.

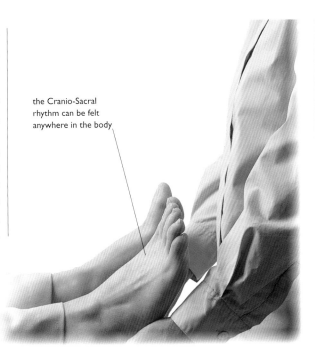

the Cranio-Sacral rhythm can be felt anywhere in the body

RIGHT *Firstly, the practitioner will spend a few minutes tuning into the Cranio-Sacral rhythm and evaluating the system. This will often be felt by holding the feet: an assessment is made of the quality and rate of the rhythm and general feel of the body.*

PATHFINDER

Cranio-Sacral therapy is a whole body therapy that claims to affect the whole system by ensuring an even and rhythmic flow of cerebrospinal fluid in the brain and spinal column. It is best known, however, for its effect on convalescents and those with musculoskeletal problems, headaches, stress, and certain learning difficulties.

ARTHRITIS SEE PP. *346–7*

BACK PROBLEMS SEE PP. *344–5*

DEPRESSION SEE P. *261*

HYPERACTIVITY SEE P. *351*

REPETITIVE STRAIN INJURY (RSI) SEE PP. *342–3*

SCIATICA SEE P. *348*

STRESS SEE PP. *262–3*

BELOW *Areas of the body will then be palpated in turn. Here the solar plexus is being assessed and compared with other areas. The practitioner will start to encourage the body to release any restrictions or tensions by holding the area very lightly and letting the hands meld with the rhythm.*

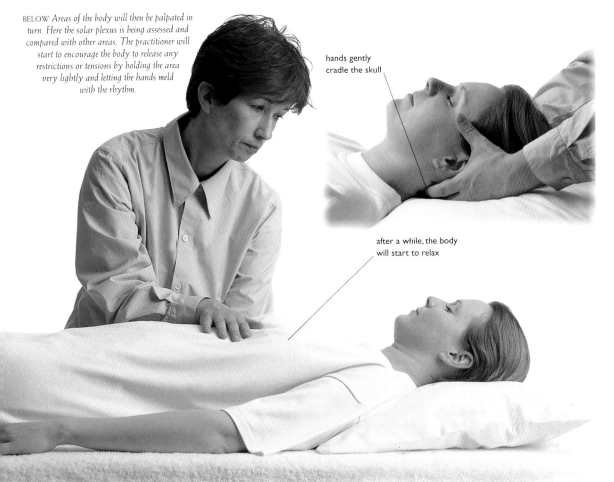

hands gently cradle the skull

after a while, the body will start to relax

LEFT *Here the cranium is being cradled lightly. Again an assessment is made by finding asymmetries of the bones of the skull and any restrictions in the flow of the cerebrospinal fluid.*

PRECAUTIONS

■ As a Cranio-Sacral therapist need not have any osteopathic or medical training – and therefore will lack certain medical knowledge – it is important to check with your family doctor if you are at all worried by your general health.

■ Cranio-Sacral therapy is not suitable for anyone suffering from severe mental or psychological disturbance.

CHIROPRACTIC

ABOVE *Daniel David Palmer had no formal medical training, but the therapy he developed is one of the most widely accepted complementary treatments.*

Chiropractic is neuromusculoskeletal manipulation, especially of the spinal column, and is used for diagnosing, treating, and rehabilitating physical problems or diseases caused by or related to the neuromusculoskeletal system. Founded by Daniel David Palmer in 1895, after he cured an office janitor of partial deafness, chiropractic is a therapy that has survived many years of bitter struggle with the orthodox medical establishment. Today it is generally accepted as one of the treatments of choice in cases of back pain. However, there is something of a split between those who confine themselves to treating musculoskeletal problems by spinal manipulation and chiropractors who claim to be able to cure other disorders, including organic disease.

The word "chiropractic" comes from the Greek words cheiro, meaning "hand," and praktikos, meaning "doing" – so the term means, literally, "doing by hand." Chiropractic was invented and developed by Daniel David Palmer, who was born near Toronto, Canada, in 1845, but later moved to Davenport, Iowa, U.S.A., where he worked as a grocer and a "magnetic healer," often using early osteopathic techniques. Like Andrew Taylor Still, the inventor of osteopathy (*see pages 106–13*), Palmer was dissatisfied with both the approach and the success rate of medicine as practiced in his time, and he read medical books extensively, although he did not undertake any orthodox medical training.

Immediate Relief

In 1895, one Harvey Lilliard, the janitor of the building in which Palmer had his office, told Palmer that he had suddenly become partially deaf some 17 years earlier. Lilliard explained that he had been bending over in a cramped position when he had felt something "go" in his neck. Palmer persuaded Lilliard to allow him to manipulate his neck, because he felt certain that one of the janitor's cervical (neck) vertebrae was out of alignment. Apparently the manipulation was successful immediately, and Lilliard's hearing returned to normal. Encouraged by this success, Palmer later investigated the case of a man who had heart trouble. He examined the man's spine, and, to quote from his book *The Chiropractor's Adjuster*, published in 1910, "found a displaced vertebra pressing against the nerves that enervate the heart. I adjusted the vertebra and gave immediate relief . . . ."

These two incidents convinced Palmer that the cause of many medical disorders is pressure on or impingement of a nerve as it leaves the spinal column – either as a result of a vertebra having become misplaced or of swelling in the soft tissues around it. As he developed his theory, Palmer came to the belief that the correct alignment of the spinal column is vitally important if good health is to be maintained. If the nerves that connect the brain to the body and its organs become impeded in any way – and the most obvious place at which they can be impeded is where they leave the spinal cord, between the vertebrae – the flow of nerve impulses to those areas will become sluggish. In turn, Palmer believed, this would result in damage to the tissues supplied by any affected nerve, and, consequently, to a medical disorder.

Imprisoned

Palmer continued to treat a wide range of diseases and complaints with his new method and, in doing so, infuriated local doctors who lost business as a result of his competition – to such an extent, in fact, that in 1896 he was imprisoned, at their urging, for practicing medicine without a licence. (Other chiropractors who followed in Palmer's footsteps were sent to prison, having been convicted of the same charge, but a stop was put to this practice at the start of the 20th century, when a judge decided that a chiropractor called Shegato Morikubo was not pretending to practice medicine; he was practicing chiropractic.)

Palmer went on to found the Palmer Infirmary and Chiropractic Institute, in Iowa, in 1898 to promote his ideas and train others in them. One such person was his son, Bartlett Joshua Palmer, who further developed the diagnostic side of the treatment system and installed one of the early X-ray machines in the Institute in 1910; X-rays have been used by chiropractors ever since.

By 1910, Palmer estimated that there were around 2,000 practitioners of chiropractic, and by the time he died in 1913, there were schools of chiropractic throughout America. Chiropractic soon spread outside America to Australasia and Europe, and the British Chiropractic Association was set up in 1925 – although it was not until 1965 that the Anglo-European College of Chiropractic was founded, in Bournemouth, Britain, to train practitioners in that country instead of America.

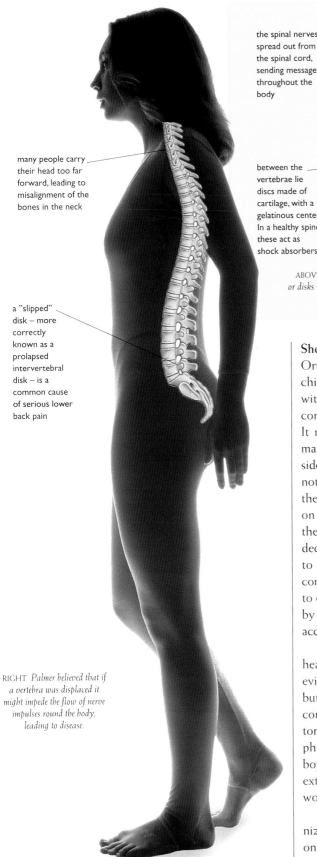

THE SPINAL COLUMN

the spinal nerves spread out from the spinal cord, sending messages throughout the body

the nerve fibers of the spinal cord pass through the center of the protecting vertebrae

vertebrae are the small bones that make up the spinal column

between the vertebrae lie discs made of cartilage, with a gelatinous center. In a healthy spine these act as shock absorbers

many people carry their head too far forward, leading to misalignment of the bones in the neck

a "slipped" disk – more correctly known as a prolapsed intervertebral disk – is a common cause of serious lower back pain

ABOVE If any misalignment or damage occurs to the vertebrae or disks that make up the spinal column, it can cause pain not only in the affected area but in other parts of the body.

RIGHT *Palmer believed that if a vertebra was displaced it might impede the flow of nerve impulses round the body, leading to disease.*

Sherman Antitrust Act

Orthodox medicine was against the development of chiropractic from the start, and continued to oppose it with some vehemence for many years, but the therapy continued to thrive as an alternative health care system. It received a considerable boost in the 1960s, when many people, disillusioned with modern drugs and their side-effects, turned to more holistic approaches that did not involve drug therapy. However, also in the 1960s, the American Medical Association (AMA) Committee on Quackery looked into chiropractic and decided that the therapy was unscientific and could be harmful, and decreed that it was inappropriate for orthodox doctors to cooperate with chiropractors. The chiropractic community was outraged, and took the AMA and others to court in 1976, claiming that it was being victimized by the medical profession and was being denied proper access to medical facilities.

In 1987, Susan Getzendanner, the federal judge who heard the case, decided that the AMA had ample evidence in the 1960s to justify its claims of quackery, but that it had broken the Sherman Antitrust Act concerning restraint of trade by boycotting chiropractors. Her judgment did not endorse chiropractic or its philosophy, but it did prevent the AMA from trying to boycott the therapy. Since then, the AMA has been extremely careful to avoid any confrontation with the world of chiropractic.

The United States Department of Education recognizes the Commission on Accreditation of the Council on Chiropractic Education, which is the accrediting agency for the chiropractic profession in the U.S.

Orthodox medicine has mixed feelings about the efficacy of chiropractic. On one hand, there are well-documented studies that show the beneficial effect of chiropractic treatment for some musculoskeletal problems, notably low-back pain. In 1995, the General Medical Council in Britain reported that patients receiving chiropractic treatment for low-back pain had a higher incidence of recovery than those treated at a hospital physiotherapy out-patients clinic. Chiropractic was also one of the treatments recommended by the Clinical Standards Advisory Group of Great Britain for low-back pain, along with physiotherapy and osteopathy (*see pp. 106–13*). And research in America – by the Rand Corporation, the Florida Department of Labor, and the Oregon Workman's Compensation Board – has been unanimous in finding that chiropractic treatment of back problems means less time off work for employees than when treatment is by orthodox means. Research worldwide corroborates these findings. On the other hand, many chiropractors claim to be able to treat a wide range of diseases as diverse as high blood pressure, asthma, digestive disorders, and hyperactivity in children. Chiropractors who make such claims are viewed with considerable skepticism by most orthodox doctors.

CHIROPRACTIC THEORY

It is difficult to be precise about chiropractic theory, because, across the profession as a whole, chiropractors differ significantly in what they believe. Daniel David Palmer took a holistic view of the human body, as do many people today, but he also believed that inside each person was an "Innate Intelligence" – similar to chi or life force in other therapies – that maintains the body in a state of health. Palmer thought that "in 95 percent of cases" disease develops because the flow of nervous impulses from the brain to the rest of the body is impeded by spinal "subluxations" as they leave the spinal column. This reduction in the flow of nerve impulses prevents "innate intelligence" from passing around the body, or reduces the amount of it that does so. And any organ or part of the body that is deprived of sufficient "innate intelligence" will become diseased or function badly. Palmer disagreed with the use of drugs in medicine, which he said treated the symptoms, rather than the cause, of disease, and he also rejected surgical treatment.

Subluxations

In orthodox medicine, this term "subluxation" is used to mean a partial or incomplete dislocation of any two bones at a joint. However, Palmer and some modern-day chiropractors use the term to refer to any misalignment or maladjustment of the vertebrae that impinges on spinal nerves as they leave the spinal cord between the vertebrae, and so affects the spinal nerves and the areas of the body that each nerve supplies. Developing this theme, the American Association of Chiropractic Colleges has recently broadened this defi-nition: "a subluxation is a complex of functional and/or structural and/or pathological articular changes that compromise neural [nervous system] integrity and may influence organ system and general health." The cause of this spinal misalignment is considered to be anything from poor posture, a muscle spasm, an accident, or a sports injury to a birth defect.

B.J. Palmer, David Daniel Palmer's son, introduced X-rays to chiropractic as a diagnostic tool and was so enthusiastic about the benefits of their use that at one

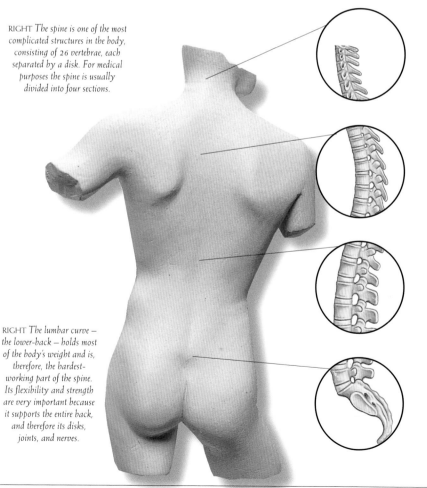

RIGHT *The spine is one of the most complicated structures in the body, consisting of 26 vertebrae, each separated by a disk. For medical purposes the spine is usually divided into four sections.*

The neck, or cervical spine, is composed of seven vertebrae. They work with the muscles in the shoulders. Together they curve forward, forming a C shape, and protect the spinal cord.

The shoulder muscles help the body to balance and to move the head easily.

The middle back, or thoracic spine, supports the upper body and curves in the opposite direction from that of the cervical spine. It is not very flexible because its vertebrae are attached to the ribs – which protect vital organs like the heart, liver, lungs, and spleen.

RIGHT *The lumbar curve – the lower-back – holds most of the body's weight and is, therefore, the hardest-working part of the spine. Its flexibility and strength are very important because it supports the entire back, and therefore its disks, joints, and nerves.*

The low-back or lumbar spine curves forward in a flexible C shape. Below it lies the sacrum and coccyx vertebrae, which fuse after the body reaches maturity.

STRAIGHTS AND MIXERS

The group of chiropractors who believe in subluxations can be subdivided into two groups, commonly known as the "straights" and the "mixers." The straights follow Palmer's doctrine that subluxations of the vertebrae can cause or contribute to most disorders, but they do not claim to be able to diagnose or treat diseases – only to detect and cure subluxations. Mixers, however, concede that diseases can develop from other causes, like bacteria and viruses, but say that subluxations affect the body's health by lowering resistance to disease.

Dr. Louis Sportelli, of the American Chiropractic Association, says, "the deviation or malposition of a spinal vertebra may cause a neurological imbalance within the body, setting the stage for a lowered resistance." Because of this claim, mixers often prescribe vitamins, homeopathic drugs, and nutritional advice in an attempt to boost the immune system.

Those chiropractors who still believe in subluxations also believe in the flow of nerve energy or innate intelligence and that this can become blocked, so preventing the body from healing itself. Because of this belief, they claim to be able to treat disorders other than those of the musculoskeletal system.

BELOW *Few chiropractors use this technique in isolation. Many mixers also recommend nutritional supplements or homeopathic remedies to their patients.*

time chiropractors took numerous X-rays of their patients' spines at nearly every treatment session. Many of these were unnecessary, and they were not only expensive but probably harmful. Critics of chiropractic say that too many X-rays are still being taken today.

For many years, chiropractors claimed to be able to see subluxations on X-ray even when orthodox doctors could see no signs of any misalignment or impinged nerves. This fact led not only to bad feeling building up between doctors and chiropractors, but to a division in chiropractic. Some chiropractors claimed that they could "feel" a subluxation and backed Palmer's late-19th-century theory in full or in part, while others moved away from it and instead concentrated their expertise on musculoskeletal problems of the spine.

The latter group have been termed by Simon Homola, an eminent retired chiropractor and author, "rational chiropractors." They believe in working along-side orthodox doctors in their own area of expertise and make no extravagant claims about what they can treat. Nor do they believe in the theory of subluxations.

The difficulties chiropractors experience when considering these matters have not been eased in the U.S.A. by the fact that, from 1973 to 2000, Congress authorized health insurance companies to pay for chiropractic treatment only if a subluxation could be seen on X-ray. To confuse matters further, the group of chiropractors who believe in subluxations divide into "straights" and "mixers" (*see above*).

Preventing Low-Back Pain

* Exercise regularly.
* Keep objects close to the body when lifting them.
* Place a pillow or rolled-up towel behind the small of the back when driving long distances.
* Put work tables at a comfortable height.
* Use a chair with good lower-back support.
* Wear comfortable, low-heeled shoes.
* Wear a lumbar corset if you lift things frequently at work.
* When you sit for a long time, rest your feet on a low stool.

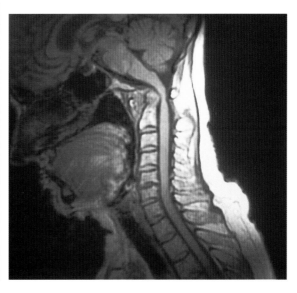

LEFT *If vertebrae are out of alignment, a subluxation is present.*

■ Manipulation of the spine, and especially of the cervical area, can be dangerous. If the neck is twisted too far, it is possible to tear the walls of the vulnerable vertebral arteries where they pass up to the neck. The result can be an aneurysm or blood clots, which, in turn, can cause a stroke or other neurological symptoms, such as vertigo and slurring, or even be fatal.

■ There have been cases of neurological damage following chiropractic manipulations of the neck. In 1992, researchers at Stanford Stroke Center found that 55 people had been referred to neurologists in California following manipulation. They were suffering from permanent nerve damage, and one died. The vast majority of chiropractic manipulations are safe, but any manipulation – like an anesthetic or surgery in orthodox medicine – carries a risk, so it is important that it is not undertaken lightly or unnecessarily.

■ The spine should never be manipulated if there are any signs of a neurological involvement, such as a loss of sensation in the legs or impaired bladder control. Bone diseases, such as osteoporosis or cancer, a recent fracture, or serious circulatory problems, such as aneurysms or a history of thrombosis, are also contraindications for the use of spinal manipulations. If in doubt, consult your doctor.

CHOOSING A PRACTITIONER

Before 1965, all qualified, licenced chiropractors were trained in North America. However, there are now many accredited schools around the world and these are associated with the World Federation of Chiropractors. In Europe, a chiropractic BSc course takes five years of full-time study, and an additional year is required to become an honorary Doctor of Chiropractic. In America, it takes four years to train as a Doctor of Chiropractic, and an undergraduate course is necessary before the training starts. The course does not include surgery or pharmacology, but emphasizes anatomy and physiology, manipulation techniques, and radiology, among other things. There are so many chiropractors in North America that chiropractic is now the largest health care alternative to orthodox medicine in the United States.

Two Schools of Thought

The majority of people visit a chiropractor because of spinal problems, and the majority of chiropractors concentrate their expertise in this area. The British Chiropractors' Association, for example, defines chiropractic as "concerned with the diagnosis and treatment of mechanical disorders of joints, particularly spinal joints." However, some chiropractors are still adherents of Palmer's view – both of "innate intelligence" and of his definition of subluxations. Such chiropractors claim not only that there is a possibility that they can help in a wide range of problems, from cancer to dysmenorrhea (period pains), but also that it is necessary to have frequent treatments to maintain good health – they are still against medical drugs and surgery except in extreme cases.

This means that there are two main schools of thought within the profession. Because of this, you must decide which you prefer. If you require treatment for a spinal problem or some other musculoskeletal problem, – the treatment you will receive may well be similar to that given by physical therapists (physiotherapists in Britain) or osteopaths. If you would prefer a more holistic, mystical treatment, you may wish to choose a physical treatment based more on, and with a closer relationship to, Eastern philosophies, than upon Western scientific evidence and medical orthodoxy.

Some Words of Advice

Should you decide that you wish to consult a chiropractor for a musculoskeletal problem, your family doctor will probably be able to suggest one; otherwise, chiropractors are to be found in most communities and you should be able to find one in your local telephone book. However, you should avoid any chiropractor who claims to treat diverse diseases, such as infections and heart problems, or who recommends that you have frequent treatments to keep your spine free of subluxations, unless you wish for a more philosophical approach – which will certainly be more expensive. Some chiropractors in America have been criticized for using aggressive marketing techniques, such as naming subluxations as "the Silent Killer" and urging people to have frequent check-ups before they have any signs of a problem.

LEFT *A qualified chiropractor should have at least a BSc from a recognized college of chiropractic, and be a member of a professional body such as the British Chiropractic Association or the Chiropractors' Association of Australia.*

LEFT *Many chiropractors suggest that you need chiropractic check-ups as often as you need regular dental examinations, so that you may avoid and prevent spinal problems even if you don't have them now. You may wish to consider such suggestions carefully.*

PRECAUTIONS

Ensure that your chiropractor is appropriately certified. Note that a chiropractor with a license as a Doctor of Chiropractic in the U.S. must have:

■ completed a minimum of two years at a college or university with a strong emphasis on science;

■ graduated from an accredited chiropractic college;

■ passed the National Board Examination or other examinations required by each state Board of Examiners;

■ met individual licencing requirements of the state health care system in which he is practicing.

CONSULTING A CHIROPRACTOR

On your first consultation, your chiropractor will take a detailed medical and family history, including details of any past injuries or diseases. You will be asked about your lifestyle, work environment – whether, for example, you have to drive or sit for long periods or perform monotonous repetitive tasks, your physical activities, such as playing sports, and, possibly, your diet. After this, you will be asked to undress to your underwear and the chiropractor will examine your general posture and spinal curvature in various positions, whether standing, sitting, or lying. The practitioner may ask you to perform certain actions or may move your joints passively through their range of movement. Your reflexes will be tested and muscles palpated for signs of tension or spasm. Your legs may be measured, too, to ascertain whether they are of equal length.

Chiropractors use a specially designed couch to examine and treat their patients. This is designed so that the practitioner can lower a patient from standing to lying without the patient moving, and is composed of separate parts that can be lowered or raised to aid treatment. After the physical examination, the chiropractor may take an X-ray if he feels that your condition warrants this. The X-ray is normally taken when you are standing, so that it shows your spine under normal conditions. Other routine medical tests may also be performed, such as taking your pulse and your blood pressure. Having completed the examination, the chiropractor will decide whether your problem is suitable for chiropractic treatment and, if so, what form the treatment will take. If the chiropractor feels that you have any underlying systemic disease, you will be referred to your family doctor.

Treatment itself normally starts at the second session and lasts for about a half-hour. The number of sessions required will depend on the nature of your problem, its longevity, and your overall fitness. The chiropractor's aim is to correct any misalignment of the spine; restore a full range of movement to the joints; relax and lengthen tense muscles, tendons; and ligaments; to correct faulty posture; and to relieve any pain caused by over-stimulated nerves. As well as using specific treatment techniques, your chiropractor will also give you general advice on relaxation methods, correct posture; and preventive back care.

Tips will also be given to you on how to stay healthy, and avoid re-injury, and suggestions made for periodic chiropractic maintenance care that you may need.

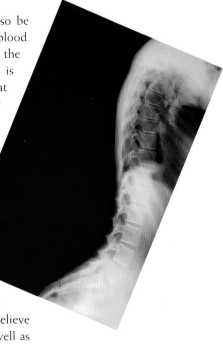

ABOVE *Chiropractors often take X-rays of back problems.*

TREATMENT TECHNIQUES

The principal, although not the only, procedure used by chiropractors is a form of manipulation known as "adjustment." An adjustment – and there are around 55 of them in a chiropractor's repertoire – consists of a sudden, short, controlled thrust against a joint. The chiropractor will move the suspect joint to the limit of its range of movement and then make a rapid thrust beyond this point to stretch the joint capsule and surrounding tissues. It is important that the patient is relaxed for this to be effective – the speed of the thrust is to ensure that the patient's muscles have no time to contract and so restrict the movement. A "crack" or popping sound may be heard during the thrust: this is caused by gases in the synovial fluid (the lubricating fluid inside each joint capsule) and is harmless.

Most chiropractors will treat only a joint that they believe is misaligned or subluxated, but some may treat the whole spine or concentrate only on one area – the cervical region, for example. From the patient's point of view, it is important to remember that all manipulations involve a degree of risk, however small, so you should ensure that adjustments are carried out only when necessary and by experienced practitioners.

If an adjustment is contraindicated for any reason, such as the possibility that it might cause the patient excessive pain or anxiety, a joint can be stretched by placing a roll or wedge in the correct position beneath the spine when the patient is lying down. However, doing this takes time, and the results are not achieved as quickly as those brought about by manipulation.

Like osteopaths and physical therapists (physiotherapists), chiropractors also use a number of soft-tissue techniques – such as massage, heat, ice, and kneading – to relax a patient's muscles before a manipulation, to release trigger points (painful knots of muscle fibers), and to lengthen tendons and muscles.

BELOW *Your chiropractor may use the "adjustment" technique on you.*

McTIMONEY CHIROPRACTIC

HISTORY

John McTimoney (1914–1980) founded the McTimoney method of chiropractic in Banbury, Britain, in 1951. Born in Birmingham, Britain, in 1914, he worked as a silversmith, engraver, and jeweler before, having been injured in a fall, he started to gradually lose the full use of his arms and found that walking was becoming increasingly difficult. Progressively more frustrated by the inability of orthodox medicine to improve his condition, McTimoney decided to try chiropractic. He was treated by an American named Ashford, who had trained under Daniel David Palmer in Iowa, U.S.A., and he was so impressed with the results that he decided to give up his job and become a chiropractor himself. This he did, having been tutored by Dr. Mary Walker, even though his qualifications were not formally recognized in Britain at that time.

McTimoney was an adherent of Palmer's holistic view of chiropractic, believing that subluxations impair nerve function and so affect the correct functioning of the body. Once in practice, he continued to try to improve both his technique and his understanding of the therapy. His approach altered to a "whole body" one. He came to the view that although the spine was the primary source of misalignments, or subluxations, the other joints of the body could also be put out of alignment by everyday stresses and strains, and that, in order to achieve a complete realignment, all the joints of the body should be treated – not just the spine. Unusually, McTimoney also treated animals with his technique and is considered to be a pioneer in this field.

In 1972, John McTimoney opened the McTimoney School of Chiropractic to train students in Oxford, Britain. It is also possible to train in animal chiropractic there. In 1979 the McTimoney Chiropractic Association was established to support the school and maintain high standards of practice.

Chiropractic is not considered suitable for broken or fractured bones, or those with diseases like cancer of the bone, osteoporosis, rheumatoid arthritis, or other conditions arising from severe pressure on the spinal cord – for example, fractured vertebra, tumor, or lesion – or disorder of the blood circulation. However, McTimoney Chiropractic is seen as a "safer" option than ordinary chiropractic because of its lighter touch.

McTIMONEY PRACTICE

Followers of the McTimoney school of chiropractic use the same techniques as other chiropractors, but in a much more gentle way. They favor a technique pioneered by B.J. Palmer known as the "toggle-recoil" thrust. In this, the practitioner pushes the joint in the

BELOW McTimoney was the first person successfully to apply chiropractic methods to animals.

JOINTS AND MOVEMENT

a pivot joint such as those in the neck permit a rotating movement only

the vertebrae, sandwiched between cartilaginous disks, allow only limited movement

ball and socket joints, as in the shoulder, allow the widest range of movement: backward, forward, sideways, and rotation

ellipsoidal joints at the wrists and ankles allow all types of movement except pivotal

hinge joints are the simplest of the mobile joints, allowing only bending and straightening. The knee and elbow are modified hinge joints, permitting some rotation too

ABOVE In mobile joints the bone surfaces are coated with cartilage to reduce friction and sealed in a fibrous capsule. This is lined with a membrane which produces a sticky lubricating fluid, to allow for ease of movement.

desired direction with one rapid movement and then releases it. The tendons and ligaments of the joint are stretched by the rapid push and their natural elasticity is thought to assist the bones to realign as they recoil when released.

Unlike other chiropractors, McTimoney practitioners examine and treat your entire body in the course of each session to ensure correct skeletal alignment. They rarely use X-rays or other diagnostic tools, preferring to rely on what they feel with their hands. Depending on age and a variety of other factors, most practitioners recommend between two to six sessions at weekly intervals to start with, and then regular check-ups to maintain correct skeletal alignment.

Orthodox medicine views the McTimoney and McTimoney-Corley chiropractic systems in the same light as mainstream chiropractic. However, there is an additional degree of skepticism among doctors in that they doubt whether such a gentle approach to manipulation can have significant effects.

McTimoney-Corley Chiropractic

Hugh Corley was a student of John McTimoney, but later developed McTimoney's whole body approach even further, to include gentle fingertip manipulations of the vertebrae and self-help exercises for patients to perform at home between treatment sessions. Corley set up the McTimoney-Corley School of Chiropractic in 1984. It provides a four-year part-time training scheme, to which another year must be added in order to become a full member of the McTimoney Chiropractic Association.

The gentleness of these two kinds of chiropractic therapy makes them especially suitable for babies and the elderly.

BELOW McTimoney chiropractors rely almost entirely on what they can feel with their hands to make a diagnosis.

BELOW *In contrast with the more vigorous methods of conventional chiropractic, the McTimoney-Corley approach uses gentle fingertip manipulation to realign the vertebrae.*

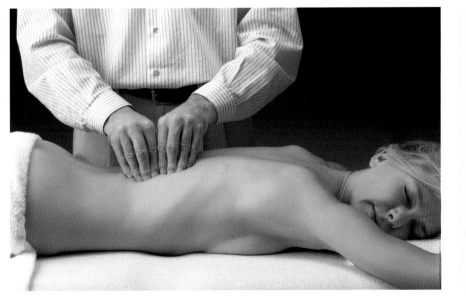

SELF-HELP

Chiropractic is not a self-help treatment. No manipulations should ever be undertaken by anyone other than an expert in the field. However, a chiropractor may well recommend that certain exercises and relaxation techniques are performed at home between sessions and after a course of treatment has been concluded.

PATHFINDER

Chiropractic is a proven treatment for problems of the musculoskeletal system, and headaches caused by muscular tension. Practitioners who adhere to Palmer's original ideas also claim that it can help migraines, gynecological problems, high blood pressure, hyperactivity in children, and many other disorders.

As a treatment for musculoskeletal problems, it has been integrated with orthodox medicine in many areas including:

ASTHMA *SEE PP.* *294–5*

BACK PROBLEMS *SEE PP.* *344–5*

BEDWETTING *SEE P.* *352*

BRONCHITIS *SEE P.* *299*

COUGHS *SEE P.* *297*

DIZZINESS *SEE P.* *271*

EARACHE *SEE P.* *282*

FAINTING *SEE P.* *270*

HEADACHE *SEE PP.* *268–9*

HYPERACTIVITY *SEE P.* *351*

INDIGESTION *SEE P.* *310*

INFERTILITY *SEE P.* *324*

MENSTRUAL PROBLEMS *SEE PP.* *322–3*

MIGRAINE *SEE P.* *269*

OSTEOPOROSIS *SEE P.* *358*

PNEUMONIA *SEE P.* *296*

PREGNANCY PROBLEMS *SEE PP.* *326–7*

REPETITIVE STRAIN INJURY (RSI) *SEE PP.* *342–3*

SCIATICA *SEE P.* *348*

KINESIOLOGY

HISTORY

George Goodheart, Jr, an American chiropractor, developed his interest in the possibilities of diagnosis through muscle testing almost by chance. In 1964, he saw a patient who had repeatedly failed physical examinations for laboring jobs because his shoulder-blade kept popping out. Goodheart found that the muscle holding the shoulder-blade in position had tiny bumps at the point where it joined the ribs. These disappeared when they were massaged and the muscle became stronger, keeping the shoulderblade in position. This discovery led him to research other factors that affected muscle performance and to develop applied kinesiology.

The term "kinesiology" is used in many different ways to mean a number of different things. In orthodox health practice, kinesiology is the study of human movement, and kinesiologists work in rehabilitation centers, and in industry. As far as complementary and alternative medicine is concerned, however, "kinesiology" is a catch-all term to describe a group of holistic, interdisciplinary therapies that share a belief that a pattern of weaknesses in specific muscles, identified by "muscle testing," indicates a diagnosis, and that a variety of techniques – including massage, manipulation, postural training, acupuncture, and "energy-balancing" – can be used to treat the cause, be it physical or emotional.

In orthodox, traditional science, "kinesiology" refers to the study of human movement – *kinesis* is a Greek word meaning "motion." Physical therapists (physiotherapists) and physiologists study biomechanics (the application of mechanical forces in human biology), the physiology of exercise, and the control of muscles by the brain as part of their training, while athletics coaches, physical education instructors, and others can obtain university degree courses and diplomas in kinesiology – dance movement therapists, for example, study kinesiology as part of their training (*see pages 226–9*).

Qualified kinesiologists of the traditional type work at hospital rehabilitation centers, treat those with developmental difficulties, emotional problems, and physical disabilities in clinics, and work in industry to maximize the efficiency of the way people use machinery.

In complementary and alternative medicine, however, the general term "kinesiology" is used to cover a wide range of diagnostic and healing systems, all of which utilize a technique called "muscle testing" (*see page 128*). This was devised by American chiropractor Dr. George Goodheart, Jr during the late 1960s and early 1970s, and he, with others, went on develop a therapy called "applied kinesiology." Later, a number of variants of the therapy emerged, all of which are known by the collective name of "specialized kinesiology."

APPLIED KINESIOLOGY

Dr. Goodheart spent many years developing and refining Applied Kinesiology (AK) in consultation with

ABOVE *Classical statues represent a physical ideal – all the muscles are in perfect working order.*

friends and colleagues, founding the International College of Applied Kinesiology (ICAK) in 1974, and becoming Research Director. ICAK prides itself on a rigorous, disciplined approach to kinesiology and contrasts the scientific approach of AK to the less substantiated claims and practices of some types of specialized kinesiology, characterizing these as "abuses" of kinesiology. AK is practiced by health care professionals, such as osteopaths, chiropractors, dentists, and a few medical doctors, who have qualified in their own fields and then undertaken a postgraduate diploma course culminating in an examination set by ICAK.

The Theory

AK depends on the theory that dysfunction in muscles may have any of a number of causes, including trapped nerves, spinal problems, tiny nodules within muscles and connective tissue, an imbalance in the meridians of traditional Chinese medicine (*see pages 20–1*), toxic chemicals, an inadequate diet, problems with the circulatory and lymph systems, food sensitivities, and neurological problems. In many cases, the result of such problems is "deafferentation." Afferent nerves carry information from sensors, including those in the muscles, to the spinal cord, brain, and organs along the path of the nerves, but in deafferentation the relay stations along these pathways do not work properly. This is one explanation for the close link that AK practitioners maintain exists between dysfunction in specific muscles and internal organs and glands to

ABOVE *Goodheart believed that poor diet was one cause of inadequate muscle function.*

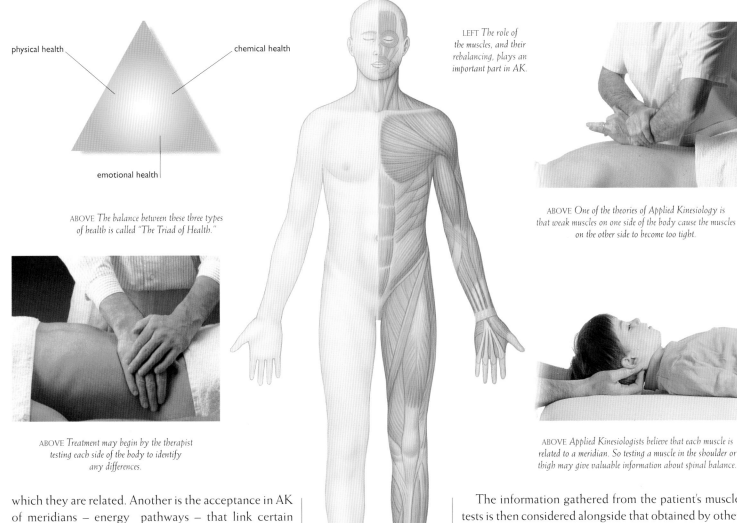

physical health

chemical health

emotional health

ABOVE *The balance between these three types of health is called "The Triad of Health."*

LEFT *The role of the muscles, and their rebalancing, plays an important part in AK.*

ABOVE *One of the theories of Applied Kinesiology is that weak muscles on one side of the body cause the muscles on the other side to become too tight.*

ABOVE *Treatment may begin by the therapist testing each side of the body to identify any differences.*

ABOVE *Applied Kinesiologists believe that each muscle is related to a meridian. So testing a muscle in the shoulder or thigh may give valuable information about spinal balance.*

which they are related. Another is the acceptance in AK of meridians – energy pathways – that link certain muscles to certain organs and glands.

The aim of treatment in AK is to restore health and the overall balance of body systems, and to improve the performance of muscles and nerves. This is done by addressing any problems such as an inadequate diet or chemical toxicity, and through correcting any structural damage or postural problems by manipulation and training, using acupuncture or acupressure (*see pages 20–31*) to balance energy flow, and massage to break down any nodules and to improve muscle and nerve function.

The Practice

AK combines elements of a number of complementary therapies with the diagnostic and treatment techniques of orthodox medical and paramedical practice, making the therapy interdisciplinary and holistic. Its aim is to obtain an overall view of the patient's neurological system in action by means of muscle testing (*see page 128*), and, in particular, to observe how muscles respond to a variety of physical, chemical, and mental stimuli. The balance between physical, chemical, and emotional health is termed "The Triad of Health."

WATCHPOINT

Applied Kinesiology is the most established form of kinesiology. Many others, however, are practiced. They include less orthodox forms (see "Specialized Kinesiology," overleaf), which some Applied Kinesiologists feel give kinesiology a bad name because they have not been tested well enough and may have little or no credibility.

The information gathered from the patient's muscle tests is then considered alongside that obtained by other means, including clinical history, a physical examination and, if necessary, laboratory investigations, before a diagnosis is reached. It is this combination of diagnostic methods – employed by health professionals – that distinguishes AK from many methods of "specialized kinesiology." Practitioners prioritize problems and treat the most important ones first.

AK is practiced by health professionals from a variety of disciplines so treatment varies according to the individual practitioner. Most use manipulation and massage of the affected muscles in one form or another, often in combination: some practitioners emphasize osteopathic and cranial techniques (*see pages 110–17*); some prefer chiropractic (*see pages 118–25*); others concentrate on techniques that work on muscles and fascia, such as Rolfing (*see pages 134–5*) and Hellerwork (*see pages 138–41*); while many practitioners favor acupuncture and acupressure (*see pages 20–31*). Muscle testing is also repeated during treatment. Other measures may include advice about diet and how to avoid any chemical substance that may be having an adverse effect on the body.

ABOVE *According to AK theory, energy flows through the body along invisible channels known as meridians.*

MUSCLE TESTING

Tests of individual muscles' strengths, weaknesses, and responses to changing circumstances play an important part in kinesiology, although Applied Kinesiologists stress that they only form one part of the diagnostic process. The technique was originally developed by Dr. Robert Lovett and physical therapists (physiotherapists) Henry and Florence Kendall in America. The Kendalls published a book on the subject in 1949 that listed around 100 tests. Later, George Goodheart built upon their work, as did his colleagues. Dr. Alan Beardall, founder of clinical kinesiology, developed around 300 more tests.

Kinesiologists maintain that muscle testing is as much an art as a science, partly because the practitioner directly influences the test and so becomes part of it. Specialized kinesiologists speak of "asking the body" for information and, to an extent, act intuitively, while Applied Kinesiologists approach muscle testing in a more rigorous way, following a disciplined, precise, and consistent sequence of steps.

The procedure starts with the examination of a large group of muscles, such as those of the thigh or arm – these are said to be indicator muscles. The kinesiologist pushes against the indicator muscles to assess the quality of response: if the limb "locks" in position, the muscles are generally strong; if it feels "spongy", one or more of the muscles has a weakness. On the basis of this information, individual muscles are isolated and assessed in the same way, until any problem is located and identified.

This part of muscle testing is known as the "physical challenge," and may continue with a test of how the muscle's response changes according to touch, heat, cold, or other sensory stimuli. Then there may be a "chemical challenge," in which the muscle's response is tested when the patient has tasted food, or smelt some chemical – in specialized kinesiology, the

1 *Rotating the humerus (upper arm bone) is a way of testing the strength of the muscle in front of the shoulder blade, known as the subscapular muscle.*

2 *Raising the patient's arm enables the therapist to test the muscle at the front of the neck, the pectoralis major clavicular muscle.*

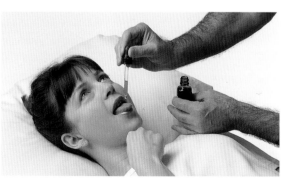

3 *If these muscles are strong enough, they can be used as "indicators." If the patient suffers from an unidentified allergy, for example, she might be asked to eat some of the suspect food. The indicator muscle would then be tested again to see if its response had changed.*

ABOVE *Undergoing kinesiology can result in the reliving of stressful experiences.*

patient may patient may merely be asked to hold a phial containing a chemical or homeopathic preparation. There may also be an "emotional challenge;" in this case, the patient is asked to visualize some stressful experience, relationship, or event from the past.

SPECIALIZED KINESIOLOGY

Since George Goodheart developed Applied Kinesiology, many of his colleagues and students, as well as others, have developed new therapies which deviate from the strict principles and practices endorsed by ICAK. These are said to be forms of "specialized kinesiology." Most of the therapies rely on muscle testing to some extent, but thereafter take a different approach to the details of diagnosis and treatment. One common thread is that muscle testing is a biofeedback mechanism by means of which energy imbalances can be detected in mind, body, or spirit. These can then be corrected – a process known as "energy balancing" – often by reference to the traditional Chinese theory of the "Five Elements" (see page 35).

CLINICAL KINESIOLOGY

Dr. Alan Beardall, an American chiropractor and Applied Kinesiologist, developed clinical kinesiology – also known as "human biodynamics" – only for use by health professionals, in the early 1980s. He extended Goodheart's work, devising around 300 more muscle tests, and mapped nearly all the muscles of the body, noting their meridians, associated organs, and reflexes, before his death in 1987. Beardall saw the human body as a "bio-computer," in which the muscles played the part of a computer's micro-circuits: just as an electrical signal is either "on" or "off," muscles are either "strong" or "weak." (Continuing the computer analogy, he believed that the information produced by the bio-computer was stored in different ways, just like computer files, and that "desktop" material, held at a superficial level, should be dealt with before "filed" material stored at a deeper level.) One of Beardall's innovations was the development of the "pause lock," also known as the "leg lock." This puts the body into "circuit retaining mode," so that information about individual muscles that are weak is held in the body as a whole, making assessment easier. To do this, the patient's legs are rotated outward and spread a short distance apart.

Diagnosis in clinical kinesiology also involves other techniques apart from muscle testing. Beardall devised more than 1,000 "hand modes" – also known as "finger modes." These are modifications of four basic movements in which the thumb is applied to the tip of each finger in turn; the effect is to make particular muscles either strong or weak, thus telling the therapist whether the patient's emotional, physical, or chemical characteristics need attention. Information is also gained from testing a series of points on the patient's skull, the theory being that these points represent different areas of the body.

Treatment methods are much more varied than those used in Applied Kinesiology. Massage, manipulation, homeopathic medicines, nutritional supplements, and acupressure are used, as in AK, but clinical kinesiologists also use gemstones, Bach flower remedies and essential oils, and nutritional supplements which Beardall developed in order to promote healing.

PRECAUTIONS

■ While all Applied Kinesiologists are health professionals, few are medical doctors; even fewer specialized kinesiologists have medical qualifications. If you suffer from any medical condition or suspect that you may do so, consult your family doctor before seeing a kinesiologist.

■ You should inform a kinesiologist before diagnosis or treatment begins if you suffer from any debilitating disease, are in pain, are convalescing, or have any chronic problems.

■ Kinesiologists stress that the patient must be completely involved in his or her treatment: the practitioner and the patient are partners in the therapy.

■ Anybody can call themselves a kinesiologist, though only those who have obtained a diploma from ICAK can claim to be an Applied Kinesiologist. Make sure that any kinesiologist you consult has received adequate training and is accredited by an appropriate organization.

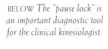

BELOW *The "pause lock" is an important diagnostic tool for the clinical kinesiologist.*

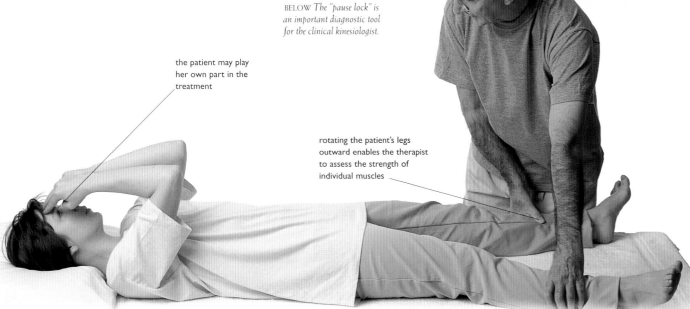

the patient may play her own part in the treatment

rotating the patient's legs outward enables the therapist to assess the strength of individual muscles

NEUROVASCULAR AND NEURO-LYMPHATIC REFLEXES

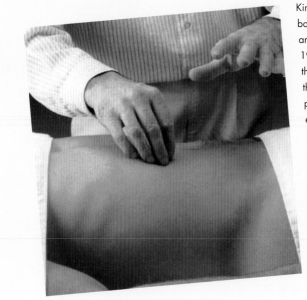

Kinesiologists believe that lightly massaging certain areas of the body can increase the efficiency of the organs with which they are associated. Neuro-lymphatic reflexes were discovered in the 1930s by an American osteopath called Frank Chapman (like the system of blood vessels, the "lymph system" is something that permeates all the tissues of the body and removes the waste products produced by chemical processes occurring within each cell). Chapman found that rubbing certain areas, mainly in and around the spaces between the ribs, stimulated particular organs. In the same decade, American chiropractor Terence Bennett discovered neurovascular reflexes. These are particular points on the head that, when held gently, increase the flow of blood to certain organs and glands, and so improve their efficiency.

LEFT *Rubbing certain areas can help remove waste products.*

TOUCH FOR HEALTH (TFH)

One of George Goodhearts's colleagues while he was developing Applied Kinesiology was Dr. John Thie, another American chiropractor. Thie wanted to make the benefits of Applied Kinesiology available to everybody, including people who were not health professionals, and in 1973 he published *Touch for Health: A New Approach to Restoring Our Natural Energies*, in which he endeavored to do just that. Later, together with Goodheart and a third chiropractor, Sheldon Deal, he established the Touch for Health Foundation, which trains instructors to teach what is essentially a self-help technique. (After a while, however, Goodheart became unhappy about the use of AK principles by lay people, while Deal went on to develop advanced kinesiology – *see opposite.*)

TFH is based on the concept of "wellness" – originally it was known as "Health From Within," rather than "TFH" – and incorporates psychotherapeutic concepts that were introduced by Thie's wife Carrie, a family therapist, and influenced by associates such as Joseph Heller (*see pages 138–41*) and Ida Rolf (*see pages 134–7*). It provides a daily routine which balances the four sides of the pyramid that represents the holistic model of health – the sides being, to quote Dr. Thie, "structure, chemistry, the mind (conscious and unconscious), and emotion ... the base of this pyramid, on which all else is founded, is spiritual truth and love." The process involves "goal setting," in which each individual chooses what he or she wishes to happen and holds a clear view of it, and then uses muscle testing as part of the technique of balancing energy flows.

TFH is now practiced by many thousands of people around the world, and its "Instructor Training Program" is available in more than 50 countries. It has also been the main building block for a large number of different types of kinesiology, each with variations in philosophy and technique. Examples include "applied physiology," developed by TFH instructor Richard Utt; "wellness

HOLISTIC HEALTH

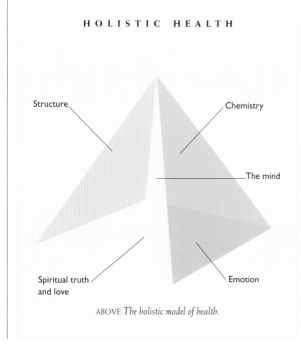

Structure

Chemistry

The mind

Spiritual truth and love

Emotion

ABOVE *The holistic model of health.*

kinesiology," devised by Dr. Wayne Topping, another TFH instructor; "biokinesiology," formulated by John Barton; "foundation kinesiology practice," developed by Maggie La Tourelle; and "Christian kinesiology," the brainchild of the Reverend Jim Reid, once the Baptist Chaplain of the "Las Vegas Strip."

ADVANCED KINESIOLOGY

Dr. Sheldon Deal, another American chiropractor, was instrumental in the development of Applied Kinesiology and also influential in the Touch for Health movement. Like John Thie, he wished to make Applied Kinesiology techniques available to lay people who had no knowl-edge of manipulative therapies, and developed a synthesis of AK techniques that he had been teaching since the early 1980s. One principle of advanced kine-siology is that some parts of the body "mimic" other ones, perhaps because of their similarity in shape. A problem that manifests itself in the area of the sacrum, for example (a bone in the lower back), may, in fact, be due to something that directly affects a bone at the back of the skull which is of a similar shape.

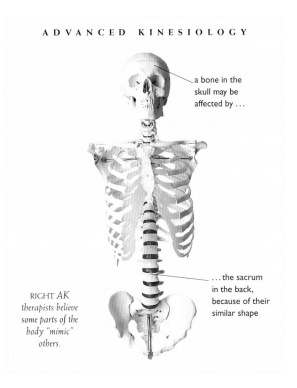

a bone in the skull may be affected by ...

...the sacrum in the back, because of their similar shape

RIGHT *AK therapists believe some parts of the body "mimic" others.*

EDUCATIONAL KINESIOLOGY (EDU-K) AND BRAIN GYM

Another TFH instructor who went on to pioneer a different form of kinesiology was educational therapist Dr. Paul Dennison. Having worked at a remedial learning center for many years, helping dyslexic and other children with learning difficulties to acquire basic skills, he started to use muscle testing to isolate imbalances that affect mental performance. Drawing also on the theories of orthodox neurology, he devised a series of exercises that improve communication between the left and right sides of the brain; the importance of this "crossover" has long been acknowledged by orthodox medicine.

Dr. Dennison developed two main techniques: "Dennison laterality repatterning" and "brain gym." He also uses "goal setting," which is a mainstay of Touch for Health. Kinesiologists would say that lateral patterning "balances" the two sides of the brain; orthodox neurologists would say that it opens up new nerve pathways between them, maintains them, and strengthens them. One technique that has proved extremely successful in

practice is the "cross-crawl," in which each hand is placed in turn on the opposite knee, while at the same time the subject hums or moves his or her head to one side. Another involves describing a figure eight with each hand alternately.

Brain gym consists of a series of exercises that not only help balance the two sides of the brain, but also increase the supply of nutrients to the brain as a whole and balance an individual's energy to maximize both mental and physical performance.

Educational kinesiology has proved its worth in the treatment of children with dyslexia and learning difficulties. It is endorsed by the U.S. National Learning Foundation and used by adults in all walks of life to improve performance and to bring out an individual's abilities.

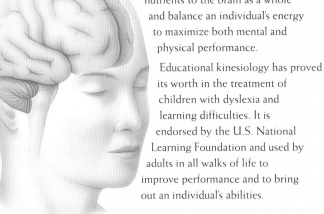

ABOVE *Balancing the brain can maximize both mental capacity and physical performance in an individual.*

RIGHT *Educational kinesiology can help a child's performance at school.*

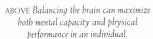

PROFESSIONAL KINESIOLOGY PRACTICE (PKP)
Another synthesis of applied kinesiology methods, designed for both lay people and health professionals, has been developed by New Zealand medical doctor, applied kinesiologist and TFH instructor Dr. Bruce Drewe and his wife, Joan. PKP does not include manipulative therapies, such as those used by osteopaths and chiropractors (*see pages 110–27*), but does utilize other skills that are not generally taught in TFH courses. In particular, PKP emphasizes the importance of "finger mode" testing, as originally developed by Dr. Alan Beardall (*see page 129*), regarding the information that this provides as a database that can be drawn upon by the person using the "bio-computer."

HYPERTON-X

Also known as "hypertonic muscle release", hyperton-X was developed in the early 1980s by Frank Mahony, a Touch for Health instructor who had also worked with Dr. Paul Dennison on educational kinesiology. Mahony discovered that there was a link between hypertonic – "over-tight" – muscles and mental and physical performance. By identifying muscles that are hypertonic by means of muscle testing and then releasing the tension in them, the flow of cerebrospinal fluid (which bathes the brain and fills the spinal cord) can be altered. Doing so, the theory has it, improves the biochemical efficiency of the body and increases the quality of communication between mind and body. Hyperton-X is primarily, though not exclusively, used to improve sporting performance and to help in the treatment of sports injuries.

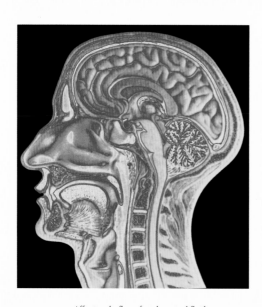

ABOVE *Affecting the flow of cerebrospinal fluid can improve communication between mind and body.*

LEFT *Frank Mahony developed Hyperton-X, which can help heal sports injuries.*

PATHFINDER

As far as medical conditions are concerned, kinesiology is best thought of as an aid to diagnosis. Its main role in treatment is to promote good health or "wellness" – both physical and psychological – and to resolve minor problems before they become major ones. Such problems include:

ADDICTIONS SEE P. 258

ALLERGIES SEE PP. 338–9

ANXIETY SEE PP. 256–7

ARTHRITIS SEE PP. 346–7

BACK PROBLEMS SEE PP. 344–5

EATING DISORDERS SEE P. 265

HYPERACTIVITY SEE P. 351

REPETITIVE STRAIN INJURY (RSI) SEE PP. 342–3

STRESS SEE PP. 262–3

LEFT *Health kinesiologists believe that allergies can be caused by energy distortions that occur when the principles of feng shui are not taken into account when arranging a room.*

Health Kinesiology

Dr. Jimmy Scott developed health kinesiology after working on the faculty at the University of California Medical School in San Francisco, and his branch of kinesiology has now spread throughout the world. Health kinesiologists use muscle testing to uncover allergies and nutritional deficiencies and to investigate "geopathic" causes of stress and illness – that is, factors such as electromagnetic radiation, energy distortions caused by a lack of attention to the principles of feng shui when planning a room and so on. Treatment is likely to involve recommendations about lifestyle changes, such as dietary changes and exercise programs, acupressure, the use of magnets in therapy and homeopathic remedies.

LEFT *Magnets are used in health kinesiology.*

EMOTIONAL STRESS RELEASE

Dr. George Goodheart noted that the skin of people who are suffering from severe stress often appears red above the eyebrows and discovered that light pressure over these areas while a patient thought through or re-lived the cause of his or her stress would increase the patient's ability to cope with stress. He called this technique "emotional stress release," and it has since become an important weapons in kinesiologists' armouries. The pressure should be maintained for ten minutes or so for it to be effective.

The rationale for the success of this technique is that ESR stimulates the neurovascular reflexes which affect the stomach – an area often been said to be the seat of our emotions.

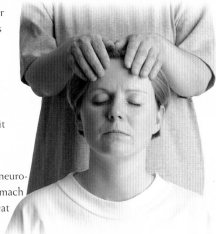

ROLFING

ROLFING

The biochemist Dr. Ida P. Rolf devised Rolfing (or "Structural Integration") after years of research into how trauma is stored in the muscles and connective . tissues of the body. Her therapy system goes deeply into them in order to restructure and balance the body – focusing on realignment with its center of gravity, and also with that of the Earth. She concluded that gravity assists balance and movement when the body is aligned correctly with it, and that psychological and physical problems can thereby be relieved.

One of the pioneers in bodywork therapies, Dr. Ida Rolf devised her therapy system of "structural integration," later trademarked Rolfing, after many years of patient research and experimentation. She came to the conclusion that a combination of memories of physical and emotional trauma, stored in the muscles and connective tissue, and a misalignment of the musculoskeletal system with the body's center of gravity were responsible for many physical and psychological problems. Her therapy system of deep massage, which focuses on loosening and stretching connective tissue, has been taken up by almost 1,000 practitioners throughout the world.

Dr. Ida P. Rolf (1896–1979) was born in New York in 1896 and was awarded a doctorate in biochemistry by the College of Physicians and Surgeons at Columbia University in 1920. She became interested in the mechanics of the human body after being treated for a rib problem by an osteopath.

Rolf's researches convinced her that the physical shape and form of the human body both affected and was affected by an individual's psychological make-up and physiological responses, and that the body reacts to and "remembers" past experiences. She believed that these "memories" are held in the myofascial system rather than just in the muscular system – "myo" refers to muscle; fascia is the white, fibrous connective tissue that encloses and connects each muscle and muscle fiber and coalesces into bands to form tendons and ligaments. Rolf suggested that throughout their lives people develop poor posture and acquire the habit of moving incorrectly as a result of the stress caused by psychological or physical traumas and that these become "set" in the fascia. Her treatment was aimed at freeing the fascia so that the body could return to its natural state.

Rolf also believed that the pull of gravity has a profound effect on the musculoskeletal system. When the upright body is aligned with gravity, the force of gravity assists balance and movement. But if the body is out of alignment – as, for example, it is when someone has poor posture – the pull of gravity acts as a stress on the system, which must work harder to stay upright and thus loses its natural balance.

The Rolf Institute
Rolf spent many years devising her treatment system – properly known as "Structural Integration", but more commonly called Rolfing® – and started to demonstrate it to other bodywork practitioners, such as chiropractors and osteopaths, in the 1950s. As interest in holistic treatment increased throughout the 1960s, Dr. Rolf became more and more well known, and in 1971 she established the Rolf Institute of Structural Integration, in Boulder, Colorado, U.S. There are now certified Rolfers in Europe as well.

The Theory
The muscles of the human body normally work in pairs. As one muscle contracts, shortening to perform an action, an opposing muscle relaxes and lengthens. For example, if you bend your elbow, the biceps – the muscle at the front of the upper arm – contracts, and the triceps – the muscle at the back of the upper arm – lengthens. When your arm is hanging loosely by your side, both muscles are relaxed, but both retain a certain amount of muscle tone, or tension.

When the body is upright and its center of gravity runs straight through the center of the body, the muscles need only retain a small amount of tension to maintain the position. But if, for example, the head is poked forward, the body will not be in alignment with the force of gravity. The muscles of the neck and upper back have to contract in order to hold the head up, against the force of gravity, and prevent the chin from falling onto the chest. At the same time, the opposing muscles will be relaxed but will not be lengthened, and so will hold little muscle tone.

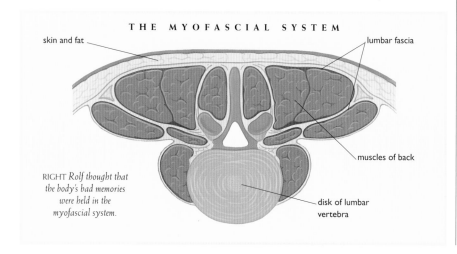

THE MYOFASCIAL SYSTEM

skin and fat

lumbar fascia

muscles of back

disk of lumbar vertebra

RIGHT *Rolf thought that the body's bad memories were held in the myofascial system.*

THE PRACTICE

Dr. Rolf compared the body to a tower of children's bricks: if the bricks sit neatly and squarely, one on top of the other, the tower is stable; on the other hand, if one or more bricks are out of alignment, the whole structure is unstable and comes under stress. Rolfers aim to realign the body so that each part sits in its correct position in relation to the section above and below it.

When she came to work out just how to realign the body, Rolf decided that the major impediment to doing so was the presence of rigid, knotted fascia. During childhood, fascia is pliable and flexible, and she theorized that in adult life it could be re-educated back into its childhood state. With this premise in mind, Rolf worked for many years to develop a system of deep massage that could maneuver the fascia back to its earlier, flexible state. In her massage system, each section of the body is worked on in turn to soften and stretch the fascia so that the section is correctly aligned with the building block above and below it. By the end of a course, the aim is to have loosened the fascia throughout the body, so that the muscles can work freely and correctly with, rather than against, the force of gravity.

RIGHT *Rolf's famous "tower of bricks" analogy. In a child's building, as long as everything is correctly balanced, all is well, but once any single block is out of place, the whole structure will topple. The same applies to the human body.*

ORTHODOX VIEW

Most doctors view Rolfing simply as a form of deep massage that has many of the same effects as massage (*see pp. 96–105*). As yet, the therapy is not widely known and little scientific research has been conducted into it. However, a paper in the journal *Physiological Therapy*, in 1988, showed that Rolfing could reduce lordosis – sway-back – in young men. And in 1988, researchers at the University of Maryland found that Rolfing reduced stress and improved neuromuscular function.

If this posture is maintained over a long period, the muscles will stay shortened, in an over-contracted state. The fascia surrounding each muscle fiber and muscle will also shorten and lose its flexibility. As a result, the muscle will feel stiff and rigid. At the same time, the neuromuscular system will have "learned" an incorrect position, and so it will feel as if it is correct. Rolfers believe that it is the stress of maintaining an incorrect position against the force of gravity that causes most instances of structural damage to the musculoskeletal system. They also believe that such stress depletes the body's energy and self-healing abilities.

Myofascial Memory

Rolfers also believe that any trauma, physical or emotional, can have an effect on the body that persists for a long time after any actual damage has mended or been forgotten. These "memories" of past events affect the myofascial system, causing the fascia to harden, bond, and lose pliability and the muscles to retain too much tension, even at rest. Both of these effects diminish the range of movement available at a joint and force a muscle to work harder to achieve the movement that is required. But, since these effects manifest themselves gradually over time, people experiencing them adapt and believe that the loss of agility and energy are part of the normal aging process. Rolfers maintain that this rigidity in the myofascial system eventually affects not only the musculoskeletal system, but also the other main body systems – and in doing so affects both physical and emotional health.

Hot Spots

The result of this stretching and loosening of the fascia is that the muscles beneath the fascia can lengthen and relax fully. Any painful, knotted areas of fascia or muscle are pummeled and pushed until they, too, are stretched and relaxed. Painful "hot spots" such as these are the areas in which Rolfers believe that emotional and physical traumas are stored by the body. And when they are massaged and the tension released, so the forgotten cause of the physical or emotional trauma may be remembered and released in turn.

As the body is gradually realigned and the muscles and fascia relaxed, any musculoskeletal aches and pains caused by poor posture, old injuries, or inefficient movement patterns will be alleviated and hopefully will not occur when the correct posture is learned. The improvement in posture deepens breathing, reduces wear and tear on the muscles and joints, and increases energy levels. Rolfing can also have a beneficial effect on stress-related problems, alter mood, and enhance self-esteem and awareness. Many people who have completed Rolfing sessions find that they are measurably taller – and that this effect of the therapy is a permanent one.

CONSULTING A THERAPIST

Standard Rolfing treatment consists of 10 sessions, each one lasting between 60 and 90 minutes. Usually, it is recommended that you attend sessions on a regular basis, at one- or two-week intervals. Each of the first seven sessions is devoted to a particular body area: in the first one, work is done on the trunk and ribcage, to help you breathe more easily and deeply; in the next ones, the practitioner – known as a "Rolfer," Rolfing Practitioner, or Rolf Practitioner – works on the lower back, then the neck, then knees, and so on, with each session building up on the results and findings of the previous ones. (Some Rolfers take a photograph before and after each session in order to keep a record of your progress.) In the last three sessions, the Rolfer concentrates on reintegrating and aligning the newly flexible tissues.

Before your first session, the Rolfer will take a full medical and personal history, asking, for example, whether you have ever sustained any injury. Already the way in which you walk into the treatment room will have been closely observed, as will the way you move, sit, and stand. You will be asked to undress to your underwear, bathing suit, or shorts, so that the Rolfer can examine your movement and physical appearance. He or she will be looking to see whether you hold one shoulder higher than the other, whether your spine is straight, and whether you bear more weight on one foot than the other – all of these assessments, and others, too, give the Rolfer an idea of the places in your body where you hold tension or stress.

During the session itself you will be asked to lie, sit, or stand on a massage table or mat, depending on which

2 Early sessions in a course of treatment concentrate on specific parts of the body. The therapist uses her hands to loosen tight muscles.

1 At the start of each Rolfing session, the therapist will take careful note of the details of the patient's posture and body alignment.

wear underwear so your body can be examined

3 Later on in the sessions, the Rolfer will reintegrate the more supple tissues in the body,

the Rolfer will look for places of stress

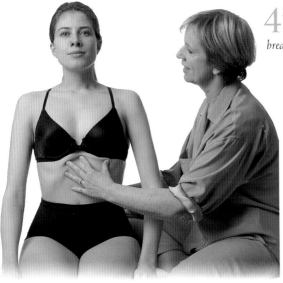

4 Expanding the ribcage will help the patient to breathe more easily.

PATHFINDER

Rolfing can also be used to treat:

ASTHMA *SEE PP.* 294–5

BACK PROBLEMS *SEE PP.* 344–5

FIBROSITIS *SEE P.* 348

HEADACHE *SEE PP.* 268–9

MIGRAINE *SEE P.* 269

STRESS *SEE PP.* 262–3

5 After a course of Rolfing you should find that it requires no extra effort to carry your head erect.

area is being worked. The Rolfer will knead, massage, and pummel your flesh, using his or her hands, fingers, knuckles, and elbows. The massage is slow and profound, and you may be asked to breathe deeply in time with the pressure. If a tender, hot spot is found, the Rolfer will concentrate on freeing any lesion or bonding in the fascia before moving on. This procedure can be intense, so it is important that you do not tense up – doing so will only increase the pain – but try to relax and allow the knot to be kneaded free. Rolfers believe that in many cases such tender spots are a "memory" of a previous traumatic event, and that the event itself may be remembered as the spot is massaged. As the knot is eased, so the memory and the tension that it has induced can be released. During the session, you may also be asked to move your body in a specific, controlled way to allow the Rolfer to manipulate the fascia and offer a new option for movement.

At the end of the first session, you may well feel a deep relaxation and sense of release – and you may be taller, too – but it is important to finish the full course to reap the full benefit of the treatment. Throughout the series you may be given some movement awareness exercises to perform between sessions. Known as "movement integration" exercises, these were developed after the main Rolfing system was devised as an adjunct to the therapy – the exercises are similar to those taught by Hellerwork practitioners (*see pages 138–41*) and are performed to re-educate your neuromuscular system into laying down correct patterns of movement. After the course of 10 standard sessions is over, you can always revisit the practitioner for a one-off refresher session.

6 Your body will be correctly aligned, your shoulders level, and your weight evenly distributed. Overall, you will look and feel more relaxed and comfortable.

SELF-HELP

By its nature, Rolfing is not a self-help technique, but a Rolfer may give some structured exercises to perform between treatment sessions. It is important to maintain the improvement made to your posture and flexibility after treatment by staying conscious of how you hold yourself and how you move. The Rolf Institute (*see Useful Addresses, pp. 368–73*) has for sale a variety of books, tapes, and videos on Rolfing structural integration, many of which are written by Ida Rolf herself and explain her theories and methods.

HELLERWORK

HELLERWORK

The American Rolfer Joseph Heller devised his own system for relieving tensions stored in the body's connective tissues, or fascia, and called it Hellerwork. It differs from Rolfing in that massage is only one aspect of the therapy, which incorporates exercises similar to those of the Alexander Technique and the Feldenkrais Method, and also dialogue between the practitioner and student/client about the way emotions affect the body. The training has three components: bodywork, movement education, and verbal dialogue – which are designed to help the student to bring his body back into a healthy upright alignment and balance.

The brainchild of a one-time space engineer and President of the Rolf Institute, Hellerwork is a form of somatic education that aims to relieve tension that has accumulated in the body's connective tissue and to restore the body to balance, whether the cause of any imbalance is the result of incorrect movements and posture that have become a habit or of emotional problems. Though little known outside America at present, it is gradually gaining in popularity as an holistic, preventive technique that can improve movement and posture skills and also increase self-awareness, self-esteem, and a sense of well-being.

Joseph Heller, the originator of Hellerwork, was once a space engineer in America who specialized in the effect of gravity on space rockets, but he was also interested in human development and the effect of deep massage on the structure of the body. In 1972, he trained under Ida Rolf (*see pages 134–37*), who had developed a system to realign the body tissues according to the pull of gravity by means of deep massage of the fascia (connective tissue). Heller became President of the Rolf Institute in 1975, but left his position three years later because he felt that massage alone would not achieve a lasting effect. Heller also worked with Judith Aston, a dance and physical education teacher who pioneered a variation of Rolfing called Aston Patterning, and studied bioenergetics (*see pages 204–5*) and Gestalt (*see pages 200–1*) among other techniques.

Heller then devised his own system: Hellerwork. Massage, however, is only one aspect of it. The second part consists of a number of exercises that bear resemblance to those of the Alexander Technique (*see pages 146–53*) and the Feldenkrais Method (*see pages 142–5*), in that they aim to re-educate everyday movements. The third component of Hellerwork derives from the fact that the body and mind are interconnected and that stress and other emotional factors affect the body tissues. Through dialogue, the client is made aware of his or her emotions and how they are reflected in the posture and motion of the body.

Heller lives and works in Mount Shasta, California, and has devised a course to train others in Hellerwork; he also continues to develop his system. There are over 400 certified Hellerwork practitioners worldwide; around 300 of them are in America.

ABOVE *Like Rolfing, Hellerwork is concerned with body alignment and using gravity to help rather than hinder us in our movements.*

THE THEORY

The three components of Hellerwork are known as "bodywork," "movement education," and "verbal dialogue." The system does not concentrate on particular areas of tension, but sees such areas as signs that the body as a whole is out of alignment and balance. These three components are designed to remedy the possible causes of problems. Hellerwork concentrates on realigning the entire body to its correct position – where the vertical line of gravity runs properly through the upright body, the joints are fully mobile throughout their range of movement, and the fascia is adequately lubricated and loose.

Bodywork

Bodywork is a form of deep massage of the fascia. Fascia is a white fibrous tissue that surrounds and connects each muscle and muscle fiber. It joins at the end of each muscle to form a tendon, which connects a muscle to a bone. Ideally, the fascia should be supple and have the ability to stretch as required, but sometimes it can become stiff and immobile. Layers of fascia can become stuck together, thus restricting movement and causing pain. Heller maintains that stiffness and tension accumulate in the fascia. Since the body's fascia is interconnected, tension in one area affects another area. Heller likens these interconnecting layers of fascia to a body stocking, which will stretch in one place if pulled in another.

Several factors can make the fascia lose its flexibility: lack of regular movement; distortion as a result of uneven physical stresses being placed upon it, as, for example, in the case of poor posture; trauma; or deep-seated emotional stress. Another factor makes this inflexibility worse: in normal circumstances, the contraction and relaxation of

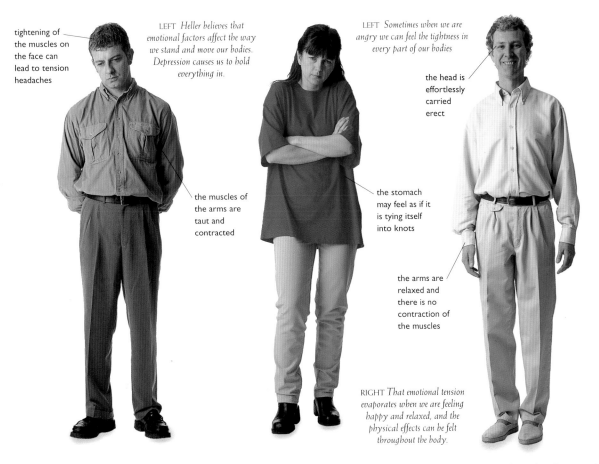

tightening of the muscles on the face can lead to tension headaches

LEFT *Heller believes that emotional factors affect the way we stand and move our bodies. Depression causes us to hold everything in.*

the muscles of the arms are taut and contracted

LEFT *Sometimes when we are angry we can feel the tightness in every part of our bodies*

the stomach may feel as if it is tying itself into knots

the head is effortlessly carried erect

the arms are relaxed and there is no contraction of the muscles

RIGHT *That emotional tension evaporates when we are feeling happy and relaxed, and the physical effects can be felt throughout the body.*

muscles make the fascia absorb interstitial fluid, which surrounds and bathes each body cell. However, if there is insufficient movement, there is no change in pressure, so the fascia does not absorb fluid and becomes stiff and dry, and therefore inflexible.

Movement Education

To function efficiently in the upright position, the human body must be straight and evenly balanced, with the line of gravitational force running down the middle of the body – from the head, through the spine to the feet. If the body is either tilted to one side or swayed back or forwards from this line, gravity exerts an increased pull on the body. The body then must work harder to stay upright and it tenses up to counter the force of gravity. The misalignment and the tension this causes adversely affects how you move. Over time, incorrect actions become a habit and the muscles and fascia become distorted and lose their flexibility.

Gravity is not the only cause of incorrect movement. After an accident or physical trauma which damages the fascia as well as other body tissues, it is a natural instinct to "guard," or protect, the area that has been damaged – by favoring the uninjured arm or leg, for example. If there is no subsequent rehabilitation, the protective procedure may become habitual, so that the damaged fascia fails to recover fully and loses its flexibility.

Hellerwork uses specific exercises to remedy these problems, worked through in a series of sessions with a practitioner. Heller also believes that the mind affects the body and vice versa. For example, emotional stress can throw the body out of alignment – depressed and anxious people tend to stand with drooping shoulders and sunken chests, while highly tense and aggressive people hunch their shoulders up and thrust their chins forward. These postures are the result of a state of mind or of character, which if not addressed has a direct physical effect on the body. These, too, can be worked through with a practitioner.

Determining State of Mind

Verbal dialogue is a psychotherapeutic technique that attempts to identify and remedy the cause of any troublesome state of mind. Practitioners lead conversations with their clients in an attempt to help them become aware of how their attitudes to the world around them and their past experiences have helped to mold how they hold themselves and perform everyday actions, and how these attitudes and experiences have had an effect on their body.

PATHFINDER

Hellerwork is a form of preventive, somatic education, not a therapy, but it can help with musculoskeletal problems caused by poor posture and/or ingrained poor movement patterns. It may also benefit people who find it difficult to relax and suffer from certain stress-related disorders:

ASTHMA SEE PP. 294–5

BACK PROBLEMS SEE PP. 344–5

FIBROSITIS SEE P. 348

HEADACHE SEE PP. 268–9

MIGRAINE SEE P. 269

STRESS SEE PP. 262–3

CONSULTING A PRACTITIONER

To find a certified practitioner in your area, consult the address section at the back of this book (*see pages 368–73*). Hellerwork is still relatively unknown and there are only 400 certified practitioners. If there is no practitioner near you – as yet, there are few outside the United States – other somatic education methods such as The Alexander Technique (*see pages 146–53*) are more widely available. Rolfing (*see pages 134–7*) has a similar philosophy to Hellerwork.

A course of Hellerwork consists of eleven ninety-minute sessions. Each session includes the three basic components of Hellerwork – bodywork, movement education, and verbal dialogue. The eleven sessions are subdivided into three main groups known as the Superficial section, the Core section, and the Integrative section. The first seven sessions focus on specific body areas. The first three of them concentrate on the superficial muscles and fascia of the body and upon early emotional development in childhood. The fourth to seventh sessions – the Core

section – focuses on the deep muscles and tissues of the body, while the verbal dialogue concentrates on the emotional changes in adolescence. The last four sessions put all the previous elements together and specifically concentrate on rotational movements in bodywork and on movement education, and the conversation concerns issues of maturity and your attitude to the outside world. The eleventh – final – session may not include any bodywork, but will focus on your particular lifestyle and how you can integrate the Hellerwork method into your life.

Before the first session, the practitioner will take a detailed history and may recommend that you see your general practitioner before starting the course. You will be photographed before and after each session to see what progress is being made. Throughout the sessions, the practitioner will talk to you about the subject being explored and may also film you so that you can see what you are doing. Hellerwork practitioners advise students to follow certain exercises at home and to have sessions after physical or emotional trauma.

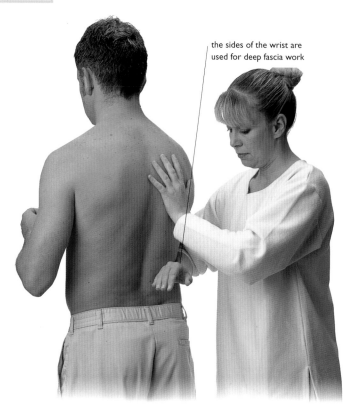

the sides of the wrist are used for deep fascia work

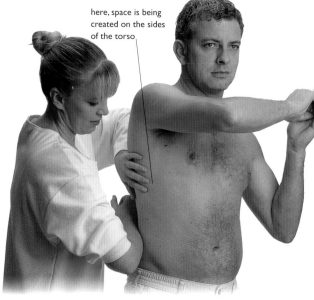

here, space is being created on the sides of the torso

The session will begin with about an hour of bodywork. You will be asked to undress to underclothes and to lie or sit on a mat or massage table. The practitioner will knead and massage with deep manual pressure to free and mobilize the fascia to its correct length.

Following the 60 minutes of bodywork there is a further 30 minutes of movement education. The exercises will concentrate on the area just massaged. Throughout the session, the practitioner will talk to you about a chosen emotional area. For example, during the Superficial sessions, the exercises and movement re-education will concentrate on the developmental movements of childhood, such as reaching out, standing, sitting, and walking. These are organized to show you the least harmful way to perform any action.

the awareness of breath is very important during the sessions

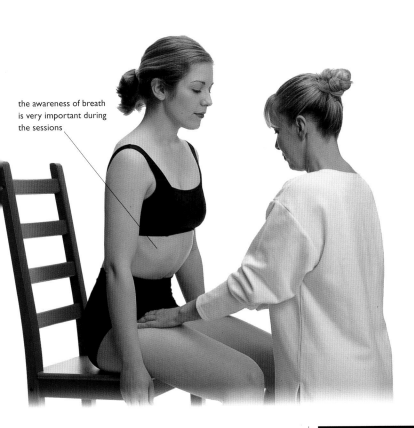

there are many muscles and fascial sheets to work on in the back

You may well be filmed performing everyday actions to enable you to see clearly how you habitually move. Once you can visualize your actions, it is much easier to change the movement to one that puts less strain on your body. Once you have completed a course of Hellerwork, you will be advised to continue with certain of the movement education exercises to maintain and increase your improvement. Hellerwork practitioners also advise a follow-up session after any physical or emotional trauma so that bad habits cannot creep in.

EFFECTS OF HELLERWORK

Hellerwork practitioners maintain that this method of somatic education can:

❖ Increase energy and fitness

❖ Enhance self-esteem

❖ Increase self-awareness

❖ Improve posture and appearance

❖ Improve coordination and balance

❖ Give a sense of well-being

❖ Slow down the aging process

WATCHPOINT

Hellerwork is not a therapy and does not aim to treat any disorders, so see your medical practitioner if you are at all worried about your health.

Deep massage is not recommended for those with certain types of cancer, osteoporosis, and some circulatory problems, such as thrombosis.

Hellerwork may not be suitable for people suffering from certain mental disorders. Deep-seated emotional problems may surface during a course of treatment and may require the attention of a qualified counselor or medical practitioner.

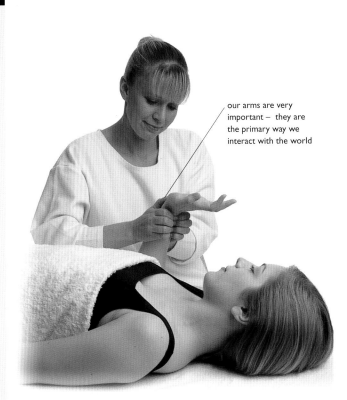

our arms are very important – they are the primary way we interact with the world

THE FELDENKRAIS METHOD

*I*n the 1940s, Dr. Moshe Feldenkrais developed the method that bears his name. Several thousand practitioners have been trained in his techniques and practice them all around the world. The Feldenkrais Method can be considered a therapy in that it teaches a form of body awareness and control that can benefit those suffering from neurological and musculoskeletal problems, as well as other challenges, but it is also a useful tool that can be used to increase self-awareness, movement skills, posture, and balance, and also to reduce stress levels and increase self-esteem and general well-being.

Dr. Moshe Feldenkrais, who devised the Feldenkrais Method, was born in Russia in 1904, but left that country when he was 13 to travel in Palestine. Later, during his 20s, he studied engineering in Paris and was then awarded a doctorate in physics at the Sorbonne, where he worked on France's early atomic research programme. During the Second World War, he escaped from Nazi-occupied France and found refuge in Britain, where he worked on an anti-submarine project before moving to Israel in 1949.

During his time in Paris, Feldenkrais had met one Jigaro Kano, a Japanese judoka who was primarily responsible for introducing the art of judo to the West, and had been awarded his black belt – judo's highest honor – in 1936. Feldenkrais was to teach judo for more than 30 years, and it was his interest in the body-training methods of this martial art, coupled with his scientific knowledge of the working of the body in mechanical terms, that led him to devise his own system of controlled exercises.

Searching for a Cure

Feldenkrais started work on his system because of a knee injury, originally the result of a football accident – he was extremely fond of the game – that kept recurring. Like F. M. Alexander (*see page 146*) who was in a similar situation, Feldenkrais tried to cure himself. He found that by integrating his own knowledge with some of Alexander's ideas about "somatic education"– a phrase coined by American Dr. Thomas Hanna, who defined somatic education as "the use of sensory-motor learning to gain greater voluntary control of one's physiological process" – he could replace learned movements that put unnecessary stress on his body with relaxed and free movements that caused no damage.

Feldenkrais studied anatomy, physiology, neurology, psychology, and other health disciplines as he slowly developed the system known as the Feldenkrais Method. In 1962, the Feldenkrais Institute was opened in Tel Aviv, Israel, to train practitioners. Feldenkrais found it difficult to train others, however, since he could not easily explain to his students the ideas that he appreciated instinctively. Nevertheless, practitioners have now been trained in the technique and use it all around the world, notably in Israel, America, Australia, and Europe. Feldenkrais died in 1984 at the age of 80.

THE THEORY

The Feldenkrais Method is a form of somatic education and therefore a preventive therapy rather than a treatment. It aims to deepen awareness in "students" (as

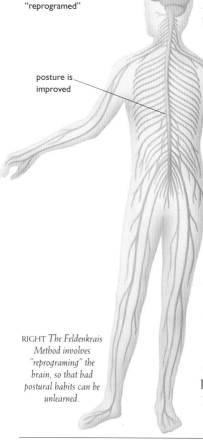

thoughts are "reprogramed"

posture is improved

RIGHT *The Feldenkrais Method involves "reprograming" the brain, so that bad postural habits can be unlearned.*

ABOVE *The first lessons often take the form of floor work as Feldenkrais believed that this "facilitated the breakdown of muscular patterns."*

THE FELDENKRAIS METHOD

Though the Feldenkrais Method is similar in some ways to the Alexander Technique (see pp. 146–53), it differs in that its emphasis is on re-educating the neuromuscular pathways rather than just the muscles – it has been likened to a Western T'ai Chi (see pp. 44–9). It is not a treatment for specific physical disorders, although patients with neuromuscular problems such as strokes, multiple sclerosis, and cerebral palsy are sometimes referred to Feldenkrais practitioners for individual lessons.However, a large number of people suffer from poor posture, stiffness, and incorrect patterns of movement that have become ingrained and instinctive, and would benefit from the greater awareness and flexibility that can result from taking lessons in this system. And, as with the Alexander Technique, many musicians, actors, and dancers have learned the Method in order to enhance their understanding of how they move and perform, and so increase their range of abilities.

people receiving therapy are known) of their habitual neuromuscular patterns, and to teach free-flowing movements that relax taut muscles and encourage the formation of new neuromuscular pathways. As children, we move with natural grace and ease, but, with time, poor postural habits and movements are learned and eventually become automatic and involuntary. The result is that the body is pulled out of its correct alignment – some muscles are too tense while others are overstretched. Meanwhile, the motor cortex of the brain becomes conditioned to believe that this state is correct and so keeps the muscles at the level of tension that maintains the incorrect alignment. To effect a lasting change in muscle tone, the brain must be reprogramed; this can be done by consciously performing a series of small, fluid movements. These open new nerve pathways so that eventually a movement that was previously only possible under conscious control becomes involuntary and automatic.

Feldenkrais devised a series of easy, fluid movements that mimic everyday actions which do just this and reprogram the brain. They are taught in group lessons in a system called Awareness Through Movement. The other part of the Feldenkrais Method, called Functional Integration, is undertaken on a one-to-one basis.

Awareness Through Movement

A Feldenkrais teacher takes a group of students through small, simple sequences of movements that gradually evolve into more complex and larger ones as the class

progresses. They may be performed as floor work, or while sitting or standing. Many of the movements are based on everyday activities like opening a door or ironing, while others are designed to increase the range of movement at a joint or to increase postural awareness. Throughout, students are told to think about the movement that is being performed: to feel and sense precisely what the muscles and joints are doing, to note how they interact with the rest of the body, and to be fully aware of each separate component of the action. Every movement should feel natural and unforced, so that the student progresses at his or her own speed without pushing, straining, or causing any pain. As Feldenkrais students become aware of how they move, and experience how easy movements are when they follow the correct pattern, their old, habitual patterns will be forgotten and correct movement becomes instinctive.

Functional Integration

This one-to-one form of the Feldenkrais Method is usually conducted with the student lying, fully clothed, on a massage table. The student is asked to relax fully and become completely passive, and to let the practitioner guide his or her movements. The teacher moves the student's body and limbs through various movements, tailored to the individual, that stimulate the sensory nerve endings in the skin and muscles. Throughout, the student is encouraged to focus on exactly how each movement feels and to appreciate how easy it is – every movement should feel pleasurable and pain-free. The sensory nerves then transmit this message to the brain; this "learns" the movement, with the result that it can reproduce it by transmitting the appropriate messages to the muscles through the motor nerves. And since the movement is so easy, relaxed, and fluid, with the student exerting no unnecessary physical effort, the muscles relax and tension is gradually reduced.

In both the group and one-to-one forms of the Feldenkrais Method, the resulting increase in co-ordination and flexibility and a decrease in muscular tension makes students feel more relaxed. They have increased energy, too, and can breathe more deeply and easily because everyday movements take less effort and cause less strain. This can have psychological and emotional benefits, such as increased self-awareness and clarity of thought and improved self-esteem.

ORTHODOX VIEW

There has been little clinical research on the long-term efficacy of the Feldenkrais Method when it comes to helping those with neuromuscular disorders. However, the Method has been shown to improve posture and flexibility and to aid relaxation.

Some orthodox doctors are happy to use the Method as a form of rehabilitation, alongside conventional physical therapy, and would not deter a patient from taking a course of lessons, since the Method is considered sound in neurological terms and its exercises safe.

the muscles are fully extended without being taut

ABOVE *Because the Feldenkrais Method also brings greater flexibility and extends the range of movement in the joints, it can be of great benefit to athletes.*

CONSULTING A THERAPIST

There are several thousand qualified Feldenkrais practitioners around the world – look in Useful Addresses (*see pages 368–73*) – each of whom has completed 1,000 hours of study to achieve certification. This training includes gaining an understanding of kinesthetic movement and its form and function, as well as courses in neurophysiology, child development, and physics.

There are various levels of Awareness Through Movement classes, ranging from ones for beginners with little flexibility to classes designed for advanced students, so make sure that you are honest with the practitioner and realistic about yourself, in order that you start at a level that is right for you; throughout, however, students are encouraged to work at their own pace. The aim of the class, which lasts about 45 minutes, is for you to concentrate on what the teacher says, noting how each individual movement feels and interacts with the rest of your body and how that particular movement makes you feel. Your aim is to discover which movements feel freer and easier and take the least

effort to perform, so it is sensible to wear loose, comfortable clothes. Feldenkrais teachers have a huge number of different series of movements in their repertoire, but each sequence starts with a basic, small movement, which may be as simple as lifting one foot an inch off the floor, and that works towards a more complex sequence once its component parts have been mastered. Generally, it is a good idea to take a course of classes, although how many you will need will depend on your individual requirements.

Feldenkrais teachers do not massage or stretch stiff muscles or joints, since they believe that the cause of any structural imbalance or damage is not rooted in the muscle or joint itself but in ingrained, inefficient patterns of movement. The practitioner will teach you how to recognize these and show you how to inhibit them and replace them with movements that cause neither tension in the muscles nor strain in the joints.

WATCHPOINT

Make sure that the Feldenkrais practitioner whom you choose is properly trained and certified. The Method is safe when taught by registered practitioners, since it is non-invasive, gentle, and works within each individual's limitations. In untrained hands, however, there are potential risks.

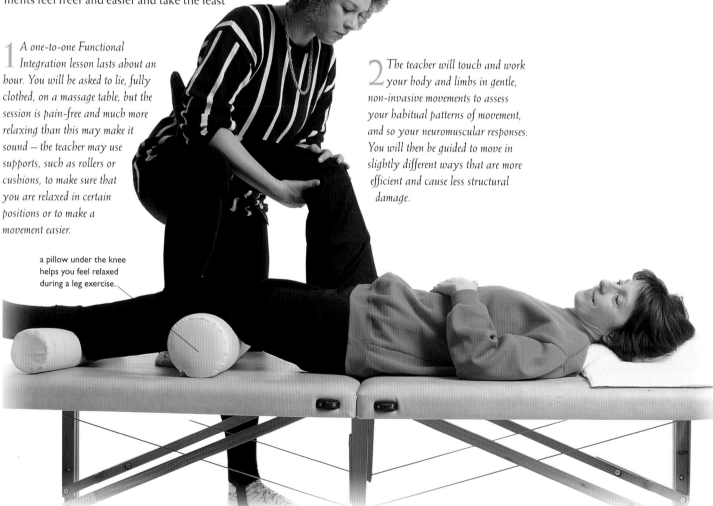

1 *A one-to-one Functional Integration lesson lasts about an hour. You will be asked to lie, fully clothed, on a massage table, but the session is pain-free and much more relaxing than this may make it sound – the teacher may use supports, such as rollers or cushions, to make sure that you are relaxed in certain positions or to make a movement easier.*

2 *The teacher will touch and work your body and limbs in gentle, non-invasive movements to assess your habitual patterns of movement, and so your neuromuscular responses. You will then be guided to move in slightly different ways that are more efficient and cause less structural damage.*

a pillow under the knee helps you feel relaxed during a leg exercise.

SELF-HELP

Feldenkrais teachers recommend that you attend a few lessons, at least, to learn the theory and practice of the Method before you use it at home. However, there are a number of books and videos available that take you through various movement sequences. You will also find details of a number of self-help exercises on the Internet; these have been written for general use by Feldenkrais practitioners to show how effective small adjustments in the way you move can be. And since the Feldenkrais Method does not involve the use of any force, it is safe as a self-help technique and is suitable for people of any age or level of fitness or flexibility.

The first step is to be aware of how you move and hold your body. Take a simple movement that you use many times a day, such as walking upstairs. Do you always lead with the same foot? Do you haul yourself up, using the hand rails? After assessing how you perform a particular action, you can try to alter it in small ways to ensure that you are always balanced – that you do not favor one leg, for example, or that you do not always carry the shopping in the same hand. If you try to keep the movements of your body symmetrical, your body will work more efficiently with less effort.

As a general rule, try to keep any sequence of movements free-flowing and effortless. If you find any movement a strain, you have probably been using an incorrect, inefficient pattern of movement that has become a habit. To effect a change, you must become aware of how you perform the movement, analyzing all of its components. Once you have come to this awareness, you can attempt to replace the incorrect sequence with one that feels balanced, free, and easy.

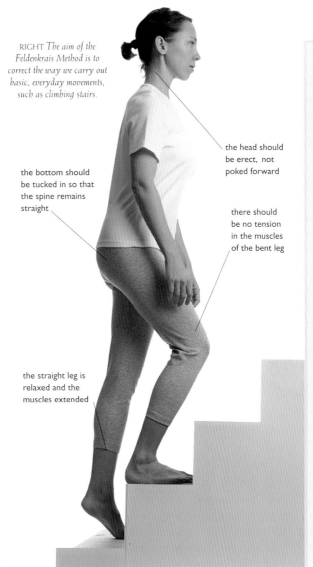

RIGHT *The aim of the Feldenkrais Method is to correct the way we carry out basic, everyday movements, such as climbing stairs.*

the bottom should be tucked in so that the spine remains straight

the head should be erect, not poked forward

there should be no tension in the muscles of the bent leg

the straight leg is relaxed and the muscles extended

PATHFINDER

The Feldenkrais Method is a form of somatic education that uses specific movements and exercises to inhibit incorrect movement sequences that have become a habit and to replace them with more-balanced and effortless ones, developing new neuromuscular pathways. It is not so much a form of treatment as a preventive therapy. It can help those suffering from neuromuscular disorders such as strokes, over-contracted muscles, and cerebral palsy. It can also alleviate stress and stress-related disorders, and improve posture, coordination, and balance, with the knock-on effect that it improves self-awareness and self-esteem and so mental outlook. It can also be used to treat:

ARTHRITIS *SEE PP.* 346–7

BACK PROBLEMS *SEE PP.* 344–5

DEPRESSION *SEE P.* 261

HEADACHE *SEE PP.* 268–9

MIGRAINE *SEE P.* 269

REPETITIVE STRAIN INJURY (RSI) *SEE PP.* 342–3

STRESS *SEE PP.* 262–3

STROKE *SEE P.* 359

poor posture can lead to rounded shoulders and neck pain

the head is carried too far forward, contributing to strain on the neck

if you sit upright, your neck is straight …

… and aligned with the rest of the spine

THE ALEXANDER TECHNIQUE

ABOVE *F. M. Alexander developed his Technique in response to problems that he was experiencing as an actor.*

Alexander found that it was "impossible to separate 'mental' and 'physical' processes in any form of human activity." Consequently, Alexander teachers instruct their students how to mentally "inhibit" bad patterns learned by the body over many years, by retargeting the messages the brain sends to the nervous system. Practicing the Alexander Technique can also provide emotional benefits:

❧ Calmness and fewer mood swings.

❧ The ability to cope better with difficult situations.

❧ A more open attitude to others.

LEFT *In the course of their lives most adults have acquired bad postural habits, which may mean that the chin or pelvis is carried too far forward. Alexander focused on lengthening neck muscles and straightening the spinal column.*

*S*ince F. M. Alexander first developed his Technique in the late 19th century, in an attempt to regain the vocal powers that were vital to his success as an actor, his methods have gained a worldwide following and reputation. The Alexander Technique is now firmly established as a beneficial and safe adjunct to treatment of a range of musculoskeletal problems, as well as an effective reducer of stress. As Alexander himself said, "Every man, woman, and child holds the possibility of physical perfection; it rests with each of us to attain it by personal understanding and effort."

The Alexander Technique is named after its founder, Frederick Matthias Alexander (1869–1955), an Australian actor. Alexander was born on a farm in Tasmania, and suffered from various respiratory disorders, including asthma, to such an extent that he was kept away from school. During the evenings he was tutored, but during the day he worked with his father's horses on the farm – later he was to say that this work had given him his sensitivity of touch.

As a young man, however, Alexander traveled to Melbourne, on the Australian mainland, to train as a reciter and actor. He became so successful, especially at reciting Shakespeare's plays, that within a short time he had set up his own theater company. Unfortunately, the nightly recitals began to take their toll and Alexander's voice became hoarse and croaky. And, to his horror, he found that he sometimes lost his voice in the middle of a show. His doctor prescribed remedy after remedy, but none of them seemed to help, and after a while Alexander realized that he would have to find a way of curing himself.

Observation and Cure

First, Alexander had to establish the source of the problem. He spent several months watching himself talk and perform by means of a series of strategically placed mirrors, and realized that when he recited he pulled his head back and down – which squashed his larynx (the area of the neck containing the vocal cords). He also realized that this action had become an ingrained habit, and that he had to do two things to rectify the problem: first, to stop holding his head back and down; second, to pull the crown of the head up and slightly forward, and so lengthen his spine.

It took some considerable persistence, but eventually Alexander managed to cure himself and his hoarseness did not recur. This success led him to realize that many common musculoskeletal and other problems could well be caused by what he called our "poor use" of the body.

Poor Use to Good Use

On hearing of Alexander's cure, other actors and reciters started to ask him for advice. Experimenting on colleagues, Alexander found that with the gentle guidance of his hands he could alter habitual poor patterns of movement that were causing the problem, to those of what he called "good use." Alexander continued his career in the theater, but his skill at resolving a variety of problems became more widely known and he was increasingly in demand. As a result, he set up a practice and, joined by his younger brother, Albert Redden Alexander, started to study sequences of movement and work out ways to combat poor use and re-educate clients into the proper use of their bodies.

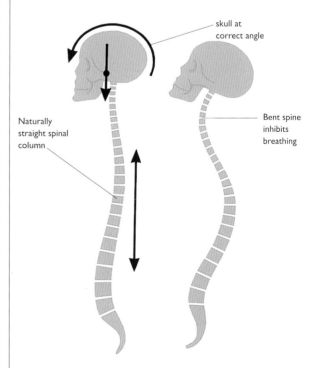

skull at correct angle

Naturally straight spinal column

Bent spine inhibits breathing

ABOVE *Alexander found that his habit of pulling his head back and down compressed his spine, chest, and ribs. This is turn put pressure on the lungs and made breathing more difficult.*

Alexander practiced in Melbourne and Sydney, before sailing to London, England, to set up a practice in 1904. He soon became very popular in London and treated many of the rich and famous. At the outbreak of the First World War, Alexander went to America and established his technique there. After the war, he spent time in both America and England before returning full time to London in 1925.

Into Orthodoxy

As Alexander's reputation grew, his methods began to win the respect of the medical profession. In fact, a group of British doctors wrote to the prestigious *British Medical Journal* in 1939, requesting that the Technique should be incorporated into medical students' training. Their plea was unsuccessful, but since then numerous doctors and educationalists have endorsed the Technique – one of the most newsworthy being Professor Nikolaas Tinbergen, who won the Nobel Prize for Medicine in 1973 and praised the Alexander Technique during his acceptance oration. One reason why the Technique enjoys such respect is that it makes no excessive claims: it does not claim to treat or diagnose specific problems, but aims to teach students of the Technique to be aware of how their body moves and how to relearn the posture and freedom that they experienced in childhood.

Alexander died in 1955, but by then he had set up a training course to teach others how to use his Technique. And since his death, the Alexander Technique has flourished, with training courses being available in most countries and the technique enjoying widespread popularity. The Technique is taught in many schools of music and acting, including the Royal School of Music and the Royal Academy of Performing Arts, London; the Sydney Symphony Orchestra, Australia; and the Juillard School and the American Conservatory in America. Studies in these institutions have shown that, as a result of learning the Technique, pupils' posture improved, they suffered less from repetitive strain injuries, and they were more relaxed during performances.

THE KEY TO GOOD BREATHING

Many of us do not breathe as efficiently as we might, and the Alexander Technique works to promote good breathing practice.

✳ Breathing is an involuntary action, and it should not be forced.

✳ Breathing through the nose ensures that air taken in is moistened and warmed before reaching the lungs.

✳ Deep breathing is linked with a toning of the muscles.

✳ Our breathing is affected by the relationship between the head, neck, and back.

✳ Freedom and space in the body means less restriction in the ribcage and lungs.

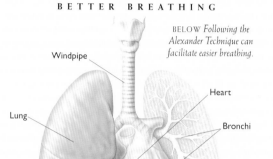

BETTER BREATHING

BELOW *Following the Alexander Technique can facilitate easier breathing.*

Windpipe

Heart

Lung

Bronchi

Bronchioles

the neck and shoulders are relaxed, so that strain is minimal

even the fingers can be "reconditioned" so that they move correctly

RIGHT *Repetitive strain injury is a frequent problem with musicians. By teaching a student to make every movement as correctly as possible, the Alexander Technique can help reduce the incidence of this.*

THE THEORY

The Alexander Technique aims to undo bad, ingrained habits and replace them with the correct, natural movement of early childhood. Young children stand and move with ease and poise, but adults often lose the ability to do this as a result of prolonged sitting, bad lifting techniques, poor posture, and the muscular tension that comes with stress, anxiety, and self-consciousness. These bad habits – known to Alexander teachers as "patterns of misuse" – become normal with time, so that the incorrect posture or movement feels "right" and the loss of flexibility and odd aches and pains are accepted as part of the aging process.

The Primary Control

Alexander believed that the relationship of the head to the neck and back governs the way the rest of the body

The reason why the head and neck are so easily moved out of the correct position is anatomical. The head rests on a simple, small pivot joint at the top of the spine, but its center of gravity is not in line with the spine. It is much farther forward: approximately in the middle of a line drawn between the top of your ear and your cheekbone. The head – and it weighs about 15lb (7kg) – is kept upright on the neck by muscles that run from the skull down the back of the neck to the shoulders. Apart from when we are lying down – or when we fall asleep sitting up – the neck muscles are always slightly contracted to pull against the weight of the head and maintain the sensitive balance that keeps it in its correct position. When the body moves, all that the neck muscles need to do is to relax, at which point the head tilts forward slightly and the

LEFT *Small children instinctively hold themselves erect and move in a free and natural way.*

CORRECTING THE ALIGNMENT OF THE SPINE

RIGHT *The alignment of the spinal column is the single most important feature of correct posture.*

RIGHT *Many adults hold their heads too low, contracting the neck, rounding the shoulders, and leading to constant strain.*

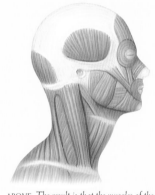

ABOVE *The result is that the muscles of the neck become too tense. The Alexander Technique aims to make students aware of these faults so that they can learn to correct them.*

functions – he called this relationship the "primary control." If the relationship between the head and neck is balanced and free, the postural muscles (those muscles that hold us upright against gravity) work without effort and tension, allowing the phasic muscles (the muscles that are activated to make a specific movement) to move the joints of the body freely. However, if the relationship is faulty, the postural muscles become tense and the phasic muscles have to work harder to achieve a movement. The result is that, over time, the body loses its grace and suppleness. Teachers of the Alexander Technique aim to restore the length, coordination, and flexibility of the spine and head – "the primary control" – and to re-establish the correct relative position of the two, whether at rest or in motion.

rest of the body follows. (If you try to stand up from a sitting position and tilt your head back at the same time, you will see how awkward and difficult it feels.)

Mood and stress

Our mental attitude affects the way we stand and move and, in turn, our posture affects our mental attitude. If someone is feeling depressed, stressed, anxious, or self-conscious, the shoulders slump, the head tilts back and sinks into the neck, and there is a tendency to shuffle. Many people hold themselves in a state of semitension all the time. Over long periods, the result is damage to the musculoskeletal system. The respiratory system, heartrate, and the smooth functioning of the digestive system are also affected, increasing stress.

PRECAUTIONS

■ The Alexander Technique is completely safe for those of any age when it is taught by a qualified practitioner.

■ If you have any doubts about your overall health you should consult your medical practitioner before a course of treatment to rule out any underlying problems.

Making and Breaking Bad Habits

Stress does affect posture, as illustrated on the left. To take an extreme example, think of someone who is startled by a car backfiring: the head moves back and down, the shoulders hunch, and the whole body tenses up in reaction to the noise. These wrong postures can become normal over time, and the Alexander Technique aims to help people to "unlearn" these bad habits. The key to the way in which bad posture (whatever its cause) becomes a habit is the system known as "proprioception". This is best summed up as the awareness of where the parts of your body are, without the need to look at them. Proprioceptors themselves are sensory nerve endings in muscles and joints that send information to the brain on the degree of contraction of muscles and the position of the joints. In response, the brain sends messages to the muscles, instructing them to either relax or contract depending on what movement is required. This loop – muscles to brain to muscles – is what maintains

ABOVE Holding the head correctly is a matter of delicate balance. The neck muscles need to work against the head's center of gravity.

our balance and poise, both when stationary and moving. When we are young, the loop works correctly and a young child performs all activities in the most efficient way. Later on in life, however, the original loop can get overridden by a new loop, which the brain has learned in response to a new pattern of messages that have been received from the proprioceptors. For example, if your head is continually held back and down, the muscles at the back of the neck will always be shortened and tense, so the receptors will not be activated. The brain will conclude that the position is the correct one – it will seem natural – and no messages will be sent to the muscles to correct it. In order to break this secondary loop, the neck muscles must be relaxed and lengthened so that the head rests in its correct position. It takes time and constant repetition, but eventually the lengthened muscles and the upright head will again feel natural, and the original loop from childhood will come back into play.

ORTHODOX VIEW

The Alexander Technique is well respected by the majority of doctors, many of whom recommend that their patients take a course of lessons.

The Alexander Technique's aims are attainable and well-documented, and there is an extensive body of research that shows that it is effective at relieving the pain and stress caused by habitual poor posture and movement. For example, an ongoing study started in 1994 at Kingston Hospital, London, England, shows that it helps to relieve chronic back pain. Research in 1992 at Columbia University, in America, showed that a group of healthy adults who attended Alexander Technique classes improved their respiratory function significantly, while a group that did not showed no change. And at Tufts University, America, a team carried out several studies between 1960 and 1980 using X-rays which showed that after learning the Technique patients' neck muscles had lengthened and showed less muscular tension.

More recently, a preliminary study took place at the University of Hertfordshire, England, in 1997 on the effect of the Technique to ease the disability and depression of patients with Parkinson's disease. The results showed a significant improvement, but further work is needed to confirm the findings.

BENEFITS OF THE ALEXANDER TECHNIQUE

The Alexander Technique is not a therapy as such, because it does not aim to treat problems. It teaches the student how to release tension held in the muscles that has been caused by habitual poor posture and unnecessary movements, and how to relearn correct use. This correction, however, can have an effect on many of the body systems, not just on the musculoskeletal system. It can give you:

✶ More freedom of movement without associated aches and pains.

✶ Improved co-ordination and balance.

✶ Increased energy levels, as less energy is required to perform everyday actions.

✶ Improved relaxation, as the muscles are not tense, but lengthened and relaxed.

✶ Improved ability to breathe correctly and deeply, thus helping with respiratory disorders.

✶ An improvement in certain gastro-intestinal problems, especially those affected by stress.

✶ Improved mental outlook, helping with depression, anxiety, and stress-related disorders.

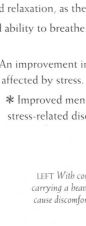

LEFT With correct posture, even carrying a heavy suitcase does not cause discomfort or misalignment.

RIGHT Dancers who have studied the Alexander Technique find they can move more gracefully.

CONSULTING A PRACTITIONER

It is fairly easy to find a certified Alexander teacher in any part of the world (see *Useful Addresses*, pages 368–73) Most of them have a private practice, though sometimes teachers are affiliated to hospitals or universities. (Certification involves teachers enrolling in a rigorous course, consisting of at least 1,600 hours' tuition over a period of around three years.)

Generally, lessons are conducted on a one-to-one basis, though some teachers offer group lessons. A typical lesson lasts about 45 minutes to an hour, and it is usually recommended that you have two lessons a week. The duration of your course of lessons depends partly on the nature of your problem, and partly on how quickly you learn the ability to inhibit existing bad habits and to relearn good ones, but a first course usually lasts for three months.

You should wear loose, comfortable clothes that do not obstruct the teacher's view of the curvatures of your spine – a T-shirt should be tucked in at the waist, for example. On your first visit, the teacher will ask you to stand, sit and move around naturally, so that your posture, balance and fluidity of movement can be assessed. The teacher will also be watching for any unnecessary tension in the muscles and any signs that pain is inhibiting movement. In short, the teacher will check for any ingrained bad habits, which you may well not be aware of.

After the assessment, you will be asked to lie, sit or stand while the teacher moves you gently into the correct position. You will be asked whether this new position feels strange and told what you need to stop doing (inhibit) and what you need to do to maintain the correct position. You will also be asked to

THREE INSTRUCTIONS

Alexander Technique teachers work according to three main principles, or "instructions," as they call them.

1 *The first instruction is to relax the muscles of the neck. Rub the muscle running down from your neck and across to your shoulder. If it feels stiff or painful, your neck muscles are over-contracted. Tense neck muscles pull the head back and down onto the spine. This compresses the spine, causing problems such as trapped nerves, low back pain, and neck pain. This position of the head also inhibits its "primary control" function, which is to initiate and lead any movement.*

2 *The second instruction, when mastered, works with the first one to maintain the head in its correct, free position. It is to lengthen your neck and "allow the head to go forward and upward" – think of the crown of your head rising up and forward, as if you were to nod your head slightly.*

3 *The third and last instruction is to broaden the back and elongate the whole spinal column. This decreases the tension in the muscles of the back and trunk, lengthens the torso, and facilitates abdominal breathing (see Breathing Techniques, pages 166–71).*

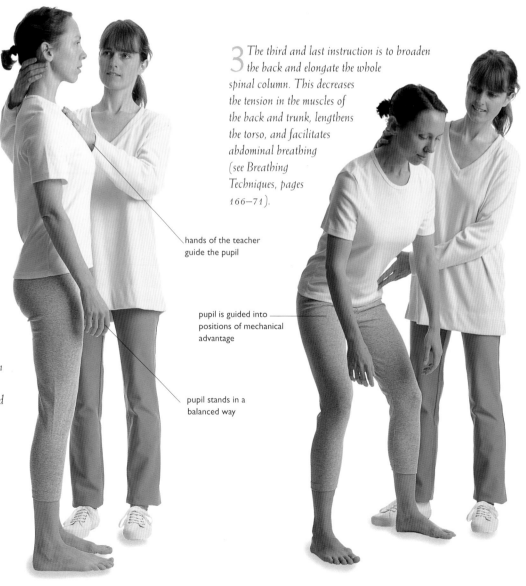

hands of the teacher guide the pupil

pupil is guided into positions of mechanical advantage

pupil stands in a balanced way

perform everyday movements, such as standing from a sitting position or walking from a standing start. The teacher will guide you into correct use of your body by means of light touch and simple verbal instructions. As you progress through the lessons, other activities that are particularly applicable to your lifestyle will be checked – be it singing, playing an instrument, swinging a golf club, ironing, or even doing such mundane things as turning a doorknob or shaking hands. The idea is that you are taught to be aware of the detail of the way in which you perform these actions, and learn how you can apply the Alexander Technique to almost any activity.

Thinking it Through

Alexander's instructions may seem relatively simple, but it can take considerable time and practice before they become second nature. To make things easier, Alexander teachers emphasize that you need to "think" any instruction. For example, instead of making a positive movement to take your head up and forward, picture the movement in your mind. This is because a positive

AIMS OF AN ALEXANDER TEACHER

❖ To make you aware of the position and relationship of your head, neck, and spine at all times.

❖ To make you aware of any undue tension in your muscles.

❖ To reveal your ingrained bad habits.

❖ To show you how to relearn and practice the correct movements until they become second nature.

❖ To give you the feeling of freedom of movement that comes with correct use of the body.

movement is likely to increase the tension in your muscles, but if you visualize the movement your neck muscles are likely to lengthen and relax, and the force of gravity will make it occur without any direct command having been sent to the muscles. The other instructions given by your teacher, during different sequences of movement, will all emphasize this need to "think": to picture the relevant part of your body relaxing, lengthening, and moving freely.

BELOW *"Thinking" movements through can help you apply the Alexander Technique to everyday movements.*

HOW TO STAND UP FROM A SITTING POSITION
Practice everyday movements using the Alexander Technique.

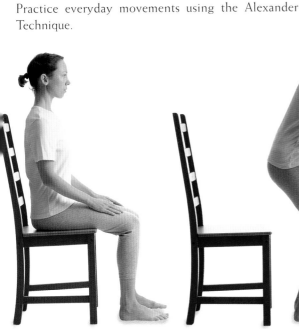

1 *Sit with your feet hip-width apart, the weight equally divided between the heel and the front of the foot. Your feet and calves should be vertical to your knees.*

2 *Without stiffening your knees and ankles, stand up. Do not arch the back or hold it rigid, concentrate on lengthening the spine: the weight is evenly distributed.*

3 *Do not lock or bend your knees. Think about your weight traveling through the center of the heel. Don't stiffen the body, or lean backward or forward from the hip joint.*

SELF-HELP

Most people find it difficult to be objective about themselves, so it is always best to learn the Alexander Technique from an accredited teacher. However, if it is not possible to take (or complete) a course of lessons, you can always learn something of the Technique, and benefit from it, with the help of the range of books, tapes and videos that are available (*see Useful Addresses, pages 368–73*). In particular, Alexander's third book, *Use of Self*, explains how the Technique evolved, and contains many useful pointers – though it is somewhat heavy going.

Meanwhile, here are some basic guidelines about how to assess your posture and start to relearn the way in which you perform your everyday activities. You will need at least one full-length mirror. Two mirrors, placed at an angle to each other – as in a shop's changing room – are ideal. Wear underclothes or a leotard, so that the outline of your body, and especially your spine, can be seen clearly.

Self-assessment

Stand naturally in front of the mirror and assess what you see. At the same time, try to sense which areas of your body feel tense or awkward. Try not to correct any problems that you think you might have by standing unnaturally straight, and attempt to be dispassionate when answering questions 1–8:

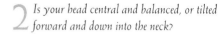

1 Are your shoulders relaxed and down, or tense, rounded, or hunched?

2 Is your head central and balanced, or tilted forward and down into the neck?

3 Is the crown of your head its highest point or is your chin jutting out or down on your chest?

4 Is your chest open and broad or curved in and collapsed?

5 Is your stomach flat or rounded?

6 Are your hips level and facing forward?

7 Are you balanced evenly on both feet with your weight distributed equally between them?

8 Is your weight distributed evenly over each foot or do you stand more on the outside or inside of each foot, or is the weight borne more over the toes or heel?

Now stand sideways to the mirror and ask yourself questions 9–10:

9 Is your body straight, or are you leaning backward or forward from the neck, hips or ankles?

10 Does your spine have a natural gentle "s" shape or is it over-arched, or looking flat?

The first part of each question gives the correct position; if you cannot answer "yes" to the questions you have a postural problem. The only way to cure faults is to keep the position of your whole body in mind throughout the day, and to make adjustments in your posture as often as necessary. (It may help you reveal the specifics of what you are doing wrong, and so work out how to correct the problem, if you exaggerate your bad stance, so that you can feel which muscles are tensing up and how it throws you off balance.)

This level of concentration is important: it is no good standing correctly in front of a mirror if you slump back into your habitual posture as soon as you walk away from

it. And correct posture must feel "right" if habits of poor use are not to recur – in other words, the nerves involved in maintaining your posture or making a movement must eventually send the correct signals out to the muscles automatically, without conscious thought. To achieve this, you must hold the correct posture – or stop holding an incorrect one – for the majority of the time, so that nerves can relearn the correct pathways and signals. Even so, a correct pose may well feel wrong for some time, and certain muscles may feel stretched or ache. This problem will pass with practice, as the muscles lengthen in time and relax to their proper position and tone.

EVALUATING MOVEMENT

Once you have evaluated your standing posture, try performing some simple actions in front of a mirror, such as standing from sitting, singing, or cleaning your teeth. As you move, watch the relationship between your head and neck in particular. Ask yourself whether what you feel you are doing corresponds to what you are actually doing. For example, when you sing does your head move down and back, so moving your chin out? Were you aware that this happens, and does it feel "right"? In fact, this movement squashes the vocal cords and inhibits breathing. The correct use is to lift the crown of your head as high as possible which elongates the neck, frees the vocal cords, and opens the chest.

If you feel and see that you move in an incorrect way every time you perform a specific activity, exaggerate the movement so that you can see and feel exactly what you are doing. Then perform the activity again, but this time do not make the movement. This takes time and effort. Constant reinforcement of the correct movement will be needed, because if you do not concentrate you will move in the old, habitual way.

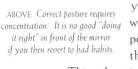

ABOVE *Correct posture requires concentration. It is no good "doing it right" in front of the mirror if you then revert to bad habits.*

As you start to learn how you use your body and how to re-educate yourself into good use, widen the scope of your study and try to assess how particular situations and emotions affect your posture. How much does your body mirror your feelings? An upright, free, and flexible body not only relieves tension in the body, but also stress in the mind (*see Relaxation Techniques, pages 158–65*).

FREEING YOUR HEAD AND NECK

Stand in front of a mirror and take a tuft of hair from the crown of your head. Pull it straight up toward the ceiling, then lift your head up as far away as possible from your neck. Try to elongate your body as well, but without going on tiptoe. Once you can feel exactly where your crown is, repeat the exercise without pulling your hair up. You will feel your neck lengthen, your shoulders relax down, your chest open, and your spine stretch.

PATHFINDER

The Alexander Technique, though not in itself a therapy, has proved to help not only problems caused by poor posture, but also other musculoskeletal problems and certain respiratory and digestive problems. It has the secondary effect of reducing both mental and physical stress, so it is recommended for stress-related disorders. Practitioners, however, stress that the Technique is not solely of benefit when there is a specific problem, it is also a preventive technique that can help everyone to move with less effort and strain, thereby increasing energy levels, reducing the chances of damage, and improving general well-being.

ADDICTIONS *SEE P.* 258
ANGINA *SEE P.* 304
ANXIETY *SEE PP.* 256–7
ASTHMA *SEE PP.* 294–5
BACK PROBLEMS *SEE PP.* 344–5
DEPRESSION *SEE P.* 261
EATING DISORDERS *SEE P.* 265
HEADACHE *SEE PP.* 268–9
MENSTRUAL PROBLEMS *SEE PP.* 322–3
MIGRAINE *SEE P.* 269
PREGNANCY PROBLEMS *SEE PP.* 326–7
PEPTIC ULCER *SEE P.* 311
REPETITIVE STRAIN INJURY (RSI) *SEE PP.* 342–3
SCIATICA *SEE P.* 348
STRESS *SEE PP.* 262–3

TRAGER WORK

O*ne of the "somatic education" systems (concerned with the structure and function of the body), Trager Work was devised by Milton Trager, a one-time acrobat and boxer with chronic back problems who became first a physical therapist and then a medical doctor. Trager Workers believe that they can link up to the energy force that surrounds us all and reprogram the subconscious in order to dissipate unnecessary muscular tension, and that small, slight movements can be taught and practiced to replace harmful learned responses with beneficial ones.*

Milton Trager, born in Chicago, USA, in 1908, suffered from chronic back problems throughout his childhood. Despite this, however, he became an acrobat and a boxer when he grew up. One day Trager gave his trainer a massage, and the trainer was so impressed with the results that he suggested that Trager used what appeared to be a special gift to help others. Trager went on to cure his own back problem, as well as his father's sciatica, and then started to use massage to treat other people, addressing problems ranging from chronic pain and muscular tension to the effects of polio and other neuro-muscular disorders.

ABOVE *Milton Trager added the concept of meditation to his method of re-educating the body.*

Trager qualified as a physical therapist (physiotherapist) before the Second World War and then studied to become a doctor of medicine after leaving the armed forces. Moving to Hawaii, he then ran an orthodox medical practice, but continued to use a hands-on approach with many of his patients, as he slowly developed his own techniques and approach to bodywork – in essence, Trager was a somatic educator, in the manner of F.M. Alexander (*see pages 146–53*), rather than a therapist. In 1958, Trager became one of the first initiates of Maharishi Mahesh Yogi, who was later to promote transcendental meditation to, among others, the Beatles. As a result of this, Trager incorporated a type of meditative state that he called a "hook-up" into his method.

In 1975, Trager set up practice in California and founded the Trager Institute in 1980 to train others in his technique. Trager died in 1997, but more than 1,000 qualified Trager Work therapists stand as his legacy. They are to be found throughout the world, though the majority of them practice in America.

THE THEORY

Trager believed that when one is in a deep state of meditation it is possible to "plug in" to the energy force that surrounds everything. This energy can then be "caught" by the "client" (as someone who is the recipient of Trager Work is called), both by means of the practitioner's hands and by the very fact of his or her presence; the energy bypasses the client's conscious mind to affect the subconscious. Trager believed that many chronic physical problems and chronic pain persist because the subconscious mind is sending false messages to the muscles and tissues, keeping them in a state of unnecessary tension. In order to effect a permanent change and break the vicious cycle, he believed that the subconscious must be repeatedly bombarded with new messages conveying a pain-free sense of relaxation, forging new links between the body and mind.

Learned responses

Over time, any action or sequence of actions that is repeated sufficiently often becomes a pattern of "learned responses." For example, when you are learning to drive a car, each step and action has to be consciously thought through before the correct action is taken, but with time and practice driving becomes automatic. Unfortunately, however, not all learned responses are either useful or healthy. Trager Work aims to replace old, harmful patterns with new patterns that are relaxed and free. Trager Work achieves its effect by the use of small, slight movements that are free and pleasurable – for this reason the Trager Institute's logo bears the Chinese characters that mean "a dancing cloud." The result is that good patterns are reinforced and the body is allowed to free itself from learned responses.

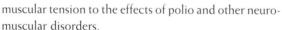

ABOVE *Maharishi Mahesh Yogi, the celebrated exponent of Transcendental Meditation, was the inspiration behind Trager's "hook-up" concept.*

PRECAUTIONS

■ Trager Work is a system of somatic education not a treatment method, so it does not diagnose or treat specific diseases and is not a substitute for medical attention. If you have any medical problem or suspect that you might have one, check with your family doctor before embarking on Trager Work sessions.

■ Trager Work may not be suitable for some cancer patients or those with a history of thrombosis. If in doubt, consult your doctor.

BELOW *The Trager Work practitioner moves your limbs gently and rhythmically, so that you experience greater freedom of movement and a feeling of lightness.*

PATHFINDER

Trager Work is a form of somatic education that aims to relieve the body and mind of unwanted stress and tension and allow them to work harmoniously with each other and the outside world. While it does not claim to cure or treat specific disorders, Trager Work is a preventive therapy and can be therapeutic, especially in the case of stress-related problems and musculoskeletal and neuromuscular disorders.

ANXIETY *SEE PP.* **256–7**

BACK PROBLEMS *SEE PP.* **344–5**

HEADACHE *SEE PP.* **268–9**

MIGRAINE *SEE P.* **269**

FIBROSITIS *SEE P.* **348**

SCIATICA *SEE P.* **348**

STRESS *SEE PP.* **262–3**

STROKE *SEE P.* **359**

CONSULTING A PRACTITIONER

Make sure that you choose a certified Trager Work practitioner (*see Useful Addresses, pages 368–73*), who will have studied the theory and practice of the therapy in detail, as well as undertaken courses in anatomy and physiology.

A session lasts from 60 to 90 minutes, and the first one starts with an assessment. This is not an orthodox medical assessment, but an attempt to learn about your lifestyle, why you are there, whether you are in any pain, and whether any of your movements are restricted or your muscles are tense. Practitioners recommend a series of at least six sessions to start with for maximum benefit, followed by less frequent sessions to maintain the results.

There are two parts to Trager Work, the first one being table-work, and the second Mentastics. You will be asked to lie down in a warm room on a firm, padded table. Wear loose, comfortable clothes such as underwear or a leotard. The practitioner starts by relaxing him or herself and going into the active, meditative state that Trager called "hook up" (Trager believed that in this state, the practitioner could sense with greater accuracy the tone, tension, and resistance of the body's tissues to movement). The practitioner will then use rhythmical rocking, vibrating, kneading, and stretching movements to discover areas of resistance or tension; no oils, lotions, or talcum powder are used. When an area of resistance or tension is found, a Trager Work practitioner will lessen any pressure on that area – as opposed to the procedure in Hellerwork (*see pages 138–41*) or Rolfing (*see pages 134–7*) in which the pressure would be increased. Your body will be moved in many small different ways, but as undue pressure is never used, the treatment will be pain-free. And as your body is moved, you will be encouraged to relax and start to let go physically and emotionally.

After the table-work has been done, your practitioner will move on to teach you Mentastics. These are simple exercises, which you can practice during the session and also use at home, that reinforce the subconscious messages relayed to your mind and body during table-work. The movements are similar to those performed on you during table-work, in as much as they are rhythmical stretching and rocking exercises.

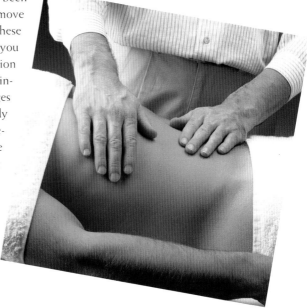

RIGHT *Once the therapist has identified any areas of tension or weakness, he will work on them even more gently.*

ZERO BALANCING

A relatively modern technique, this was developed by "Fritz" Frederick Smith, a medical doctor who is also an osteopath, acupuncturist, and Rolfer, and a student of Eastern philosophies and Western bodywork. Zero Balancing describes a series of energy fields and pathways in the human body. It uses specialized bodywork techniques and the energetic interface between practitioner and client to reorganize these energy fields, at the same time as correcting any misalignment of the musculoskeletal system.

"Fritz" Frederick Smith qualified as an osteopath in America in 1955 and became a doctor of medicine in 1961. But he was not convinced that either orthodox medicine or osteopathy contained the whole truth about how illness develops and health can be maintained, so he went on to study Eastern medical philosophies and other Western therapeutic techniques, becoming a licensed acupuncturist (*see pages 20–31*) and a certified Rolfer (*see pages 134–7*). Dr. Smith's studies gave him a new view of how the body works, based on energy fields, and in the early 1970s, he devised a therapy that combines Western bodywork techniques and Eastern ideas of energy and healing, and called it Zero Balancing. Since retiring from medical practice in 1991, Smith has concentrated on developing and teaching Zero Balancing.

THE THEORY

Zero Balancing has been described as a form of structural acupressure (*see Acupuncture, pages 20–31*) and its application to the physical structure of the body, mainly the skeleton. Zero Balancers believe that energy can be tapped, strengthened, or freed by integrating and balancing the body's innate energy with its physical structure.

Energy fields

Practitioners maintain that there are three main energy fields in the human body. The first, and most important, is the energy that is held within the skeleton. This energy is outside our voluntary control,

but is essential for health and our ability to adapt to the changing circumstances of the outside environment. There are three pathways within the skeleton: the first, and main, pathway flows from the skull, down the spine, through the pelvis and hips to the feet; the second begins at the shoulders and passes down the transverse processes of the vertebrae to the pelvis, where it joins the main pathway; the third path goes from the shoulder girdle through the arms to the hands.

The second energy field also has three pathways, but instead of affecting our interactions with the outside world, it defines us as individuals. The inner energy pathway lies in the muscles, which produce a flow of energy when they contract. Some goes to increase the levels of skeletal energy, but it also helps to integrate the left and right sides of the brain, assisting them to work in harmony. The flow of energy in the middle pathway corresponds most nearly to the Chinese meridians. One of its functions is to enable each individual to fulfil his or her emotional, mental, and spiritual needs. The outer pathway is found just under the skin. Called the "Wei Chi," it is the body's "energy boundary." This field can either absorb or repel external forces and tries to prevent the body from losing too much energy and so depleting overall energy levels.

The third and last energy field is all-encompassing and permeates the whole body and the space around it. Its function is to help the body to adapt physically and emotionally to different circumstances.

Foundation joints

Zero Balancers recognize that certain joints, known as the "foundation joints," can affect all the energy fields. These joints are the ones involved in maintaining balance and conducting gravitational force through the body. They comprise the intervertebral joints, the costovertebral joints (between the ribs and the vertebrae), the sacroiliac joint (between the sacrum at the base of the spine and the pelvis), and the intertarsal joints (between the bones of the foot). The joints also play an important part in the transmission of energy throughout the whole body.

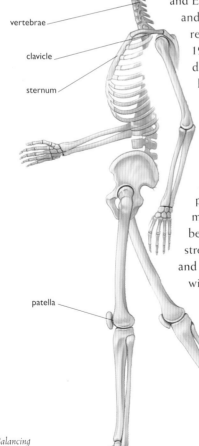

skull

vertebrae

clavicle

sternum

patella

RIGHT Zero Balancing techniques work mainly on the skeleton.

CONSULTING A PRACTITIONER

Zero Balance practitioners are usually qualified therapists in another field, such as massage, acupuncture, or one of the bodywork therapies, who have learnt Zero Balancing to enlarge their repertoire of treatments. At present, a few therapists practice Zero Balancing in the U.S., U.K., Switzerland, and Mexico.

You should wear loose comfortable clothes for a session, which generally lasts for about a half-hour; you are normally advised to have at least three sessions. The practitioner will take a short medical history and ask why you have come for treatment. Your shoulder girdle, upper back, and sacroiliac joint will then be examined while you are seated, and next you will be asked to lie down fully clothed, on the treatment couch.

The practitioner will use specific "fulcrum" techniques. Your lower back, hips, and feet will be worked on first, then your ribs, neck, and shoulders; finally, the practitioner will return to the lower body in order to balance and align joints and soft tissues – the last movement, or fulcrum, is designed to reintegrate the whole of the body.

The practitioner is not aiming for a specific outcome during treatment, but rather to release the energy flow, and correct structural misalignment. Many people report feeling taller, more relaxed, and less anxious following treatment, and musculoskeletal aches and pains are often eased.

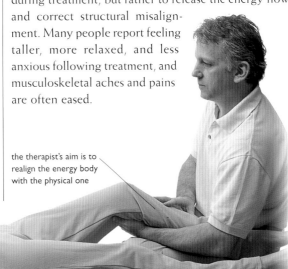

the therapist's aim is to realign the energy body with the physical one

PATHFINDER

Zero Balancing aims to balance the skeletal system and to encourage the free flow of energy throughout the body. It may be of use for muscular or skeletal pain, as well as for reducing stress and increasing the ability to relax – and so may be helpful to those suffering from stress-related disorders.

ANXIETY SEE PP. 256–7
BACK PROBLEMS SEE PP. 344–5
FIBROSITIS SEE P. 348
HEADACHE SEE PP. 268–9
MIGRAINE SEE P. 269
STRESS SEE PP. 262–3

ABOVE AND RIGHT Zero Balancing theory maintains that an invisible energy body surrounds the physical body like a glove.

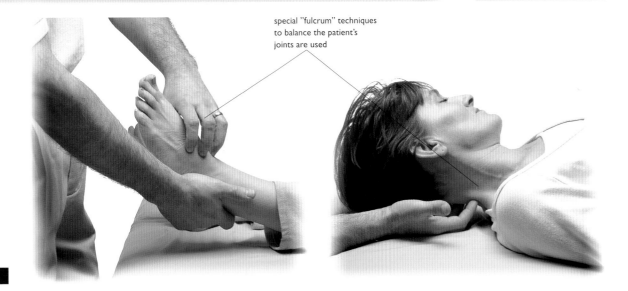

special "fulcrum" techniques to balance the patient's joints are used

PRECAUTIONS

■ Zero Balancing is not a substitute for orthodox medical treatment of any condition. Consult your doctor if you are in any doubt about your health.

■ The therapy is not recommended for anyone who has severe emotional, psychological, or physical illness.

Zero Balancers use a bodywork method known as the "fulcrum" to connect – or "interface" – the practitioner's energy fields and physical structure with that of the client's energy and structure. (A fulcrum is a means by which influence is brought to bear.) The aim of the bodywork fulcrum is to release retained energy, increase the body's energy fields, and to balance any misalignment of the musculoskeletal system and maintain it in its proper position.

During a session, the practitioner will be watching carefully for "working signs." These show that the client's energy fields are being reorganized. Such signs may include, among many others, rapid eyelid movements, shallow breathing followed by a deep breath, twitches, bowel rumblings, and altered facial expressions. Treatment is not result-oriented. Rather, the practitioner aims to release the energy flow and correct structural misalignment, and then to see what response there is.

RELAXATION TECHNIQUES

Our perception of stress, and our response to it, was a vitally important survival tool when human beings first walked the Earth. And even today, a certain amount of stress is part and parcel of the human condition. But when stress cannot be released, it can have alarming consequences. It is now generally accepted that stress is a contributory factor in numerous disorders, and a direct cause of some medical problems. The answer, doctors and complementary therapists believe, is to avoid stress if possible – and if this is impossible, to dissipate it by means of relaxation techniques.

The term "holism" was coined in the 20th century, but the idea that the whole is more important than its parts has been understood since time immemorial. Perhaps it was because early healers did not know or understand the workings of the human body that they concentrated on the whole person – both in a physical and mental sense – rather than an isolated part of that person. This was holistic medicine. It was only as medical practitioners began to understand the intricate internal workings of the body, and develop the ability to conquer various specific problems and diseases, that orthodox medicine lost sight of the importance of treating the whole body, including the mind, as well as the part.

However, in the middle of the 20th century there was a resurgence of interest in "alternative" and "holistic" therapies. Many people had become disillusioned with conventional medicine, with its iatrogenic diseases (*iatros* is the Greek word for doctor, and the term literally means "caused by doctors"), technology, the side-effects of drugs, and an impersonal approach.

As a result of public pressure and the upsurge in "modern" diseases, such as heart problems and ulcers, some doctors started to look into the effect of lifestyle and mental outlook on common diseases. It was soon found that high stress levels contributed to or caused many physical diseases, such as cancers, degenerative heart conditions, digestive problems, and other chronic disorders. And in 1976, Professor Hans Seyle, of Montreal, Canada, wrote *The Stress of Life*, in which he put forward the view that psychological factors have

ABOVE *Cavemen had to respond to stressful situations whenever they went hunting.*

a considerable effect on physical disorders; that the mind affects the body, and vice versa. This concept has now become part of mainstream medical thinking: medicine has come full circle.

Recognition of the dangers of stress was one thing, but the question still remains: what can you do to reduce stress levels? The answer is to practice relaxation techniques, for relaxation and stress are the opposite sides of the same coin. The "progressive muscular relaxation" techniques described over the next few pages were devised by American physiologist Dr. Edmund Jacobson in the 1930s. Importantly, he made it clear that relaxation is not only a state of the body, but of the mind, too: when the mind is calm and at ease, the body is relaxed. However, in order to understand how relaxation techniques work, it is necessary to know what stress is and how it works.

THE MECHANISM OF STRESS

The term "stress" is taken from the vocabulary of engineering and describes the changes that occur in the body when the mind perceives a threat or challenge, whether it is real or imaginary. The changes are triggered by the release of chemical messengers, called catecholamines, into the bloodstream and by nerve impulses, and they prepare the body for quick, decisive action. What this action will be is not yet decided, which is why the response is known as "fight-or-flight" – it is a survival mechanism.

THREE STAGES

In physiological terms, the "fight-or-flight" response

BELOW *Having a baby may be considered a cause of "good stress," one that few parents would want to avoid.*

THE FIGHT-OR-FLIGHT RESPONSE

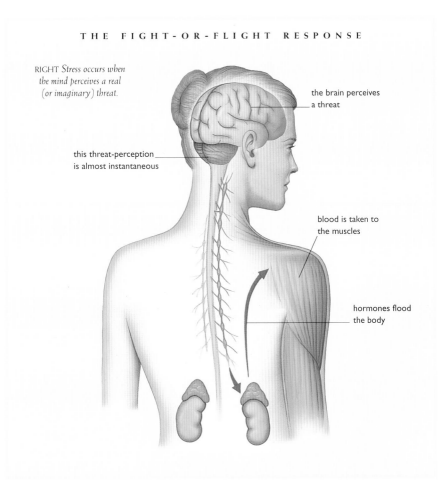

RIGHT *Stress occurs when the mind perceives a real (or imaginary) threat.*

the brain perceives a threat

this threat-perception is almost instantaneous

blood is taken to the muscles

hormones flood the body

WHAT IS RELAXATION?

In a relaxed state the heart and breathing rate is slow and steady, blood pressure is low, the muscles are relaxed, and the internal organs and intestines have adequate nutrients and a good supply of blood. And a special family of hormones – the endorphins – is released when we are relaxed. These hormones affect our mood and give us a sense of well-being as well as acting as the body's own painkillers. (Endorphins are also

ABOVE *Stress and relaxation – opposite sides of the coin.*

released during exercise.) Relaxation is not only a state of the body, but also of the mind. When the mind is calm, the body is relaxed. If the body is tense, the mind is alert; if the mind is troubled, the body becomes tense. But when both body and mind are relaxed, as when in a deep sleep, the body can maintain health by strengthening the immune system and repairing any tissue damage. Relaxation and stress are both necessary for a healthy and varied life, but if stress predominates for too long, physical and psychological problems can develop.

breaks down into three stages: "ready," "steady," and "go."

READY: A threat is sensed and evaluated by the brain; this process is nearly instantaneous and is involuntary: it does not require conscious control.

STEADY: The subconscious brain prepares the body for action by producing catecholamines that are carried in the bloodstream to receptors in various glands in the body. At the same time that this is happening, a specialized part of the nervous system called the "sympathetic system" floods the body with impulses.

GO: The brain is now fully alert, the muscles supercharged with energy, and the body is prepared to take decisive action.

A Matter of Degree

The fight-or-flight response has served humans very well for many thousands of years. If a hunter met a hyena, say, he or she would be ready in a flash to fight or run: the outcome would either be victory, wounds or death, or escape. Then the hunter's body would return to its normal state – a state of balance, known today as "homeostasis" – because the event had resulted in a definitive outcome.

In modern society, however, the type of threat that we face is rarely so direct and physical. The stress is usually caused by emotional or psychological factors, and the fight-or-flight stress response is inappropriate – you cannot hit your boss if you have to stay late at work. Nevertheless, it is a function of human physiology that we do use this response, to a degree. And as many such stresses are continual and cumulative rather than short-lived, many people stay in a perpetual state of readiness – neither fully relaxed nor sufficiently physically active to bring about its release. Over time, the result can be high blood pressure, heart and circulatory problems, an inhibited immune system, digestive problems, tense muscles, and psychological problems.

Learning to Relax

Relaxation is the other side of the coin. It is the normal state to which the primitive hunter's body returned after the encounter with the hyena. The hunter achieved relaxation because the stress of the encounter had been dissipated by physical action. Similarly, physical exercise, whether a run, a game of squash, or just a long walk, will dissipate your stress hormones and leave your body feeling relaxed and at ease – even if a bit stiff. But many people find it difficult to achieve an adequate amount of regular exercise. If you are one of them, it is important to learn how to use both physical and mental relaxation techniques to disperse your stress.

WHAT ARE YOUR STRESS LEVELS?

Individual responses to stress vary. Some people can cope with much greater levels of stress than others – in fact they thrive on it. Others are easily affected and take longer to recover. Each person has their own "elastic limit," which is the point at which the damage that stress does to the body becomes irreparable.

In the 1960s Thomas H. Holmes and Richard H. Rahe, working at the University of Washington School of Medicine, compiled a list of the most common events that produced major stress, calling them "life changes." Each event was scored according to its effect. They found that the majority of people who scored too many points in any one twelve-month period found it difficult to cope with the stress, their ability to relax was impaired, and the probability of illness was increased.

ABOVE *It is important for people of all ages to keep fit and active.*

YOUR RESULTS

Calculate your stress points, and then add on an appropriate number for any life event that puts you under stress but is not included in the index:

✳ 50 to 100 points – low stress levels; nearer 100 points there is a 10% increase in the risk that you will develop an illness over the next two years.

✳ 100 to 200 points – moderate levels of stress; there is a 10% to 35% increase in the risk that you will develop an illness over the next two years.

✳ 200 to 300 points – high stress levels; there is a 35% to 50% increase in the risk that you will develop an illness over the next two years.

✳ 300 plus points – extremely high stress levels; there is a dangerously high probability that you will develop an illness over the next two years.

HOLMES AND RAHE'S 'LIFE CHANGE INDEX'

Points	Rank	Event
100	1	Death of partner
73	2	Divorce
65	3	Marital separation
63	4	Jail term
63	5	Death of family member
53	6	Personal injury
50	7	Marriage
47	8	Fired from work
45	9	Marital reconciliation
45	10	Retirement
44	11	Change in health of family member
40	12	Pregnancy
39	13	Sex difficulties
39	14	Gain new family member
39	15	Business readjustment
39	16	Financial change
37	17	Death of close friend
36	18	Change to new line of work
35	19	Change in amount of arguments with partner
33	20	Large mortgage
29	21	Child leaves home
29	22	Trouble with in-laws
28	23	Personal achievement
26	24	Partner begins/ends work
26	25	Begin/end work
25	26	Change in living conditions
24	27	Change personal habits
23	28	Trouble with employer
20	29	Change in work hours or conditions
20	30	Change in residence
20	31	Change in school
19	32	Change in recreation
19	33	Change in church activity
18	34	Change in social activity
17	35	Small mortgage loan
16	36	Change in sleep habits
15	37	Change in number of family get-togethers
15	38	Change in eating habits
13	39	Vacation
12	40	Christmas
11	41	Minor law violation

Adapted from Holmes and Rahe's Life Change Index; *Journal of Psychosomatic Research,* 1967, Volume 11, pp. 213–18, © Pergamon Press.

SIGNS AND SYMPTOMS OF STRESS

While a large number of medical conditions are stress-related, the presence of various signs and symptoms can indicate that a person's stress levels are too high. Individuals vary in their reaction to stress, but if you frequently experience any four signs or symptoms in each of the three categories that follow, or any eight of them on occasions, it is likely that you need to work on relaxation techniques to reduce your stress levels.

Emotional signs

* Irritability and/or over-excitability
* Feeling depressed
* Intolerance of others and/or yourself
* Aggressiveness and/or anger
* Suspiciousness
* Fussing over small things
* Restlessness and/or impulsiveness
* Tension
* Anxiety about minor things
* Despondency
* Loss of concentration and/or memory
* Feelings of frustration
* Feelings of panic
* Nightmares or disturbed dreams
* A feeling of being apart
* Hesitating over decisions
* Frequent crying
* Loss of interest in sex
* Feeling of loss of control
* Illogical worries and/or fears

ABOVE *Impaired concentration is a sign of stress.*

Behavioral signs

* Increased smoking
* Increased alcohol consumption
* Increased use of medication
* Increased casual sex
* Overeating
* Obsessive dieting or taking of laxatives
* Gnashing or grinding of teeth
* An eye tic
* Finger or foot tapping
* Frowning
* Nail-biting
* Scratching the scalp or hair twiddling
* Pacing the floor
* Excessive concern about time
* Loss of interest in personal appearance
* Loss of sense of humor
* Increased lethargy
* Prone to accidents
* Difficulty in getting to sleep
* Difficulty in getting back to sleep
* Difficulty in waking

ABOVE *People smoke more when the pressure is on.*

Physical signs

* Headaches
* Dry mouth and/or throat
* Indigestion
* Nausea
* Butterflies in the stomach
* Constipation
* Diarrhea
* Unusual gain or loss in weight
* Unusual gain or loss of appetite
* Skin problems – eczema, hives, rashes
* Ulcers
* High blood pressure
* Palpitations
* Excessive sweating and/or cold sweats
* Rapid or irregular breathing
* Tightness in the chest
* Increased incidence of allergies
* Frequent colds or flu
* Premenstrual tension (PMT)
* Impotence or frigidity

ABOVE *Tension in the body creates headaches.*

LEFT *Compulsive clock-watching indicates a tense individual.*

A BASIC RELAXATION TECHNIQUE

This technique, generally called "progressive muscular relaxation," is used in slightly different forms by the majority of relaxation therapists – in fact, in many therapies, such as visualization (*see pages 206–7*) and meditation (*see pages 60–3*), a relaxation routine is an important preliminary. However, the technique is easy to learn and use at home.

This relaxation routine involves contracting and relaxing each of the large muscle groups of the body in turn, starting at your feet and ending with your face, until each is free of tension. Some people find it difficult to master the art of allowing the muscles to "let go" – but it can usually be done if you persevere.

Preliminaries

The technique demands that you focus inwardly on yourself, rather than on your surroundings, so find somewhere where you will not be disturbed by children, a telephone, or any other noise for at least an hour – background noise will ruin your carefully created atmosphere. Wear loose, comfortable clothes, but make sure that your feet are warm – wear a pair of socks if necessary. Make sure that the room is warm and softly lit, then lie down on your back on a firm bed or a comfortable mat. Put a small cushion under your head – some people find it more comfortable to place a cushion beneath their knees, too. You can either rest your arms by your side or across the stomach, whatever is more comfortable for you.

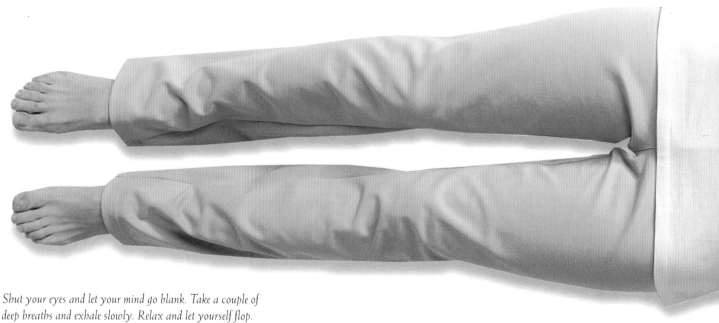

1 *Shut your eyes and let your mind go blank. Take a couple of deep breaths and exhale slowly. Relax and let yourself flop.*

2 *Starting with your right foot, curl your toes up tight and scrunch up your foot. Hold for a count of ten, then let go and relax your foot. Repeat until your foot feels warm and floppy.*

3 *Next, tense the calf muscles of your right leg; hold for a count of ten and then let go. Repeat until your lower leg feels heavy and relaxed.*

4 *Continue up your leg to your right thigh. The muscles here are large and sometimes tense, so it may take some time to relax your thigh completely.*

5 *Repeat steps two to four on your left leg. Are both legs now floppy and relaxed? If not, tense up both legs and hold the contraction for as long as you can before letting go. If necessary, repeat until you feel that both legs are immovable and heavy.*

6 *Clench your buttock muscles as tightly as you can; hold for a count of ten and let go. Repeat with your stomach muscles. You should feel as though you are sinking into the bed or mat.*

7 *Breathe in deeply and evenly three times, in order to work the muscles around your chest and to increase the level of oxygen in your blood, then breathe out slowly: sigh the air away and imagine any mental tension ebbing away with it.*

8 *Starting with your right arm, make a fist and grip tight; hold for a count of ten and let go. Repeat until your hand feels warm and floppy. Work up your arm (as you did with your leg) to the forearm and from there to the upper arm. Repeat with the left arm, then, if necessary, tense the whole of both arms as described for the legs in step five.*

PRECAUTION

■ Avoid lying flat on your back in the later stages of pregnancy, although this technique can be used if your body is slightly turned to one side.

This technique can take time to master – so be patient. But as you become more aware of how to relax and release tension, you will find that you have the ability to relax any muscle group at will. When you have reached this stage you may not need to contract the muscles first, but will be able to "let go" at will, anywhere, at any time. This will enable you to stay calm and relaxed even when you are in a stressful situation – but you must stay in tune with your body, so that you can pinpoint where you hold tension and when you start to tense up. If you find yourself tensing up while driving a car, for example, make a positive effort to "let go" and feel the tension drain away. Stop the car, relax your grip on the steering wheel, and rest back in your seat – doing so will clear your mind as well as release the tension in your arm and shoulder muscles.

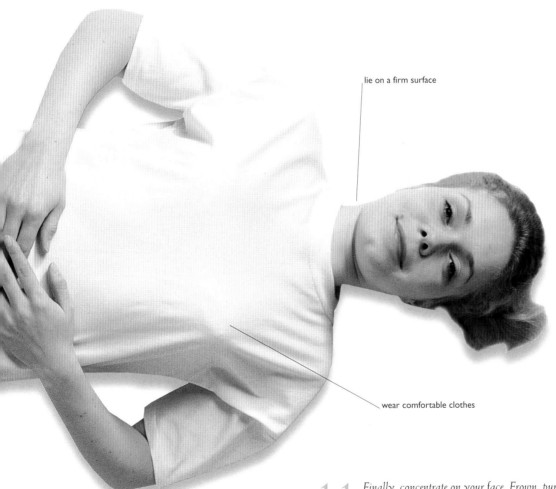

lie on a firm surface

wear comfortable clothes

9 *Much of the tension in the body is held in the shoulder and neck muscles, so it takes much time and attention to make them relax fully. Hunch both shoulders up as far as possible toward the ceiling; hold tight for as long as possible and then let them flop back on to the bed. Hunch your shoulders hard up toward your ears (you should still be lying down); hold and let go. Repeat the sequence as many times as is necessary to make your shoulders feel heavy and relaxed.*

10 *Rock your head from side to side to loosen your neck muscles – the weight of your head will do most of the work for you.*

11 *Finally, concentrate on your face. Frown, purse your lips, pout, grimace, bare your teeth, grin – in fact pull faces. Hold each "face" for a few seconds and then let go.*

12 *Take a few more deep, even breaths and imagine any residual tensions fading away with each exhalation. Repeat to yourself, "I feel more and more relaxed." Feel your body sink into the bed.*

13 *You will probably be feeling sleepy by now, so rest quietly for around 15 minutes. When this time is up, don't jump up and start racing around. Instead, come to slowly, making a catlike stretch, and shake before getting up to start doing anything else.*

OTHER WAYS TO COMBAT STRESS

There are many ways of relaxing and reducing stress, and different methods suit different personalities. Some people need hard exercise to dissipate stress, while others need solitude and quiet. Most people know what works for them, but in a stressful situation the tendency is to put off a game of tennis or "time out" until the crisis is over. Unfortunately, crisis often follows crisis, so the physiological effects of stress stay with the body, slowly building up to upset the balance required to maintain health. Here are some practical ways of avoiding stress and relaxing when it is impossible to use the basic relaxation routine.

Take Exercise

As we have seen, stress, be it mental or physical, alters the chemical balance in the body to prepare it for action. Exercise of any type utilizes this physiological preparation and returns the body to homeostasis. Take a brisk walk, play squash, go for a run, cycle, swim, ride, or rollerskate. If you are stuck at home, put some music on and dance, or do some strenuous gardening or housework – but do something.

Stand Straight

Someone who is tense tends to stand stiffly, with hunched shoulders, a gritted jaw, and clenched hands. And when you are depressed and anxious, your shoulders become rounded, your head drops forward, and your back curves. In both cases, the signs of stress are evident, and over time the posture becomes a habit, feels "normal" and is difficult to change. But the muscles are not in correct alignment and become either overstretched or taut. This adds to the tension present from stress and a vicious circle is set up: mental stress is producing physical stress and vice versa.

A number of special techniques can improve posture, such as the Alexander Technique (*see pages 146–53*), Osteopathy (*see pages 110–15*), and Trager Work (*see page 158*) to name a few. Find out about the different techniques and find one that suits you – as with all the therapies in this volume, it is vital that you find one that you feel comfortable with. Doing so is important, because good posture not only reduces tension in the muscles, but has the psychological effect of making you feel better and gives others the impression that you are a confident person.

ABOVE *Regular exercise will help combat the effects of a stressful lifestyle.*

ABOVE *A hot bath will ease the stresses and strains of the day.*

Take Time Out

Try to ensure that you have time for yourself each week, however hectic your lifestyle. Do not wait for others to suggest an evening off, because if you seem to be coping, people will assume that you are all right. Use the time to pamper yourself and do what you want: have a massage (*see pages 96–105*), soak in a hot bath with aromatherapy oils (*see pages 104*), curl up with a good book, visit a friend – just do whatever makes you feel good.

Laugh

We all know instinctively that laughter releases tension, both in ourselves and in those around us. Research has shown that this belief has a basis in fact, and therapists now encourage their patients to laugh – some hospitals and hospices make use of comedy programs for this purpose. Put laughter back in your life – keep a few of your favorite comedies on video, take time out to meet friends who make you laugh, try and see the funny side of things!

ABOVE *Laughter is a good stress-buster.*

Learn to Say "No"

Most of us want to please others, so we are inclined to agree to do things that we either do not want to do or that will overstretch us. Force yourself to say "no" to people, be it your employer, friend, partner, or children. If you become exhausted and resentful – stressed – you will end up being little use to anyone. People respect those who know their own mind and are straightforward and decisive.

Stimulate your Mind

Many jobs are mundane much of the time and this fact can bring its own stresses and frustrations. If changing your employment is not a possibility, ensure that you are adequately stimulated in your time off. Take up an exciting hobby or sport, stretch your intellect with an evening class, or get involved in the local community. A boring, repetitive job can leave you feeling exhausted at the end of the day, with a desire just to flop in front of the television, but this is not true relaxation and in time the stresses will show.

Try Not to Worry

Everyone worries, but doing so is normally ineffectual. Learn from the past and try not to worry too much about the future. Plan for it instead, perhaps using visualization techniques (*see pages* 206–9), but then leave the future to take care of itself. Worrying increases stress, reduces sleep, creates wrinkles, and gives you a care-worn, bad-tempered demeanor. One way to lessen worry is to prioritize what you have to do in order of importance. Tackle the most important task first, because the stress of having an unsolved problem or unfinished business is usually worse than that caused by facing it.

If there is nothing that can be done to resolve a situation and its outcome is out of your control, you should find a way of accepting it and coping with it. Try meditation (*see pages* 60–5), yoga (*see pages* 54–9) or seeing a counselor (*see pages* 188–93).

Make Love

A satisfying and fulfilling physical relationship with a partner releases tension and stress marvelously well, and feeling desired is both stimulating and relaxing.

Get a Pet

In recent years a considerable body of research has been published that shows that owning a pet, especially a dog, relieves symptoms of stress. Stroking and petting a dog lowers your blood pressure and pulse rate. If you have a pet, make more time to make a fuss of it.

THE MECHANICS OF STRESS

✳ A challenge or threat is sensed by the brain.

✳ Hormones are produced which raise heartrate, increase breathing rate, elevate blood pressure, and make more energy available to the muscles.

✳ The brain is now fully alert and the body is prepared to take decisive action with maximum efficiency.

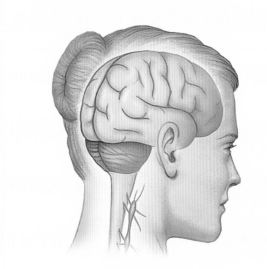

BELOW Stroking a cat reduces stress.

ABOVE *Making a list of potential tasks can stop needless worrying.*

PATHFINDER

The ability to relax is vital in maintaining health, since undissipated stress can cause some diseases and contribute to others. Relaxation is not only preventive, but beneficial in the treatment of most disorders, since it improves the quality of life and strengthens the immune system. It is a valuable part of the treatment of many conditions. For example, a report in the US journal *Psychological Reports*, in 1985, claimed that relaxation reduced the incidence of seizures in epileptics by 30%; and the *British Journal of Psychiatry* reported, in 1986, that relaxation helped patients suffering from anxiety.

ACNE SEE P. *276*

ANGINA SEE P. *304*

ANXIETY SEE PP. *256–7*

ARTHRITIS SEE PP. *346–7*

ASTHMA SEE PP. *294–5*

BRONCHITIS SEE P. *299*

DEPRESSION SEE P. *261*

DIARRHEA SEE P. *312*

FEAR OF DENTAL TREATMENT SEE P. *286*

GASTROENTERITIS SEE P. *309*

HEADACHE SEE PP. *268–9*

HIV AND AIDS SEE PP. *340–1*

INFERTILITY SEE P. *324*

INSOMNIA SEE P. *264*

LABOR PAINS SEE P. *328*

LARYNGITIS SEE P. *292*

MENOPAUSE SYMPTOMS SEE PP. *330–31*

MIGRAINE SEE P. *269*

NAUSEA AND VOMITING SEE P. *308*

PALPITATIONS SEE P. *307*

PHOBIAS SEE P. *260*

PREGNANCY PROBLEMS SEE PP. *326–7*

STRESS SEE PP. *262–3*

BREATHING TECHNIQUES

Doctors recognize that the ability to relax and breathe correctly is an important tool in combating stress and helping patients with respiratory and other disorders. However, they do not see it as in any way a cure for most underlying problems – though correct breathing may be a useful adjunct to conventional treatment in conditions such as asthma, or problems that may have psychological overtones, such as anxiety attacks.

While orthodox medicine does not recognize the concept of a "life force," or believe in the concept of meridians, there is general acceptance that the breathing techniques taught in Eastern healing systems are likely to be as effective as those taught in conventional Western medicine.

In both traditional Eastern medicine and modern Western orthodox medicine, the importance of correct breathing techniques is held to be paramount. In Eastern medicine, this is considered to be because whenever we breathe in or out we inhale or exhale a "life force"; in Western medicine it is because correct breathing maximizes both the amount of oxygen in the blood and the amount of carbon dioxide, a waste product, that is removed from the blood. Few people breathe correctly – that is, deep, slow, calm breathing – but it is relatively easy to learn how to do so, and to make it a habit.

In normal circumstances we do not notice that we are breathing: it is an automatic activity, requiring no conscious control. However, we have the ability to bring breathing under conscious control if we wish, and this ability was recognized and utilized by the physicians and healers of ancient Eastern medicine. They considered correct, controlled breathing to be vital for health, since breath was the bridge between the outside world and the body. They also believed that the whole world, including human beings, was comprised of a "life force," known, depending on the specific healing system, as "prana," "chi" or "qi," or "ki." This "life force" is an invisible, subtle energy of waves and minute particles that not only forms all things but can also change them. When we breathe correctly, we inhale and exhale this energy, which flows freely and maintains physical and mental health. But if respiration is inadequate and shallow, life energy does not flow freely and so stagnates – the result is disease. This ancient philosophy is still the basis of Eastern medicine today (*see Acupuncture, pages 20–31; Shiatsu, pages 32–7; Ayurveda, pages 78–85*).

The Western View

The picture is somewhat different in the West, where the wise men, shamans, and witch doctors of early times were certainly aware that various breathing techniques could induce trances, improve performance, and affect health, but their techniques were ignored as orthodox medicine developed. In fact, it was not until the middle of the 20th century, when correct, deep breathing was found to be a useful way of combating stress, that breathing techniques came to be appreciated once more. And while few orthodox doctors in the West believe in a "life force," they now recognize that correct breathing calms the body and mind, while shallow, rapid breathing increases the symptoms of stress. As a result, correct breathing is now taught in many orthodox hospitals for

ABOVE *The Eastern principles of healing breathing continue in meditation techniques today.*

respiratory problems, childbirth, and as part of stress management.

This unanimity between Western orthodoxy and Eastern medicine – even though the agreement is on the effect of correct breathing techniques rather then their mechanism – is becoming even more significant in the modern world. The reason is that the heavily polluted air found in many towns and cities is low in oxygen and negative ions (*see Negative Ion therapy, page 171*).

THE PHYSIOLOGY OF BREATHING

Oxygen is the vital fuel of life. It powers all human activity, from the metabolism of a single cell to the contraction of a muscle. Breathing is the activity that takes oxygen into the body from the air – in rough terms, 20 percent of air is made up of oxygen and 80 percent of nitrogen – and expels carbon dioxide, which is the waste product produced by the use of oxygen. And since the body does not store oxygen, with the exception of a small amount that is held in the muscles, its supply must be continuous.

As we inhale, air is sucked into the lungs, where it passes through tubes of descending size – the trachea,

ABOVE *The polluted air in our cities can affect our breathing mechanisms.*

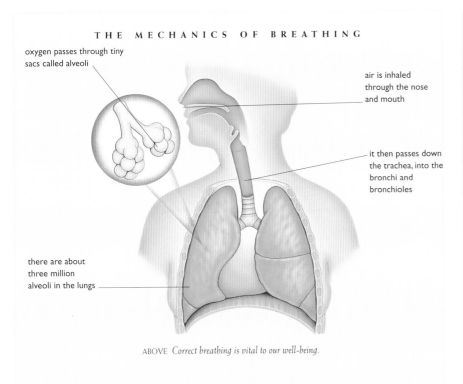

THE MECHANICS OF BREATHING

oxygen passes through tiny sacs called alveoli

air is inhaled through the nose and mouth

it then passes down the trachea, into the bronchi and bronchioles

there are about three million alveoli in the lungs

ABOVE *Correct breathing is vital to our well-being.*

INCORRECT BREATHNG

When you breathe calmly and deeply, the lungs are washed with air by each breath to ensure that the body receives, the correct amount of oxygen for its needs. But most people only use about half the capacity of their lungs, and take air in principally to the upper lobes. The result is that the alveoli are not filled with fresh oxygenated air, so the blood receives too little oxygen and too little carbon dioxide is exhaled. By contrast, when you become stressed or anxious, your breathing tends to become shallow and rapid – hyperventilation. If this type of breathing continues for too long, the blood loses too much carbon dioxide and becomes less acidic. This, in turn, affects the functioning of the nerves and muscles, and leads to symptoms such as palpitations, faintness, panic attacks, general tiredness, headaches, and muscular tension.

RIGHT *Hyperventilation can cause headaches.*

bronchi, and bronchioles – until it reaches tiny sacs called alveoli. These sacs – there are about three million of them in the lungs – have very thin walls and are surrounded by small blood vessels, called capillaries. The oxygen in the air passes through these walls, enters the capillaries, and is picked up by a chemical called hemoglobin, which is contained in the red blood cells. At the same time, carbon dioxide is released from the hemoglobin, and this passes into the alveoli to be expelled from the lungs during expiration.

Oxygen Balance

Normally, breathing is automatic, and the levels of oxygen and carbon dioxide in the blood are kept steady by an intricate series of checks and balances. However, the body's requirements can change in certain circumstances: if you run for a bus, for example, there is an increase in the amount of oxygen required by the muscles and in the level of carbon dioxide; and so you breathe more rapidly to compensate. If you are asleep or resting, less oxygen is required,

20% oxygen

80% nitrogen

ABOVE *The air we breathe is made up of roughly 20 percent oxygen and 80 percent nitrogen.*

so your rate of breathing slows.

Unfortunately, other factors can disturb this system, with the result that there is either insufficient oxygen in the blood – a condition known as "hypoxia" – or an excess of carbon dioxide. Hypoxia can be due to external factors, such as high altitude, where the air contains less oxygen, or to internal problems – these include anemia, in which an underlying disorder results in an inadequate amount of hemoglobin in the blood, and ischemic hypoxia, which occurs as a result of poor circulation or heart failure. Another cause of hypoxia, though only to a very mild degree, is incorrect breathing. But whatever the degree of hypoxia, the result is that the blood does not carry sufficient oxygen to the vital organs. The effect of this varies according to the degree of hypoxia: in severe cases, damage can be caused to the liver, kidneys, heart, and brain; and if the brain is starved of oxygen for more than a few minutes, it dies. Even mild hypoxia caused by incorrect breathing can have deleterious effects (*see box above*).

PRECAUTIONS

■ Asthmatics should avoid, or use only with care, breathing techniques involving the inhalation of steam.

■ Asthmatics should always keep their conventional medication with them for use in an emergency.

HOW TO BREATHE CORRECTLY

Correct breathing allows the full capacity of the lungs to be utilized, not just that of the upper lobes – and is sometimes known as "abdominal" or "diaphragmatic" breathing. The lungs are encased by the ribcage, with the spinal column behind them and the breastbone in front. Below them is a large sheet of muscle, called the diaphragm, which separates the chest from the abdominal cavity. When breathing correctly it is this muscle – with some help from the intercostal muscles that run between all the ribs – that contracts to push out the chest wall and so expand the lungs, with the result that air is sucked in to them. When the diaphragm and intercostals relax, they return to their former position, allowing the chest wall to collapse slightly, expelling air from the lungs. On contracting, the diaphragm moves down and the abdomen rises slightly; on relaxing the diaphragm rises and the abdomen flattens.

In incorrect breathing, the diaphragm is not used to its full potential, and the intake of our lungs tends to rely on the intercostal muscles between the upper ribs. However, it is not difficult to re-educate yourself in the habit of correct, primarily diaphragmatic, breathing. To learn the technique, you should put aside 15 minutes for practice each day. Rehearse the techniques given below until they become second nature and are maintained whatever your activity or situation.

LEARNING CORRECT BREATHING WHILE LYING DOWN

Lie on a firm bed or a cushioned mat in loose, comfortable clothes, making sure that there is nothing tight, such as a belt, at your waist. Try to relax as much as possible – it is helpful if you choose a room where it is unlikely that you will be distracted.

1 *Place both your hands on the bottom edges of your ribs, with the tips of your fingers nearly touching in the middle.*

2 *Take a deep, slow breath in through your nostrils, visualizing air being sucked into the lung spaces under your fingers – if you are breathing properly, your fingers will move up, out and apart and your stomach will rise as you breathe in, but your shoulders will remain stationary. Hold the breath for a count of seven.*

PANIC ATTACKS

A panic attack is a sudden feeling of acute anxiety. It is quite normal for the body to prepare for flight or fight (*see pages 158–65*) by raising the heartrate and breathing rate, but in a panic attack, both are raised to abnormal levels and breathing becomes extremely shallow and rapid. The result is hyperventilation: too much carbon dioxide is exhaled and so the blood becomes acidic. The resulting symptoms are faintness, palpitations, muscular tension, and, sometimes, numbness.

As an immediate first-aid treatment, breathe deeply and slowly in and out of a paper bag held over your mouth and nostrils. This will increase the level of carbon dioxide in the blood and lessen the symptoms. In the long term, relaxation techniques (*see pages 158–65*) can lessen the frequency and duration of panic attacks and cognitive behavioral therapy (*see pages 198–9*) is often effective in treating the root cause of the problem.

ABOVE *Blowing into a paper bag can reduce the feelings of panic.*

WATCHPOINT

If you feel slightly faint and light-headed while breathing deeply, stop for a while and breathe calmly and the feeling will pass – it is a common response to an unusually large quantity of oxygen reaching the brain and other organs.

3 *Release the breath over the course of a count of ten – no muscular effort is required, so there is no need to push the air out of the lungs. Your fingers and stomach will return to their starting position.*

4 *Repeat the sequence three times before breathing naturally and instinctively for a few minutes. Then repeat the deep breathing sequence – but no more than twice more.*

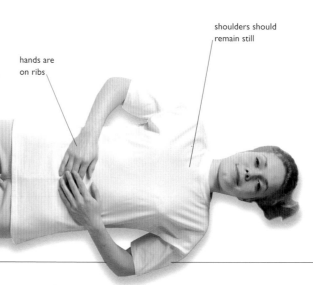

shoulders should remain still

hands are on ribs

CORRECT BREATHING WHEN SITTING

Once you have mastered the art of abdominal breathing when lying down, it is useful to extend the technique for use in other situations, whether at work or in the home. Correct breathing can give you a quick energy boost during the day and help you to keep calm and relaxed in stressful situations.

Learning to breathe deeply and quietly when sitting has obvious benefits for people who work at a desk during the day, but it is particularly useful for asthma sufferers, since it can reduce both the severity and frequency of attacks. If you are asthmatic, practice the technique given below, and when you have mastered it try repeating the exercise when sitting astride a chair with your arms over its back. Then try to relax and follow the routine as soon as you feel your chest tighten or an attack starts.

Sit comfortably in an upright chair with your spine straight and supported. Undo a tight belt if you are wearing one.

CORRECT BREATHING WHEN WALKING

Learning how to breathe correctly when walking is always important for general well-being and health.

1 Relax your shoulders and put your hands on your lap. If your shoulders feel tense, bunch them up as tightly as possible toward your ears, hold for a count of five, and then let them flop down.

2 When you are ready, take a deep breath using the same method described for lying down. Feel your diaphragm push down and out and your stomach swell. Concentrate on filling the lower lobes of each lung – your shoulders should stay motionless.

3 If you find that your shoulders are moving, place your hands over the bottom of your ribcage, as in the previous exercise, to check that its lower part is expanding under your fingers.

4 Repeat a few times so that the movement becomes habitual and can be performed anywhere. When you have done this, try the routine when standing.

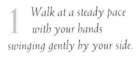

1 Walk at a steady pace with your hands swinging gently by your side.

2 Breathe in deeply – as previously described – while taking around four paces. Then hold your breath for two paces and exhale during a further four paces. If this proves difficult, start with a two-one-two sequence of breathing in and out during paces and gradually build up to a sequence of four.

3 Repeat this sequence four times and then return to normal breathing. Repeat the whole sequence a few times during your walk.

FORCED EXPIRATION

🍃 Once in a while – perhaps after sitting for a long time on a subway train or in heavy traffic – it is useful to force as much polluted air as possible out of the lungs. When we breathe normally, there is always residual air left in the lungs, especially in the lower lobes. To ensure that these alveoli are filled and emptied occasionally helps them to function efficiently.

🍃 Take as big a breath as possible through your nostrils until you feel that your lungs are at bursting point. Immediately this point is reached, contract your stomach muscles hard, forcing the air out through your nostrils.

🍃 Attempt to empty your lungs completely – you may have to jerk your stomach muscles tight a few times to achieve this. Do not contract your shoulders or the muscles of your ribcage as this will tighten the bronchioles and impede the smooth flow of air from the alveoli.

EASTERN BREATHING TECHNIQUES

Eastern healers not only understand the importance of breathing correctly, but also believe that air itself has healing properties. Their therapies involve breathing in "life force" known as "qi" (or "chi") in China (*see Acupuncture, page* 20–5) or "ki" in Japan (*see hara breathing, Do-in, page* 38) and visualizing (*see Visualization, page* 206–9) the healing air flowing into the lungs and spreading throughout the body – especially to the area that requires treatment. During exhalation the disease is visualized flowing out of the problem area and lungs, and away.

In India the "life force" is known as "prana" and Sun and Moon or "prana" breathing technique is practiced by yogi (*see pages* 54–9). Simply, it involves sitting cross-legged in a quiet location and pinching both nostrils shut with your right thumb and forefinger. Release the pressure on your right nostril and breathe in deeply. Hold your breath for the same length of time that you breathed in and then pinch the right nostril and breathe out through the released left nostril – again for the same length of time. As this becomes easy, try to lengthen the amount of time the air is held in the lungs and the length of exhalation to twice the time that is taken to inhale.

LEFT *Eastern techniques are seen to be healing as well as calming.*

Blue or purple colors are very calming

COLOR BREATHING

The use of color as a therapy has always been an integral part of Ayurvedic medicine (*see pages* 78–85). One method used in Ayurvedic medicine and by modern color therapists (*see pages* 248–9) is to breathe deeply as in the basic "healing breath" technique above, but at the same time to visualize a particular healing color flowing into your lungs and bathing your body. Then exhale while visualizing the complementary color.

NEGATIVE ION THERAPY

Air contains electrically charged particles called ions that carry either a negative or positive charge. The number of ions and the proportion of negative to positive ions in the atmosphere changes from area to area and with the climate. For example, rural, mountainous, and coastal areas have a greater proportion of negative ions in the atmosphere than positive ones, and the air around running water – near a waterfall or fast-flowing river, for example, or even after a heavy rainstorm – is also rich in negative ions. However, urban areas have more positive ions, since negative ions are destroyed by smoke and pollution, and also by central heating units in offices and homes.

In the early 20th century, researchers discovered that the proportion of negative to positive ions in the air affects mood and mental stability. When the air is rich in positive ions, people become irritable and tense and find it difficult to concentrate; they also suffer from headaches, general malaise, and lethargy. (There is a rise in the crime rate as well as requests for medical assistance when dry, warm winds, which are rich in positive ions, blow – such as the Sharav in Israel and the Sirocco in North Africa.) But an atmosphere rich in negative ions has the reverse effect: there is less general malaise and people feel cheerful, energetic, and positive. Air rich in negative ions has also been found to be beneficial in the treat-

ment of burns and certain skin problems, such as eczema, and to ameliorate depression, anxiety states, headaches, and respiratory problems. As a result of these findings, "ionizers" were developed. These are machines that release negative ions into the atmosphere while at the same time removing pollutants. Ionizers are available from specialist shops and health centers and come in a range of different sizes – from small portable ones that are suitable for the home and car, to large ones for open-plan offices. Many hospitals and workplaces now have ionizers in each room.

Even without an ionizer, it is possible to increase the number of negative ions and decrease the number of positive ions in your home. Place bowls of water by any radiators or air conditioning units to humidify the air – or buy a humidifier – and make sure that you use the central heating or air conditioning as little as possible. Open all your windows after a heavy shower to let fresh air rich in negative ions into the house. And if you are feeling tense or irritable or you have a headache, take a long shower, breathing in deeply while you do so.

ABOVE *The air near running water is charged with negative ions.*

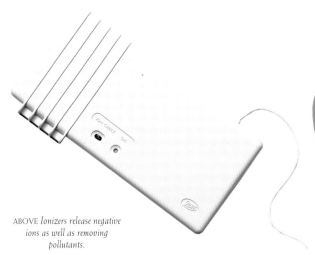

ABOVE *Ionizers release negative ions as well as removing pollutants.*

BELOW *Air full of positive ions can cause a lack of concentration.*

PATHFINDER

The ability to breathe correctly and deeply, utilizing the whole of both lungs, benefits the body – physically and mentally. Correct breathing is particularly important if you suffer from stress-related disorders, such as panic attacks and high blood pressure, and respiratory problems, such as bronchitis and asthma. Air rich in negative ions can help mood and energy levels and ameliorate certain skin problems and psychological problems.

Eastern healers and color therapists also believe that air has its own healing force and that specialized breathing techniques, as well as correct breathing, can be helpful in the treatment of most disorders.

ACNE *SEE P.* 276
ARTHRITIS *SEE PP.* 256–7
ASTHMA *SEE PP.* 294–5
BRONCHITIS *SEE P.* 299
COUGHS *SEE P.* 297
DIABETES *SEE PP.* 336–7
DIZZINESS *SEE P.* 271
FAINTING *SEE P.* 270
HEADACHE *SEE PP.* 268–9
HICCUPS *SEE P.* 301
HIGH BLOOD PRESSURE *SEE P.* 302
HYPERVENTILATION *SEE P.* 301
INFERTILITY *SEE P.* 324
INSOMNIA *SEE P.* 264
MIGRAINE *SEE P.* 269
NAUSEA AND VOMITING *SEE P.* 308
PHOBIAS *SEE P.* 260
STRESS *SEE PP.* 262–3
TINNITUS *SEE P.* 281

HYDROTHERAPY

The virtues of water (used internally and externally, both hot and cold, and in the form of liquid, steam, or ice) as a therapeutic agent have been known for thousands of years — baths were not just social centers but the equivalent of health farms for the ancient Romans. Today, hydrotherapy has become a form of treatment that is curiously underused in many countries. In Germany and France, however, it is recognized as having considerable value, to the extent that the therapy is available in state-funded healthcare systems and is acknowledged as valuable by private health-insurance schemes. And, by its very nature, hydrotherapy can easily be adapted for use at home, as a self-help therapy. Baths, saunas, whirlpool baths, and simple compresses can all play a part.

The term "hydrotherapy" was coined in the 19th century, but water had been valued for its healing properties for many centuries before then. The ancient Greeks, for example, believed that water had healing and health-maintaining properties, and the Romans made water treatment a part of their everyday lives by building public baths next to natural springs. And Antonius Musa, a Greek-born freeman of Rome, is known as the "father of hydrotherapy," because in 23 B.C.E. he was rewarded with tax immunity, a gold ring, and money for successfully treating the liver ailment of Emperor Augustus by prescribing cold baths. In fact, Roman baths were the precursor of today's leisure centers, health clubs, and spas, since their facilities included treatment rooms, massage areas, a library, and gymnasia – they were the social hubs of the communities they served.

ABOVE *Brighton's proximity to the sea made it a popular health resort.*

Sea Water and Spas

Bathing remained popular until the 15th century, when an epidemic of syphilis and other infections, which were thought to be transmitted in water, made water treatments less popular. But by the middle of the 18th century there was a resurgence of interest in the healing properties of water, and especially of sea water. In 1754 one Dr. Richard Russell tested the sea water at a tiny village called Brighthelmstone, in England, and was so impressed with its benefits that he wrote a book called *A Dissertation on the Uses of Sea Water in the Diseases of the Glands*. Brighthelmstone quickly became a fashionable health spa and was renamed Brighton – patronized by royalty, it became the first seaside health resort.

Spas (the word "spa" derives from the town of Spa, in Belgium, whose therapeutic waters had been famous since Roman times) soon sprang up all over Europe and the rich and fashionable rushed to "take the waters." Competition between spas became fierce, and some outrageous claims were made about the therapeutic powers of each and every mineral water.

"Taking the waters" also became popular in America. The hot springs of Saratoga Springs, in the mountains of New York State, became North America's first fashionable spa in the late 18th century. By the mid-19th century various medical establishments had been set up around the springs, notably the Remedial Institute, which offered a variety of therapeutic water treatments.

Hydrotherapy can ease pain and reduce inflammation, congestion, and fever. It can also help relieve muscle spasms and the tension held in muscles and soft tissues, so reducing joint stiffness and allowing an improved range of movement – it is especially beneficial for osteoarthritis and rheumatoid arthritis.

Hydrotherapy also has considerable psychological benefits, too. It can reduce stress and induce relaxation, which, in turn, stimulates release of the body's own painkillers and mood enhancers – the endorphins – bringing about feelings of well-being.

BELOW *Hydrotherapy can reduce the inflammation associated with arthritis.*

HOW HYDROTHERAPY WORKS

Despite claims that water has an innate power to heal, its main effect when used for healing purposes depends on its temperature, and its ability to provide weight-bearing support to the human body. Hot water dilates – increases in size – the superficial blood vessels, increases the flow of blood to the skin and muscles, and reduces the flow of blood to the internal organs. Conversely, cold water

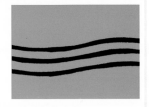

Cold water can stimulate.

constricts the flow of blood to the skin, increases blood flow to the internal organs, and inhibits the biochemical reactions that cause inflammation. Hot water soothes and relaxes, while cold stimulates – both ease muscle tension and spasms.

An improved circulation boosts the immune system, which helps the body to combat disease and infection. It also increases the amount of oxygen and other nutrients available to the cells of the body, which is necessary for them to function and repair themselves when damaged. And this circulatory improvement also makes the lymphatic drainage system and sweat glands

more efficient at removing waste products (caused by biochemical reactions) from the body.

Hot water soothes and relaxes.

PRIESSNITZ AND KNEIPP

Vincenz Priessnitz (1799–1851) discovered that many of his aches and pains could be cured with cold compresses. As his reputation spread, Priessnitz opened a hydrotherapy center run on Spartan lines. It offered many harsh, cold treatments, ranging from wet bandaging, cold stomach packs, and icy douches for the genitals to the dreaded "fire-engine treatment." In this, patients – or victims – gripped an iron rail while freezing water was poured onto them from a height of 20 feet (6m). The rich took to this treatment with relish, and numerous therapists visited Gräfenberg to study Priessnitz's techniques and then spread his message throughout Europe and America.

The main rival to Priessnitz was the Bavarian priest Father Sebastian Kneipp (1821–1897). His hydrotherapy treatments were less forceful than those of Priessnitz and were also used in combination with herbal treatment, but they seemed to be just as effective. Doctors distrusted Father Kneipp, but patients flocked to him and "kneipping" became very popular, and remains so in Europe.

HYDROTHERAPY TODAY

The emergence of technology-based medicine after the First World War convinced many doctors that hydrotherapy had only a limited part to play in treatment programs. As a result, in many countries – France and Germany being exceptions – the therapy was not available to all and came to be restricted to those who could afford to visit a health farm. However, physical therapists (physiotherapists in Britain) have always prescribed hydrotherapy, often in specialist hospital hydrotherapy departments, and the therapy has become increasingly important during post-operative convalescence and rehabilitation, especially when weight-bearing exercises might cause damage; it also plays a part in the orthodox treatment of neurological problems and paralysis and conditions such as cystic fibrosis and cerebral palsy.

Recently, hydrotherapy has made something of a comeback in America and Britain, as an alternative therapy that does not require the use of drugs and as a way of combating the stresses of modern life. But in continental Europe it has continued to be used widely and is available to all. In Germany and France, such treatments are often combined with herbalism.

ABOVE *Hydrotherapy can play a part in the treatment of neurological problems.*

LEFT *The Romans evolved a whole culture around bathing.*

HYDROTHERAPY TECHNIQUES

There are a number of different approaches to hydrotherapy, and, as a result, a number of different techniques – these are listed below and in the following pages.

Generally, the physical therapists (physiotherapists in Britain) who work in orthodox medicine treat specific problems and conditions. For example, they tailor exercises for use in a hydrotherapy pool to the needs of individual patients (for that reason, they are not listed here); they also use cryotherapy, sitz baths (generally only to improve poor circulation of the feet), high-powered jets, compresses (sometimes containing mud, similar to that used in thalassotherapy), and wraps.

Other, less orthodox forms of hydrotherapy are confined to health farms, spas – where their prime purpose is to relieve stress, offer general physical improvement, and promote a feeling of well-being – and clinics in which treatment is based, broadly or strictly, on naturopathic principles. (Father Sebastian Kneipp was one of the founders of naturopathy, as well as an advocate of hydrotherapy. He reputedly cured himself of tuberculosis by standing in the River Danube.)

Cryotherapy

The use of ice or freezing water in treatment, known as "cryotherapy," was pioneered by Vincenz Priessnitz, though as practiced today cryotherapy is not nearly so physically challenging and unpleasant as it was in his day. Physical therapists use it to numb and freeze the skin and subcutaneous tissues over areas of the body that have been injured structurally, as, say, by a sprain. Cryotherapy can be given in the form of ice

ABOVE *The pool is an integral part of a stay in a health farm.*

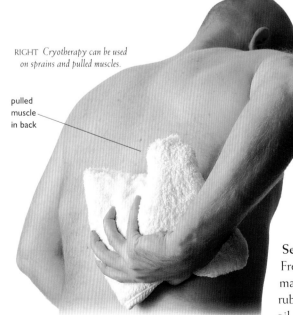

RIGHT *Cryotherapy can be used on sprains and pulled muscles.*

pulled muscle in back

rubs and massages, cold compresses, cold baths or jets of water.

Uses of cryotherapy

* Gives temporary pain relief by slowing the transmission of nerve impulses. If pain is the cause of loss of mobility, a greater range of movement can be achieved during treatment.
* Reduces inflammation because it constricts blood capillaries, especially in post-traumatic swelling.
* Encourages the dispersal of lymph and fluid from the tissues.
* Reduces muscle spasms and so aids relaxation.

Self-help

Freeze sprays, ice wraps, and packs are available from many pharmacies, but an ice cube can always be rubbed over painful, hot, and swollen areas – rub some oil over the skin first to prevent ice burn. In an emer-

SITZ BATH SELF-HELP

It is not difficult to give yourself a sitz bath at home, by using a washing-up bowl or baby bath to immerse your feet. The bowl can either be placed on a small, plastic stool inside the bathtub or you can sit sideways in the tub and place the bowl on a stool beside it. The only problem is that you have to keep on emptying and filling the tub and bowl with hot and cold water alternately. More conveniently, a similar treatment, called a pediluvium, can be given to the feet alone to improve venous return and reduce swollen ankles, by using hot and cold foot baths.

gency, a bag of frozen peas straight from the freezer can be wrapped in a towel and placed over the injured area for 10 minutes. This is well worth remembering as an instant treatment for the very painful muscle spasm of a pulled muscle in the lower back.

Sitz bath

A sitz bath is given using in a bowl-shaped bath just big enough for the hips. Two hip baths placed next to each other are used – one contains sufficient hot water to cover the abdominal area while the other is filled with cold water. The patient sits in the hot tub, with his or her feet in the cold tub (with the knees out of the water). After three minutes the position is reversed: the patient sits in the cold tub, keeping the feet in the hot tub for two minutes. The whole process is repeated several times, often with the back and pelvic areas being massaged during immersion. Alternatively, some naturopaths advocate transferring bodily from hot to cold every two minutes, using one sitz bath at a time. The purpose of a sitz bath is to relieve tissue congestion and to improve the circulation of blood and lymph in the pelvic region.

Uses of sitz baths

* Improves circulation in the legs and feet.
* Reduces pelvic and abdominal congestion and improves the circulation of blood and lymph in the area.
* Helps to reduce hemorrhoids and relieve constipation, cystitis, and menstrual problems.
* Can stimulate liver and kidneys to improve function.

Jacuzzis or whirlpool baths

The sides of jacuzzis and whirlpool baths are fitted with jets that propel pressurized bubbles through the water to massage the skin and underlying tissues. The force of the massage can be adjusted by the operator – by increasing the pressure and size of the bubbles – so that either a relaxing, soothing sensation is given or the large muscles are pummeled and probed. The process generally takes about 20 minutes.

Whirlpool baths and jacuzzis are available for the home; there are also devices that fit into a normal bath.

Uses of jacuzzis

A gentle massage:
* improves skin tone, relaxes the muscles and improves the circulation;
* relaxes the body physically and mentally by easing tension and anxiety;
* combats exhaustion and insomnia;
* helps if you are feeling run-down.
   More vigorous pummeling:
* reduces muscle spasm and tension;
* eases back and neck pain;
* improves the circulation and helps in the elimination of toxins, so reducing edema (accumulation of fluid);
* helps to regain flexibility of muscles and increase the range of movements in joints, so is ideal for all forms of arthritis.

RIGHT *Hydrotherapy can easily be practiced yourself.*

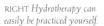

A power shower, especially if it is hand-held, can be used as a home alternative to treatment with high-powered jets. Stand under a warm shower for a few minutes to warm the skin and the muscles. Imagine the tension draining away, and enjoy the relaxing effect of the water cascading over your skin. Then aim the jets of water at any tight muscles or painful areas. Pay particular attention to the muscles of the back, neck, and shoulders, which often tense up and give rise to headaches. Let the water pulse over the muscles for a comfortable period.

HIGH-POWERED JETS

The use of high-powered jets of water, which may be hot or cold, depending on an individual's treatment regime, is based on Vincenz Priessnitz's "fire-engine treatment" (*see pages 172–3*). Today, however, the treatment is less severe: you may have to hang onto a bar, but the hydrotherapist will direct the cold water at your body from a little way above it and from the side. Strong jets of water are aimed at the areas that require attention, to pummel, stimulate, and massage, the skin, subcutaneous tissues, and underlying muscles. In a variation of the treatment, called "the Scottish douche," the jets of water are aimed at the back and the muscles around the spine from around 12 feet (3m) away, in order to stimulate the nervous system.

Uses

* Stimulates the skin and soothes taut muscles, so improving skin and muscle tone.
* Helps the elimination of toxins from the tissues.
* Improves the circulation.

Therapy with high-powered jets is especially useful in the treatment of asthma, partly because the water releases negative ions into the air. It is also useful in the treatment of arthritis, circulation problems, and musculoskeletal problems, and can relieve stress and headaches.

LEFT *Your shower at home can soothe aches and pains.*

Hydrotherapists in orthodox medicine

As part of their training, physical therapists (physiotherapists in Britain) study hydrotherapy as a treatment for various conditions such as arthritis, paralysis, cerebral palsy, sports injuries, and for rehabilitation. Physical therapists are fully trained and state-registered, and patients are normally referred to them by doctors.

Naturopathic hydrotherapists

Naturopathy is founded on the belief that the body has its own healing system and vitality, and that to prevent and cure disease the whole body must be treated. It is practiced throughout the Western world. Naturopathic treatments are as noninvasive as possible. Nutrition, hydrotherapy, massage, shiatsu, acupressure, reflexology, osteopathy, chiropractic, herbal medicines, and yoga may all be recommended by a naturopath. Naturopathic hydrotherapists, who usually practice at health farms and spas as well as specialist naturopathic clinics, stress the importance of a healthy, organic diet, fresh air, exercise, and rest. They use hydrotherapy as one of their tools to rebalance the body and to stimulate the body's own healing abilities. Qualified practitioners are recognized and licensed in some countries, such as Germany, and in some American states. To find a practitioner write to a recognized center (*see Useful Addresses, pages 368–73*) or visit a reputable health club or spa.

A naturopathic hydrotherapist will take a full history of your health, lifestyle, and outlook on life, and tailor the therapy to your specific needs. Treatment may include drinking pure water or water containing various minerals or herbs, jet massages, sitz baths, hot and cold compresses and baths, thalassotherapy, cryotherapy, Turkish or steam baths, and saunas.

BELOW *Sports injuries can benefit from hydrotherapy techniques.*

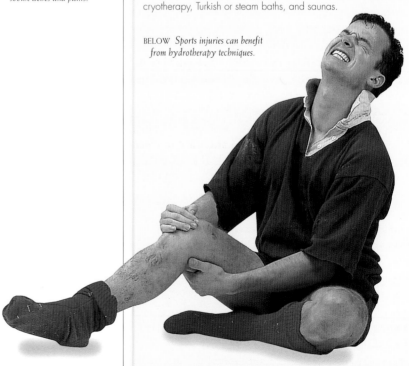

THALASSOTHERAPY

The use of sea water and sea air in treatment is known as "thalassotherapy" – *thalassa* is the Greek word for the sea. Sea water contains minerals, in particular salts, and is also believed by some thalassotherapists to have innate healing properties as a result of the "imprints" it contains of other beneficial substances with which it has come into contact. Sea air also has a greater proportion of negative ions in it than the air over land, and these help reduce the levels of histamines, which are produced during allergic reactions, and improve mood.

ABOVE
Seaweed extracts tone the skin.

And seaweed contains minerals such as iodine, which can encourage sweating and cleanse and tone the skin.

Sea-water baths or jets are also used to cleanse and tone the skin as well as to improve the circulation. Seaweed may be added to a bath – known as a "kelp bath" – to induce sweating and encourage the elimination of toxins from the body. Seaweed may also be used as a poultice on specific areas of the body.

- Helps relieve hayfever and allergies.
- Improves mood and lifts depression and irritability.
- Increases and speeds the elimination of toxins by stimulating the lymphatic and circulatory systems.
- Helps arthritis and other musculoskeletal problems.
- Home thalassotherapy kits are available, in the form of mineral lotions that can be added to a bath, seaweed wraps, and kelp extract tablets.

WATCHPOINT

Do not undergo any form of thalassotherapy treatment that involves the use of seaweed or seaweed derivatives if you are allergic to iodine or have an open wound.

ABOVE *A bath is one of the easiest self-help treatments to indulge in.*

Hot and cold baths

A hydrotherapist may prescribe lying in a hot bath (at about 100°F/38°C) for at least 20 minutes to ease stiff joints and muscles, or in a warm or cool bath to treat a variety of other problems. Some therapists, and in particular naturopaths or adherents of kneipping (*see pages 172–3*) add either herbs, muds, minerals, or oils (*see Aromatherapy, pages 104–5*) to these baths, the particular ones selected being dependent on the patient's individual problem.

Among these substances are mineral muds and Epsom salts. Mineral muds occur naturally in some areas, such as the Dead Sea, in Israel and Jordan, and in Austria and Italy, and many of them have some curative value. A hot mud bath is surprisingly pleasant and soporific, though a cold jet shower is needed afterward to clean the mud off. The different substances that can be added to baths have varying effects. Epsom salts, for example, induce sweating; mineral muds are claimed to cleanse and soothe the skin, eliminating impurities and toxins, and improving the circulation. The latter effect can be useful in the treatment of certain skin conditions, circulatory disorders, mental fatigue, insomnia, and stress.

Uses

Hot baths:

* relax the muscles and ease stiff joints;
* improve the circulation to the skin

and subcutaneous tissues;

* can be very beneficial to those suffering from arthritis, and general aches and pains.

Cold baths:

* reduce fever;
* reduce inflammation;
* improve blood supply to the internal organs.

Self-help

Add aromatic herbs (*see pages 104–5*) or pleasant-smelling lotions to your bath water and relax, undisturbed and soothed, for around 20 minutes.

Epsom salts can be bought at most health shops and large pharmacies (they may be sold under their chemical name of "magnesium sulfate"). For an average-sized bath, pour around 5lb (2.5kg) of the salts under hot running water. Lie in the bath for at least 15 minutes. Be careful when you stand up at the end, in case you feel slightly faint. Finish the treatment with a cool shower followed by a vigorous rub with a warm towel. A cold bath can be taken either on its own or after a hot bath – in the latter case the effects are similar to those of sitz baths (*see pages 174–5*). You should not stay in a cold bath for too long, however, in case you lower the core temperature of your body – about 10 minutes is the maximum.

ABOVE *Epsom salts can be added to a bath for a relaxing soak.*

BALNEOLOGY

Literally, "balneology" means the study of the science of bathing and medicinal springs. However, the term is often used today to describe the treatment of various disorders by means of bathing. As such, it covers most of the treatments listed on these pages.

Depending on the desired effect and the philosophy of the hydrotherapist, the bath may either be hot or cold and may or may not have a variety of substances added to it; the water itself may either be pure or from a spa or be sea water.

COMPRESSES AND WRAPS

The use of alternating hot and cold compresses is a standard treatment in both orthodox and alternative hydrotherapy (in practice, the words "compress" and "wrap" are interchangeable; in theory, the former is tighter than the latter).

In a "whole body compress," the patient lies on a treatment table and is first covered with hot, wet towels and then wrapped in a sheet; finally, blankets are placed on top to keep the heat in. After about twenty minutes the hot towels are replaced with cold, wet towels. The body reacts to this change in temperature by increasing the blood flow to the internal organs, which not only improves the efficiency of the internal organs, but also stimulates the immune system. Smaller areas of the body can be treated in the same way by alternating hot and cold wraps made from absorbent cotton or lint. However, in the treatment of an injury or inflammation, cold wraps alone may be used.

Whole Body Compresses

* stimulate the immune system, so improving resitance to infection and disease, and speeding up recovery;
* increase the blood supply to the internal organs and so improve their efficiency, benefiting in particular the digestive system, and helping relieve flatulence and chronic constipation.

Specific Wraps

* reduce inflammation and swollen joints;
* ease sinus trouble;
* relax muscle spasms;
* increase the blood supply to the area.

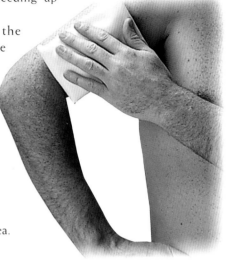

RIGHT *Heated cloths can reduce swelling in joints and muscles.*

COLONIC IRRIGATION

The use of hydrotherapy on the lower bowel – colonic irrigation – depends on the belief that pieces of impacted fecal matter sometimes stick to the lining of the colon and that their constituents can then be reabsorbed by the bloodstream. These toxins, the theory goes, then cause a variety of symptoms, from lethargy, constipation, and headaches to halitosis, allergies, and digestive disorders. Cleansing the bowel with purified water flushes the waste matter and its toxins away, and the symptoms with them.

The removal of impacted feces by means of water was practiced by the ancient Chinese, Egyptians, and Indians, and probably by many other civilizations, too. The technique was used in the spas of 19th-century Europe, and has become increasingly popular in the West in recent years.

Colonic irrigation is available at numerous health farms and clinics and many people claim to benefit from it; a number of home colonic irrigation kits are also on the market. However, most doctors do not endorse the technique, unless the procedure is conducted under strict medical supervision and for a specific reason, such as when feces become impacted in chronic constipation. The reason for their disapproval is that irrigation removes the essential "healthy" and protective bacteria that occur naturally in the intestines at the same time as the feces and toxins. Doctors believe that a good diet, high in fiber, will cure and prevent constipation and its associated ills without further intervention.

However, the procedure has other risks. The putting of tubes into the rectum and colon could lead to perforation and unless the equipment is properly sterilized, there is a risk of cross-infection. Also, the infusion of large amounts of fluids (i.e. water) into the colon could lead to fluid-electrolyte imbalances within the body, which are potentially very hazardous.

BELOW *Colonic irrigation has become very popular.*

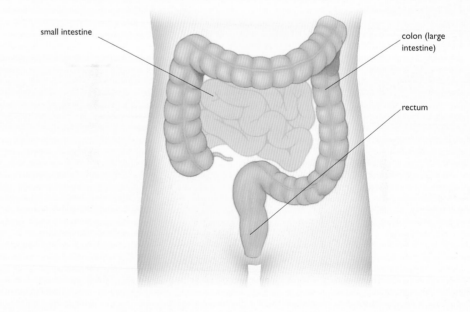

small intestine

colon (large intestine)

rectum

Self-help

The use of cold water as a treatment has been covered earlier (*see Cryotherapy, page 174*), but it is equally easy to use hot water in the form of compresses and wraps for use in the home. A warm hot-water bottle (make sure that it is not too hot) can be placed over the affected area to relieve pain from a sore stomach or stiff back, while a hot, wet cloth can be placed over the sinuses to ease pain and encourage them to discharge.

SAUNAS, STEAM BATHS, AND TURKISH BATHS

A sauna is not strictly a bath, since dry heat is used rather than steam (as in a steam bath or Turkish bath), but the effect is the same as that produced by steam. Some people do not like breathing in hot air, whether dry or wet, and in such cases a steam cabinet may be the better option, because the patient's head is outside the cabinet and is not exposed to hot air. A cold shower or bath is taken after these heat treatments in order to constrict the surface blood vessels, stop the sweating, and stimulate the skin.

A Turkish bath differs from a steam bath in that you will be scrubbed clean, massaged, and rubbed, and then left under warm towels to relax.

Uses

* Cleanses, relaxes, and invigorates.
* Induces sweating to rid the body of impurities and reduce edema (accumulation of fluid in the tissues).
* Improves the blood supply to the skin and subcutaneous tissues, so improving skin tone and the supply of nutrients and oxygen that are necessary for tissue repair.
* Relaxes tense and aching muscles, so increasing joint flexibility.

SELF-HELP

Many leisure centers, health farms, and spas have Turkish baths and saunas. Follow the directions closely and remember to have a cool shower or swim afterward.

WATCHPOINT

Turkish baths, steam baths, and saunas can be dangerous if you suffer from heart or circulatory problems. If you are in any doubt, consult your doctor.

LEFT *The steam from a Turkish bath will encourage sweating and improve skin tone.*

PATHFINDER

Hydrotherapy has many uses in maintaining and improving health. It improves the circulatory and lymph systems, reduces inflammation, eases stiff muscles and joints, and tones the skin and muscles. Because of the buoyancy of water, hydrotherapy also allows people to exercise muscles that could not be worked on dry land, thereby increasing strength, mobility, and confidence. It can also be used to treat:

ACNE *SEE P.* 276
ALLERGIES *SEE PP.* 338–9
ARTHRITIS *SEE PP.* 346–7
ASTHMA *SEE PP.* 294–5
BACK PROBLEMS *SEE PP.* 344–5
BRONCHITIS *SEE P.* 299
BURSITIS *SEE P.* 349
CATARRH *SEE P.* 285
CHICKENPOX *SEE P.* 353
CHILBLAINS *SEE P.* 277
COLD SORES *SEE P.* 275
COUGHS *SEE P.* 297
CRAMP *SEE P.* 349
CYSTITIS *SEE P.* 316
DEPRESSION *SEE P.* 261
FIBROSITIS *SEE P.* 348
FLU *SEE P.* 298
GOUT *SEE P.* 337
LABOR PAINS *SEE P.* 328
MEASLES *SEE P.* 355
MIGRAINE *SEE P.* 269
MUMPS *SEE P.* 352
NEURALGIA *SEE P.* 267
PSORIASIS *SEE P.* 272
SHINGLES *SEE P.* 266
SINUSITIS *SEE P.* 284
STROKE *SEE P.* 359
TOOTHACHE *SEE P.* 288
VARICOSE VEINS *SEE P.* 306

FLOTATION THERAPY

Even though some people find the prospect of floating in water for two hours in a confined space extremely daunting, many of those who have tried flotation therapy swear by the experience. And research has shown that the use of a flotation tank can not only reduce stress levels by bringing about an extremely deep state of relaxation, but it can also have beneficial psychological results. At the moment, flotation therapy is available only in health clinics and specialized centers, but its adherents believe that it will soon be widespread. The flotation tank is completely enclosed and soundproofed, and the flotation session takes place in complete or semi-darkness. However, you can switch on a light at any time, and open the door.

The "sensory isolation flotation tank," now known more commonly simply as a "flotation tank," was developed in 1954 by Dr. John C. Lilly, an American neurophysiologist and psychoanalyst. Lilly, who is probably best known for his work into the relationship between human beings and dolphins, was trying to investigate how the human brain reacted when it was deprived of all external stimuli. At the outset of his experiments, Lilly had assumed that the lack of any stimulation would just make the brain "go to sleep." Instead he discovered that, freed of physical stimulation, the mind became more open to suggestion, capable of increased powers of imagination, and that problem-solving abilities improved.

In the 1970s, American researchers started to look further into the therapeutic effects of flotation tanks. They soon discovered that a session of "flotation

SELF-HELP

Flotation tanks for the home are available from specialist health shops and by mail order. Before buying, check that the door opens easily from the inside and that there is a full safety warranty. It would be sensible to ask your hydrotherapist for advice before making your purchase.

therapy," as it came to be called, helped people to achieve a state of deep relaxation. Soon flotation tanks were installed in clinics in a number of U.S. cities, and their use gradually spread to Europe, too. However, flotation therapy is still not as popular as therapists think it will be eventually, perhaps because of a general dislike of being shut up in a confined space.

HOW A FLOTATION TANK WORKS
Though the mechanism by which flotation therapy has psychological effects is not known, the way in which it reduces stress is more clearly understood. Lying in a flotation tank for up to two hours in an environment that contains no physical stimuli means that there are no external factors against which the body can react. As a result, the levels of stress hormones, such as epinephrine (adrenaline) and cortisol circulating in the bloodstream

RIGHT *A session in a flotation tank can be calming and therapeutic.*

are much reduced. At the same time, levels of endorphins – the body's own natural painkillers and "feel-good" hormones – rise. The combination of these two factors brings about a state of deep relaxation, and this lowers the heartrate and the rate of breathing, and reduces muscular tension generally.

USES OF FLOTATION THERAPY

The stress-reducing qualities of flotation therapy make it a useful preventive treatment that helps maintain good physical and mental health by making stress-related disorders less likely to develop. But, since it results in the production of endorphins, flotation therapy can also play a part in the treatment of chronic pain – that is, the long-lasting, nagging pain that remains when any acute pain has dissipated. Tense muscles cause chronic pain, for example, and pain in turn causes muscles to tense – a vicious cycle. The endorphins produced by the body as a result of flotation therapy can block the transmission of this pain to the brain – as no pain is felt, the muscles relax and the circle of pain is broken. As a result, flotation tank therapy is useful in cases involving chronic pain, including musculoskeletal disorders such as arthritis, headaches, and low back pain.

Because of its ability to alter psychological states, flotation therapy is often used to enhance meditation (*see pages 60–5*) and as an aid in psychotherapy (*see pages 188–95*), especially in the treatment of obsessive and addictive behavior.

LEFT *Flotation therapy can relieve persistent, chronic pain.*

PRECAUTIONS

■ Do not undergo flotation therapy if you have a history of psychosis or other psychological disorders, including claustrophobia.

■ Inform your hydrotherapist if you are suffering from anxiety and/or panic attacks, and ensure that he or she remains close by throughout the treatment.

■ Epsom salts can make some skin conditions worse, so check with your doctor before undergoing flotation therapy if you have a skin condition – a skin patch test may be necessary.

FLOTATION TANKS

A flotation tank is approximately 8ft (2.4m) long and 4ft (1.2m) wide. It is filled with about 10in (25cm) of water, kept at skin temperature – 98.6°F (35°C) – to reduce any distracting skin sensations. In fact, the tank is not so much full of water as of an extremely dense solution of Epsom salts, giving the water its buoyancy – the concentration of salt in a flotation tank is greater than that in the waters of the Dead Sea. Fresh air circulates inside the tank, and an intercom system allows you to speak to your therapist.

CONSULTING A PRACTITIONER

Most flotation tanks are found at health clinics or specialized flotation centers. The resident hydrotherapist (*see pp. 174–81*) will take a short medical history to check your suitability for the treatment – if you suffer from severe psychological problems or claustrophobia, for example, you should not use a flotation tank unless under strict medical supervision. If you are receiving flotation therapy as part of the treatment of an addiction or of obsessive behavior, your psychotherapist will also be present, and will be able to talk to you through a two-way microphone and speaker system.

Otherwise, after you have taken a shower and entered the tank, you can choose to float in silence or select an audio tape to suit your requirements – whether to learn a new language or for therapeutic purposes. Some centers also have video screens inside their flotation tanks, though many therapists frown on the use of them unless their purpose is to aid learning through visualization (*see pp. 214–17*). After two hours, the session finishes and you leave the tank and take another shower. However, you can finish the session before the two hours are up if you feel uncomfortable and choose to do so.

PATHFINDER

A session of up to two hours in a flotation tank reduces the levels of the stress hormones, increases the levels of the endorphins – the body's painkillers and "feel-good" hormones – and heightens mental alertness, responsiveness, and problem-solving abilities. The effects can last from a few hours to a few days, but the benefits are prolonged with subsequent sessions. Flotation therapy relieves pain and treats stress-related disorders, and certain psychological problems.

ADDICTIONS *SEE P.* 258
ANXIETY *SEE PP.* 256–7
HEADACHES *SEE P.* 288
STRESS *SEE PP.* 262–3

ABOVE *Flotation therapy can be used as part of the treatment for alcoholism.*

THE BATES METHOD AND VISION THERAPY

When William Horatio Bates, the New York ophthalmologist who devised the Method that bears his name, saw a small child being fitted with glasses he said, "It's enough to make the angels weep." His method of eye exercises was intended to do away with the need to wear glasses — he believed that glasses "imprison" our eyes, and that his techniques, in which the muscles around the eyes are allowed to relax and let the eyes heal themselves of a variety of disorders, were more natural. Since Bates's death, "vision therapists" have built on his work to provide other alternative forms of eye treatment.

William Bates was a young doctor when he came to the view that people should be encouraged to "throw away their glasses and see with their own eyes." Later, as an ophthalmologist, he was to devote his life to the natural treatment of eye disorders. In 1920, Bates published *The Cure of Imperfect Eyesight by Treatment Without Glasses*, which set out his techniques, and the book has been in print ever since.

Bates died in 1931, but a revised version of his book, called *Better Eyesight Without Glasses*, was published in 1940, and his second wife, Emily, continued to promote his Method with the assistance of Dr. Harold Peppard. In 1932, Gayelord Hauser published a book called *Keener Sight Without Glasses*, which linked elements of the Bates Method with considerations about diet. Today, the Bates Method is used throughout the world and still has many adherents, despite a book written in 1956 by Dr. Philip Pollack, an optometrist from Manhattan, New York City, U.S.A., called *The Truth About Eye Exercises*, which debunked it. However, "vision therapists" – some of whom also call themselves "developmental" or "behavioral" optometrists – have built on his original work and prescribe "learning lenses" for conditions such as dyslexia, and "3D-viewing," "pyramid" or "pinhole" glasses for eyestrain and other causes of impairment of vision.

THE THEORY

In one published article, Bates said, "Once you begin to wear glasses, the strength of the lenses must be increased periodically (because your eyes are getting weaker). Glasses ... act as a crutch and do not treat the cause of poor eyesight." He developed the theory that the lenses of the eyes do not change shape, and that the majority of vision problems are the result of either stress or emotional problems, which cause the muscles around the eye to become too tense. The answer, he believed, to problems ranging from short-sightedness, long-sightedness, astigmatism, and even cataracts and glaucoma, was to encourage, through the use of special eye exercises, the muscles to relax. Orthodox ophthalmologists maintain that defects in vision are the result of either a congenital (present at birth) defect in the shape of the eyeballs or the structure of the lenses, or of degenerative changes to them.

Modern vision therapists, in general, take an opposing view. They tend to believe that eye problems are due to a weakness in the muscles around the eyeballs, and prescribe exercises to strengthen them. Some vision therapists also advise the use of special glasses, involving bifocal and prism lenses, as well as hand-eye co-ordination exercises to treat learning disabilities as well as problems with vision.

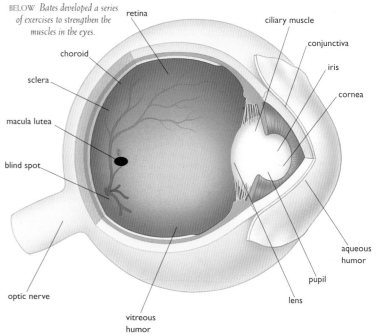

BELOW *Bates developed a series of exercises to strengthen the muscles in the eyes.*

retina
ciliary muscle
conjunctiva
choroid
iris
sclera
cornea
macula lutea
blind spot
aqueous humor
optic nerve
pupil
lens
vitreous humor

CONSULTING A PRACTITIONER

The Bates Method is primarily a self-help technique that is taught by individual practitioners, or learned by people who read Bates's books. The Method can be condensed into four separate techniques: palming; splashing; focusing; and swinging.

PALMING – *Place your palms over your eyes, making sure that no pressure is involved, so that all light is shut out from them. Then make a conscious effort to relax your whole body. Stare at the dark, wrapping yourself up in it and focusing purely on the blackness for about 15 minutes. Do this twice a day.*

SPLASHING – *In the morning, splash your eyes with first warm, then cold, water – up to 20 times. Do the same thing at night, but start with cold water.*

FOCUSING – *Hold something, such as a pencil, in your hand at arm's length out in front of you. Close one eye and focus on it for 10 seconds. Then take another object in your other hand, and, keeping the first object at arm's length, hold the second one a hand's length from your face. Focus on that for 10 seconds, then blink before focusing on the object held at arm's length. Repeat the whole exercise five times, two or three times a day.*

SWINGING – *Focus your eyes on some distant object – something in the view from your bedroom window, say. Sway from side to side – in a leisurely way, rather than energetically – while holding your focus. But, as you sway from side to side, you should blink your eyes: your left eye as you move to the left and your right eye as you move to the right. Continue for five to ten minutes, but repeat as often as you can during the day.*

PATHFINDER

The Bates Method, in particular, and vision therapy, in general, claim to cure a variety of eye problems by – in the first case – relaxing the muscles around the eyes, and – in the second case – by strengthening the same muscles and, sometimes, by using a variety of specially designed glasses. Both the Bates Method and vision therapy may be helpful for those with the conditions noted below; neither, however, should be used if glaucoma or any other disease involving the eyes is suspected, rather than a defect in vision that has had a gradual onset and is related to the aging process. If in doubt, consult your doctor.

CATARACT *SEE P.* 279
EYESTRAIN *SEE P.* 280
GLAUCOMA *SEE P.* 279

WATCHPOINT

The Bates Method is not a suitable form of treatment for any serious form of eye condition, such as glaucoma or cataracts. If you are in any doubt about your condition, consult your family doctor.

HUXLEY'S BRAVE NEW WORLD

British novelist Aldous Huxley, whose best-known books are probably *Brave New World* and *The Island*, had suffered from problems with vision for all his life: the corneas of his eyes had been scarred since childhood. But Huxley was treated by Margaret Dorst Corbett, who ran two schools that used the Bates Method, and he claimed that her treatment had changed his life. He became an enthusiastic promoter of the system. Huxley died in 1963, still convinced of the merits of the Bates Method. However, skeptics point to a newspaper report of a speech he made in 1952, when it seemed for a while as if he was reading the speech from his notes; in fact, he had memorized it, and when his memory let him down he had to resort to a magnifying glass.

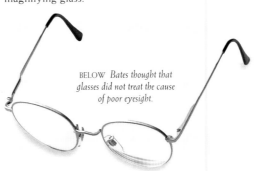

BELOW *Bates thought that glasses did not treat the cause of poor eyesight.*

PART THREE

MIND AND
SPIRIT THERAPIES

INTRODUCTION

ABOVE *Freud constructed a theory of human personality and the techniques of psychoanalysis.*

The concept of psychological illness, which is completely taken for granted today, has developed from the work of Sigmund Freud in the last century, even though ideas about its origins and treatment have diverged considerably since then. There is now a baffling variety of treatments available for problems which are considered to have mental or emotional origins – with over 300 different types of psychotherapy alone on offer. In addition, there are mind and spirit therapies that are claimed to treat a wide range of problems rather than psychological ill-health as such.

With the growing understanding of the links between mind and body and the way in which one influences the other, it is now increasingly accepted that mind and spirit therapies may alleviate symptoms that are apparently physical in nature, as well as those that are caused by some organic illness. Many people are referred by their doctors for some type of psychotherapy to treat a range of problems from phobia to depression, from addiction to obsessive behavior and many more. Counseling and approaches such as dance, art and music therapies may also be recommended as an adjunct to other types of treatment for both physical and psychological ill-health. Many individuals who are apparently well choose to consult a counselor or therapist for help with difficulties such as relationship or family problems or because they want to change their attitudes, behavior or to possibly achieve some kind of personal growth.

While many of the therapies around today are now very much part of mainstream medicine, others are regarded by orthodox doctors as less effective or soundly based and a few as somewhat dubious. Any therapy that works on the mind has potential risks, especially for those who have some form of psychological illness or who may have unrecognized difficulties which could surface during treatment. For this reason, it is vital that the therapist who treats you is the right one and that he or she has a sound understanding of your problems as well as of the aim of the treatment. If you are choosing a therapist for yourself rather than consulting one recommended specifically by your doctor, you must spend time establishing the background and training of the person concerned, what the treatment involves and the way in which it is designed to work. Even if you have been referred by a health professional, you still need to be sure that the choice of therapist is right for you, and be prepared to change if you have real doubts about the person's ability to address your problems for whatever reason.

Psychotherapy and counseling of all kinds are 'talking' therapies, but the way in which they are conducted, the time they take and their approaches and purposes differ considerably. Some are organized on a one-to-one basis, others in groups with a therapist and some may use either or both depending on circumstances. Broadly speaking, the cognitive therapies are more tailored towards solving problems in the here and now, psychoanalysis delves extensively into your early life and emotions, while the humanistic therapies are often tailored towards developing self awareness and personal growth. Counseling will normally be most appropriate in specific fields such as relationship worries or family problems.

Within these generalizations, however, there is a wide range of theoretical approaches, with therapists

BELOW *A one-to-one session is a common way to talk through any issues.*

therapist

patient

ABOVE *As a non-verbal technique, music therapy can help people communicate by other means.*

ABOVE *Art therapy is both a treatment and self-help techniques.*

ABOVE *Therapeutic tapes can also aid the relaxation process.*

ABOVE *The hypnotic state can be described as extreme mental and physical relaxation.*

drawing to greater or lesser degrees on the various different schools of thought. As well as finding the treatment best suited to your psychological needs, you also need to consider whether you will feel personally comfortable in a given clinical situation – confrontation, role-playing and drama, which are a feature of some therapies, are not for everyone.

You should be able to have an initial consultation before you and the therapist decide to proceed, in which you should have the opportunity to assess the person and their approach for yourself and the therapist should

SUMMARY

Once you have found the right therapist and begun regular consultations, it is important to understand that however skillful, they cannot work magic. Much of the work will have to be done by you and without your full engagement in the treatment process and co-operation with your therapist, little or nothing is likely to be achieved. At times you may be tackling difficult and painful issues, which may mean some consultations are distressing or even infuriating, but there is no doubt that the majority of people can learn and benefit from such encounters, emerging stronger and psychologically healthier as from the experience.

also be able to say whether they are in a position to offer the kind of help you need. At this point too, it is wise to ask how many sessions are likely to be needed, over what period of time, how soon can you might expect to reap the benefits and, if appropriate, the cost of treatment.

There are many other types of therapy in which 'talking' is not used as a treatment tool: dance, music and art therapies, for example; biofeedback and autogenic training, sound, light and color therapies also use non-verbal techniques. Hypnotism is different again in that while talking is involved, it is the effect of the altered state of consciousness induced by the therapist which is of prime importance in treatment.

Some of these therapies cannot be practiced on a self-help basis, though many will involve your being given exercises and homework to do between sessions. Similarly, you may be taught how to do self-hypnosis and how to apply the skills learned in biofeedback and autogenic training on your own, though individuals vary in how well they are able to achieve the required mental states by themselves. You may also be taught dream work and visualization, and considerable commitment may be needed from you in such cases.

PSYCHOTHERAPY AND COUNSELING

Psychotherapy and counseling are umbrella terms used to describe the plethora of treatments by which trained practitioners help those who have mental and emotional problems. The origins of psychotherapy stem from the work of Austrian psychiatrist Sigmund Freud and his followers, which has done as much to define the 20th century as Einstein's theory of relativity and the application of Marxist theories of communism. In the face of the failure of conventional medicine to cure even such everyday problems as depression, anxiety, and phobias, psychotherapy and counseling have diversified and flourished to an extraordinary extent. Today they form an important part of modern medical care, and a large number of hospitals, doctors' offices, and health clinics employ psychotherapists and counselors.

Until the 19th century, human mental and behavioral disorders were ascribed to the operation of malign external influences, or to imbalances within the body. It was believed that demonic possession, witchcraft, and evil spirits were what drove people mad, and that disorders of the blood could lead to ill-temper, depression, timidity, or impetuosity. The brain itself was regarded as a mechanism, separated entirely from the soul – the essence of our humanity – which had its seat somewhere else in the body. In preindustrial times, people with emotional or behavioral problems were helped either by their priest or by other members of their community. However, in the 19th century, following the Industrial Revolution and the increasing secularization of society, there arose new institutions and professions devoted to problems of mental illness. Science replaced religion as the main framework for understanding madness and the insane became subject to much greater social control.

Psychoanalysis

Most of us are familiar with such terms as "ego," "id," and "Oedipus complex" *(see page 192)*, since Freud's ideas have become part of everyday speech. However, it is not just in the field of language that Freud made a major contribution to the modern world. He transformed both the ways in which we think of the human mind and our understanding of human personality.

Freud's investigations into the disturbed mind inevitably led to the use of psychoanalysis as a form of psychotherapy. The very act of uncovering repressed memories and desires provided the means of curing their effects. Over the years he developed a number of techniques – such as "free association" and "transference" – which are still very much in use today *(see page 192)*. After about 1910, however, the psychoanalytic movement

began to split apart. Carl Jung developed his own school of "analytical psychology" *(see page 194)* and Alfred Adler propounded "Adlerian psychoanalysis" *(see page 195)*. Other followers of Freud, such as Melanie Klein *(see page 195)*, broke away to work in the fields of child psychology and the psychology of learning.

However, Freudian psychoanalysis and its offshoots were soon to be joined by other approaches to the study and manipulation of the mind. Psychotherapy in its various forms entered a phase of extraordinary growth that continues to this day.

Behavioral Therapy

The first significant challenge to Freud's theories of human personality and psychoanalysis came from the field of animal behavior, and in particular from two American researchers, John B. Watson and B. F. Skinner *(see pages 196–7)*. In their view, human behavior was entirely the product of conditioning. That is, desirable behavior could be produced and undesirable behavior discouraged through a system of rewards and punishments. The "unconscious" mind, with its dark motives and repressed desires, was simply irrelevant. Therapy could be achieved by manipulation of behavior and attitudes through application of the correct reward and punishment regime *(see pages 196–9)*.

In certain areas, including education and the treatment of such phenomena as obsessions, phobias, and addictive behaviors, Watson and Skinner's ideas and techniques are still influential. More importantly, however, they prepared the ground for the "cognitive" therapies that were to emerge after World War II. These, too, rejected the necessity to delve deeply into past experiences and their effects on the unconscious mind, and concentrated on the need to address problems in the "here and now."

CHOOSING A THERAPIST

With so many different types of therapy and counseling available, it can be extremely difficult to know which one to choose. Much will depend on the problem that you wish to solve, your own particular personality, and how much time and money you have available.

The table below gives the main branches (or "orientations") of therapy and counseling – fuller descriptions of theory and technique can be found in the following pages. You should study these, as well as consulting friends and your doctor, before deciding which type of therapy is suitable for you. The better informed you are beforehand, the more likely you are to make an appropriate choice. Whatever you decide, it will help if you bear the following points in mind.

✳ The best person to refer you to a psychotherapist or counselor is a qualified medical practitioner. That way you can be sure that the therapist will be appropriately trained, and that the form of therapy is likely to be suitable for your needs.

✳ Be clear about what you want to achieve from therapy. If your problem is related to a specific area – problems at work or with relationships – then some form of cognitive therapy will be more appropriate than a psychoanalytic or humanistic approach. If you are more concerned with your general lifestyle and are looking for personal growth and development, then a humanistic approach would be more suitable for you. If you want to investigate your personality and its development at a deep and profound level, then psychoanalytic therapy may be the answer.

✳ Choose a form of therapy that suits your personality. If you are outgoing and enjoy the company of other

people, then some form of group therapy might be most appropriate. If you hate the very idea of standing up in front of others, or of role-playing, then one-to-one counseling would be best. If, on the other hand, lack of self-confidence is one of the problems you want to address, you might benefit from a course of therapy that allows both individual and group sessions at the appropriate stages of treatment.

✳ Remember that you are not stuck with a particular type of therapy or counseling, even when you have started a course of consultations. There is nothing to stop you trying out two different counselors from different "orientations" at the same time (assuming that you can afford the time and money) before settling on the one that suits you best.

✳ The relationship with your analyst or counselor is vital. If you feel that your counselor is not sympathetic to you and is not helping you, then you are free to stop the course at any time – no criticism of the counselor is implied if you do so. Even counselors have their own attitudes and personalities. They cannot change these to suit a client: the best they can do is to try to use the most appropriate aspects of their own personalities in the ways that will most help their clients. If you cannot develop a relationship of mutual trust, then it is better to end the consultations and start again.

ABOVE *In one-to-one counseling it is essential for the patient and therapist to have a relationship of confidence and trust.*

PATHFINDER

People undergoing psychotherapy and counseling range from those with a generalized dissatisfaction with life to those with quite serious mental disturbance. The main uses of psychoanalytical techniques are in the treatment of:

ADDICTION *SEE P.* 258

ANXIETY *SEE P.* 256

DEPRESSION *SEE P.* 261

EATING DISORDERS *SEE P.* 265

ECZEMA AND DERMATITIS *SEE P.* 273

HIV AND AIDS *SEE PP.* 340–41

HYPERVENTILATION *SEE P.* 301

LABOR PAINS *SEE P.* 328

MISCARRIAGE *SEE P.* 325

POST-DELIVERY PROBLEMS *SEE P.* 329

PSORIASIS *SEE P.* 272

STRESS *SEE P.* 262–3

STROKE *SEE P.* 359

TYPES OF THERAPY AND COUNSELING

Psychoanalytic Therapies
(see pages 188–95)
Freudian psychoanalysis
Jungian pschoanalytic psychotherapy
Adlerian psychotherapy
Psychodynamic counseling

Behavioral and Cognitive Therapies
(see pages 196–99)
Behavioral therapy
Cognitive and cognitive-analytical behavior therapy
Rational-emotive behavior therapy (REBT)
Reality therapy
Personal construct therapy
Brief (solution-focused) therapy

Humanistic therapies
(see pages 200–3)
Gestalt therapy
Person-centered therapy
Transactional analysis
Primal therapy and rebirthing

Transpersonal and Integrative Therapies
(see pages 204–5)
Neurolinguistic programing

Transpersonal therapy
Psychosynthesis
Bioenergetics

Family Therapy
(see pages 296–7)
Relationship counseling

Group Therapy
(see pages 208–9)
Psychodrama
Encounter groups

MODERN PSYCHOTHERAPY AND COUNSELING

BELOW *Freudian psychoanalysis failed to heal the psychological wounds opened by World War II, and psychotherapy began to take new directions to cope with these modern challenges.*

After World War II, the nature of psychotherapy and counseling began to change, particularly on the west coast of the U.S. Doubts about the validity of classical Freudian analysis began to intensify. All too often, psychoanalysis seemed to be an interminable process, lasting many years and with no discernible improvement at the end of it. As was often pointed out, Freud drew his experience and research data from a limited practice with a small number of cases in prewar Vienna. His findings were unlikely to apply – at least without substantial modification – to a world that had recently been through the major trauma and social upheavals of a world war. Psychologists and psychotherapists began to look for quicker, more pragmatic, ways of dealing with people and their mental and emotional problems.

This development contributed to the emergence of two separate strands of therapeutic thinking. The first included the theories generally grouped under the heading of "cognitive" therapies. The second contained the so-called "humanistic" and "person-centered" therapies.

Cognitive Therapies

The term "cognitive" relates to knowing, perception and awareness, and cognitive therapies tend to concentrate on people's perceptions and misperceptions of themselves and the world around them. The basic ideas behind cognitive therapies sprang from the work of clinical psychologists in the U.S. during the 1950s and 1960s. As a result of their work, they concluded that many abnormal states of mind were the results of, rather than the causes of, undesirable patterns of behavior and irrational and habitual patterns of thought. They therefore devised therapies aimed at replacing these negative and harmful behaviors and attitudes with more positive and beneficial ones (*see pages 198–9*).

BELOW *During any course of psychotherapy or counseling, you will build up a strong rapport with your chosen therapist.*

In due course, the cognitive therapies produced offshoots in the form of "rational-emotive" and "rational-emotive behavior" therapies, reality therapy, and in such hybrids as cognitive-behavioral and cognitive-analytical therapies. Cognitive therapy is also the fundamental technique used for brief, or problem-focused, therapy and for therapies that are designed to reduce different types of stress.

Both cognitive and behavioral therapies have a structured, problem-solving, or symptom reduction approach to psychological treatment, with the therapist playing a very active role.

The Humanistic Movement

Humanistic psychotherapy encourages people to explore their feelings and take responsibility for their own actions. The emphasis is on achieving one's potential and on self-development. Although the humanistic trend in psychotherapy is mainly associated with developments in therapy and counseling in the U.S. in the 1950s, its origins can be traced back to the influential "Gestalt" movement (*see page* 200).

Gestalt therapy (*see pages* 200–1) was created in the 1940s by Frederick and Laura Perls. An essential feature of this therapy is its extreme hostility to theorizing and its concern with working with a person's immediate experience. Gestalt emphasized the "here and now" and stressed that the "client" should be seen as an holistic individual to be understood in the context of the whole environment as he or she perceives it. Gestalt also developed an array of new techniques, often involving drama and role-playing, that were to be freely borrowed by later schools of therapy.

The humanistic trend was further developed by two American psychotherapists, Carl Rogers and Abraham Maslow, in the 1950s. Carl Rogers introduced the

ABOVE *American psychotherapist Carl Rogers pioneered the idea of "person-centered" psychotherapy in the 1950s.*

concept of "person-centered psychotherapy" (*see page* 202), in which the role of the therapist is non-directive and aimed largely at allowing clients to work through and solve their problems for themselves. Maslow constructed his theories around a hierarchy of basic human needs, from food and security to self-confidence and self-respect, that must be met if people are to achieve a sense of self-fulfilment. The improvement and enhancement of self-esteem and self-confidence are crucial to this type of therapy, as is the whole notion of personal growth and development.

Psychotherapy and Counseling Today

Other forms of humanistic therapy include transactional analysis (TA), and primal therapy and rebirthing. TA (*see page 202*) proposes that everyone has three "ego states," composed of a child, adult, and parent within them. In each social interaction, one ego state dominates. Primal therapy and rebirthing (*see page 203*) are based on the theory that suppressed birth or infancy traumas can resurface in later life as neuroses, depression, and many other psychological problems.

Recent years have seen an enormous proliferation of types of psychotherapy and counseling, each with its own particular blend of theory and practice. The integrative therapies borrow freely from other types of therapy, while the transpersonal therapies interweave a strand of spirituality into their therapeutic practices (*see pages 204–5*). There is, particularly in the U.S., a brand of psychotherapy to suit all.

PRECAUTIONS

When carried out by a properly qualified practitioner, all recognized forms of psychotherapy and counseling are safe. However, you should always take the following precautions:

■ Do not undertake any form of therapy or counseling if you suffer from a serious mental disorder.

■ Always ask which professional association he or she belongs to, and, if in doubt, contact the association to check. Counselors should generally have two to three years' training in the appropriate therapy; psychotherapists should have four to five years' training, and psychoanalysts should normally have trained for considerably longer, often with orthodox medical training as well. All practitioners should have undergone analysis or counseling themselves.

■ Establish from the outset the likely duration and cost of treatment. Check whether you are expected to pay for the initial consultation before you attend.

Most doctors now accept the value of psychotherapy or counseling, particularly where emotional distress has been caused by a particular event or change in lifestyle. Bereavement, news of terminal illness (such as cancer), marital breakdown and sexual dysfunction, and addictions are all routinely treated by counseling. Counseling is also automatically offered to survivors of traumatic events, such as major accidents, or kidnappings. Large companies often offer counseling to staff who have been made redundant. Student counseling services are widely available, and are backed up by medical expertise. Most surgeries and health clinics have counselors, and almost all hospitals have counseling services available.

Medical opinion is more divided on the value of particular types of therapy. Cognitive and behavioral therapies have proved useful for dealing with anxiety, phobias, depression, and relationship and sexual problems. Almost all doctors would concede that people suffering from emotional distress can be helped by sympathetic counseling, and, as a result, require less conventional care.

There is less research evidence for the efficacy of long-term psychoanalysis than the shorter cognitive-behavioral techniques. Traditional psychoanalysis is also relatively time consuming and expensive, making it less cost effective, and so is less used, particularly in Britain.

PSYCHOTHERAPY AND COUNSELING TODAY

Both psychotherapy and counseling have become an integral part of the social landscape. In orthodox medical practice, clients are regularly referred to counseling services for specific problems, such as addiction, bereavement, post-traumatic stress, marriage break-down, sexual problems, student anxieties, delinquency, stress, and a variety of other emotional and behavioral problems. Counseling is widely accepted as a valuable adjunct to orthodox medical treatment in the care of terminal cancer patients. Therapy is available for individuals, groups, families, or couples. In most cases, these services are available through normal health care channels and are paid for by health services or insurance.

There are also more and more people who seek therapy outside the normal health services. In today's increasingly fragmented societies, people often turn to therapy to counteract feelings of alienation or loneliness, or general dissatisfaction with their present lifestyles and relationships. It is on this fertile ground that the fringe therapies flourish. While most alternative therapists are honest, not all are so scrupulous. Lack of government regulation has allowed members of such quasi-religious sects as the Church of Scientology to present themselves as therapists. Potentially dangerous encounter-group therapies such as EST (Erhard Seminar Training) have also flourished.

In general, however, psychotherapy and counseling have proved their value. Whether you are seeking help for a specific problem, or are simply dissatisfied with one or more areas of your life and personality, you should be able to find in the next few pages of this book a type of therapy that suits your needs.

Counseling aims include:

• Self-awareness

• Self-acceptance

• Self-actualization

• Enlightenment

• Problem-solving

• Psychological education (gaining ideas and techniques with which to understand and control behavior)

• Acquisition of social skills

• Cognitive change (modification of beliefs or thought patterns associated with self-destructive behavior)

• Behavioral change (modification of self-destructive patterns of behavior)

• Systematic change (changing the way social systems, e.g. families, operate)

• Empowerment (working on skills that will enable the client to confront social inequalities

• Restitution (making amends for destructive behavior)

RIGHT *Counseling helps many people resolve feelings of fear, depression, and alienation in the modern world.*

FREUDIAN PSYCHOANALYSIS

Freud's great achievements were the construction of a comprehensive theory of human personality, in both an ordered and disordered state, and the development of the basic techniques of psychoanalysis. Modern Freudian psychoanalysis still draws heavily on both. Freud was undoubtedly a genius, but his approach reflected the intellectual and social fashions of the time. For example, the idea of libido as a general life energy reflects 19th-century biological theories. Also, the view that emotional problems had a sexual cause was widely held by his contemporaries.

The Theory of Personality

Freud considered that we are all ruled by three separate entities within the mind – the "id," the "ego," and the "superego." The id resides in the unconscious part of the mind, and is the source of our most basic urges, desires, feelings, and impulses. The ego represents the conscious part of the mind, and is responsible for thought, self-awareness, judgement, and decision-making. The superego is also part of the unconscious mind. It acts as an overall censor and controller of our thoughts and actions – it is, to all intents and purposes, our conscience. These three factions are motivated by a unitary life-force known as the "libido," which Freud considered to be mainly driven by sexual energy.

Mental problems arise when the ego, id, and superego are in conflict. If one of the three is consistently thwarted or frustrated by one or both of the others, the suppressed feelings emerge as emotional, behavioral, or even physical disorders. In Freud's view, most of these problems arose from experiences in early childhood, and were often related to the psychosexual development of the child. Partly from his own experience of undergoing psychoanalysis, he identified his famous "Oedipus complex," according to which the son strives constantly to oust the father in his mother's affections. The resulting conflicts and frustrations can emerge in myriad ways in later life.

Psychoanalytic Techniques

For Freud, the essence of therapy through psychoanalysis was the uncovering of subconscious and repressed material, usually through extensive exploration of the patient's past. He originally tried hypnosis (*see pages 210–15*) for this, but soon became dissatisfied with the results. He developed instead a technique known as "free association" in which

ABOVE The development of the id, ego, and superego were essential to Freud's theory of psychoanalysis.

RIGHT *Austrian psychologist Sigmund Freud (1856-1939) is regarded as the founding father of psychoanalysis.*

the patient was encouraged, while relaxed, to say more or less anything that came into their heads, and to follow any train of thought, no matter how whimsical or meandering it seemed. He also sought to uncover repressed material in the patient's subconscious mind through the analysis of dreams, which he had used a great deal during his own psychoanalysis (his best-known book, *The Interpretation of Dreams*, appeared in 1899), and through revealing slips of the tongue – "Freudian slips."

A further key element of Freudian analysis is the phenomenon of transference. During the course of treatment, the patient comes to identify the doctor with objects of love or hate from the past – often of their own family members. This can lead to the formation of strong emotional attachments, to which the analyst responds by assuming the role assigned to him or her. Freud regarded this relationship as crucial to the success of therapy, and an essential tool in the uncovering of the patient's unconscious psyche.

CONSULTING A PSYCHOANALYST

In popular mythology, the analyst is something of a figure of fun – a bearded "shrink" with a thick central European accent who is usually as mad as, if not madder than, his patient. Patients fare little better: as portrayed by Woody Allen and other film-makers, they are generally entirely dependent, infantile human beings given to calling their analyst at the slightest sign of crisis, whatever the time of day or night.

The reality, of course, is quite different. For one thing, many analysts today are women, and very few were born, or educated, anywhere other than the country in which they practice. Many are young. They are among the most intensively trained of all medical specialists. They are also, through their professional associations, regulated by strict rules of conduct and behavior.

Finding a suitable analyst may be difficult. It is probably best to rely on a recommendation from your doctor, or a trusted friend. If you know anything about the different schools of analysis – Freudian, Jungian, Adlerian, Kleinian, Lacanian, to name but a few – then it is worth finding out which one the analyst follows. However, analysts are almost as variable as their patients, and such labels present only a very broad picture of the field of psychoanalysis.

Before embarking on analysis, you should be aware that treatment is likely to continue for several years and can be expensive in terms of time and money. Two to five sessions of 50 minutes a week for two years is generally considered the minimum, and five years or more is common. Many people, however, are prepared to sacrifice such luxuries as a new car or part of their annual holiday for the peace of mind and support that they perceive analysis as providing.

What Happens in Analysis?

The first consultation is devoted to a discussion of the frequency of sessions, cost, and likely course of treatment. You will be asked to explain why you think you need analysis, and what you hope to gain from it. At this stage the analyst should state frankly if he or she does not feel able to help you. You, in turn, should feel free to decide that you do not wish to work with this particular analyst.

Subsequent consultations should all follow a similar pattern. The analyst will attempt to relax you and make you comfortable (the proverbial couch is still used, but an armchair is more common). You will then be encouraged to talk freely about whatever comes into your mind. Throughout the session, the analyst will guide you towards areas that he or she thinks might be of interest. Part of the analyst's skill lies in picking up cues about topics that might deserve further investigation – you might appear to be avoiding certain topics, or become hesitant and confused, or angry when particular subjects arise. The direction in which the analyst pushes you will be determined by the school to which the analyst belongs. Freudian analysts will try to take you back in time, to your early experiences and traumatic events; Jungian analysts will take a broader approach,

UNDUE INFLUENCE?

While Sigmund Freud was undoubtedly the father of psychoanalysis, his reputation has not survived the century since the publication of the case of Anna O. intact.

Critics point out that, by its very nature, psycho-analysis is unscientific – in the sense that no controlled experiments are possible and that any data collected are much influenced by the perception of the psychoanalyst.

In addition, doubt has recently been cast on the nature of Anna O's relationship with Freud. Some critics go as far as to say that some of what is said in the book *Studies in Hysteria* was either exaggerated or invented by Freud.

OEDIPUS COMPLEX

A psychoanalytical term coined by Freud to describe the unconscious sexual feelings of a son for his mother and a jealous hatred of his father, the Oedipus complex is regarded as a normal desire and applies just as much to girls as to boys. Jung described the female equivalent, in which a girl desires her father, as the Electra complex.

LEFT *One-to-one counselling can be intense for the patient.*

concentrating on present feelings and emotions and on your dreams and fantasies, as well as on your early memories. Some analysts will be more interested in early sexual feelings, some in feelings of power-lessness or helplessness, and others in the actual words you use. In all cases, however, the aim is to explore your unconscious and to identify the conflicts and unresolved emotions that are causing problems in the waking present. Identifying and confronting these may bring about a cure, but, even if not, you will have a much deeper knowledge and under-standing of yourself.

As treatment continues, you are likely to find that you are experiencing strong emotions – love, hate, and intense like or dislike – toward your analyst. You will become strongly dependent on him or her. This is the phenomenon known as "transference," and the analyst will encourage the relationship to develop. Transference represents the displacement of all the feelings you have about people from your past – parents, siblings, friends, and lovers – onto your analyst. In this way, these feelings can be explored and analysed in the present.

ABOVE *For Carl Gustav Jung (1875–1961) the unconscious was filled with psychological truths held collectively by the whole of humanity.*

ABOVE *Jung viewed mystical expereience and religion as integral parts of the human personality.*

JUNGIAN ANALYTICAL PSYCHOTHERAPY

Carl Gustav Jung (1875–1961) was a Swiss psychiatrist, and an early follower of Sigmund Freud's tech-niques. He was one of those who attended the first conference of the International Psychoanalytical Association in Vienna in 1908, and is considered to have been one of the founding fathers of the psychoana-lytic movement and its findings.

The movement began to show signs of fission. By 1911, Jung had parted company with Freud, to found the movement he called "analytical psychology." The main source of disagreement was the importance Freud attached to infantile sexuality in childhood development and in the later appearance of neuroses. Jung was in

many ways as profound a thinker as Freud, and much more eclectic: he was sympathetic to religious and mystical experience (for which he was much teased by Freud) and incorporated these into his theories of human personality. His ideas have been influential in the devel-opment of many of the humanistic and "New Age" psychotherapies.

Jungian Theory

Jung took a much more holistic view of human nature than Freud, and this affected his attitudes toward therapy. As he said himself: "The object of therapy is not the neurosis but the man who has the neurosis." Furthermore, he believed that neurosis itself came not from "...some obscure corner of the uncon-scious, as many psychotherapists still struggle to believe; it comes from the totality of a man's life and from all the experiences that have accumulated over the years and decades, and finally, not merely from his life as an individual but from his psychic experience within the family or even the social group."

Central to Jung's theory of personality was the idea that people are motivated by the will to live and by a lifelong desire for self-fulfilment and "wholeness" – a process he called "individuation" – rather than simply by sex. He also believed that our subconscious minds are populated by shared myths and memories – the "collective unconscious" – as well as by individual expe-riences, instincts, and desires. He also coined the terms "introvert" and "extrovert" to describe the two basic personality types and the different ways in which they approached the rest of the world.

Jungian Analytic Techniques

As an analyst, Jung was pragmatic and flexible. He was

BELOW *The interpretation of dreams is central to Jungian analytical psychotherapy.*

very aware of the dangers of bringing his own assumptions to bear on a particular case and considered that every individual case should be treated differently and according to its own merits. As he wrote: "The patient is there to be treated and not to verify a theory."

He also took the view that neurosis represented an attempt to resolve unrecognized problems and, as such, provided an opportunity for growth and self-realization. At least part of the role of therapy was to build on a patient's neuroses and turn them to positive advantage.

Like Freud, Jung believed in the importance of the transference relationship, which he saw not just as a means of resolving past conflicts, but also as a crucial tool in the exploration of the significance of the conflict and in putting it to creative use. He also believed in the use of free association and in the significance of dreams.

Superficially, Jungian analysis is very similar to Freudian analysis, depending on verbal communication between patient and analyst in a relaxing environment. However, the analyst's responses will often lead the patient in very different directions to those determined by Freudian analysis, and the emphasis will be much more on emotional problems as they affect the present life and circumstances of the patient. Treatment is similarly protracted. A minimum of one or two 50-minute consultations a week for six months is required, and two years or more is usual.

ADLERIAN PSYCHOANALYSIS
Alfred Adler (1870–1937) was an Austrian eye-specialist who became interested in Freud's work and switched to psychiatry. Like Jung, he was one of the founders of the psychoanalytical movement, and he also rebelled against the Freudian identification of the libido with the sex drive.

Adler went on to found his own school of psychoanalysis. He was interested in the effects of inherited disorders and disabilities on mental states, but he is best known for his theory that the primary motivating force is not sex but the will to dominate. It was Adler who first coined the phrase "inferiority complex."

Adler's psychoanalytic technique displays some similarities to later cognitive therapies (see pages 198–9). Transference is not one of the main tools of analysis, although establishing and maintaining a good working relationship with the client is important. The emphasis initially is on understanding how the client's mind works – his or her "psychodynamics" – and on helping clients to develop insight and understanding of their own minds and personalities. From there, the analyst moves on to help clients understand what basic mistakes they may be making in their lifestyles and in their relationships, and encourages them to seek out new alternatives and express their freedom to choose.

KLEINIAN PSYCHOANALYSIS
The Austrian psychiatrist Melanie Klein (1882–1960) was a leading figure in psychiatric circles from the 1920s until her death, and another early disciple of Freud's who came to disagree with him over the importance of infantile sexuality. She eventually broke with Freud, and, between the two world wars, evolved her own theories of personality and neurosis which have been influential in psychoanalytic practice ever since. Echoes of her work can be found in the theories of both the leading child psychologists, Jean Piaget and Erik Erikson.

Klein specialized in child psychoanalysis and believed that childhood development was influenced as much by the need to make sense of the outside world, and to form social relationships within it, as it was in coming to terms with their own bodies and developing sexuality. Kleinian analysis attempts to identify the areas in which this process has gone wrong or is incomplete and correct them accordingly.

PSYCHODYNAMIC THERAPY
Alone among the psychoanalytic therapies, psychodynamic therapy or counseling can be used to address specific rather than general problems – family relationships, for example (see pages 206–7) – and can last a relatively short time. Some 20 to 40 sessions may be sufficient to deal with a particular issue.

Psychodynamic therapy seeks to make sense of the present, in terms of the patient's way of life and the problems that arise in day-to-day living. To do this will often involve probing into the past, to search out the roots of current malaise. The techniques of transference and free association are still used, as in other forms of psychoanalysis, and other techniques may be borrowed from several different schools, depending on the inclination and experience of the therapist.

The aim is to give the patient an awareness of the causes of present difficulties and give him or her the confidence to exercise their freedom to change their lives for the better.

ABOVE Melanie Klein developed a technique of analyzing children at play in order to gain insight into their fantasies and anxieties.

BELOW Psychodynamic therapy seeks to resolve the mental conflicts and destructive inner drives of the patient.

BEHAVIORAL AND COGNITIVE THERAPIES

ABOVE *Ivan Pavlov (1849–1936) found that conditioned reflexes in dogs were applicable to human behavior.*

The behavioral and cognitive therapies are more direct and pragmatic than either psychoanalytical or humanistic techniques. They are based on the straightforward notion that undesirable patterns of behavior – for example, shyness or irrational fears and phobias – are the cause of personality problems and not the result of them. Cure the undesirable behavior, and the whole personality can be restored to good health. A whole range of techniques is used, from the relatively crude system of "rewards" and "punishments" applied by the behaviorists to the more subtle manipulation of people's perception of themselves and their association with the world around them. Nevertheless, these therapies all offer a way of tackling specific problems and they have the advantage of offering measurable progress in a reasonably short period of time.

BEHAVIORAL THERAPY

Behaviorism was an attempt to explain human pyschology through studies of the behavior of animals. The ideas on which behavioral therapy are based came originally from the work of Ivan Pavlov, a Russian physiologist and winner of the 1904 Nobel Prize for medicine. During his work with dogs, Pavlov found that he could induce them to salivate by consistently ringing a bell whenever they were given food. Eventually, the sound of the bell was sufficient to cause salivation, even when it was not accompanied by food. Pavlov termed this reaction a "conditioned reflex": the dogs' behavior had been conditioned by learning and experience.

In the ensuing years, a number of researchers, notably the Americans John B. Watson and B. F. Skinner, began to apply these findings to the study of human behavior. They could see no reason why what applied to animals should not apply to people, and argued that if our behavior is the product of learning and the environment, then it should be possible to change it by behavior modification.

The popularity of behaviorism coincided with the growth of the advertising industry, with its needs for controlling and manipulating consumers' desires for certain products. Watson eventually abandoned his academic studies in order to become an advertising executive.

Positive Reinforcement

Behavioral therapists believe that poorly adapted behavior and negative attitudes feed back into the environment, making it worse and reinforcing the stimuli that caused the problems in the first place. But, if we can change our behavior for the better, we also change our environment for the better, setting in motion a spiral of continual positive reinforcement and behavioral improvement.

Therapists see no reason to delve into the past to find out why a particular pattern of behavior has formed – although memories, dreams, and fantasies may be part of the patient's self-image that needs to be changed. The aim of therapy is simply to correct the undesirable behavior patterns and perceptions, and to encourage the formation of behaviors and attitudes that are well-adapted and productive.

BELOW *Behavioral cognitive therapies are used to treat undesirable patterns of behavior and stress-related disorders.*

heightened stress levels and heart rate

irrational response to situation

CONSULTING A BEHAVIORAL THERAPIST

As with other forms of therapy, the actual techniques used vary according to the experience and preferences of the particular practitioner and the nature of the specific problem to be cured. However, the basic techniques used in behavioral therapy are very much the same.

Therapy begins with a comprehensive personality assessment, using a method known as "BASIC ID diagnosis." The letters stand for Behavior (your public, observable, behavior patterns and habits); Affect (a psychological term for feelings, moods, and emotions); Sensation (how you experience the world through your senses, including aches and pains, and other pleasant or unpleasant sensations); Imagery (how you view yourself and your personality); Cognition (your personal "philosophy" of the world, your ideas and understanding); Interpersonal relationships (how you relate to other people); and Drugs and biology (what medication or other drugs you might be taking, your state of health, and any concerns you may have about it).

Once this assessment has been carried out, the therapist will help you to identify the areas that need attention, and discuss ways of dealing with them. Specific goals will be set rather than general ones. For example, the therapist will suggest dealing with problems with family relationships by focusing on a specific situation in which the problems occur. You will be asked to examine how your own attitudes and behavior may be making the situation worse, and will be taught how to approach it in a different and more positive way.

You may be asked to act out the situation, modeling your behavior on alternatives that your therapist has shown you. You will be asked to put what you have learnt into practice at home, and will be given "homework" to do. You may be required to negotiate some form of contract with your therapist, in which you agree to pursue certain goals in your daily life, and to keep records of how you have performed. You may be encouraged to adopt a regime in which you are rewarded for success but not for failure – there may even be some form of punishment or disincentive involved.

Other techniques that may be used by behavioral therapists include desensitization and aversion

FUNCTIONAL ANALYSIS

Behavioral modification requires functional analysis of patterns of problem behavior, with the aim of knowing what stimulates specific responses. For example, the therapist of someone who wished to stop smoking would analyse where and when the person smokes, what he does when he smokes, and the pleasures he experiences.

conditioning. Desensitization is an effective way of dealing with phobias and other irrational fears. The patient is relaxed and gradually, over a period of time if necessary, introduced to the fear-provoking stimulus. The familiarization process usually starts as a mental or visualization exercise, but is soon put into practice, bit by bit, in real life. The technique can be used to deal with such things as a fear of flying, or heights, or lifts, or dentistry.

Aversion therapy is a method of discouraging pleasurable but destructive habits by associating them with unpleasant experiences. For example, drugs that cause immediate feelings of nausea when alcohol is taken are sometimes used as a form of aversion therapy in the treatment of alcoholism.

Behavior therapy may be individual or group based, or it may take place in the context of family or marriage (including sexual) counseling (*see pages 206–7*). In addition to its value in the treatment of phobias, depression, obsessive-compulsive disorders and stress-related conditions, it is often used in an educational context and in therapy for children with behavioral disorders.

BELOW *Behavioral therapy can help treat phobias of many kinds.*

ORTHODOX VIEW

Behavioral and cognitive therapies are the most studied and widely evaluated of the different psychotherapeutic approaches. Studies generally show that patients have benefited from counseling, particularly in the treatment of anxiety, depression, phobias, panic attacks, marital and other relationship problems, and sexual problems. No one technique seems to be notably more successful than any other.

Most doctors would now agree that behavioral and cognitive therapies are useful, even if only because everyone feels better if they have a sympathetic ear to turn to. They can also lessen the burden of generalized, unspecific complaints that doctors often have to deal with, and reduce the frequency of minor psychosomatic complaints. Many medical practices and most hospitals now have psychotherapists, or specially trained nurses and general practitioners, attached to their staff, and emotional and lifestyle problems are routinely referred to them as part of wider treatment.

Behavioral and cognitive therapies are also commonly in the network of private, government-funded, and voluntary counseling agencies found in today's developed societies. They are the basis for services such as marriage guidance, bereavement, post-traumatic stress and substance abuse counseling.

ABOVE *Cognitive therapies alter patients' self-perception and challenge their attitudes and feelings.*

COGNITIVE THERAPIES

The term "cognitive therapy" is something of a misnomer, because, in reality, it comprises a range of related therapies that share many of the same basic assumptions but differ in emphasis and in details of technique. The boundaries between them are not rigidly defined, and experienced psychotherapists are quite likely to draw on several different therapies at times when the patient seems likely to benefit.

Underlying all the cognitive therapies is the assumption that it is our perceptions of ourselves and others, and of the events that give rise to them, that cause emotional and behavioral problems, and not the events themselves. Childhood experiences may be important, but only insofar as they affect our current beliefs about ourselves and the world around us. Therapy is therefore aimed at altering the patient's belief system in such a way that the problems are eliminated.

Cognitive techniques lend themselves to brief, solution-based therapies, as well as to longer-term counseling. These techniques also share with the humanistic therapies (*see pages 200–3*) a belief in the power of the mind to bring about healing changes in people's attitudes and emotions.

Cognitive-Analytical Therapy

This approach draws on psychoanalytic as well as cognitive techniques. It accepts the importance of the unconscious mind, and encourages the development of a "transference" relationship between therapist and patient (*see page 192*). However, counseling takes place within a structured and focused framework, and the emphasis is on encouraging patients to understand the origins of their attitudes and beliefs and the effect they have on present feelings and behavior, so that they and the therapist can work together to change them for the better. Treatment is likely to consist of several months of weekly 50-minute sessions but may continue for much longer.

BELOW *The cognitive therapist identifies the thought processes which are causing the patient's dysfunctional behavior.*

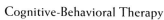

Cognitive-Behavioral Therapy

Cognitive-behavioral therapy grew out of behavioral therapy (*see pages 196–7*) during the 1950s and 1960s, mainly in the U.S., and was developed by clinical psychologists rather than psychotherapists. A key element in this therapy is known as "cognitive restructuring," in which patients are required to question and remodel their basic outlook on life. Self-defeating and self-denigrating thoughts are replaced by positive ones, and specific problems are addressed in the context of the whole.

The patient's involvement in the process is vital: if you consult a cognitive-behavioral therapist, you will be set certain goals and will be required to do "homework" in order to achieve them. Techniques from behavioral therapy, such as relaxation and desensitization, are also used. Treatment may last for as little as three months of weekly 50-minute sessions.

Rational-Emotive Behavior Therapy

Similar in many ways to cognitive-behavioral therapy, rational-emotive behavior therapy (REBT) was developed in 1955 by American psychotherapist Albert Ellis. Practitioners believe that most emotional distress is the result of irrational or harmful beliefs. They use a technique called "disputing" to help patients to question their current attitudes and expectations, and to replace those that are erroneous or unhelpful with new, more positive and productive ones. For example, many people have unrealistically high expectations of themselves, and feel guilt and shame when they fail to live up to them. The REBT therapist teaches patients (or "students") to recognize their own strengths and weaknesses, and so build a more rational and useful image of themselves.

If you consult an REBT therapist, you will be encouraged to experiment with alternative beliefs and may be asked to take part in role-playing and "shame-attacking" exercises, and will be given "homework" designed to bring about cognitive restructuring. Behavioral techniques, such as the awarding or withholding of rewards, may be used to ensure your involvement in the therapy. Treatment may be face-to-face or in groups, and is likely to take several months of weekly sessions.

1 *In the pragmatic approach adopted by behavioral therapists, clients are taught to adapt their behavior so that they can achieve their goal.*

2 *Here, the therapist shows that it is much more effective to present a happy face rather than a gloomy face to the world.*

Reality Therapy

As with other forms of cognitive therapy, reality therapy, developed by the American psychologist Dr. William Glasser, is based on the idea that emotional distress is caused by an erroneous or maladjusted belief system. Reality therapists believe that human behavior is designed to satisfy five basic needs: survival; the need to belong; the desire for power; the urge for freedom; and the need for pleasure and entertainment. When our behavior fails to satisfy these basic needs, we tend to assume what is known as a "failure identity," leading to weakness and irresponsibility, and to depression, anxiety, and other emotional problems.

Therapy is designed to make people aware of their responsibility for their own actions, and to recognize the

ABOVE *Talking things through can help the patient gain a better view of the world.*

failings of their current behavior patterns and beliefs in helping them to fulfil their five basic needs. Once patients have accepted that they have the freedom to choose, the therapist will guide them into exploring other ways of behaving and feeling that work better for them. Ultimately, this leads to the formation of a "success identity" and the resolution of feelings of inadequacy, frustration, or despair. Treatment usually lasts for several months and requires considerable commitment from the patient.

3 *The therapist shows the client how to "rehearse" a situation that is expected to be emotionally difficult for them.*

4 *By "rehearsing" such scenes the client can learn in advance how to handle the situation and be prepared for any eventuality.*

Personal Construct Therapy

This form of cognitive therapy was devised in the 1950s by the American psychologist George Kelly. It is based on the theory that we perceive the world not as it is, but as we construct it from personal experience. Our behavior is a response to this constructed world rather than a response to reality, and if our behavior gives rise to emotional or mental disorders, it is because we have constructed a "wrong" view of the world. Kelly developed the repertory grid as a way of recording the unique constructs of individuals. He also devised a number of therapeutic methods, the best known being fixed-role therapy, whereby the client adopts ways of behaving which are different from his or her usual style.

Therapy is designed to help patients restructure their view of the world. Treatment begins with a questionnaire, designed to analyze comprehensively your current expectations, beliefs, thoughts, and attitudes about yourself and the outside world. Sources of problems are identified and your hopes, needs, and desires are explored. Various cognitive and behavioral techniques are then used to demonstrate alternative ways of perceiving and reacting – you may, for example, be asked to think and behave as though you were someone completely different for a week. By the end of treatment, you should have reconstructed your picture of the world in such a way that you can exist comfortably with it.

Brief Solution-Focused Therapy

Where there is a very specific problem to be tackled – a phobia, for example, then solution-focused therapy offers a fast way of dealing with it. The nature of the problem is discussed and the best ways of dealing with it in the light of the patient's strengths and weaknesses are agreed. In the next two sessions, the relevant cognitive and behavioral techniques are practiced and put into action; the patient is given a plan of action to follow. The final session is to check on progress and to agree on strategies for the future.

PATHFINDER

Cognitive and behavioral therapies have been used successfully to treat the following conditions:

ADDICTION SEE P. 258

ANXIETY SEE PP. 256–7

ASTHMA SEE PP. 294–5

BEDWETTING SEE P. 352

DEPRESSION SEE P. 261

FEAR OF DENTAL TREATMENT SEE P. 286

HYPERACTIVITY SEE P. 351

HYPERVENTILATION SEE P. 301

MALE REPRODUCTIVE PROBLEMS SEE PP. 332–3

OBESITY SEE PP. 334–5

RSI SEE P. 342

STRESS SEE PP. 262–3

confused, anxious thoughts

poor self-image

ABOVE *Reconstructing your view of yourself can help ease depression and anxiety.*

HUMANISTIC THERAPIES

The humanistic therapies reflect a significant strand of late 20th-century thought. All share, in one way or another, the belief that psychological disturbance is due to the failure of the individual to realize his or her potential or to false perception and an inability to achieve personal growth. All believe that the goal of therapy is to encourage patients to reintegrate their personalities, to become more aware of themselves and their worlds, and to take responsibility for themselves and their actions.

While the humanistic therapies – which include Gestalt, person-centered psychotherapy, transactional analysis, and primal therapy and rebirthing – have some things in common with the behavioral and cognitive therapies (*see pages 196–9*), they bear virtually no resemblance to classical psychoanalytical psychotherapy (*see pages 192–5*). Past experiences and unconscious motives, fears, and desires are recognized only insofar as they affect thoughts and feelings in the here and now. The therapist is not a figure of authority – a teacher, judge, or interpreter – but a warm and caring companion, whose relationship with the patient is one of mutual respect.

GESTALT THERAPY

The term "gestalt" is German for "the whole," and it is a central tenet of Gestalt psychology that we perceive the world as a mosaic of interlocking experiences, people, and events rather than as a set of unrelated parts. In Gestalt, the whole is always more than the sum of its parts.

Gestalt psychology became popular in Europe in the first half of the 20th century and was opposed to the mechanistic approach followed by the American behaviorist school of Watson and Skinner (*see page 196*). The Gestalt psychologists were primarily interested in human perception and thought rather than stimulus-response conditioning, and considered many aspects of perception, memory, and learning processes to be "wholes" which are complete in themselves and that cannot be analyzed into smaller components. Therefore, when something is learned, the individual's entire perception of the environment has been changed. Gestalt psychologists were responsible for ideas such as "mental set," a state of preparedness to perform certain kinds of mental task rather than others, and attempted to define laws of perceptual organization.

In the 1940s, Frederick ("Fritz") and Laura Perls began to apply Gestalt concepts to psychotherapy in the U.S., synthesizing European "insight" with American values to produce a confrontational, anti-intellectual therapy. In the 1960s, they opened the Esalen Institute on the Big Sur coast of California, which, throughout a turbulent decade, became possibly the most influential and innovative center for psychotherapy in the world. While Gestalt psychotherapy has perhaps had its heyday, it is still widely practiced, and its influence and the techniques its practitioners developed are still in evidence in most of the humanistic schools.

Gestalt Theory

The Gestalt theory of personality is complex and often not easy to understand. Essentially, Gestalt views the self as an organic entity that interacts with and is part of the environment – the world as a whole. The self can

ABOVE *Gestalt therapy helps the patient reintegrate into their environment and grow in their personal relationships.*

only have identity by differentiating itself from the outside world and must establish the boundary between the self and the "not self" – between "I" and "thou." Like any organism, the self exists by taking in nourishment from its surroundings. Personal growth depends on the recognition of what is nourishing in the environment and what is harmful or toxic, which in turn requires an awareness of the Gestalt – the whole picture of the environment and the self's relationship to it.

Maintaining the Boundary

Problems arise when personal growth becomes distorted because of disturbances to the boundary: if it becomes too rigid, the individual becomes isolated and alienated; if it becomes indistinct, the individual may be excessively dependent and incapable of accepting responsibility or making choices.

Problems may also be the result of lack of awareness of the environment as a whole. Normally, the environment is perceived as a background pattern against which particular events or experiences emerge from time to time to occupy the foreground. Once the foreground issue has been resolved, it melts into the background again and is replaced by a new issue. If the foreground issue is not dealt with satisfactorily, however, it will not melt away and will continue to occupy the foreground at the expense of other issues that require attention. If the foreground issues pass too rapidly into the background, they remain unresolved; if they pass too slowly, they pile up on each other.

Here and Now

In a healthy person, the Gestalt is constantly changing as a result of external events and changing internal needs. As a result, it is the "here and now" that matters, and not the past or future. Both past and future affect our present perceptions, but they should form part of our awareness of our current situation – living in the past or future is a distortion of the Gestalt. Similarly it is what we want now and how we are trying to achieve it that are important, and not our interpretation or rationalization of events. To allow our behavior to be determined by "should" and "ought" is to attempt to make ourselves conform to an image rather than being aware of ourselves as we really are.

Finally, from its existentialist roots, Gestalt psychology takes the idea that we are all free to choose and we need to learn to live our lives according to our own needs rather than striving to fulfil the wishes and expectations of others.

ORTHODOX VIEW

Most doctors would regard the humanistic and person-centered therapies, with their emphasis on personal growth and fulfilment, as largely irrelevant to conventional medicine.

There is, however, a school of thought that considers that the classical, psychoanalytical view of human personality and personality disorders is out of date, and that humanistic theories might well have something to contribute to the emergence of new models of human thought and emotion.

CONSULTING A GESTALT THERAPIST

In Gestalt therapy, patients and therapists are equal. The therapist is there to facilitate and represent the dialogue between "I" and "thou," helping to define the boundaries of the patient's individuality and to explore the ways in which he or she is currently responding to others and the world in general. The therapist does not lead or take responsibility for the patient – to do so would be to collude with the patient's inability or refusal to take individual responsibility. It is for the patient to decide what areas of personality need exploration or "work." Much of the therapy may consist of dialogue, in which observation and awareness of body language are significant, but many other techniques have been developed to help remove unresolved issues from the foreground of consciousness, and to increase awareness.

Perhaps the best known of Gestalt innovations is the "empty chair" technique. In this, the patient is encouraged to imagine that the person or issue with which they have an unresolved conflict is sitting in an empty chair, and then to hold a conversation with it as though he, she, or it was actually present. Alternatively, the patient may occupy two chairs representing two sides of a personal conflict. Unexpectedly deep emotions may be released by this process. Another technique used by Gestalt therapists is to encourage the patient to hit chairs and sofas with padded sticks, called "battacca bats," in order to experience emotions of rage or frustration. Also used is the "therapy marathon," in which participants undergo group therapy over a period of two days and nights without sleep. In a less extreme form, Gestalt therapy also uses "encounter groups" as a way of furthering self-awareness through supervised physical and emotional interaction with other members of the group.

patient holds conversation

patient's issue in empty chair.

ABOVE *The Gestalt therapist acts as a facilitator, enabling the patient to explore, often through dialogue, their unresolved feelings.*

LEFT *The "empty chair" technique produces a potent cathartic release in the patient.*

PERSON-CENTERED PSYCHOTHERAPY

Person-centered therapy is sometimes equated with the humanistic therapies as a whole. But, although there are many similarities in basic concepts, range of techniques, and aims, there are several ways in which person-centered therapies are unique.

Two American psychologists, Abraham Maslow and Carl Rogers, set out the basic tenets of person-centered therapy in the 1950s. Maslow asserted the futility of trying to apply dogmatic theories and practices to the treatment of emotional problems: everyone is different and perceives the world differently. The therapist must understand and enter the patient's frame of reference to be of any help. Maslow believed that personal fulfilment depended on the satisfaction of a number of fundamental needs that become more important in a systematic progression. Lower, "basic" needs such as those for food and security are important first. "Higher" needs such as self-esteem become important once the lower levels have been satisfied. Children must be satisfied at one level before

attacking stance

immediate defensive position

ABOVE *The person-centered therapist encourages the patient to define the course they think their therapy should take.*

they can move on to the next, and the top of the pyramid may take at least 30 years to reach, or may never be met. Maslow's needs in ascending order are physiological (for example, adequate food, water, and shelter), safety (to be secure and free from danger), social (to have friends and be accepted by others), self-esteem (self-confidence and self-respect) and self-actualization (to develop all one's potential).

Conditional to Unconditional

The task of the person-centered therapist is to create a climate of warmth, freedom, and security, to understand the patient's internal frame of reference, and to demonstrate uncondi-

CLIENT-CENTERED THERAPY

Carl Rogers gave real meaning to the term "person-centered" psychotherapy. He considered the "client" (rather than "patient") to be the only person who can develop solutions to his or her problems. He believed that the role of the therapist is to facilitate such development by simply understanding the client's problems and creating a relaxed environment in which the client can express themself freely.

Rogerian therapy emphasized giving unconditional positive regard, which would free the client from approval-seeking so that he could explore his own self-actualization.

TRANSACTIONAL ANALYSIS (TA)

Of all the humanistic therapies, TA is one of the most appealing because of its apparent simplicity. First elaborated by the Canadian-born psychologist Eric Berne in the 1960s, and popularized as Games People Play, TA is based on the premise that all interactions between people involve the assumption of specific roles. The basic roles – or "ego states" – are those of parent, adult, and child (the "PAC" model). At different times, and in different circumstances, these roles are adopted to become "victim" or "martyr," "poor me" or "generous me," "helpless me" or "superior me." If I address you from one of my ego states and you reply in turn, this exchange is known as a transaction. Transactional analysis takes place when the ego-state model is used to understand sequences of transactions, and explains how we replay childhood strategies in adult life.

Which roles are adopted and when depend on the individual's "life script," which originates in childhood and serves as a blueprint for present behavior, self-image, and relationships with others. As grownups, we are unlikely to be aware of the life script we have written, but we continue to follow it. To realize our full potential, we need to gain autonomy over our

parent   adult   child

ABOVE *According to TA we all adopt different roles or "ego states" depending on our childhood experiences.*

life scripts, which can be achieved through awareness, spontaneity, and the capacity for intimacy.

The philosophical assumptions underlying TA are that everyone decides their own destiny, but these decisions can be changed. Several TA concepts have become widely known, including the idea of the "inner child" and the notion of life-stage transition crises.

Confrontation and Contract

TA therapy is more directed and sometimes more confrontational than most humanistic therapies. The therapist will deliberately challenge the patient about the roles he or she adopts and encourage active re-evaluation of the patient's life script. There may be a contract between therapist and patient determining areas of behavior and attitudes that need to be changed. The techniques of Gestalt therapy *(see pages 200–01)* are often used in TA, although Gestalt therapists would argue that it is better to absorb TA theories into Gestalt practice.

Transactional analysis therapy has a wide variety of applications. In addition to individual, group, couple, and family counseling, it has been used successfully in education, and management and communications training.

tional positive regard. Therapy is successful when the patient has learned to replace conditional positive self-regard with unconditional positive self-regard, and is able to view him or herself in a more positive light.

Therapy may consist mainly of empathetic conversation, but more often it will involve any of the range of techniques used by other humanistic therapies, such as art (*see pages 238–41*), dance (*see pages 226–31*), psycho- drama, encounter groups and role-playing (*see pages 206–9*), dreamwork (*see pages 224–5*), and so on. Patients are often also given assignments to work on at home.

PRIMAL THERAPY AND REBIRTHING

In 1970, the American psychotherapist Arthur Janov published *The Primal Scream*. In it, he laid the basis for what was to become primal therapy. Janov's thesis was simple and persuasive. He argued that our fundamental need during the earliest years of life is love. The infant craves the attention, physical affection, and demonstrable emotional love of its parents. If this is not forthcoming or is felt to be inadequate, the child feels a terrible sense of hurt. Soon anger at the hurt becomes the dominant emotion.

These childhood traumas remain with us. They manifest themselves in adult life as neuroses or obsessions, as depression, anxiety, feelings of inadequacy, problems with relationships, and sometimes crippling despair. Primal therapy is a way of coming to terms with painful childhood traumas by reliving them and so releasing the pent-up feelings they have caused.

Cathartic Experience

Primaling requires deep relaxation, often brought about by breathing exercises (see pages 166–71) and biodynamic massage (see pages 204–5). The experience can let loose strong emotions. Patients often report great emotional pain and anguish, sometimes expressed as a need to scream the "primal scream." They also report that the experience is cathartic – they feel cleansed and "lightened."

In primal therapy the role of the therapist varies with the individual practitioner. Some therapists will direct the patient towards particular childhood experiences; others will allow the patient to work his own way gradually toward confrontation with his private demons.

Some therapists will work to establish a strong client–therapist relationship; others will act merely as passive agents. Primal therapy has been claimed to be valuable in the treatment of adults who have a history of childhood deprivation or abuse, and has also been used to successfully treat severely traumatized children.

Rebirthing

Patients receiving primal therapy often report that, as they go deeper into therapy, they find themselves reliving earlier and earlier experiences. Ultimately, they may find themselves reliving the greatest of human traumas, the experience of birth.

LEFT *Love, or lack of love, in childhood may be a primary shaping force of personality.*

PATHFINDER

Humanistic therapies have been used successfully to treat the following disorders:

ADDICTION: *SEE P. 258*

ANXIETY: *SEE PP. 256–7*

DEPRESSION: *SEE P. 261*

HYPERACTIVITY: *SEE P. 351*

HYPERVENTILATION: *SEE P. 301*

OBSESSION: *SEE P. 259*

STRESS: *SEE PP. 262–3*

These therapies are also used to treat learning difficulties, developmental disorders, manic depression, obsessive–compulsive disorders, posttraumatic stress, and relationship and sexual problems.

may not want to face experiences

painful thoughts and feelings

LEFT *Primal therapy emphasizes catharsis and can be a painful experience for the patient.*

TRANSPERSONAL AND INTEGRATIVE THERAPIES

T*he transpersonal and integrative therapies are basically humanistic in approach, but they combine humanistic theories and practices with those from other branches of psychotherapy, or introduce an element of spirituality, religion, or mysticism into their thinking. The transpersonal therapies in particular would appeal to those with an interest in adding a spiritual dimension to their lives.*

NEUROLINGUISTIC PROGRAMING (NLP)

Neurolinguistic programming, or NLP, is unusual among psychotherapies in that it is based not on a theory of personality and behavior but on a set of therapeutic tools. It was also founded by two American academics whose main interests were not related to psychology: John Grinder, a professor of linguistics, and Richard Bandler, a graduate in information sciences.

In the mid-1970s, Grinder and Bandler became interested in the question of how it was that certain individuals could all claim considerable success while working with entirely different systems of therapy. They thought that by studying the ways in which these individuals worked, they might be able to extract the successful elements from their techniques and build them into a set of therapeutic models. Their initial observations were drawn from various fields, including family therapy (*see pages 206–07*), Gestalt therapy (*see pages 200–01*), hypnotherapy (*see pages 218–23*), and anthropology. To this they added their own experience of linguistics and communications.

Dual Components

The resulting system, neurolinguistic programing, has a number of different components, each with its related therapeutic techniques. For example, the linguistic component seeks to explore the deeper meaning and significance of the words that people use. A person who describes something as "always" the case may take a different view if challenged as to whether they really mean "always" or merely "most of the time" or "some of the time." The patient may be made aware of wider possibilities as a result. The neurological component deals with the ways in which thinking affects physical states and vice versa, and also with the ways in which people represent their experiences internally – whether visually or verbally, for example.

NLP also relates body movements, such as posture and eye movements, to the ways in which people access

ABOVE *Body cues, such as eye movement and gesture, are used in NLP to determine the way we access and process information.*

and process information. Awareness of these movements both extends the "vocabulary" of communication and allows areas for the exercise of therapeutic techniques. During an NLP session a person will be taught how to change particular patterns of speech and body language in order to communicate more effectively and bring about personal change.

Some of the techniques evolved by NLP have been adopted by other forms of therapy, for example the "swish" technique that involves replacing negative images with positive ones (*see Visualization, pages 214–5*), and techniques for lowering or increasing the intensity of feeling roused by internal representations (*see Hypnotherapy, pages 218–223*).

NLP claims to offer "one-session" cures for many common psychological problems, such as phobias and undesirable behavior traits. While these claims may be exaggerated, NLP certainly seems to be able to effect cures within as little as three sessions that would have taken months of therapy using other techniques.

TRANSPERSONAL THERAPY

Transpersonal therapy is a recent development popular mainly in the U.S. which attempts to introduce a spiritual dimension into psychotherapy. Encompassing elements from psychosynthesis (*see page 205*) and the more mystical aspects of Jungian analysis (*see page 194*), in particular the use of archetypes, it also draws upon ideas and techniques from areas such as meditation (*see pages 60–3*), the "chakras" (*see Ayurveda, pages 78–85*), dreamwork (*see pages 224–5*), visualization (*see pages 214–7*), healing (*see pages 86–7*), Buddhism, and astrology.

The aim of therapy is to encourage people to transcend their own personalities, through creative and ritualistic techniques, and become aware of their oneness with the universe. By finding his own spiritual path, a person can achieve the realization of an ultimate state. Therapy may be individual or in groups, and may continue indefinitely.

ABOVE *Transpersonal therapy encompasses elements of Eastern philosophy and ritual.*

PSYCHOSYNTHESIS

The Italian psychiatrist Roberto Assagioli founded psychosynthesis in the early 20th century. Like transpersonal therapy, it emphasizes the spiritual side of our nature, and attempts to "synthesize" our normal state of consciousness with higher, altered states, integrating them into a single, spiritual whole. A range of creative techniques is used, including painting, dance, writing, and therapy, which may be individual or in groups, and is often long-term.

RIGHT *Psychosynthesis makes use of creative techniques such as free drawing and painting.*

PATHFINDER

Transpersonal therapies, with their spiritual dimension, are best thought of not as forms of treatment of specific disorders but as a means of self-improvement and fulfilling one's potential. Neurolinguistic programing, being an integrative therapy that incorporates the most successful elements of many other forms of psychotherapy, has been used in the treatment of childhood behavioral disorders, developmental disorders, learning difficulties, manic depression, posttraumatic stress, and relationship and sexual problems, as well as the following conditions:

ADDICTION *SEE P.* 258
ANXIETY *SEE PP.* 256–7
DEPRESSION *SEE P.* 261
HYPERACTIVITY *SEE P.* 351
HYPERVENTILATION *SEE P.* 301
OBSESSION *SEE P.* 259
STRESS *SEE PP.* 262–3

BIOENERGETICS

Bioenergetics (also known as Bioenergetic Analysis) is a body-oriented psychotherapy which, like elements of Gestalt therapy (see pages 200-201) and neurolinguistic programming (see facing page), draws heavily on the theories of the psychologist Wilhelm Reich. It is sometimes referred to as Reichian psychotherapy, and the system was developed by a student of Reich, the American psychotherapist, Dr. Abraham Lowen, in the 1960s.

Reich believed that our bodies, particularly the muscular system, both reflected and formed part of our response to deeply felt emotion. As children, for example, we may have learnt to clench our muscles and adopt defensive postures as a way of repressing unacceptable emotions or behavior, or as a way of warding off pain. As adults, we continue to show the same response whenever a similar situation occurs. This is known as "body armoring."

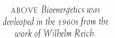

ABOVE *Bioenergetics was developed in the 1960s from the work of Wilhelm Reich.*

Body posture and muscular tension are thus an important form of communication which, when interpreted by a skilled therapist, can provide valuable clues as to the existence and nature of repressed, often unconscious, childhood memories. However, whereas other therapies seek to use this knowledge as a way of increasing self-awareness, or as a form of behavior that can fruitfully be modified, bioenergetics uses it to explore and release the emotions roused by the memory of the traumatic experience itself.

Grounding

Therapy is usually conducted in groups of a dozen or more, and consists of a series of exercises intended to raise consciousness of, and then release, the tension in various areas of the body – typically, the chest, shoulders, pelvis, and jaw. Much importance is attached to the way you stand, since firm "grounding" is believed to provide a balanced platform for the body and emotions. Various "stress" positions are adopted to focus and concentrate emotional energy, which can then be released through exercises such as wringing a towel or hitting a bed with a racquet. Psychotherapeutic techniques are also used. Painful, repressed memories may surface during the process, but so too can happy and pleasurable ones.

Biodynamic Massage

Reich was also particularly interested in the flow of energy through the body, and in what blocks and releases this.
His theories of energy flows have been incorporated into a system of massage, known as biodynamic massage, developed in the 1960s by Gerda Boyesen. This is a particularly important tool in primal therapy and rebirthing (see page 203).

RIGHT *A balanced posture is believed to provide "grounding" for both physical and emotional balance.*

FAMILY THERAPY AND RELATIONSHIP COUNSELING

*I*n virtually all cultures, the basic unit of society is the family. However, the shape of family life has certainly changed during the last 50 years as divorce has become more common and increased mobility has led to wider separation of family members. Nevertheless, almost all of us grow up in the context of a family, and extend the family when we have children of our own. Family therapy treats the family as a single entity, seeking to cure the problems of individual family members by treating the family as a whole. Specialist counselors treat marital and sexual problems.

Family therapy is based on the premise that the family forms an organic unit, in which anything that affects one part of the unit will affect the rest as well. If one member of a family is in emotional distress, the whole family suffers in one way or another, and the family's response to this distress is crucial in determining whether the problem gets better or worse.

In a healthy and well-adjusted family, the relationships between family members, and between the family and the outside world, are in a constant state of flux. As people grow and change, and pass through the major lifestages and events – births, marriages and deaths, childhood, adolescence, and adulthood, and often separations and divorce – the family must continually adapt and adjust. Family members are constantly renegotiating their roles, whether as parents, children, or siblings. And the family as a whole responds to changing circumstances and influences from the outside world.

When something goes wrong with this process of adjustment, one or other member of the family may start showing signs of emotional or psychological distress. This is a symptom of a malaise in the family as a whole, and to cure it, the whole family needs to be treated as a unit, not just the individual who is suffering.

BELOW Family problems can manifest themselves in behavioral disorders in children.

ABOVE Family therapy is concerned with the treatment of the individual through the family unit.

All for One

Childhood behavioral disorders or learning difficulties are one of the ways in which family problems can manifest themselves as individual disturbance. External events, such as financial difficulty, change of lifestyle, or a move to an unfamiliar place, combined, for example, with the birth of a sibling, may lead a child to feel insecure and unloved. Disordered behavior becomes a way of getting parental attention. Therapy in such cases requires a change in the attitude and behavior of all family members, as well those of the disturbed child. Similarly, adolescent eating disorders, such as anorexia or depression, are often best dealt with by family rather than individual therapy.

FORMS OF THERAPY

All forms of family therapy aim to help the family to communicate more effectively, and to have a better understanding of each other's needs and concerns.

Many different techniques may be used to achieve this, depending on the orientation of the therapist involved. The role of the therapist is to act as a catalyst for change within the family (or "system") as a whole rather than to enter into an alliance or a close relationship with a specific family member.

A psychoanalytical family therapist, for example, will usually have trained in one of the main psychoanalytical schools of thought (*see pages 192–5*), and will concentrate on releasing repressed or buried emotions by identifying the traumatic events or circumstances that gave rise to them. This form of therapy may be lengthy and may involve individual as well as family counseling sessions.

Therapists trained in behavioral or cognitive techniques (*see pages 196-9*) will examine the ways in which members of the family behave toward each other, and the perception they have of themselves and their relationships with each other and the rest of the world. Therapy will usually involve teaching the different family members new, more helpful and productive ways of behaving in the family setting. Family members may, for example, be asked to imagine themselves as if they were their parent or sibling, and to act out the other's role. They may be encouraged to experiment with different behaviors, both for the benefits they may bring and as a way of deepening mutual understanding and trust. Therapy should be treated as a continuous, ongoing, process which extends well beyond the consulting room and should form part of the backdrop to normal day-to-day family life.

Behavioral and cognitive therapies may be quite short. In brief solution-focused therapy (*see page 199*), attention is focused on a single issue rather than on the psychological health of the family as a whole, and as few as three or four sessions may be enough to bring about significant improvement. Most counseling that is offered by social and welfare agencies is behavioral and cognitive rather than psychoanalytical or humanistic.

Family therapy is also practiced in Gestalt and other forms of humanistic and person-centered therapy (*see pages 200–3*). Here the emphasis is more on teaching the members of the family how they can provide mutual respect and support so that each of them can achieve greater self-realization and healthy personal growth.

MARITAL AND RELATIONSHIP THERAPY
Marital breakdown is increasingly common in modern Westernized societies. Where a family is involved, strained relationships and separation can cause distress to the whole family as well as to the couple concerned.

LEFT *A rocky relationship can be helped by marriage counseling.*

PATHFINDER

Family therapy has been shown to be successful in the treatment of developmental disorders and, specifically, the following conditions:
ADDICTION SEE P. *258*
DEPRESSION SEE P. *261*
EATING DISORDERS SEE P. *265*
HYPERACTIVITY SEE P. *351*
Marital, relationship, and sexual therapies are used to treat relationship breakdown and sexual dysfunction.

Marital and relationship counselors work with all couples, including straight, lesbian or homosexual partners. Most commonly, behavioral and cognitive techniques are used, but psychoanalysis and humanistic therapies are also practiced.

Successful marital therapy depends on commitment from both partners. If either of the partners is uncertain about the other's level of commitment to the relationship, there will be a degree of mutual mistrust that may itself cause the relationship to break down.

Once commitment has been established, therapy will generally be aimed at improving communications between partners and strengthening awareness of each other's point of view. Couples will be led to understand that disagreements usually arise not because one person is right and the other wrong, but because each is approaching the problem from a different perspective.

Sexual Therapy
When marital and relationship problems are due to sexual dysfunction – impotence, frigidity, or painful intercourse, for example – specialist sex therapy may be advised. This may involve bolstering the partners' self-esteem and removing fears of sexual inadequacy as well as exercises designed to restore physical affection and intimacy. A counselor will help couples improve their verbal and physical communication, and give advice on commonly encountered sexual problems. Cognitive-behavioral methods are particularly successful at dealing with psychosexual disorders. Again, it is important that both partners are committed to the relationship and learn to discuss their sexual needs and problems openly with each other.

talking through problems is the first step

ABOVE *Marital therapy addresses current dynamics in the relationship and helps the couple face the future.*

GROUP THERAPIES

Most forms of therapy can be practiced in a group setting as well as on an individual basis. Group therapy can be particularly effective for people trying to come to terms with a specific problem that is shared by other members of the group — for example, drug or alcohol addiction, or experience of abuse as a child. A group can provide valuable support and the realization that the sufferer is not alone is in itself therapeutic. Group therapy is often available on a voluntary basis through various support and self-help groups. It is also widely used as a tool for personal growth and for the improvement of interpersonal and social skills.

When people begin to attend group therapy sessions, they usually re-create the problems that led them into therapy in the first place. The group is designed to offer a warm, sympathetic environment that offers participants emotional support and allows them to test out new modes of behavior and new ways of relating to people.

Groups are usually small — around six to 12 members — and are supervised by trained group therapists. The methods used vary widely, ranging from simple discussion groups to role-playing and psychodrama. Some groups are centered around a particular psychological or emotional problem, such as eating disorders, trauma, alcohol or drug addiction, or coping with serious illness and disease. Others are intended more as forums for bringing about lifestyle changes, the building of self-esteem, and generally improving the quality of relationships and other aspects of emotional life.

There are three main orientations in group therapy: psychodynamic, humanistic, and cognitive-behavioral. Psychodynamic groups focus on gaining personal insight. The humanistic approach is devoted to ideas of personal development or self-actualization. The cognitive-behavioral tradition is concerned with effecting behavioral change and is used in cases of assertiveness training and dealing with behaviors such as overeating or anorexia, for example.

Individual therapists also vary greatly in style. Some aim for calm and rational discussion, while others encourage the display of as much emotion as the participants can bear. Some are content to play a largely passive, guiding, role while others actively direct the session and set definite therapeutic goals.

Group therapy may consist of weekly sessions over a long period, or it may be intensive with several sessions a week over a short period of time. Some "encounter groups" may meet for 24 hours or longer.

Group Therapy In Action

Most groups have fairly strict rules. Things said and done during group sessions are not meant to be discussed with people outside the group, and members are often discouraged from socializing with each other outside the context of the group. Anything that affects the dynamics of the group should happen within the confines of the group. Participants are also expected to make a commitment to the group, and should not miss, be late for, or withdraw from group sessions. Often, people wanting to enter group therapy will have one or more initial assessment sessions on a one-to-one basis so that the therapist can judge their suitability for participation in the group.

ENCOUNTER GROUPS

Encounter groups are part of a therapeutic technique developed by Carl Rogers (*see page* 202). Their primary aim is self-knowledge and personal growth and development. Participants are encouraged to display their emotions, however painful, and to relate both physically and emotionally to each other. Some groups practice nudity as a way of breaking down barriers.

While encounter groups have proved useful in a variety of contexts, from team-building and task-orientation to business and administration, they also have drawbacks. The encounter group may arouse strong and harmful emotions, which the group may not be well equipped to deal with. There is also a danger that participants can identify so completely with the group that they alter their behavior to conform with group expectations and aspirations. In the process, their other relationships — with colleagues, family, and friends — may be ignored and suffer as a result. Religious and pseudo-religious cults often use encounter group methods to foster complete dependence on the group and its leader, and to detach individuals from their families and the outside world in general.

ABOVE Group therapy sessions can support those who are fearful of expressing and facing their problems.

The first few sessions of group therapy are usually aimed at building trust between members of the group. You are encouraged to talk about the particular problem that you have – your reasons for wanting therapy – and other group members are encouraged to provide feedback by commenting on what you have said. The group will offer support and encouragement, sometimes gently confronting you over anything that seems inappropriate or wrong. You will be able to try out new ways of expressing yourself, new behaviors, and new perceptions of yourself. You may be asked to try these out in your day-to-day life and then report back with your experiences. Above all, the group offers a warm, caring, and sympathetic environment in which the healing process can take place.

PSYCHODRAMA

Psychodrama is a form of group therapy developed in the U.S. in the 1930s by Jacob L. Moreno, a Viennese-trained psychiatrist, based on his experiences of watching children at play. It was not until the 1960s, however, that his work began to receive widespread attention. As psychotherapy developed and flourished, aspects of his work were adopted and adapted by therapists working in a variety of different schools, from Gestalt and person-centered therapies (*see pages 200–203*) to cognitive ones (*see pages 196*). Psychodrama is now recognized as a powerful therapeutic tool, which, when used alongside other therapy techniques, can be seen to bring about considerable improvements in behavior in a short period of time.

In a group psychodrama session, the therapist – always a trained psychodramatist – assumes the role of director, and guides the players through the different phases of the action. In the first phase, the "warm-up," a "protagonist" will be chosen to represent the theme of the session, and other members of the group will take the roles of important auxiliary figures in the drama. The remaining group members will become the audience, representing the world in general.

In the second phase, the "action," the chosen problem is acted out on stage by the protagonist, who tries various ways of resolving it. In the third phase, the "sharing," all members of the group are invited to discuss their reactions to the action, and to suggest further ways of dealing with the problem. Sessions take at least 90 minutes and sometimes longer.

A Laboratory of Life

Psychodrama allows people to externalize their inner conflicts and emotions in such a way that they can be examined without pain or fear. The element of play-acting allows actions to be performed and feelings to be expressed without the threat of unwanted consequences. New behaviors, and new ways of relating to others can be experimented with in a non-judgmental environment free from threat. It encourages a crea-tive and inspi-rational approach to people's problems.

PATHFINDER

Group therapies have been used successfully for a wide range of conditions. When used generally to promote emotional and mental health, group therapies are used in self-confidence and assertiveness training; interpersonal and social skills training; and personal growth and development. They are also of value in the treatment of the following conditions:

ADDICTION SEE P. *258*

ANXIETY SEE PP. *256–7*

OBSESSION SEE P. *259*

STRESS SEE PP. *262–3*

LEFT *Gestalt therapy helps the patient reintegrate into their environment and grow in their personal relationships.*

TECHNIQUES USED IN PSYCHODRAMA

Participants in psychodrama groups act out their problem situations in their lives. The protagonist is encouraged to act out his conflicts in the "here and now" rather than emotionally distancing himself by talking about them in the past tense. Psychodramatists have developed numerous techniques that help in the dramatic representation of inner conflicts and emotional problems. These include:

■ BEHAVIOR REHEARSAL: Anticipated events that give rise to fear or unease are treated as though they could be re-enacted. Different ways of dealing with the situation are tried out and discussed, and the best way is rehearsed until the protagonist has perfected the performance. Similar techniques can be used to re-enact experiences that may have been hurtful or humiliating in the past and to experiment with better ways of dealing with similar situations in the future.

■ ROLE REHEARSAL: The protagonist is asked to imagine himself in the role of a significant other person and then to act out the other's feelings on stage. When carefully guided by the therapist, people often develop a deeper understanding of others in their lives, and acquire a fresh and more profound perception of their own personalities and behavior.

■ MULTIPLE ROLE PLAYING: In this, the protagonist identifies different aspects of his own personality and dramatizes them in such a way that they engage in dialogue with each other. This can lead to the recognition of the reasons for inner conflicts and uncertainties, and to a more fruitful fusion of the different parts.

■ STAGE TECHNIQUES: Several useful dramatic techniques may be used. One is the "aside," in which the protagonist comments on the action to the audience in a way that is not meant to be heard by the rest of the cast. Another is the "soliloquy" in which the actor verbalizes inner feelings and uncertainties in solo speech on stage. There is also "speaking behind the back," when players speak about someone on stage as though they were not there.

AUTOGENIC TRAINING

One of the simplest and most flexible of the mind–body therapies, autogenic training is sometimes referred to as the Western form of Eastern meditation. In fact, it often appeals to people who want the benefits of meditation but who are reluctant to accept the belief systems and spiritual doctrines that form part of Eastern practice. Originally regarded as a form of stress relief, autogenic training has been shown in recent years to provide a wide range of health benefits for a significant number of conditions. Like other mind and spirit therapies, it also provides the basis for personal growth and self-fulfilment, and the expansion of the capabilities of the mind.

Autogenic training (AT) was first developed in Germany in the 1920s. Its founder was a Berlin psychiatrist and neurologist, Johannes Schulz, who had used hypnosis and had been impressed by its benefits. His work on AT was an attempt to devise a system that anyone could use, but which still brought about these same benefits. Dr. Schulz devised six silent verbal exercises for the mind which were refined by his colleague, Dr. Wolfgang Luthe, into the basic techniques that are in use today. As word of the success of the technique spread, other doctors from around the world began to take an interest, and during the last 20 years there has been a steady growth in the number of practitioners throughout Europe and North America.

Today, there is a considerable body of research attesting to the effectiveness of AT. The therapy is available in the U.K. in a number of hospitals, where it has been found to be invaluable in reducing the stresses of labor. It is also widely used in industry, for example to reduce jet-lag in airline pilots and crew and in corporate staff training programs. In the U.S., autogenic therapy has been used as part of the training program for astronauts. Autogenic training is often described as a "rest, relaxation, and recreation" system that is designed to optimize performance and concentration and reduce stress.

ABOVE *U.S. astronauts receive autogenic training to help maintain mental balance and precision in the most demanding of circumstances.*

WHAT IS AT?

AT shares several features with other mind–body therapies, particularly relaxation (see pages 158–65), meditation (see pages 60–67), and self-hypnosis (see pages 222–3). It involves the creation of a state of "passive concentration," in which the mind can attend to various parts of the body in turn, without alarm or concern. The technique is fairly precise and in order to practice AT, you will first need to be trained in the correct postures, the suggestions and phrases you need to use, and the methods used for achieving passive concentration. It is

also essential to practice autogenic exercises regularly between classes, for about ten minutes, three times a day. After several months of practice, you should be able to maintain a state of positive concentration for about half an hour at a time.

It has been suggested that some of the beneficial effects of AT – particularly increased creativity, and improved sporting performance and communication skills – stem from its ability to bring the two sides of the brain into better balance. This allows expression to the imaginative and intuitive right side of the brain, which normally plays little part in day-to-day activities.

increased concentration

improved sporting performance

ABOVE *Improved sporting performance is just one of the benefits claimed by practitioners of autogenic training.*

CONSULTING A PRACTITIONER

The first stage in AT is training with a qualified instructor. This usually takes place in small groups in a series of weekly 90-minute sessions over a period of eight weeks.

At the initial consultation, the practitioner will take details of your medical history and ask questions about your general lifestyle. You will then be advised on the postures to adopt when using AT – these are designed to cut down awareness of the outside world. There are three main postures:

✳ Lying flat on your back on the floor, as relaxed and comfortable as possible;

✳ Sitting in a comfortable chair with your hands on the arms or on your thighs;

✳ Sitting on the edge of a hard chair with rounded shoulders and drooping head.

At no stage are these exercises directed toward the cure of a specific disorder. The whole idea is that the mind and body are themselves capable of curing or alleviating whatever is wrong once they are set free of the constraints of the active mind.

The basic autogenic training can then be extended to incorporate more advanced techniques. For example, autogenic modification involves adopting formulas that focus on particular issues and is used to direct the technique into more specific areas. Autogenic neutralization can be used to deal with behavioral problems and promote positive personal development; and autogenic meditation can be used to explore the deeper levels of

PATHFINDER

Research has shown that autogenic training can be effective in the treatment of a variety of conditions, and the beauty of the technique is that, after instruction from a qualified teacher, it can be used on a daily basis as a self-help technique.

ANXIETY SEE PP. 256–7
ASTHMA SEE PP. 294–5
DEPRESSION SEE P. 261
ECZEMA AND DERMATITIS SEE P. 273
HEADACHES SEE P. 268
HIGH BLOOD PRESSURE SEE P. 302
HIV AND AIDS SEE PP. 340–41
IBS SEE PP. 314–5
INSOMNIA SEE P. 264
RAYNAUD'S DISEASE SEE P. 306
STRESS SEE PP. 262–3

smooth, regular breathing

relaxed limbs

The aim is to reach an altered state of consciousness similar to meditation that enables the body's self-healing processes to operate. This is followed by a series of exercises:

1 The first involves paying passive attention to the limbs, starting with your right arm. You will be asked to carry the thought that your right arm is heavy. The heaviness is then extended to your left arm, and then moves to the right leg and to the left. They should be relaxed after this.

2 You are then asked to think of the limbs as being warm; begin with your arms as before and then move onto your legs.

3 In the third exercise you are asked to think of your heartbeat as smooth and regular.

4 The fourth exercise calms breathing, making it regular and easy.

5 The fifth exercise concentrates on soothing and warming the solar plexus and the abdomen.

6 Finally you are asked to think of your forehead being cooled, as though a cool hand were being pressed on a fevered brow.

PRECAUTIONS

AT is very safe, with no long-term adverse side-effects. However, initial training in AT techniques with a qualified instructor is essential because AT is a powerful tool that may unleash buried feelings of frustration or anger. It is therefore important to have expert advice available. If you have an existing medical condition, such as psychiatric problems, pregnancy, or a heart condition, always consult your doctor before undergoing AT, and ensure that the instructor is medically qualified. Remember, too, that AT is an adjunct to medical treatment, rather than a substitute for it. Occasionally, trainees have reported headaches or chest pains after practicing AT. These may need further investigation.

ABOVE *Progressive relaxation aims to free the mind from the constraints of everyday life so that it can focus on the healing process. Regular practice is necessary, and programs should always be undertaken under the supervision of a trained instructor.*

SELF-HELP

Once you have mastered the techniques of AT, it becomes one of the most versatile and useful of all the therapies that can be employed to reduce stress and promote well-being. Because of the variety of postures that can be used, it is possible to practice AT almost anywhere – on a train journey, in the office, at home, or lying on the beach.

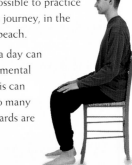

As little as ten minutes' practice a day can provide noticeable physical and mental benefits, and a few more than this can pay further dividends. As with so many other forms of self-help, the rewards are proportional to the effort.

BIOFEEDBACK

It is ironic that one of the newest and most technology-dependent forms of therapy should tread closely in the footsteps of ancient Eastern healing traditions. Yet this is exactly what biofeedback does. Using the full panoply of Western monitoring machinery, biofeedback is a process used to teach people how to influence aspects of their physiology that were, until recently, considered to be outside conscious control: for example, brainwaves, heartrate, blood pressure, and skin temperature. Biofeedback is now widely accepted as an effective relaxation technique — but also offers the ability to control a wide range of ailments, from stress-related conditions to asthma and migraines.

Biofeedback originated in the work of the so-called "behaviorist" school of psychologists in the years before the World War II. These researchers, using animals such as rats and pigeons, set out to demonstrate that most aspects of behavior are conditioned, and that desired behaviors can be reinforced by rewards (*see pages 196–7*).

At the time, it was assumed that only behavior that was under voluntary control could be influenced in this way. However, in the late 1950s and during the 1960s, it became apparent that processes previously considered to be involuntary could also be altered at will in response to conditioning. People could be trained to produce relaxing alpha brain waves, and laboratory rats could be trained to control such things as blood pressure, heartbeat, and bloodflow to different parts of the body.

Before long, scientists began to reason that what worked in rats might well work in the human body. The availability of sophisticated monitoring equipment, such as the electroencephalograph (EEG) and the electromyograph (EMG), meant that researchers had plenty of machines with which to test their theory. And the results lived up to expectations. To the Eastern yogi or Buddhist monk, this would have come as no surprise. But to the more sceptical West, it flew in the face of the conventional wisdom that "involuntary" aspects of human physiology were outside the domain of the conscious mind.

Nevertheless, the time was ripe. The explosion of interest in alternative medicine during the 1970s and 1980s created an ideal climate for this blend of science

ABOVE *In the same tradition as many ancient Eastern healing techniques, biofeedback has evolved from an understanding that our physical, mental, and emotional functions are all interconnected.*

and holistic idealism, and interest in biofeedback grew rapidly — not least because it appeared to validate many of the assumptions on which holistic medicine is based. Today biofeedback is practiced widely in the U.S., and is becoming increasingly common throughout the rest of the Western world.

WHAT IS BIOFEEDBACK?

The concept of feedback comes from electronics, where it refers to a method of controling systems by feeding back to them the results of previous output. For example, a thermostat is a feedback device — one that responds to the external temperature by turning a heat source on or off. Biofeedback is the application of this principle to biological systems, and in particular to the human body.

Biofeedback needs, first of all, a method of monitoring the physiological function that is to be controled. At its simplest, this may be no more than a fingertip blood flow meter, but more sophisticated equipment is also used — an EEG to measure brain activity, an EMG to measure muscular tension, an ECG (electrocardiograph) to measure heartbeat, and monitors to record electrical skin resistance (ESR) and perspiration, skin temperature, and so on. The patient is attached to the biofeedback device by probes or electrodes.

Information about changes in the body must then be displayed to the subject in an easily understood form. This might be a board of flashing lights, or sounds of varying pitch, or a simple rhythmic tone. Increasingly, as computers become even more sophisticated, the output from the monitoring equipment is displayed as images on a VDU.

The subject is then trained (the process being called "biogenic training") to achieve the desired result – a reduction in the number of flashing lights or a lowering of pitch – by an act of will. Most people find that they are able to learn the particular state of mind that works for them in the space of just a few hours, and should then be able to enter it whenever they wish, even without the aid of monitors.

Biofeedback was originally regarded as an effective form of relaxation therapy, and stress relief is still one of its main uses. However, in the U.S. in particular, it is also regarded as a holistic therapy leading to greater self-awareness and the achievement of personal goals.

CONSULTING A PRACTITIONER

After an initial consultation, the practitioner – almost always a doctor – will choose the function to be monitored and attach you to the the appropriate equipment. You will then be asked to concentrate on the display, whether it be visual or auditory, and to concentrate on changing it.

In practice, you need to be in a state of relaxed awareness to undergo biogenic training. The doctor will use various techniques to help you relax, perhaps by talking soothingly to you, or by helping you to "visualize" comforting images. Some therapists reinforce the training by offering "rewards" of one type or another.

Biogenic training takes time: at least six sessions of about a half hour each are usually required. Unfortunately, while many people perform very well while attached to the machinery in the therapist's consulting room, they gradually lose the ability to do

ABOVE *An example of normal EMG readings from a biofeedback monitor.*

so when they return home – it can be difficult to recreate the correct frame of mind in a day-to-day setting. It is important, therefore, that the doctor devotes some part of the course to training when the equipment is switched off. Self-help techniques (*see below*) may also be useful.

SELF-HELP

A number of special monitoring devices are available for use in the home. They range from the "Relaxometer," used to measure skin resistance, and "temperature trainers," used to measure blood flow in the underlying tissues, to simple EEG and EMG machines.

Even without special machinery, it is important that you practice the biofeedback skills you have learned on a regular daily basis. Without doing so, it is unlikely that the therapy will have lasting effects.

PATHFINDER

Biofeedback has proved of value in treating many stress-related conditions, including anxiety, insomnia, high blood pressure, tachycardia, and tension headaches. It is the best known treatment for Raynaud's Disease and trench foot, and has been successful in combating migraines and low back pain. Asthma and incontinence are among other disorders that have been successfully treated. There is also evidence that biofeedback can be used in the treatment of eating disorders, smoking, and addiction to alcohol. Conditions that respond well to biofeedback techniques include:

ALLERGIES *SEE P.* 339

ANXIETY *SEE PP.* 256–7

ATHEROSCLEROSIS *SEE P.*305

BACK PROBLEMS *SEE P.* 345

DIABETES *SEE P.* 336

FEAR OF DENTAL TREATMENT *SEE P.* 286

HIGH BLOOD PRESSURE *SEE P.* 302

IRRITABLE BOWEL SYNDROME (IBS) *SEE P.* 315

MIGRAINE *SEE P.* 269

RAYNAUD'S DISEASE *SEE P.* 306

STRESS *SEE P.* 262–3

STROKE *SEE P.* 359

TINNITUS *SEE P.* 281

URINARY INCONTINENCE *SEE P.* 317

PRECAUTIONS

Biofeedback is very safe. However, if you are undergoing any sort of medical treatment, you should consult your doctor before undergoing therapy. Biofeedback should not be used as a substitute for proper medical attention since it may mask the symptoms of a more serious condition.

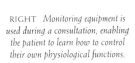

RIGHT *Monitoring equipment is used during a consultation, enabling the patient to learn how to control their own physiological functions.*

VISUALIZATION

ANCIENT IDEAS

Visualization was known to the ancient Romans, though not put to the therapeutic purposes for which it is employed today. Ovid, the Roman poet, advised a lovesick youth to imagine the object of his affections in unflattering situations in order to overcome his infatuation.

ABOVE *Ovid can be said to be an early advocate of visualization.*

In essence, visualization is a form of constructive daydreaming. It harnesses the imagination to create a sense of well-being, to replace negative attitudes with positive ones, and to enhance the natural healing powers of the body. Visualization is one of the most enjoyable and relaxing forms of therapy. At its simplest, it involves no more than the creation and exploration of pleasant or satisfying images produced by the mind. When used in a more focused way, the images can be chosen to deal directly with emotional problems or with particular diseases and disorders. Visualization forms a part of many relaxation and mind and spirit therapies.

Although relatively new in the West, visualization has been used in Eastern medicine for thousands of years. It is an integral part of Chinese medicine, and is an equally ancient tradition among Tibetan Buddhists, who are taught to visualize a healing deity to bring about a cure. Shamanic societies, using witch doctors, medicine men, and healing priests, have all made use of the power of the imagination in curing (or causing) disease.

Even in the West, the value of visualization was not completely ignored. The Roman poet, Ovid, in his book *Cures for Love*, recommends that a lovesick young man should overcome his infatuation by imagining his beloved in unflattering situations: if she sings badly, then imagine her singing; if she has bad teeth, then picture her smiling. Visualization was also used by some hypnotists in the 19th and early 20th centuries. Nevertheless, it was not until the 1960s, partly as a result of research in biofeedback therapy (*see pages 212–3*), that visualization began to be regarded as a valuable form of therapy in its own right.

Today, visualization has become widely accepted in complementary medicine, and is often used in conjunction with other mind and body therapies such as hypnotherapy (*see pages 218–23*), autogenic therapy (*see pages 210–11*), and biofeedback and relaxation techniques (*see pages 158–65*). It has also entered into mainstream medical practice to a limited extent. Some cancer specialists, especially in the U.S., Europe, and Australasia, recommend it as part of an overall program of therapy, claiming that adherents enjoy a better quality of life. Visualization techniques have also been used for some time to help sporting competitors to improve their performance.

WHAT IS VISUALIZATION?

Most people are able to conjure up mental images. These may be remembered scenes from past times, or they may be purely imaginary. Visualization provides techniques for turning these images to good use.

There are two main ways in which images are used. The first is passive or receptive visualization. In this, the subject is in a relaxed state, and the image is allowed to surface gently in the mind. Exploration and examination of the image in all its details – including scents and sounds – may provide clues to subconscious emotional problems and can suggest ways of dealing with them. Receptive visualization can be a tool for self-discovery.

The second form is active visualization. This involves selecting and concentrating on an image that has direct

LEFT *Imagine a restful landscape of great beauty to help combat stress.*

relevance to a specific emotional or physical problem. If you are suffering from stress, you can relax deeply by concentrating on calm and soothing scenes. If you suffer from asthma, you might imagine a mountain stream, with clear running water and fresh clean air. This form of visualization is often accompanied by the use of auto-suggestion, for example, "I am feeling warm and comfortable, and my breathing is deep and even" (*see self-hypnosis, pages 222–3*).

Active visualization may go much further than this. You can create a picture of a battle going on inside your body and imagine yourself as a participant. Cancer patients, for example, might think of themselves as white blood cells engaged in pitched battle with cancerous cells in a tumor, and watch triumphantly as the defeated enemy is eliminated from the body.

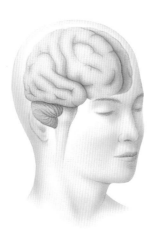

ABOVE *Active visualization stimulates the right-hand side of the brain.*

How Does It Work?

The cerebral cortex is the largest part of the brain, and is concerned with information processing. It is divided into two hemispheres, each associated with different kinds of mental activity. The dominant hemisphere, usually the left side, is concerned with logic, language, and mathematics, while the right is thought to be the seat of imagination, creativity, and intuition. Visualization has been shown to stimulate the right hemisphere of the cerebral cortex. The production of images in the mind may send messages from the cerebral cortex to the autonomic nervous system, which controls "involuntary," automatic processes such as heartbeat, digestion and body temperature, and also through the pituitary gland to the hormonal system. But how the imagination affects these processes is unclear.

CONSULTING A THERAPIST

After an initial consultation to assess your needs and to choose appropriate images, you will be asked to sit or lie down in a comfortable position, relax, and close your eyes. Often, the practitioner will lead you through some simple relaxation exercises (see pp. 162–3) to free the body from tension and stress.

The therapist will then guide you as you build up the image in your mind. You will be asked to fill in the scene as completely as possible, and describe it in detail – including any associated sounds and smells. You will be encouraged to focus entirely on the picture you are building up in your mind, ignoring any distractions and extraneous events. The therapist may also lead you in repeating various positive suggestions or affirmations that represent the direction that the therapy is designed to take.

At the end of the session, you will be told to open your eyes and take a few moments to become aware of your surroundings again. You will usually be encouraged to repeat the process at home, sometimes with the aid of a tape, at least

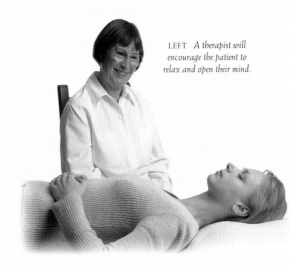

LEFT *A therapist will encourage the patient to relax and open their mind.*

once a day between sessions. According to the theory, if visualization is repeated enough, expectations rise and the patient acts as though the image were a reality.

A few people have great difficulty in forming and concentrating on mental images, and visualization may not be the best form of therapy for them. Equally, some people experience benefits from visualization straight away, although most require several sessions before real improvement becomes apparent. However, once the technique has been learnt and maintained, a therapeutic image can be conjured up almost instantly and used to deal with imminent problems, such as the recurrence of pain.

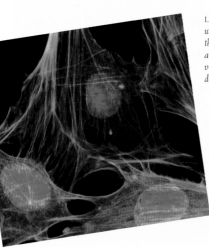

LEFT *Cancer patients who use visualization in their treatment programs are encouraged to visualize white blood cells destroying cancer cells.*

ORTHODOX VIEW

Although the mind/body relationship cannot as yet be scientifically explained, studies suggest that visualization is a valuable stress-reducing technique. Harnessing the power of the imagination to affect these automatic processes may enable the body to find other ways of dealing with pain and diseases. Most doctors accept that visualization, in so far as it promotes relaxation and relief from stress, has definite health benefits. Many would also agree that a positive attitude in dealing with disease can enhance the effectiveness of other forms of therapy. It is on this basis that some specialists recommend visualization alongside chemotherapy or radiation therapy in the treatment of cancer and the management of chronic pain.

Nevertheless, most doctors would be profoundly skeptical about the ability of mental images, however vivid, to influence directly the progress of organic diseases.

SELF-HELP

Before beginning a session of visualization at home, find somewhere quiet and peaceful, where you are not likely to be disturbed for at least 15 minutes. Make sure you are comfortable – a high-backed chair with head and neck support is ideal – and relax fully. It may help to use a simple relaxation technique (*see pages 162–3*), or put yourself into a light trance if you are familiar with self-hypnosis (*see pages 222–3*). Then begin to concentrate on your chosen image.

Visualization is a very personal form of therapy, so choose images that are appropriate for the problem that you want to deal with. Take care not to choose situations with unpleasant associations – don't imagine yourself in a flower-filled garden if you suffer from hayfever, for example, or in a dark tunnel if you are claustrophobic.

1 *Imagine that you are looking at a large screen and project onto it a picture of the way you are now. Make the image as unpleasant as possible. If you are overweight, picture yourself on a beach in an ill-fitting bathing suit. Imagine that you would like to swim in the sea, but are afraid to do so for fear that people will mock the rolls of fat around your body, and that the exercise will leave you panting and out of breath. Watch your friends or family playing on the beach and wish that you could join them.*

While it is better to learn visualization from an experienced practitioner, there are some simple exercises that you can perform without guidance and use to extend the lessons you have learnt during therapy. Remember that visualization is a creative process. Don't rely simply on literal representations of a scene, but use symbols, personal associations, and memories. Experiment with different images and techniques until you find the ones that work best for you.

To Change Unwanted Habits

Visualization can help to change undesirable habits, such as smoking, drinking too much, and overeating. A useful technique is known as the "swish" method, described in the following steps:

ABOVE *Mentally projecting a positive self-image is part of the healing technique of visualization.*

2 *Then replace this image with one depicting how you would like to be: slim and fit, and participating in the activities going on around you. You feel happier and have much greater self-confidence.*

3 *Return to the negative image once more, but this time, place a small "picture-within-a-picture" image of the positive situation in the bottom right-hand corner of the screen.*

4 *As you watch, allow the small, positive picture to grow rapidly and brighten until it covers and obscures the negative picture. Allow the negative image to fade away completely.*

5 *After doing this, blank the screen once more, and repeat the exercise five or six times, blanking the screen or opening your eyes at the end of each "swish."*

6 *Before you end the session, try conjuring up the images once again. The positive image should be easier to call up, and brighter and clearer than the negative image. If not, repeat the exercise, and consider making changes to the images you are using. Perform this exercise at least once a day, and preferably two or three times, until you have achieved the desired result.*

PRECAUTIONS

■ Take care not to visualize situations that may contain elements that could disturb you.

■ Do not attempt to use visualization to control symptoms without being sure that they are not indications of underlying disease that needs treatment. Consult your doctor if you are not sure what the symptoms mean.

For Pain Relief

Pain, which can range from mild discomfort to excruciating agony, is the body's way of signaling that something is wrong. It may have a clear origin or no apparent explanation. The mind is considered to be capable of determining our ability to tolerate pain. How much pain is experienced depends on the amount of endorphins, the body's natural painkillers, that are in circulation. The level of endorphins is affected by our psychological state: someone who is depressed produces fewer endorphins and consequently may perceive the pain as being worse. There are a number of useful ways of using visualization to control pain.

One technique that can be used effectively in the control of chronic pain, particularly when it becomes severe, makes use of the image of a dial. The dial technique, with appropriate imagery, can also be useful in other situations. For example, sexual problems can sometimes be solved by imagining the numbers on the dial as stages of sexual arousal, which can be stimulated by sexual fantasies or by imagining desire as a fluid cascading through the body. This response will then become more natural until the response is automatic and the problem cured.

1 *Assess your current level of pain and rate it on the dial on a scale of one to ten, where ten represents the worst pain you normally experience. Keep the image of the dial in your mind.*

2 *Imagine yourself entering a dark tunnel, which represents your pain. The pain itself will get slightly worse as you enter the tunnel, and the pointer on the dial should move slightly higher.*

3 *As you walk through the tunnel, you notice a pinpoint of light at the far end. This grows gradually in size and brightness as you approach and, at the same time, you feel an easing of your discomfort. The hand on the dial slowly moves down.*

4 *Continue to walk along the tunnel until the level of pain is at a tolerable level – two or three on the dial, say. Do not expect to remove the pain altogether, since this is seldom successful, and failure can undermine the positive effects of the imagery. At this point, allow yourself to emerge from the tunnel into the brightness.*

5 *Before opening your eyes, tell yourself how much more comfortable you feel and will continue to feel.*

ABOVE *Visualizing ice around a painful area can help with pain control.*

ABOVE *The "dial technique" can be used to control and overcome pain.*

Another method is to concentrate on the idea of numbness. If you picture your hand surrounded by ice, you will gradually feel it growing numb. Once this has been achieved, you can move your hand and place it over the painful area and imagine the numbness being transferred to the site of the pain.

FOR MEDICAL CONDITIONS

Specific diseases and disorders can often be helped by visualizing the actual healing processes going on in the body. This requires some basic knowledge about the disease process itself, so you may need to read or seek advice about your particular condition.

For eczema, for example, imagine that your discomfort is due to insects crawling around your skin. Then picture the insects being swept away by cooling, healing water, and watch the bloodflow in the skin increase to speed up the healing process.

For high blood pressure, picture the heart as a muscular sac and the arteries as muscular tubes. Watch how the heart responds to signals from the brain by speeding up, and raising blood pressure, or by slowing down and lowering blood pressure. Then gradually picture the "slowing down" signals outnumbering the "speeding up" signals and feel your blood pressure diminishing.

For infections, picture the white blood cells as they tackle and kill the invaders and eliminate them from the body. If you are taking antibiotics, watch as the drugs destroy the alien bacteria.

For depression or the symptoms of premenstrual syndrome (PMS), imagine that you are carrying all your problems up a hill in a backpack. Gradually unload the contents of your backpack into a chest or casket, and then lock it, leaving you unencumbered in beautiful surroundings.

PATHFINDER

Visualization is often used as a pain-control technique. However, it can also be useful in aiding the healing process in the following specific disorders:

ALLERGIES SEE PP. 338–9
ANXIETY SEE PP. 256–7
ASTHMA SEE PP. 224–5
COLD SORES SEE P. 275
DEPRESSION SEE P. 261
EATING DISORDERS SEE PP. 264–5
ECZEMA AND DERMATITIS SEE P. 273
HIGH BLOOD PRESSURE SEE P. 302
HIV AND AIDS SEE PP. 340–1
LABOR PAINS SEE P. 328
MENSTRUAL PROBLEMS SEE P. 322
OBESITY SEE PP. 334–5
POST-DELIVERY PROBLEMS SEE P. 329
PREMENSTRUAL SYNDROME SEE P. 323
PSORIASIS SEE P. 272
SHINGLES SEE P. 266
STRESS SEE PP. 262–3

ABOVE *Visualizing the healing process can be beneficial for skin complaints such as eczema.*

HYPNOTHERAPY

Hypnosis is a strange, dreamlike state of consciousness, that has been used for centuries to promote healing. It is best explained as a state of extreme physical and mental relaxation, whereby the patient experiences a sense of detachment from reality and a heightened suggestibility. Hypnotherapists consider that the workings of the mind have a direct effect on the body and aim to stimulate subconscious problem-solving and healing mechanisms to affect mental and physical processes. Hypnotherapy has managed to distance itself from its more dubious antecedents and is increasingly accepted as a legitimate form of therapy.

It seems likely that the hypnotic trance has been a common experience since the earliest days of the human race. There is no doubt that it has played its part in both pagan and religious rituals and it is known to have been used by the ancient Greeks to cure hysteria and by the Druids (who called it the "magic sleep") to cure warts. However, the history of the use of hypnotism as a form of therapy is usually traced back to the 18th century and to the work of an Austrian doctor called Franz Anton Mesmer.

Mesmer originally practiced in Vienna, where he found that he had the ability to cure all sorts of diseases without the use of surgery or medication. He attributed this to the existence of a form of "animal magnetism" that flowed through the body, and based his treatments on various – often highly flamboyant – rituals to restore the proper flow of this "magnetic fluid." Word of his successes soon spread and, in 1778, he was invited to Paris by Louis XVI. His popularity alarmed the medical establishment of the day, and a commission to examine the claims of "mesmerism" was set up in 1784. This duly reported that the cures that the method undoubtedly achieved were due not to magnetism, but to the patients' imaginations. Mesmer and his "animal magnetism" gradually fell into disrepute, and little more was heard of the matter.

Medicine of the Imagination

The commission had, however, missed an important point – if a "medicine of the imagination" worked, then why not practice a medicine of the imagination?

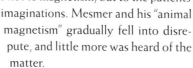

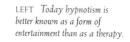

LEFT *Today hypnotism is better known as a form of entertainment than as a therapy.*

ABOVE *Hypnotism was developed from an earlier controversial technique, mesmerism, and was used by Freud in his early career.*

This point was not lost on some of Mesmer's followers and a few doctors continued to experiment. At the University College Hospital in London, in the early 19th century, a surgeon called John Elliotson began to use hypnotic techniques to anesthetize patients during surgery. Despite the fact that Elliotson was a highly respected physician, he was treated with derision and was dismissed from his post. A respected Scottish surgeon, James Baird, also became interested in mesmerism, conferring a degree of respectability on the practice by changing the name from mesmerism to hypnosis, from the Greek *hypnos*, meaning "sleep." In fact, the term is rather misleading, because numerous studies have shown that the pattern of brain activity during hypnosis is quite different from that observed during sleep.

In 1891, a committee of the British Medical Association gave cautious approval to the use of hypnosis for certain forms of therapy. But none of this was enough to overcome the traditional hostility of the medical profession, and interest in Britain remained at a very low level throughout the first half of the 20th century. Hypnotism became the stuff of stage performances – the province of showmen and charlatans.

Serious Men of Science

Interest in France was more lively. At the Medical Faculty of the Salpêtrière Hospital in Paris, Professor Jean-Martin Charcot investigated the subject at length and argued persuasively that hypnotism should be taken seriously. His ideas were taken up by Ambrose Liébeault and Hippolyte Bernheim, who founded a "school of hypnotism" in Nancy in the 1890s. These men were certainly not charlatans: on the contrary, they were serious men of science and their views commanded serious respect from their colleagues and the public.

Among those who became interested in hypnosis was Sigmund Freud (*see pages 188 and 192*), who studied under both Bernheim and Charcot. Freud used hypnosis for a time in the treatment of mental illness, but preferred to

AUTO-SUGGESTION

A hypnotic technique popularized in the 1920s by French pharmacist Emile Coué, auto-suggestion is a way of changing your behavior by firmly repeating ideas to yourself.

The best-known example of this is, "Every day, in every way, I am getting better and better." This technique can be used to control undesirable habits or to cope with anxiety, as the repetitive nature of the chant calms the patient. The patient will soon respond to minimal repetition.

work with the patient fully conscious and developed psychoanalytical techniques of his own. Ironically, these were not so very different from the techniques now used in modern hypnotherapy.

In America, hypnotism never fell into quite the same disrepute as it did in Britain, and research and experiment carried on quietly throughout the early 20th century. In 1933, the first modern book on the subject – *Hypnosis and Suggestibility*, by C. L. Hull – was published. The modern form of hypnotherapy, widely used in the West, was developed by Milton H. Erickson, a U.S. psychotherapist, in the 1950s and 1960s.

As long ago as 1953, the British Medical Association recommended the use of hypnotherapy for the treatment of physical and psychological disorders and, three years later, the American Medical Association did the same. The growth of interest in complementary therapies during the 1980s stimulated a great expansion in the number of practitioners and it is widely available today in many hospitals.

WHAT IS HYPNOSIS?

When we are fully alert, our conscious minds are working full time. The conscious mind acts as a filter to the deeper subconscious mind, censoring and interpreting subconscious impulses so that they conform to our particular view of the world at the time. In a hypnotic trance, the two streams – conscious and subconscious – become disassociated: each carries on separately without reference to the other, but the mind increasingly focuses on the inner subconscious stream. Daydreaming, intense absorption in some task to the exclusion of all others, and the half-waking, half-sleeping state that often precedes and follows true sleep are all very similar to, if not actually examples of, hypnosis.

Hypnotherapists usually find it convenient to divide hypnosis into three different stages. The first is a light or shallow trance. In this, the eyes are closed, but subjects remain fully aware of the outside world and are conscious of events going on around them. Nevertheless, even in a light trance, subjects will accept suggestions to give themselves a more positive self-image and increased self-confidence.

The second stage, a medium trance, can produce far more dramatic effects. Heart rate and other physiological processes slow down, and the brain produces alpha waves, the brain waves associated with quiet, receptive states. Aches and pains may be banished, allergic reactions cease, and the mind becomes deeply receptive to suggestions. Most hypnotherapy is performed on subjects in a medium trance.

Age Regression

The third stage is a deep trance. The subject is completely anesthetized and is capable of extraordinary feats of memory. The hypnotist can guide the subject back to his or her earliest youth – even to the moment of birth – and the subject will recall events and scenes in minute and vivid detail. This technique, known as age regression, is used to uncover hidden or suppressed memories that may be responsible for a variety of mental or physical problems so that they can be treated.

The deeper into hypnosis the subject goes, the closer he/she drifts towards the state of sleep. However, since the subject is not asleep, he/she will generally remain aware of his/her surroundings and remember his/her experience. Amnesia will usually only occur if this has been suggested to the subject while he/she is in a trance.

Most people are capable of entering a hypnotic state and of these, about 10 percent are highly hypnotizable and can be taken into a deep trance. However, much depends on the willingness of the person to be hypnotized.

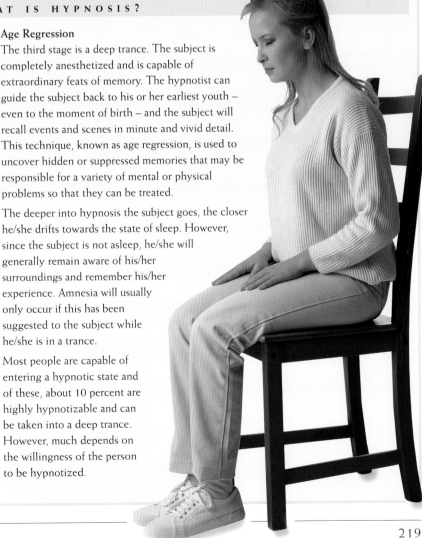

IMAGINATION

Imagery is often regarded as the language of the subconscious, and the use of imagery is a very powerful means of self-development when under hypnosis. The patient can train herself to use her imagination in a positive way, which can in turn improve her performance. Negative feelings can also be controlled by the use of imagination, and unwanted feelings can be modified or disposed of. (*See also Archetypes, p. 194, Visualization, pp. 214–7, and Dreamwork, pp. 224–5.*)

CONSULTING A THERAPIST

Most hypnotherapists agree that all hypnosis is self-hypnosis. The hypnotist's role is to guide you into a trance. You cannot be hypnotized against your will, and you can rouse yourself from a trance whenever you really wish to do so. Nor can you be made to do anything under hypnosis that you find offensive or repugnant. People are sometimes worried that they surrender all control of their thoughts and actions to the hypnotist and that an unscrupulous practitioner might take advantage of them. In fact, the worst that can happen is that people can lose their inhibitions – much as they might do under the influence of alcohol – and they may then be persuaded to do something that that they later regret; but this will not happen if you choose a responsible hypnotherapist in the first place.

A course of hypnotherapy will usually begin with a full consultation. The therapist will find out details of your medical history and discuss any current physical or psychological problems. He will also explain what will happen during hypnosis, and the number of sessions that are likely to be required.

HYPNOTHERAPY TECHNIQUES

Hypnotherapy treatment usually consists of weekly one-hour sessions, the number of which will vary according to the problem. The techniques used to induce a trance vary from one practitioner to another, but the basic principles are much the same.

Classical Induction

You will be asked to relax, perhaps by imagining yourself in some favorite place, or by remembering a time when you were contented and at ease. The therapist will then talk to you in a calm, controlled, and relaxing manner. This may take the form of constant repetition of a particular phrase, or it might involve a description of a walk along a sunny river bank, for example. You may be asked to concentrate on a particular spot on the wall, or to stare at a pendulum or even simply the tip of a pencil.

After a while your eyelids will start to feel heavy and the therapist will encourage you to close them, talking all the time in the same slow, soothing fashion. After a while, you begin to feel more and more detached from the everyday world. Sounds, except for the hypnotist's voice, seem to be coming from far away. You will feel comfortable, peaceful, and relaxed. After about 15 minutes you will be in a light trance. This may be sufficient for certain purposes – people who want to give

ABOVE During hypnotherapy the patient will be asked to concentrate on an object such as a pendulum in order to induce the trance state.

up smoking often only need a single session in a light trance for the treatment to succeed. However, for most forms of therapy, a medium or deep trance is required.

A common method of taking the subject into a deeper trance is to use the image of a staircase or an elevator. The hypnotherapist will ask you to imagine yourself at the top of the stairs, and will slowly count from one to ten as you go down. Alternatively, he will ask you to think of yourself descending in an elevator, and will count down from ten to one as you pass successive floors. You will be asked to "go deeper" into your inner self as this is going on.

Under Hypnosis

At this stage, the hypnotist can simply plant the required suggestions in the subject's mind – allergic symptoms, such as the itching skin of eczema, or the breathlessness of asthma, can often be cured by the straightforward suggestion that they are going away. However, most reputable hypnotherapists would regard this as dubious practice. Most physical and psychological disorders have underlying causes that need to be discovered and dealt with if a successful cure is to be effected. An important part of therapy is therefore the uncovering of repressed feelings of anxiety or anger and their replacement with positive feelings of confidence and a belief in the ability to cope. It is also vital that the suggestions continue to work when the subject is roused from the trance. Post-hypnotic suggestions may take some time

BELOW The practitioner will make sure the patient is in a trance before beginning the treatment.

PAST-LIFE THERAPY

Some hypnotherapists and psychotherapists use age regression techniques (see p. 219) to enable patients to express what appear to be memories of previous lives: The patient is encouraged to remember past events that may be of current significance, and may find herself recalling times and places of which she has no knowledge. Although these regressions are sometimes thought to be evidence of reincarnation, it is more likely that they are symbolic representations of buried thoughts or emotions, and it is inadvisable to interpret events recalled in this way literally.

However, whatever their source, these "memories" can lead to catharsis, a sudden release of anxiety or tension that results from uncovering repressed trauma, and may help resolve emotional disorders such as anxiety or phobias.

LEFT *Hypnosis may uncover underlying anxieties which are the cause of the patient's disorder.*

RIGHT *Positive feelings implanted by the hypnotherapist should remain with the patient once the session is over.*

to take root, and several sessions may be required before negative feelings can be converted into positive ones.

The hypnotherapist will also plant suggestions that make it easier for you to enter a trance in the future, and will teach you techniques of self-hypnosis – most courses of hypnotherapy require you to reinforce the effects of sessions with the therapist with regular periods of self-hypnosis (*see pages 213–4*). This is particularly true in the case in the control of chronic pain – as in severe arthritis, for example – or where self-hypnosis not only offers pain relief but helps to alter attitudes to pain and counteracts the anger or depression that chronic pain can cause.

CHOOSING YOUR THERAPIST

It is always better to go to a fully qualified hypnotherapist who has the training and experience to deal with any psychological problems that may emerge in the course of therapy. Just as hypnotherapy can be a powerful aid in curing diseases and disorders, so, in the wrong hands, it can actually make matters worse. A hypnotist who merely cures the symptoms without investigating the underlying cause may simply be laying the foundations for a new set of symptoms to emerge: you may be cured of your eczema but find that you develop crippling migraines instead. An untrained hypnotist may also fail to recognize when symptoms are due to a serious physical condition. A stomach ache may be due to tension and stress, and may be helped by hypnosis, but it may also be a symptom of an ulcer which, if untreated, can become life-threatening.

As a general rule, you should avoid hypnotists who advertise, even if they only offer cures for smoking or eating disorders. Your doctor is the best person to ask for advice. Many doctors are trained in hypnotherapy themselves, although not all of them practice, and they will normally be able to recommend a good hypnotherapist in your area.

RIGHT *In a relaxed trance state the hypnotized subject is asked to imagine a calm setting.*

ORTHODOX VIEW

On the whole, hypnotism has been long regarded as somewhat disreputable, first because of its use on the stage as a form of entertainment and second because the mechanism behind it is still not understood. However, there is incontrovertible scientific evidence to show that hypnosis does work, although it cannot be explained how, and hypnotherapy is gaining increasing acceptance in the medical profession. Studies have shown that some patients are able to anesthetize themselves using hypnosis, and higher levels of endorphins, the body's natural painkiller, have been recorded following hypnotherapy.

Hypnotherapy appears to work by encouraging the use of the patient's inner resources. Suggestions and imagery are the tools most often used in hypnosis, and often form a part of behavioral and cognitive therapy (*see pp. 196–9*).

Hypnosis is used most successfully in the treatment of phobias or addictions, but it has also been shown to be effective in providing pain relief for surgery, dentistry, and childbirth. Hypnosis is a naturally occuring state, but there are precautions (*see pp. 222*). However, it is not suitable as a substitute for conventional treatment and your doctor's advice should always be sought before embarking upon it. Most doctors would advocate self-hypnosis as a relaxation technique.

PRECAUTIONS

■ Hypnotherapy is a particularly safe form of treatment, with no recorded significant side effects. However, it would be wise to be wary of hypnotherapists who advertise or who are not trained in psycho-therapeutic techniques. Always seek your doctor's advice before consulting a hypnotherapist.

■ Do not undergo hypnotherapy or self-hypnosis if you suffer from epilepsy: there is a small risk of inducing a fit. Hypnotherapy should be avoided if you have a history of psychosis or severe depression.

■ Do not use self-hypnosis to treat pain or other problems that might indicate an underlying medical problem.

ABOVE *Listing what you hope to achieve from hypnosis can be the first step to achieving your goals.*

SELF-HYPNOSIS

Most people can learn to hypnotize themselves. Self-hypnosis is commonly used to reinforce the post-hypnotic suggestions planted by a professional hypnotherapist. This is not only because these suggestions often need to be strengthened gradually over a period of time – particularly if they involve substantial changes in attitudes or lifestyle – but also because your own motivation and commitment to change can be vital to the success of the treatment. If, at heart, you really don't want to change your behavior or lifestyle, or have a deep-rooted fear of doing so, then self-hypnosis is very unlikely to have any effect.

It is also important that you don't expect too much. The effectiveness of hypnosis, like other forms of therapy, varies widely from one person to another. Some people have reported an extraordinary degree of improvement in a very short time, but these are the exceptions. Most people find that improvements are gradual and often, to begin with, imperceptible. A few people will experience no apparent benefits at all.

Most therapists recommend that you should practice self-hypnosis at least once a day, for about 20 to 30 minutes, although this can be reduced once you become more expert at sinking into a trance. If possible, establish a routine, so that your sessions take place at the same time each day, preferably at a time when there will be a minimum of distractions. Choose a quiet room with a comfortable armchair and, if necessary, take the phone off the hook and warn other members of the family to keep away.

Preliminaries

Before embarking on self-hypnosis, it can help a great deal if you spend some time analyzing exactly what it is you want to improve, and what benefits the changes will bring. If you want to give up smoking, for example, you might make a list of the following benefits:

✻ Improved general health and fitness;
  ✻ Decreased risk of lung cancer, heart disease, and other smoking-related disorders;
    ✻ More money to spend on other things such as clothes or holidays;
  ✻ Absence of the smell of stale tobacco from clothes, hair, and the home;
✻ A feeling of freedom from the spell of an addictive habit.

It is also worth examining any underlying benefits – or "secondary gains" – that you derive from the behavior you want to change. Does it earn you attention or sympathy from those around you, for example, or does it enable you to avoid facing up to something you find

unpleasant? If so, it can be difficult to achieve your goal without addressing the underlying problem.

You should also prepare, very precisely, the suggestions you want to plant. These should always be phrased in a positive rather than a negative way. You should not say, for example, "I will not feel anxious and nervous at meetings with business colleagues," because the words "anxious" and "nervous" will only reinforce the feelings of anxiety and nervousness you already have. Instead, you should say, "I can feel relaxed and confident at meetings with business colleagues." If the suggestion includes mention of a specific meeting, then post-hypnotic suggestion will come into play: "When I enter the meeting on Monday morning, I will feel relaxed, calm and confident" will trigger these feelings when you enter the meeting room.

The "staircase technique" is very similar to the one used by professional hypnotherapists.

﹡ Close your eyes and imagine yourself at the top of a staircase with ten or twenty steps leading down to a beautiful place of great peace and calm.
﹡ Slowly descend the staircase, counting the steps as you go. Try to synchronize the counting with your breathing – go down, say, one step on every second outward breath.
﹡ Tell yourself as you descend that you are feeling increasingly relaxed and comfortable, and that when you reach the bottom you will be contented and at peace. Say to yourself that you are going deeper and deeper into your inner self.
﹡ When you reach your special place, explore it in every detail before finding somewhere to sit. Then repeat your suggestions so as to fix them deep in your subconscious mind.
﹡ To come out of hypnosis, simply reverse the process, climbing back up the stairs and counting downward from ten or twenty to one. Before opening your eyes, suggest that you are going to feel alert and refreshed.
The "eye-fixation" technique is also part of the hypnotherapist's repertoire that can be used just as well at home.

﹡ Sit in a comfortable armchair and relax. Find a spot on the wall, or a small object, positioned just above your line of sight, and stare at it.
﹡ Keep your gaze fixed firmly on the spot, and concentrate on it to the exclusion of everything else. After a while it may begin to move, or change shape. Keep staring, noticing how it changes.
﹡ Soon your eyelids will begin to feel heavy. Eventually, you may be unable to keep them open.
﹡ Enjoy the feeling of relaxation that begins to spread through you. Notice how your breathing slows down. Repeat suggestions to deepen relaxation: for example, "With each breath, I am feeling a little more relaxed;" and "With each breath I am moving deeper into myself."
﹡ Rehearse your suggestions to create positive feelings.
﹡ Come out of hypnosis when you are ready by counting down from three to one. Before opening your eyes, suggest to yourself that you will feel alert and refreshed on awakening.

Self-hypnosis in Practice

The technique of self-hypnosis can be learned from books or tapes, but it may be useful to consult a hypnotherapist first. Begin by making a list of the suggestions that you want to repeat under hypnosis. If you find it difficult to repeat your suggestions as you slip more deeply into a trance, it may help to write them out as a list, and read it through several times. You can then suggest that your subconscious mind can help by retaining and repeating the suggestions under hypnosis.

Another technique is to record your suggestions on tape, and to play them back during self-hypnosis. Alternatively, your hypnotherapist, if you have one, may give you a tape to take home, or at least advise you on the best way to make your own. Once you are calm and relaxed, use one of the following techniques, or a combination of them, to induce a trance.

ADDICTION SEE P. 258
ALLERGIES SEE PP. 338–9
ANXIETY SEE PP. 256–7
ASTHMA SEE PP. 294–5
DEPRESSION SEE P. 261
EATING DISORDERS SEE P. 265
ECZEMA AND DERMATITIS SEE P. 273
FEAR OF DENTAL TREATMENT SEE P. 286
HIGH BLOOD PRESSURE SEE P. 302
INSOMNIA SEE P. 264
IRRITABLE BOWEL SYNDROME SEE PP. 314–5
LABOR PAINS see P. 328
MENSTRUAL PROBLEMS SEE PP. 322–3
MIGRAINE SEE P. 269
NAUSEA AND VOMITING SEE P. 308
OBESITY SEE PP. 34–5
OBSESSION SEE P. 259
PHOBIAS SEE P. 260
PSORIASIS SEE P. 272
STRESS SEE PP. 262–3

LEFT *Although usually used by a hypnotherapist, the "eye-fixation" technique can be done at home.*

DREAMWORK

When we dream we are unconscious, but our minds are far from still. Visual images, feelings of fear or delight, and a variety of other sensations, create a rich and detailed inner landscape. Dreams have been the vehicles for visions, revelations, prophecies, and inspiration. So it is not surprising that they have been a source of fascination since the earliest days of the human race, nor that scientists have seen them as one of the keys to the understanding of the human mind and personality. What sets dreamwork apart as a form of therapy is that it regards the dream ego rather than the waking ego as being the real "self," and dreamworkers are concerned with regaining "wholeness" — the reintegration of conflicting parts of the ego — by following the implicit messages contained within our dreams.

ABOVE *Jung believed that dreams are our main contact with the "collective unconscious."*

Nearly all forms of dreamwork are based on the theories of the Swiss psychologist Carl Gustav Jung, the founder of analytic psychology (*see pages 194–5*). Jung believed that dreams are not simply a reflection of the individual subconscious, but draw on the shared past of the human race – the collective subconscious – and represent the aims and aspirations of the individual. He thought that people are motivated, above all, by the desire to achieve "wholeness" and completeness, a process he called "individuation." The problem is that the conscious mind has been conditioned by upbringing, background, and a host of other experiences and works according to a different set of objectives to these. The conscious mind overrules the subconscious, but at the cost of such mental disturbances as neuroses and phobias. These conflicts are reflected in our dreams, the theory goes, and analysis of our dreams can help to identify and remove the causes of conflict.

Jung's ideas were incorporated into the movement known as Gestalt therapy (*see pages 200–1*), which flourished, particularly in California, in the 1960s. Dreamwork developed, chiefly under Frederick Perls, as an offshoot of Gestalt, with a particular emphasis on group therapy. The popularity of the technique grew gradually over the years, and there are now numerous dreamwork groups, particularly on the West Coast of the U.S.

Dreamwork has been slow to spread to the U.K. and the rest of Europe, but there are now practitioners in most European countries.

RIGHT *Dream symbols express the dreamer's motivations and life experiences and can only be interpreted through self-analysis.*

WHAT IS DREAMWORK?

The actual techniques used by dreamworkers vary from one group and from one teacher to another. However, all dreamwork techniques generally share the same basic concepts.

✳ Dreams represent the mind's attempts to absorb and assimilate recent experiences and to reconcile them with previous experiences and with "archetypes" (*see page 194*) present in the subconscious.

✳ The integration center is the source of our dreams, and can be identified with the "self." It is this rather than the conscious ego that represents the true self, and it is only by allowing expression to the true self that we can achieve wholeness and fulfillment of our potential (individuation).

✳ It is not the function of dreams to resolve conflicts arising in the conscious ego. Rather, it is the conscious ego that should serve the dream, and the dream source from which it originates.

✳ We should not apply standard interpretations to specific symbols in our dreams. We should interrogate our dreams to let them speak for themselves so that we can learn from them.

✳ We should not allow others to interpret our dreams for us. If we attempt to interpret somebody else's dream, we are liable to project our own subconscious personality onto theirs.

✳ Each dream is regarded as a "whole," and every part of a dream image in some way or other can be interpreted as a projection of ourselves. This applies as much to a cliff, a tree, a dog, or a feeling of anxiety, as it does to the dream ego that is observing the scene.

✳ The self is composed of opposing elements – positive and negative, and masculine and feminine – we must not attempt to exclude or suppress those we consider bad, but recognize and embrace them.

LEFT *The visual imagery of a dream may seem disparate and confusing, but dreamworkers believe that every detail is in some way a projection of the self.*

PATHFINDER

Since Dreamwork does not claim to be a curative therapy, no cross-references to particular conditions are included here. However, Dreamwork can help certain people realize their own subconscious drives toward "wholeness" and "completeness" and, in so doing, alleviate neuroses and phobias. Dreamwork is an important tool in the psychoanalytical therapies.

DREAMWORKING IN PRACTICE

The first requirement for any form of dreamwork is to remember your dreams. Dreams fade quickly in the light of day, so you should keep a pen and paper beside your bed, and write down the contents of your dream immediately on waking. You will then be able to work constructively with your dreams.

Various techniques are used, both in group and individual sessions. The most basic is a set of questions that you can ask about any dream. This might include, for example:

✳ What are you doing in the dream and what feelings do you associate with each action?

✳ What similarities and contrasts are there between events and objects in the dream?

✳ How does this dream relate to events in your real life?

✳ What would you most like to change in the dream?

✳ What do you most like in the dream?

✳ What is most fascinating, frightening, worrying about this dream?

✳ What is still unresolved or unfinished in this dream?

You can then set about examining the dream in more depth, perhaps by looking more closely at the dream ego. What are you, the dream ego, doing in the dream and what are you not doing? Why? What are your attitudes? Your motives? Your emotions? How else might you have behaved in the dream?

ABOVE *Keeping a dream diary is an essential part of any dreamwork.*

You can then rewrite the dream. Decide how you would have liked your dream ego to have behaved and revise the dream. Does this resolve any unresolved issues? Is the result better than the original and, if so, why?

A useful and entertaining way of examining a dream involves play-acting. Imagine that you are one of the elements of the dream – animate or inanimate – and pretend you are that element. Describe what you are feeling, and what your role is in the scene. Act out the role if possible. Then act out a dialogue – using two chairs which you occupy alternately – between two different elements, exploring the relationship between them and the dream ego. If conflicts arise, pull up a third chair and occupy it with the "unresolved issue," which should also contribute fully to the whole debate.

In group situations, or in the hands of an experienced practitioner, there are further methods of dream exploration. The first is dream re-entry, in which you reexperience the dream while in a meditative state. You can consciously change the way your dream ego reacts and continue doing so until the dream has a satisfactory resolution. The second, dream enactment or dream theater, involves the recruitment of other members of the group to play roles from your dream. Both are powerful and effective dreamworking tools.

DANCE MOVEMENT THERAPY

Throughout history, men and women have used dance not just for ritual purposes but as a method of self-expression and as a focus for the community. Dance movement therapy is a way of expressing ideas and emotions through movement and has developed since World War I, into an adjunct to conventional medicine that has acknowledged benefits in the treatment of psychiatric and behavioral disorders, learning difficulties, and physical disabilities. As such, dance/movement therapy is widely available in hospitals and clinics in the U.S. and is increasingly being accepted as a mainstream therapy in Europe.

Dance is one of our most fundamental forms of self-expression and always has been – whether in the form of the intricate heel and toe taps of traditional Celtic dancing or the less-regimented rain and war dances of Native Americans. This concept was clearly understood by Rudolf Laban, a choreographer who provided the link between folk dances and the dance movement therapy of today. Laban (1879–1958), from what is now Bratislava, in Slovakia, devoted his life to what was later called "the art of movement." As well as devising a system of movement notation that is still in use today, he encouraged whole communities to take part in "dance dramas," believing that these had important emotional, psychological and spiritual benefits; these beliefs reflected the ideas of Jung (*see page 194*) on the use of expressive movement in psychotherapy. Laban also established a network of dance studios, in which his principles were taught to professional dancers, athletes and therapists alike.

Dance Movement Therapy Evolves

Laban was forced to flee Nazi Germany, where he had been working as Director of Movement at the Berlin State Opera, just before the onset of the Second World War and settled in Britain to continue his work. In Washington D.C., U.S., in the 1940s, psychiatrists found that patients benefitted considerably by attending classes held by dance teacher Marian Chace. Later, Chace was asked to hold hospital classes for patients who had previously been considered to be too disturbed to take part in other communal activities; she went on to use her therapy in the treatment of schizophrenia. In California, a dancer called Trudi Schoop also started to hold classes for disturbed patients.

Dance movement therapy increased in popularity over the subsequent decades, and in 1966 the American Dance Therapy Association (ADTA) was established. The ADTA established a number of university and college training courses leading to Master's degrees in dance movement therapy – involving courses in psychotherapeutic theory and practice, kinesiology (the study of muscles and human motion, human development and disease processes, as well as dance and movement – and now maintains a register of qualified practitioners and has laid down a code of ethics for them. Today, there are many registered dance movement therapists practicing in psychiatric hospitals.

ABOVE *Marian Chace developed Rudolf Laban's ideas about the healing qualities of dance.*

RIGHT *Dance movement therapy can be a useful technique for people who have trouble expressing themselves verbally.*

HOW DANCE MOVEMENT THERAPY WORKS

The ADTA defines dance movement therapy as "the psychotherapeutic use of movement as a process which furthers the emotional, cognitive, and physical integration of the individual." This definition depends on the idea that the way an individual moves reflects his personality and state of mind, and that by changing patterns of movement the therapist can affect the patient's mood and physical and mental functioning.

At first sight, this idea may seem to be rather far-fetched. But children are noted for the uninhibitedness of their movement, which may denote exuberance, contentment, or depression, and it is only the social conventions that break the spontaneity of the link between emotion and movement during adolescence and early adulthood. Even so, the link survives: most people find it easy to accept that body language exists, however unconscious and subtle it may be, and that it is an important medium of communication, both in terms of conveying information and receiving it.

ABOVE *During childhood the link between emotion and body movement is uninhibited.*

provides a more positive self–image

eases worries about the state of health

improves the flexibility of limbs

LEFT
Older people may benefit from dance therapy as a means of expressing their fears and staying fit.

EURHYTHMY

Rudolf Steiner (1861–1925) was an Austrian scientist who developed a philosophical system called "anthroposophy" that encompassed many areas of human life and activity, such as medicine, agriculture, drama, movement, and even architecture. Steiner believed that each individual has not just a physical body but an "etheric" vegetal body ("vegetal" refers to functions that are common to animals and plants, such as growth, circulation, and generation), an "astral," or "soul," body, and an "ego," or "spirit." As far as anthroposophical medicine is concerned, practitioners – who are trained as medical doctors – believe that the smooth interaction of these bodies is vital to the maintenance of good health and that anthroposophical techniques can help repair any irregularities.

One such technique is a movement therapy known as "eurhythmy," which smooths the interaction between the physical body and the ego. It is a dance-like art form, but music and speech are expressed in choreographed movements, each of which corresponds to specific musical notes or sounds – this characteristic gives eurhythmy its other names of "visible speech" and "visible song." The therapy is practiced routinely by children educated at special "Steiner schools."

Dance movement therapists use the rhythm and movement of dance, generally accompanied by music, to revive this link. Movement is often used to bypass the conscious mind and make contact with the subconscious, emotional part of the brain. The aim is to express hidden emotions in a non-verbal way through dance or movements. A patient's movements are watched closely to see whether they reveal any subconscious emotional problems, and the therapist then encourages him to reveal them more fully. Eventually, after further therapy, the patient will have explored any problem in depth and gained insight into it, and will then be able to come to terms with it at a conscious level. While dance movement therapy is a useful tool in the treatment of emotional problems, it can also be used in other circumstances. It helps the elderly to maintain flexibility, suppleness, and vitality, for example, and to express fear and grief, and it helps the intellectually impaired to learn and to develop relationships.

Dance movement therapy is often used in conjunction with occupational therapy or physiotherapy to promote a positive self-image. Even the physically disabled may benefit by being enabled to extend their functions through posture, gesture, mime, rhythmic sequences, and movement differentiation.

ORTHODOX VIEW

The body of research into dance movement therapy that has built up since World War II shows fairly conclusively that the therapy is an effective way to treat emotional and psychological disturbances, as well as being a useful adjunct to the treatment of physical disabilities and some chronic illnesses.

This being the case, the medical profession accepts the worth of dance movement therapy. The therapy is therefore provided by most government-funded health care systems and private insurance schemes.

CONSULTING A PRACTITIONER

Because dance movement therapy is seen as having an important role to play in mainstream, orthodox medicine, patients are often referred to a dance movement therapist by a doctor. However, a number of accredited dance movement therapists accept patients who have not been referred, on a private basis.

Therapy sessions can be on a one-to-one basis or as part of a group – group sessions are often more valuable in the case of the elderly and those with learning difficulties and psychiatric disorders, since in the first case they create a feeling of comradeship and in the second and third cases they promote socialization skills. One-to-one therapy sessions are more appropriate in the case of emotional problems.

A course of therapy, which may take anything from six weeks to several years, starts – after a warm-up, to protect muscles and sinews from strain – with the therapist trying to assess how patients express themselves through dance, often using the dance notation developed by Rudolf Laban (see page 226). Formal dance routines are sometimes used in the first instance, though some therapists prefer to ask for spontaneous movements in the patients' own time – as if acting out a dream, for example.

EUTONY

The movement therapy called eutony was developed by Gerda Alexander – no relation to F.M. Alexander, originator of the Alexander Technique (see pages 146–53) – in Copenhagen, Denmark, in the 1930s. Today, eutony is still relatively little known but is most commonly available in Canada, France, Germany, and Scandinavia.

Gerda Alexander focused above all on sensory self-awareness of the body, believing that to become a "master of proprioception" (see pages 146–53) was healing in itself. Patients – called "pupils" – are analyzed in terms of their muscle tone as either "hypertonic" (too much tone), "normotonic'" (normal), or "hypotonic" (too little tone), and taught to manipulate "blocked energy" while learning sensory self-awareness. The result is said to be not only increased coordination and good posture, as in the Alexander Technique, but calm and serene spirituality, which we all have the potential to enjoy as part of our collective unconscious. For this reason, eutony is sometimes used by its adherents as a psychotherapeutic tool.

Sessions last 60–90 minutes, with the number of treatments varying according to the individual's needs. Eutony is considered to work best for musculoskeletal disorders and is well regarded by medical practitioners who have encountered it.

A number of techniques are used to encourage patients to bring out their innermost emotions, the most important of which is Laban's use of "mirroring." In this, the therapist "reflects" a patient's movements, copying them and overemphasizing them in order to encourage the patient to express through dance the emotions that the movements convey more fully. The theory is that emotion is expressed as a physical sensation in the body, and that when a patient is encouraged not to "hold back," which dance movement therapy does, the initial sensations, called "streamings," become more and more intense until the emotion is laid bare. Afterward, the therapist talks through the experience of the dance session, helping the patient to come to terms with whatever has caused the problem.

therapist observes movements

client expresses emotions through movement

emotions come to the surface more readily

ABOVE *The dance therapist (left) observes a patient's movements and the emotions that may surface through them.*

PERSON-CENTERED EXPRESSIVE THERAPY

American psychologist Carl Rogers developed person-centered psychotherapy, one of the humanistic therapies, in the 1950s (*see page 202*), and moved on to use it with encounter groups (*see page 208*) in the 1970s. His daughter Natalie Rogers, a psychotherapist who had been using art and movement therapy in her practice, started working with him at this time and later began to experiment with the use of expressive arts therapy with groups.

By 1985, Rogers had developed a therapy used in groups based on her father's philosophy of psychotherapy that combined movement therapy with the use of music, writing, and art, and opened the Person-Centered Expressive Therapy Institute (PCETI) in California, U.S. Rogers has used her techniques with groups of children with emotional disturbances, with troubled college students, and adults with psychiatric disorders. She also promotes her therapy as a method of empowering people from all walks of life.

PCETI trains therapists in Rogers' technique and awards a Master's degree in it. There are now PCETI centers in Britain, Mexico, Russia, and Argentina, as well as in America.

certain gestures are repeated

PRECAUTIONS

Dance movement therapy is safe in most cases, but confronting repressed emotional problems can be a disturbing process with significant psychological consequences. Consult your doctor before starting therapy if you are in any doubt; also do this if you have a medical condition, such as circulatory or musculoskeletal problems, that may be exacerbated by vigorous movement.

PATHFINDER

Dance/movement therapy is primarily seen as a psychotherapeutic tool, and is used in the treatment and rehabilitation of people with emotional or psychological problems.

Dance/movement therapy has been shown to be of benefit in treating chronic pain, circulatory disorders, hearing difficulties, learning difficulties, intellectual impairment, psychosis, schizophrenia, sexual abuse, and visual impairment. It has also been used to treat the following disorders:

ADDICTION *SEE P. 258*

ALZHEIMER'S DISEASE *SEE P. 356*

ARTHRITIS *SEE PP. 346–7*

ASTHMA *SEE PP. 294–5*

DEPRESSION *SEE P. 261*

EATING DISORDERS *SEE P. 265*

HYPERACTIVITY *SEE P. 351*

STRESS *SEE PP. 262–3*

BELOW *A discussion with the therapist afterward will help consolidate the patient's experience of the session.*

MUSIC THERAPY

ANCIENT LINKS

Music concerns the art of organizing sounds to produce melody, harmony, and rhythm. Musical cultures evolved in ancient civilizations such as those in China, Persia, and India as well as in Europe. Music has long been used for self-expression and as a healing remedy, and there are accounts of the healing properties of music in the Bible. The ancient Greeks thought so highly of music's curative powers that the god Apollo was dedicated to music and medicine.

ABOVE *As God of both music and healing, Apollo shows that the Ancient Egyptians and Greeks believed in music as a curing force.*

Music is the purest form of artistic expression, appealing directly to our moods, feelings and emotions. All the world's religions use chants or hymns or incantations as an integral part of ritual, contemplation or prayer. Music epitomizes harmony, rhythm and form — concepts that lie at the heart of much holistic medicine. As a result, music is regarded as a valuable form of therapy by conventional and complementary practitioners alike and has been used since the 1940s as a therapeutic tool to treat those with psychological illness and disabilities. Active music-making is now often used as an aid to socialization and self-expression, particularly among those who have difficulty in communicating, and simply listening to music has proved successful in the relief of tension and stress, and in the treatment of depression.

Music must be as old as language. Speech is basically musical, and rhythm, phrasing, and cadence are even more fundamental to language than the meanings of the words themselves. The use of music as therapy therefore probably predates the appearance of any written records. It is known that the ancient Egyptians and Greeks thought highly of the curative powers of music – in Greece, Apollo was the god of both music and healing. It was also in Greece that Pythagoras formulated the rules of harmonics and used them as the basis for a school of philosophy and medicine.

Music and the chanting of musical sounds have always been a vital part of Eastern medicine. Hindus, Buddhists, Chinese, Japanese, and Indonesians all share the use of the sound "om" in healing meditation and prayer, while Christians and Jews have the similar incantation "amen"; Muslims say "amin." The chanting of mantras lies at the heart of Indian Ayurvedic medicine (*see pages 78–85*) as well as transcendental and other forms of meditation (*see pages 60–63*).

In the West, music has been used throughout history, but in a relatively unfocused way. Mothers throughout the world have sung lullabies to calm a fretful child, and the keening of women at a wake is a traditional means of giving vent to feelings of grief and loss. However, it was only in the 20th century that serious attention was paid to the use of music in a therapeutic setting, initially as a form of treatment for traumatized veterans of World War II. Today, music therapy is a conventional adjunct to other forms of psychotherapy and is available in many hospitals and clinics. Together with the more general sound therapy (*see pages 234-5*), it is also a flourishing branch of holistic complementary medicine, with an emphasis on integration of the personality and wholeness of self as well as on direct healing.

WHAT IS MUSIC THERAPY?

At the simplest level, music has the power to soothe and calm, and to enhance or alter moods. Advertisers, supermarkets, film-makers and many others all exploit this for one purpose or another. Hospitals are increasingly using music as a means of creating a relaxed atmosphere in which other forms of treatment can be carried out more easily and with greater success.

Many practitioners of music therapy, however, go well beyond this. Sound, like light, is a form of vibrational energy (*see page 234*). Just as different parts of the body respond to the vibrations of different colors of light, so too do they respond to different tones or pitches of sound. While any form of sound – not just music – can be used for healing, music has particular value because it is harmonic. Such therapists believe that exposure to music can help to bring the tissues and organs of the body into harmony.

LEFT *Singing is universally recognized to have a soothing effect on babies.*

CONSULTING A THERAPIST

Many patients are referred to a music therapist by a doctor or psychiatrist. However, it is easy to join a workshop – even for a single session – or to arrange for private sessions on a one-to-one basis.

Therapy usually involves group sessions at least once a week, each lasting an hour or more. You will be encouraged to join the rest of the group in playing musical instruments or singing – it doesn't matter whether or not you are musical: rhythmic shaking of a tambourine can be as satisfying as playing a recorder or a flute. Music is usually improvised under the leadership of the therapist, and can be geared to the needs of the individual patient. Active music therapy is mainly used in the treatment of those who have difficulty in expressing themselves and relating to other people. It may also be valuable in the care of sufferers from Alzheimer's Disease. It can help the elderly and disabled to keep moving, and to maintain mind and body coordination.

Passive music therapy – simply listening to music – is usually offered on an individual basis, and the choice of music is carefully tailored to the patient's tastes and to the condition being treated. It has been used for emotional disorders, such as anxiety and depression, and in the treatment of autism and developmental disorders.

THE TOMATIS METHOD

Recently, a great deal of interest has been shown in a form of passive music therapy developed by a French doctor and sound researcher, Alfred Tomatis. The technique is based on the theory that sounds travel by a variety of different pathways to the central nervous system (CNS), where they can have a profound effect on the cerebral cortex of the brain. The Tomatis method, also known as Auditory Integration Therapy (AIT), involves playing music – usually Mozart or Gregorian chants – that subtly, almost imperceptibly, filters out certain frequencies during the course of the session. These minute alterations stimulate attention and activity in the brain and lead to greater awareness of external stimuli.

Originally confined to France, the Tomatis method is now spreading more widely. The first center in the U.K. opened in 1995. It is claimed to be effective in the treatment of mental disabilities, attention deficit disorder (hyperactivity), and other developmental disorders, autism, dyslexia, tinnitus, and vertigo.

ABOVE *The music of Mozart is claimed to affect the cerebral cortex of the brain.*

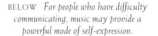

BELOW *For people who have difficulty communicating, music may provide a powerful mode of self-expression.*

ORTHODOX VIEW

The benefits of music therapy in relieving stress and improving relaxation are widely accepted, as is its value in the care of the elderly. Some studies have shown that music can affect the rhythm of breathing and heartbeat, and can alter blood pressure. However, much seems to depend on the involvement of the patient: live music seems to be more effective than tapes or CDs.

Most doctors would agree that music can help patients to relax and that it is a valuable form of communication for the disabled. However, few would accept that music can have direct effects on physical disease. The idea that sickness can be cured by the application of vibrational energy, is still alien to orthodox medicine.

SELF-HELP

Music therapy is ideal for self-help. At its simplest, it requires no equipment and no expense. With a straight-forward sound system, the possibilities are hugely extended, and if you can spare the time and have the patience to learn a musical instrument, you can enrich your life in ways that are only indirectly therapeutic. Self-help books and tapes are widely available, and workshops are generally easy to find and cheap to attend if you want to start by learning some of the basic techniques – even a single session will prepare you for rewarding do-it-yourself practice.

Music therapy has non-musical goals: it aims to help you release tensions and express yourself in a non-verbal way, and to improve cognitive, physical, communicative, social, and emotional skills. The rhythm of music is thought to reduce stress by affecting the body's physiological processes. It is also thought to encourage the manufacture and release of endorphins, the body's natural painkillers. Music therapy is of particular benefit to children, who are more likely to react to it in a spontaneous and uninhibited manner.

SINGING

Use your voice. Sing something cheerful in the bath in the mornings to put you in the right frame of mind for the day to come. Sing around the house or the garden, or in the car. Learn the words of your favorite songs so that you can sing along to them when they are played on the radio.

LEFT *Singing while performing everyday chores is one of the simplest forms of music therapy.*

TONING

Use the technique known as "toning" to release inhibitions and reduce stress. As children, we give voice to our emotions. We shout, scream, and sing as a matter of course. As adults, we feel inhibited about vocalizing our feelings, with the result that our emotions are repressed. Toning involves singing at the most primitive level, using grunts and groans, and cries and sighs, as a way of venting and releasing pent-up emotions. There are toning therapists who can teach you how to use your voice in this way.

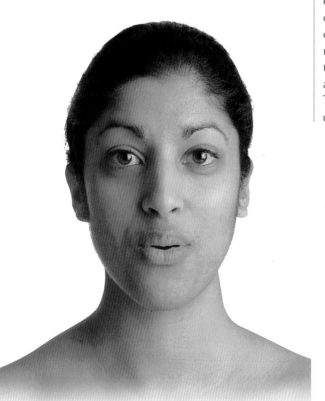

LEFT *Primal vocal expression enables a patient to release pent-up anger and emotions.*

PRECAUTIONS

Music therapy is very safe, and without any adverse side-effects. However, the following points should be borne in mind.

■ Music therapy is not a substitute for proper medical treatment. If you are suffering from a serious mental or emotional disturbance, you should seek professional help.

■ When listening to music at home using earphones, take care to keep the music at a comfortable volume. Prolonged playing of loud music can cause permanent hearing damage.

THERAPEUTIC TAPES

Special therapeutic tapes – sometimes requiring active participation from the listener – are readily available either by mail order or from specialist bookshops. They may not suit all tastes, and may take a little time to get used to. However, it is worth persevering: many people have reported that they have experienced a deep sense of calm, and achieved profound relaxation, with the aid of therapeutic tapes.

RIGHT *Specially recorded therapeutic tapes may be helpful in the process of relaxation.*

PERSONAL CHOICE

Choose music from your own collection that accurately reflects your current mood or the mood you want to experience, and simply listen to it. This works best if you are relaxed and comfortable, and are able to concentrate fully on the music – listening through earphones is better than listening to loudspeakers. If you want to feel confident, listen to brisk, jolly music; if you want to feel romantic, choose something soft and melodic. You can use this technique not just to alter your moods, but to explore and examine them. If you are feeling angry, playing angry music can allow you to look for the roots of your anger and exorcize them.

MAKING A THERAPY TAPE

Perhaps the most effective, and satisfying, form of do-it-yourself music therapy is the technique known as "entrainment." This is designed first of all to gain your complete involvement in the music, and then to lead you gradually from an undesirable mood into a more fulfilling and productive one. You will need two or three 30–45 minute tapes and a good selection of cassettes or CDs.

1 Start by choosing music that reflects the mood you are in. If you are feeling depressed, for example, and want to elevate your mood, then begin with around 10 minutes of sad, doleful music. Pop music, classical music, or jazz will all do, according to your own tastes and preferences.

2 Next, pick three or four extracts that are somewhere between your present mood and the mood you wish to achieve. Start with the gloomiest and work up to the most cheerful. The transition from one mood to the next should be gradual, without abrupt changes of tempo.

3 End with three or four more pieces that represent your desired state – uplifted, confident, and cheerful. Make similar tapes for when you are feeling angry or stressed and want to relax, or for when you are restless and want to be calm and concentrated.

Play these tapes whenever you want to alter your mood. Remember that the more absorbed you are in the music, the more effective the therapy will be.

PATHFINDER

Music therapy, like art therapy (*see pages 236–9*) is widely used in the treatment of mental disturbance, such as psychoses and Alzheimer's Disease, learning and other developmental disorders in children, and in the care of the chronically ill and the elderly. It also reduces stress in surgical and intensive care wards.

More generally, it can be used to improve social and communication skills, particularly among those whose verbal skills are impaired.

Music therapy can also be of help in treating the following conditions:

ALZHEIMER'S DISEASE
SEE P. *356*

ANXIETY SEE PP. *256–7*

COLIC SEE P. *350*

DEPRESSION SEE P. *261*

HYPERACTIVITY
SEE P. *351*

LABOR PAINS SEE P. *328*

STRESS SEE PP. *262–3*

LEFT *Listening through headphones will enable you to immerse yourself fully in the music.*

SOUND THERAPY

*S*ound can be used in different ways in therapy. It can be listened to; it can be created; and it can be focused directly on specific areas of the body. Unlike music therapy, which is mainly concerned with the effects of melody, harmony, and rhythm on our moods and emotions, sound therapy attempts to restore balance in the body and affect the body's healing processes by applying sounds of specific frequencies to parts of the body whose vibrational patterns are disturbed. Although a relative newcomer to the world of complementary medicine – at least in its present form – sound therapy has already been successful, and most practitioners believe that it has a bright future.

The use of sound as a form of therapy first began to attract attention at the end of the 19th century, when it was discovered that sounds could produce changes in the physiology of the human body such as increasing the rate of blood flow. Most attention was paid to the healing power of music (*see pages 230–33*), particularly in cases of psychological and emotional disturbance. Recently, however, the use of sound in a non-musical context has become a fully-fledged form of therapy.

Interest in the use of sound for healing purposes surfaced through scientific investigation. In 1925 the French physicist de Broglie postulated that the electron, which revolves about a positively charged nucleus in an atom, was not a particle, but a non-material wave. Matter, when reduced to its smallest component, is only energy. This means that everything in the universe is in a state of vibration, including the human body. It stands to reason, therefore, that if the human body is vibrating itself, then any imbalances or problems within it will respond to sound waves, or other vibrations. Out of this scientific concept evolved vibrational medicine, whereby machines using sound waves as a form of therapy have been in operation since the 1950s.

The vibrational technique known as cymatics, pioneered by the British doctor and osteopath Peter Manners, has become particularly popular in the U.S., but is gaining adherents worldwide. Another recent form of therapy, part music and part sound, is the Tomatis method (*see page 231*). In the early 1990s another

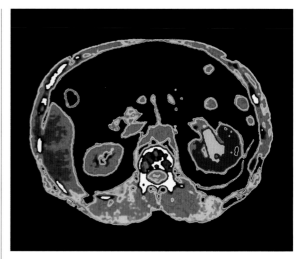

ABOVE In orthodox Western medicine ultrasound is used to shatter kidney stones.

technique, physio-acoustic methodology (PAM) was developed in Finland, whereby computer-generated sound waves, played through speakers in a special chair in which the patient sits, are claimed to be able to lower blood pressure and also to reduce muscle tension.

WHAT IS SOUND THERAPY?

Sound, like light, is a form of vibration that travels through space as a wave motion. However, while light consists of oscillations in an electromagnetic field, sound is due to the movement of molecules in the air – sound cannot travel in a vacuum. Audible sound is only a part of the full sound spectrum. Very high frequency sounds – ultrasound – and very low frequency sounds are outside the range of the human ear.

Ultrasound is used to shatter kidney stones without surgical intervention. It is also the basis for the ultrasound scanner, one of the most useful of modern diagnostic aids. Sound is also routinely used in physical therapy (physiotherapy) to reduce inflammation of the joints, and to ease muscular aches and pains.

BELOW Sound therapy is mostly used to treat bone and joint problems and can be particularly effective on back pain.

However, sound therapists, like light and color therapists (see pages 240–41 and pages 246–9) go further. They believe that every tissue in the body vibrates with a characteristic frequency and that sickness in any part of the body manifests itself in disturbances of the normal frequency of vibration. They believe that they can restore the normal balance of vibrational energy by applying sound of the correct frequency directly to the organs and tissues concerned, and restore the body to harmony and health.

CONSULTING A PRACTITIONER

The techniques used by sound therapists vary widely from one practitioner to another. They also depend on whether the therapy is designed to treat a specific condition or is simply intended to relieve stress and create a sense of well-being.

Most commonly, after an initial consultation, the therapist will apply sound to specific areas of the body using a special hand-held device that delivers the relevant sound frequencies from a prerecorded tape. This is the method used in cymatics. Other therapists prefer to use the sounds of their own voices. They direct the sounds – chants, incantations, shouts, and groans, for example – at different areas of the patient's body. The experience is bizarre, but apparently effective.

CYMATICS THERAPY

Cymatics concerns the use of a hand-held machine that transmits sound waves through the skin. It is placed over the part of the body to be treated and set to a frequency matching cells in a healthy body.

The frequencies are highly complex, and are designed specifically for the organ or tissue being treated. The patient may or may not feel the vibrations, or hear the sounds, during treatment. Each session lasts for 10 to 15 minutes, and there is no set length for the duration of a course of treatment.

CHANTING

A technique that is rapidly gaining popularity in the West, chanting is common to many cultures. Through weekly, hour-long treatments, the patient is taught how to use tone in the voice to create pure sounds that are said to resonate through the body and bring about a state of physical and emotional well-being. Chanting is also used to boost self-confidence.

PRECAUTIONS

■ Sound therapy is generally very safe. However, there are some cases in which it should be avoided, or undertaken only after consulting your doctor.

■ Do not undergo sound therapy if you have a heart pacemaker.

■ Always consult your doctor before having sound therapy if you suffer from heart or kidney disease.

■ Never aim loud sounds directly at the head. Damage to the internal ear can lead to partial or total deafness.

SELF-HELP

It is possible to buy hand-held applicators, together with prerecorded tapes, for use in the home. These can be very useful, particularly in the case of sprains, and aching muscles and joints. They provide an alternative to physical manipulation, which many people find painful or uncomfortable. However, the results are likely to be less effective than those achieved by a trained physiotherapist during an integrated course of treatment.

The technique known as "toning" (see Music therapy, page 232) is a form of sound therapy that can be practiced at home. In this, the idea is to let your voice resonate throughout your body, resulting in increased harmony and wholeness, and a deepened sense of well-being.

PATHFINDER

Sound therapy has proved particularly valuable in the treatment of muscle, joint, tendon, and ligament disorders. It can reduce pain and inflammation in arthritic and rheumatic complaints. It helps to reduce discomfort and improve the recovery time for hip replacement operations. Sound therapy is also used to treat the following conditions:

ARTHRITIS SEE PP. 346–7

BACK PROBLEMS SEE PP. 344–5

FIBROSITIS SEE P. 348

LABOR PAINS SEE P. 328

REPETITIVE STRAIN INJURY SEE PP. 342–3

SCIATICA SEE P. 348

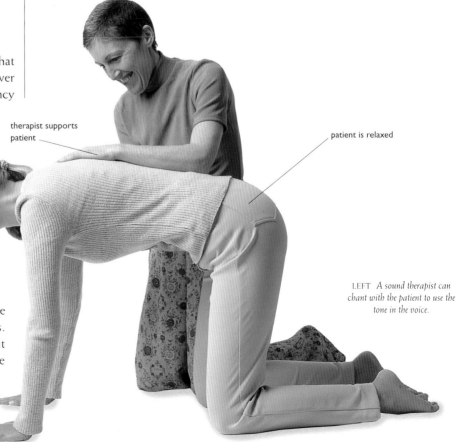

therapist supports patient

patient is relaxed

LEFT A sound therapist can chant with the patient to use the tone in the voice.

ART THERAPY

VISUAL IMAGES

Art has always been used to express feelings that sometimes cannot be put into words. However, it was not until the early 20th century that the importance of artistic self-expression and the potential of art as a psychotherapeutic tool was recognized. Following World War II, art therapy was used in the rehabilitation of traumatized war veterans. Today it is practiced in a variety of settings, from prisons to schools, and is of particular benefit to those who might otherwise have problems articulating their views, such as children, the emotionally disturbed, and those who have learning difficulties.

ABOVE *Art therapy helped disturbed people who had seen the horrors of World War II.*

The creative therapies — art and music therapy — are unusual in that they span the divide between orthodox and complementary medicine. They incorporate the holistic, individual-centered approach to healing of other mind and spirit therapies, emphasizing personal growth and fulfillment, but at the same time they are used in hospitals and clinics throughout the world to treat mental illness, psychosomatic diseases and developmental problems, and in the care of the elderly and terminally ill. Art therapy is also widely recognized as one of the best ways of revealing deep and strong emotions that an individual might otherwise not dare to express.

The use of art – painting, drawing, sculpture, and so on – in the treatment of mental and emotional disorders dates back to the early years of the 20th century. Rudolf Steiner incorporated art, as well as music and dance, into his system of anthroposophical medicine (*see page 227*). Steiner numbered Jung (*see page 194*) and Montessori among his correspondents and acquaintances, and his ideas on such things as education and psychology were highly influential. Both Freud (*see pages 188 and 192*) and Jung recognized that artistic expression provided an insight into the subconscious mind, and other psychoanalysts and educationalists soon realized the importance of artistic self-expression as part of normal childhood development.

After World War II, art therapy found its way into hospitals as a means of helping survivors to overcome wartime traumas and readjust to normal life. Traditionally, it took the form of an artist working informally with the patients in a hospital. However, psychotherapists rapidly came to appreciate the potential of art therapy in psychiatry, and professional therapists started to appear. The British Association of Art Therapists was founded in 1963, and art therapists were state-registered in 1997.

In the U.S., the work of Margaret Naumberg led to increasing recognition of art therapy in the postwar years. It is now widely practiced throughout the country.

WHAT IS ART THERAPY?

As children, we all draw, paint, and make models in clay, Plasticine, or mud. In part, this is a way of exploring and familiarizing ourselves with the world around us. But it is also an important means of self-expression, particularly when verbal skills are not well developed.

Children use drawing and painting to express their feelings and emotions in a free and uninhibited manner. Art provides them with a safety valve for feelings of anger or frustration, and may sometimes express deeper emotions such as a fear of being abandoned or the withdrawal of parental love. For children with emotional disturbances or learning difficulties, art may be one of their few means of self-expression.

From the age of about ten onward, much of this childhood spontaneity is lost. Painting becomes more formal, realistic, and restrained. The capacity for self-expression through the medium of art is lost by most adults, and it is this that art therapy attempts to restore.

It is important that you are not put off by any perceived or actual inability to draw or paint. The point is not to produce a work of art, or even something pleasing to look at. The essence of art therapy is to give free rein to the subconscious to express itself through color, shape, and form. The resulting images will reflect any inner conflicts, fears, and other suppressed emotions, and will enable you to confront and deal with them.

Buried Emotions

Most people find it useful to do art therapy in the presence of a trained therapist, who can provide guidance in interpreting the images or shapes that are produced. The therapist can also help in cases in which the images are horrific, frightening, or shocking. Some people have deeply buried emotions of hate, fear, rage, or alienation which find an outlet in artistic creation, and these can be difficult to confront on your own. Problems may often become apparent through art therapy that might

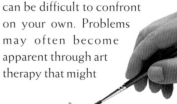

LEFT *Art therapy aims to recover some of the spontaneity of expression which we all enjoyed as children.*

LEFT *Members of a group therapy session are encouraged to paint with freedom and expression.*

ORTHODOX VIEW

The value of art therapy in the treatment of psychological and emotional disorders has been established by extensive research. In fact, it is common for doctors working in mainstream, conventional medicine to refer those patients whom they believe would respond to art therapy to a specialist therapist.

Art therapy is used extensively in hospitals, prisons, and other institutions. It only gives grounds for skepticism in the world of orthodox medicine when it comes to the use by some therapists of elements of Jungian analytical psychology. Not all doctors agree that the self-interpretation of symbols derived from drawings and painting has any validity.

LEFT *Creative art may assist in bringing deeply rooted psychological conflicts to the surface, where they may be dealt with.*

not have been revealed so soon by other forms of psychotherapy, such as psychoanalysis. As a result, they can be dealt with at an early stage before they become serious.

Besides its use in the treatment of psychological problems, art therapy is increasingly popular as a means of achieving greater self-awareness and self-fulfillment. Here the emphasis is on the transformation of negative images into positive ones, as well as on the resolution of inner conflicts and emotional problems. Working on images to alter them can be a powerful agent for flexibility and change.

Therapeutic Roles

There are two different schools of thought about the role of the therapist in art therapy. The first holds that the therapist is there merely to help and guide. The focus is on the patient and the picture. It is thought that attempts at interpretation by the therapist interfere with the patient's inner dialogue and discourage the complete freedom of expression that is necessary for the therapy to work. The act of painting is itself regarded as therapeutic, since it allows the patient to express and come to terms with inner conflicts and emotions.

Other therapists, however, regard art therapy as part of the more general process of psychotherapy. Painting becomes a non-verbal means of communication between the therapist and the patient, and is used in much the same way as verbal self-expression. Its chief function is to allow the therapist to identify the sources of problems in the subconscious and to help the patient to deal with them.

Symbols of the Subconscious

Another strand in art therapy is derived from Jungian analytical psychology. In this, drawings and paintings, like dreams, are thought to contain symbols that can be interpreted in terms of subconscious forces and archetypes (*see page 194*). Generally, patients will be encouraged to work out the interpretations for themselves, and decide the significance of symbols to themselves personally, but with guidance from the practitioner, rather than the practitioner providing the interpretation for the patients. You, and you alone, are considered to hold the key to the symbols that have emerged from your unconscious.

CONSULTING A PRACTITIONER

Most art therapists work in hospitals, mental institutions, educational establishments, or prisons, and it is often the case that patients are referred to them by a psychologist or doctor. If you want to start a course of private therapy, your doctor will usually be able to recommend a practitioner. If not, the appropriate associations will be able to supply names of therapists practicing in your area.

The first thing the therapist will do is to conduct a preliminary interview. This involves consulting any notes about previous and current medical treatment, and asking a series of questions designed to shed light on your lifestyle, problems, general emotional health, and your expectations from treatment. This is also an opportunity for you to find out exactly how the therapy will proceed and to discuss the sort of medium that you want to work in – whether it be watercolor, crayon, pastels, or clay.

Therapy itself may be conducted on a one-to-one basis, but it can also take the form of group therapy with up to eight or ten participants. Sessions usually last an hour or more and take place weekly over a period of at least six months. Whether you are being treated individually or in a group, your therapist will probably suggest various techniques to help you relax, and to free the imaginative and intuitive part of your mind from the normal conscious constraints. Visualization (*see pp. 214–7*) is sometimes used. You will be encouraged to imagine a scene in as much detail as possible and then to put it on paper, focusing all the time on the picture in your mind and not on what you are painting. Other techniques involve taking a familiar object and looking at it in an unusual way, for example, upside down, and then drawing it very slowly, concentrating on each line and curve and on the different textures.

BELOW *An art therapist will give guidance on relaxation and visualization techniques.*

SELF HELP

Practicing art therapy on your own is an excellent form of relaxation. The equipment you need is simple, inexpensive, and easy to carry around. Painting, drawing, or modeling help to reduce stress, and generally lead to greater self-awareness and emotional well-being. Joining an art course – it doesn't have to be a specialized art therapy course – may help, but it is not necessary. Remember that you do not need to be talented. The object is not to produce works of art, but to release inner tensions and improve emotional balance by learning to communicate with your unconscious mind.

When you have finished, look carefully at your work and try to see if there seems to be any dominant shape or color, or a particularly noticeable shape or symbol. If so, think about what might it signify in terms of your emotions and feelings.

Keep your paintings or drawings so that you can identify any recurring elements or themes even though their meanings may not be clear. Do they fluctuate wildly between gloomy or somber and cheerful and vital, and how does this relate to your moods? Do they change and evolve over a period of time, and if so, how does this reflect changes in your lifestyle or personal circumstances?

BELOW *Painting equipment is inexpensive and accessible to all.*

1 *Find somewhere in your home where you can rely on being undisturbed for a half hour or so, and make sure that you are fully relaxed. You need to allow free play to your imagination and intuition. The techniques of visualization, relaxation (see pages 158-65), and meditation (see pages 60-63) may all be useful if you know them.*

2 *Try to free your hands from the control of your conscious mind, so that images can flow directly from your mind onto the paper. It may help to start off by drawing with your left hand if you are right-handed, or with your right if left-handed. Alternatively, draw a familiar object from an unfamiliar perspective, as described above.*

3 *Paint or draw whatever comes into your head. You should not rush, but neither should you allow your conscious mind to intervene. Do not try to evaluate your painting in esthetic terms, and don't use an eraser or make corrections. It doesn't matter if the result seems to be a meaningless splodge of garish colors, or a tangled mess of scrawled curves and lines.*

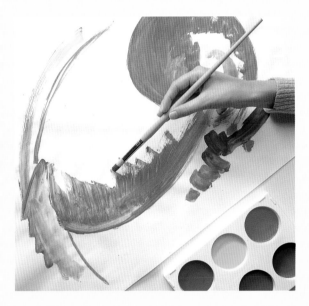

manipulating clay can be very therapeutic

PATHFINDER

Art therapy is routinely used in the treatment of such problems as eating disorders, and drug and alcohol abuse. It is also used in rehabilitation clinics, psychiatric hospitals, and homes for the elderly and the chronically ill, and can help sufferers from AIDS and Alzheimer's Disease. Finally, it is an important part of the treatment of children with learning difficulties, or emotional and behavioral problems.

Art therapy is also used to treat the following conditions:

ADDICTION SEE P. *258*

ALZHEIMER'S DISEASE SEE P. *356*

DEPRESSION SEE P. *261*

EATING DISORDERS SEE P. *265*

HIV AND AIDS SEE PP. *340–41*

HYPERACTIVITY SEE P. *351*

OBSESSION SEE P. *259*

PHOBIAS SEE P. *260*

STRESS SEE PP. *262–3*

PRECAUTIONS

Art therapy has been shown to be of great value in the treatment of a wide range of emotional and psychological disorders. It is a useful self-help aid to relaxation, and even helps achieve a deeper understanding of your personality and changing moods.

However, art therapy should not be used as a form of self-help treatment of any psychological problem. If you think that you have any such condition, consult your doctor or a registered therapist.

4 *Change the medium you are working in if you are not comfortable with it. If you are not happy painting or drawing, or modeling in clay, try cutting out pictures that appeal to you from magazines, or use colored pieces of paper, and make a collage out of them.*

LIGHT THERAPY

A s well as increasing vitality and bestowing a general sense of well-being, light plays an important part in regulating the body's "biological clock," which controls sleep and hormone production. Research has shown that exposure to bright sunlight has definite benefits for both physical and mental health. Light therapy, using natural sunlight or an artificial substitute, is now used widely by the medical profession to cure seasonal depression – SAD, or seasonal affective disorder – as well as a variety of skin complaints. It can also be used to manipulate the body's biological clock, and is therefore sometimes used to combat the effects of jetlag.

We know from ancient writings that the Egyptians, Greeks, and Arabs all recognized the therapeutic value of sunlight. However, the origins of modern light therapy lie in the 19th century and the development of naturopathy. The combination of sunlight, fresh air, and exercise was regarded as a more or less universal panacea. In particular, there was much interest in the use of light in the treatment of tuberculosis, or "consumption" as it was then generally called. In 1903, a Danish doctor, Niels Finsen, received the Nobel Prize for Medicine for his work on the effects of ultraviolet light on tuberculosis.

Throughout the 20th century, light therapy and its sister discipline, color therapy (see pp 246–9), continued to be developed. Today, now that much more is known about the effects of light on human physiology, light therapy has earned itself a genuine place in the medical repertoire.

ABOVE Seasonal affective disorder (SAD), characterized by fatigue and depression, is thought to be caused by lack of sunlight in winter.

HOW LIGHT THERAPY WORKS

Sunlight is described as full-spectrum light; that is, it contains all the colors of the spectrum mixed together to form white light. Artificial white light, for example from a fluorescent tube, has the same characteristics. Light therapy differs from color therapy in that only full-spectrum light is used.

Sunlight contains much more than just visible light. Gamma rays, X-rays, and ultraviolet light (UV) are all forms of radiation with shorter wavelengths than visible light, while infrared radiation has longer wavelengths.

Sunlight owes much of its effect on the body to the pineal gland, a structure lying deep in the brain. For centuries, the function of the pineal gland was a mystery. It was regarded as the "third eye" and was considered by the French philosopher René Déscartes to be the seat of the soul. Today, we know that the pineal gland plays an important role in the regulation of hormonal balance. It influences the production of seratonin, a hormone that affects our moods, and it also produces melatonin,

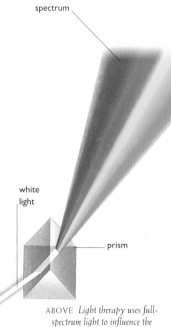

spectrum

white light

prism

ABOVE Light therapy uses full-spectrum light to influence the functioning of the pineal gland.

particularly in darkness.

The connection between melatonin and light was not recognized until the 1980s, but researchers soon realized that suppression of melatonin production by subjecting people to bright light might provide a cure for the puzzling condition known as seasonal affective disorder (SAD) or "winter blues," as well as offering a way of overcoming jetlag. Since then, many people have been saved from the debilitating lethargy and depression that accompany prolonged periods of darkness or poor light.

Exposure to full-spectrum light also increases the rate at which vitamin D is formed in the body. Vitamin D is essential for the absorption of certain minerals, including calcium, magnesium, and phosphorus, all of which are important in building and maintaining the strength of bone. Natural light can therefore help such conditions as arthritis and osteoporosis.

People undergoing light therapy have also reported a wide range of other beneficial effects, from lowered blood pressure and reduced blood-cholesterol levels to relief of

RIGHT *Arthritis is just one common complaint against which light therapy has claimed benefit.*

depression and arthritic pains. Natural light can kill bacteria, making it effective against such skin infections as acne. It may even affect the libido, rejuvenating the sex drive, and it has been used both to relieve the stresses of premenstrual syndrome (PMS) and as a substitute for hormone replacement therapy (HRT) during the menopause. Light therapy can also help insomniacs through its regulation of melatonin production. Almost everyone feels an increase in vitality and general well-being.

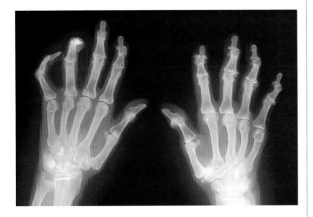

ABOVE *Arthritis is just one common complaint against which light therapy has claimed benefit.*

SELF-HELP

There are a number of ways to bring a little more light into your life.

■ In winter, try to spend as much time as possible out of doors. Go for walks or do some gardening.

■ In summer, try to spend a few minutes at least soaking up the sun without applying a sun-block. If you are lying in the sun for any length of time, you should of course apply a sun-block appropriate to your skin as soon as the few minutes are over.

■ Light therapy can be performed indoors at home if you purchase a home therapy unit. You should try to spend around 20 minutes a day underneath the lamp.

■ Vitamin D supplements should be eliminated from your diet if you are embarking on a course of light therapy. Together with the body's increased production of vitamin D, they could lead to toxic levels in the tissues.

BELOW *Hobbies such as gardening are a good way of maximizing exposure to sunlight.*

PATHFINDER

Light therapy can play a part in the treatment of various disorders, though there is some disagreement about how effective it is.

ACNE *SEE P.* 276
ARTHRITIS *SEE PP.* 346–7
DEPRESSION *SEE P.* 261
INSOMNIA *SEE P.* 264
MENOPAUSE *SEE PP.* 330–31
OSTEOPOROSIS *SEE P.* 358
PSORIASIS *SEE P.* 272
PREMENSTRUAL SYNDROME *SEE P.* 323

CONSULTING A PRACTITIONER

A course of light therapy typically involves one session a week, usually lasting an hour. Requirements vary, of course, according to circumstances and the time of year. Light is measured in a unit called the lux. Daylight averages about 5,000 lux; at least 2,500 lux are required to have a beneficial effect on the body. The amount of lux available in offices is generally less than 1,000.

Consult an eye specialist if you have an eye disorder or disease, before embarking on light therapy.

You should remove any spectacles or contact lenses before treatment begins, since these interfere with the passage of light into the eye. Then take off your shoes and as much of your outer clothing as you like and lie on your back beneath a fluorescent lamp, or array of lamps. The lamps emit full-spectrum, or bright white light from which UV rays have been filtered, so burning or damage to the skin is not a danger. You should keep your eyes open for at least part of the time – 20 minutes, say – for maximum benefit.

In some centers, foot reflexology (*see pp. 68–73*) is offered as an accompaniment to light therapy. If so, the therapist will need to discuss your medical history with you in order to determine the right pressure points to use. Most people find the experience very pleasurable, and often curative as well. If nothing else, the gentle foot massage serves to counteract the potential boredom of lying on your back for an hour with nothing else to do.

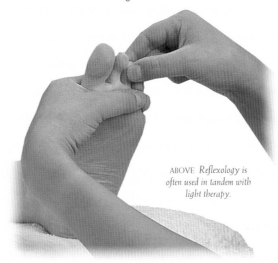

ABOVE *Reflexology is often used in tandem with light therapy.*

PRECAUTIONS

So long as light therapy is not overdone, and the precautions given below are observed, it is a safe form of treatment. However, it is not a substitute for medical treatment of any physical condition or disorder.

■ Consult your doctor if you have any symptoms.

■ Do not expose yourself to direct sunlight for longer than the recommended time for your type of skin.

BIORHYTHMS

There is no doubt that the human body is governed by a number of natural rhythms and biological cycles: the reproductive cycle in women, for example, and the circadian rhythm – from the Latin words circa and die, meaning "about a day" – that causes chemical changes in the brain in response to light and brings about "jetlag" when disturbed. But biorhythm theory maintains that a number of other cycles interweave inexorably throughout life from the moment of birth, governing our physical, emotional, intellectual, intuitional, esthetic, and spiritual abilities. By monitoring the state of each cycle, adherents of biorhythm theory believe that potential problems can be avoided and variations in mood and ability can be explained.

The theory of biorhythms is by no means an ancient one – in fact it is just over 100 years old and originated in Europe. Curiously, two doctors, working independently, both have a claim to have discovered biorhythms: Wilhelm Fleiss and Hermann Swoboda.

The Magic Numbers

Fleiss was a numerologist – someone who believes that numbers have magical properties and studies their influence on life – and a friend and a frequent correspondent of Sigmund Freud (see pages 192-193). Working in Berlin, Germany, at the end of the 19th century, he observed no matter what number he selected, he could create an equation that would give that number as a result if his calculation included either or both numbers 23 or 28.

This, Fleiss believed, meant that 23 and 28 had magical properties – unfortunately, he was in error on this point (see Orthodox View box, far right) – and in his book The Rhythm of Life: Foundations of an Exact Biology, which drew on his correspondence with Freud and was published in 1906, he demonstrated that the same numbers had considerable relevance to any number of biological and physical phenomena. Arguing that there must be a similar connection with the workings of the human mind and body, he deduced that there must be two rhythms to life, based on 23 and 28 days. Then, noting that 28 days fitted women's menstrual cycle, he called this the "female" period and 23 days the "male" period.

Synchronicity

Meanwhile, in an example of what Jung, (see page 194), called "synchronicity," Dr. Hermann Swoboda was coming to similar conclusions at the University of Vienna, Austria. Swoboda analyzed his patients' moods, dreams, and outbreaks of illnesses, and he, too, discovered that there were two distinct cycles of 23 and 28 days. However, Swoboda termed the former the "physical" cycle and the latter the "emotional" one. (Today it is Swoboda's terminology, rather than that of Fleiss, that is generally used.)

Three Cycles

The work of Fleiss and Swoboda was developed further in the 1920s by Alfred Teltscher, a teacher of engineering in Innsbruck, Austria. Having examined his students' work, he observed that their intellectual abilities seemed to fluctuate over a 33-day period – he christened this the "intellectual cycle."

At this point, and for many years afterward, the theory of biorhythms was limited to three cycles: physical, at 23 days; emotional, at 28 days; and intellectual, at 33 days. As such, it was promoted in the 1970s by two separate authors, Bernard Gittleson and George S. Thommen. Biorhythm theory quickly became popular, especially in Japan, where Professor K. Tatai, Head of Behavioral Sciences at Tokyo University, combined the three cycles into the standard biorhythm chart that we

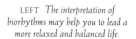

LEFT The interpretation of biorhythms may help you to lead a more relaxed and balanced life.

WHAT ARE BIORHYTHMS?

Many bodily functions, such as waking and sleeping, follow periodic patterns of behavior. Biorhythms are internal cycles said to regulate emotional, physical, and intellectual functioning. They start from zero and are calculated from your date of birth. When expressed as a graph, each cycle raises to a high point, then descends below the zero line. As the cycles vary in length, they meet occasionally.

When cycles cross the zero line, they give rise to "critical" or "caution" days when something negative is likely to occur. If several cycles intersect, you are thought to be particularly vulnerable.

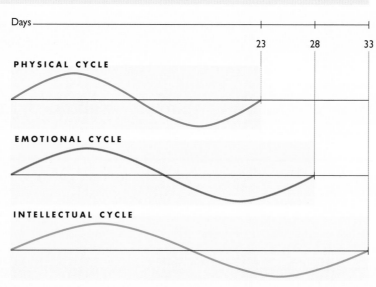

Days

23 28 33

PHYSICAL CYCLE

EMOTIONAL CYCLE

INTELLECTUAL CYCLE

see today. Specialist companies can work out your biorhythms for you, or you can calculate your own, generally by using a computer program.

The Next Step

In recent years there has been a revival of interest in biorhythms, and an extension of biorhythm theory to take in further cycles. In part this has been caused by the increase in use of personal computers and the World Wide Web, since it is relatively simple to write a program to plot an individual's biorhythms. They depend on the notion that everybody's biorhythms start at zero at the moment of birth. (In the three-cycle theory, this also means that after 58 years and 66 days the three cycles are all at zero once more – biorhythmists call this "rebirthing.") Expressed as a graph, each cycle rises from the zero line to a high point, then swoops down, crossing the zero line – at a "switch point" (see page 244) – to descend to a low point; at various places on its path it is intersected by the graph of the other cycles. The point at which a graph crosses the zero line represents a "critical" day, on which an accident or some negative life-event is more likely to occur; this is considerably more likely if several graphs are crossing the line on the same day.

This revival has led to the discovery of more cycles. A 38-day "intuitional" cycle governs how predictable and how cautious we are; a 43-day "esthetic" cycle controls our interest in things that are beautiful and harmonious; and a 53-day "spiritual" cycle determines our inner stability and state of relaxation. In addition,

some biorhythmists believe that further cycles can be found in different combinations of the three basic cycles: the "mastery" cycle derives from a combination of the intellectual and physical cycles; the "passion" cycle is the combination of the physical and emotional cycles; and the "wisdom" cycle represents the combination of the emotional and intellectual cycles.

Biorhythms Today

The appeal of biorhythm theory is clear: biorhythms appear to provide a way of predicting an individual's future that is based on science. They are used increasingly by corporations and municipal bodies in the U.S. and Germany, and, in particular, in Japan. In the early 1960s, for example, the Tokyo Institute of Public Health published a study showing that bus and taxi drivers had significantly more accidents on their "critical" days. However, this research was not confirmed by a 1979 study by the British Transport and Road Research Laboratory, which found no significant correlation. Later, a taxi company warned its drivers when they were having a "critical" day and found that the rate of accidents fell by 50 percent. This may, of course, have been because the drivers were more cautious, having been warned that an accident was likely to happen.

ABOVE *City firms now use biorhythms to help predict an individual's future.*

INTERPRETING BIORHYTHMS

Knowledge of biorhythms cannot prevent accidents but practitioners claim it may help you to avoid potentially difficult situations. Your biorhythm chart can not only tell you about your potential positive aspects and weaknesses on a given day, but help you plan your schedule so that you only undertake important tasks and confront troublesome situations on the most propitious days. For example, it would make sense to write an important business paper – or an essay, if you are a student – on a day on which your intellectual and emotional cycles are high. By the same token, it might be inadvisable to run a road race on a day when your physical cycle is low. Take special care on and around critical days, in order to reduce the chances of a mishap.

A Biorhythm Chart

The horizontal axis of a biorhythm chart indicates the days of the month, and is known as the "caution line." The vertical axis runs above and below the caution line, indicating, respectively, the high and low of each cycle. The lines representing the cycles themselves swoop from high to low and back again, criss-crossing each other because of the different length of each cycle.

The high and low points of each cycle are not necessarily opposites but, to an extent, complementary. For example, the force represented by a particular cycle is at its strongest when at the highest point, but it does not become negative at its lowest point, but more passive. However, when two cycles are both at a high point – a "double high" – or all three cycles are at the top of the chart – a "triple high" – mood, confidence, and performance are all high; similarly a "double low" or "triple low" is likely to indicate low performance, stress, and a depressed mood.

The Emotional Cycle

* High: feel emotions intensely; open to emotional experiences; creative; positive; motivated; interested.
* Low: flat and low; negative;lack of ideas and creativity; uninterested in emotions, and emotional encounters.

The Physical Cycle

* High: filled with physical energy; active; strong; enthusiastic; heightened reflexes; resistant to minor infections.
* Low: lethargic; slothful; wanting to rest and recharge batteries; slower reflexes; lower immunity to minor infections.

LEFT *Self-confidence and vitality are characteristics of the emotional cycle moving to its height.*

SWITCH POINTS

The point at which any line crosses the caution line is known as a "switch point," and the day on which this happens (as well as the day before and the day after, according to some) is said to be a "critical day," in which performance in the area indicated will be poor. Vulnerability is increased when two cycles are at a switch point, and becomes extreme when three cycles meet at a switch point.

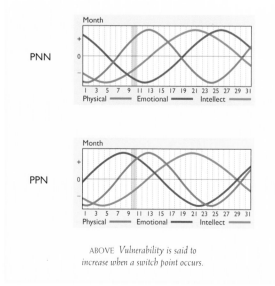

ABOVE *Vulnerability is said to increase when a switch point occurs.*

ABOVE *Strenuous physical challenges may best be undertaken when the physical cycle is high.*

CONSULTING A PRACTITIONER

Biorhythms are primarily a self-help tool, though some naturopaths use them as part of their consultations. In this case, therefore, the "practitioner" is generally a mail-order company, which will draw up your biorhythm chart on the basis of the day and approximate hour of your birth.

If you have access to a personal computer, you will find that numerous programs that generate biorhythm charts are available at relatively little expense. You can use these to prepare charts for you and for other members of your family. And, if you have access to the Internet, you will easily be able to find sites that will prepare your biorhythm chart and allow you to download it at no expense – simply type "biorhythms" into a search engine.

RIGHT *You can generate biorhythm charts on your personal computer.*

PATHFINDER

There is no place for biorhythms in the treatment of any physical or psychological disorder. However, in the same way that astrological horoscopes bring comfort and reassurance to many people, the use of biorhythms may help to explain mood changes. As such, biorhythms may be useful in combating mild (that is, having no clinical significance) anxiety, depression and stress.

ANXIETY; SEE PP. 256–7
DEPRESSION; SEE P. 261
FEAR OF DENTAL
TREATMENT SEE P. 286
STRESS-RELATED
DISORDERS;
SEE PP. 262–3

The Intellectual Cycle

✻ High: good problem-solving ability; increased rationality; mentally alert and sharp; creative.

✻ Low: intuitive rather than rational; mentally dulled, and sluggish.

RIGHT *Work tasks may be carried out more effectively when the intellectual cycle is high.*

RIGHT *When the intellectual cycle is low, the mind is dull and sluggish.*

COLOR THERAPY

ABOVE *The bright colors in abstract paintings can affect the mood in different ways.*

Everyone is aware of how colors can affect moods and emotions. This is not just a matter of everyday experience, but has been amply borne out by scientific research. Color therapy uses this sensitivity to color to identify and correct any imbalances in the body's internal energy patterns that might lead to emotional or physical ill health. Therapists believe that each organ and body system has its own characteristic vibrational energy, and disorders can be healed by applying color of the corresponding vibrational energy, either to the whole body or to the organ concerned.

The use of color as a therapy has a long history. The ancient Egyptians built healing temples of light and color, as did the ancient Greeks. The use of color became deeply embedded in Chinese and Indian medicine, and it remains an integral part of Ayurvedic medicine (*see pages 78-85*) to this day.

In Europe and the U.S., interest in the therapeutic use of color developed during the second half of the 19th century. In 1878, Dr. Edwin Babbitt published *The Principles of Light and Color*, in which he recommended various techniques for the use of color in healing. It was not until 1933, however, that a definitive work, *The Spectro Chrometry Encyclopedia*, by the Hindu scientist Dinshah Ghadiali, was published. Around the same time a form of color therapy, known as "Syntonics," was developed in the U.S. by Dr. Harry Riley Spitler. He found that he could produce profound physiological and psychological changes in his patients by altering the color of light entering their eyes.

Interest has grown steadily in the intervening years, particularly in the U.S., where today there are hundreds of practitioners using a wide variety of color-related therapeutic techniques. Interest in color therapy in Europe and the U.K. has been slower to take off, but as knowledge and experience have grown, color therapy has become assured of a place in the repertoire of complementary medicine.

WHAT IS COLOR THERAPY?

Color therapists believe that, because all matter is a form of energy, the application of energy to the body will have effects for good or ill. Light is a form of energy, and because it can be split into colors, it is possible to deliver this energy at very precise levels and in easily controlled doses. In sickness, the body is deficient in one or more of the color types. The aim of color therapy, therefore, is to restore the correct energy balance by applying the correct colors to the body. Colors are also

COLORS AND THEIR MEANING

Each color is associated with one of the seven chakras of the body, and every color has its complementary color. Single colors or combinations of complementary colors can be used to treat imbalances in the chakras or illness associated with that bodily region.

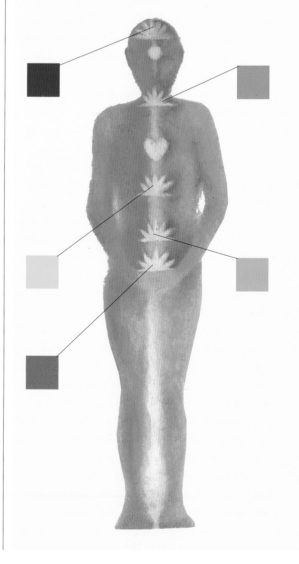

considered to be particularly relevant to specific organs, and disorders in these organs can be treated using the appropriate colors.

Many color therapists adhere to the ancient traditions of Indian medicine, in which the body's energy is thought to be focused at seven points known as "chakras" into which light is believed to stream. Each chakra is associated with particular organs or body systems, and is identified with a particular color. Various tests will be used to ascertain which colors are required to keep the chakras working in harmony.

Red: associated with the base chakra in the sacral region. It promotes vitality, strength, sexuality, willpower, and alertness. Red is used to counteract anemia, lack of energy, impotence, and low blood pressure. Its complement is turquoise.

Orange: associated with the spleen chakra, which regulates circulation and metabolism. Orange promotes happiness and joyousness. This color is used to treat depression and kidney and lung problems, such as asthma and bronchitis. Its complement is blue.

Yellow: associated with the solar plexus chakra, which is concerned with intellect and judgment. Yellow stimulates mental ability and concentration, and aids detachment. This color can be used to treat rheumatism and arthritis, as well as stress-related illnesses. Its complement is violet.

Green: the color of the heart chakra. Green is the color of nature and represents purity and harmony. It is a great healer, used to balance and stabilize the body. Its complement is magenta.

Turquoise: no chakra is associated with this color. It is soothing, purifying, and calming. It is used to combat inflammatory diseases and to boost the immune system. Its complement is red.

Blue: associated with the throat chakra, which deals with willpower and communication. Blue is a calming color, good for curing insomnia. It can be used for throat problems, asthma, stress, and migraine, and it is good for improving verbal skills. Its complement is orange.

Violet: the color of the crown chakra, which is concerned with the energy of the higher mind. It is the color of dignity, honor, self-respect, and hope. It is used to bolster self-esteem and counter feelings of hopelessness, as well as in the treatment of mental and nervous disorders. Its complement is yellow.

Magenta: a color of the highest order, connected with spirituality, meditation, and letting go. It is an agent for change, for the clearing out of old attitudes and obsessions, and for making a break with the past. Its complement is green.

Black, white, gray, and brown are also colors with recognized associations. Black is not used in color therapy and gray only very rarely (for excess of pride and arrogance). Brown is occasionally used (in the form of clothing) as an antidote to selfishness. White light forms the basis for light therapy (see pages 246–7).

CONSULTING A THERAPIST

There are so many different varieties of color therapy that it is difficult to describe what is likely to happen when you visit a therapist precisely. For example, some therapists claim to be able to diagnose your condition simply by looking at you. These are the psychics, who maintain that they can "see" a person's "aura" (multicolored layers that surround an individual) and tell instantly what colors are needed. Photographic techniques are also used sometimes, based on what is known as Kirlian photography (a high-frequency photographic technique developed in Russia in the 1940s).

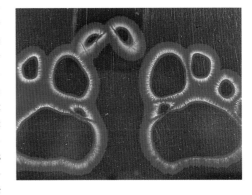
ABOVE *The process of Kirlian photography can help the color therapist see the "aura" around a patient's body.*

Not all diagnostic techniques rely on the interpretation of the aura. Many color therapists use more conventional methods. They will discuss your medical history, your emotions, your energy levels during the day, and the nature, and history of any specific complaints. Some may also read your horoscope. Others make their diagnosis from the color of the eyeballs, urine, stools, and fingernails. If these are tinged with red, for example, the patient is in need of blue. Still others use a method called "color dowsing," in which the therapist runs a finger down a chart of the patient's spine and marks any vertebrae that give rise to a pricking or tingling sensation. Each vertebra is associated with a particular therapy color and its complementary color, thus enabling the therapist to draw up the appropriate treatment regime.

Even this does not exhaust the list of possible diagnostic techniques. Many color therapists believe that we know instinctively what colors we need to restore our internal balance. In a simple test, known as the Lüscher test, you are asked to rank the eight major colors in order of preference. The result can tell the trained therapist a great deal about your personality, your state of health, and the workings of your conscious and subconscious minds and can pinpoint any stresses and imbalances in your system that may be actual or potential sources of disease. Even simpler is the method known as Aura-Soma (see page 249), which is increasingly popular as a form of self-treatment.

Once the therapist has made a diagnosis, she will calculate how much of the missing color is required and how frequently it should be given. There is a wide variety of techniques for the application of color. Most commonly, you will be asked to lie down on your back, usually wearing a white robe, and you will then be

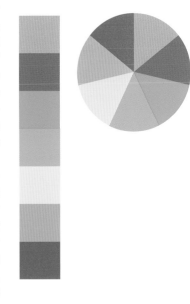
ABOVE *Our instinctive response to different colors, whether negative or positive, can be used by a color therapist as a diagnostic technique.*

bathed in light of the relevant color. Sometimes, your whole body is bathed in light, but for certain specific treatments, only a small area may be exposed. Normally two colors will be set in the lamp: the main therapy color and its complementary one – both are used in healing. Treatment usually consists of a long period of exposure to the main color, followed by a shorter session with its complement. However, some systems use rhythmic alteration of colors to achieve different results. The light is often beamed out in a particular shape, too, since geometric shapes can also have a powerful effect on the body and mind, particularly when linked with color. Sessions usually last for about an hour.

A relaxing alternative to this type of color therapy is the use of a bath illuminated by colored lights at the sides. Any colors can be used, but the most common are blue and orange, its complement, which act to reduce stress and muscle tension. Similar effects can be achieved by lying down for 30 minutes or so wrapped in a piece of colored silk.

There are a number of other ways of treating the body with color. In Indian medicine, it is common to use gems and crystals to focus color onto particular parts of the body. Some Western practitioners use massage with muslin bags containing chrome salts. These are placed in the sun or under a colored lamp for an hour or so before treatment. You are likely to be taught several other useful techniques, which you can use at home. These include diet – eating foods of a particular color; so-called "rainbow" healing, in which you drink water that has been energized in a colored container; "color breathing;" and the use of color in your clothing and other aspects of daily life.

PRECAUTIONS

■ Color therapy should not be used as a substitute for conventional treatment of physical disease.

■ It may be a useful adjunct to such treatment in certain cases, but you should always consult your doctor before embarking on any course of color therapy.

■ Check, too, that you know which of the many possible approaches to therapy the practitioner you choose favors.

SELF-HELP

There are several ways in which you can practice color therapy at home. If you are not undergoing a course of treatment with a therapist, simply pick the color that you feel would make you more cheerful, or more relaxed, and use that.

Rainbow Healing

This is a simple and cheap way of applying color to the body. Water, when exposed to sunlight in a colored container, takes on some of the vibrational energy of that particular color. Special colored containers can be bought, but they can easily be improvized using colored cellophane. Simply drink this water at regular intervals throughout the day.

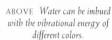

ABOVE *Water can be imbued with the vibrational energy of different colors.*

Color Breathing

This is a form of meditation or visualization, in which you imagine yourself inhaling and exhaling colors. It can be practiced in bed before going to sleep, or when waking in the morning.

1 *Find somewhere comfortable to sit or lie down and relax.*

2 *Keep your breathing deep, regular, and calm.*

3 *Imagine yourself surrounded by intense light of the color you choose. Be aware of the healing properties of the light.*

4 *As you breathe in, imagine that you are inhaling this color, and follow it as it spreads from your lungs to your solar plexus and then throughout your body.*

5 *As you breathe out, imagine that you are exhaling the complementary color.*

LEFT *Some colors are complimentary – blue and orange, for example.*

LEFT *Color breathing can be easily practiced at home.*

Diet

Introduce food of your chosen color into your diet. If you need yellow, eat bananas and yellow-fleshed fruits, corn, butter, saffron rice, and so on. Your color therapist can help you choose a balanced diet.

ABOVE *Fruit and vegetables provide a vast source of bright and vibrant color.*

Clothes and Decoration

Just as we often wear clothes that reflect our moods, so the color of the clothes we wear can alter the way we feel. Wear bright clothes to counteract depression, lack of self-confidence, or low self-esteem, and wear calming colors to suppress irritability or stress. The same principles apply to the way you decorate your home. You may not be able to undertake major redecoration, but a new bedspread or pillow covers, a new lampshade, or a new set of drapes can make a great deal of difference.

LEFT *A few well-chosen objects of the right color can have a powerful effect on our mood.*

AURA-SOMA

The Aura-Soma remedies are a collection of small "balance" bottles, each containing a layer of colored essential oil on top of a layer of colored spring water containing herbal extracts. Most contain two colors, and there are about 90 combinations in all. You are simply asked to pick out the four bottles that most appeal to you, and then to splash the mixtures onto your skin (or around your aura) every day. There is no set length of of time for treatment – you just carry on for as long as the technique appears to be doing you good.

Aura-Soma remedies were developed in 1984 by Vicky Wall, a British chiropodist who acquired psychic powers after going blind. She described the treatment as "non-intrusive, self-selective soul therapy." Aura-Soma is mainly practiced in the U.K., although there is a small number of therapists in the U.S. and Australia.

RIGHT *Choose the balance bottles that appeal most to you.*

LEFT *The right color clothing can enhance self-confidence and bring about a positive outlook.*

PATHFINDER

The main areas in which color therapy has proved successful are those that involve mood, emotion and some aspects of mental performance. However, adherents of the therapy claim that it can be used to treat a variety of conditions, including the following:

ALLERGIES *SEE PP. 338–9*

ANEMIA *SEE P. 303*

ANXIETY *SEE PP. 256–7*

ARTHRITIS *SEE P. 346–7*

ASTHMA *SEE PP. 294–5*

DEPRESSION *SEE P. 261*

HIGH BLOOD PRESSURE *SEE P. 302*

HIV AND AIDS *SEE PP. 340–41*

HYPERACTIVITY *SEE P. 351*

INSOMNIA *SEE P. 264*

LOW BLOOD PRESSURE *SEE P. 303*

MIGRAINE *SEE P. 269*

NAUSEA AND VOMITING *SEE P. 308*

NEURALGIA *SEE P. 267*

OBSESSION *SEE P. 259*

STRESS *SEE PP. 262–3*

4

COMMON
AILMENTS

INTRODUCTION

*I*n the following section, you will find information on conditions and symptoms both major and relatively minor, with detailed guidelines about what can be done about them by your doctor, by alternative therapists and, in many cases, by you yourself using simple, self-help techniques. In a few instances, where you are certain that the cause of your symptoms is not serious and likely to be self-limiting, such as a cold or an occasional attack of slight indigestion, there may be no point in consulting your doctor.

ABOVE *Wild plants and herbs are often used in tandem with the alternative therapy.*

BELOW *A one-to-one session with your chosen therapist can help alleviate worries you may have.*

In the majority of cases, however, your first port of call should be your family doctor, who may be able to prescribe effective treatment and/or rule out any serious condition which might require further investigation or protracted medical treatment. In any case, you should normally be given some kind of diagnosis of the cause of your problem, even though, in some instances, this may amount to little more than a description or medical label. There may be occasions when your doctor can offer little in the way of effective conventional treatment – as with many instances of low back pain, hair loss or irritable bowel syndrome, for example, but it may still be possible to refer you to other sources of help.

Even if you are receiving conventional treatment of some kind, perhaps for a chronic condition such as arthritis, however, there are certain to be many other ways in which your symptoms can be relieved or made easier to bear. No reputable alternative practitioner is likely to suggest that you stop or alter any existing treatment without your doctor's agreement; nor, in most cases, will they offer a rapid cure, and you should be wary of anyone who does. Nevertheless, over a course of therapy, it may be possible to alleviate or even eradicate the underlying cause of your symptoms, especially if these are related to problems such as stress, poor posture or aspects of your lifestyle.

Consulting a Therapist
When you are being treated by your doctor for a particular health problem, it is wise to let him or her know when you are planning to consult an alternative therapist. Not all conventional doctors are open-minded about possible benefits, however, especially when it comes to

CONTENTS

newer or less widely-known approaches, and you may meet with discouragement or even downright hostility when you tell him or her that you are thinking of (or are already) using some form of alternative therapy. If this happens, you should ask the reasons for their objections and make a point of listening to the answers. It may be that your doctor believes that the treatment you have in mind has no proven value or that they simply have no time for alternative medicine in any shape or form. In such cases, it is up to you whether to take their advice, but there is no real reason why you should, provided you are not expecting miracles. On the other hand, your doctor may have a good reason for advising you against a particular therapy, perhaps because it carries particular risks in your case (and may even worsen your condition or just not be right for you), and this type of warning must obviously be taken seriously.

HOW TO USE THE COMMON AILMENTS SECTION

This is a clearly set out, easy-to-use guide to the most common ailments experienced and tells you, at a glance, the information that you need to know about each complaint. As well as listing more general ailments – those that may affect people of any age and sex – there are sections specific to the male and female reproductive systems, the well-known childhood illnesses, and those associated with the onset of old age. Each spread is laid out in a similar fashion so the information can be accessed immediately each time. In each instance, the ailment itself is described in detail, giving information more clearly. The "Conventional Treatment" box tells you what to expect if you go to your doctor or hospital with your particular problem; the "Caution" box makes clear the situations in which the alternative therapies are not suitable and where they should not be used; the "Datafile" box gives examples of typical groups of people that may be prone to this particular ailment and a selection of statistics about the complaint. There is also a more comprehensive therapies box, where each therapy that may help the ailment is listed and cross-referenced to the part of the book in which it appears. This section also features helpful photographs, showing typical symptoms and the therapies actually being applied to individuals.

Each ailment has a descriptive introduction

Symptoms are listed clearly for ease of reference

A "Data File" gives the latest facts and figures about this ailment

The Conventional Treatments tell you what to expect a doctor to prescribe

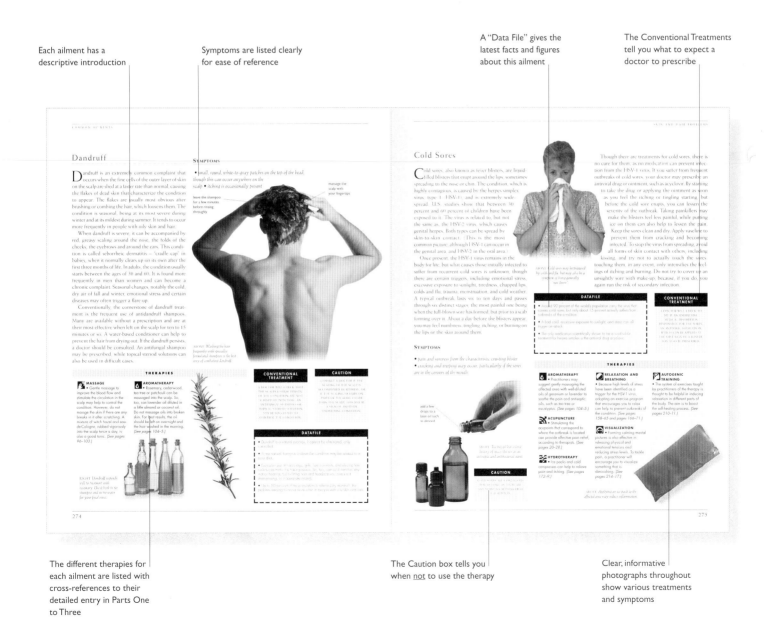

The different therapies for each ailment are listed with cross-references to their detailed entry in Parts One to Three

The Caution box tells you when <u>not</u> to use the therapy

Clear, informative photographs throughout show various treatments and symptoms

Having said that, many more doctors today are willing to accept that conventional medicine does not have all the answers, and are more than happy for their patients to take some responsibility for managing their own health, both through alternative therapy and self-help approaches.

Where there are known contraindications to specific types of therapy for a particular condition, you will find these explained in the relevant sections on the following pages.

As you can see from the section headings listed on page 252, the ailments dealt with in these pages are for the most part arranged according to the part or system of the body affected. So, for example, you will find conjunctivitis in the section covering eyes and ears, while diabetes is to be found in the section on the endocrine system. Those conditions and problems which arise at a specific time or stage in your life are dealt with separately in the sections on childhood, reproduction, and old age. In general, therefore, it is a simple matter to find what you are looking for by referring to the section which relates to your symptoms. Thus, nausea is to be found under "Digestion," cystitis under "Urinary system," allergies under "Immune system," and so on. On the rare occasions when you are not sure where to find your particular ailment, just check in the index beginning on page 376.

How to Use the Section

Once you have found the relevant page, you will be led through a description of the ailment, including possible causes and symptoms. This can generally only be a guide, and if you are not sure whether you have correctly identified your problem, you should seek a professional diagnosis. Often, however, you will be in no doubt, and you will then be able to work your way through the information and advice given. Where appropriate, there is a brief outline of the probable conventional treatment, if there is any, and of any tests or investigations which may be required before it can be begun.

The most likely symptoms and some possible alternative causes are explained, and your attention is drawn to symptoms which may be a sign of something serious or where immediate medical attention may be required. For example, a sharp pain in the eye or blurred vision, a fever above 102 degrees, or moderate to severe chest pains all require immediate expert medical attention. You will also find 'Datafile' boxes relating to many of the conditions, which include facts about incidence (how common it is), risk factors, whether the disease is contagious and so on.

ABOVE *If you have a cough, for example, its type will be closely observed by an alternative practitioner.*

It is always worth trying the simple self-help tips whenever they are suggested for your particular ailment. Something as easy as raising the pillow end of the bed can alleviate a cough or the symptoms of heartburn for example, while taking a vitamin C-rich drink with a meal instead of tea can aid iron absorption in people with anemia. Sometimes the recommended self-help approaches may be a little more demanding: making the right long-term changes in your diet may be helpful for a variety of conditions, including atherosclerosis, constipation, and PMS, for example. Holistic practitioners will also include advice on diet as part of their approach to treatment. Exercise too has an important role to play in the prevention and alleviation of a huge range of health problems, particularly those related to the heart, blood, and circulation, but it can also be helpful for people with diabetes, depression, obesity, and weight problems, and during pregnancy and the menopause, to name but a few. However, if you are not in good health, or have a condition such as heart disease or angina, and especially if you have never exercised before, it is wise to get advice from a health professional before you start. Again, you

LEFT *Both conventional and alternative practitioners will advocate drinking plenty of fluids – whether you are seriously ill or not.*

will find tips and advice on suitable lifestyle modifications where appropriate in the section related to your particular problem. Many alternative therapies involve specialized movement and exercise – including yoga, t'ai chi, the Alexander Technique and dance therapy, for example – and you should tell your therapist of any health problem which might be relevant to your ability to participate.

As explained in the previous chapters on the different alternative therapies, it is often essential to consult a qualified practitioner who will assess your needs and tailor the treatment to you as a unique individual. It's also the case that it is simply impossible to attain the full benefit of many types of treatment without the help of a fully trained and experienced practitioner. Nevertheless, some therapies do lend themselves more easily than others to home

ABOVE *A healthy diet, full of fresh fruit and vegetables, is essential for everyone's well being.*

SUMMARY

The claims of conventional medicine are today being questioned by increasing numbers of people. The idea is borne out of the fact that modern medicine is simply not as efficient or effective as we have have been led to believe and adverse drug reactions and side-effects tell their own story. Our growing understanding of holistic treatment has encouraged us to examine the healing practices and cultures from around the world, and from each we can gather valuable information about diet, lifestyle, illness, health, and well-being. This section, which details the ailments that most people will come across at some point in their lives, provides a starting point for those who do wish to try alternative therapies instead of the more conventional medical treatment. It is important to remember, however, that in some cases medical intervention is crucial, so if you are at all worried about anything, do consult your doctor. Used sensibly, however, this section can give you and your family something different to experiment with if, for example, a child has a cold or a sore throat that can be treated using alternative methods. All these alternative therapies have the same focus; to boost immunity, help prevent more serious conditions such as cancer or heart disease, encourage emotional well-being and relaxation, enhance strength, and keep the body's systems functioning the way that they should, and hopefully as awareness of these will help give you an improved quality of life. Alternative therapies are more likely to make you feel better, more vital and more alert; they have fewer side-effects and work actively to prevent illness. With all this information at our fingertips it is now possible to encourage our bodies to work at their optimum level.

treatment by the individual concerned. In particular, you may well be able to obtain symptomatic relief by applying some of the simpler techniques used by professional therapists and this is certainly worthwhile. This will be even more effective if you have already been taught elements of the technique concerned during a course of therapy, but the simple instructions given in the "Therapies" panel for each ailment on the following pages are easy to apply even for the complete novice. Among the therapies which can be adapted for self-treatment in this way are aromatherapy, hydrotherapy, acupressure, shiatsu, ayurveda, massage, visualization, color therapy, relaxation and breathing therapies, and yoga. Naturally, such self-help methods can only make use of a very restricted range of the treatments which would be offered in a professional consultation, but they can still make a difference.

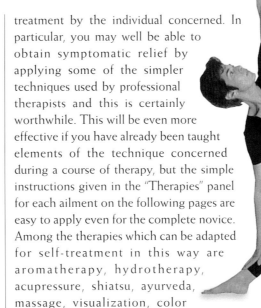

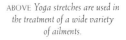

ABOVE *Yoga stretches are used in the treatment of a wide variety of ailments.*

As well as advice on which therapies can be used at home and how, the "Therapies" panels also give a brief summary of other treatments which can only be given by a trained therapist but which may be beneficial for particular ailments. If you are interested, you can then refer back to the relevant section in an earlier chapter to find out in more detail what is involved, and what you can expect from a particular therapy.

Whatever the nature of the ailment you are suffering from at any given time, taking positive steps to help yourself is bound to offer very real benefits, psychological as well as physical. Following simple self-help advice is unlikely to actually cure any condition, but it may often ease pain and discomfort and sometimes make it less likely that the problem will recur. Alternative remedies have much to offer for conditions which may be chronic and, in some cases, quite serious or even life-threatening. With problems affecting the musculoskeletal system, for example, or those which are in some way stress-related, they are frequently at least as effective as conventional medicine and often more so. The information in this chapter will guide you toward the steps you can most usefully and safely take toward improving your own well-being so that you are an effective partner with the professionals in managing your personal health.

ABOVE *As an alternative therapy which is relatively accessible to all, massage is helpful for many ailments relevant to it.*

MIND AND EMOTIONS

Anxiety

Anxiety is a psychological state characterized by excessive unease or fear. In certain circumstances, the condition is completely normal and can be positively beneficial, because the body is preparing itself for fighting, or running away from danger – the so-called "fight or flight" syndrome (*see Stress, pages* 262–3). Sometimes, however, anxiety can become acute and constant, with no apparent trigger, and requires medical advice and attention.

Physical symptoms of anxiety include palpitations, difficulty in breathing, dry mouth, nausea, frequent urination, rapid pulse, headache, fatigue, dizziness, muscular tension, sweating, churning stomach, an irritable bowel, tremor and shake, and skin that is cold to the touch. Mental or emotional symptoms include feelings of unease, fear, dread, irritability, panic, nervous anticipation, inner terror, worrying about trivia, difficulty in concentration, difficulty in falling asleep, and inability to relax. The condition is often associated with depression and may be accompanied by suicidal feelings. Conventional treatment involves the prescription of anti-anxiety drugs, antidepressants, or sleeping tablets, usually for only a short time to help you over a difficult period.

Your doctor may advise you to increase the amount of exercise you do, particularly walking and swimming. Exercise promotes the release of endorphins, the body's natural painkillers, which induce feelings of relaxation

ABOVE *Many people turn to cigarettes in times of stress, but this is well-known to be harmful to health.*

BELOW *Anti-depressants and other conventional drugs should be treated as only a short-term solution.*

and well-being. If you smoke, you should cease. Reduce the amount of alcohol you drink, and cut out caffeine in the form of coffee, tea, and various fizzy drinks. All these substances are stimulants and exacerbate anxiety. Follow a healthy diet, and avoid junk food.

Professional counseling may be suggested to help to resolve underlying problems and dilemmas. Anxiety that is rooted in a specific problem or dilemma can be treated very effectively by resolving the problem. More generalized anxiety often has its roots in low self-esteem and feelings of inadequacy. In this case, a professional counselor will concentrate on teaching you to refocus upon yourself and help you to think more positively about your character and your achievements.

Complementary health practitioners are usually well-versed in treating minor anxiety conditions, which may respond to a number of therapies.

SYMPTOMS

- *listlessness, weakness, and tiredness* • *headaches* • *tension, nervousness, and irritability* • *depression* • *unexplained pains*
- *dizziness* • *sighing breaths* • *panic or palpitations*
- *nausea, vomiting, diarrhea, or frequent urination* • *insomnia*

THERAPIES

ACUPRESSURE
• A practitioner will show you the acupoints that work the most effectively for you in controlling your anxiety and how to stimulate them. You can then apply pressure to these points whenever you start to experience the first symptoms of anxiety in order to prevent a full-blown attack. (*See pages* 29–31.)

AROMATHERAPY
• Massages with essential oils can be relieving, calming and refreshing. Try massaging with a blend of essential oils of lavender, geranium and bergamot in sweet almond oil or peach kernel oil. Other suitable oils include Roman chamomile, frankincense, lavender, neroli, rose and ylang ylang. (*See pages* 104–5.)

BREATHING TECHNIQUES
• Deep, slow, relaxed breathing is a vital element in controlling anxiety and in relieving an anxiety attack. A practitioner will teach you the appropriate techniques, which you should practice regularly, rather than only on a fire-fighting basis. (*See pages* 166–71.)

PSYCHOTHERAPY AND COUNSELLING
• Practitioners may recommend a course of cognitive-behavioral therapy. You will be taught how to understand your thinking patterns, so that they can react differently to the situations that are causing them anxiety. (*See pages* 196–9.)

BIOFEEDBACK
• Anxiety was one of the first complaints to be tackled by biofeedback practitioners. In respiration biofeedback, patients listen to their own amplified breathing patterns and are taught how to regulate them to relieve anxiety symptoms. (*See pages* 212–13.)

MASSAGE
• Regular massage can relieve muscle tension and reduce stress and anxiety. (*See pages* 96–103.)

YOGA
• This is particularly effective in combatting anxiety, because it helps both the body and mind to relax. The poses work best if practised regulary – 15 minutes a session is a minimum. (*See pages* 52–9.)

BELOW *Just having someone to talk to can help relieve anxiety problems.*

the therapist will help you to understand your difficulties

you can unburden yourself to someone who is not going to criticise you

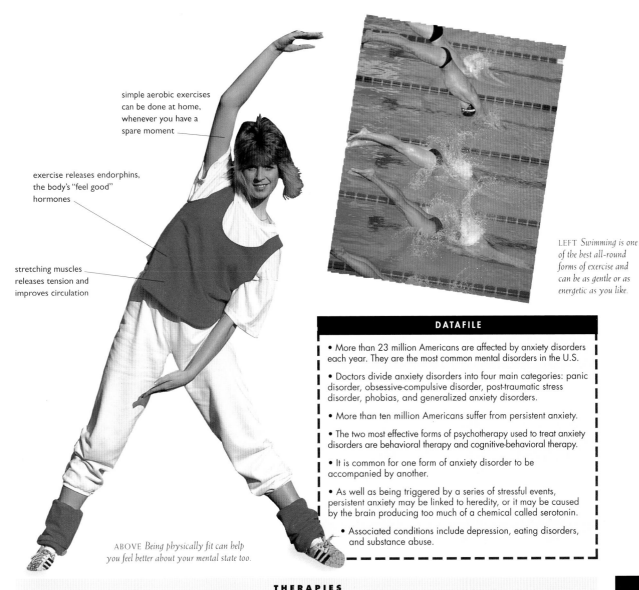

simple aerobic exercises can be done at home, whenever you have a spare moment

exercise releases endorphins, the body's "feel good" hormones

stretching muscles releases tension and improves circulation

LEFT Swimming is one of the best all-round forms of exercise and can be as gentle or as energetic as you like.

ABOVE Being physically fit can help you feel better about your mental state too.

DATAFILE

• More than 23 million Americans are affected by anxiety disorders each year. They are the most common mental disorders in the U.S.

• Doctors divide anxiety disorders into four main categories: panic disorder, obsessive-compulsive disorder, post-traumatic stress disorder, phobias, and generalized anxiety disorders.

• More than ten million Americans suffer from persistent anxiety.

• The two most effective forms of psychotherapy used to treat anxiety disorders are behavioral therapy and cognitive-behavioral therapy.

• It is common for one form of anxiety disorder to be accompanied by another.

• As well as being triggered by a series of stressful events, persistent anxiety may be linked to heredity, or it may be caused by the brain producing too much of a chemical called serotonin.

• Associated conditions include depression, eating disorders, and substance abuse.

THERAPIES

REFLEXOLOGY
• Reflexology works on the meridians and acupoints (see pages 20–21) of the feet and hands. A once-weekly treatment for six weeks may prove effective in reducing anxiety. (See pages 66–71.)

HYPNOTHERAPY
• A deep sense of meditation and relaxation is achieved through hypno-therapy, with the added benefit of the practitioner being able to address the specific causes of anxiety while you are in this deeply relaxed state. Six to eight sessions should prove valuable. (See pages 218–23.)

RIGHT With skilful massage across the neck and shoulders, you can literally feel the tension easing.

MEDITATION
• The therapy aims at relaxing the mind and so triggering the body's natural relaxation responses. You should practice the technique twice daily, for 5–10 minutes at a time. (See pages 60–3.)

COLOR THERAPY
• A therapist will probably concentrate on using blue, violet and white, together with their complementary colors, in order to restore your mind and body to a state of balanced harmony. Colors to avoid would be red and orange. (See pages 248–51.)

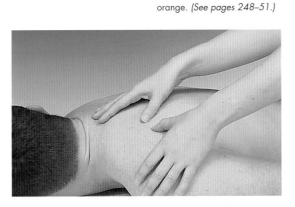

OTHER THERAPIES
• Practitioners believe the following can alleviate anxiety: shaolin (see pages 42–3); qigong and t'ai chi ch'uan (see pages 44–5 and 46–51); polarity therapy (see pages 64–5); metamorphic technique (see pages 72–3); Bowen technique (see pages 76–7); healing (see pages 86–7); kinesiology (see pages 126–33); Alexander technique (see pages 146–53); Trager-work (see pages 154–5); Zero Balancing (see pages 156–7); flotation therapy (see pages 180–1); autogenic training (see pages 210–11); visualiza-tion (see pages 214–17); music therapy (see pages 232–5).

CAUTION

IF ANXIETY PERSISTS FOR LONG PERIODS, BECOMES ACUTE AND PREVENTS YOU FUNCTIONING PROPERLY EITHER AT HOME OR AT WORK, OR IS ACCOMPANIED BY SUICIDAL FEELINGS, CONSULT A DOCTOR WITHOUT DELAY. HE MAY REFER YOU TO A SPECIALIST COUNSELOR, PSYCHOLOGIST OR PSYCHIATRIST FOR HELP.

CONVENTIONAL TREATMENT

YOUR DOCTOR MAY PRESCRIBE A TRANQUILIZER, SEDATIVE, OR MILD PAINKILLER TO HELP TO BREAK THE VICIOUS CIRCLE OF WORRY THAT ANXIETY MAY CAUSE. DRUGS, HOWEVER, ARE NOT A LONG-TERM SOLUTION TO THE PROBLEM.

Addictions

Put at its simplest, addiction means that a dependence on a substance, or, in some cases, an activity, takes over life. It is a physical and psychological state, particularly associated with a number of drugs, the most common being caffeine, nicotine, alcohol, tranquilizers, and sleeping tablets, and including numerous illegal substances, such as cannabis, cocaine, and heroin. Among the disorders related to the misuse of such substances, the experts make a clear distinction between substance abuse and substance dependence. Substance abuse victims cannot control their cravings. Though they repeatedly try to stop using the drug, they fail. Substance dependence victims share the same symptoms, but, in addition, have built up a tolerance for the drug, so that increasing amounts of it are necessary for the desired effect. In both cases, the addict may experience physical "withdrawal" symptoms without the drug in question, such as the delirium tremens that is a result of alcoholism.

Addicts need help and support. Without this, attempts to rectify the condition fail far more often than not. Coming to terms with the existence and extent of the problem is an essential first step, and professional counseling can contribute greatly to achieving this. Further medical back-up may include the prescription of antidepressants, sleeping tablets and, in some cases of drug addiction, substitute drugs where the original one has caused chemical changes in the brain.

SYMPTOMS

• *irritability* • *irrationality* • *mood swings* • *anger* • *irregular heartbeat* • *trembling* • *tremor* • *nausea* • *craving for the drug* • *headache* • *depression* • *anxiety* • *restlessness* • *sweating* • *abdominal pain* • *vomiting* • *diarrhea* • *loss of appetite* • *failing memory*

DATAFILE

• A teenager can become an alcoholic in six to 18 months of heavy drinking, as opposed to five to 15 years for an adult.

• Alcohol and drug abuse affect an estimated 25.5 million Americans.

• Almost 62 million Americans have tried smoking cannabis at least once in their lives.

• Cannabis impairs driving skills for at least four to six hours after smoking a single cigarette; long-term use has been shown to have damaging physical and psychological effects.

• Drinking alcohol as an aid to sleep can easily lead to dependence.

• Once someone has smoked just four cigarettes, he has a 90 percent chance of becoming a regular smoker.

• Alcohol has a more damaging effect on women than on men.

LEFT *Drinking small quantities of red wine is known to be good for you, but in excess it can damage your health, your ability to perform at work, and your relationships.*

CAUTION

ADDICTIONS ARE BEST TREATED BY A MEDICAL PRACTITIONER. NO DRUG SHOULD BE SUDDENLY WITHDRAWN WITHOUT MEDICAL SUPPORT.

CONVENTIONAL TREATMENT

YOU MAY BE ADVISED TO UNDERGO PROFESSIONAL COUNSELLING AND TO JOIN A SELF-HELP GROUP SUCH AS ALCOHOLICS ANONYMOUS. VITAMINS AND ANTICONVULSANTS MAY BE PRESCRIBED.

THERAPIES

FLOTATION THERAPY
• Therapists claim that flotation can lower blood pressure, reduce the levels of stress-related biochemicals in the body, lessen pain, and remove feelings of tension and stress. *(See pages 180–1.)*

HYPNOTHERAPY
• Studies show that the therapy is widely effective in dealing with nicotine addiction. Practitioners also claim that it can help to alleviate depression and reduce anxiety. *(See pages 218–23.)*

AUTOGENIC TRAINING
• This relaxation therapy is thought to help people who are trying to avoid, or cut out, drugs such as sleeping pills and tranquilizers. *(See pages 210–11.)*

ACUPUNCTURE
• Acupuncture on the ear is considered by some practitioners as particularly helpful when dealing with painful withdrawal symptoms, because it is thought to stimulate the production and release of endorphins, the body's natural pain-relievers. *(See pages 20–8.)*

YOGA
• By devoting time every day to yoga routines, you may be able to purge mind and body and achieve a state of deep relaxation. Therapists claim that yoga can boost self-

esteem by inspiring a sense of discipline and achievement. *(See pages 52–9.)*

ALEXANDER TECHNIQUE
• Learning to be calm can help in coming to terms with addiction. Teachers of the Alexander technique will show you how to stand and sit correctly for maximum physical and mental ease. *(See pages 146–53.)* Relaxation techniques may also be helpful. *(See pages 158–65.)*

AROMATHERAPY
• Massage with a detoxifying oil, such as juniper, is recommended. Alternate with chamomile, clary sage, and ylang ylang, all of which are antidepressants. *(See pages 104–5.)*

PSYCHOTHERAPY AND COUNSELING
• Both are often suggested in conjunction with other treatment programs. Cognitive-behavioral therapy and group therapy are both considered potentially beneficial. *(See pages 196–9, and pages 208–9.)*

MASSAGE
• Practitioners argue that full body massage can help to boost self-esteem and that the touching the therapy involves signals support for the recipient. The therapy is widely used to help in the treatment of addiction in the U.S. *(See pages 96–103.)*

MEDITATION
• Focussing mentally on a thought, sound, image or object helps to stimulate physiological self-control. A therapist will advise you on which are the best techniques for use. *(See pages 60–3.)*

OTHER THERAPIES
• Practitioners believe the following therapies can help to alleviate addictions: acupressure *(see pages 29–31)*; kinesiology *(see pages 126–33)*; dance movement therapy *(see pages 226–31)*; art therapy *(see pages 238–41)*.

ABOVE *With many addictions, the most difficult thing is admitting that you have a problem and need help. Counseling and support groups help sufferers realise that they are not alone.*

Obsession

An obsession is a persistent idea or thought that dominates someone's mind. An overwhelming urge to act upon an obsession is known as a compulsion. When someone becomes overwhelmed or dominated by obsessive ideas or compulsive acts, the medical term for the condition is obsessive-compulsive disorder. The behavior totally disrupts victims' lives: they may be unable to go out because they feel the need to return to their homes time after time to check that the door is locked, for example. Washing the hands repeatedly through fear of germs, checking that lights are turned off, and manic tidiness are other common examples of the disorder.

True obsessive-compulsive disorder is quite rare, though minor obsessional symptoms are commoner. Orthodox doctors usually suggest a form of behavioral therapy to deal with the problem, sometime accompanied by the prescription of antidepressants.

SYMPTOMS

• *the mind is obsessed by recurrent thoughts about the same subject, to the exclusion of nearly everything else, including work and family* • *fear of contamination* • *raw skin caused by repeated hand washing or repeated housework* • *agresssive thoughts and behavior* • *depression*

ABOVE *Even cleanliness can be taken too far. A constant desire to wash your hands may be a symptom of some deeper anxiety.*

CONVENTIONAL TREATMENT

IF THE PROBLEM LOOKS LIKE BECOMING EXTREME, YOU MAY BE PRESCRIBED A COURSE OF TRANQUILIZERS AND REFERRED TO A PSYCHIATRIST.

CAUTION

THOSE WITH AN OBSESSIVE-COMPULSIVE DISORDER CAN CONCEAL THE PROBLEM FROM ALL BUT THE PEOPLE THEY LIVE WITH. IF YOU SUSPECT SOMEONE IS SUFFERING FROM THE CONDITION, TRY TO GET HIM TO SEEK PROFESSIONAL HELP WITHOUT DELAY.

the counselor will listen sympathetically and make constructive suggestions

you can talk freely without fear of ridicule

LEFT *Talking to a professional counselor may help identify the cause of the problem.*

THERAPIES

HYPNOTHERAPY
• A hypnotherapist will put you into a trance and, while you are deeply relaxed, will suggest ways in which you can deal with your problems. She may also advise on self-hypnosis techniques you can use for yourself to help to relax deeply when the need arises. *(See pages 218–23.)*

SHIATSU
• Therapists believe that this form of massage can be useful in alleviating obsessional thought patterns, particularly among the under 50s. *(See pages 32–7 and Do-in, pages 38–41.)*

YOGA
• By encouraging feelings of mental and physical well-being, yoga has helped many people suffering from obsessions or compulsive behavior. It will also help you to relax. A teacher can show you which positions are best and how to execute them. *(See pages 52–9.)*

ART THERAPY
• Practitioners believe that the therapy helps by encouraging sufferers to "let go" of some of the underlying fears, tensions and anger that are characteristic consequences of their condition. In particular, they advocate the use of modeling clay, or other malleable materials. *(See pages 238–41.)*

AUTOGENIC TRAINING
• A therapist can teach you the six mental exercises and three physical positions that form the basis of this effective relaxation therapy. *(See pages 210–11.)*

COLOR THERAPY
• Therapists believe that colors of specific hues and shades are effective in improving physical, emotional and spiritual health. They claim that color illumination with a soft magenta light has proved its effectiveness in treating cases of obsession. The therapy also involves counseling and the teaching of appropriate relaxation techniques. *(See pages 248–51.)*

PSYCHOTHERAPY AND COUNSELING
• A behavioral therapist will show you ways to help to manage the anxieties that are an integral part of the disorder more positively. Response prevention, which is designed to show that irrational fears do not come true, is also part of the therapy. *(See pages 196–9.)*

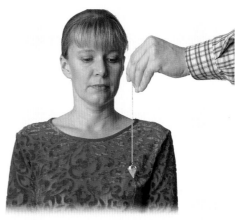

ABOVE *Hypnotherapy reaches the subconscious part of your mind and enables you to deal with concerns of which you are unaware.*

Phobias

Phobias are deep, irrational fears usually classified as anxiety disorders that, if left untreated, can cause severe anxiety, pain attacks, and possible depression. They can take many different forms, but among the most common are agoraphobia, the fear of open spaces, claustrophobia, the fear of being in an enclosed space, and social phobia, fear of any social gathering. Another common phobia is the fear of certain creatures, notably snakes and spiders.

Though antidepressants and tranquilizers can provide effective short-term relief, many doctors hesitate to prescribe them on their own, in case they become addictive. Rather, they will refer sufferers to a specialist psychologist, who may treat the condition through the use of a technique called desensitization. This involves repeated and increasing exposure to the feared situation or object, so that you gradually learn how to overcome your fears and the phobic response abates.

LEFT People who also suffer from phobias often feel trapped within their fears and need a helping hand to control what seems to others to be an irrational response to the world.

CONVENTIONAL TREATMENT

YOU MAY BE PRESCRIBED ANTIDEPRESSANTS OR TRANQUILIZERS ON A SHORT-TERM BASIS. IN THE LONGER TERM, YOU MAY BE ADVISED TO UNDERGO DESENSITIZATION BY SATURATION THERAPY, WHICH WORKS BY EXPOSING A SUFFERER TO THE CAUSE OF THE PROBLEM FOR GRADUALLY INCREASING PERIODS OF TIME.

SYMPTOMS

• *increased heartbeat* • *excessive sweating* • *high blood pressure* • *trembling and shaking* • *nausea* • *fainting* • *hyperventilation (rapid breathing)*

RIGHT AND BELOW *Many people dislike the sliminess of snakes or the scuttling run of spiders, but in the phobia sufferer they cause physical symptoms of distress.*

DATAFILE

• Phobias are thought to be caused by a combination of psychological factors and life events.

• Approximately 27 million Americans – nearly 15 percent of the population – suffer from an anxiety disorder at some point in their lives.

• Panic attacks are characterized by repeated, unprovoked attacks of terror, accompanied by chest pain, heart palpitations, shortness of breath, dizziness, weakness and sweating. They tend to be short-lived, lasting for 10 to 20 minutes.

• The commonest form of phobia is agoraphobia, the fear of open spaces. Another common variant is claustrophobia, the fear of crowded places or of being confined in small spaces.

THERAPIES

AROMATHERAPY
• Body massages with essential oils can be effective in treating phobias, some of the most effective oils being bergamot, chamomile, clary sage, geranium, jasmine, juniper, lavender, marjoram, melissa and ylang ylang. *(See pages 104–5.)*

RELAXATION TECHNIQUES
• These are of inestimable value to anyone suffering from a phobia and you are well advised to learn the techniques and to practice them. Use them whenever you feel a panic attack approaching, as they can relieve its symptoms, particularly hyperventilation. *(See pages 158–65.)*

BREATHING TECHNIQUES
• Deep, regular, relaxed breathing from the diaphragm is an essential part of learning to control your physical responses to a perceived threat, which is what your phobia is to you. *(See pages 166–71.)*

HYPNOTHERAPY
• A hypnotherapist will take you back to the time when when the phobia first demonstrated itself and then will work with you to overcome the fear. He or she may also ask you to visualize the phobia stage by stage as a way of coming to terms with it and overcoming it. *(See pages 218–23.)*

ART THERAPY
• Practitioners think that phobias often have their roots in childhood terrors and fears and that depicting them through drawing and painting can help to overcome them. *(See pages 238–41.)*

PSYCHOTHERAPY AND COUNSELING
• As well as desensitization techniques *(see above)*, cognitive-behavioral therapy can encourage the development of more positive patterns of thinking and behavior. *(See pages 196–9.)*

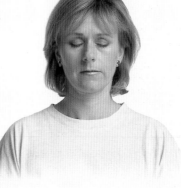

RIGHT *Simple exercises with controlled breathing can relax you sufficiently to reduce your anxiety.*

Depression

Depression covers a range of feelings, from temporary "blues" to a state of extreme dejection and melancholy with an accompanying mood of hopelessness and feelings of inadequacy. It may be triggered by an outside cause, such as bereavement, divorce or job loss; or it may be due to a combination of factors such as early psychological losses, poor upbringing, genetic predisposition, or biochemical imbalance. Sometimes, the condition can alternate with spells of euphoria and hyperactivity (manic-depressive disorder). SAD (Seasonal Affective Disorder), which typically occurs in the winter, is another variant.

Most people suffer from depression at some point in their lives but at times it may require medical treatment. A doctor may treat mild depression with a short course of tranquilizers or sleeping pills. Sensible self-help measures include increasing exercise, to boost energy levels, and talking through the problem with someone close to you. More severe depression may require a course of antidepressants and counseling, though it can take weeks – or months – for these to be effective.

DATAFILE

• The risk of depression increases with age: 17 year olds are four times more likely to be depressed than 8 to 12 year olds.

• Major depressions occur in 10–20 percent of the world's population in the course of a lifetime.

• One person in 50 with a depressive illness needs hospital treatment. One in 20 suffer from winter depression (Seasonal Affective Disorder, or SAD), thought to be caused by overproduction of the hormone melatonin. Cases of SAD are on the increase but can be treated by phototherapy (bright light therapy).

• Half of all people with depression experience recurrences.

SYMPTOMS

• *profound and prolonged change of mood* • *overwhelming sense of failure and self-blame* • *suicidal thoughts and feelings* • *loss of zest for life* • *slow speech* • *confusion* • *constant fatigue* • *loss of appetite* • *poor concentration* • *aching limbs* • *poor sleep and waking early in the morning, several hours before you need to* • *cessation of periods* • *generalized, unexplained anxiety* • *loss of libido*

you have no enthusiasm for anything

you are physically exhausted and can't be bothered exercising

LEFT *Depression means more than "feeling a bit down." Your self-esteem is at an all-time low, you find it difficult to motivate yourself to do anything, and you cannot believe that anyone else cares.*

CAUTION

IF SYMPTOMS ARE SEVERE, OR LAST FOR LONGER THAN TWO WEEKS, SEEK MEDICAL ADVICE. IF YOU FEEL AT ALL SUICIDAL, SEEK MEDICAL HELP IMMEDIATELY.

CONVENTIONAL TREATMENT

YOU MAY BE PRESCRIBED ANTIDEPRESSANTS TO RELIEVE THE CONDITION, IF IT IS SEVERE, AND REFERRED TO A COUNSELOR OR PSYCHIATRIST. MILD DEPRESSION IS TREATED WITH SHORT COURSES OF TRANQUILIZERS OR SLEEPING PILLS.

THERAPIES

MASSAGE
• Relaxing massages may help to relieve the feelings of loneliness and isolation that sometimes bring on depression. (See pages 96–103.)

HYDROTHERAPY
• According to practitioners, sauna baths and vigorous body rubs have proved effective in treating the symptoms of depression. (See pages 172–9.)

ACUPUNCTURE
• A practitioner will stimulate the acupoints on the various meridians considered to affect mood. (See pages 20–8.)

AROMATHERAPY
• Antidepressant oils that can be used in massage include neroli, jasmine, geranium, melissa and rose. Ylang ylang, lavender, clary sage or chamomile have both a sedative and antidepressant effect. (See pages 104–5.)

DANCE THERAPY
• Dance exercise combined with music in a social setting can raise endorphin levels and help relieve depression. (See pages 226–9.)

PSYCHOTHERAPY AND COUNSELING
• A practitioner will teach you how to think positively by showing you how to identify pessimistic thoughts and then how you can change them. (See pages 196–9.)

YOGA
• Relaxing and stretching poses and deep breaths can be useful. (See pages 52–9.)

OTHER THERAPIES
• The following therapies may alleviate the condition: qigong and t'ai chi ch'uan (see pages 44–5; 46–51); meditation (see pages 60–3); reiki (see pages 74–5); craniosacral therapy (see pages 116–17); Feldenkrais method (see pages 142–5); Alexander technique (see pages 146–51); relaxation techniques (see pages 158–65); visualization (see pages 214–17); hypnotherapy (see pages 218–23); music therapy (see pages 232–5); art therapy (see pages 238–41); light therapy (see pages 242–3).

RIGHT *Dance therapy can help lift the symptoms of depression.*

Stress

Some degree of stress in life is beneficial. When it becomes a problem, this is more often than not the result of continuous mental or physical pressures that individuals find impossible to meet. The trigger point, or threshold, obviously varies from person to person. Some people thrive on stress, perceiving every difficulty and hurdle in life as a challenge. Others find it difficult or impossible to accommodate or cope with such changes. For them, such things become stressful, rather than challenging.

Some people thrive on a degree of stress, but excessive stress, or suffering from stress over a period of time, is generally not good for the health. What happens is that certain situations – the stressors – may set off what is termed the "fight or flight" response in your body. Perceiving an emergency, the brain sends out alarm signals via chemical messengers called neurotransmitters. These signals trigger the production of hormones whose function it is to put the body on alert and prepare it for trouble. Your pulse rate accelerates, your heart pounds, your knees may shake and your stomach may become upset. But, because the stressor is usually mental or emotional, there is no appropriate physical release. The long-term result is a depletion of the body's supply of stress-related hormones, making it more vulnerable to illness and disease. Common examples of stress-related disorders include back pain, raised blood pressure, and indigestion.

Having recognized the problem, there is much that you can do for yourself to help to resolve it. Look at the main causes of stress in your life and decide how you can reduce their levels: this is important for your

you may suffer from headaches or notice tightness of the jaw muscles, as if your teeth were permanently clenched

the stomach is traditionally the seat of the emotions, and digestive upsets are a common symptom of stress

your muscles may feel tight and tense

CAUTION

NO ONE CAN TOLERATE HIGH LEVELS OF STRESS OVER LONG PERIODS OF TIME WITHOUT SERIOUS RISK TO THEIR PHYSICAL OR MENTAL HEALTH. REDUCING STRESS IS AN ESSENTIAL PART OF A HEALTHY LIFESTYLE.

LEFT *A certain amount of stress is considered to be good for you – otherwise you would be living your life on an emotional plateau – but there are times when there is just too much to do and you don't feel you can cope any longer.*

THERAPIES

YOGA
• A teacher will show you which postures will help to promote relaxation, so achieving a balance between body and mind. You will also be taught breathing routines, such as alternate nostril breathing, that will similarly help you to relax. (See pages 52–9).

T'AI CHI CH'UAN
• This therapy's slow, flowing movements are said to release physical and mental tensions and adjust the body's energy flow. The breathing techniques you will also learn promote relaxation and inner calmness. (See pages 46–51 and Qigong, pages 44–5.)

MASSAGE
• Regular massage is a proven counter to the effects of stress. The rubbing, kneading and pummelling the therapy involves will relieve muscle tension and also trigger the release of endorphins, which will have an uplifting effect. (See pages 96–103.)

ACUPUNCTURE
• This therapy is considered to be particularly useful when tackling physical problems that arise as a result of stress. The exact nature of the treatment depends on the problems. (See pages 20–8.)

AROMATHERAPY
• Massages with essential oils are excellent de-stressors. Among the most effective oils are basil, chamomile, geranium, lavender, neroli and rose. Strengthening oils include rosemary, ginger and lemongrass, while frankincense calms and deepens breathing. (See pages 104–5.)

ROLFING
• The therapy is claimed to be effective in relieving stress, but you should note that it is physically demanding. (See pages 134–7 and Hellerwork, pages 138–41.)

MEDITATION
• By practicing meditation regularly, practitioners argue that you can reduce stress levels substantially. The physical evidence for this includes lowered blood pressure and a slower pulse rate. A therapist wil identify the techniques that are best for you. (See pages 60–3.)

LEFT *Essential oils from plants are used in aromatherapy to reduce stress.*

health both in the short term and in the long term. Look at your workload and decide how to cut it down if you need to. The magic words are Prioritize, Delegate and Eliminate. Do only what is truly important to you. Can someone else take over some of your tasks? Can you simply cross some of your tasks off your daily list? Concentrate on problem-solving in order to reduce stress. Unresolved problems continue to produce stress and any therapy that you choose, therefore, is diminished in its benefits.

Increasing the amount of exercise you take will undoubtedly help, though you should not undertake a program of vigorous exercise without consulting your physician. Try, for example, a combination such as riding, yoga and walking, or squash and t'ai chi. Eating regularly and healthily is also of importance. You should feel better within two weeks if you improve your diet, cutting out caffeine, alcohol, and nicotine, and eat plenty of fresh fruit and vegetables.

a healthy diet promotes an overall feeling of well-being and enables you to deal better with the ups and downs of life

fresh, health-giving food need not be boring or take long to prepare

LEFT *It's very easy to reach for the chocolate or to eat quickly prepared junk food when under stress.*

SYMPTOMS

• *disturbed, fitful sleep* • *insomnia* • *waking up much earlier than usual and falling asleep during the day* • *change in appetite* • *weight gain or loss* • *reduced zest for life* • *irritability* • *confusion* • *forgetfulness* • *feeling anxious or panicky* • *headache* • *migraine* • *stomach ache* • *anger* • *dizziness* • *impotence* • *increased heart beat* • *in children:* • *naughtiness* • *listlessness* • *restlessness* • *being withdrawn* • *refusing to socialise* • *bedwetting* • *uncontrollable rages* • *stealing*

DATAFILE

• The three best recognized causes of stress are bereavement, divorce, and moving home.

• The most widely used scale of causes of stress was formulated by two American researchers, Thomas Holmes and Richard Rahe, in 1967. It rates life changes, starting with bereavement, in units up to 100. To calculate your stress rating, tick any event that has occurred to you in the last two years. Add up your score. Between 150 and 300 units gives you a 50 percent chance of a serious change in your health within the next year. More than 300 units increases the risk to 80 percent.

CONVENTIONAL TREATMENT

A DOCTOR MAY RECOMMEND TIME OFF FROM WORK SO THAT YOU CAN RELAX AND REDUCE YOUR STRESS LEVELS. SHE MAY PRESCRIBE ANTI-ANXIETY DRUGS, ANTIDEPRESSANTS OR SLEEPING TABLETS TO HELP TIDE YOU OVER, BUT IT IS INADVISABLE TO TAKE THESE FOR LONG PERIODS.

THERAPIES

REFLEXOLOGY
• Practitioners believe that the overall treatment promotes relaxation. By additionally working on the appropriate reflex areas, they also claim that they can treat specific physical symptoms that are associated with stress. (See pages 66–71.)

DANCE THERAPY
• Dance movement therapy is particularly effective in lifting the spirits and channelling the nervous energy in a positive direction of enjoyment. Three half-hour sessions a week can substantially reduce stress levels. (See pages 226–31.)

HYPNOTHERAPY
• Hypnotherapists believe that suggesting ways of coping with your problems while you are in a state of trance means that you can trigger these at will

when confronted by them. (See pages 218–23.)

MUSIC THERAPY
• Simply relaxing at home listening to music is often an effective way of unwinding. Attending actual therapy sessions also helps you to relax and relieve your feelings by sharing with others, according to practitioners. (See pages 232–5.)

AUTOGENIC TRAINING
• A therapist will teach you a specific program, which normally draws on elements of relaxation techniques, meditation and self-hypnosis. Some therapists may incorporate yoga into the overall package. The idea is to lessen the body's reaction to stress by reducing the pressure on it. (See pages 210–11.)

LEFT *Because reflexology is a holistic therapy, treating the whole body and encouraging it to heal itself, it is particularly effective at relieving stress, whatever the cause.*

PSYCHOTHERAPY AND COUNSELING
• A cognitive-behavioral therapist aims to help you identify your personal triggers and deal with the stresses they cause by teaching you how to modify aspects of your personality that make you vulnerable to them. (See pages 196–9.)

BIOFEEDBACK
• By teaching you how to monitor your reactions to stress, therapists argue that you can use this knowledge to cope with and eventually control them. (See pages 212–13.)

RELAXATION AND BREATHING
• Learning how to relax your muscles and breathe deeply and calmly will both help you to manage stress more effectively. (See pages 158–65 and pages 166–71.)

OTHER THERAPIES
• Practitioners believe the following may help alleviate the condition: shiatsu/do-in (see pages 32–41); shaolin (see pages 42–3); polarity therapy (see pages 64–5); metamorphic technique (see pages 72–3); reiki (see pages 74–5); Bowen technique (see pages 76–7); therapeutic touch (see pages 90–1); craniosacral therapy (see pages 116–17); kinesiology (see pages 126–33); Feldenkrais method (see pages 142–5); Alexander technique (see pages 146–53); Tragerwork (see pages 154–5); Zero Balancing (see pages 156–7); hydrotherapy (see pages 172–9); flotation therapy (see pages 180–1); visualization (see pages 214–17); art therapy (see pages 238–41); biorhythms (see pages 244–7); and color therapy (see pages 248–51).

Insomnia

Whatever our age, we all need our sleep, because too little means that we think less clearly, and suffer from fatigue and irritability. Insomnia is characterized by the inability to fall asleep, repeatedly waking through the night, or waking too early in the morning and being unable to fall asleep again. It can be caused by worry, emotional stress, exhaustion, anxiety, depression, fever, overindulgence in alcohol or withdrawal, jet-lag, pain and drinking excessive amounts of caffeine. Although the after-effects of insomnia are unpleasant, they are not seriously damaging to health, and you will fall asleep eventually.

To deal with the complaint, relearning good sleeping patterns is of paramount importance. A bedroom is for sleeping – so banish radio, TV, newspapers, books, and anything that is work-related. You need to regard the bedroom as a place of slumber rather than as a place of work. Make sure that the bedroom is sufficiently dark, so that you are not woken in the early morning by sunlight – buy thicker curtains, if necessary. Your bed should be firm enough to support you without dipping and soft enough to be comfortable. Keep a pen and paper by the bed to record worries that crop up as you are falling asleep. Writing them down so they can be tackled in the morning is a useful technique.

Try to go to bed at the same time each night and to get up at the same time each morning. Noticeable time variations may lead to sleep disturbance. If you are not sleepy, get up because otherwise you will come to associate lying in bed with being awake, not falling asleep.

If you are often tired, but are sleeping fairly well, it may help to cut out caffeine, nicotine and alcohol. You may need sleeping tablets to help you over the first two weeks of cutting out alcohol while the body gets used to doing without it, but you should soon notice an improvement. There is no need to worry if you find yourself sleeping less with age – we need less sleep as we become older and it may be better to sleep, say, five

LEFT *You can help relieve your own sleep problems by making sure your bed is comfortable, that you are warm but not too warm and that your bedroom is well ventilated.*

or six hours at night and to take a brief nap in the afternoon after lunch or cat nap during the day.

SYMPTOMS

• over-active mind, preventing sleep • nightmares causing repeated wakening • restlessness in bed • waking up in the morning still feeling tired

CAUTION

SLEEPING PILLS AND TRANQUILIZERS ARE NOT A LONG-TERM SOLUTION TO THE PROBLEM OF INSOMNIA. IN FACT, SOME CAN AUGMENT THE PROBLEM BY DISRUPTING THE NATURAL SLEEP CYCLE. ANYONE REGULARLY RELYING ON DRUGS FOR SLEEP SHOULD CONSULT A DOCTOR.

CONVENTIONAL TREATMENT

A DOCTOR WILL TRY TO IDENTIFY THE UNDERLYING FACTORS CONTRIBUTING TO INSOMNIA, WHICH ARE USUALLY PSYCHOLOGICAL, SUCH AS ANXIETY, BUT SOMETIMES PHYSICAL, SUCH AS NIGHT SWEATS OF TB, THYROTOXICOSIS, ORTHOPNEA OR HEART FAILURE. SLEEPING TABLETS SHOULD NOT BE TAKEN FOR LONGER THAN TWO WEEKS. THE DOCTOR MAY ALSO ARRANGE FOR YOU TO HAVE COUNSELING.

DATAFILE

• More than 100 million Americans of all ages regularly fail to get a good night's sleep.

• Many disorders of sleeping and waking interfere with quality of life and personal health.

• Your proper sleeping position is usually the position you are in when you wake up.

• Insomnia may be fleeting, long-term or chronic, and may be a sign of depression.

• Daytime symptoms of insomnia include sleepiness, anxiety, impaired concentration and memory, and irritability.

• Large numbers of people who take sleeping tablets find within a few weeks that they cannot manage without them.

• Most people sleep for between 6.5 and 8.5 hours a night. About 16 percent sleep for more than 8.5 hours, while 18 percent manage with fewer than 6.5 hours. Someone who sleeps for 8 hours at the age of 30 is likely to only need 7 hours at the age of 60.

THERAPIES

LEFT *Massage by yourself – or with your partner – is a relaxing precursor to sleep.*

MASSAGE
• Massaging the legs, abdomen, the back, and the shoulders is recommended to induce sleep. *(See pages 96–103.)* Aromatherapy massage using lavender oil is also recommended. *(See pages 104–5.)*

HYPNOTHERAPY
• Practitioners may teach methods that are claimed to be very effective for inducing sleep. *(See pages 118–23.)*

RELAXATION AND BREATHING
• Relaxing the muscles and breathing deeply from the diaphragm before going to bed can help alleviate insomnia. *(See pages 158–65 and pages 166–71.)*

OTHER THERAPIES
• Therapies recommended by practitioners include: acupuncture *(see pges 20–28)*, shiatsu/do-in *(see pages 32–41)*; qigong/t'ai chi ch'uan *(see pages 42–51)*; shaolin *(see pages 42–3)*; yoga *(see pages 52–9)*; polarity therapy *(see pages 64–5)*; reflexology *(see pages 66–71)*; autogenic training *(see pages 210–11)*; biofeedback *(see pages 212–13)*.

Eating Disorders

Eating disorders are serious emotional and physical problems that, if untreated, can have life-threatening consequences. The conditions are on the increase, particularly among men and pre-teens. Anorexia nervosa, known as the "slimmer's disease," primarily affects teenagers. It is characterized by self-starvation and progressive weight loss. Bulimia nervosa, by contrast, involves secretive binge eating, followed by deliberate purging through self-induced vomiting, the taking of laxatives and diuretics, or through compulsive exercise. Binge Eating Disorder is binging without the purging, though the sufferer may sporadically fast or diet.

Anorexia and bulimia are believed to share a number of causes. The conditions generally arise as a result of family dynamics and emotional tensions or personality problems, notably feelings of insecurity, low self-esteem and fear of sexuality. Some experts believe that the conditions might be sparked off by biochemical imbalances within the body. Prompt medical treatment is vital, as otherwise chronic illness may set in. Any alternative therapy should be used in conjunction with orthodox treatment: it cannot substitute for it, or replace it.

SYMPTOMS

• *refusal to eat* • *being absent at mealtimes* • *embarking on a slimming diet when there is no obvious need to do so* • *rushing away from the table directly after eating in order to induce vomiting* • *unexplained loss of weight* • *pallor* • *fatigue* • *obsessional exercising*

CAUTION

PEOPLE SUFFERING WITH ANOREXIA AND BULIMIA ARE NOTORIOUSLY RELUCTANT TO SEEK PROFESSIONAL HELP FOR EITHER CONDITION BECAUSE OF THEIR COMMITMENT TO LOSING WEIGHT. IF YOU SUSPECT THAT A FRIEND OR FAMILY MEMBER IS EITHER ANOREXIC OR BULIMIC, DO EVERYTHING THAT YOU CAN TO OBTAIN PROFESSIONAL HELP, VIA THEIR FAMILY DOCTOR, FOR THEM. IN THE MEANTIME, FEED THEM AS NORMAL AND DISCUSS THE PROBLEM OPENLY IF POSSIBLE.

CONVENTIONAL TREATMENT

HOSPITALIZATION WHEN THE SUFFERER IS DANGEROUSLY UNDERWEIGHT; ALSO FOOD SUPPLEMENTS, SUPERVISED MEALTIMES, AND PSYCHIATRIC COUNSELING.

RIGHT *Sufferers from eating disorders frequently have a very distorted vision of themselves, seeing themselves as grossly overweight when they are nothing of the sort. Most sufferers are teenage girls, but the problems are becoming more common in boys too.*

DATAFILE

• 86 percent of people with eating disorders report onset by the age of 20.

• About 10 percent of all people with eating disorders are men.

• Infertility and loss of sexual desire are common consequences of anorexia nervosa.

• The illness can last from anywhere between one and 15 years – and even longer in some cases.

• Around six out of every hundred teenage girls are anorexic.

THERAPIES

ACUPUNCTURE
• Once the sufferer has recognized the existence of an eating disorder, acupuncture and acupressure can both be helpful in stimulating the appetite and boosting the immune system. *(See pages 20–8 and pages 29–31.)*

ALEXANDER TECHNIQUE
• This therapy has tremendous healing powers for those ill at ease with themselves. The technique teaches a calm awareness and acceptance of the body. *(See pages 146–53.)*

PSYCHOTHERAPY AND COUNSELING
• Psychological and psychiatric support are likely to offer sufferers the best prospects of long-term help. Counseling will focus on promoting a positive body image, increased self-esteem and eliminating self-destructive behavioral patterns. Group and family therapy are particulary effective in dealing with eating disorders. *(See pages 192–207.)*

AROMATHERAPY
• Massage with mood-enhancing, relaxing essential oils may relieve symptoms. Recommended oils include bergamot, lavender, neroli and ylang ylang. *(See pages 104–5.)*

DANCE MOVEMENT THERAPY
• The therapy is considered to provide a good outlet for pent-up feelings, encouraging the realization of a sense of purpose and awareness of individual identity. *(See pages 226–31.)*

HYPNOTHERAPY
• A practitioner may try to induce a positive feeling towards eating through the use of post-hypnotic suggestion. *(See pages 218–23.)*

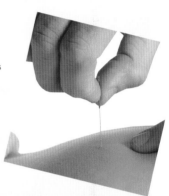

ABOVE *According to acupuncture theory, inserting needles at specific points re-establishes a healthy relationship between the organs of the body, enabling the stomach, liver and spleen, for example, to function better.*

VISUALIZATION
• By cultivating a positive self-image, practitioners believe that the technique will help to boost self-esteem and so combat the lack of confidence that is part of the condition. *(See pages 24–7.)*

OTHER THERAPIES
• Other therapies practitioners believe can help alleviate the condition include: massage *(see pages 96–103)*; kinesiology *(see pages 126–33)*; and art therapy *(see pages 238–41)*.

BRAIN AND NERVES

Shingles

Shingles is an acute, painful inflammation of the spinal nerve ganglia. The characteristic sign, which does not always appear, is a prominent and painfully itchy rash which often forms a girdle around the middle of the body, though it can also appear on the face, neck, arms and legs, depending on the nerves affected. The rash normally goes after two or three weeks, sometimes causing scarring, but the pain shingles causes, known as post-herpetic neuralgia, can persist for much longer.

Shingles is caused by the virus that causes chicken-pox, which can lie dormant in a nerve root for years, reactivating when the immune system is low, or in response to acute stress. Prompt medical treatment is important to shorten the course of the disease and reduce the chances of post-herpetic neuralgia striking.

SYMPTOMS

• *sensitivity and pain* • *fever* • *sickness* • *rash of yellowing blisters* • *scabs* • *pain and tenderness after the rash clears up*

DATAFILE

• Some 850,000 Americans contract shingles each year.

• About 20 percent of people who suffer from chickenpox as children are likely to suffer from shingles later in life.

• Associated pain and tenderness can persist for months and sometimes for years after the actual attack.

• The condition most frequently occurs in people over the age of 50.

• The condition recurs in around five percent of cases.

• The traditional belief that if the shingles rash stretches all the way around the body the victim will die is an old wives' tale.

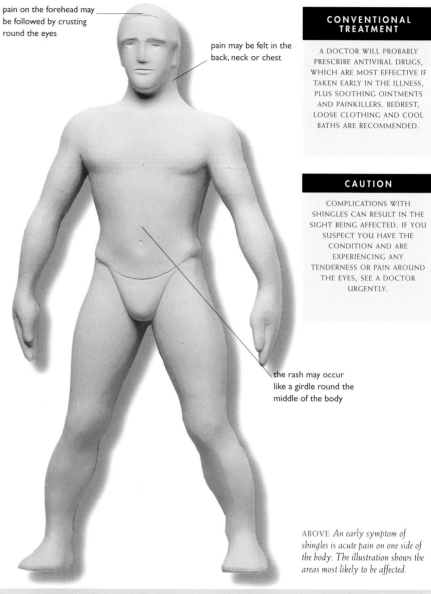

pain on the forehead may be followed by crusting round the eyes

pain may be felt in the back, neck or chest

the rash may occur like a girdle round the middle of the body

ABOVE *An early symptom of shingles is acute pain on one side of the body. The illustration shows the areas most likely to be affected.*

CONVENTIONAL TREATMENT

A DOCTOR WILL PROBABLY PRESCRIBE ANTIVIRAL DRUGS, WHICH ARE MOST EFFECTIVE IF TAKEN EARLY IN THE ILLNESS, PLUS SOOTHING OINTMENTS AND PAINKILLERS. BEDREST, LOOSE CLOTHING AND COOL BATHS ARE RECOMMENDED.

CAUTION

COMPLICATIONS WITH SHINGLES CAN RESULT IN THE SIGHT BEING AFFECTED. IF YOU SUSPECT YOU HAVE THE CONDITION AND ARE EXPERIENCING ANY TENDERNESS OR PAIN AROUND THE EYES, SEE A DOCTOR URGENTLY.

THERAPIES

ACUPUNCTURE
• The neuralgic pain that is part of the condition can be treated once the rash has subsided by stimulation of the acupoints along the Stomach, Large and Small Intestine and Governor meridians. Practitioners may also stimulate the acupoints next to the rash. *(See pages 20–8.)*

AROMATHERAPY
• Massage with any combination of two or more of the following essential oils will prove soothing and beneficial, though you should avoid affected areas: bergamot, chamomile, geranium, eucalyptus, melissa, lavender and tea tree. *(See pages 104–5.)*

REFLEXOLOGY
• Practitioners believe that gentle stimulation of the appropriate reflex points on the feet will help the body to fight the virus and have a revitalizing effect. *(See pages 66–71.)*

VISUALIZATION
• To help recovery, a practitioner may suggest imagining that the skin is completely healed and glowing with health. *(See pages 214–17.)*

HYDROTHERAPY
• Ice packs and cold compresses can relieve the pain and itching caused by a shingles rash. *(See pages 172–7.)*

LEFT *An aromatherapy massage or compress soaked in appropriate essential oils can help relieve the pain of shingles.*

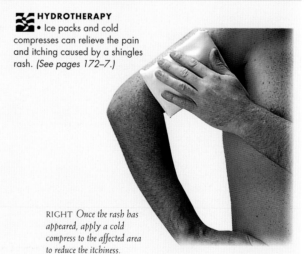

RIGHT *Once the rash has appeared, apply a cold compress to the affected area to reduce the itchiness.*

Neuralgia

Neuralgia is a general term for pain originating in a nerve, though the condition is subdefined according to which nerve is affected. Inflammation of the trigeminal nerve – indicated by intense, spasmodic pain in one side of the jaw or the cheek – is termed trigeminal neuralgia. Other common forms are postherpetic neuralgia, which can occur after shingles, and glossopharyngeal neuralgia. Other viral infections can also cause the condition. The level of pain involved can vary in intensity from a shortlived mild tingling to recurrent or constant agony. Cold and damp conditions often exacerbate the pain, as does stress and anxiety.

Conventional treatment usually involves finding the cause of neuralgia and the prescription of painkillers and appropriate medications. Some doctors favor the administration of mild electrical impulses to anesthetize the affected nerve, a procedure known as TENS therapy, generally done at home. Another method is the injection of a so-called "nerve block" into the nerve to destroy its hypersensitive fibers. You should cut out coffee and smoking because caffeine and nicotine can make some types of neuralgia worse.

SYMPTOMS

• *mild to severe pain* • *site of pain varies depending on nerve affected* • *pain can be intermittent, recurrent or constant*

CONVENTIONAL TREATMENT

STRONG PAINKILLERS WILL BE PRESCRIBED TO ALLEVIATE SYMPTOMS, WHILE IN SEVERE CASES, THE NERVE MAY BE KILLED BY INJECTION, OR SURGICALLY REMOVED.

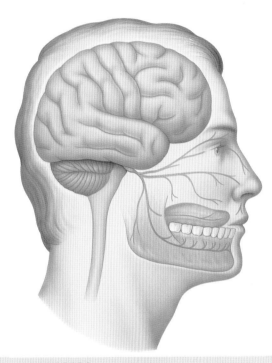

LEFT *The trigeminal nerve carries messages from the brain throughout the face and jaw area. Damage to or malfunction of the nerve causes the severe pain known as trigeminal neuralgia.*

THERAPIES

FLOTATION THERAPY
• While in flotation therapy, the mind and brain are completely at rest without actually being asleep: this, claim practitioners, provides the optimum conditions for the body's own healing properties to take over and counteract pain. *(See pages 180–8.)*

COLOR THERAPY
• A color therapist deduces from your aura how the pain has originated and, in this way, how best to treat it. *(See pages 248–51.)*

HYDROTHERAPY
• Practitioners advocate the application of hot and cold packs to the affected area to ease the pain of the condition. *(See pages 172–9.)*

AROMATHERAPY
• Massaging essential oil of eucalyptus, lavender or chamomile into the affected area will help to relieve pain, as will massage with a blend of mustard and pepper oils in a grapeseed carrier oil. *(See pages 104–5.)*

ACUPUNCTURE
• To help with trigeminal neuralgia, a practitioner may suggest stimulating acupoints on the governor, gall bladder, bladder, Large Intestine and Liver meridians. Further stimulation of the corresponding points on the opposite side of the body to the site of the pain may also be advised. *(See pages 20–8.)*

ACUPRESSURE
• For trigeminal neuralgia, a practitioner will demonstrate how to apply a gentle inward pressure at the inner end of the eyebrow on the affected side of the face. The alternative is to press downward lightly with both index fingers at the points near the corners of the mouth. *(See pages 29–31.)*

YOGA
• Deep, relaxed breathing and the easier, beginners' poses will prove helpful in coping with pain. *(See pages 52–9.)*

REFLEXOLOGY
• A reflexologist will concentrate on energizing all the systems of the body so that the body's natural pain killing properties soothe the neuralgia. Reflexology is also said to be effective in boosting the immune system, which should contribute to banishing the cause of the neuralgia. *(See pages 66–71.)*

MASSAGE
• Light massage of the affected area will help to reduce the neuralgic pain and stimulate the entire body to resolve its cause. Gentle, sweeping strokes are recommended. *(See pages 96–103.)*

ABOVE *If you smoke and suffer from neuralgia, it will almost certainly be of benefit to give up cigarettes.*

RIGHT *Gentle pressure on a point near the corner of the mouth will relieve the pain of trigeminal neuralgia.*

Headache

Headaches are among the commonest of all medical conditions. For the most part, they are due to muscular tension in the head, neck or shoulders, accompanied by a dilation and contraction of blood vessels in the head. The pain can occur in any part of the head, usually worsening toward the end of the day, and their severity can vary widely from a dull ache to an intense, stabbing pain.

Specific types of headache vary depending on their cause. The great majority are the result of tension, anxiety, stress, and fatigue, though they can also be a symptom of astigmatism, sinusitis, dental problems, tooth grinding, digestive upsets, raised temperature, raised blood pressure, sunstroke, food allergies, alcohol abuse, drinking too much coffee, hormonal swings, and, on rare occasions, a number of brain conditions, including meningitis, a subarachnoid hemorrhage, or a brain tumor. Headache is also a common consequence of a head injury.

Tension headaches affect around 75 percent of all headache sufferers. Typically, they involve a steady ache, rather than a throbbing, and affect both sides of the head simultaneously. Research shows that men and women are afflicted with them equally. To relieve the pain, you can try applying heat to the area of the head or neck where it is at its most severe, or an ice bag wrapped in a towel. A gentle fingertip massage over the area just in front of and above the ears, or pressing the area at the top of the nose between the eyebrows may help, as can lying down and relaxing. Regular exercise and practicing relaxation techniques will not only help to reduce the stress that may be triggering the headaches, but also will decrease the severity of the pain. Your doctor may prescribe painkilling analgesics to the same end.

DATAFILE

• An estimated 45 million Americans suffer from chronic headaches that are severe and sometimes disabling.

• Headache sufferers in the U.S. make more than eight million visits a year to doctors' offices.

• Nearly 90 percent of men and 95 percent of women have had at least one headache attack.

• Most headaches are tension headaches.

• Cluster headaches are so-called because they can recur on a daily basis, the attacks lasting in total for up to several months. Cluster headaches are six to nine times more likely to strike at men rather than women, heavy drinkers and smokers being the most susceptible. They are usually accompanied by allergy symptoms such as nasal congestion or a runny nose.

SYMPTOMS

• pain and throbbing in the head • sensation that a tight band is pressing around the head • a feeling of pressure at the top of the head • bursting or throbbing sensations • eye and neck pain • dizziness

LEFT *There are innumerable causes and degrees of headache, and the effects can range from mild discomfort to debilitating pain.*

THERAPIES

ACUPUNCTURE
• Headaches are believed to be the result of an energy blockage in the head. Depending on the cause of the headache, practitioners will stimulate the relevant acupoints. (See pages 20–8.).

ACUPRESSURE
• A therapist will identify which acupoints work the best for you. Apply a light, firm fingertip pressure, release and apply again. Many people get relief by pressing both sides of the face, a little outward from the eye socket at the point where the eyebrow tapers off. (See pages 29–31.)

YOGA
• Because headache is often associated with muscular tension and stress, yoga is ideal for its relief and prevention. Poses such as Shoulderstand may help. (See pages 52–9.)

MASSAGE
• Massaging the back of the neck, the upper part of the shoulders, and the tight band of muscle on either side of the spine just below the neck can help, as can a friction rub behind the ears. (See pages 96–103.)

ABOVE *Applying pressure to the little dents in the temples is an easy self-help remedy for headache, based on thousands of years of Eastern tradition.*

OSTEOPATHY
• An osteopath may advise manipulation to free contracted muscles at the base of the skull, thought to be the cause of the majority of headaches, and to improve the mobility of the neck joints. (See pages 106–13 and Chiropractic, pages 118–25.)

BIOFEEDBACK
• You will be taught techniques that are thought to relieve muscle tension and also deal with the dilation of the blood vessels in the head that is one of the characteristics of a headache. (See pages 212–13.)

SHIATSU
• Treatment involves gentle stretching and massaging of the shoulders and gentle massage of the neck. (See pages 32–7 and Do-in, pages 38–41.)

CAUTION

MOST HEADACHES HAVE A BENIGN CAUSE AND ARE SELF-LIMITING, BUT SOME MAY INDICATE SEVERE ILLNESS. CONSULT YOUR DOCTOR IF THE HEADACHE COMES ON SUDDENLY AND IS VERY SEVERE, OR IS ASSOCIATED WITH A FEVER, RASH, STIFF NECK, OR INTOLERANCE OF BRIGHT LIGHTS, OR IF THERE ARE ASSOCIATED PROBLEMS SUCH AS: WEAKNESS OR NUMBNESS IN THE FACE, ARMS, OR LEGS, INCOORDINATION, DROWSINESS, OR CHANGE IN PERSONALITY.

CONVENTIONAL TREATMENT

IF HEADACHES ARE FREQUENT AND SEVERE, YOUR DOCTOR MAY PRESCRIBE ANALGESICS TO REDUCE THE PAIN.

Migraine

Migraine is characterized by an intense throbbing, pulsating or pounding pain in the forehead, temple, ear, jaw or around the eye, usually on one side of the head only. There are two types of migraine: common and the rarer classical. An attack can last for a few hours, or up to several days.

Migraine can be triggered by a variety of factors, including stress, hormonal changes of the menstrual cycle, late nights, bright lights, loud music, oral contraceptives, nicotine, sudden changes in the weather or temperature, and certain foods, such as chocolate, cheese, oranges and wheat, and additives. Four times as many women as men suffer from the condition, while statistics show that it tends to run in families. Its exact cause is not fully understood, but changes in the bloodflow in the brain are thought to be a key element: sufferers seem to have blood vessels in the head and neck that over-react to various pain triggers, with a migraine attack as the ultimate result. Early warning signs of an attack are thought to be due to a narrowing of these vessels, while the full-blown pain of migraine proper is believed to be the result of their subsequent dilation, or expansion.

There is no cure for migraine, although many attacks can be controlled by avoiding triggering factors and the use of drugs. The most successful treatments are those that prevent an attack, or stop it in its earliest stages.

CAUTION

IF YOU SUDDENLY HAVE A MIGRAINE ATTACK IN ADULT LIFE, NEVER HAVING HAD ONE BEFORE, YOU SHOULD CONSULT YOUR FAMILY DOCTOR WITHOUT DELAY, AS THIS MAY BE THE SYMPTOM OF A MORE SERIOUS UNDERLYING DISORDER.

CONVENTIONAL TREATMENT

IF THE ATTACKS ARE FREQUENT AND SEVERE, MEDICATION MAY BE PRESCRIBED. THIS INTERFERES WITH THE WIDENING OF THE BLOOD VESSELS IN THE HEAD, SO DECREASING THE PAIN OF AN ATTACK. TO ENABLE THE BODY TO MAKE THE BEST USE OF THE MEDICATION, IT IS IMPORTANT TO TAKE IT AT THE FIRST SIGN OF AN ATTACK.

BELOW *A number of foods are notorious "triggers" of migraine and sufferers soon learn to avoid them. The foods illustrated here are all rich in tyramine, an amino acid which narrows and then dilates blood vessels and therefore affects blood supply to the brain.*

red wine
oranges
cheese
chocolate

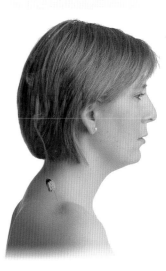

ABOVE *Because we don't fully understand what causes migraine, it can be controlled but not cured.*

SYMPTOMS

• *common migraine: slowly developing severe headache, lasting for a few hours to two days and made worse by the smallest movement or noise; nausea and vomiting*
• *classical migraine: headache preceded by an aura which includes visual disturbances (such as temporary loss of vision, double vision, flashing lights), weakness in a limb, strange taste or smell, tingling, vertigo; headache accompanied by nausea, vomiting, and aversion to light and noise*

THERAPIES

REFLEXOLOGY
• Practitioners apply pressure to the tips of the big toes, the areas that correspond to the head. They may also stimulate the points on the side of the feet that are believed to be linked with the neck and the spine. *(See pages 66–71.)*

AROMATHERAPY
• Massaging a few drops of neat lavender oil into the temples and around the back of the neck is an effective headache treatment, according to practitioners. *(See pages 104–5).*

HYDROTHERAPY
• Hot baths, saunas, steam baths, or alternate hot and cold showers may all be suggested to release tension and promote relaxation. Ice packs on the head or neck can also be effective in relieving pain. *(See pages 172–9.)*

RELAXATION AND BREATHING
• Both techniques are good for easing tension in the muscles. *(See pages 158–65 and pages 166–71.)*

OTHER THERAPIES
• Practitioners believe the following may help: meditation *(see pages 60–3)*; polarity therapy *(see pages 64–5)*; metamorphic technique *(see pages 72–3)*; reiki *(see pages 74–5)*; therapeutic touch *(see pages 90–1)*; cranial osteopathy *(see pages 114–15)*; Rolfing *(see pages 134–7)*; Hellerwork *(see pages 138–41)*; Feldenkrais method *(see pages 142–5)*; Alexander technique *(see pages 146–53)*; Tragerwork *(see pages 154–5)*; and Zero Balancing *(see pages 156–7).*

THERAPIES

ACUPUNCTURE
• Stimulation of the acupoints on the meridians for stomach and large and small intestines are said to be effective, as is moxibustion. *(See pages 20–28.)*

ACUPRESSURE
• The three most effective pressure points for the treatment of migraine are on the hand, at the end of the crease between finger and thumb; at the top of the neck beneath the skull; and close to the spine: on the feet, the web between the big and second toe. *(See pages 29–31.)*

BIOFEEDBACK
• Practitioners believe that the techniques they teach will help to reduce attacks and their severity. *(See pages 212–3.)*

OTHER THERAPIES
• Practitioners believe the following therapies may help: autogenic training *(see pages 210–11)*; hypnotherapy *(see pages 218–23*; color therapy *(see pages 248–51).*

THERAPIES RECOMMENDED FOR HEADACHE RELIEVE MIGRAINE AS WELL

Fainting

Medically termed a syncope, fainting is a sudden loss of consciousness. It can be caused by fear, an emotional shock, or stress. It tends to happen in warm conditions, because this causes a temporary shortage of blood supply to the brain. The attack may be heralded by dizziness, feeling faint, and looking pale. Someone who has fainted should lie flat and recover – it is dangerous to hold them up as this delays the restoration of circulation to the brain. Complete recovery usually occurs after a few minutes. Fainting is commonest in otherwise healthy young women.

SYMPTOMS

- *sweating* • *nausea* • *shallow, rapid breathing*
- *weak pulse* • *impaired vision* • *ringing in the ears* • *weakness and confusion* • *pallor*

lying with your feet above your head helps restore an adequate blood supply to the brain

BELOW *The effect of gravity is instrumental in "bringing someone round" after a fainting fit.*

CONVENTIONAL TREATMENT

SOMEONE WHO HAS FAINTED SHOULD BE ALLOWED TO LIE FLAT AND RECOVER.

DATAFILE

- Fainting often occurs as a result of a vasovagal attack, in which overstimulation of the vagus nerve causes slowing of the heartbeat and a fall in blood pressure – which reduces the flow of blood to the brain. These attacks are commonly caused by pain, stress, shock, fear, or being in a room with too little oxygen.

- Other causes include prolonged standing, low blood pressure, heart problems, injury, profuse bleeding, and antihypertensive drugs.

THERAPIES

ACUPRESSURE
- Strong stimulation of the acupoint two-thirds of the way up between the top lip and nose will aid recovery. (*See pages 29–31.*)

SHIATSU
- It may be that your circulation is not as efficient as it could be and in this case regular shiatsu massage will prove valuable in preventing further fainting attacks. (*See pages 32–7 and Do-in, pages 38–41.*)

YOGA
- Tension and stress respond well to both the spiritual elements and the physical poses of yoga: practice regularly in order to ward off further fainting attacks. (*See pages 52–9.*)

MASSAGE
- Muscular tension, stress of all types and poor circulation all respond well to all body massage. A combination of strokes should be used. (*See pages 96–103.*)

AROMATHERAPY
- A few drops of rosemary oil, massaged into the temples, may prevent loss of consciousness. (*See pages 104–5.*)

OSTEOPATHY
- Tension around the neck joints may affect the nerves and blood vessels to the head. Osteopathy – or chiropractic – may well succeed in preventing further fainting attacks by resolving the underlying problem. (*See pages 106–13 and pages 118–25.*)

BREATHING TECHNIQUES
- Fainting can be caused by breathing too shallowly and too quickly, as many of us do when we are stressed. A therapist will show you how to concentrate on deep, even, regular breathing. (*See pages 166–71.*)

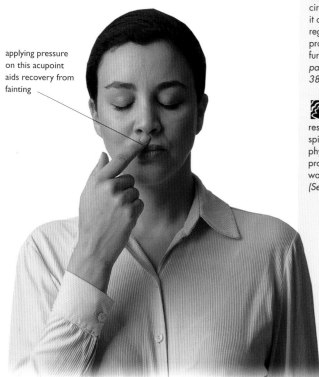

applying pressure on this acupoint aids recovery from fainting

LEFT *The stimulation of this acupressure point can aid recovery after fainting.*

Dizziness

Dizziness is a non-specific term, which may be used by patients to describe a number of sensations: anxiety, near-fainting, nausea, or vertigo. Vertigo is a sensation that either the sufferer or the room is moving and generally signifies a problem with the inner ear or the part of the brain to which the inner ear is connected.

Determination of the cause depends on obtaining an account of the circumstances during which the attack took place, and associated symptoms, such as fever, respiratory tract infection, vomiting, headache, deafness, ringing in the ears, blurred vision, or weakness or numbness anywhere in the body. Common causes of dizziness include: inner ear infections (viral labyrinthitis, *see page 283*), benign postural vertigo, near-syncope (a near faint), anxiety (*see pages 256–7*), and Ménière's disease, as well as drugs and alcohol.

If experiencing dizziness, sit or lie down until the attack passes. Do not attempt to drive or carry on with your job. You should consult a doctor if the dizziness is prolonged, if it recurs, or if it interferes with any activity, particularly if this involves heights or operating heavy machinery.

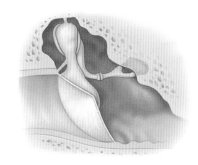

LEFT *The complex and delicate mechanism of the inner ear is fundamental to our sense of balance. An infection in the ear is one of the common causes of dizziness.*

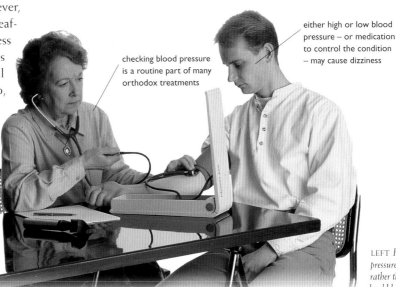

checking blood pressure is a routine part of many orthodox treatments

either high or low blood pressure – or medication to control the condition – may cause dizziness

LEFT *High or low blood pressure is really a symptom rather than a condition, and should be investigated.*

CAUTION

IF ATTACKS OF DIZZINESS ARE PROLONGED OR DISABLING, BECOME FREQUENT OR ARE ACCOMPANIED BY RECURRING HEADACHES WITH NAUSEA AND VOMITING, YOU SHOULD CONSULT A DOCTOR AS SOON AS POSSIBLE.

CONVENTIONAL TREATMENT

DIZZINESS CAUSED BY A NEAR FAINT SHOULD BE TREATED BY THE PERSON LYING FLAT OR PUTTING THEIR HEAD BETWEEN THEIR KNEES. FURTHER TREATMENT WILL DEPEND ON THE UNDERLYING CAUSE. CONSULT YOUR DOCTOR.

THERAPIES

ACUPUNCTURE
• An acupuncturist will question you about your lifestyle and other health conditions in order to establish the cause of your dizzy spells and treat accordingly. (See pages 20–8.)

ACUPRESSURE
• A therapist will show you how to stimulate two main pressure points, one on the foot and the other in the neck, just below and behind the bottom of the ear lobe. (See pages 29–31.)

SHIATSU
• You are less likely to suffer from dizziness if the circulation of blood around your body is working efficiently. Shiatsu massage concentrates on supporting the circulation and enhancing the immune system. (See pages 32–7 and Do-in, pages 38–41.)

YOGA
• Yoga is a gentle therapy that will help you to establish better control of your body. It will also tone up your circulation, thus helping to prevent further attacks of dizziness. (See pages 52–9.)

REFLEXOLOGY
• Both relaxing and invigorating, reflexology can do much to eliminate dizzy spells. A practitioner will first try to establish the cause of your dizzy spells and advise on diet and lifestyle. (See pages 66–71.)

MASSAGE
• Thorough whole-body massage is ideal for toning up the body and preventing further attacks of dizziness. (See pages 96–103.)

OSTEOPATHY
• In cases in which dizziness has been caused by a misalignment of the upper neck joints, osteopathy or chiropractic can prove enormously helpful in both alleviating the problem and preventing another attack of dizziness. It involves manipulation of the upper neck and further down the spine. (See pages 106–13 and pages 118–25.)

CRANIAL OSTEOPATHY
• A practitioner will manipulate parts of the skull to correct what are termed cranial rhythmic impulses. Because the therapy is extremely gentle, it is particularly suited to the very young and the elderly. (See pages 114–15.)

BREATHING TECHNIQUES
• A therapist will teach you how to breathe deeply and slowly from the diaphragm in order to prevent becoming dizzy. Take it slowly at first, or the unaccustomed deep breathing may actually cause you to feel dizzy. (See pages 166–71.)

LEFT *According to chiropractic theory, displacement of any part of the skeletal frame may press against nerves, affecting their function and causing "an aberration known as disease". This may take the form of dizziness, which can then be remedied by chiropractic treatment.*

SKIN AND HAIR

Psoriasis

A noncontagious skin disorder that occurs in many different variations and degrees of severity. The most common form is plaque psoriasis, which consists of swollen skin lesions covered with silvery-white scales. Other types display characteristics such as pus-like blisters, severe sloughing of the skin, drop-like dots, and smooth inflamed lesions. The cause of the condition is unknown, although it is generally thought that there is a genetic component as psoriasis tends to run in families. Once the disease is triggered – trigger factors include infections, skin injury, vaccinations and certain medications – the body's immune system is thought to activate the excessive skin-cell reproduction characteristic of the disease. Common sites include the elbows, knees, shins, scalp and just below the breasts.

There is no known cure for psoriasis. It is what doctors call a chronic condition – this means that it recurs – though individual outbreaks can be treated successfully. However, psychological complications can result: embarrassment, frustration, fear, depression, and loss of self-esteem are all common factors. For this reason, stress management is usually advised, along with adopting a healthy diet and cutting back on the amount of alcohol you drink.

For the psoriasis itself, the treatment will vary, depending on the nature of the psoriasis, its extent or severity, the sufferer's past medical history, lifestyle, age, sex, and the site of the condition. For mild to moderate psoriasis, suitable medications include traditional coal tar, while moisturizers will help to keep the skin supple. Ultraviolet light therapy may also be advised. If the condition does not improve, more powerful medications, such as steroid creams, may be tried.

ABOVE *The main symptom of psoriasis is an inflamed, scaly look to the skin caused by overproduction of new skin cells.*

CONVENTIONAL TREATMENT

A DOCTOR MAY PRESCRIBE COAL TAR OR DITHRANOL OINTMENT IN THE FIRST INSTANCE. IF THE ATTACK IS SEVERE, TOPICAL STEROIDS MAY BE ADVISED. ULTRAVIOLET LIGHT THERAPY CAN BE BENEFICIAL.

CAUTION

IF YOUR DOCTOR ADVISES YOU TO USE STEROID CREAMS TO TREAT PSORIASIS, THIS MEANS CONTINUED MEDICAL SUPERVISION AS THE DRUGS INVOLVED ARE POWERFUL AND EXCESSIVE DOSES MAY LEAD TO SIDE-EFFECTS.

SYMPTOMS

- *pain with cracks appearing in the dry areas of the hands and the feet* • *pustules on the palms of the hands or the soles of the feet* • *glazed, scaly plaques in moist areas of the body* • *distortion and pitting of the nails in some cases*

DATAFILE

- Psoriasis affects one percent of the American population.

- The condition is slightly more prevalent among women than it is among men. The average age of onset is 28 years of age, though psoriasis can appear at birth and as late in life as 90.

- Between ten to 15 percent of psoriaisis sufferers are aged under ten.

- In the U.S., between 150,000 and 260,000 new cases of psoriasis occur each year.

- More than 1,500,000 people are treated by U.S. doctors for psoriasis annually.

LEFT *Because psoriasis is frequently triggered by stress or, as some hypnotherapists believe, is the result of repressed emotions, relaxing techniques such as self-hypnosis can be very effective in the treatment of the condition.*

THERAPIES

HYDROTHERAPY
• A practitioner may recommend hot baths with Epsom salts to stimulate the circulation and eliminate the build-up of waste products that many complementary therapists believe contribute to the onset of the disease. *(See pages 172–9.)*

LIGHT THERAPY
• Both conventional and complementary therapists agree that treatment with ultraviolet light is beneficial. The risks of skin cancer and skin aging are minimal in the short term: indeed, research suggests that ultraviolet treatment may be safer than the sunbathing. *(See pages 242–3.)*

ACUPUNCTURE/ ACUPRESSURE
• Therapists believe that, by stimulating the appropriate acupoints on the relevant meridians, the symptoms of psoriasis can be relieved. *(See pages 20–28 and pages 29–31.)*

HYPNOTHERAPY
• Self-hypnosis can be taught as a valuable relaxation technique. *(See pages 218–23.)*

PSYCHOTHERAPY AND COUNSELING
• Worry, anxiety, and other psychological problems are among the factors that can trigger a psoriasis attack. Therapists attempt to set such fears at rest by showing you how to come to terms mentally with the condition. *(See pages 188–91.)*

VISUALIZATION
• According to its practitioners, creating a mental picture of the illness and envisaging the treatment you are receiving actually at work can help to strengthen the body's self-healing powers. It is also an effective way of combating worry and anxiety. *(See pages 214–7.)*

REFLEXOLOGY
• Practitioners consider manipulation of the relevant reflex areas on the feet to be beneficial for inflammatory skin conditions. *(See pages 66–71.)*

Eczema and Dermatitis

Eczema is an inflammation of the skin that occurs in conjunction with a persistent itchiness and, often, with weeping blisters that subsequently form dry scabs and crusts. The two commonest forms are contact eczema, also known as dermatitis, which develops within minutes and is caused by allergic reaction, and atopic eczema, which is thought to run in families, especially if there is a family history of asthma or hay fever.

Eczema tends to be a disease of childhood and commonly improves or remits completely in adolescence and early adult life. Conventional treatment of eczema centers on generous use of moisturizing emollients and bath oils together with avoidance of precipitating factors such as soaps and detergents and allergens. Corticosteroid creams and ointments may be prescribed for moderate to severe disease to break the cycle of itching, scratching and skin thickening. Antibiotics may be required for secondary skin infections. Severe cases of eczema may be referred to a dermatologist, who will review the treatments and may conduct tests for specific allergens in order that they can be avoided in future. If stress is a factor in the onset or exacerbation of eczema, then measures to reduce stress may help.

The microscopic appearance of skin affected by dermatitis is in actual fact indistinguishable from that of eczema, but the term tends to be reserved for allergic skin rashes with an external cause. Almost any substance can cause dermatitis in a sensitized individual, but some of the commonest are nickel in watches and jewelry, cosmetics and antiperspirants, household cleaning products and detergents, pets, and garden plants.

SYMPTOMS

• *in contact eczema, a pink or red rash, which may or may not itch* • *atopic eczema causes the skin to itch, scale, swell, and sometimes blister*

the skin may be red and inflamed

some forms of eczema are extremely itchy

BELOW *Contact eczema or contact dermatitis may be caused by an allergic reaction to common household products such as detergent.*

ABOVE *The condition can be relieved by the application of moisturizing creams, by putting sodium bicarbonate in a hot bath to lessen itching, and by taking vitamin and mineral supplements.*

DATAFILE

• Eczema usually runs in families and is often associated with allergies, asthma, and stress.

• Wearing rubber gloves, unwashed new clothes, or plated jewelry can cause contact eczema, along with common chemical irritants such as detergents, soaps, some synthetic fibers, antiperspirants, and nail polish remover.

• If you have atopic eczema, the chances of being allergic to nickel in jewelry, or of suffering from dry skin in the winter, are higher than average.

• Eczema can occur in single episodes, or become chronic.

• The best way to prevent a rash caused by contact with toxic plants like poison ivy is to wash the exposed skin with soap and water as soon as possible after contact.

• Eczema in infants is often caused by an allergy to certain proteins in wheat, milk, and eggs.

• A person may contract eczema at any age and at any place on the skin, though it is found mainly on the scalp, hands, feet, and legs.

THERAPIES

ABOVE *A reflexologist might seek to alleviate eczema by treatment designed to strengthen a patient's constitution and improve his general health.*

ACUPUNCTURE
• Practitioners believe that eczema is associated with exposure to heat, damp, and wind. Treatment is based on counteracting the effects of these elements and on correcting any blood and energy deficiencies that may have resulted. This involves stimulating the acupoints on the relevant meridians. *(See pages 20–8.)*

REFLEXOLOGY
• Massaging the reflex areas relating to the affected areas, plus the ones related to the solar plexus, adrenal and pituitary glands, liver, digestive system, kidneys, and the glands involved in reproduction, is advocated. *(See pages 66–71.)*

AROMATHERAPY
• A massage using extremely diluted lavender, bergamot and geranium essences may help to reduce inflammation and relieve itching. Such treatment must be carried out by a professional therapist because if the dilution is insufficient the oils may make the inflammation worse, rather than better. *(See pages 104–5.)*

PSYCHOTHERAPY AND COUNSELING
• Therapists aim at helping to reduce the physiological changes that are stress-related. They believe that it is these changes that trigger the itchiness characteristic of the condition. *(See pages 188–91.)*

HYPNOTHERAPY
• Practitioners claim that the therapy can help to control itching, particularly in cases of atopic eczema affecting children. *(See pages 218–23.)*

AUTOGENIC TRAINING
• The relaxation exercises you learn as part of autogenic training help the body to relax at will and mobilize its own healing powers. The therapy is claimed to be particularly effecive in cases of eczema. *(See pages 210–11.)*

OTHER THERAPIES
• Other therapies practitioners believe may help alleviate the condition include: relaxation techniques *(see pages 158–65)*; breathing techniques *(see pages 166–71)*; and visualization *(see pages 214–17)*.

Dandruff

Dandruff is an extremely common complaint that occurs when the fine cells of the outer layer of skin on the scalp are shed at a faster rate than normal, causing the flakes of dead skin that characterize the condition to appear. The flakes are usually most obvious after brushing or combing the hair, which loosens them. The condition is seasonal, being at its most severe during winter and at its mildest during summer. It tends to occur more frequently in people with oily skin and hair.

When dandruff is severe, it can be accompanied by red, greasy scaling around the nose, the folds of the cheeks, the eyebrows and around the ears. This condition is called seborrheic dermatitis – "cradle cap" in babies, when it normally clears up on its own after the first three months of life. In adults, the condition usually starts between the ages of 30 and 60. It is found more frequently in men than women and can become a chronic complaint. Seasonal changes, notably the cold, dry air of fall and winter, emotional stress and certain diseases may often trigger a flare-up.

Conventionally, the cornerstone of dandruff treatment is the frequent use of antidandruff shampoos. Many are available without a prescription and are at their most effective when left on the scalp for ten to 15 minutes or so. A water-based conditioner can help to prevent the hair from drying out. If the dandruff persists, a doctor should be consulted. An antifungal shampoo may be prescribed, while topical steriod solutions can also be used in difficult cases.

SYMPTOMS

• *small, round, white-to-gray patches on the top of the head, though this can occur anywhere on the scalp* • *itching is occasionally present*

leave the shampoo for a few minutes before rinsing throughly

massage the scalp with your fingertips

RIGHT *Washing the hair frequently with specially formulated shampoos is the best way of combating dandruff.*

THERAPIES

MASSAGE
• Gentle massage to improve the blood flow and stimulate the circulation in the scalp may help to control the condition. However, do not massge the skin if there are any breaks in it after scratching. A mixture of witch hazel and eau-de-Cologne, rubbed vigorously into the scalp twice a day, is also a good tonic. *(See pages 96–103.)*

AROMATHERAPY
• Rosemary, cedarwood, tea tree or patchouli can be massaged into the scalp. So, too, can lavender oil diluted in a little almond or coconut oil. Do not massage oils into broken skin. For best results, the oil should be left on overnight and the hair washed in the morning. *(See pages 104–5.)*

RIGHT *Dandruff responds well to treatment with rosemary. Use it both in the shampoo and in the water for your final rinse.*

CONVENTIONAL TREATMENT

A DOCTOR WILL CHECK THAT THE SCALES CHARACTERISTIC OF THE CONDITION ARE NOT CAUSED BY INFECTION. AN ANTIFUNGAL SHAMPOO OR TOPICAL STEROID SOLUTION MAY BE SUGGESTED TO CONTROL THE CONDITION.

CAUTION

CONSULT A DOCTOR IF THE SCALING OF THE SCALP IS ACCOMPANIED BY REDNESS, OR IF THE SCALING OCCURS ON PARTS OF THE BODY OTHER THAN THE SCALP. THIS MAY BE A SIGN OF ANOTHER UNDERLYING CONDITION.

DATAFILE

• Dandruff is a natural process. It cannot be eliminated, only controlled.

• Some natural therapists believe the condition may be related to a poor diet.

• Excessive use of hairsprays, gels, hair colorants, and electric hair curlers can make the flaking worse. So, too, can cold weather, dry indoor heating, tightly-fitting hats and headscarves, infrequent shampooing, or inadequate rinsing.

• Up to 50 percent of the population is affected by dandruff, the problem tending to occur more often in people with oily skin and hair.

Cold Sores

Cold sores, also known as fever blisters, are liquid-filled blisters that erupt around the lips, sometimes spreading to the nose or chin. The condition, which is highly contagious, is caused by the herpes simplex virus, type 1 (HSV-1), and is extremely widespread. U.S. studies show that between 30 percent and 60 percent of children have been exposed to it. The virus is related to, but not the same as, the HSV-2 virus, which causes genital herpes. Both types can be spread by skin-to-skin contact. (This is the most common picture, although HSV-1 can occur in the genital area, and HSV-2 in the oral area.)

Once present, the HSV-1 virus remains in the body for life, but what causes those initially infected to suffer from recurrent cold sores is unknown, though there are certain triggers, including emotional stress, excessive exposure to sunlight, tiredness, chapped lips, colds and flu, trauma, menstruation, and cold weather. A typical outbreak lasts six to ten days and passes through six distinct stages, the most painful one being when the full-blown sore has formed, but prior to a scab forming over it. About a day before the blisters appear, you may feel numbness, tingling, itching, or burning on the lips or the skin around them.

ABOVE *Cold sores may be triggered by colds and flu, but may also be a symptom of being generally "run down".*

Though there are treatments for cold sores, there is no cure for them, as no medication can prevent infection from the HSV-1 virus. If you suffer from frequent outbreaks of cold sores, your doctor may prescribe an antiviral drug or ointment, such as acyclovir. By starting to take the drug or applying the ointment as soon as you feel the itching or tingling starting, but before the cold sore erupts, you can lessen the severity of the outbreak. Taking painkillers may make the blisters feel less painful, while putting ice on them can also help to lessen the pain. Keep the sores clean and dry. Apply vaseline to prevent them from cracking and becoming infected. To stop the virus from spreading, avoid all forms of skin contact with others, including kissing, and try not to actually touch the sores: touching them, in any event, only intensifies the feelings of itching and burning. Do not try to cover up an unsightly sore with make-up, because, if you do, you again run the risk of secondary infection.

SYMPTOMS

- *pain and soreness from the characteristic crusting blister*
- *cracking and weeping may occur, particularly if the sores are in the corners of the mouth.*

CONVENTIONAL TREATMENT

A DOCTOR WILL CHECK TO SEE IF AN UNDERLYING MEDICAL DISORDER IS RESPONSIBLE FOR THE SORES. AN ANTIVIRAL MEDICATION, WHICH CAN BE APPLIED AT THE FIRST SIGN OF A BLISTER, MAY ALSO BE PRESCRIBED.

THERAPIES

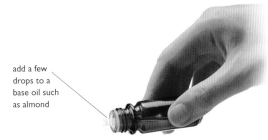

add a few drops to a base oil such as almond

ABOVE *Tea tree oil has a long history of successful use as an antiseptic and antibacterial agent.*

AROMATHERAPY
- Practitioners may suggest gently massaging the affected area with well-diluted oils of geranium or lavender to soothe the pain and antiseptic oils, such as tea tree or eucalyptus. *(See pages 104–5.)*

ACUPUNCTURE
- Stimulating the acupoints that correspond to where the outbreak is located can provide effective pain relief, according to therapists. *(See pages 20–28.)*

HYDROTHERAPY
- Ice packs and cold compresses can help to relieve pain and itching. *(See pages 172–9.)*

RELAXATION AND BREATHING
- Because high levels of stress have been identified as a trigger for the HSV-1 virus, adopting an exercise program that encourages you to relax can help to prevent outbreaks of the condition. *(See pages 158–65 and pages 166–71.)*

VISUALIZATION
- Forming calming mental pictures is also effective in releasing physical and emotional tensions and reducing stress levels. To tackle pain, a practitioner will encourage you to visualize something that is diminishing. *(See pages 214–17.)*

AUTOGENIC TRAINING
- The system of exercises taught by practitioners of the therapy is thought to be helpful in inducing relaxation in different parts of the body. The aim is to boost the self-healing process. *(See pages 210–11.)*

RIGHT *Applying an ice pack to the affected area may reduce inflammation.*

CAUTION

COLD SORES ARE CONTAGIOUS FOR AS LONG AS THERE ARE ANY MOIST SECRETIONS FROM THE BLISTERS.

Acne

Acne is a common inflammatory skin disorder, characterized by blackheads and pustules, that most frequently occurs in teenagers around the time of puberty as a result of hormonal fluctuations. It can also affect adults who are suffering from stress. As well as hormonal fluctuations, most dermatologists believe that heredity and hygiene may all play a part.

The trigger is an increase in the body's production of the sex hormones at puberty, which stimulates the sebaceous glands to produce excessive amounts of sebum, the fatty oil that lubricates the skin. As a result, the glands can become blocked and inflamed, causing blackheads and pimples to appear. If the blocked glands become infected, the condition can worsen, with sebum and pus building up under the skin to form larger pimples or cysts, which can leave scars and pitting. The face, neck, shoulders, upper chest, and back are the areas commonly affected.

The treatment of acne depends on its severity. Mild acne that is unlikely to lead to scarring is treated with topical exfoliants and facial washes. Over-the-counter drying creams and lotions based on benzoyl peroxide or salicyclic acid may help moderate acne. More severe cases are treated with topical or orally administered antibiotics, or isotretonin drugs (derived from vitamin A). A doctor will advise you to wash often and thoroughly, though over-vigorous scrubbing should be avoided, as this can lead to more irritation. You should keep the skin free from oil or oil-based make-up. Some doctors may advise changing your diet, avoiding fatty and oil foods, although others believe that diet has little or nothing to do with the condition. Natural therapists, on the other hand, recommend cutting out sugar and refined carbohydrates. They may also suggest daily friction rubs on unaffected areas, plus a twice-weekly trunk pack, to improve overall skin condition. To help heal damaged skin, an infusion of comfrey leaves makes an excellent facial wash.

DATAFILE

• More than 80 percent of U.S. teenagers are affected by acne.

• Girls get the condition earlier than boys, but it tends to be more severe in the latter.

• The french fries and chocolate parents usually blamed for acne are not the culprits. The specific cause is increased hormone production that is unrelated to food consumption.

• Garlic has a minor effect as a natural antibiotic when rubbed onto spots.

• The condition is not confined to adolescence.

SYMPTOMS

• blackheads and small pimples on the face, shoulders, back or chest • the pimples fill with pus • inflamed, painful cysts deep in the skin in severe cases • their legacy can be permanent scarring and pitting

keeping the face scrupulously clean and avoiding oil-based cosmetics will help combat acne

acne may occur all over the upper body

CONVENTIONAL TREATMENT

A DOCTOR MAY SUGGEST A SPECIFIC LOTION TO COMBAT THE ACNE, AN ANTIBIOTIC COURSE, UV LIGHT THERAPY, OR THE USE OF ABRASIVE TREATMENT TO MINIMIZE THE SEVERITY OF AN ATTACK AND THE EFFECTS OF SCARRING.

CAUTION

DO NOT PICK AT OR SQUEEZE ACNE SPOTS. NOT ONLY WILL THEY BECOME LARGER AND MORE INFLAMED: SOME DEGREE OF SCARRING IS MORE LIKELY TO OCCUR. DO NOT USE A SUN LAMP AND DO NOT SUNBATHE A LOT WITHOUT TAKING YOUR DOCTOR'S ADVICE, AS EXCESSIVE EXPOSURE TO ULTRAVIOLET LIGHT CAN DAMAGE THE SKIN.

LEFT *Acne is frequently a source of embarrassment for both boys and girls during the teenage years.*

THERAPIES

HYDROTHERAPY
• Facial steam treatment is recommended by practitioners to help to open blocked skin pores and clear the sebum. You may also be recommended to try hot Epsom salts baths. Thalassotherapy, a sea-water variant of hydrotherapy, can also be effective. *(See pages 172–9.)*

RELAXATION AND BREATHING
• Therapists argue that acne sufferers can only benefit from reducing stress levels. You will be shown how to breathe more effectively first and then taught exercises to help you to relax. *(See pages 158–65 and pages 166–71.)*

LIGHT THERAPY
• Ultraviolet (UV) light therapy can be beneficial, but should be undertaken only under the supervision of a qualified practitioner. *(See pages 242–3.)*

BELOW *Eating a healthy diet is the single most effective way of promoting healthy skin.*

increase your intake of fresh fruit and vegetables

Chilblains

Small, itchy, red swellings on the skin, chilblains are caused by the skin's abnormal reaction to cold. They usually appear on the toes and fingers, though they may affect the lobes of the ears and other parts of the body, and occur when, due to poor circulation, the blood vessels shrink so much that the skin's supply of blood and oxygen is severely restricted. Damp or draughty conditions, diet and hormonal imbalance, genetic factors, malnourishment, diabetes, and the more common problem of ill-fitting shoes can be contributory factors.

To help prevent chilblains, keep your body, feet and legs warm, especially if your circulation is poor. Start the day with a warm bath to get the circulation going, keep exposure to cold to a minimum, and regularly rub moisturizing cream into areas likely to become chilled. Do not smoke, as nicotine reduces the circulation in the skin, and take regular exercise.

Chilblains usually clear up in two to three weeks without treatment. If they do develop, do not scratch them – this will only make them worse. Instead, apply a soothing lotion, such as witch hazel or calamine, which will take away most of the discomfort, and, at night, rub some lanolin ointment well into the feet to help to retain heat. If the chilblain has ulcerated, apply an antiseptic dressing: if you have diabetes, or are undergoing medical treatment, consult your doctor. Diabetics and the elderly may be prescribed medications to boost their circulation.

ABOVE *Soaking the feet in a basin of warm water will stimulate blood flow to the affected area*

CONVENTIONAL TREATMENT

A DOCTOR WILL EXAMINE THE SWELLINGS TO EXCLUDE OTHER CONDITIONS AND PRESCRIBE A CREAM TO STOP THE IRRITATION. IF THE CHILBLAINS ARE ON THE TOES AND THE RESULT OF A POOR CIRCULATION, THE NERVES CONTROLLING THE BLOOD SUPPLY MAY BE OPERATED ON.

SYMPTOMS

• *pain and itching* • *inflamed swellings on the skin* • *sensation of heat in affected areas*

THERAPIES

HYDROTHERAPY
• Practitioners recommend alternate hot and cold hand or footbaths daily. These help to stimulate the circulation. Bathe the hands or feet in warm water for around three minutes, then dip them in cold for one minute. Repeat for about 20 minutes, always finishing with the cold water. Hands benefit from alternate hot and cold compresses between the shoulderblades and the base of the neck: for feet, the best place is the lower back. (*See pages 172–9.*)

MASSAGE
• By boosting the circulation in the skin, regular massage of the hands and feet can help to prevent chilblains. (*See pages 96–103.*)

ACUPRESSURE
• Practitioners advise the use of acupressure to help to ease pain and discomfort. (*See pages 29–31.*)

AROMATHERAPY
• Massaging the feet in a footbath containing hot water mixed with a little mustard oil relieves symptoms. Lemon, lavender, chamomile, cypress, peppermint, or black pepper oils are also effective massage elements. (*See pages 104–5.*)

Abscesses and Boils

Abscesses and boils are localized bacterial infections, usually of the skin. The body responds to the presence of the bacteria by increasing the blood-flow to the area of infection (which accounts for the redness, heat and swelling). Specialist white blood cells leave the blood vessels for the tissues and engulf the bacteria. Pus is a mixture of dead tissue, white blood cells and living and dead bacteria.

Small amounts of pus can be reabsorbed by the bloodstream, but, once an abscess has reached any significant size, the only way it will resolve is by discharging. The most effective way of draining an abscess is to lance it to release the pus, though a hot compress may be soothing and hasten the natural discharge of an abscess or boil.

A large abscess results in large numbers of bacteria entering the bloodstream, causing fever and illness. Surgical drainage together with antibiotics is the only effective treatment for this serious condition. Repeated abscess formation may be a complication of chronic conditions such as diabetes or kidney malfunction.

SYMPTOMS

• *boil: painful red lump, possibly discharging* • *boil/abscess with bacteremia or septicemia: high fever, vomiting, muscle aches, headaches*

CONVENTIONAL TREATMENT

AS WELL AS LANCING THE ABSCESS TO RELEASE PRESSURE AND LESSEN THE PAIN, A DOCTOR MAY IDENTIFY THE BACTERIA INVOLVED AND PRESCRIBE ANTIBIOTICS TO STOP THE SPREAD OF INFECTION. URINE AND BLOOD MAY BE TESTED TO ESTABLISH WHETHER UNDERLYING DISEASES SUCH AS DIABETES ARE REDUCING THE RESISTANCE TO INFECTION.

THERAPIES

HYDROTHERAPY
• If the abscess is on the trunk, or the upper part of the legs, Epsom salts baths may help. Abscesses in other areas can be treated with alternate hot and cold compresses. (*See pages 172–9.*)

REFLEXOLOGY
• Stimulation of the appropriate reflex points on the feet by a trained practitioner is said to help with the condition. (*See pages 66–71.*)

EYES AND EARS

Conjunctivitis

Popularly known as "pink eye," conjunctivitis occurs when the conjunctiva, the delicate membrane that covers the whites of the eyes and the inside of the eyelids, becomes inflamed. The classic symptoms are a redness and burning sensation in the eyes, an acrid discharge, and a strong sensitivity to light. Sometimes, especially after a night's sleep, the eyes are sticky and crusted. One or both eyes can be affected.

Most cases of conjunctivitis are caused by bacterial or viral infections, though allergies like hay fever, foreign bodies in the eye, and environmental irritants, such as tobacco smoke and aerosol sprays, can all trigger the condition. If the cause is an infection, the condition is highly contagious. You should touch your eyes only when necessary and wash the hands before and afterwards to cut down the risk of the infection spreading. You should also make sure that no one else uses your towels and face clothes and use a clean pillow case each night. Wear sunglasses if you find daylight irritating. Bathing your eyes in tepid, boiled water with a little added salt may help. Blink into the water a couple of times to saturate the eye properly.

With medical treatment, bacterial or viral conjunctivitis is curable in a week or so. A doctor may prescribe antibiotic eyedrops or ointment to fight the infection. Allergic conjunctivitis will clear up once the allergen triggering it has been detected and dealt with: antihistamines may be used to help to treat the condition.

CAUTION

CONSULT YOUR DOCTOR IMMEDIATELY IF YOU HAVE ANY DIFFFICULTY SEEING, OR IF THE EYE IS VERY PAINFUL. THE SYMPTOMS SHOULD RESOLVE SPONTANEOUSLY WITHIN 48 HOURS. IF THEY DO NOT, CONSULT YOUR DOCTOR.

SYMPTOMS

• *eyes become red and sore with accompanying irritation, dryness and grittiness* • *discharge from the eyes, which may vary from watery to pus-like, depending on what is causing the conjunctivitis* • *swelling and puffiness of the eyelids*

DATAFILE

• Common eye disorders in children include astigmatism, when an additional curvature on the surface of the cornea or lens makes it hard to focus, farsightedness, nearsightedness and strabismus, or "crossed eye", which occurs when one eye turns in, out, up, or down independent of the other.

• Glaucoma is the leading cause of blindness in the U.S.

THERAPIES

HYDROTHERAPY
• Applying cool compresses to the eyes three to four times a day for ten to 15 minutes a time can help to reduce itching and swelling and generally relieve the discomfort. A cold face plunge can also help to clear some of the symptoms. *(See pages 172–9.)*

AROMATHERAPY
• Apply warm compresses, impregnated with a few drops of lavender, chamomile, or rose oil, to the affected area. These can help to draw out infection and encourage healing. *(See pages 104–5.)*

BELOW *Conjunctivitis can be highly contagious and you should touch your eyes as little as possible when you are suffering from it.*

rubbing your eyes risks spreading the infection

LEFT *Wash your hands thoroughly after touching your eyes.*

ABOVE *Bathing the eye with chamomile encourages healing.*

Glaucoma

Glaucoma occurs when the internal pressure in the eye increases enough to damage the nerve fibers in the optic nerve. The increase in pressure happens when, for reasons that are unknown, the passages that normally allow the fluid in the eyes to drain become clogged or blocked. The result is damage to vision and, if the condition is left medically untreated, blindness.

The incidence of glaucoma increases with age. People with a family history of glaucoma, African Americans, the very nearsighted and diabetics are at a higher risk of developing it. Chronic glaucoma, which can take months or even years to become noticeable, is the most common form. Prompt diagnosis and treatment is vital to control glaucoma. Diagnosis requires a comprehensive optometric examination. Once this has been made, treatment includes eyedrops and medicines to lower the pressure in the eyes. In some cases, laser treatment or surgery may be advised to reduce the pressure.

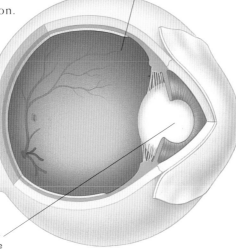

with glaucoma, increased pressure in the eye may not allow fluids to drain away properly

the result is damage to the optic nerve, which means that 'sight messages' are not sent to the brain correctly. In other words, vision is impaired

with cataracts, the damage is to the lens, which in extreme cases has to be replaced

SYMPTOMS

• *chronic glaucoma: develops gradually and painlessly without symptoms* • *acute glaucoma: sudden blurred vision; loss of side vision; seeing colored rings around light; pain or redness in the eyes*

CONVENTIONAL TREATMENT

TREATMENT FOR CHRONIC AND ACUTE GLAUCOMA MAY INVOLVE EYEDROPS, PAINKILLERS, AND SURGERY. THE AIM IS TO REDUCE THE PRESSURE INSIDE THE EYE THAT IS CAUSING THE CONDITION.

THERAPIES

LEFT Cranial oesteopathy can help relieve pressure on the eyes.

CRANIAL OSTEOPATHY
• Therapists believe that, by gently massaging the cranium, the amount of fluid within the head can be more adequately dispersed and the build-up of pressure in the eyes relieved as a result. *(See pages 115–16.)*

BATES METHOD
• The relaxing visual exercises taught as part of the Bates method are thought by practitioners to be effective counters to deterioration of sight, although they cannot cure glaucoma. *(See pages 182–3.)*

Cataract

A cataract is the development of an opacity within the lens of the eye. It is caused by chemical changes to the proteins within the lens. Although they may be congenital, cataracts are commoner with advancing age. They may be related to the total dose of UV light that the eye has received in life, as they are commoner in tropical countries. Cataracts may be related to chronic disease, notably diabetes, or renal failure, severe myopia (shortsightedness), or corticosteroid drugs.

Most often, cataracts affect people aged over 55, though they are also occasionally found in younger people. There are no warning signs of pain and discomfort to show that one may be forming, though other symptoms may be present. These include blurred or hazy vision, spots appearing in front of the eyes, increased sensitivity to glare, or the feeling of a film forming over the eyes. Nor is there any treatment that can prevent one from forming, though optometrists can prescribe changes in eyeglasses or contact lenses to mitigate its effects. If the condition develops to the point where sight is impaired, the affected lens may be surgically removed and a plastic, artificial lens substituted.

SYMPTOMS

blurred or hazy vision • *a change in the perception of colors* • *spots in front of the eyes* • *increased sensitivity to glare* • *the feeling of a film forming over the eyes*

CONVENTIONAL TREATMENT

YOUR VISION WILL BE TESTED AND SPECIAL EYEGLASSES OR CONTACT LENSES PRESCRIBED TO MITIGATE THE EFFECT OF CATARACTS. EVENTUALLY, SURGICAL REMOVAL MAY PROVE NECESSARY.

THERAPIES

ACUPRESSURE
• Massaging the acupoint on the bone below the pupil of the eye may help to relieve the problem temporarily. *(See pages 29–31.)*

BATES METHOD
• According to practitioners of the Bates method, the problems of cataracts can be compounded by what they consider bad visual habits. You will be taught a system of eye exercises to counter these. *(See pages 182–3.)*

Eyestrain

Eyestrain is not strictly a medical term and means differing things to different people. It can be experienced as burning tightness, sharp pains, dull pains, watering, blurring, double vision, headaches, and other sensations. One of the major causes of the condition is prolonged or constant use of a computer: others include protracted working in artificial light, reading in poor light and watching television for hours in the dark.

If you work on a computer, you should spend no more than two hours at a time in front of the screen, followed by at least an hour away from it. Optometrists advise getting your eyes tested on at least an annual basis: their argument is that, though working on a computer probably does not cause sight problems in itself, it can bring to light or exacerbate existing shortsightedness. To make your workstation vision-friendly, you should relocate any lamps that cast glare on the screen, and, if necessary, add a glare-reduction filter to it. A white screen with dark letters is best – if yours has a dark background, room light should be reduced by half. Clean the screen frequently.

When reading, make sure that there is sufficient light, and, when watching television at night, always have a side light on in the room. In either case, you should relax your eyes by looking away from what you are reading or watching for a few seconds at regular intervals. If you are suffering from straightforward eyestrain, a doctor will probably suggest you bathe the eyes and use eyedrops to relieve the condition. Placing pads soaked in a cool infusion of feverfew over the eyelids and resting for up to 20 minutes can also help.

LEFT *Staring constantly at a computer screen is a common cause of eyestrain in the modern world. Take at least a ten-minute break every hour.*

SYMPTOMS

• *feeling of tightness around the eyes* • *difficulty in focussing* • *recurrent headaches, particularly across the forehead and behind the eyes*

BELOW *Dr. Bates recommended holding two pencils or other objects at different distances from the eyes and focussing first on one, then on the other.*

CAUTION

IF YOU WORK WITH A VDU, MEDICAL ADVICE IS THAT YOU TAKE REGULAR BREAKS AWAY FROM THE SCREEN AND HAVE YOUR EYESIGHT TESTED ON AT LEAST AN ANNUAL BASIS, ESPECIALLY IF YOU ALREADY WEAR EYEGLASSES OR CONTACT LENSES.

CONVENTIONAL TREATMENT

A DOCTOR WILL ADVISE YOU TO BATHE THE EYES AND USE EYEDROPS TO RELIEVE ANY ACHES, PAINS AND OTHER PHYSICAL SYMPTOMS. YOU WILL BE ADVISED TO HAVE YOUR EYES TESTED TO SEE IF YOU NEED EYEGLASSES, OR A CHANGE IN PRESCRIPTION.

commercial eyewashes are sold with a little cup to help you use them

LEFT *A simple eyewash, available from pharmacies, relieves tired eyes. Alternatively, gently press used teabags of green tea or chamomile against the eyes.*

THERAPIES

BATES METHOD
• Practitioners of the Bates method recommend a series of basic exercises that will "re-educate" the eyes and get rid of the bad habits that contributed to causing the eyestrain. *(See pages 182–3.)*

AROMATHERAPY
• Massage a mixture of one drop of lemon, or rose, oil diluted with two tablespoons (30ml) of a carrier oil into the temples. *(See pages 104–5.)*

ACUPRESSURE
• Therapists believe that massaging key acupoints on the face will relieve the condition. Massage the bridge of the nose with the thumb and index finger of one hand. Then, use both thumbs to massage both sides of the top of the nose, while keeping the other fingers flat on the forehead. Finally, massage beneath the eyes with the index fingers, just below the cheekbones. *(See pages 29–31.)*

Tinnitus

A condition where the sufferer is intermittently aware of a ringing, buzzing or whistling noise in one or both ears that has no external source is termed tinnitus. There are a number of possible causes, though wax in the ear, middle ear infection with blockage of the Eustachian tubes, and inner ear damage, particularly of the cochlea, are the most common. The condition has been linked to high blood pressure, anemia and arterial disease, and can be aggravated by psychological problems, notably anxiety and depression, and overuse of drugs such as aspirin and quinine, persistent loud noise, smoking, and alcohol abuse. The problem is often the result of the deafness that comes with ageing.

Unless the cause is a simple one – wax in the ears, for instance, which can be dissolved, or syringed away – there is no cure for tinnitus, and often the cause is never known. In some cases, the intensity of the ringing sounds can be moderated by the use of drugs. A doctor may suggest trying a masker, which fits into the ear like a hearing aid and masks the noise associated with tinnitus with so-called "white noise."

SYMPTOMS

• *tinkling, buzzing or ringing in the ears*

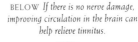

BELOW *If there is no nerve damage, improving circulation in the brain can help relieve tinnitus.*

massage head with appropriate essential oils such as rosemary

ABOVE *Working in a noisy environment or excessive exposure to loud music can damage the nerves in the ear and lead to tinnitus.*

CONVENTIONAL TREATMENT

IN SOME CASES, THE INTENSITY OF THE NOISES ASSOCIATED WITH TINNITUS CAN BE CONTROLLED BY DRUG THERAPY. ALTERNATIVELY, A MASKER MAY BE FITTED TO THE AFFECTED EAR OR EARS.

DATAFILE

• The noise of a typical pop concert can impair hearing in less than half an hour.

• Herbalists believe that feverfew is effective in treating tinnitus and that, taken daily, it may help to ward off attacks.

THERAPIES

ACUPUNCTURE
• According to practitioners, low-pitched sounds in the ears are indicative of Kidney disharmony, while high-pitched ones suggest Liver disharmony. Treatment is at the appropriate acupoints along the relevant meridians. *(See pages 20–28.)*

CRANIAL OSTEOPATHY
• Manipulating the interlocking joints, or sutures, of the cranium is said by therapists to alleviate the condition, though orthodox doctors are skeptical about its effectiveness. *(See pages 114–15.)*

RELAXATION AND BREATHING
• By teaching techniques to ease tension and relieve the symptoms of anxiety and stress, therapists help sufferers to lower their awareness of the noise associated with the complaint. *(See pages 158–65 and pages 166–71.)*

BIOFEEDBACK
• Learning how to relax muscles in the forehead through biofeedback training helps to reduce stress levels and so helps with the noise of tinnitus, according to therapists. In a Californian experiment, 80 percent of participants in a 12-session, six-week trial reported a reduction in noise levels. *(See pages 212–13.)*

PSYCHOTHERAPY AND COUNSELING
• A counselor's aim is to help you come to terms with the condition, and so to prevent the vicious circle of chronic anxiety developing. *(See pages 188–91.)*

Earache

Earaches can be very mild or very painful. Their most common cause is an inflammation of the middle ear (otitis media). This often results from a blockage in the Eustachian, or auditomeatory, tubes, which run from the back of the throat to the middle ear and allow secretions from the middle ear to drain away into the nose and throat. If the tubes become blocked, fluid gathers, pressure rises and the middle ear becomes painful and often infected as a result. Symptoms of an acute infection include intense, throbbing pain and fever; signs of a chronic infection are intermittent discomfort and intermittent discharge of pus. Other possible causes of earache include changes in air pressure while flying, something stuck in the ear, too much ear wax, dental problems, glue ear (a chronic accumulation of fluid in the middle ear) in children, deafness, and ear injuries.

Acute ear pain should be treated by a doctor. The treatment will depend on its cause, but generally includes taking an analgesic for pain relief and, if earache is the result of an infection, a course of antibi-

ABOVE Using the middle three fingers, apply gentle pressure to a point just in front of your ear.

otics. If the condition is related to sinus or nasal congestion, an antihistamine or the use of a decongestant may be advised. Self-help measures for pain relief include applying a warm compress to the ear. To open up the Eustachian tubes and help them to drain, try propping up your head while you sleep, using a cool-mist vaporizer, especially at night, and gently (to avoid bursting the eardrums), but firmly, blowing through your nose while holding both nostrils closed until you hear a pop. You can do this several times a day.

Children between the ages of six months and three years are very prone to earache and ear infections: over ten million children in the U.S. are treated for ear infections every year. However, as a child grows, the Eustachian tubes start to curve downward, allowing the fluids produced in the middle ear to drain more freely.

SYMPTOMS

- *pain* • *fever* • *soft wax or pus may drain from the ear*
- *partial deafness*

BELOW Earache is most prevalent in children and can be very distressing. In addition to the pain – usually caused by an infection accompanying a cold – both hearing and balance may be affected.

THERAPIES

CRANIAL OSTEOPATHY
• Gentle mainpulation of the bones of the skull or selected points may help to relieve the pressure caused by fluid build-up by promoting drainage. *(See pages 114–15.)*

CHIROPRACTIC
• In some cases of recurrent ear infection, chiropractic may be helpful to help to drain the build-up of fluid. *(See pages 118–25 and Osteopathy, pages106–13.)*

MASSAGE
• Therapists believe that massaging the affected ear can help to keep the Eustachian tube open. Apply gentle pressure and draw a line along the back of the ear and down the back of the jawbone, followed by gently pushing and releasing the flap of skin in front of the ear several times. Alternatively, place the fleshy part of your palm just below the thumb over

the ear and rotate around the ear. *(See pages 96–103.)*

ACUPRESSURE
• Pressing firmly with three fingers on the area in fror of the ear, and gently with the middle fingers in the hollows behind the earlobes may relieve earache, but only if there is no underlying infection. *(See pages 29–31.)*

CONVENTIONAL TREATMENT

TREATMENT VARIES ACCORDING TO THE CAUSE OF EARACHE, BUT USUALLY INCLUDES THE PRESCRIPTION OF ANTIBIOTICS OR DECONGESTANTS. IF THE EUSTACHIAN TUBES BECOME PERSISTENTLY BLOCKED, PRESSURE-EQUALIZING TUBES MAY BE SURGICALLY INSERTED THROUGH THE EARDRUM TO AID DRAINAGE.

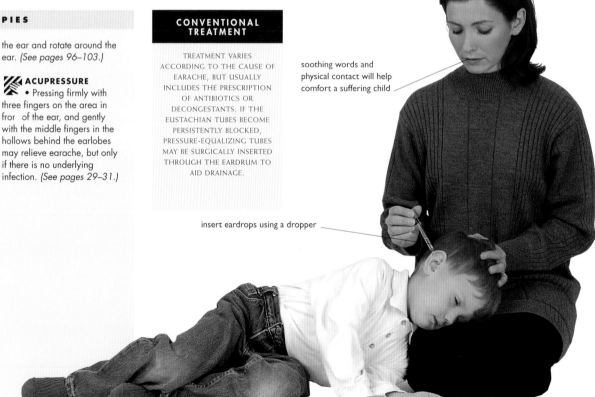

soothing words and physical contact will help comfort a suffering child

insert eardrops using a dropper

Labyrinthitis (Otitis interna)

Labyrinthitis is an inflammation of the fluid-filled chambers of the inner ear, causing disruption of the sense of balance. As well as vertigo, the condition may cause nausea, vomiting, abnormal, jerky eye movements, and a ringing, hissing or buzzing in the ears (see Tinnitus, page 281). The cause is usually an infection, possibly associated with mumps or flu; or a result of Ménière's disease or otosclerosis.

You should rest in bed until the dizziness subsides, then gradually resume your normal activities. You should not drive until a week after the symptoms have completely disappeared. If the condition is caused by a virus, some complementary therapists advise looking at the diet and increasing the consumption of foods such as oily fish to boost the immune system.

Depending on the cause, a doctor may prescribe diuretics to reduce the fluid accumulation in the inner ear and antinausea medications, if you feel nauseous. An intensive course of antibiotics will be prescribed if the condition is caused by a bacterial infection. Here, prompt treatment is important, because otherwise the inner ear can be permanently damaged.

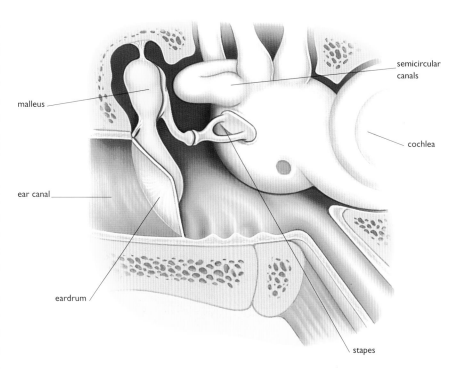

ABOVE *The ear is a complicated and delicate structure. Infections can cause a variety of unpleasant symptoms.*

SYMPTOMS

• *giddiness, dizziness, faintness, and possible falling* • *nausea and vomiting* • *partial deafness* • *ringing, buzzing or hissing in the ears*

HYDROTHERAPY
• According to some therapists, the application of alternating hot and cold compresses may help relieve symptoms, but they cannot treat the underlying causes of the condition. (See pages 172–9.)

ACUPUNCTURE
• Stimulating the relevant acupoints will improve the flow of qi and boost the local circulation to combat the condition, according to practitioners. (See pages 20–28.)

CONVENTIONAL TREATMENT

A DOCTOR MAY PRESCRIBE APPROPRIATE DROPS OR OINTMENTS, OR PACK THE EAR CANAL WITH A DRESSING SOAKED IN AN ANTIBACERIAL OR ANTIFUNGAL AGENT.

CAUTION

CALL YOUR DOCTOR IF, DURING TREATMENT, YOU SUFFER FROM A LOSS OF HEARING IN EITHER EAR, PERSISTENT VOMITING, FAINTING FITS, A RAISED TEMPERATURE, OR IF NEW, UNEXPLAINED SYMPTOMS DEVELOP.

LEFT *Applying a warm compress, followed by a cold one, to the affected area can help relieve earache.*

NOSE

Sinusitis

Sinusitis is an inflammation of the nasal sinuses, the hollow cavities within the cheekbones, around and behind the nose, and sometimes of the frontal sinuses, behind the forehead. The inflammation is normally caused by inadequate draining of the sinuses as a result of allergy, infection, and obstruction. The result is a build-up of mucus, creating intense pressure and pain.

Acute sinusitis may be triggered by a bacterial infection – usually as a complication of a common cold – or an allergy. Chronic sinusitis is recurrent. It can also be caused by bacterial infection, but may occur because of problems in the immune system, or physical obstructions, such as nasal polyps, in the nasal cavities. Tobacco smoke, dry air, and other pollutants can trigger either form of the disease.

Signs and symptoms include nasal congestion, with a green-yellow mucus discharge that sometimes can be blood-tinged; a feeling of pressure inside the head; a headache that is at its worst in the morning; cheek pain that resembles toothache; and tiredness, lack of energy, and eye pain. With medical treatment, acute sinusitis usually clears up in three weeks, but chronic sinusitis can take between four to six weeks to clear fully.

There are several self-help measures to treat the condition. Warm, moist air may relieve the congestion, so use a vaporizer, or try steam inhalations. Warm compresses may relieve pain in the sinuses and nose. Hot lemon drinks are thought to loosen mucus; garlic, onions and horseradish to reduce mucus production. Add mustard and aromatic herbs, such as oregano, to your food. Extra zinc and vitamin C can, in some cases, help to build up the body's resistance to infection.

SYMPTOMS

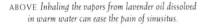

- nasal congestion with thick, stretchy mucus
- nosebleeds and sneezing • loss of sense of smell
- headache • feelings of pressure in and around the head • severe pain around the eyes and in the cheeks, which can feel like toothache

ABOVE *Inhaling the vapors from lavender oil dissolved in warm water can ease the pain of sinusitus.*

LEFT *Peppermint is also helpful in clearing nasal congestion.*

CONVENTIONAL TREATMENT

YOUR DOCTOR MAY PRESCRIBE NASAL SPRAYS, NOSE DROPS, OR ORAL DECONGESTANTS TO REDUCE THE CONGESTION, ANTIBIOTICS FOR ANY BACTERIAL INFECTION, AND ANTIHISTAMINES FOR ALLERGIES. SURGERY IS SOMETIMES NEEDED TO CLEAR NASAL OBSTRUCTIONS.

CAUTION

CALL A DOCTOR IF YOU ARE SUFFERING FROM A FEVER, BLEEDING FROM THE NOSE, SEVERE HEADACHE, FACIAL SWELLING, BLURRED VISION OR OTHER EYE SYMPTOMS.

THERAPIES

SHIATSU
• Pressure on the tsubo midway between the two bones of the thumb and index finger in the fleshiest part of the hand, on the one between the eleventh and twelfth thoracic vertebrae, and on the tsubo lateral to the base of the nose on a line directly below the pupils may help with sinus congestion. (See pages 32–7 and Do-in, pages 38–41.)

REFLEXOLOGY
• To ease the congestion and relieve the pain, a practitioner will stimulate the sinus points on each toe repeatedly. The thumb slowly moves up each toe, from base to tip. (See pages 66–71.)

ACUPRESSURE
• A practitioner may advise stimulating acupoints on the Large Intestine meridian by pressing firmly either side of the nostrils at the base of the nose. (See pages 29–31.)

ACUPUNCTURE
• Inserting needles into the appropriate acupoints will improve the flow of qi and restore the balance of yin and yang. The acupoints on the governor and the large and small Intestine meridians are the ones treated, plus the ones on the spleen meridian if there is an allergy involvement. (See pages 20–28.)

AROMATHERAPY
• Massage the face with a well-diluted mixture of lavender, thyme, eucalyptus, peppermint, pine and tea tree oils to relieve pain, clear blockage and stuffiness, and act as an antiseptic to help clear the infection. (See pages 104–5.)

HYDROTHERAPY
• Alternate hot and cold compresses on the base of the skull and on the forehead can relieve the condition, as will a daily cold sitz bath. Alternate hot and cold footbaths may also help. (See pages 172–9.)

CRANIAL OSTEOPATHY
• Practitioners believe this therapy can ease sinusitis by boosting the drainage of sinus fluids. (See pages 214–15.)

Catarrh

Catarrh is the medical term used to describe the over-production of thick mucus in response to an inflammation or irritation of the membranes that line the passages of the throat, nose, and lungs. It gives rise to sneezing, a blocked or runny nose, coughs or earache, and loss of the senses of taste and smell. The condition is often triggered by colds and flu; other triggers include smoking, dust inhalation, chronic sinusitis, upper respiratory tract infection, and allergy. A series of colds in quick succession may lead to chronic catarrh.

Conventional treatment may involve the prescription of antibiotics if the catarrh is the result of a bacterial infection, or antihistamines if it is an allergic response. You may also be advised to use decongestant nose drops to relieve the symptoms of the complaint. Steam inhalations may be useful (use with care if you are asthmatic). If the attack is in response to an allergy, help yourself by avoiding the triggering allergens. You should also keep rooms well-ventilated and cut back on dairy products, sugar and sugary foodstuffs in favor of a nutritious wholefood diet including plenty of fresh fruit, salads, vegetables, fish, nuts, honey, and wholegrain cereals.

avoid food with a high sugar content and cut down on dairy products

choose lots of fresh fruit and vegetables, and wholegrain cereals

ABOVE *Eating a healthy diet is one of the best ways to reduce catarrh, in particular cutting back on dairy foods.*

CONVENTIONAL TREATMENT

CONSULT A DOCTOR IF THE BLOCKAGE LASTS LONGER THAN TWO TO FOUR WEEKS, OR IF THE DISCHARGE IS BLOODSTAINED. YOU MAY BE PRESCRIBED ANTIBIOTICS OR ANTIHISTAMINES, DEPENDING ON WHAT IS CAUSING THE CATARRH.

CAUTION

SITZ BATHS, HOT SHOWERS, SAUNAS, AND STEAM BATHS SHOULD BE AVOIDED IF YOU ARE PREGNANT.

SYMPTOMS

• *blocked, possibly runny nose, or excessively runny nose* • *cough* • *earache* • *possible nosebleeds* • *ulcers may develop on the septum, the bone separating the nostrils*

BELOW *Another cause of the blocked-up feeling we associate with a cold is the over-production of mucus known as catarrh.*

blowing your nose too hard or too often can lead to nosebleeds

THERAPIES

ACUPRESSURE
• Pressure is applied to the acupoints at the back of and on either side of the skull, and on the web of the hand, to relieve the symptoms of the complaint. *(See pages 29–31.)*

ACUPUNCTURE
• A practitioner will stimulate the acupoints on the large Intestine, Stomach and Lung meridians. *(See pages 20–28.)*

MASSAGE
• To help drain the sinuses, facial massage may be suggested. If mucus has become lodged in the bronchial tubes, stroking the upper back plus vibratory petrissage over the shoulder muscles and vibratory friction over the lower tip of the breastbone may help. *(See pages 96–103.)*

HYDROTHERAPY
• Treatments such as mustard footbaths, sitz baths, long, hot showers, saunas, steam baths, hot and cold compresses, and friction rubs may all be recommended by hydrotherapists. *(See pages 172–9.)*

REFLEXOLOGY
• A reflexologist may recommend massaging the reflex areas relating to the sinuses and nose. In addition, he may suggest massaging the areas relating to the head, eyes, upper lymph nodes and the digestive system. *(See pages 66–71.)*

BELOW *Acupressure on the hand can help shift catarrh.*

MOUTH AND THROAT

Fear of Dental Treatment

Fear of dental treatment is an extremely common phenomenon. Sufferers develop intense feelings of anxiety and panic: they feel, for example, that they are completely in the hands of the dentist, that dentists are always impatient, and that dentists do not care about the pain their patients are in. Children can be particularly affected, especially if they sense that their parents themselves are scared of dentists and treatment.

Most modern dentists are aware of the nervousness that affects many of their patients. They may offer home visits, sedation, and anesthetics, or offer or advise hypnosis and other forms of relaxation therapy to help to combat the problem.

SYMPTOMS

- *rapid pulse* • *profuse sweating* • *raised blood pressure*
- *trembling* • *nausea*

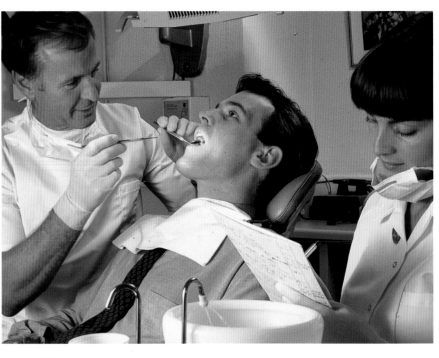

ABOVE *A good dentist will try to put you at ease by explaining what he is doing and pausing if you show any sign of discomfort.*

RIGHT *Certain types of music have been proven to have a therapeutic effect in relieving anxiety.*

DATAFILE

- Some studies show that nearly 80 percent of Americans suffer from some feelings of fear about dental treatment, while, according to the American Dental Hygienists' Association, 12 to 15 percent of them totally avoid any kind of dental treatment because of severe dental anxiety.

CONVENTIONAL TREATMENT

HOME VISITS, SEDATION AND ANESTHETICS MAY BE OFFERED TO COMBAT FEAR OF TREATMENT. COGNITIVE-BEHAVIORAL THERAPY, HYPNOSIS, AND RELAXATION TECHNIQUES MAY ALSO BE RECOMMENDED.

THERAPIES

AROMATHERAPY
- Bergamot, chamomile, clary sage, geranium, jasmine, juniper, lavender, marjoram, melissa, and ylang ylang, which are all sedative, are among the best oils to try. Use them for massage, combined with a light carrier oil, such as sweet almond. Carry a bottle of the diluted oils with you and apply to the temples or pulse points before dental treatment. *(See pages 104–5.)*

AYURVEDA
- Individual treatment is prescribed according to specific individual needs. *(See pages 78–85.)*

BIOFEEDBACK
- Therapists will show you how to systematically tense and relax 16 of the larger muscles in the body over a period of 15 to 20 minutes, while sitting in a dental chair. During this time, the muscular tension is registered electronically and displayed so that you can monitor your state of relaxation. The aim is to increase your personal control over your physiological responses. *(See pages 212–13.)*

PSYCHOTHERAPY AND COUNSELING
- A cognitive-behavioral therapist will encourage you to confront your fear by talking openly about it and formulating what are termed negative cognitions in words. You will then be helped to reformulate problems by breaking them down into specific difficulties, each of which are tackled in turn. *(See pages 196–9.)*

LEFT *Sedative oils can help relax you before a trip to the dentist.*

HYPNOTHERAPY
- A hypnotherapist will use her hypnotic skills to help you to reprogram the way you think and so overcome your fears of dental treatment. Consult a reputable hypnotherapist if you decide to use this method of overcoming your phobia. *(See pages 218–23.)*

BIORHYTHMS
- Therapists believe that, on a personal level, there are three main cycles that influence our lives – the emotional, lasting 28 days, the physical, lasting 23 days, and the intellectual, lasting 33 days. The cycles and the phases within them can be used to plot the days on which sufferers are best equipped to deal with their phobia. *(See pages 244–7.)*

MUSIC THERAPY
- Many dentists now play soothing background music during treatment. The theory is that this will help to relax the person being treated and so calm nerves and fears. *(See pages 232–5.)*

RELAXATION AND BREATHING
- Learning and practicing quick and easy relaxation techniques and being shown how to breathe deeply helps to calm the nerves and relieve stress. *(See pages 158–65 and pages 166–71.)*

Dental Discomfort

(following treatment)

Discomfort after dental treatment is usually caused by injury – perhaps to a nerve – or bruising around the tooth that has been treated. This may occur immediately after treatment has been completed, or pain may follow initial discomfort after an anesthetic has worn off. There may also be some bleeding from the gums.

If the pain persists, you should consult a dentist immediately, as this may signal an infection. The dentist will check for this with X-rays and treat the infection accordingly.

SYMPTOMS

• *pain* • *bleeding gums* • *swollen gums if underlying infection*

ABOVE *Applying oil of cloves gently to the affected area should help.*

massage oil of cloves on the painful area

LEFT *Severe pain after dental treatment is unusual, but you should consult your dentist if you are worried. The treatment may have damaged a nerve.*

THERAPIES

AROMATHERAPY
• Oil of clove or macerated cloves can be gently massaged into and around the affected area. This will help to prevent infection, reduce the inflammation and soothe discomfort. *(See pages 104–5.)*

ACUPUNCTURE
• The World Health Organization lists acupuncture as a therapy that can help in the treatment of this condition. *(See pages 20–28.)*

Grinding of Teeth

Habitual grinding, or clenching, of the teeth is medically known as bruxism. It is usually a subconscious habit, but is audible to others. At its most common in the elderly and among children, and most often occurring during sleep, its appearance may be linked to anxiety and alcohol consumption. It is bad for the teeth, injuring and irritating the pulp, and eventually damaging the latter to the extent of killing the nerve if the condition is left untreated. The habit is rather like rocking a pole that is implanted into the ground until it has been thoroughly loosened, particularly if the condition is left untreated.

Dentists have devised an appliance they call a bite plate to be kept in the mouth during sleep. It prevents grinding, is not uncomfortable, and will save teeth and peridontal tissue.

BELOW *You may think you are sleeping peacefully, but grinding your teeth can cause serious long-term damage.*

ABOVE *Wearing a bite plate at night keeps the teeth apart.*

THERAPIES

ACUPUNCTURE
• Stimulation of the relevant acupoints may help to relieve the pain or promote sedation. *(See pages 20–8.)*

ACUPRESSURE
• Applying pressure on the acupoint in the hollow under the cheekbone may relieve the condition. *(See pages 29–31.)*

AUTOGENIC TRAINING
• This therapy is claimed to be successful in relieving excessive muscular tension in the facial region *(See pages 210–11.)*

OTHER THERAPIES
• Osteopathy *(see pages 106–13)* and chiropractic *(see pages 118–25)* may help.

Toothache

• sensitivity to cold, hot or sweet things • pain when you bite can be a sign that the tooth or a filling is broken • swelling and inflammation of the surrounding gum, which may also bleed

An aching or pain in a tooth is generally the result of tooth decay, otherwise known as dental caries. It occurs when bacteria in plaque, a soft, sticky, almost invisible film that forms on the teeth every day, react with starchy and sugary foods to produce acids. These acids eat away at the tooth enamel and the root surface. Without treatment, little cavities become big ones: the tiniest untreated cavity can ultimately grow to destroy a whole tooth.

If a tooth is sensitive to cold, heat or sweet things and the resulting pain lasts for more than a few minutes, the nerves in the tooth may be inflamed due to advanced decay and consequent bacterial infection. If left untreated, this infection may spread to the bone to form a pus-filled abscess, in which case a course of antibiotics will be needed in order to cure it in addition to standard dental treatment. If pain is absent except when you bite, the tooth or a filling may be broken. In either case, you should make an immediate dental appointment. To stop the problem arising – or, at the least, to catch it before it becomes more serious – you should schedule a regular dental check-up at least every six months, but your dentist will advise how frequent this needs to be.

sensitivity to hot and cold drinks is an early warning sign of gum problems

RIGHT *If teeth are particularly sensitive, this may be an indication of some problems ahead.*

ABOVE *One of several acupressure points to relieve toothache is situated just below the cheekbone.*

BELOW *Some people tend naturally to build up more plaque than others and may need frequent visits to a dental hygienist.*

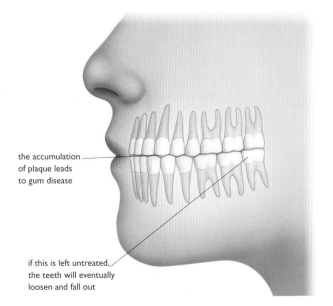

the accumulation of plaque leads to gum disease

if this is left untreated, the teeth will eventually loosen and fall out

CAUTION

TOOTHACHE IS A SYMPTOM OF AN UNDERLYING DENTAL PROBLEM WHICH CAN ONLY BE RESOLVED BY CONSULTING A DENTIST. THIS SHOULD BE DONE AS QUICKLY AS POSSIBLE, AS OTHERWISE THE CONDITION WILL ONLY BECOME WORSE.

DATAFILE

• 96 percent of the U.S. population have cavities in their teeth.

• 50 percent of Americans do not have regular dental check-ups.

• Around 50 percent of Americans aged over 65 have lost their teeth, and many wear false teeth.

• Americans spend upwards of $2 billion a year on toothpaste, mouthwashes, dental floss, and other dental products.

• 75 percent of Americans suffer from some form of gum disease.

THERAPIES

ACUPRESSURE
• Applying pressure to the acupoint on the back of the hand, between the thumb and the index finger, may help to relieve the pain of a toothache. Other possible acupoints include the ones at the bottom of the cheekbones directly below the pupil, and the point directly in front of the ear in the depression that deepens when the mouth is opened. There are two more useful acupoints above and below this one. (See pages 29–31.)

AROMATHERAPY
• Peppermint, cajuput, or clove oils applied directly to the affected area act as a natural analgesic, while oil of coriander can reduce inflammation and pain. Rubbing a little lavender oil on to the face and jaw can also ease the discomfort and distress. (See pages 104–5.)

ACUPUNCTURE
• Practitioners believe that stimulation of the appropriate acupoints can relieve the pain, but this may only be temporary. (See pages 20–8.)

HYDROTHERAPY
• Sucking an ice cube, or applying an ice pack to the cheek, are frequently used forms of pain relief. (See pages 172–9.)

CRANIAL OSTEOPATHY
• Soothing manipulation of the skull bones may be effective in the treatment of toothache. (See pages 114–15.)

Gum Disease

Gum disease is an infection of the tissues surrounding and supporting the teeth, and is a major cause of tooth loss in adults. In the U.S., about three out of four adults aged over 35 are affected by some form of the condition. It is caused by plaque, a sticky bacterial film that constantly forms on the teeth. The bacteria create toxins that can damage the gums and, eventually, spread to the bones. Tartar below the gumline can also contribute to the development of the disease.

In the first stages of gum disease – this is called gingivitis – the gums can become red, swollen and tender. They may also bleed, especially when or after you brush the teeth. Other tell-tale signs may include gums that have pulled away from the teeth, bad breath, pus between teeth and gums, loose teeth, and a change in the way your teeth fit together when you bite. If you notice any of these symptoms, you should consult a dentist as soon as you can, since, at this early stage, the condition is usually reversible.

You should floss daily, brush your teeth before every meal, consider using an electric toothbrush, and arrange to have your teeth cleaned and checked regularly by a dental hygienist or dentist. You should avoid spicy foods, and ones that are high in sugar. The free flow of saliva and the action of the tongue and lips on the teeth and gums are important for maintaining dental hygiene. Saliva production is reduced in dehydration, so drink plenty of water and cut down on between-meal snacks. To soothe and heal inflamed, bleeding gums, try rinsing the mouth with a solution of warm water mixed with a tablespoon of aloe vera gel, or apply the gel directly to the affected area.

Because gingivitis is usually painless, you may not recognize that you are suffering from it. If left untreated, gingivitis can worsen and progress to another, more serious form of gum disease called periodontitis. If this is not treated promptly by a dentist or periodontist, the gums and bone that support the teeth can become seriously damaged, with the result that they may have to be extracted.

SYMPTOMS

• *red, swollen and tender gums, which bleed easily during and after brushing* • *bad breath* • *gums pulling away from the teeth* • *loose teeth* • *a changed bite*

RIGHT *It is important to clean your teeth both regularly and correctly. Brushing too violently may hurt the gums and make the problem worse.*

CONVENTIONAL TREATMENT

YOUR DENTIST WILL RECOMMEND A SUITABLE TOOTHBRUSH AND, IF NECESSARY, SHOW YOU THE MOST EFFECTIVE BRUSHING AND FLOSSING TECHNIQUES. YOUR TEETH SHOULD BE SCALED AND CLEANED AS PART OF ANY ROUTINE DENTAL CHECK-UP.

CAUTION

GINGIVITIS SHOULD ALWAYS BE TREATED PROMPTLY OTHERWISE IT CAN PROGRESS TO A MORE SERIOUS FORM OF GUM DISEASE, PERIODONTITIS.

THERAPIES

AYURVEDA
• Practitioners may suggest drinking diluted lemon juice and massaging the gums with coconut oil. Dabbing bleeding gums with cutch (tannin-rich extract of an Indian plant, i.e. acacia) may also be recommended. *(See pages 78–85.)*

ACUPUNCTURE
• Gingivitis features as one of the conditions the World Health Organisation has recommended can be treated with acupuncture. *(See pages 20–8.)*

RIGHT *Ayurvedic practitioners may recommend a very diluted lemon-juice mouthwash or to rub your gums with coconut oil. However, lemon juice can harm the enamel on your teeth, so consult a dentist before doing this.*

Tonsillitis

Tonsillitis is an inflammation that affects the tonsils, which are two small collections of lymph tissue at the back of the throat. It can occur at any time, but is particularly common during childhood. First-graders are particularly vulnerable, because school brings them into contact with large numbers of viruses to which they have not had the chance to build up their natural resistance.

The condition, which is infectious and takes three to five days days to develop, can be caused by either a virus or by bacteria (often by the streptococcal bacterium). The infected tonsils become red and swell: sometimes, flecks of white or yellow pus appear on their surfaces. Sometimes, too, the adenoids, nodules of tissue at the back of the nose, may become infected and inflamed, while, in rare cases, complications such as quinsy (an abscess that forms around the tonsils), kidney inflammation, or rheumatic fever may develop.

In normal circumstances, the worst of the illness is usually over within 48 hours. During this time, the best thing to do is to go to bed, drink extra fluids and try not worry too much about eating. Blackcurrant tea, hot blackcurrant juice, hot lemon and honey drinks or honey and apple cider vinegar may relieve a sore throat. Cod liver oil tablets, along with vitamin C and garlic, can also help with the healing process.

Consult a doctor if symptoms, notably a high temperature, last for longer than two days; if any phlegm that may be coughed up is green or yellow; if a fine red neck rash appears; if a child becomes pale, listless and will not drink enough to pass urine; or if the symptoms appear in anyone aged over 40. A doctor may recommend taking painkillers and, if a bacterial cause is considered likely, prescribe an antibiotic. An antibiotic can be effective only if the cause is bacterial: antibiotics have no effect on viruses. Surgery to remove the tonsils is no longer common medical practice, except if the tonsillitis is serious, recurrent and persists past adolescence.

SYMPTOMS

sore throat • pain on swallowing • swollen and tender neck glands • high temperature • headache, earache, general weakness and malaise • bad breath and a white-coated tongue • fever in some cases

THERAPIES

AROMATHERAPY
• A gentle massage with diluted eucalyptus oil may help to ease discomfort. Thyme oil is a powerful antiseptic and also has a local soothing effect. Add to a light carrier oil and massage into the neck. Tea tree oil, applied neat to the tonsils on the end of a cotton bud, may help to fight the infection and relieve discomfort. *(See pages 104–5.)*

AYURVEDA
• Mustard oil is recommended by therapists to reduce pitta and kapha, and have a neutral effect on vatha. *(See pages 78–85.)*

HYDROTHERAPY
• A practitioner may recommend the use of a humidifier, as dry air can exacerbate the condition, plus the use of a cold throat compress and stomach pack. *(See pages 172–9.)*

LEFT *A warm blackcurrant drink is a pleasant way for children (and adults) to soothe an inflamed throat.*

DATAFILE

• Tonsillitis is more common in children than in adults.

• Tonsils are not a useless part of the body, as was once popularly believed, but are part of the body's system of protection from infection.

• Tonsillitis usually develops suddenly as a result of a streptococcal infection, but may also be caused by a viral infection.

• Frequently, tonsillitis clears up without treatment.

CONVENTIONAL TREATMENT

BEDREST, DRINKING PLENTY OF FLUID, PAINKILLERS IN RECOMMENDED DOSES. IF SYMPTOMS PERSIST FOR MORE THAN THREE DAYS, A DOCTOR MAY PRESCRIBE ANTIBIOTICS, BUT ONLY IF THE CAUSE OF THE TONSILLITIS IS ESTABLISHED AS BACTERIAL. SURGERY MAY BE RECOMMENDED, BUT ONLY IN SERIOUS, PERSISTENT AND RECURRENT CASES.

CAUTION

CONSULT A DOCTOR IF SYMPTOMS, PARTICULARLY A RAISED TEMPERATURE, LAST FOR LONGER THAN TWO DAYS WITHOUT IMPROVEMENT.

ABOVE *Garlic has wide-ranging medicinal properties and will help fight the infection of tonsilitis.*

Sore Throat

Sore throat is a symptom which may be caused by a number of different infectious organisms. Most sore throats (70–80 percent) are caused by viruses, the remainder by bacteria. There is no ready way to distinguish between viral and bacterial sore throats, though viral infections tend to be milder and may be associated with a cough. High fever and lots of pus on the tonsils make a bacterial cause more likely. Antibiotics may slightly shorten the duration of a sore throat caused by a bacterium.

Scarlet fever, rheumatic fever, and post-streptococcal glomerulonephritis are all complications of bacterial throat infections caused by the Group A streptococcus. They are much rarer in the developed world than they used to be, but most doctors would test for a bacterial sore throat and give antibiotics if necessary. Glandular fever is a viral illness in which sore throat is the predominant symptom. The pain is usually severe and the tonsils are inflamed and covered in thick white pus. The virus affects the body systemically, is debilitating, and may cause enlarged lymph glands, liver, and spleen.

Normally, an uncomplicated case of sore throat should resolve itself within a few days, though, if the infection is prolonged and accompanied by high fever and malaise, it it vital to see a doctor.

As well as reducing the painful inflammation, complementary treatments aim at strengthening the body's natural defenses against the illness by boosting the immune system. Gargling with salt water helps to ease symptoms and reduce inflammation, while gargling with honey water may help to deal with infection and encourage healing, as will a hot honey and lemon drink, or a white cabbage-juice gargle. Conventionally, painkillers, antiseptic lozenges and gargles will all help to soothe the affected area.

You should avoid airborne pollutants, which will aggravate the soreness, as will breathing cold and dry air. Rest the voice and keep warm. If the infection lasts for longer than four days, a doctor should be consulted. He or she may prescribe antibiotics to treat any bacterial infections and to prevent other problems from developing.

CONVENTIONAL TREATMENT

PAINKILLERS, ANTISEPTIC LOZENGES, THROAT SPRAYS, AND ANTISEPTIC GARGLES WILL HELP TO SOOTHE INFLAMMATION AND IRRITATION. IN THE EVENT OF BACTERIAL INFECTION, A COURSE OF ANTIBIOTICS WILL BE PRESCRIBED TO ENSURE PROTECTION AGAINST RHEUMATIC FEVER.

CAUTION

IN PREGNANCY AVOID USING THE FIRST SHIATSU PRESSURE POINT GIVEN HERE. SEE A DOCTOR IN CASE UNTREATED STREP THROAT LEADS TO SCARLET OR RHEUMATIC FEVER, WHICH CAN SERIOUSLY DAMAGE HEALTH.

LEFT *Gargling is the classic remedy for a sore throat. Salt water reduces inflammation, while honey water fights infection.*

SYMPTOMS

hoarseness and thirst • pain makes it difficult to swallow • possibly a burning sensation • mild fever • enlarged and tender lymph glands in the neck • general feelings of ill-health and tiredness • possible earache

DATAFILE

• Noninfectious forms of sore throat can be caused by prolonged irritation, resulting from excessive use of the voice, eating spicy foods, dusty working conditions, industrial fumes, overindulgence in alcohol, and smoking.

• Mild viral infections are by far the more common, and are usually uncomplicated to treat.

• Bacterial infections, such as strep throat, are more serious and require medical intervention, particularly if a child is affected as there is a risk of rheumatic fever developing. The uncomplicated viral form of sore throat should disappear in three to six days with no specific treatment.

THERAPIES

AROMATHERAPY
• Massage a little lavender oil, blended in a light carrier oil, into the neck. The oil has antiseptic, antibacterial and painkilling properties. Dab the throat with diluted tea tree oil on a cotton bud. The tea tree oil is an analgesic and infection fighter, which will help to ease the symptoms and treat the cause. Heavily diluted eucalyptus oil is a good alternative. *(See pages 104–5.)*

SHIATSU
• Therapists concentrate on massaging the pressure points – known as tsubos – between the ribs and on the hands. The first pressure point is located between the first and second ribs, one inch below the middle of the clavicle. Press with one thumb for seven to ten seconds. The second is midway between the two bones of the thumb and the index finger in the fleshiest part of the hand. Again, press hard with one thumb for seven to ten seconds. *(See pages 32–7 and Do-in, pages 38–41.)*

HYDROTHERAPY
• The use of a humidifier may help, as dry air can make a sore throat worse. Cold stomach packs and throat compresses may help to stimulate the immune system and aid circulation. *(See pages 172–9.)*

Laryngitis

Laryngitis is an inflammation of the larynx, the part of the trachea, or windpipe, where the voice box is located. There are two types: acute laryngitis, which is infectious, can strike suddenly and lasts for only a day or so, and chronic laryngitis, which may last for days or weeks and recur at intervals.

In both types, the larynx and vocal cords become swollen and sore, with hoarseness and sometimes complete loss of voice as a result. Acute laryngitis is usually a complication of a sore throat, cold or other upper respiratory tract infection, and should last for only a few days. It can also be an allergic reaction to inhaled pollen. Chronic laryngitis is more persistent, and may be caused by long-term irritation from tobacco smoke, dust or other pollutants, overuse of the voice and excessive coughing, or emotional strain or stress.

Orthodox treatment is simple and straightforward. The first thing to do is to rest the voice. Talk as little as possible, do not shout and, if you smoke, stop. Drink extra fluids and rest in bed if you feel ill. Painkillers, throat sprays, medicated lozenges, and gargles can help to ease symptoms. In acute laryngitis, if there is a risk of the infection spreading, a doctor may prescribe antibiotics. Contact a doctor if the raised temperature associated with the condition persists for more than three or four days, if your voice is hoarse for more than three weeks, or if you cough up blood or green or yellow phlegm. For chronic laryngitis, consult a doctor if the hoarseness lasts for more than three weeks, or if pain in the throat or ear develops.

Complementary therapies concentrate on alleviating symptoms. Gargling with salt water or drinking a glass of honey and lemon or honey and apple cider vinegar may help to reduce any inflammation and infection, while also encouraging healing. A steam inhalation (use with care if you are asthmatic) of sandalwood or thyme is thought to similarly ease inflammation and reduce infection. Avoid alcohol, as this will only lower your resistance to infection.

SYMPTOMS

• acute laryngitis: throat is inflamed and coated with mucus; painful dry cough which produces no phlegm; voice becomes hoarse and speaking may be painful • chronic laryngitis: surface of the larynx dry and inflamed; swollen vocal cords, making it difficult to raise the voice above a whisper; permanent, irritating cough

DATAFILE

- There are two types of laryngitis: acute and chronic.
- Acute laryngitis usually clears up in a day or two.
- In chronic laryngitis, there is hoarseness, the feeling of "a frog in the throat" and tenderness that continues unabated for some time.
- Resting the voice is one of the best cures for laryngitis.
- If, as a result of over-using the voice, nodules and polyps form on the vocal cords, these can be removed. They are not malignant.

CONVENTIONAL TREATMENT

PAINKILLERS, COUGH SYRUP, THROAT LOZENGES, SPRAYS AND INFUSIONS WILL ALL HELP TO ALLEVIATE THE SYMPTOMS. IF THERE IS A RISK OF INFECTION SPREADING TO THE LUNGS, ANTIBIOTICS WILL BE PRESCRIBED. IF THE HOARSENESS PERSISTS, YOUR DOCTOR MAY ARRANGE FOR A SPECIALIST EXAMINATION TO DETECT ANY POLYPS AND NODULES ON THE VOCAL CORDS, WHICH CAN THEN BE SURGICALLY REMOVED. SUCH ABNORMALITIES CAN RESULT FROM EXCESSIVE USE OF THE VOICE, AND ARE NOT CANCEROUS.

CAUTION

CONSULT A DOCTOR IF THE HOARSENESS ASSOCIATED WITH ACUTE BRONCHITIS PERSISTS FOR MORE THAN THREE OR FOUR DAYS. FOR CHRONIC BRONCHITIS, CONSULT A DOCTOR IF SYMPTOMS PERSIST FOR LONGER THAN 21 DAYS. CHILDREN WITH ACUTE LARYNGITIS NEED CAREFUL MONITORING, BECAUSE THE MUCUS MAY BLOCK THE NARROW LARYNGEAL OPENING, CAUSING CROUP. SOME HAY FEVER OR ASTHMA SUFFERERS MAY BE ALLERGIC TO LAVENDER (SEE THERAPIES BOX).

THERAPIES

AROMATHERAPY
• Massage the throat with a drop of lavender or tea tree oil in a light carrier oil. For this, you need only three to four drops of the chosen oil, added to an eggcup of carrier oil. For young children, halve the quantities of essential oil. (See pages 104–5.)

RELAXATION TECHNIQUES
• If chronic bronchitis is being triggered by stress, making the time for a short relaxation session once or twice a day is a good way of unwinding. The basic aim is to release excessive tension from the muscles. (See pages 158–65.)

BREATHING TECHNIQUES
• You can build on relaxation techniques by mastering other techniques that will teach you how to breathe better. Most people use only about half their lung capacity when they breathe: these techniques help you to make your breathing more efficient and so helps to alleviate the symptoms of the condition. (See pages 166–71.)

BELOW *Lemon juice and hot water, sweetened with a little honey, is a home remedy for sore throats. The lemon's vitamin C content helps boost the immune system and the fruit also has antibacterial and anti-inflammatory properties.*

Mouth Ulcers

Affecting more than one in five adults in the U.S., mouth ulcers are small, shallow, round or oval sores, often with a slightly raised yellowish edge, a pale gray base and a thin, inflamed border. They can appear on the inside of the lips, cheeks or floor of the mouth, and can be caused by viral infections, brushing the teeth too vigorously, badly-fitting dentures, accidentally biting the side of the mouth, or eating very hot food. They can also be triggered by stress, or being run down and can be a feature of Crohn's disease, ulcerative colitis, coeliac disease, or food allergy. Women may be particularly prone to mouth ulcers around the time of menstruation.

Conventional antiseptic or painkilling pastilles and mouthwashes will help to relieve pain, as will rubbing the affected area with a little aloe vera gel, or rubbing the tongue with a piece of fresh ginger. You should consult a doctor if the ulcers are persistent or recurrent, or if the sores appear in the grooves alongside the gums. In persistent cases, hydrocortisone pellets, pastes, or antibiotics may be prescribed. If the condition is being caused by ill-fitting dentures or jagged teeth, you need to consult a dentist.

SYMPTOMS

• *pain, often even before the ulcer appears* • *soreness and sensitivity to hot or spicy food* • *discomfort when you chew or swallow* • *dry mouth* • *possibly bad breath*

THERAPIES

RELAXATION TECHNIQUES
• The appearance of mouth ulcers may be stress-related, in which case learning how to relax will help in treating the condition. *(See pages 158–65.)*

OTHER THERAPIES
• Stress-related ulcers may be relieved by trying the therapies recommended for reducing stress. *(See pages 262–3.)*

CAUTION
CONSULT YOUR DOCTOR IF ANY LUMP IN THE MOUTH PERSISTS FOR MORE THAN TWO WEEKS, PARTICULARLY IF IT IS HARD, OR IF WHITE PATCHES APPEAR INSIDE THE MOUTH OR THROAT.

CONVENTIONAL TREATMENT
IF SELF-HELP MEASURES FAIL, A DOCTOR MAY PRESCRIBE STRONGER OINTMENTS OR PELLETS WHICH CAN BE PLACED AGAINST THE ULCER TO RELIEVE THE PAIN AND SPEED HEALING. BLOOD TESTS MAY BE NEEDED TO CHECK FOR ASSOCIATED DISORDERS AND A COURSE OF VITAMIN SUPPLEMENTS PRESCRIBED.

ABOVE AND RIGHT *Ginger has been used as a folk medicine throughout the world for thousands of years. It is an antiseptic and reduces irritation.*

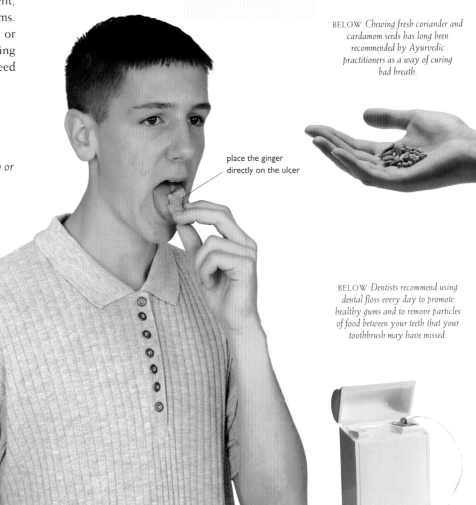

place the ginger directly on the ulcer

BELOW *Chewing fresh coriander and cardamom seeds has long been recommended by Ayurvedic practitioners as a way of curing bad breath.*

BELOW *Dentists recommend using dental floss every day to promote healthy gums and to remove particles of food between your teeth that your toothbrush may have missed.*

LUNGS AND BREATHING

Asthma

Asthma is a common condition in which the muscles of the bronchi (the lungs' air tubes) contract in spasm, leading to shortness of breath, coughing, and wheezing. For most sufferers, asthma is an allergic disease in which an attack is triggered by a foreign invader, or allergen. Common allergens include pollen, tobacco smoke, house dust, pet hair, and foods. There are, however, other triggers, such as stress, viral infection, pollution, physical exertion, or breathing in very cold air. In asthma sufferers the bronchi are chronically inflamed and hypersensitive. The bronchi narrow as a reaction to the trigger, causing the wheezing and breathlessness characteristic of the disease. The body also releases chemicals, such as histamine, to combat allergens, causing a coughing reflex, which further constricts the bronchi, and the cycle starts over again. For some asthma sufferers, attacks have no obvious causes.

Some forms of allergic asthma can sometimes be cured by desenitization; otherwise, asthma can be controlled. A doctor will prescribe a bronchodilator inhaler or nebulizer to relieve the symptoms of an acute attack, and anti-inflammatories to combat the underlying lung inflammation. A RAST test may also be advised to identify specific allergic triggers so that they can be avoided as much as possible in the future. One common allergen, the house dust mite, can be controlled by keeping the house as dust-free as possible. Use synthetic bedding, and avoid thick carpets and heavy curtains in the bedroom. Vacuum regularly and wash bed linen once a week. Do not keep pets and ban smoking. Pollen sufferers should avoid walking through long grass and keep windows closed on hot summer days.

For more than 40 percent of asthmatics, exercise or physical exertion can be a trigger. However, unlike allergen-induced asthma,

SYMPTOMS

- *shortness of breath* • *raised pulse rate and sweating*
- *wheezing, especially when you breathe out* • *coughing up phlegm or feeling congested* • *chest tightness*

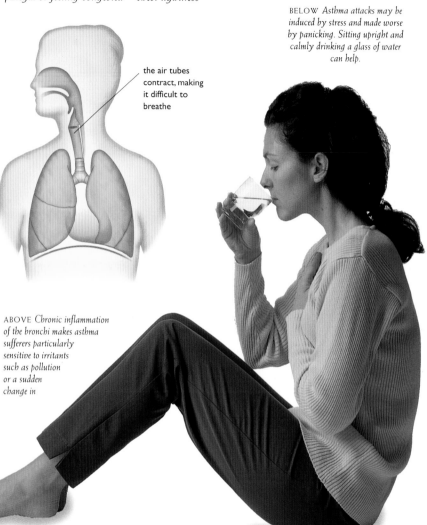

the air tubes contract, making it difficult to breathe

ABOVE *Chronic inflammation of the bronchi makes asthma sufferers particularly sensitive to irritants such as pollution or a sudden change in*

BELOW *Asthma attacks may be induced by stress and made worse by panicking. Sitting upright and calmly drinking a glass of water can help.*

THERAPIES

ACUPRESSURE
• Acupressure works to improve the flow of qi ("life energy") around the body, and may help to relieve asthma symptoms. (See pages 29–31.)

MASSAGE
• Massaging the back with long, flowing strokes and then kneading the shoulders can be helpful, according to therapists. Cupping on the middle and upper back is also a useful technique. (See pages 96–103.)

ACUPUNCTURE
• Therapists believe that needling the end of the meridians for the lungs, kidney, bladder, stomach, and spleen will relieve asthma symptoms. Needling two points on the back or a point on top of the breastbone is also thought to be effective, as is auricular acupuncture (See pages 20–28.)

MEDITATION
• Meditation can lower bodily tension by inducing inner calm. (See page 60–63.)

ALEXANDER TECHNIQUE
• A practitioner of the technique will teach you how to stand upright and improve your posture. This allows the chest to expand fully, so relieving strain and improving breathing. It may also help to clear the airways. (See pages 146–53.)

AROMATHERAPY
• Diluted eucalyptus, juniper, and wintergreen oils can be applied to the chest nightly. (See pages 104–5.)

CHIROPRACTIC
• An asthma attack may make the upper thoracic vertebrae out of alignment, which can put pressure on the lungs and precipitate another attack. Regular soft tissue massage, especially between the shoulderblades, and chiropractic adjustment to the vertebrae, are recommended. (See pages 118–25 and Osteopathy, pages 106–13.)

most exercise-induced asthma does not cause prolonged and intense brochoconstriction and does not do permanent damage to the lungs. In fact, regular exercise, such as swimming, can help to increase lung capacity and strengthen the heart. To exercise safely, carry your bronchodilator with you while you work out. Warm up well before exercise, and avoid exercise on cold, dry days, or if the air quality is poor. Exercise in short bursts and stop to use your inhaler if you begin to wheeze or cough.

Many asthma attacks are brief, but they can sometimes continue for several days. The attack usually begins a few minutes after contact with a triggering agent, but can occur six to eight hours later. Symptoms of asthma may be experienced only intermittently, reflecting changing allergens in the environment, or when a viral infection is present. In its severest form, asthma patients suffer chronic shortness of breath.

During a severe attack, it is important to stay calm. Sit upright, with hands on knees for support. Loosen tight clothing and try to breathe slowly and deeply. Sip a cup of warm water and take a dose of bronchodilator. Call a doctor if the symptoms do not respond quickly.

CONVENTIONAL TREATMENT

ALL ASTHMATICS NEED REGULAR, EFFECTIVE MEDICAL MONITORING. ONCE THE CONDITION HAS BEEN DIAGNOSED, A DOCTOR WILL PRESCRIBE A COMBINATION OF LONG- AND SHORT-TERM DRUG TREATMENTS – AN ANTI-INFLAMMATORY, USUALLY A STEROID, TO CONTROL THE BRONCHI INFLAMMATION AND A BRONCHODILATOR (IN THE FORM OF A NEBULIZER OR AN INHALER) TO OPEN THE AIRWAYS DURING AN ACUTE ASTHMA ATTACK. A PEAK FLOW METER, WHICH MEASURES HOW FAST YOU EXHALE, HELPS TO MONITOR THE STATE OF THE LUNGS AND MAY GIVE WARNING OF THE ONSET OF A SERIOUS ATTACK.

ABOVE *An asthma attack may be triggered by an allergic reaction to a variety of substances, including animal hair and cigarette smoke. If you can identify your particular "trigger", your best course is to avoid it as much as possible.*

THERAPIES

COLOR THERAPY
• During an asthma attack, try the following color combinations: purple on the face, throat and chest to slow the heartrate; scarlet on the kidneys to stimulate the kidneys and adrenals; orange on the throat and chest to act as an antispasmodic. After an attack, try lemon on the front of the body to dissolve blood clots, and magenta on the chest and kidneys to balance emotions and increase energy. *(See pages 248–51.)*

HYDROTHERAPY
• Place a hot, wrung-out towel over the chest and back to relax the breathing muscles. Alternate with a cold compress. Fill a bowl with hot water and add a few drops of eucalyptus oil, lavender or chamomile essential oil to the water. Place a towel over your head and the bowl and inhale the steam but take care – if you start to splutter and cough, stop. Try drinking some hot water with the juice of one clove of garlic. *(See pages 172–9.)*

PSYCHOTHERAPY AND COUNSELING
• Cognitive behavioural therapy can reduce the frequency of attacks in children and help deal with related problems, such as bedwetting, which further increase anxiety. For adults, therapy to combat anxiety can be a key to reducing the seriousness and frequency of attacks. It can also teach you to control stress and cope with the panic associated with asthma attacks. *(See pages 196–9.)*

RELAXATION AND BREATHING
• Learning to relax muscles, especially in the shoulders and abdominal region, while breathing from the diaphragm, can help improve lung function. Try breathing in slowly through the nose, holding the breath half as long again, then slowly exhaling. *(See pages 158–65 and 166–71.)*

ROLFING
• Deep tissue massage will help to break up restrictive patterns in nerves and muscles, which builds up with chronic asthma. *(See pages 134–7 and Hellerwork, pages 138–41.)*

OTHER THERAPIES
• Other therapies thought to help include: shiatsu/do-in *(see pages 132–41)*; autogenic training *(see pages 210–22)*; hypnotherapy *(see pages 218–23)*; and dance movement therapy *(see pages 226–9)*.

VISUALIZATION
• Try to visualize the bronchi in the lungs and form an image of the bronchi tightening during an attack. In this way, you can learn a degree of control over the lungs and, as a result, control your symptoms. Other visualizations can aid relaxation and reduce anxiety. *(See pages 210–11.)*

YOGA
• Studies have shown that yoga can improve lung function and exercise capacity among asthmatics. The combination of stretching and controlled breathing in yoga will strengthen all muscles, including respiratory muscles, encourage relaxed breathing, and help clear airways. Using yogic breathing techniques during an attack will also reduce panic and slow your pulse rate. *(See pages 52–9.)*

LEFT *Yoga's concentration on controlled breathing is shown to be beneficial to asthma sufferers.*

CAUTION

ALWAYS KEEP ASTHMA MEDICINES TO HAND. IF AN ATTACK DOES NOT RESPOND QUICKLY TO SELF-ADMINISTERED TREATMENT, CONSULT A DOCTOR IMMEDIATELY. ASTHMA SUFFERERS SHOULD SEEK MEDICAL ADVICE FOR COUGHS THAT PERSIST LONGER THAN TEN DAYS, OR IF A COUGH IS ACCOMPANIED BY FEVER, DIFFICULTY WITH BREATHING, BLUE LIPS, OR DROWSINESS.

DATAFILE

• There are around 15 million asthma sufferers in the U.S. alone, and over 200 million worldwide. Asthma cases have risen by 75 percent since 1980, with the incidence among very young children increasing by 160 percent.

• More sufferers are found in industrialized nations than in developing countries.

• Drinking a strong cup of coffee may stave off a mild asthma attack. Caffeine is thought to open up the lungs' airways.

• Cockroaches are another common allergen, especially in inner city areas. Up to 58 percent of Americans with allergic asthma are sensitive to these.

Pneumonia

Pneumonia is an acute inflammation of the lung, caused by either a bacterial or virus infection. The disease may affect a part of one lung – lobar pneumonia – or both lungs together. Bronchopneumonia, a generalized infection of both lungs, can be caused by any one a large number of organisms. It is more common in the elderly and in those with preexisting lung disease such as asthma or bronchitis.

Pneumonia either begins as, or is preceded by, an upper respiratory tract infection, such as a cold. The onset of the actual disease can be rapid and dramatic, starting with sudden, violent cold shivers, followed by high fever and profuse sweating. There will be a painful cough and rapid, rasping breathing. Sudden chest pain, aggravated by breathing and coughing, can also be experienced, often only on one side of the body.

This is a serious disease that requires treatment by a qualified medical practitioner. Conventionally, an initial diagnosis is confirmed by chest X-ray, with the subsequent treatment depending on the cause of the disease. Antibiotics are usually prescribed for pneumonia that is bacterial in origin: they may be prescribed for viral pneumonia as well, but only if a secondary infection is suspected. Bacterial pneumonia treated with the appropriate antibiotic usually last between seven to ten days: viral pneumonias, which are usually less serious, normally take a week to heal. In both types, two or three weeks of convalescence may be needed.

In addition to what a doctor will prescribe, there are things you can do for yourself to make yourself feel more comfortable, and encourage the healing process. The first essential is bedrest. Drink plenty of fresh juices and cool water to flush the system, while there are various infusions and inhalations that can be tried to help clear the lungs of the fluid that is blocking them.

Pneumonia is not usually a life-threatening disease for the young and middle-aged, provided that they are reasonably physically fit. However, the disease can be fatal among the elderly, babies and toddlers, and people who are already ill from other causes. This is why prompt medical attention is vital.

SYMPTOMS

- *rapid, shallow breathing* • *chest pain, often only on one side of the body* • *fever, sweating, and violent shivering attacks* • *persistent cough with mucus that possibly may be blood-stained* • *sore throat and headache*

alternate between hot and cold compresses on the forehead and neck

ABOVE *Ginseng has been used in China for thousands of years to strengthen the body's vital energy.*

DATAFILE

- Viruses are thought to cause around half of all types of pneumonia.

- Children under the age of one, people aged over 60, diabetics, smokers, and heavy drinkers are most at risk of contracting the disease.

- There are more than two million cases of pneumonia in the U.S. a year and between 40,000 and 70,000 Americans die annually of the disease.

- The commonest form of bacterial pneumonia is the pneumococcal variety. There are more than 50 other possible causes.

- Anyone who allows himself to get run down is potentially more vulnerable to pneumonia.

THERAPIES

OSTEOPATHY
• Soft-tissue manipulation may help to loosen phlegm and support the body's own self-healing process. Osteopathy should be carried out only by a qualified practitioner. (See pages 106–13 and Chiropractic, pages 118–25.)

HYDROTHERAPY
• Applying a hot-water bottle to the chest and the back daily for half-an-hour may help to ease congestion. Applying hot and cold compresses to the base of the skull and the forehead, swapping them around alternately, can help to soothe headache. (See pages 172–9.)

AROMATHERAPY
• Massages of *niaouli* or *cajeput* may help to ease symptoms. but these should not be given if there is fever present. (See pages 104–5.)

MASSAGE
• Therapists recommend massge of the back and chest to dislodge phlegm. (See pages 96–103.)

LEFT *Aromatherapy oils can be massaged in to ease symptoms.*

Coughs

Coughing can be symptomatic of a mild illness, such as a cold, or simply a natural, involuntary response to clear the air passages of foreign material. Other illnesses of which coughing is a symptom include sinusitis, croup, bronchitis, pneumonia, flu, the first stages of measles, asthma, whooping cough, or an excess of catarrh produced from the nose or sinuses in response to irritation or as a result of infection.

A dry cough is caused by inflammation of the bronchial tubes, itself the result of an infection or an allergy. A loose, wetter cough may be caused by the mucus from infections or colds, or occur as a reaction to pollutants in the atmosphere, a foreign object, or nervousness constricting the throat. A constant nighttime cough, or one which recurs with each cold and is hard to get rid of, may be an indication of asthma. Heavy smokers often suffer from an early-morning cough.

Persistent coughs, accompanied by chest pains or other symptoms, such as a fever, may be indicative of a serious respiratory illness. In such a case, consult a doctor. Otherwise, many coughs respond well to home treatment. Simply raising the end of the bed can help to ease coughing at night, as will inhaling jasmine or pine, or burning the essential oil in a room. Carrot juice mixed with honey and a little warm water is a traditional remedy that can be taken by the spoonful throughout the day.

RIGHT *There are many different kinds of cough and the majority usually respond well to home remedies.*

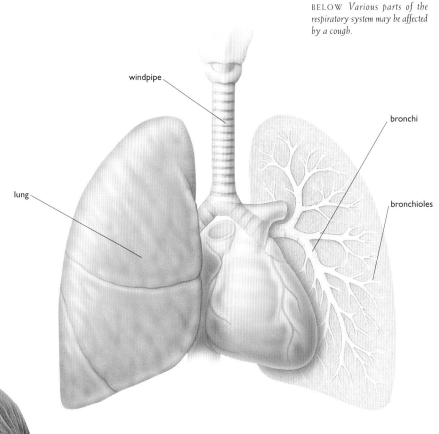

BELOW *Various parts of the respiratory system may be affected by a cough.*

windpipe

bronchi

lung

bronchioles

a dry cough is the result of an inflammation in the lungs

a damp cough may be a reaction to a foreign body

CONVENTIONAL TREATMENT

A DOCTOR WILL CHECK TO ENSURE THAT THE COUGH IS NOT A SYMPTOM OF A MORE SERIOUS UNDERLYING CONDITION. IF NOT, YOU WILL BE ADVISED TO KEEP WARM AND TAKE A SUITABLE COUGH LINCTUS UNTIL THE CONDITION PASSES.

CAUTION

IF A COUGH IS ACCOMPANIED BY A FEVER, YOU HAVE DIFFICULTY IN BREATHING, YOUR LIPS ARE BLUE, YOU SUFFER FROM DROWSINESS OR HAVE DIFFICULTY IN SPEAKING, YOU SHOULD CONTACT A DOCTOR. YOU SHOULD ALSO CONTACT ONE IF A COUGH LASTS FOR MORE THAN TEN DAYS.

THERAPIES

AROMATHERAPY
• Massaging frankincense or sandalwood into the chest and back can help relieve symptoms. The latter is especially good for dry coughs. (*See pages 104–5.*)

HYDROTHERAPY
• Apply hot and cold compresses to the chest and upper back. (*See pages 172–9.*)

ACUPUNCTURE
• Practitioners believe that coughs are caused by an imbalance in the energy flow in the lungs, which they correct by stimulating the acupoints on the Lung meridian in the arms. (*See pages 20–28.*)

OTHER THERAPIES
• Other therapies that may help include: Ayurveda (*see pages 78–85*); Osteopathy (*see pages 106–13*); Chiropractic (*see pages 118–25*); Relaxation techniques (*see pages 158–65*); Breathing techniques (*see pages 166–71*).

297

Flu

A viral infection of the respiratory tract, flu, more properly known as influenza, is transmitted by contaminated droplets, usually via sneezing and coughing. Incubation of the virus takes one or two days, during which time it is infectious and can be spread rapidly. The problem with the condition is that the viruses that cause it are like chameleons, quickly adapting to changed conditions. This is why flu vaccinations are not 100 percent effective as they can only protect people against specific strains of the disease. Their effectiveness lessens the older you are: statistics show that, in the elderly, only 50 percent of those vaccinated are fully protected. Two new super-vaccinations scheduled for launch may offer complete protection. Vaccinations are recommended for the very old, women intending to become pregnant, diabetics, bronchitis sufferers, and those with weak immune systems.

Flu usually lasts about a week. The symptoms are similar to those of the common cold, but are more severe. In addition to sneezing, coughing and fever, flu sufferers experience muscular aches and pains, headache, sweating and shivering, sore throat, and painful breathing, as well as nausea and loss of appetite.

Doctors recommend bedrest, upping fluid intake, and taking painkillers. Antihistamines and decongestants may help to reduce mucus. Some practitioners advise "megadosing" with powdered vitamin C as soon as the infection becomes apparent but, although vitamin C undoubtedly encourages healing, helps to fight infection, and boosts the action of the immune system, there is no hard evidence that megadoses are effective.

In some cases, secondary infections, such as bronchitis, set in after flu. Fighting off this type of infection takes a heavy toll on the body, and patients may feel symptoms of fatigue and mild depression for several weeks as a result.

DATAFILE

- There are three classes of virus – A, B, and C. Type C confers immunity on the patient. Types A and B may change their structure every two or three years, so that our bodies cannot build up resistance against them.

- New strains of the virus spread rapidly around the world, infecting millions of people and causing many deaths. Widespread epidemics occur approximately every ten years.

- Antibiotics are not effective against viral infections, such as flu. They will work against secondary bacterial infections, such as bacterial bronchitis.

- Children are most at risk, due to low exposure to virus strains.

- More people died in the flu epidemic of 1918 than were killed on the battlefields during the whole of the First World War.

SYMPTOMS

- *fever, and sometimes shivering* • *sore throat and cough*
- *runny nose and sneezing* • *breathlessness and weakness*
- *headache, stiff and aching joints, muscular pain* • *nausea and loss of appetite* • *insomnia and depression*

breathing difficulties are one of the more distressing symptoms of flu

LEFT *Although the symptoms are superficially similar, flu is more than a bad cold. It can cause muscular aches and pains, sweating, and shivering.*

THERAPIES

ACUPRESSURE
• Bladder pressure points to the right of the spine will clear and balance the respiratory system. Large Intestine 4 relieves congestion and headaches: squeeze your right thumb and forefinger together, forming a ridge on your hand above the thumb. The point is in the middle of that ridge, just above the end of the crease formed by thumb and forefinger. Lung 7, on the wrist just below the pad of the thumb, clears upper respiratory tract infections. *(See pages 29–31.)*

ACUPUNCTURE
• Moxibustion is recommended by acupuncturists. The moxa herb is lit and held over the acupoint to generate heat and improve the flow of qi. *(See pages 20–28.)*

AROMATHERAPY
• Massage tea tree and geranium oil into the chest and head to reduce symptoms and fight infection. *(See pages 104–5.)*

AYURVEDA
• Impregnate a cloth with a mixture of 1 part mustard oil to 40 parts alcohol. Press the cloth to your forehead to reduce fever. You can also try sunflower, coriander and bitter orange. *(See pages 78–85.)*

HYDROTHERAPY
• To relieve the aches and pains associated with flu, stand in the shower and direct warm water on to your calves for a few minutes, then blast briefly with cold water. Add a few drops of eucalyptus to a sponge and rub over your body in the shower or bathtub, breathing in the soothing vapors. *(See pages 172–9.)*

MASSAGE
• Massage the bridge of your nose with your thumbs to help clear the sinuses. Massaging the feet is also comforting. According to therapists, it helps to bring energy down from the head to aid healing. *(See pages 96–103.)*

CAUTION

DO NOT GIVE A CHILD OR TEENAGER ASPIRIN IF THEY HAVE FLU. THE COMBINATION OF ASPIRIN AND VIRAL INFECTION IS ASSOCIATED WITH REYE'S SYNDROME, A DISEASE AFFECTING THE BRAIN AND LIVER. TAKE SMALL DOSES OF ACETAMINOPHEN INSTEAD. PREGNANT WOMEN SHOULD AVOID ASPIRIN.

CONVENTIONAL TREATMENT

BEDREST, DRINKING PLENTY OF FLUID, PAINKILLERS, SUCH AS ASPIRIN OR PARACETOMOL, ANTIHISTAMINES AND DECONGESTANTS ARE RECOMMENDED TO REDUCE MUCUS. IF SECONDARY INFECTION SETS IN, A DOCTOR MAY PRESCRIBE ANTIBIOTICS.

Bronchitis

An inflammation of the mucus lining of the bronchi (the lungs' air tubes). There are two varieties – acute and chronic. Acute bronchitis usually follows a bout of flu or a cold, often in conjunction with a cold, damp, or polluted environment. Bronchitis can be viral or bacterial in cause. However, only bacteria, which may infect after the onset of viral infection, cause thick, yellow-green (infected) mucus. Chronic bronchitis can follow repeated acute attacks, but generally develops gradually, particualrly in smokers and the elderly. The mucous membrane becomes permanently thickened, blocking the tubes and causing breathlessness and a persistent cough. It is also linked to long-term inhalation of dust, smoke, and environmental pollutants.

Both types of bronchitis require medical supervision to diagnose whether the causes are bacterial, viral, or if the condition is chronic. A doctor will only prescribe antibiotics if the causes are bacterial and a sputum test may be needed to confirm this. A straightforward case of bronchitis lasts about one week and will require bedrest, fluids and painkillers such as acetaminophen, to reduce pain and fever. The cough may persist for a while longer.

CONVENTIONAL TREATMENT

BEDREST AND PAINKILLERS ARE RECOMMENDED TO REDUCE FEVER AND PAIN. EXPECTORANTS MAY HELP TO LOOSEN PHLEGM AND CLEAR THE LUNGS. A DOCTOR WILL PRESCRIBE ANTIBIOTICS IF THE CAUSE OF THE INFECTION IS BACTERIAL OR TO GUARD AGAINST SECONDARY BACTERIAL INFECTION. A YEARLY FLU VACCINATION IS ADVISED FOR PATIENTS WITH CHRONIC BRONCHITIS. THEY ARE ALSO STRONGLY ADVISED TO LOSE EXCESS WEIGHT AND, IF THEY SMOKE, TO STOP.

CAUTION

CALL A DOCTOR IF A PATIENT'S TEMPERATURE RISES ABOVE 102°F, OR IF HE STARTS TO COUGH UP BLOOD.

DATAFILE

• Quitting smoking will reduce your risk of contracting bronchitis – smokers are 50 times more susceptible to the disease.

• Acute bronchitis is usually caused by the same viruses that cause the common cold or flu.

• Male bronchitis sufferers outnumber females by ten to one.

SYMPTOMS

• *Cough, dry at first, but later bringing up yellow-green phlegm* • *chest pain* • *fever* • *breathlessness and wheezing*

ABOVE *A home-made steam bath can be contrived from covering your head with a towel and breathing in the fumes from a bowl of hot water infused with eucalyptus.*

THERAPIES

ACUPUNCTURE
• Practitioners believe acupuncture causes the muscular walls to dilate to allow the remaining lung tissue to function efficiently. Acupuncturists in China have recently claimed that up to 50 percent of bronchitics benefit from their acupuncture treatments. Chronic sufferers need to have therapy repeated regularly to maintain its effect. (See pages 20–28.)

ACUPRESSURE
• Clasp your hands together, touching your upper wrist with your forefinger. The point is found on a line with the thumb, in a small depression. Unclasp your hands and apply pressure to this point. Press on a point on the crease of the inside of the elbow, on the thumb side. (See pages 29–31.)

AYURVEDA
• Apply a cloth impregnated with mustard oil to the forehead to reduce a fever. First rectify the oil with alcohol (one part oil to 40 parts alcohol). (See pages 78–85.)

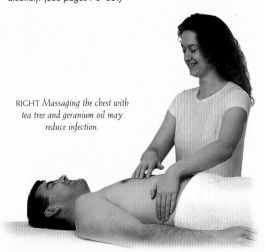

RIGHT *Massaging the chest with tea tree and geranium oil may reduce infection.*

MASSAGE
• Tapping the back and chest can help dislodge phlegm and improve the breathing of chronic bronchitics. (See pages 96–103.)

OSTEOPATHY
• Massage of the soft tissues of the neck, shoulders, chest and back aids relaxation and makes breathing easier. (See pages 106–13 and Chiropractic, pages 118–25.)

HYDROTHERAPY
• Steam, in the form of a sauna, steam bath or inhalator (use with care if asthmatic), will ease chest congestion. Put a few drops of essential oil on a tissue and take into the sauna or steam bath, or add a few drops of an essential oil to the inhalator: eucalyptus (expectorant), tea tree (antiseptic) or thyme (antiseptic and expectorant), or lavender (relaxes muscles and aids breathing). (See pages 172–9.)

RELAXATION AND BREATHING
• A therapist can teach methods to improve lung capacity and help you use your lungs and chest more efficiently. Ayurvedic breathing exercises and yoga (see pages 52–9) are particularly useful. Chronic sufferers will find relaxation techniques and deep breathing helpful in controlling the anxiety associated with breathlessness. (See pages 158–65 and 166–71.)

Common Cold

The common cold is a highly contagious viral infection that is at its most prevalent in winter, though common all the year round. A cold can be caused by many different viruses – up to 200 have been identified – which, as they are constantly changing, means that it is practically impossible to build up a complete immunity to infection, though adults are usually less vulnerable. People particularly at risk are the elderly, young children and babies, and people who are already suffering from another illness or disease.

The virus affects the whole of the upper respiratory tract, the walls of which swell and produce excess mucus, giving rise to the typical symptoms of a stuffy or runny nose, throat discomfort, malaise, and occasional coughing. The mucus is loaded with viruses, so the air breathed out, coughed, or sneezed may infect others in the vicinity.

A cold takes one to three days to develop and usually runs its course in three to seven days. Children and the elderly are susceptible to further infections, such as sinusitis, ear inflammations, and bronchitis. There is no medical cure, so the best thing to do is to get plenty of rest, drink lots of fluids, such as ginger tea and hot lemon and honey, and take regular doses of painkillers if necessary. Nose drops are not generally recommended, because although these may bring some immediate relief, they can cause the nose to become more blocked in the long term.

peppermint oil can be massaged on the face

ABOVE *Peppermint is a good decongestant and can ease the symptoms of a cold.*

SYMPTOMS

• *sneezing* • *runny nose* • *raised temperature* • *sore throat* • *dry cough* • *headache* • *lack of appetite and energy*

THERAPIES

AROMATHERAPY
• A facial and throat massage with diluted tea tree, peppermint or rosemary essential oils may help relieve cold symptoms. *(See pages 104–105.)*

ACUPRESSURE
• A range of pressure points relieve cold symptoms. Try the point on the middle of the sole of the foot, just behind the ball, and the point below the brow ridge at the corner of the eye nearest the bridge of the nose. *(See pages 29–31.)*

AROMATHERAPY
• Try a steam inhalation (asthmatics should use with care) with antiviral essential oils, such as eucalyptus, lavender, or tea tree. An inhalation of peppermint oil can also ease congestion and coughs. *(See pages 172–9.)*

YOGA
• Practitioners believe that yoga boosts the immune system and reduces the frequency of catching colds. Breathing techniques can also increase the resistance of the respiratory tract. Do not perform yoga stretches while you have a fever – do static relaxation poses and gentle pranayama (yogic breathing). *(See pages 52–9.)*

RELAXATION TECHNIQUES
• Relaxation will improve your breathing and make it easier to deal with a cold. Lie on your back with arms and legs slightly apart. Close your eyes and relax your body stage by stage, beginning from the toes and working up to your head. Inhale deeply throughout. *(See pages 158–65.)*

DATAFILE

• Susceptibility to cold viruses is closely linked to high stress levels.

• The disease is transmitted through infected mucus, so keep away from people who are coughing and sneezing and wash your hands frequently.

• Eat well, take regular exercise, and get plenty of sleep to boost your natural resistance to infection.

CAUTION

VISIT YOUR DOCTOR IF A FEVER CONTINUES OVER 101°F FOR MORE THAN 72 HOURS OR YOU HAVE SYMPTOMS OF SECONDARY INFECTIONS IN THE LUNGS, EARS OR SINUSES. DO NOT GIVE ASPIRIN TO CHILDREN OR TEENAGERS. YOU SHOULD ALSO CONSULT A DOCTOR IF A CHILD STARTS CRYING AND WILL NOT STOP, IF SHE BECOMES DROWSY AND UNRESPONSIVE, IS SICK MORE THAN TWICE, OR SEEMS TO BE HAVING BREATHING DIFFICULTIES.

CONVENTIONAL TREATMENT

RECOMMENDED TREATMENT INCLUDES BEDREST IF YOUR TEMPERATURE IS RAISED, PLENTY OF FLUIDS, ANTIHISTAMINES TO REDUCE INFLAMMATION, DECONGESTANTS, AND COUGH MEDICINES AS NEEDED.

catching your sneeze can help stop germs spreading

LEFT *A runny nose and sneezing are classic symptoms of a cold.*

BELOW *Like sore throats, the symptoms of a cold may be relieved by drinking hot lemon or ginger tea.*

Hyperventilation

Hyperventilation is the act of breathing more rapidly and shallowly than normal. This causes the level of carbon dioxide in the blood to drop, leading to faintness, numbness, and muscle tension. Acute attacks of hyperventilation can be brought on by emotional or physical trauma. Attacks also occur as a result of anxiety, after physical exertion, or at high altitude. It may also be the body's response to high levels of acidity in the blood – as a result of aspirin overdose, for example – untreated diabetes, or kidney failure.

If you begin to hyperventilate, stay calm. Loosely cover your nose and mouth with a paper bag: breathe slowly into it and rebreathe the air about 10 times to increase carbon dioxide levels. Breathe normally for a couple of minutes then repeat the process if necessary.

SYMPTOMS

• *lack of air* • *numb arms, legs, mouth* • *visual changes*
• *muscle tension in forearms and calves* • *loss of consciousness*

CONVENTIONAL TREATMENT

RECOMMENDED TREATMENT INCLUDES COGNITIVE-BEHAVIORAL THERAPY; BETA-BLOCKER DRUGS TO HELP CONTROL PHYSICAL SYMPTOMS.

CAUTION

IF YOU EXPERIENCE CHEST PAINS AND/OR PAIN THAT SPREADS TO THE ARM, NECK, OR JAW, SEEK MEDICAL HELP.

LEFT *To relieve an attack of hyperventilation, breathe slowly into a paper bag about 10 times.*

THERAPIES

BREATHING TECHNIQUES
• Controlled breathing techniques will help you to reduce anxiety before stressful events. *(See pages 166–71.)*

PSYCHOTHERAPY AND COUNSELING
• Cognitive-behavioral therapy helps to dispel the fear associated with hyperventilation and panic attacks. Humanistic and transpersonal therapies are also recommended *(See pages 196–205.)*

MEDITATION
• Learn meditation and practice it every day to relieve stress and encourage positive thoughts. *(See pages 60–63.)*

RELAXATION TECHNIQUES
• Hyperventilation is often triggered by anxiety. If you are stressed, daily muscle relaxation sessions may help you deal with the condition. *(See pages 158–65.)*

Hiccups

Irritation of the nerves in the diaphragm that leads to a sudden inhalation of air. The diaphragm contracts and the vocal cords close, producing the characteristic sound. A bout of hiccups usually last only a few minutes, with a brief interval between attacks.

Hiccups can result from eating too quickly, drinking too many carbonated drinks, alcoholism, stress, excitement, stomach irritation, toxins, temperature changes, or pregnancy. Although they can hurt, hiccups are not themselves harmful. In rare cases, however, they may be a symptom of hiatus hernia, pneumonia, or pleurisy.

There is no shortage of home remedies for hiccups. One of the most reliable is to swallow a teaspoon of dry sugar slowly. Alternatively, eat a small piece of dry bread slowly; suck on a piece of lemon; drink a glass of water quickly; swallow a small amount of finely cracked ice; hold your tongue with your thumb and index finger and gently pull it forward; or ask a friend to say "boo" and surprise you into breathing normally.

SYMPTOMS

• *a sound caused by abrupt contraction of the diaphragm and closure of the vocal chords* • *may be chest pain*

THERAPIES

RELAXATION AND BREATHING
• Relaxation and breathing techniques may help to relieve hiccups. Deep slow breathing is the best way to get an attack to pass. Try holding a paper bag over your nose and mouth and breathe in and out slowly. Playing long notes on a wind instrument may also help. Bend your head backward and hold your breath for a count of ten. Exhale immediately and drink a glass of water. *(See pages 166–71.)*

MASSAGE
• Massage the back of the roof of your mouth with a cotton swab. A finger works just as well. *(See pages 96–103.)*

CAUTION

SEEK EMERGENCY AID IF THE HICCUPS ARE ACCOMPANIED BY ABDOMINAL PAIN AND SPITTING UP OF BLOOD OR BLOOD IN THE STOOLS.

CONVENTIONAL TREATMENT

HICCUPS DO NOT REQUIRE MEDICAL TREATMENT UNLESS THE BOUT LASTS FOR MORE THAN EIGHT HOURS IN AN ADULT OR THREE HOURS IN A CHILD. A PROTRACTED BOUT OF HICCUPS CAN LEAD TO EXHAUSTION.

ABOVE *Slowly swallowing a teaspoonful of dry sugar is a frequently recommended remedy for hiccups.*

DATAFILE

• An American farmer suffered from hiccups for 65 years – the longest known bout of hiccups in history.

• Some researchers believe that hiccups are triggered automatically by a "hiccup center" in the brain in order to stop you choking on food or drink.

HEART, BLOOD, AND CIRCULATION

High Blood Pressure

Blood pressure is raised when the pressure exerted by the blood on the walls of the arteries in which it travels is greater than normal. This indicates that the heart is working harder than usual to pump blood around the body. In healthy people, blood pressure falls when resting and rises in response to stress, physical exertion, or perceived danger. Sustained high blood pressure (hypertension), even when at rest, can damage the cardiovascular system, which increases the risk of stroke, coronary artery disease, and heart failure, as well as damage to the brain, kidneys, and eyes.

It is difficult to diagnose mild hypertension, because the condition is symptomless. For this reason, doctors advise everyone aged over 40 to have their blood pressure monitored, especially if there is a family history of hypertension or if other factors, such as kidney disease, diabetes, or being overweight put you at risk. If the pressure is above normal limits on three separate check-ups, then hypertension is the likely cause.

Adopting a healthy lifestyle is the most effective way to combat mild hypertension. Switch to a low-fat, high-fiber diet, rich in fruits and vegetables, and keep your weight at a healthy level. Stop smoking, and reduce consumption of alcohol, salt, and caffeine. Some practitioners recommend dietary supplements of potassium, calcium, and magnesium. Regular exercise and relaxation techniques will also help.

SYMPTOMS

• *mild hypertension – no symptoms* • *severe hypertension – headaches, breathlessness, dizziness and disturbed vision, fatigue, insomnia*

CAUTION

IF YOU HAVE BEEN PRESCRIBED ANTIHYPERTENSIVE DRUGS, CONSULT YOUR DOCTOR BEFORE TAKING DIETARY SUPPLEMENTS OR HERBAL REMEDIES, OR BEFORE STARTING AN EXERCISE PROGRAM.

CONVENTIONAL TREATMENT

A DOCTOR MAY RECOMMEND LIFESTYLE AND DIET CHANGES (MAINTAINING A HEALTHY WEIGHT, STOPPING SMOKING, EXERCISING REGULARLY) AND DRUG THERAPY, INCLUDING BETA-BLOCKERS, DIURETICS, AND VASODILATORS.

ABOVE *Qigong and t'ai-chi practitioners believe that these therapies are very helpful for blood pressure problems. They enable you to achieve more with less effort.*

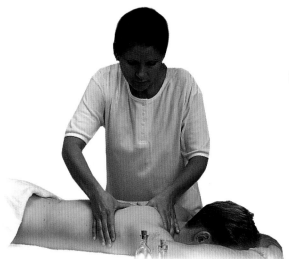

LEFT *The soothing effects of an aromatherapy massage can help to lower blood pressure.*

THERAPIES

AROMATHERAPY
• A slow, stroking massage with sedative essential oils, such as marjoram, lavender, geranium, sandalwood, rose, or clary sage, is recommended to help reduce high blood pressure by relaxing muscle tension. *(See pages 104–5 and Massage, pages 96–103.)*

BIOFEEDBACK
• During therapy, you learn how to monitor your blood pressure as you relax and thereby how to reach and recognize a relaxed state whenever the need arises. *(See pages 212–13.)*

BREATHING TECHNIQUES
• Slow, even breathing encourages muscle relaxation and helps to reduce stress levels. *(See pages 166–71.)*

QIGONG
• Meditation and gentle exercise are thought to lower blood pressure by improving the flow of chi. T'ai chi ch'uan is thought to work similarly. *(See pages 44–5 and pages 46–51.)*

VISUALIZATION
• Patients learn how to create mental pictures of soothing, comforting scenes, which create calm and relaxed feelings and reduce stress. *(See pages 214–7.)*

OTHER THERAPIES
• Practitioners believe the following therapies may help the condition: acupuncture *(see pages 20–28)*; meditation *(see pages 60–63)*; reflexology *(see pages 66–71)*; healing *(see pages 86–7)*; therapeutic touch *(see pages 90–91)*; autogenic training *(see pages 210–11)*; hypnotherapy *(see pages 218–23)*; color therapy *(see pages 248–51)*.

BELOW *A healthy, low-fat diet plays a major part in blood pressure control. Being overweight is a common cause of high blood pressure.*

DATAFILE

• 50 million Americans suffer from hypertension. It is estimated that one-third of them are unaware of their condition.

• Some practitioners advise eating raw garlic to reduce blood pressure.

• Normal blood pressure is not an absolute but a range, depending on the sex, age, and general fitness of the patient. Most doctors woud recommend lifestyle changes for those whose blood presssure is consistently 140/90 mm Hg or above.

• The condition is more common among the middle-aged (about 10 percent are affected) and among men.

Low Blood Pressure

Low blood pressure (hypotension) can lead to a reduction in the supply of blood to the brain, which can cause dizziness and fainting. It may be caused by the heart's failure to maintain the pressure, a loss of fluid from the circulation, pregnancy, general ill health, diabetes, lack of food, heat exhaustion, antidepressant drugs, or an excessive dose of an antihypertensive drug. Severe hemorrhage, burns, and gastroenteritis can also reduce blood pressure. A sudden drop when standing up is known as postural hypotension: the best way to combat this is to change position slowly.

If you suffer frequently from low blood pressure, your doctor may want to run some tests to identify the cause.

SYMPTOMS

• *dizziness and fainting* • *dilated pupils*

THERAPIES

HYDROTHERAPY
• Therapists believe that a cold shower or bath boosts the circulation by causing the blood vessels to constrict and then dilate as the blood starts pumping again normally. They may also recommend sitz baths, unless you have a heart condition. A flannel wrap treatment may also be recommended for circulatory problems. *(See pages 172–9.)*

AROMATHERAPY
• Regular massage with stimulating oils, such as black pepper, lemon or sage, can help to control blood pressure. *(See pages 104–5.)*

OTHER THERAPIES
• The following therapies may help to alleviate the condition: therapeutic touch *(see pages 90–91)* and color therapy *(see pages 248–51).*

CONVENTIONAL TREATMENT

IN SEVERE, PERSISTENT CASES, A DOCTOR MAY PRESCRIBE DRUGS TO RAISE BLOOD PRESSURE.

LEFT *Inhaling rosemary and peppermint oil can bring quick relief from the symptoms of low blood pressure.*

Anemia

Anemia is a reduction in the blood's ability to carry oxygen, caused by low levels of either hemoglobin (an oxygen-carrying chemical) or red blood cells in the blood. At first, the effects of anemia are unnoticeable. As the condition progresses, however, the sufferer may appear pale, feel tired, and become dizzy or faint. Severe anemia can lead to an irregular or increased heartrate as the heart pumps more blood to try to compensate for the lack of oxygen.

Most cases of anemia are related to iron deficiency, which can be treated with iron supplements and increasing the amount of food containing iron. Pregnancy, breast-feeding a baby and blood loss from the gastrointestinal tract, due to an ulcer or cancer, can also deplete stores of iron. Lack of dietary iron is rarely a primary cause of anemia, but can exacerbate the problem. Anemia may also be caused by deficiencies in folic acid or vitamin B12, or as a result of genetic defects. Alcohol, some infections, and certain antibiotics or anti-inflammatory drugs can also cause anemia.

SYMPTOMS

• *weakness and fatigue* • *breathlessness* • *pale skin and lips* • *headaches and dizziness* • *fainting* • *irritability* • *recurrent infections* • *lack of concentration* • *loss of appetite*

DATAFILE

• Iron is an essential component of hemoglobin.

• In the U.S., 20 percent of women of childbearing age have iron-deficiency anemia, often due to heavy menstrual bleeding.

• Over-reliance on aspirin, which causes stomach bleeding, may be a cause of iron-deficiency anemia.

THERAPIES

AYURVEDA
• Practitioners believe that anemia is due to an imbalance of pitta, one of the three essential energies. They recommend purification, or panchakarma, through diet, massage, and purging using a mild laxative rich in iron called punarnava mandura. *(See pages 78–85.)*

HYDROTHERAPY
• High-powered water jets may be recommended as a method of stimulating the internal organs. *(See pages 172–9.)*

SHIATSU
• Practitioners attempt to rebalance energies along the spleen and stomach meridians in order to treat both anemia and underlying menstrual problems. *(See pages 32–7 and Do-in, pages 38–41.)*

YOGA
• Yoga may help to restore hormonal imbalances that lead to heavy menstrual bleeding. During your period, practice breathing and relaxation techniques only, not the stretches. Inverted asanas (poses) should not be performed during menstruation. *(See pages 52–9.)*

ACUPUNCTURE
• Acupoints on the back, lower trunk, arm and leg will be stimulated. Moxibustion may also be given in the same areas. *(See pages 20–28.)*

CAUTION

ALWAYS SEEK MEDICAL ADVICE IF YOU SUSPECT YOU ARE ANEMIC, BECAUSE THE CONDITION CANNOT BE TREATED SUCCESSFULLY WITHOUT ESTABLISHING ITS UNDERLYING CAUSE. DO NOT PRACTICE INVERTED YOGA POSES IF YOU ARE PREGNANT OR SUFFER FROM HIGH BLOOD PRESSURE.

CONVENTIONAL TREATMENT

A DOCTOR MAY RECOMMEND BLOOD MONITORING, ADVICE ON DIET, AND SUPPLEMENTS OF IRON, FOLIC ACID, OR VITAMIN B12, AND TREATMENT OF THE UNDERLYING CAUSE, FOR EXAMPLE, HORMONES TO LESSEN MENSTRUAL BLEEDING.

ABOVE *Iron-rich foods and supplements are frequently recommended to combat anaemia.*

Angina

Angina is a constricting chest pain that occurs in spasms as a result of a reduction in the bloodflow through the coronary arteries supplying the heart. This happens because the arteries carrying the blood are too narrow for an adequate flow in certain conditions and circumstances.

The pain is like someone sitting on the chest, or like drawing a tight band around it. It usually starts across the upper part of the front of the chest, from which it can spread to the jaw, down the left arm, and sometimes down the right arm as well. The pain most commonly occurs after a heavy meal, physical exertion, during cold weather, and as a result of emotion, brought on, say, by an argument, or a sudden shock. Groups likely to be susceptible to the condition include smokers, the overweight, and diabetics. Attacks usually last a few minutes: if the angina is left untreated, they usually recur. With treatment, the frequency of the attacks can be reduced and, at best, they may stop completely. In the event of an attack, the first thing to do is to sit down and rest, or, if you are walking in the street, to stand still. If the attacks are linked to emotional stress, you should try to reduce this as much as possible. If they happen during physical exertion, stop what you are doing and do not attempt to resume it, as further activity during an attack can be harmful. Taking a mild sedative may help, if this is feasible. Look out for patterns in the attacks and try to avoid the situations that trigger them. If you smoke, stop. Cut back on rich, heavy meals. Try to keep your weight normal – or lose it if you need to.

Because the risk of heart attack increases if the arteries continue to narrow, anyone who suffers a first attack of angina should consult a doctor as soon as possible. If the condition has been medically diagnosed, you should also call the doctor if the pain lasts longer than usual. Pain lasting for longer than ten minutes should be treated as a medical emergency. Conventional treatment is to prescribe drugs to dilate the arteries, so improving the flow of blood to the heart. Other medications may be prescribed to lower the blood pressure, while a program of moderate, controlled exercise to strengthen the heart may also be suggested. In severe cases, surgery may be advised.

SYMPTOMS

• *constricting pains in the upper chest, which can spread up the neck, down the left arm and, sometimes, down the right arm as well* • *pains often accompanied by feelings of exhaustion, choking, suffocation, and nausea*

CONVENTIONAL TREATMENT

DRUGS SUCH AS GLYCERYL TRINITRATE OR BETA-BLOCKERS MAY BE PRESCRIBED TO PREVENT OR TO TREAT ATTACKS. ASPIRIN MAY BE PRESCRIBED TO REDUCE THE RISK OF A CLOT FORMING IN THE NARROWED CORONARY VESSELS. YOU MAY ALSO BE ADVISED TO GO ON A LOW-FAT DIET. IF THERE IS A DANGER OF THE CORONARY ARTERIES BECOMING COMPLETELY BLOCKED, A CORONARY BYPASS OPERATION OR ANGIOPLASTY MAY BE NECESSARY.

CAUTION

NO CHEST PAINS SHOULD BE TREATED BY COMPLEMENTARY THERAPIES UNTIL THEIR CAUSE HAS BEEN FULLY ESTABLISHED. PROLONGED OR SEVERE CASES OF ANGINA CAN BE A PRECURSOR OF A HEART ATTACK AND SHOULD RECEIVE URGENT MEDICAL ATTENTION.

RIGHT *Do not ignore the symptoms of angina. Left untreated, attacks are likely to recur and may eventually lead to a heart attack.*

although pain starts in the chest, it may spread to the jaw

pain may also travel down the left arm

THERAPIES

ACUPUNCTURE
• Acupuncturists believe that angina often arises because of excessive yang in the body. Treatment is aimed at restoring the correct balance of yin and yang, and to relieve pain, and aid relaxation. *(See pages 20–28.)*

OSTEOPATHY
• Tensions in the neck, shoulders and back can serve to aggravate the chest pains. Both osteopathy and chiropractic can relieve these muscular tensions. *(See pages 106–13 and Chiropractic, pages 118–25.)*

RELAXATION TECHNIQUES
• Practicing basic relaxation techniques will help you to unwind and release the stress and other mental tensions that may be contributing to the attacks. *(See pages 158–65.)* Other recommended relaxation therapies include yoga *(see pages 52–9),* meditation *(see pages 60–63),* the Alexander technique *(see pages 146–53)* and autogenic training *(see pages 210–11).*

QIGONG
• This gentle form of exercise is recommended for relaxation and breathing control, and has been scientifically proven to boost the functioning of the cardiovascular, nervous, and respiratory systems. *(See pages 44–5 and T'ai chi ch'uan, pages 46–51.)*

REFLEXOLOGY
• Massaging the appropriate reflex areas in the feet is thought to help to reduce raised blood pressure and so help in the treatment of angina. *(See pages 66–71.)*

Atherosclerosis

Atherosclerosis is a degenerative disease of the arteries. Fatty deposits that develop on the artery walls harden and enlarge into raised circular areas called plaques, which eventually, if left untreated, partially or wholly block the affected arteries. The condition starts in early adult life and increases with age. Along with thrombosis (where blood becomes solid and forms a clot), it is the main cause of heart disease and strokes. Contributory factors to its development include smoking, high blood pressure, stress, heredity, diabetes and, according to some experts, high cholesterol levels in the blood.

The condition is symptomless until it reaches the stage when the constriction actually starts to interfere with the blood circulation. What happens then varies, depending on where the atherosclerosis is sited. If the coronary arteries are affected, the heart can be deprived of the oxygen and nutrients it needs to work properly. Without treatment, this can lead to angina and, eventually, to a heart attack. Similarly, atherosclerosis in the cerebral arteries can lead to a stroke.

Conventionally, drugs may be prescribed to improve bloodflow, reduce the risk of blood clots forming, lower cholesterol levels and lessen the strain on the heart. If the coronary arteries are seriously affected, bypass surgery or angioplasty may be necessary. Self-help measures include following a low-fat diet, giving up smoking , and learning to manage stress. Taking aspirin in prescribed doses is also recommended: aspirin reduces the stickiness of the blood platelets, making them less likely to come together to form a clot. Avoid overeating: part of any excess food that is eaten is deposited as fat in the arteries. Exercise may help – but you should consult your doctor before starting any exercise program – especially if you have not exercised regularly for a prolonged period.

SYMPTOMS

• *narrowed coronary arteries: chest pain on exertion*
• *blocked coronary arteries: sudden onset of severe, persistent chest pains* • *narrowed cerebral arteries: temporary disturbances of balance, vision, speech, and use of the arms and legs* • *blocked cerebral arteries: speech impairment, loss of use of limbs, unconsciousness*

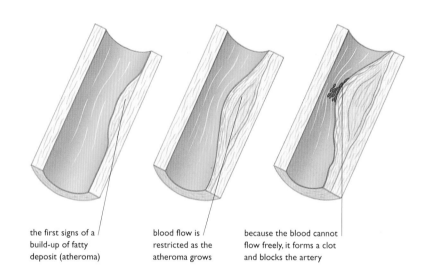

the first signs of a build-up of fatty deposit (atheroma)

blood flow is restricted as the atheroma grows

because the blood cannot flow freely, it forms a clot and blocks the artery

CONVENTIONAL TREATMENT

BLOOD TESTS, X-RAYS AND OTHER EXAMINATIONS TO ASSESS THE SEVERITY OF THE CONDITION AND WHICH ARTERIES ARE AFFECTED. ANTICOAGULANTS MAY BE PRESCRIBED TO LESSEN THE RISK OF BLOOD CLOTS FORMING, TOGETHER WITH OTHER DRUGS TO IMPROVE BLOODFLOW AND LOWER CHOLESTEROL LEVELS. SURGICAL OPTIONS IN EXTREME CASES ARE A BYPASS OPERATION OR ANGIOPLASTY.

THERAPIES

AROMATHERAPY
• Regular massage with juniper and lemon may help to break down fatty deposits in the body. Massage with essential oils of peppermint, lavender, rose and marjoram, may help to strengthen the heart, though, if you are pregnant, avoid the marjoram. (See pages 104–5.)

T'AI CHI CH'UAN
• Gentle t'ai chi ch'uan will not put extra strain on the heart. The aim is to encourage an even flow of energizing qi around the body. (See pages 46–51 and Qigong, pages 44–5.)

YOGA
• Basic yoga positions – particularly the Corpse pose – will help you relax and discharge tensions and stress. (See pages 52–9.)

MEDITATION
• Focusing the mind through meditation can induce deep calm, so helping to combat persistently raised stress levels. (See pages 60–63.)

BIOFEEDBACK
• Training in biofeedback means that you will have the ability to tell when you are getting stressed and also to monitor how successful you are in becoming relaxed. (See pages 212–13.)

MASSAGE
• Regular massage may reduce stress levels and help to stimulate the circulation. (See pages 96–103.)

DATAFILE

• Atherosclerosis can lead to angina and heart attack, if the coronary arteries supplying the heart with blood are affected.

• Atherosclerosis can cause transient ischemic attacks (TIAs) and stroke, if the cerebral arteries are involved.

• It can cause pain in the calves on walking, or a sudden onset of severe pain in the affected leg, which goes cold and turns pale, if the femoral arteries are affected.

LEFT *Left untreated, atherosclerosis grows gradually worse and can lead to a heart attack or stroke. Drugs to reduce the risk of blood clotting are commonly prescribed.*

Raynaud's Disease

In Raynaud's disease, the blood vessels serving the fingers – and sometimes the toes – contract and go into spasm in response to cold. The condition is more common in women than in men, its onset usually occurring in young adulthood, with attacks lasting usually for no more than 15 to 30 minutes. It tends to improve with age. However, Raynaud's phenomenon, a related condition, can be more serious, since it may be a sign of an underlying disease.

In an attack, the affected areas suddenly turn white and numb. In severe cases, they may then turn blue and, finally, red. They may be painful, tingling, and burning. The hands and feet should be kept warm and protected from cold. Smokers should give up, since smoking exacerbates the problem. Consult a doctor if the symptoms are extreme, or do not respond to warming.

SYMPTOMS

• *tingling sensations, burning, and numbness in fingers and toes* • *affected areas turn white, blue, then red* • *in extreme cases, gangrene may set in*

CONVENTIONAL TREATMENT

TO EXCLUDE THE POSSIBILITY OF AN UNDERLYING DISORDER, X-RAYS AND BLOOD TESTS MAY BE TAKEN. VASODILATORS MAY BE PRESCRIBED TO IMPROVE THE CIRCULATION.

THERAPIES

AYURVEDA
• Massage the hands and feet with a mixture of warm mustard and sesame seed oils. This will help to stimulate the circulation. (See pages 78–85.)

AROMATHERAPY
• Oils, such as black pepper, lemon and rosemary, can be massaged into the affected areas to increase circulation and warmth. *(See pages 104–5.)*

OSTEOPATHY
• Careful manipulation of the spine and the neck may help to improve the blood circulation to the body's peripheries. *(See pages 106–13.)* Chiropractic can produce the same results. *(See pages 118–25.)*

HYDROTHERAPY
• Warm water dilates blood vessels, increasing the bloodflow and boosting the circulation. A therapist will advise on the best course of treatment. *(See pages 172–9.)*

BIOFEEDBACK
• Practitioners teach how, by focusing mentally on warming up the fingers and toes, you can actually achieve this with the aid of a hand-held temperature sensor. *(See pages 212–13.)* Autogenic training will teach a series of mental exercises to help you think yourself well. *(See pages 210–11.)*

BELOW *The oil from black peppercorns can help improve circulation.*

Varicose Veins

An often painful condition, with worse discomfort at the end of the day, varicose veins are swollen, lengthened and twisted veins just below the skin's surface. The condition becomes increasingly common from the late teens onwards, while, in women, it frequently starts during pregnancy. Other factors include obesity, constipation, prolonged periods of standing or sitting, a sedentary lifestyle, and heredity. The most common area where they appear is the legs, but veins inside the rectum can also become varicose (known as hemorrhoids), as can those around the vulva (during pregnancy), the scrotum, and the esophagus.

The primary reason for varicose veins arising is obstruction of the bloodflow. This causes the one-way valves of the veins to lose their efficiency, allowing the blood to flow backwards. The result is increased pressure on, and consequent distension of, the veins. If this is associated with pregnancy, the condition may abate after childbirth, but otherwise it may persist intermittently. Sufferers are advised to take plenty of exercise, to avoid standing for long periods, and try to relax for short spells with legs raised on a pillow or cushion. If you are overweight, you will be advised to diet. Support socks, tights or stockings can also help: for maximum effectiveness, these should be put on first thing in the morning before the veins fill with stagnating blood. Varicose veins are not always painful: most people who have them surgically removed do so for cosmetic reasons.

SYMPTOMS

• *extremely sore, swollen, and tender veins* • *bruising and discoloration* • *burning sensation* • *irritated and flaky skin* • *ulcers* • *swollen legs and aching calves*

THERAPIES

AROMATHERAPY
• Rosemary oil, blended with a light carrier oil, can be massaged into the legs to improve the circulation. Similarly, essential oils of juniper and lavender can be diluted and massaged into the surrounding area. *(See pages 104–5.)*

HYDROTHERAPY
• Alternating hot and cold baths and splashes may be suggested to improve the circulation, as may hot and cold compresses. Sponging or spraying the legs with cold water for several minutes two times a day may bring relief. *(See pages 172–9.)*

YOGA
• The inverted positions may help to reduce blood pressure in the legs. Do not attempt these if you are pregnant or if you have high blood pressure *(See pages 52–9.)*

CAUTION

IF INJURED, A VARICOSE VEIN CAN BLEED PROFUSELY. SEEK MEDICAL HELP IF THIS OCCURS. AVOID HYDROTHERAPY IF YOU ARE SUFFERING FROM A HEART CONDITION.

CONVENTIONAL TREATMENT

A DOCTOR MAY PRESCRIBE INJECTING THE VEINS WITH A CHEMICAL TO SHRINK OR CLOSE THEM, OR SURGERY IN SEVERE CASES IN THE LEGS TO STRIP OUT THE VEINS.

ABOVE *Massaging rosemary oil into the legs can help with varicose veins. The herb's stimulating properties improve blood circulation.*

BELOW *Standing for long periods is a common cause of varicose veins. Relaxing for a few minutes with your legs raised can help.*

Palpitations

An awareness of your heartbeat is termed a palpitation. Palpitations can be regular or irregular. They are often brought on by strenuous exertion, such as running for a bus or up a flight of stairs, or while experiencing anxiety, fright, shock, or anger. Other triggers include excessive smoking, drinking too much alcohol, coffee or tea, viral infections, an overactive thyroid, heart disease, hyperventilation, and indigestion.

Palpitations are very common, usually harmless and, indeed, frequently go completely unnoticed. The "missed heartbeat" of which sufferers often complain is not, in fact, a dropped beat at all: rather, it is due to what doctors term an ectopic beat, which occurs earlier than usual, causing a longer, compensatory gap before the next beat. Ectopic beats are usually benign but, if frequent or if associated with other symptoms such as dizziness, fainting, chest pain or shortness of breath, should be investigated by a medical professional.

Frequent or prolonged palpitations should always be medically investigated, since they can be a symptom of thyroid or heart disorders. If either is suspected, a doctor will arrange for an electrocardiogram to be taken to check for heart problems, or blood tests to detect any thyroid disorder. Palpitations caused by heart disease usually respond to beta-blockers and anti-arrhythmics. If the trigger is an emotional one, psychotherapy or a course of relaxation techniques may be suggested.

SYMPTOMS

• *pounding in the chest following exercise or exertion* • *uncomfortable awareness of a rapid heart rate when anxious* • *sensation of a seemingly "missed" heartbeat*

CAUTION

A FAST, IRREGULAR HEARTBEAT IS ALWAYS ABNORMAL AND MUST BE BROUGHT TO THE ATTENTION OF A MEDICAL PRACTITIONER.

CONVENTIONAL TREATMENT

FREQUENT OR PROLONGED PALPITATIONS SHOULD BE INVESTIGATED BY A DOCTOR TO CHECK THAT THEY ARE NOT A SYMPTOM OF A MORE SERIOUS COMPLAINT SUCH AS A THYROID DISORDER OR HEART DISEASE.

BELOW *If you smoke and suffer from palpitations, give up cigarettes at once.*

you may experience shortness of breath

unaccustomed exercise may cause the heart to pound uncomfortably

stopping exercising abruptly may lead to nausea

LEFT *The heart always beats faster and more strongly during and immediately after exertion. This is harmless and normal – it is only if the pounding is painful or does not stop within a few moments of stopping exercise that it should cause concern.*

THERAPIES

MASSAGE
• Regular slow stroking of the limbs may help to ease palpitations by reducing stress levels, lowering raised blood pressure, and encouraging relaxation. (*See pages 96–103.*)

AROMATHERAPY
•If palpitations are triggered by emotional causes, a regular massage using calming oils such as ylang ylang, marjoram, lavender, and mandarin may help. So, too, may peppermint, aniseed, melissa, rosemary, and neroli, used separately or combined in a good carrier oil. (*See pages 104–5.*)

ACUPRESSURE
• Applying pressure to the pericardium and heart meridian acupoints on the wrist is thought to be calming in its effect. (*See pages 29–31.*)

AUTOGENIC TRAINING
• If the palpitations are triggered by anxiety, or other psychological conditions,

autogenic practitioners believe that the mental exercises the therapy involves should enable you to control the conditions. It is a well-accepted approach to relaxation. (*See pages 210–11.*) Biofeedback techniques may also help in controlling stress- and anxiety-related palpitations. (*See pages 212–13.*)

YOGA/RELAXATION TECHNIQUES
• Learning how to breathe is a key step in promoting relaxation. Yoga breathing exercises can be extremely helpful. (*See pages 52–9.*)

The techniques taught by practitioners to reduce stress by relaxing the muscles are also useful. (*See pages 158–65.*)

PSYCHOTHERAPY AND COUNSELING
• Some form of psychotherapy may be suggested if the palpitations have emotional triggers. (*See pages 188–91.*)

BELOW *Massaging the legs can lower blood pressure and relieve tension in the muscles after exercise.*

DIGESTION

Nausea and Vomiting

Vomiting is the body's natural reaction to the ingestion of harmful substances or toxins produced by illnesses or drugs. Nausea is the sensation that you are about to vomit. The causes of vomiting include gastroenteritis, shock, head injury, migraine, food poisoning, gallstones, overindulgence in food or drink, disturbances in the inner ear, such as those that can result from travel, and even emotionally distressing sights and noxious smells. Hormonal changes during pregnancy and menstruation can also cause both conditions. In addition, vomiting may be an indicator of more serious medical problems, such as appendicitis, glaucoma, ulcers, hepatitis, and meningitis. If you feel nauseous, combined with headache and abdominal pain, without vomiting, then the cause may be psychological rather than physical. However, persistent nausea can be an indicator of liver disease.

If food poisoning is thought to be the cause of vomiting, a doctor will probably suggest avoiding solid food for 24 hours and rehydrating with a salt–glucose solution. In severe cases, a doctor may prescribe antiemetic drugs to suppress the vomit reflex. Over-the-counter medication is available specifically for travel sickness. Home remedies for nausea include chewing on raw or candied ginger and drinking ginger, peppermint, or clove tea. Swallowing some crushed or cracked ice is said to relieve morning sickness.

CONVENTIONAL TREATMENT

A SINGLE, SHORT BOUT OF VOMITING DOES NOT REQUIRE MEDICAL ATTENTION, BUT RECURRENT VOMITING WILL NEED FURTHER INVESTIGATION TO ENSURE THERE IS NO UNDERLYING MEDICAL PROBLEM. IN SOME CASES, A DOCTOR WILL PRESCRIBE ANTIEMETICS. SOME DOCTORS MAY ADVISE TAKING VITAMIN B6 TO HELP WITH MORNING SICKNESS AND TRAVEL SICKNESS.

CAUTION

SEEK MEDICAL ADVICE IF VOMITING CONTINUES FOR MORE THAN 12 HOURS, ESPECIALLY IN CHILDREN; THE VOMIT CONTAINS BLOOD; OR IF IT IS ACCOMPANIED BY ABDOMINAL PAIN, HIGH FEVER, DROWSINESS, HEADACHES, OR AVERSION TO LIGHT. DO NOT TAKE MEDICATION FOR NAUSEA AND VOMITING IF YOU ARE IN THE FIRST TRIMESTER OF PREGNANCY. DO NOT CHEW GINGER OR DRINK GINGER TEA IF YOU HAVE A PEPTIC ULCER.

BELOW *Ginger, peppermint, or clove tea may all relieve nausea. Ginger is particularly recommended for morning sickness; cloves should not be taken in early pregnancy.*

a headache can often occur with nausea

try and rehydrate with plenty of fluids

DATAFILE

• Persistent nausea may indicate liver problems, which need prompt medical action to resolve them.

• Nausea following a fall or blow to the head is an indication of concussion.

• A cup of ginger tea soothes the sickness associated with colds and influenza and helps fight infections.

• Aromatherapists recommend an orange oil massage to prevent travel sickness.

• A British medical journal reported results showing ginger to be more effective than antihistamine drugs in preventing motion sickness.

THERAPIES

ACUPRESSURE
• The classic acupressure point to relieve nausea and sickness is Pericardium 6, which is located on the inside of the wrist, three finger breadths away from the wrist crease between the two tendons. Press on the point firmly with the thumb for three minutes. Sufferers from chronic travel sickness are advised to wear special wrist bands – snugly fitting elastic bands with small plastic balls to press on the P6 point. *(See pages 29–31.)*

HYPNOTHERAPY
• If you are prone to morning sickness, a course of hypnotherapy treatment in advance of your next pregnancy may help to prevent the condition, or, at the least, lessen its frequency. Research shows that hypnotherapy can also prevent nausea associated with chemotherapy. *(See pages 228–33.)*

RELAXATION
• If nausea is caused by stress and anxiety, use relaxation exercises to relieve your tension. This therapy may also be helpful to reduce the panic associated with prolonged or violent vomiting. *(See pages 158–65.)*

COLOR THERAPY
• Therapists believe the color green relieves the nervous tension that is a common cause of persistent nausea. They will treat you with colored lights or colored silks, and can also teach self-help methods, such as color visualization, to aid healing. *(See pages 248–51.)*

LEFT *As a color, green can help with persistant nausea.*

Gastroenteritis

A common irritation and inflammation of the digestive tract. In the U.S., gastroenteritis, or stomach flu, is second only to the common cold in frequency. The most common causes are infecting organisms, such as viruses, bacteria, and parasites, but other possibilities include allergies, reaction to some medications, stress and tension, and overindulgence in alcohol.

The symptoms of gastroenteritis vary greatly from person to person, but include nausea, vomiting, diarrhea, abdominal pain, headache, mild fever, and muscle aches. Viral gastroenteritis lasts between 24 and 48 hours, but bacterial or parasitic infections can last more than a week and require treatment with antibiotics. For mild cases, doctors recommend bedrest and avoiding solid foods. As soon as you stop vomiting, begin drinking small amounts of clear liquids. After 24 hours without symptoms, progress to full liquids, such as soups, and then to solid, mild foods. Avoid raw fruit, alcohol, and fatty foods for several more days.

LEFT *Live plain yoghurt is often recommended after an attack of gastroenteritis.*

DATAFILE

• There are 90 million cases of gastroenteritis each year in the U.S.

• Gastroenteritis causes between five and ten million deaths each year worldwide.

• Most cases of gastroenteritis are caused by viruses.

• Poor food hygiene is a cause of many cases of gastroenteritis, so avoid poorly prepared or refrigerated foods, especially in warm weather.

CONVENTIONAL TREATMENT

REST IN BED AND DRINK SMALL AMOUNTS OF LIQUID AS OFTEN AS POSSIBLE TO AVOID THE RISK OF DEHYDRATION. DOCTORS MAY PRESCRIBE ANTIEMETICS TO STOP SEVERE VOMITING OR OTHER DRUGS TO TREAT PERSISTENT DIARRHEA. THEY MAY ALSO RECOMMEND ANALYSIS OF FECES TO ELIMINATE THE POSSIBILITY OF UNDERLYING INTESTINAL INFECTIONS, SUCH AS AMEBIC DYSENTERY.

CAUTION

CONSULT A DOCTOR IF DIARRHEA CONTINUES FOR MORE THAN 72 HOURS (24 HOURS FOR A BABY OR SOONER IF A BABY REFUSES TO DRINK OR BECOMES LISTLESS), OR IF THERE IS MUCUS OR BLOOD IN THE FECES.

SYMPTOMS

• *fever* • *abdominal pain* • *nausea and vomiting* • *diarrhea*
• *shock and unconsciousness in severe cases*

you may experience fever and/or a headache

nausea and stomach ache may be accompanied by diarrhoea

THERAPIES

AROMATHERAPY
• Therapists recommend a stomach massage using five drops of chamomile essential oil, three drops of dill, two drops of ginger, and two drops of peppermint diluted in one ounce of carrier oil. This may help to soothe and relieve pain. *(See pages 104–5.)*

RELAXATION TECHNIQUES
• Gastroenteritis caused by emotional upsets can be prevented by taking steps to reduce stress and relax. *(See pages 158–65.)* Techniques include visualization *(see pages 214–17)*, deep breathing *(see pages 166–71)*, and meditation *(see pages 60–63)*.

YOGA
• Certain yoga exercises and breath and cleansing practices are thought to improve bowel tone and function, and will help to relieve gastroenteritis brought on by stress. Inverted postures in particular are claimed to help to stem the release of apana (downward flow) and so help to cure diarrhea. However, you should not practice these if you suffer from raised blood pressure, are menstruating, or if you are pregnant. *(See pages 52–9.)*

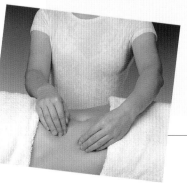

RIGHT *An aromatherapy stomach massage can help relieve the symptoms of gastroenteritis.*

Indigestion

Indigestion, also called dyspepsia, is a general term for a mixed collection of symptoms, including abdominal pains, nausea, heartburn (a burning sensation behind the breastbone), hiccups, belching, and flatulence. The most common causes of this abdominal discomfort are eating too much, eating too quickly, or eating rich, fatty, or spicy foods. These all lead to an increase in the production of gastric acid, which irritates the lining of the stomach. Heartburn occurs when gastric acid flows back into the esophagus. Heavy smokers and drinkers, pregnant women, the overweight, and people under stress are particularly prone to indigestion. Persistent indigestion may be an indication of a more serious complaint, such as a peptic ulcer, gallstones, or gastro-enteritis, and requires further medical investigation.

There are many antacid products on the market, which can provide short-term relief. They work by introducing an alkaline substance to the stomach in order to neutralize the acid. In severe cases, your doctor may prescribe drugs, known as H2 blockers, to reduce stomach acid concentration. Natural remedies include teas made from chamomile, licorice root, or peppermint. The best way to avoid the problem is to eat small amounts of food at regular intervals and eat slowly. Keep an eye out for trigger foods, such as chillies or curries, and drinks, and avoid them.

SYMPTOMS

• *abdominal discomfort* • *nausea* • *burning sensation behind breastbone ("heartburn")* • *hiccups*
• *flatulence ("gas")*

CONVENTIONAL TREATMENT

RECOMMENDED MEASURES INCLUDE OVER-THE-COUNTER ANTACIDS, DIETARY AND LIFESTYLE CHANGES (FOR EXAMPLE, CUTTING OUT SPICY FOODS, ALCOHOL, AND TOBACCO). IN SEVERE CASES, DRUGS MAY BE PRESCRIBED TO REDUCE STOMACH ACID AND TESTS CARRIED OUT TO DISCOVER IF IT IS THE RESULT OF AN UNDERLYING CONDITION.

ABOVE *Unhealthy eating habits are the most common cause of indigestion. You are likely to suffer after consuming too much rich food or alcohol.*

CAUTION

PROTRACTED, RECURRENT BOUTS OF INDIGESTION MAY BE THE SYMPTOMS OF A MORE SERIOUS UNDERLYING CONDITION. CONSULT A DOCTOR IF INDIGESTION DOES NOT CLEAR UP IN A REASONABLY SHORT SPACE OF TIME.

BELOW *Licorice has soothing properties and makes an excellent tea for indigestion sufferers.*

DATAFILE

• Cutting down on caffeine and tobacco may ease indigestion.

• Eat slowly and chew each mouthful to help you digest food.

• Do not drink too much with a meal. Both Ayurveda and Chinese medicine recommend avoiding iced drinks with food.

• If you get heartburn at night, try elevating the head of the bed by about 30 degrees to alleviate the symptoms.

THERAPIES

ACUPRESSURE
• Therapists recommend specific acupoints to relieve stomach pains and indigestion, including heartburn. Lie on your stomach and place the palm of the right hand over the solar plexus. Place the palm of the left hand between your pubic bone and belly button. Turn your head to one side and begin long, deep breathing. *(See pages 29–31.)*

ACUPUNCTURE
• Practitioners believe that acupuncture on the stomach, large intestine and spleen meridians can reduce stomach acidity and increase the formation of protective mucus. It is thought to be particularly effective for indigestion caused by stress. Practitioners report that around 60 percent of their patients gain some long-term relief through acupuncture, though treatment may need to be repeated after six to twelve months. *(See pages 20–28.)*

CHIROPRACTIC
• This treatment focuses on manipulating the lower thoracic area of the spine, in order to clear blood and nerve supplies to the digestive organs. *(See pages 118–25 and Osteopathy, pages 106–13.)*

YOGA
• Yoga followers believe eating too much food overloads the system, and so they aim to consume just two double handfuls of food and two double handfuls of liquid at a sitting, and to leave the stomach one-third empty at the end of a meal. They also use yogic postures and breathing to reduce stress and balance the body's energies. *(See pages 52–9.)*

LEFT *A qualified acupuncturist can treat indigestion by reducing stomach acidity and promoting the production of beneficial mucus.*

Peptic Ulcer

A peptic ulcer is a shallow, rounded sore in the lining of the digestive tract that may be found in the stomach wall (a gastric ulcer) or in the first section of the small intestine (a duodenal ulcer). The symptoms of an ulcer are pain and discomfort (especially related to food), nausea, and vomiting. In the severest cases, the ulceration will cause the wall of the digestive tract to become perforated. If this occurs, the tract's contents will leak into the abdominal cavity, causing a potentially fatal condition called peritonitis. A perforated ulcer generally requires surgical repair. If the ulcer bleeds chronically (indicated by black, tarry stools), anemia may result.

The exact cause of peptic ulcers was for a long time unknown, but there is increasing evidence that many are caused by a bacterium called *Helicobacter pylori*. Other causes include non-steroidal anti-inflammatory drugs such as ibuprofen, alcohol, overuse of aspirin, and severe stress such as trauma or surgery.

Antibiotics to elimate *Helicobacter pylori* may be successful in the first instance. Antacids may relieve symptoms, and drugs known as H_2 blockers may be prescribed to reduce stomach acid. If you are prone to ulcers, stopping smoking, reducing alcohol consumption, and the avoidance of foods that precipitate symptoms may help to reduce recurrences.

SYMPTOMS

• *gnawing or burning pains* •
belching • *bloating* • *vomiting* •
weight loss • *anemia*

RIGHT
*Chamomile oil can
relieve ulcer symptoms.*

DATAFILE

• Non-steroidal anti-inflammatory drugs, such as ibuprofen, also contribute to ulcers.

• People with blood group O are more likely to get ulcers.

• Doctors estimate that 10 percent of people suffer from a peptic ulcer at some time in their lives.

• Antibiotic treatment of certain ulcer types protects nearly 90 percent of patients from future attacks.

• Pain from gastric ulcers is typically brought on by eating; pain from a duodenal ulcer feels like hunger pangs.

• In up to 90 percent of cases, peptic ulcers recur within two years of the initial attack.

BELOW *Although peptic ulcers are primarily caused by stress, poor eating habits can also contribute. Drinking chamomile tea instead of ordinary tea or coffee is known to help the digestion.*

eating too quickly impedes digestion

certain foods can irritate an ulcer

LEFT *A reflexologist will concentrate on the stresses and imbalances that are causing the ulcer. But there are specific points on the foot which are related to stomach problems.*

THERAPIES

ACUPUNCTURE
• Research by Chinese psychologists has shown that acupuncture can reduce the acidity of the stomach, one of the contributing factors to a peptic ulcer. Results have been positive for both duodenal and gastric ulcers. *(See pages 20–28.)*

AROMATHERAPY
• Therapists recommend massaging essential oils of chamomile, frankincense, geranium, and marjoram into the abdomen to relieve ulcer symptoms. *(See pages 104–5.)*

REFLEXOLOGY
• Reflexologists focus on the instep area of the foot to treat the abdomen and other internal organs. Specific reflexes, such as the gall bladder, adrenal, colon, and ileo-caecal valve are also found in ths area. *(See pages 66–71.)*

SHIATSU
• Practitioners believe that applying pressure to the urinary bladder meridian, which runs down the spine and has connections to the internal organs, can affect the digestive organs, including the stomach. *(See pages 32–7 and Do-in, pages 38–41.)*

YOGA
• Practitioners recommend many basic balancing asanas (postures), but advise against seated poses. The abdominal lock is recommended for hyperacidic conditions, such as ulcers: bend forward and exhale through your mouth, then close your throat so no air can enter. Expand your chest, as though inhaling and suck in your abdomen, forming a deep hollow. Relax the muscles as you do so. Hold until you need to breathe, then release and inhale slowly. *(See pages 52–9.)*

ALEXANDER TECHNIQUE
• By correcting bad posture and chronic muscular tension, practitioners argue that the technique can relieve strain on the digestive system. *(See pages 146–53.)*

Diarrhea

Bouts of diarrhea cause frequent loose or liquid bowel movements that are urgent, explosive, or impossible to control, and which may be accompanied by stomach cramps and flatulence. Diarrhea occurs when the walls of the intestine fail to reabsorb sufficient water from the feces as they pass through the gut. An infection, such as dysentry, will cause the body to secrete excess gastroinstestinal fluid which the large intestine then fails to reabsorb. Inflammatory bowel diseases, such as ulcerative colitis, affect the functioning of the colon.

These diseases are just two of a long list of possible causes of diarrhea. Eating large amounts of food with laxative properties, such as ripe fruit or pulses, can bring on a bout. Stress and anxiety take their toll on the digestion, and diarrhea can often result from a stressful or frightening situation. Drugs, such as antibiotics, and vitamin supplements can trigger diarrhea in some people. Bacteria, parasites, viruses, and food allergies can all cause diarrhea, as well as vomiting, as the body attempts to get rid of these alien invaders.

For most adults, a short bout of diarrhea is not in itself serious. But the resulting loss of fluids and body salts can lead to dehydration, which is life-threatening, so it is important to drink liquid throughout the attack. To rehydrate the body, drink fruit juice to replace the electrolytes lost from diarrhea, or add half a teaspoon of salt and eight level teaspoons of sugar to a quart of water. Babies with persistent diarrhea can become dehydrated very quickly, especially if they are also vomiting. Give the baby plenty of cooled, boiled water and consult a doctor. Prolonged or recurrent diarrhea, especially if there is blood or mucus in the feces, may be an indication of a more serious condition, such as Crohn's disease, ulcerative colitis, irritable bowel syndrome, diverticular disease, or, in a few cases, bowel cancer.

SYMPTOMS

- *runny, watery feces and forceful bowel movements*
- *abdominal cramps* • *depending on the cause, vomiting and flatulence*

RIGHT *Depending on the cause of diarrhoea, it may be accompanied by headaches, nausea, or fever.*

a headache may occur with a diarrhea attack.

CONVENTIONAL TREATMENT

DRINK PLENTY OF WATER DURING AN ATTACK TO PREVENT DEHYDRATION. A DOCTOR MAY PRESCRIBE A SALT AND GLUCOSE SOLUTION TO RESTORE LOST BODY SALTS AND FLUIDS. IF THE DIARRHEA IS PERSISTENT AND ACCOMPANIED BY STOMACH CRAMPS AND VOMITING, ESPECIALLY IF YOU HAVE RECENTLY RETURNED FROM VACATION, A DOCTOR MAY REQUEST A FECES SAMPLE TO CHECK IF THE CAUSE IS A BACTERIUM OR PARASITE, WHICH CAN BE TREATED WITH ANTIBIOTICS. IN SEVERE CASES, A DOCTOR MAY REQUEST A COLONOSCOPY OR BARIUM ENEMA TO INVESTIGATE WHETHER THE CAUSE IS IRRITABLE BOWEL SYNDROME OR AN INFLAMMATORY BOWEL DISEASE.

CAUTION

CONSULT A DOCTOR IF ADULT DIARRHEA PERSISTS FOR MORE THAN 48 HOURS, OR IF A BABY SUFFERS PERSISTENT DIARRHEA, ESPECIALLY COMBINED WITH VOMITING. IF YOU SUFFER FROM FREQUENT BOUTS OF DIARRHEA, WITH BLOOD OR MUCUS IN THE FECES OR ALTERNATING WITH CONSTIPATION, CONSULT A DOCTOR. SHE MAY RECOMMEND FURTHER INVESTIGATION TO ELIMINATE SERIOUS UNDERLYING DISEASES.

DATAFILE

- In the U.S., 100 million cases of diarrhea occur every year. Ninety percent of sufferers do not seek any medical attention.

- In the West, diarrhea is the most common reason for missing work, while in the developing world, it is a leading cause of death.

- Diarrheal diseases can quickly reach epidemic proportions, especially if sanitation and hygiene are poor.

- The serious side-effect of diarrhea is dehydration, so try to drink plenty of water during an attack.

THERAPIES

ACUPRESSURE
- Practitioners apply pressure to points along the stomach and spleen meridians to treat diarrhea. Curve the fingers, placing the fingertips under the edge of the ribs directly below the nipple. Hold the indentations at the base of the ribcage while you breathe deeply for one minute. *(See pages 29–31.)*

ACUPUNCTURE
- Studies in China report that acupuncture speeds recovery from bowel infections and reduces the risk of complications. Some researchers believe that acupuncture works by stimulating the production of chemicals that kill invading bacteria. *(See pages 20–28.)*

BREATHING TECHNIQUES
- Emotions, such as fear and anxiety, can provoke sudden bouts of diarrhea. Relaxation and breathing therapies are thought to reduce stress hormone levels, which rise while you are experiencing negative emotions. They can also help to keep your digestive system running efficiently. *(See pages 166–71 and Relaxation, pages 158–65.)*

YOGA
- Specific exercises and yogic breath and cleansing practices are very helpful for improving bowel tone and function. *(See pages 52–9.)*

BELOW *It is easy to become dehydrated when suffering from diarrhea, so be sure to drink lots of water.*

Constipation

Constipation is a condition caused by feces being retained in the rectum for several days, becoming dried out and hardened and more difficult to pass (and likely to cause hemorrhoids and fissures). Abdominal swelling, and a feeling of fullness even after defecation, add to the discomfort. Common causes include ignoring the need to defecate, not drinking enough fluids, not eating enough fiber, a sedentary lifestyle, and anxiety. It may be a side-effect of aging, due to loss of muscle tone, and a consequence of pregnancy. Some medicines, such as painkillers, heart medicines, antihistamines, and antidepressants, plus the habitual use of laxatives or iron tablets, can also cause constipation. Consult your doctor if you have a change in bowel habits, particularly if it is associated with symptoms such as blood in the feces.

Drinking more fluids, eating more fiber, and getting more exercise will all help to alleviate the condition.

eat plenty of green vegetables

introduce grains into your diet

LEFT *Fiber is a natural laxative, so make sure there is plenty of it in your diet.*

SYMPTOMS

• *infrequent, difficult bowel movements* • *pain during defecation* • *weight loss* • *swollen stomach* • *some sufferers experience headache, lethargy, loss of appetite, coating on the tongue, and flatulence*

DATAFILE

• The long-term use of laxatives can itself be a cause of constipation. The body becomes accustomed to its daily dosage and ceases to function without the drugs.

• Normal frequency of bowel movements ranges from twice a day to twice a week. A person suffering from constipation may not have a bowel movement for a week or more.

• Constipation is the most common chronic digestive complaint. Research suggests that 15 percent of people in the West may suffer from the condition.

CAUTION

ON RARE OCCASIONS, CONSTIPATION MAY BE AN INDICATION OF A MORE SERIOUS CONDITION, SUCH AS IRRITABLE BOWEL SYNDROME, DIVERTICULOSIS OR CANCER. CONSULT YOUR DOCTOR IF CONSTIPATION LASTS LONGER THAN TWO WEEKS, OR IF IT IS INTERSPERSED WITH BOUTS OF DIARRHEA OR BLOOD IN THE FECES.

LEFT *A sedentary occupation is a common cause of constipation. Try to fit more exercise into your daily routine.*

CONVENTIONAL TREATMENT

A DOCTOR WILL ENCOURAGE YOU TO BECOME MORE ACTIVE AND TO INCREASE THE AMOUNT OF FIBER AND FLUIDS IN YOUR DIET. HE MAY ALSO PRESCRIBE MILD LAXATIVES FOR INFREQUENT BOUTS OF CONSTIPATION.

THERAPIES

ACUPUNCTURE
• Practitioners stimulate acupoints along the large intestine and liver meridians to treat constipation. They believe this will restore the normal functioning of the intestines. *(See pages 20–28.)*

AROMATHERAPY
• Supplement an abdominal massage *(see Massage, right)* with essential oils diluted in a carrier oil. Therapists recommend a few drops of marjoram, rosemary, or fennel oil, diluted in grapeseed oil, to treat constipation. *(See pages 104–5.)*

AYURVEDA
• Practitioners recommend basti, or enema therapy, for vata disorders, such as constipation, which are concentrated around

the colon. The full purging treatment includes massage and steam baths. Enema therapy is not recommended if you suffer from hemorrhoids. *(See pages 78–85.)*

MASSAGE
• Abdominal massage stimulates the bowel, which may bring some relief. Lie with the upper half of your body supported by pillows and a pillow beneath your knees. Using a firm, gentle pressure, make large stroking movements up the right side of the abdomen, across the ribcage, and down the left side. Switch to small, circular movements, working your way along the same path. Continue the massage for ten minutes. *(See pages 96–103.)*

YOGA
• The half-shoulderstand asana is recommended for constipation, particularly in conjunction with rapid abdominal breathing. The latter uses the movement of the abdomen to expel air and draw air into the body. Follow the pose with jogging in place and the embryo pose, in which you lie on your back and draw the knees into the chest. *(See pages 52–9.)*

REFLEXOLOGY
• Massaging the reflex areas relating to both the small and large intestines, and, additionally, the areas concerned with the adrenal glands, liver, solar plexus, and lower spine is recommended by practitioners. *(See pages 66–71.)*

RIGHT *Marjoram and rosemary are two of the essential oils aromatherapists recommend to treat constipation.*

Irritable Bowel Syndrome (IBS)

In this common condition, the muscles of the intestines do not function properly and go into spasm intermittently. This causes the contents of the large intestine to be pushed through either too quickly, leading to diarrhea, or too slowly, leading to constipation. A frequent symptom of IBS is alternating bouts of diarrhea and constipation. IBS sufferers also experience abdominal pains and distension, caused by excessive production of gas, which are both byproducts of a poorly functioning digestive system. Additional physical symptoms include flatulence, nausea, lack of appetite, and excessive mucus in the feces. Many people also report psychological symptoms of depression, anxiety, and nervousness. This may in part be due to the distressing and embarrassing nature of the symptoms or, as some nutritionists believe, due to malabsorption of minerals and vitamins essential for brain functioning.

The colon can become irritated and go into spasm for many reasons. There is some evidence that food intolerances and allergies may be a factor. The over-population of certain organisms in the intestines, such as a yeast-like microorganism called *Candida albicans*, are another possibility. A bacterial imbalance may sometimes be triggered by the use of drugs, such as antibiotics, and can lead to IBS symptoms. Stimulants, such as caffeine, nicotine, sugar, and alcohol, are often triggers for IBS. There is also a strong connection between the functioning of the digestive system and the psychological state, as stress appears to trigger and aggravate IBS symptoms.

The symptoms of IBS follow a similar pattern to other bowel diseases, so it is important to eliminate the possibility of other conditions, such as diverticular disease, Crohn's disease, or ulcerative colitis. A doctor will make a full examination and may request an internal examination of the bowel via the rectum

RIGHT AND ABOVE *Milk, alcohol, and sweet foods can all cause a form of allergic reaction in sensitive people, which may result in irritable bowel syndrome.*

LEFT *The digestive system is long and complicated, and there is plenty of opportunity for it to malfunction. Stress, an unhealthy diet, and excessive use of stimulants can all contribute to bowel problems.*

oesophagus

stomach

liver

duodenum

colon (large intestine)

small intestine

rectum

THERAPIES

HYDROTHERAPY
• Some alternative practitioners recommend a detoxifying process called colonic hydrotherapy to relieve the symtoms of IBS. During the treatment, a tube is inserted into the rectum and filtered water is flowed in under gentle pressure. The water stays in the colon for about two minutes, before flowing away carrying with it fecal matter from the colon. Some doctors, however, consider colonic hydrotherapy ill-advised for IBS. Consult your practitioner first. Avoid this therapy if you suffer from hemorrhoids. *(See pages 172–9.)*

HYPNOTHERAPY
• The British medical journal, *The Lancet*, has reported that hypnotherapy successfully treated cases of IBS that could not be treated by medical means. The therapist induces a general state of relaxation, then focuses the therapy on warming the abdominal area to relieve the IBS symptoms. *(See pages 218–23.)*

YOGA
• Yoga practitioners see IBS as a disturbance in the flow of prana, or life energy. This has an upward flow (udana), a downward flow (apana), and a balancing movement around the navel (samana). Diarrhea is caused by excessive apana and alternating diarrhea and constipation by samana. In general, inverted poses (avoid if pregnant or suffering from high blood pressure) are advised for the release of apana and breathing exercises for the stabilization of samana. *(See pages 52–9.)*

(a colonoscopy) or a barium enema and X-ray of the intestines. Treatment for IBS does not follow a set path, but orthodox doctors recommend a high-fiber diet and may prescribe antispasmodic drugs to control diarrhea or bulking agents to increase water absorption into the feces. They may also advise counseling to relieve stress. Alternative practitioners recommend that IBS sufferers pinpoint food sensitivities or allergies and eliminate these trigger foods from their diet. They often find a link between intolerance to milk products, wheat, or sugars, including fruit sugar, and IBS symptoms. Many alternative therapists also recommend cutting out stimulants, such as nicotine, caffeine, and alcohol, and reducing the amount of red meat and fat in the diet. As with conventional treatment, increasing dietary fiber, particularly the soluble fiber found in beans, seeds, fruit, and vegetables, is advised to control symptoms.

SYMPTOMS

Intermittent diarrhea and constipation • swollen stomach • abdominal pains • gas and stomach rumblings • headache • general malaise • depression and anxiety

BELOW *Stress has been shown to contribute to IBS, which is particularly common in young women. Symptoms may include loss of appetite and a tendency to tire easily.*

back pain

heartburn

stomach ache

gas

DATAFILE

- It is estimated that up to 15 percent of the Western population suffers, or has suffered from, IBS.

- The vast majority of IBS sufferers are women aged between 20 and 45.

- Up to 50 percent of referrals to gastroenterologists are linked to IBS.

- Naturopaths recommend that IBS sufferers replace coffee with chamomile or peppermint teas, which have antispasmodic qualities.

- Some fibers, such as wheat bran, can exacerbate IBS symptoms.

CONVENTIONAL TREATMENT

ONCE A DIAGNOSIS HAS BEEN MADE, A DOCTOR CAN HELP TO ALLEVIATE THE SYMPTOMS BY PRESCRIBING DRUGS TO CONTROL THE DIARRHEA OR MUSCULAR SPASM, AND BULKING AGENTS TO DEAL WITH CONSTIPATION. A NUTRITIONIST CAN HELP YOU TO WORK OUT A SUITABLE DIET, TAKING INTO ACCOUNT ANY FOOD ALLERGIES OR INTOLERANCES, WHICH INCREASES YOUR AMOUNT OF SOLUBLE DIETARY FIBER AND CUTS DOWN ON RED MEAT AND FAT. A DOCTOR MAY ALSO RECOMMEND COUNSELING TO HELP WITH THE PSYCHOLOGICAL ASPECTS OF THE CONDITION.

CAUTION

CONSULT A DOCTOR IF THERE IS BLOOD IN THE FECES OR YOU SUFFER FROM CHRONIC DIARRHEA; IF YOU ARE OVER 40 AND NOTICE A SUDDEN CHANGE IN YOUR BOWEL HABITS.

THERAPIES

ACUPRESSURE
• To relieve chronic diarrhea, constipation, and gas build-up, lie on your back, with knees bent and feet flat on the floor. Place the fingertips of both hands between the pubic bone and belly button. Take long, deep breaths and press one to two inches deep inside the abdomen. Take long, deep breaths as you press firmly for one minute. *(See pages 29–31.)*

AROMATHERAPY
• Therapists recommend massaging the abdomen with lavender or chamomile oils,

which have antispasmodic qualities. The massage itself may help to regulate the functioning of the bowel. *(See pages 104–5 and Massage, pages 96–103.)*

BELOW *Lavender is a safe and versatile oil whose many uses include countering the spasms that 'cause the pain of IBS.*

AYURVEDA
• A practitioner will recommend a detoxifying, purging process called panchakarma to eliminate organisms, such as *Candida albicans*, which may be the cause of IBS symptoms. He may also prescribe herbs to strengthen the body's natural defenses. *(See pages 78–85.)*

AUTOGENIC TRAINING
• This form of meditation will help to relieve IBS symptoms triggered by stress and anxiety. A practitioner will teach you how to relax both the mind and body

whenever you notice an increase in stress levels. *(See pages 210–11.)*

BIOFEEDBACK
• It is common for IBS symptoms to be triggered as a habitual reaction to certain situations. Psychologists often recommend bowel sound biofeedback to retrain and regain control of bowel functioning. *(See pages 212–13.)*

QIGONG
• You may be shown exercises designed to stimulate the flow of qi and improve the

functioning of the digestive system. *(See pages 44–5 and T'ai Chi Ch'uan, pages 46–51.)*

RELAXATION
• Learning how to release muscular tension may help in the management of the stress and anxiety that can trigger the condition. *(See pages 158–65 and Breathing, pages 166–71.)*

MEDITATION
• Meditation techniques may help you to reduce mental and physical tensions. *(See pages 60–63.)*

URINARY SYSTEM

Cystitis

Cystitis is an inflammation of the lining of the bladder. The usual cause is a bacterial infection, most often *Escheria coli*, which travels from the anus, via the uretha, to the bladder. Food allergies, accidental bruising during sexual intercourse, chemical sensitivity, and vaginal yeast infections can also all increase the likelihood of a bladder infection. Women are far more prone to the condition than men because the urethra, which carries urine from the bladder, is much shorter and its opening is closer to the anus, making it easier for the anal bacteria to spread.

Symptoms include burning pain on passing urine – this itself is unpleasantly smelly – wanting to urinate more often, though, when you try, only a few drops are passed, and pain in the lower abdomen. Sometimes, they can disappear within hours, but they can drag on for a number of weeks.

You can help yourself by relaxing and resting as much as you can and by drinking plenty of fluids. Water or mild herbal teas, such as chamomile, are best. Aim at drinking seven pints every 24 hours. Drinking cranberry juice regularly also helps to reduce the likelihood of bacterial infection in the urinary tract. Cut out meat, eggs, fish, cheese, foods containing vinegar, citrus and sour fruit from your diet – in fact, some therapists say that a 48-hour fast, followed by a raw food diet, can aid recovery from the condition. Avoid foam baths, scented soaps, and vaginal deodorants. If the pain persists, painkillers will bring some relief.

In all cases – particularly if there is blood in the urine, and if the condition is recurrent – medical advice should be sought, because there is a possibility that the infection may spread to the kidneys, which is serious. If the cystitis is bacterial in origin – this can be diagnosed by testing the urine – antibiotics are normally extremely effective. If the condition is recurrent, then further examinations and tests will be necessary to exclude, or treat, any other underlying causes. It may be worth taking an allergy test, for instance, and avoiding foods that yield a positive response.

CONVENTIONAL TREATMENT

DIAGNOSIS IS CONFIRMED BY VAGINAL EXAMINATION AND URINE ANALYSIS. IF THE CAUSE IS BACTERIAL INFECTION, A COURSE OF ANTIBIOTICS WILL BE PRESCRIBED. IF THE CONDITION IS CHRONIC, SPECIALIST INVESTIGATIONS MAY BE NECESSARY TO RULE OUT, OR TREAT, COMPLICATING FACTORS, SUCH AS KIDNEY DAMAGE.

CAUTION

ALWAYS COMPLETE THE FULL COURSE OF ANTIBIOTICS IF ONE IS PRESCRIBED, RATHER THAN STOPPING IT EARLY BECAUSE YOUR SYMPTOMS CLEAR AND YOU FEEL BETTER. IF YOU STOP, YOU MAY DEVELOP CHRONIC CYSTITIS.

SYMPTOMS

• *burning pain on urination*
• *frequent, urgent need to pass water, although little, if any, is passed* • *pain in the lower abdomen and lower back* • *nausea and possibly vomiting* • *unpleasant-smelling, cloudy urine that may contain blood*

RIGHT *Drinking plenty of fluids helps counteract cystitis. Water, cranberry juice or chamomile tea are usually recommended.*

BELOW *Eating live yoghurt and massaging rosemary oil into the legs helps the symptoms of cystitis.*

DATAFILE

• More frequent in women than in men, because of the close proximity of the urethra and vagina to the anus.

• There are two types of cystitis – acute, when the inflammation lasts only for a short time, and chronic, when the bladder may be permanently inflamed.

• Incompletely emptying the bladder when urinating may predispose towards cystitis, because urine stagnating in the bladder becomes infected easily.

• Prevalent in women of childbearing years, particularly during pregnancy.

• Stress, oral contraceptives and a poor diet may lower resistance to the infection.

THERAPIES

AROMATHERAPY
• For pain relief, rosemary oil, blended with a light carrier oil, can be massaged into the legs. Similarly, essential oils of juniper and lavender can be diluted and massaged into the surrounding area. *(See pages 104–5.)*

HYDROTHERAPY
• Alternating hot and cold baths and splashes may be suggested to improve the circulation, as may hot and cold compresses. Sponging or spraying the legs with cold water for several minutes two times a day may bring relief. *(See pages 172–9.)*

YOGA
• Lying on your back with the legs at a 45 degree angle against a wall may ease the condition. *(See pages 52–9.)*

ACUPRESSURE
• Stimulating the appropriate acupoints on the stomach meridian may relieve cystitis. *(See pages 29–31.)*

Urinary Incontinence

Urinary incontinence concerns the involuntary release of urine, ranging from a slight leakage to total loss of bladder control. There are three main forms: stress, urge, and overflow incontinence.

Stress incontinence can be caused by a sudden rise in pressure in the abdomen as a result of coughing, laughing, lifting, jumping, running, sneezing, or as a result of straining to have a bowel movement. It is commoner in women than in men and is often experienced after childbirth as a result of injury or strain to the pelvic floor muscles. In urge incontinence, which is often due to a bladder infection, or to a hyperactive or "spastic" bladder, an uncontrollable urge to urinate is followed by a complete emptying of the bladder. Overflow incontinence occurs when the outward flow of urine is impeded by a blockage, usually an enlarged prostate gland.

In most cases, the problem is curable and treatable once the type and cause of the incontinence has been identified. Your doctor may evaluate and treat the condition, or, in some cases, refer you to a urologist, a doctor who specializes in treating problems of the bladder and urinary tract. Medication, collagen injections for a certain type of stress incontinence, or surgery may be needed. Treatment may also include exercises designed to strengthen the pelvic floor muscles and other self-care measures. Try to avoid drinks, foods, and medicines that contain caffeine, and limit your consumption of carbonated drinks, alcohol, citrus juices, greasy and spicy foods, and items that contain artificial sweeteners, because these can irritate the bladder. Drink one to two quarts of water daily. Visit the bathroom often, even if you do not feel the urge to urinate, and empty your bladder as much as you can on each occasion. There is a wide range of aids, including incontinence pads, available to help you to cope with the inevitable accidents.

SYMPTOMS

- *involuntary passing of urine*

THERAPIES

RELAXATION TECHNIQUES
- Kegel exercises are designed to strengthen the pelvic floor muscles. You should squeeze and relax the muscles alternately for three seconds at a time. Start out doing this three times a day, gradually working up to three sets of ten contractions, holding each one for ten seconds at a time. Other relaxation techniques may help as well. *(See pages 158–65.)*

BIOFEEDBACK
- You can be taught how to use sensors that will help you to identify and strengthen the muscles involved in bladder control. *(See pages 212–13.)*

HYDROTHERAPY
- Hot and cold sitz baths can help, or alternating hot and cold compresses over the lower abdomen and back. These may improve both the local circulation and muscle tone. *(See pages 172–9.)*

ACUPUNCTURE
- Stimulation of the appropriate acupoints is thought to ease incontinence. *(See pages 20–28.)*

ACUPRESSURE
- Practitioners believe that this therapy may ease the problems of incontinence. Strong pressure is applied upwards in the hollow between the inner ankle bone and the Achilles tendon. *(See pages 29–31.)*

LEFT *Hydrotherapists may recommend alternating hot and cold baths. For home treatment, hot and cold compresses applied alternately are an effective substitute.*

apply the compresses to the lower abdomen

Kidney Complaints

The kidneys can be affected by several disorders, the commonest of which is kidney stones. These occur when minerals in the urine crystallize into small stones – either in the kidneys themselves, or the ureters, the tubes that carry urine to the bladder – most commonly as a result of infection, though there can be other causes. Usually, the stones are painless while in the kidneys, but they can cause short bursts of severe back pain in the overall region when they become dislodged and start to travel down, or block, the urinary tract. Sometimes, this pain can spread to the abdomen and genitals, and it can become painful to pass urine. The urine, too, may contain blood. Other kidney disorders include pyelonephritis, a bacterial complaint that is usually the result of another condition such as cystitis, and glomerulonephritis, a rarer but more serious disorder.

You should consult a doctor in the event of any suspected kidney trouble, since this can become serious without medical attention. It is important to tell your doctor if you have ever suffered from a kidney problem, as many drugs should be used with caution in such conditions. If you are suffering from kidney stones, you should avoid foods which are calcium-rich, cut back on sugar and salt, eat more green vegetables, and drink low-calcium bottled mineral water or filtered water.

Conventionally, diagnosis starts with a urine test and a physical examination of the abdomen to see if the kidneys are enlarged or tender. Blood tests, a kidney scan, x-rays and, sometimes, a kidney biopsy may be required to find out more. Treatment depends on the cause and nature of the problem. Stones can be broken down and fragmented with ultrasound, while infections usually can be cleared up by antibiotics.

SYMPTOMS

• *agonizing pain through muscle contractions; pain can spread to the lower abdomen and the genitals* • *blood in the urine* • *serious loss of kidney function if the urinary tract becomes blocked*

CONVENTIONAL TREATMENT

PHYSICAL EXAMINATION AND A URINE TEST ARE THE FIRST STAGES IN MAKING AN INITIAL DIAGNOSIS. SUBSEQUENT TESTS AND TREATMENTS DEPEND ON THE SPECIFIC CAUSE OF THE PROBLEM.

THERAPIES

ACUPUNCTURE
• Acupuncture may be given at points on the governor, conception, bladder, large intestine, kidney, and spleen meridians. Moxibustion may also be suggested. The acupuncture is intended to correct an imbalance in the body's yang: the moxibustion is thought to strengthen the kidneys. *(See pages 20–28.)*

ACUPRESSURE
• A therapist will apply pressure at the appropriate acupoints on the kidney, spleen, conception, and bladder meridians. *(See pages 29–31.)*

T'AI CHI CH'UAN
• According to practitioners, this therapy releases bodily tensions by balancing the energy flows of body and mind and has the effect of giving the kidneys an internal massage. It also improves the circulation of body fluids and the expulsion of waste. *(See pages 46–51 and Qigong, pages 44–5.)*

REFLEXOLOGY
• The reflex areas of the feet to be manipulated are the ones corresponding to the kidneys, the bladder, and the pituitary and adrenal glands, as well as the areas relating to the lymphatic system. *(See pages 66–71.)*

AROMATHERAPY
• Potentially useful oils for the treatment of kidney stones include fennel, geranium, juniper, and lemon. These can be added to a light carrier oil and massaged into the area of the bladder. *(See pages 104–5.)*

ABOVE *You may not be aware of kidney stones until they become dislodged. Then you are likely to experience short bursts of severe lower back pain.*

BELOW *Flush out the kidneys by drinking lots of liquid. Bottled or filtered water is best.*

Bladder Stones

Bladder stones mainly affect men. Most of them are made up of crystals – sometimes called gravel – of calcium oxalate, or uric acid, and are caused by the precipitation from solution of the minerals present in the urine. The stones may obstruct the outflow of urine, with infection as the result, though, more often than not, they remain unrecognized and undetected. Conventional treatment is much the same as for kidney stones. Self-help measures include adopting a high-fiber diet, exercising regularly, and drinking plenty of fluids. Cranberry juice, for instance, is thought to help to reduce the accumulation of gravel in the bladder. Reducing salt and sugar intake may also help to prevent the condition's recurrence.

SYMPTOMS

• *finding it difficult to pass urine* • *incontinence* • *burning pain on passing urine, which may be cloudy and smell unpleasant* • *small amounts of urine being passed* • *fever* • *dull abdominal ache*

BELOW *Certain t'ai chi exercises concentrate on specific areas of the body and can help the kidneys expel waste.*

breathing is regular

body is released of tensions

BELOW *A healthy, low-fat diet can help prevent the formation of stones. Drinking cranberry juice is often recommended.*

CONVENTIONAL TREATMENT

YOUR DOCTOR MAY SUGGEST ULTRASOUND TREATMENT TO BREAK UP THE STONES, OR, IF THEY ARE TOO BIG TO FRAGMENT SUCCESSFULLY, SURGERY TO REMOVE THEM.

CAUTION

IF YOU ARE SUFFERING FROM THE SYMPTOMS OF BLADDER STONES, CONSULT A DOCTOR AS SOON AS POSSIBLE.

THERAPIES

AROMATHERAPY
• Essential oils that work on the urinary tract include tea tree, sandalwood, juniper, and eucalyptus. They should be applied in repeated hot compresses over the area of the bladder. *(See pages 104–5.)*

BELOW *Cranberry juice and a high-fiber diet can prevent kidney stones.*

DATAFILE

• Up to 80 percent of kidney stones are composed chiefly of calcium.

• Around one in one thousand Americans are affected by kidney stones – ten percent being men and three percent women.

• Kidney stones range in size from less than ⅛ inch to over 1 inch in diameter.

• Differences in dietary and fluid intake may predispose certain people to develop kidney stones.

• According to some natural therapists, fresh lemon juice, drunk in a little hot water every morning, will help to flush the kidneys and break down kidney stones.

REPRODUCTION

Breast Problems

There are many medical problems that can affect the female breast. Chief among them are pain, swelling, and tenderness, often associated with the menstrual cycle or a bacterial infection; skin problems, such as eczema, acne, and other skin infections; and cysts, lumps, and tumors, which may be cancer-related in a minority of cases.

Many women experience swelling and tenderness in both breasts before or during their period. If the pain is only felt in one breast and is not period-related, then the cause may be a strained muscle, a change in contraceptive pill, a blow to the breast, or a cyst. If the pain lasts for longer than one menstrual cycle, a doctor should be consulted.

The state of the skin on the breast can also be an indication of breast health. Many women get patches of allergy-related eczema on their breasts, or even the odd pimple. Some are also prone to infections that cause the breasts to become red, hot, and swollen: these can be treated with antibiotics or hydrocortisone cream. If the skin suddenly becomes hot and swollen, or if it suddenly dimples and the nipple retracts, consult a doctor as these are both possible signs of an underlying tumor. A permanently scaly, itchy nipple should also be medically examined.

Finding a lump in the breast can be very frightening, since most women assume this is an indication of cancer. In fact, 80 to 90 percent of all breast lumps are non-cancerous. They are usually benign tumors, such as fibroadenomas, cysts, or nipple-duct tumors. Tests, such as ultrasound, needle aspiration, a biopsy, or a mammogram, will determine whether a breast lump is cancerous or not.

Examine your breasts a few days after menstruation and at the same time each month to check that they are normal and pick up any changes quickly if they occur. Stand up in front of a mirror and, keeping your fingers flat, move them gently over every part of the breast. Use your right hand to examine the left breast and vice versa. Check for any thickening, hard lumps, or knots. Then raise the arms overhead. Look for changes in shape, swelling, dimpling, or changes in

the nipples. Lie down and place a pillow under your right shoulder. Place your right hand behind your head. Then with the flat fingers of your left hand, press gently in small circular motions around an imaginary clock face. Each breast will have a normal ridge of firm tissue. Move in toward the nipple, including the nipple. Keep circling to examine every part of the breast. Repeat on the left breast. Finally, squeeze the nipple gently between the thumb and index finger.

If you notice any new cysts or lumps, changes in the tissue, or discharge from the nipple, consult a doctor. You should also have your breasts examined by a women's healthcare practitioner once a year.

SYMPTOMS

- *painful, swollen breasts* • *nipple discharge* • *cracked nipples*
- *inverted nipples* • *rashes and skin infections* • *skin dimpling*
- *lumps and cysts*

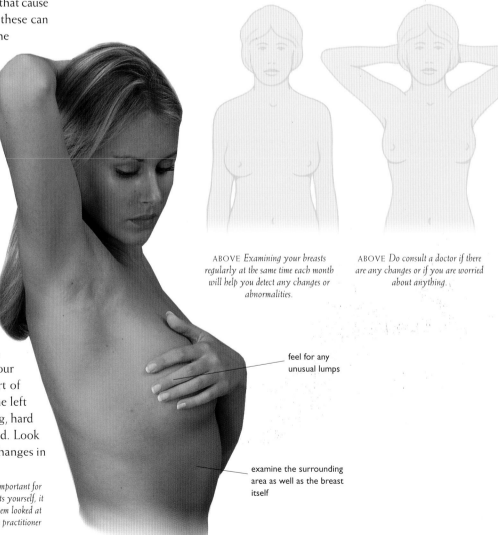

ABOVE *Examining your breasts regularly at the same time each month will help you detect any changes or abnormalities.*

ABOVE *Do consult a doctor if there are any changes or if you are worried about anything.*

feel for any unusual lumps

examine the surrounding area as well as the breast itself

RIGHT *Although it is important for you to check your breasts yourself, it is a good idea to have them looked at by a women's healthcare practitioner once a year.*

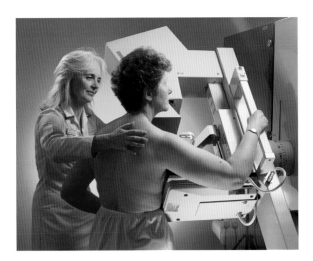

ABOVE *Regular breast screening can detect both benign and malignant lumps at an early stage.*

CONVENTIONAL TREATMENT

A DOCTOR MAY PRESCRIBE DIURETICS TO EASE BREAST SWELLING DUE TO WATER RETENTION AND TO REDUCE THE SYMPTOMS OF CYSTS. DRUGS MAY BE USED TO BALANCE ESTROGEN LEVELS TO REDUCE BREAST SWELLING. ANTI-INFLAMMATORIES CAN ALSO EASE SWELLING. CANCER SCREENING OPTIONS INCLUDE ULTRASOUND, NEEDLE ASPIRATION, BIOPSY OR MAMMOGRAM. NON-CANCEROUS CYSTS MAY BE DRAINED AND BENIGN TUMORS MAY BE REMOVED. CANCER TREATMENT INCLUDES HORMONE THERAPY, RADIATION THERAPY, AND CHEMOTHERAPY, AS WELL AS SURGERY TO REMOVE THE CANCEROUS AREA.

CAUTION

CONSULT A DOCTOR IF A LUMP, NIPPLE DISCHARGE, OR PAIN IS LOCALIZED IN ONE PART OF THE BREAST; IF A LUMP FEELS IRREGULAR, HARD, AND IMMOBILE; IF A NEW LUMP FAILS TO DISAPPEAR WHEN YOUR PERIOD STARTS, OR IF AN OLD LUMP IS GROWING OR CHANGING; IF NIPPLE DISCHARGE IS PERSISTENT AND BLOODY; IF A SKIN INFECTION DOES NOT CLEAR UP; IF THERE IS DIMPLING OF THE SKIN OR IF THE NIPPLE BECOMES INVERTED. YOU SHOULD HAVE YOUR BREASTS EXAMINED ANNUALLY BY A WOMEN'S HEALTHCARE PRACTITIONER AND SELF-EXAMINE YOUR BREASTS EVERY MONTH.

THERAPIES

ACUPRESSURE
• Practitioners believe the Stomach meridian irrigates the breast channel and so can help to treat breast conditions. Some also advise that overeating will block your stomach qi ("life force") and so lead to problems in the breast area. *(See pages 29–31.)*

AROMATHERAPY
• Blend geranium essential oil with a little carrier oil and massage into tender, swollen breasts. Some therapists recommend a full body massage with geranium oil a few days before the onset of menstruation to improve circulation and prevent water retention. *(See pages 104–5.)*

HYDROTHERAPY
• Some therapists believe detoxification through steam baths and saunas clears out the body's systems and keeps you and your breasts healthy. This advice is based on studies showing that aerobic exercise, and the sweat it produces, may reduce cancer risk by promoting lymphatic drainage and removing toxins from tissues. *(See pages 172–9.)*

RELAXATION TECHNIQUES
• Many alternative practitioners believe that relaxation is a key to preventing serious illness. Combined with a healthy diet and exercise, relaxation will keep your immune system working to its maximum potential. Relaxation techniques are also useful for dealing with the pain of breast complaints and the associated fear and anxiety, for example, if you are worried about a cyst or lump and are awaiting diagnosis. *(See pages 158–65.)*

MASSAGE
• A massage technique called manual lymph drainage is believed to stimulate the lymphatic system and help the removal of toxins from the body. Self-massage of the breasts can also be soothing if you suffer from tender breasts during your period. A gentle massage will also help you to relax prior to your monthly breast self-examination. *(See pages 96–103.)*

MEDITATION
• Use meditation techniques to help you learn to relax. Some research studies suggest that there is a link between the formation of breast cysts and stress, which unbalances the body's hormone levels. *(See pages 60–63.)*

T'AI CHI CH'UAN
• This exercise-based therapy will keep you supple and healthy. Practitioners believe that the movements ensure a good flow of energy through your body – according to Traditional Chinese Medicine, any stagnant qi will adversely affect your health, including the health of your breasts. *(See pages 46–51 and Qigong, pages 44–5.)*

REFLEXOLOGY
• Practitioners advise stimulation of the second to fifth zones on the top of the feet as an effective treatment for breast cysts. *(See pages 66–71.)*

BELOW *Yogic relaxation techniques keep the body stress-free if you are worried about the possibility of serious illness.*

DATAFILE

• Up to 40 percent of women suffer from breast cysts. The vast majority of these are non-cancerous.

• Breast cancer is the leading cause of death for women aged 35 to 50 in the U.S. and the second leading cause of cancer death in women worldwide, after lung cancer.

• 1 in 9 women develop breast cancer. Each year there are 180,000 new cases and 45,000 deaths.

• Around 300 men die each year from breast cancer.

• Women in the U.S. are five times more likely to get breast cancer than healthy women in Asiatic countries.

• The chance of developing breast cancer increases with age. At 30 you have a 1 in 2,525 chance of developing the disease, but at 35 your chances are 1 in 622.

• Many alternative practitioners recommend switching to a healthy low-fat diet and cutting down on salt and alcohol to prevent breast problems. Caffeine is also best avoided since it is associated with the formation of breast cysts.

BELOW *A breast massage with geranium essential oil in a carrier oil can improve circulation and prevent water retention.*

Menstrual Problems

The most common problems associated with the menstrual cycle are painful menstruation (dysmenorrhea), heavy periods (menorrhagia), irregular periods, or absent periods (amenorrhea).

Most women suffer from painful periods at some time in their lives. The characteristic menstrual cramps, usually felt in the pelvis and lower back, can vary in degree from month to month or year to year. They may be accompanied by headache, nausea, vomiting, diarrhea, and palpitations, as well as tiredness and irritability. Menstrual cramps are thought to be related to the release of hormone-like chemicals called prostaglandins, which cause muscles in the uterus to go into spasm.

Primary dysmenorrhea usually starts with the first period and often disappears after the sufferer has a baby or starts taking the contraceptive pill. Most symptoms can be relieved by taking drugs such as ibuprofen. In more severe cases, drugs may be prescribed to stop uterine cramps, or rebalance hormone levels. Secondary dysmenorrhea occurs when periods suddenly become painful. This may be due to fibroids, endometriosis, tumors, pelvic infection, stress, emotional shocks, or a thyroid disorder. A doctor will investigate possible causes and give suitable treatment, for example, a course of antibiotics that will eradicate infection.

Menorrhagia – excessive bleeding during a period – has many possible causes, including stress, pelvic infection, endometriosis, or the use of an IUD contraceptive. Your doctor can run a blood test to check if the cause is a hormonal imbalance and, if so, may prescribe hormones or a progesterone-only contraceptive pill. She will also examine the vagina and uterus to eliminate the possibility of uterine abnormalities.

Primary amenorrhea is the term used if menstruation has not occurred by the age of 18. The cause is most often low body weight, although deformity of the uterus or vagina and disorders, such as adrenal hyperplasia, are other possibilities. Secondary amenorrhea occurs when menstruation stops for more than six months, due to pregnancy, breast-feeding, the menopause, or taking the contraceptive pill.

SYMPTOMS

• *amenorrhea: irregular or absent periods* • *menorrhagia: heavy periods* • *dysmenorrhea: painful periods, with possible headache, nausea, vomiting, diarrhea, fatigue, and irritability*

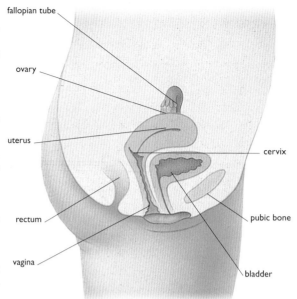

fallopian tube

ovary

uterus

rectum

vagina

cervix

pubic bone

bladder

ABOVE *Painful periods usually occur because prostaglandins cause the uterus to go into spasm, producing the characteristic menstrual cramp.*

THERAPIES

SHIATSU
• Therapists focus on stretching and applying pressure to the legs, whereby they can gain access to the three meridians, kidney, liver, and spleen, that control the blood. They believe this gives most effective relief for a range of menstrual problems, from cramping to irregular periods. (See pages 32–7 and Do-in, pages 38–41.)

YOGA
• This therapy is believed to aid menstrual problems by relieving stress, balancing hormone levels, and toning the pelvic area. Therapists recommend specific postures to encourage circulation in the pelvic region. Practice relaxation and breathing exercises only during your period. (See pages 52–9.)

VISUALIZATION
• An energizing visualization may help to counteract the drop in energy levels women experience during menstruation. Sit comfortably with your arms by your sides. Take a deep breath and visualize a big balloon above your head filled with a bright red healing energy. Imagine that you pop this balloon and release the energy. (See pages 214–7.)

THERAPEUTIC TOUCH
• By concentrating a flow of healing energy on the affected areas of the body, therapists believe that they can relieve the symptoms of many menstrual problems. (See pages 90–91.)

CAUTION

CONSULT A DOCTOR IF YOUR PERIODS SUDDENLY STOP OR BECOME PAINFUL, YOUR MENSTRUAL BLEEDING BECOMES HEAVIER THAN USUAL, OR YOU BLEED BETWEEN PERIODS.

BELOW *Relaxing in a hot bath, possibly with a few drops of lavender or marjoram oil, can help relieve the tension and symptoms of painful periods.*

Premenstrual Syndrome (PMS)

The term PMS covers a huge range of symptoms – as many as 150, according to some PMS experts. The most common are anxiety, irritability, depression, headache, bloated stomach, fatigue, and food cravings. The symptoms can appear at any time during the two weeks before a menstrual period and disappear shortly after the period begins. Some women find that symptoms of other disorders, such as arthritis and depression, worsen during this period.

The cause of PMS is not clear. Some doctors believe the symptoms are caused by hormonal imbalances, possibly related to vitamin B6 deficiency, and prescribe progesterone treatment or estrogen implants. Other conventional treatments include diuretics to reduce bloating caused by water retention, antidepressants to manage psychological symptoms, evening primrose oil capsules, vitamin supplements, and painkillers. Many sufferers have found that changes in lifestyle, such as taking moderate exercise, and altering eating habits, such as eating small meals at regular intervals, alleviate the symptoms.

SYMPTOMS

• *headache* • *tender breasts* • *swollen abdomen* • *depression*
• *fatigue* • *irritability* • *food cravings*

LEFT AND BELOW
Taking Vitamin B supplements and moderate exercise have both been shown to reduce the symptoms of PMS.

DATAFILE

• Vitamin B6, taken twice daily, can help to prevent cramps and heavy bleeding, but consult your doctor first as it can be harmful in large doses.

• A sudden change in lifestyle, such as losing a large amount of weight, can cause your periods to stop. Provided you are not underweight, your periods should start once your weight stabilizes.

• 70 to 80 percent of women find taking oral contraceptives reduces painful periods.

• Taking exercise during a period may improve bloodflow and reduce pelvic pain.

• A warm bath or hot water bottles applied to the lower back and abdomen will soothe cramps.

THERAPIES

ACUPRESSURE
• Therapists recommend applying pressure to points on the sacrum to help relieve menstrual cramps. Lie on your back with your hands, one on top of the other, under the base of the spine and apply pressure for two minutes. *(See pages 29–31.)*

ALEXANDER TECHNIQUE
• The natural tendency when women experience period pains is to tense up the body, which leads to further mental and physical discomfort. Practitioners teach their pupils to release physical tension, especially in the abdomen and lower back, through relaxation techniques and new postures and ways of moving. *(See pages 146–53.)*

AROMATHERAPY
• Clary sage, basil, and fennel oils, massaged into the lower back, may help to regulate hormone balance and the menstrual cycle. Therapists recommend a lower abdominal massage with cypress, rose, or geranium oil to treat heavy bleeding and antispasmodic oils, such as lavender, cypress and clary sage for menstrual cramps. *(See pages 104–5.)*

CHIROPRACTIC
• Manipulation and treatment of the lower back and sacrum may help to relieve the pain associated with menstruation. *(See pages 118–25 and Osteopathy, pages 106–13.)*

HYDROTHERAPY
• Warm water is a traditional way to calm and relax both the mind and the body. Run a tub of warm water and add one cup of sea salt and one cup of baking soda to the water. Soak in the water for 20 minutes to reduce cramps, irritability, and anxiety. Let the water cool a little if you suffer from heavy menstrual bleeding, since heat will increase the bloodflow. *(See pages 172–9.)*

HYPNOTHERAPY
• This is an accepted way of relieving pain and reducing stress- and anxiety-related conditions. *(See pages 218–23.)*

THERAPIES

ACUPRESSURE
• Two acupressure points on the Spleen meridian are believed to be very effective. Sit up with the soles of the feet together. Place both thumbs on the inside of the ankles, four finger widths above the anklebone, and feel for a slight indentation. Press on the point for one minute. Next, place the thumbs on the arches of the feet. Wiggle the toes back and forth and feel for a muscle that moves at the same time. Press on the muscle for one minute. *(See pages 29–31.)*

ACUPUNCTURE
• Therapy focuses on freeing the qi along the Liver meridian and usually begins after ovulation, a few days before the onset of symptoms. Moxibustion is sometimes used. Most therapists recommend treatment be given over three menstrual cycles for the best effect. *(See pages 20–28.)*

AROMATHERAPY
• A full-body massage with clary sage, neroli, jasmine, or ylang ylang is recommended for PMS. A lower back and abdominal massage with grapefruit, carrot seed, or juniper oil may ease the discomfort of water retention. For best results, aromatherapy massage should be done a few days before the onset of symptoms. *(See pages 104–5.)*

MEDITATION
• Relaxation techniques, such as meditation, may help to relieve anxiety and irritability. Many therapists believe that stress is a cause of PMS, so this may also work preventively. *(See pages 60–63.)*

YOGA
• Practitioners recommend a daily yoga session, with deep relaxation techniques, in the week before a period. *(See pages 52–9.)*

OTHER THERAPIES
• Other therapies include reflexology *(see pages 66–71),* therapeutic touch *(see pages 90–91),* and visualization *(see pages 214–17).*

Female Infertility

Infertility, the inability to conceive after at least a year of regular sexual intercourse without the use of contraceptives, is a common problem, affecting between 10 and 15 percent of couples. In most cases, the failure to conceive is due to a specific physical cause in one or other partner. *(For male infertility problems, see page 332.)*

Female infertility may occur because the endocrine system is not functioning properly, because the woman is nearing menopause, or because she has stopped taking oral contraceptives in the last three months. Even if an egg is produced, it may not be able to reach the uterus because the Fallopian tubes have been blocked or distorted by an infection. Prolapse, ovarian cysts, scarring on the cervix, and uterine abnormalities are other causes of infertility. Sometimes the mucus covering the cervix destroys the sperm before the egg can be fertilized. Some cases of infertility seem to have no physical cause, but may be related to poor diet, fatigue, smoking, or stress.

Your doctor will carry out a blood test to check hormone levels. She may ask you to record your body temperature daily to check whether you are ovulating regularly. Just before ovulation, the temperature on waking will be a little below normal, 97 or 97.8°F. After ovulation, it rises by half or one degree. If further investigation is required, you may be referred to a specialist infertility unit. Treatment includes drugs to trigger ovulation or egg production, surgery to clear Fallopian tubes, and in-vitro ("test-tube") fertilization.

SYMPTOMS

• *failure to conceive after 12 months of intercourse without use of contraceptives*

LEFT *Infertility in women may occur for a number of reasons, either physical or emotional. You may not be ovulating properly, you may be under stress or there may be blockages in the fallopian tubes which can be treated by microsurgery.*

LEFT *If you are having trouble conceiving, keeping a note of your body temperature can help you see when you are ovulating.*

CONVENTIONAL TREATMENT

A BLOOD TEST CAN CHECK HORMONE LEVELS, WHILE MONITORING YOUR BODY TEMPERATURE WILL DETERMINE WHETHER OVULATION IS TAKING PLACE. YOUR DOCTOR MAY RECOMMEND FURTHER INVESTIGATIONS AND SUBSEQUENT TREATMENT WILL DEPEND ON THE OUTCOME OF ALL THESE TESTS. OPTIONS INCLUDE SURGERY TO UNBLOCK FALLOPIAN TUBES, DRUG THERAPY TO STIMULATE EGG PRODUCTION OR OVULATION, OR IN-VITRO FERTILIZATION, WHEREBY EGGS ARE GATHERED FROM THE BODY, FERTILIZED OUTSIDE IT, AND THEN IMPLANTED IN THE UTERUS.

DATAFILE

• Drug therapy to combat infertility and in-vitro fertilization (IVF) may lead to multiple pregnancy.

• Vitamin E supplements may increase male and female fertility. Calcium, magnesium, and vitamin A are also thought to help the chances of conception.

• Fertility declines in women over the age of 35.

• Researchers report that smoking diminishes fertilization in women by two-thirds.

• Dieting and weight loss may reduce fertility.

THERAPIES

ACUPRESSURE
• The acupoint found three finger widths below the belly button is thought to tone the abdominal region and enhance fertility. *(See pages 29–31.)*

ACUPUNCTURE
• Therapists believe infertility relates to Liver qi stagnation. Acupuncture at the right time in the menstrual cycle (possibly over several months) may help to clear congestion. *(See pages 20–28.)*

AROMATHERAPY
• Therapists believe that aromatherapy can improve fertility. A back or abdominal massage with neroli, rose or jasmine may encourage a natural hormone balance, while clary sage cleanses and soothes the uterus. *(See pages 104–5.)*

CHIROPRACTIC
• To enhance circulation and improve functioning of the reproductive organs, some practitioners teach pelvic and breathing exercises and give gynecological manipulation. *(See pages 118–25 and Osteopathy, pages 106–13.)*

QIGONG
• Gentle movement therapies, such as qigong and t'ai chi ch'uan, are thought to help to ensure a smooth flow of qi, or energy, through the body and rebalance the natural cycles, such as ovulation. *(See pages 44–5, and pages 46–51.)*

RELAXATION
• The inability to conceive can be extremely stressful, but stress in itself may be a factor in infertility. Relaxation techniques to relieve mental and physical tension may be advised. *(See pages 158–65.)* Meditation, breathing, and visualization may also help. *(See pages 60–63, 166–71, and 214–7.)*

PSYCHOTHERAPY
• Infertility may have psychological as well as physical causes, especially if you are subconsciously unsure that you want to start or add to a family. Therapy can bring such issues out into the open and help you to resolve them. *(See pages 206–7.)*

RIGHT *If your problem is stress-related, relaxation techniques can help reduce tension.*

Miscarriage

The spontaneous abortion of a pregnancy prior to 20 weeks' gestation is termed a miscarriage. After 20 weeks, loss of the baby is termed stillbirth. A large number of miscarriages go unrecognized because they occur before pregnancy is diagnosed. After pregnancy is confirmed, around 20 percent of pregnancies end in miscarriage, most taking place between the sixth and tenth weeks of pregnancy. In most cases, the pregnancy fails because the fetus is not developing normally, or because it fails to implant itself in the lining of the uterus. Often there is no clear explanation, but some women are more at risk than others. These include mothers over 40, those with poorly controlled diabetes, women carrying more than one baby, and smokers.

Consult a doctor if you notice bleeding, blood clots or a dark discharge from the vagina, accompanied by cramp-like pains and back pain, since these may indicate the pregnancy is in danger. Some doctors advise bedrest at first, in the hope that the pregnancy will settle down. If the symptoms continue, you may be given an internal examination and an ultrasound to determine if you have miscarried. A full miscarriage is signified by heavy bleeding lasting up to ten days. In later miscarriages, the woman may experience a form of labor and pass part or all of the fetus, which is extremely distressing.

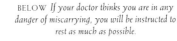

BELOW *If your doctor thinks you are in any danger of miscarrying, you will be instructed to rest as much as possible.*

CAUTION

SEEK MEDICAL ATTENTION IF YOU FEEL SEVERE ABDOMINAL PAIN BETWEEN THE FIFTH AND TENTH WEEKS OF PREGNANCY, SINCE THIS MAY INDICATE AN ECTOPIC PREGNANCY, WHICH CAN BE LIFE-THREATENING.

DATAFILE

• The risk of miscarriage falls significantly after the eighth week of pregnancy.

• About one in five pregnancies ends in miscarriage.

• Forty percent of miscarriages are caused by chromosomal abnormalities – a problem in the genetic coding – of the fetus.

• Later miscarriages are usually caused by illness or problems with the mother's uterus or cervix.

SYMPTOMS

• *bleeding, blood clots or dark vaginal discharge* • *cramp-like pains in abdomen* • *back pain* • *continuous bleeding*

THERAPIES

ACUPUNCTURE
• Therapists believe that it is important to build and conserve a woman's qi ("life force") and restore her blood supplies after a miscarriage. They apply moxibustion and acupuncture treatment to the Liver and Kidney meridians. *(See pages 20–28.)*

ART THERAPY
• A miscarriage can bring deep feelings of grief and bereavement. Drawing, sculpting, and painting can help people to express and work through these emotions. *(See pages 238–41.)*

LEFT *Art therapy can help grieving mothers come to terms their loss.*

COLOR THERAPY
• Therapists believe that the color red stimulates energy flow and assists in the manufacture of hemoglobin for new red blood cells. It is also thought to relieve the sadness and depression that follow a miscarriage. *(See pages 258–61.)*

MASSAGE
• Couples can feel very isolated after a miscarriage and unable to discuss their feelings, especially of grief. Massage between partners may help to re-establish physical closeness. *(See pages 96–103.)*

PSYCHOTHERAPY & COUNSELING
• Some people find talking to a counselor or therapist helps them come to terms with the grief and sadness that follow a miscarriage. It is often useful for patients to have these feelings acknowledged as real and important. *(See Family Therapy and Relationship Counseling, pages 206–7.)*

BELOW *The colour red is thought to relieve depression.*

Pregnancy Problems

Pregnancy typically lasts 40 weeks from the first day of a woman's last menstrual period. The time is often referred to in three parts, or trimesters. The first trimester lasts from 0 to 12 weeks, the second from 13 to 27 weeks, and the third from 28 to 40 weeks. Doctors examine the mother and baby at every stage to ensure normal development and monitor fluid retention, blood pressure, and placental growth, which may lead to complications in later pregnancy. Both conventional and alternative practitioners advise that pregnant women lead as healthy a lifestyle as possible – do not smoke, avoid stress, eat a balanced diet, and exercise regularly.

A woman's body undergoes major physical changes during the first trimester. Many women feel exhausted because the heart is working harder to increase the flow of blood to the fetus. Regular naps and exercise may help to boost energy levels. Eat a healthy diet and check you are getting enough protein and iron – anemia is another common side-effect of pregnancy. Changes in hormone levels may cause nausea and vomiting, experienced by about half of all pregnant women. Eating small amounts of food, particularly carbohydrates, may alleviate this symptom. Some doctors advise taking a vitamin B6 supplement, but be aware that large doses may be toxic. Another common problem, which tends to disappear during the second trimester, is an increased desire to urinate. Urinate as often as you feel you need to, and empty the bladder fully each time.

Hormonal changes during the first trimester can make the breasts feel tender and sore. Wearing a good support bra, even at night, may help. Hormones are also thought to be the cause of tiredness, headaches, and dizziness experienced during the initial stages, although stress and fatigue may be contributory factors. It is best to avoid taking any medication during pregnancy, so talk to your doctor before taking painkillers for headaches. Women often find as well that they retain excess fluid, especially in the hands, legs, and feet. This should be monitored carefully by your doctor, since it may be an indication of a more serious underlying condition.

Many women find the second trimester the most enjoyable part of their pregnancy. Nausea tends to diminish, they feel more energetic, and they sleep better. There are, however, new symptoms to contend with. As the uterus grows, the internal organs are pushed out of place. Hormones cause the surrounding muscles and ligaments to soften, sometimes leading to musculoskeletal aches and pains. Back pain is common, but can be minimized by strengthening the abdominal muscles and maintaining good posture at all times – take care to bend the knees when lifting things. The uterus can also put pressure on a vein called the inferior vena cava, which causes varicose veins to appear on the legs. Women often experience aches and pain in the pelvis and abdomen and cramps in the lower legs.

During the second trimester, the digestive system slows down due to hormonal influences, causing heartburn and constipation. Doctors recommend regular gentle exercise, eating more fiber, and drinking plenty of fluids to alleviate constipation; consult a doctor before taking antacids to relieve heartburn. Many women notice skin changes as well, including dark patches, especially on the nipples, red and itchy palms

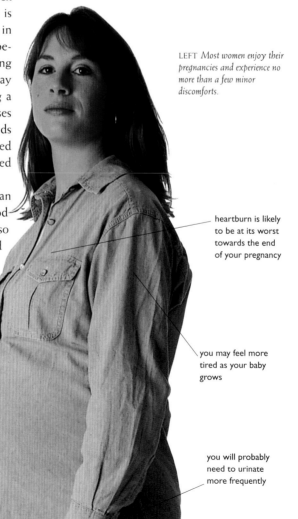

LEFT *Most women enjoy their pregnancies and experience no more than a few minor discomforts.*

heartburn is likely to be at its worst towards the end of your pregnancy

you may feel more tired as your baby grows

you will probably need to urinate more frequently

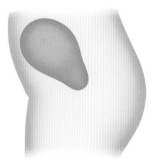

ABOVE *After about six weeks, your baby will be about 3 in. (8 cm.) long and will have developed limbs, genitals, and some facial features.*

ABOVE *By four to five months he will have doubled in size and his major organs will be functioning.*

and soles, blotchy patches, moles, heat rashes, and brittle fingernails, all of which usually disappear after delivery. Stretch marks are fine red lines that appear on the breasts, abdomen and thighs as the skin stretches to cover the growing body. These fade with time, but may not disappear after the baby is born.

As the uterus gets bigger, pressure increases on the internal organs, so backaches and heartburn both tend to worsen during the third trimester. Many women find it difficult to find a comfortable position in which to sleep or even sit, which leads to tiredness and stress. The third trimester is also the time when most medical complications occur, such as gestational diabetes, pre-eclampsia (pregnancy-induced hypertension that can lead to the life-threatening condition eclampsia), placental problems, intrauterine growth retardation (when babies do not grow as rapidly as they should); and post-term pregnancy (when pregnancies go beyond 42 weeks). All these require orthodox treatment.

SYMPTOMS

- *anemia* • *nausea and vomiting* • *painful breasts* • *fatigue*
- *insomnia* • *backache* • *constipation* • *heartburn*
- *flatulence* • *fluid retention* • *hemorrhoids* • *stretch marks*
- *skin conditions* • *varicose veins*

ABOVE *Eating healthily when you are pregnant is vital if you are to give your baby the best possible start in life.*

CAUTION

CONSULT A DOCTOR IMMEDIATELY IF DIZZINESS IS SEVERE AND OCCURS WITH ABDOMINAL PAIN OR VAGINAL BLEEDING; IF YOU SUFFER PROLONGED BOUTS OF NAUSEA; IF YOU URINATE AT FREQUENT INTERVALS FOR TWO DAYS; EXPERIENCE FLU SYMPTOMS; OR IF FLUID RETENTION HAS NOT DECREASED AFTER THREE DAYS. IF YOU HAVE NOT BEEN VACCINATED AGAINST GERMAN MEASLES, AVOID CONTACT WITH THE DISEASE.

DATAFILE

- During pregnancy, the amount of blood in your body increases by about 40 percent and the uterus grows to 150 times its normal size.

- Women should gain about 25 to 30 pounds during pregnancy. The smallest gain occurs during the first trimester, when an average weight gain would be about six pounds.

- Women feel the first fluttering movements of the baby between 16 and 20 weeks. This is also known as the "quickening."

- Ninety percent of women report that some areas of skin, particularly on or around the nipples, get darker during pregnancy.

- Increases in progesterone levels during the first trimester can make you want to sleep more than usual.

THERAPIES

ACUPRESSURE

• Acupressure on the Pericardium 6 point may reduce feelings of nausea during the first trimester. A different acupoint located one thumb width below the inside of the anklebone can help to relieve fluid retention, especially swollen ankles. There are specific acupoints which must not be stimulated during pregnancy as this may induce a miscarriage. *(See pages 29–31.)*

ALEXANDER TECHNIQUE

• A woman's center of gravity shifts forward during pregnancy as the uterus grows and breasts become larger and heavier. To compensate for this, many women arch their backs and put strain on their ligaments and muscles, which leads to back pain. The Alexander technique teaches pupils the correct posture to use when sitting, standing, picking up objects, and moving. *(See pages 146–53.)*

BREATHING

• The growing uterus displaces the bottom of the lungs so your pattern of breathing may change during the later stages of pregnancy. Using the diaphragm is the most efficient, and least tiring, way of breathing. During pregnancy the ribs and shoulders take over as the diaphragm becomes compressed by the uterus. Breathing exercises can help refocus control on the diaphragm. *(See pages 166–71.)*

CHIROPRACTIC

• Practitioners believe that treatment during pregnancy can correct vertebral misalignment and relieve the pressure that causes back pain, put joints back in their normal position and keep them mobile, and ensure that pelvic bones are aligned to make delivery easier. *(See pages 118–25 and Osteopathy, pages 106–13.)*

MASSAGE

• Practitioners argue that massage during pregnancy has many beneficial effects. It reduces emotional tension and stress, relaxes the body, and, if done by the partner, can bring the couple closer together during the pregnancy. Massaging a pregnant belly clockwise helps with digestion, and using an oil or cream with vitamin E, such as wheatgerm oil, may help reduce stretch marks. Do not massage the abdomen, legs, and feet during the first three months of pregnancy. *(See pages 96–103.)*

MUSIC THERAPY

• Sounds can be extremely relaxing both for mother and, some believe, the unborn baby. Therapists recommend slow, quiet classical music if you are feeling anxious or tense. They believe it slows the pulse and heartrate, lowers blood pressure, and decreases levels of stress hormones. Natural sounds, such as ocean waves and whale song, may also induce a sense of peace and relaxation. *(See pages 232–5.)*

RELAXATION

• Many pregnant women find a warm, scented bath the perfect place to relax. The water supports the extra weight and the warmth helps to ease aches and pains. Try a relaxation technique in the bath, focusing on tensing and then releasing different parts of the body. Get out of the bath slowly to avoid feeling faint. *(See pages 158–65 and Hydrotherapy, pages 172–9.)*

YOGA

• Yoga stretches the pelvic muscles, improves flexibility, and eases daily aches and pains. Yogic deep breathing will also keep you relaxed and stress-free during pregnancy. Pregnant women should avoid forward bending, inverted poses, and asanas lying on the stomach. It is advisable to learn a simplified and modified routine from a yoga specialist. *(See pages 52–9.)*

ACUPUNCTURE

• Stimulation of the appropriate acupoints may help to alleviate "morning sickness," the nausea and vomiting commonly experienced in pregnancy. *(See pages 20–28.)*

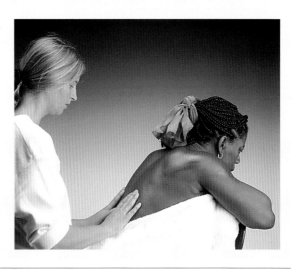

BELOW *A massage can soothe and relax a pregnant woman; it can also help digestion and stretch marks.*

327

Labor Pains

Labor falls into three distinct stages. The first stage begins after the breaking of the waters and when regular contractions of the uterus start. It ends when the cervix, the opening to the uterus, dilates fully to allow the baby to move into the vagina. The process can take anywhere between 7 and 13 hours, the contractions getting increasingly rhythmic and intense throughout. By the time the cervix is fully dilated the contractions are severe. Then the mother has to push when instructed and use breathing to help to control the movement of the baby through the birth canal. This is the second stage of labor, and may take as little as ten minutes or several hours. The third stage is the actual birth.

In the early stages of labor, the mother is encouraged to use exercise, massage, breathing and relaxation techniques, and TENS (Transcutaneous Electrical Nerve Stimulation) to cope with pain. As the contractions become more severe, there are further options for pain relief, including "gas-and-air", painkilling injections,

and an epidural (spinal) injection. Some women find that giving birth in an upright position – standing, sitting, or squatting – is a natural way to cope with labor pains.

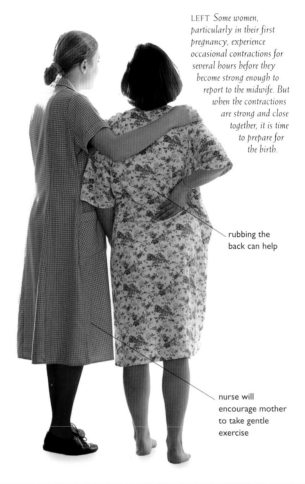

LEFT *Some women, particularly in their first pregnancy, experience occasional contractions for several hours before they become strong enough to report to the midwife. But when the contractions are strong and close together, it is time to prepare for the birth.*

rubbing the back can help

nurse will encourage mother to take gentle exercise

CONVENTIONAL TREATMENT

PAIN RELIEF, PAINKILLING INJECTIONS, OR EPIDURAL ANESTHESIA, IS THE MAIN FORM OF TREATMENT. IF LABOR BECOMES PROLONGED, A DOCTOR MAY PERFORM A FORCEPS DELIVERY OR AN EPISIOTOMY – AN INCISION TO WIDEN THE VAGINAL OPENING AND PREVENT TEARING OF TISSUES. IF THERE ARE COMPLICATIONS, THE BABY MAY BE DELIVERED BY CAESAREAN SECTION.

ABOVE *Listening to soothing music or gentle sounds like waves on the shore can relax you during labour.*

THERAPIES

ACUPUNCTURE
• There is strong evidence that acupuncture is an effective pain reliever and some hospitals will offer the therapy to help with labor pains. In China it is widely used for Cesarean sections. Moxibustion applied to an acupuncture point on the little toe is thought to help place the fetus in the correct position for birth. *(See pages 20–28.)*

ACUPRESSURE
• Therapists believe that pressure on the muscle on top of the shoulders and the sacral points at the base of the spine will relieve pain and tension. Gentle pressure on the acupoint in the webbing between the thumb and index finger is thought to speed up the process. *(See pages 29–31.)*

MASSAGE
• Massage and touch therapies can help with many aspects of birth. Some practitioners advise perineal massage prior to labor to stretch the muscles around the vaginal opening and prevent tearing of the tissues. Massaging the uterus softly releases oxytocin in the body and may help to bring on labor. Massage of the back and buttocks during labor can be relaxing, reassuring, and pain relieving. *(See pages 96–103.)*

PYSCHOTHERAPY
• You may find it helpful to discuss your fears and anxieties about giving birth with a counselor. A positive attitude to the birth will enable you to relax

more and help to lessen the pains. *(See pages 188–91.)*

RELAXATION
• Tension and fatigue increase labor pain, so relaxation is one of the keys to a comfortable birth. Practitioners can teach many techniques to use during labor. Breathing deeply and controlledly will also help you to relax. *(See pages 158–65 and Breathing, pages 166–71.)*

SOUND THERAPY
• Listening to gentle sounds or music between contractions can be soothing and relaxing for a woman in labor. *(See pages 236–7.)*

VISUALIZATION
• Therapists work with the patient before birth to create positive images of labor. They ask the patient to imagine that the contractions of the uterus are no more painful than the contractions of a bicep. The mother is encouraged to see the contractions as natural and necessary parts of labor and feel that the delivery is progressing slowly and calmly. *(See pages 214–17.)*

HYDROTHERAPY
• A warm bath during the first stage of labor can aid relaxation and relieve pain. Some therapists advocate the use of a birthing pool while in labor. *(See pages 172–9.)*

BELOW *Visualization techniques may help you feel positive about what can be a frightening experience.*

Post-delivery Problems

Giving birth can take its toll on emotional and physical health. Many women continue to suffer from pain after the birth, as the uterus contracts to its normal size. They may also suffer from backache, perhaps caused by straining during delivery, hemorrhoids, a sore abdomen following a Caesarean section, and soreness in the genital area, as a result of the stitches needed to repair a tear or for an episiotomy. New mothers often feel exhausted after a long or difficult labor; they may also be anemic if they have lost a large amount of blood.

Many postnatal symptoms are related to changing hormone levels. These include hair loss, acne, slow nail growth, a decrease in libido, and an increase in premenstrual symptoms. The drop in estrogen and progesterone is also thought to be the cause of the sadness, weepiness, and depression experienced by many new mothers. Mild "baby blues" begin about three days after delivery and last only for a few days. Postnatal depression starts within weeks of the birth and may last for a year or more. Puerperal psychosis, characterized by manic depression, hallucinations, and virtual breakdown, happens in rare, extreme cases.

Other factors, such as fatigue, physical discomfort, anxiety about caring for the baby, and feeling isolated from other people, may contribute to post-delivery problems. Such problems are not unique and nothing to be ashamed about. You should talk through any difficulties you may have with your doctor. Breast-feeding problems, for example, may be caused by an infection in the milk ducts (mastitis), which is treatable with antibiotics. If symptoms of depression persist, your doctor may prescribe antidepressants or hormonal drugs, and suggest counseling.

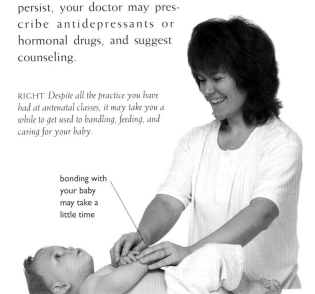

RIGHT *Despite all the practice you have had at antenatal classes, it may take you a while to get used to handling, feeding, and caring for your baby.*

bonding with your baby may take a little time

SYMPTOMS

• *pain and discomfort following Caesarean section or episiotomy* • *fatigue* • *anemia* • *headache* • *hair loss* • *acne* • *postnatal illness (low libido, low self-esteem, irritability, weepiness, depression)* • *breast-feeding problems (sore nipples and breasts, blocked milk ducts, insufficient milk)*

DATAFILE

• Breast-feeding may inhibit menstruation for anywhere between six weeks and two years, but it is still possible to get pregnant during this time.

• An epidural can occasionally lead to a severe headache that lasts up to 48 hours after the injection.

• Poor breast milk production may be caused by not drinking sufficient fluids.

• "Baby blues", or mood swings, are common after delivery, but if they persist for longer than a few weeks, a doctor should be consulted.

• Shared massages, say practitioners, can help in the bonding process between mother and baby

THERAPIES

AROMATHERAPY
• Therapists recommend massaging chamomile into the abdomen and lower back to relieve pains after labor. Lavender and chamomile, diluted in apricot kernel oil, can be applied directly to sore stitches. A massage with mood-enhancing oils, such as clary sage or jasmine, may help to ease depression and anxiety. *(See pages 104–5.)*

ACUPRESSURE
• The acupoint found four finger widths below the kneecap and one finger width outside the shinbone is thought to aid postpartum recovery. Pressing the acupoint on top of the foot between the big and second toe is thought to relieve the sweating that can occur after childbirth. *(See pages 29–31.)*

HYDROTHERAPY
• Practitioners recommend applying ice to perineal tears as soon as possible to reduce swelling. They also advise taking sitz baths to aid the healing process. *(See pages 172–9.)*

MASSAGE
• The weeks after the birth are a good time for both partners to massage each other. Regular massage helps the mother's body recover its muscle tone, and eases the strains placed on the body from childbirth. The mental relaxation of massage may relieve the emotional stresses associated with a new baby. *(See pages 96–103.)*

BELOW *Hormone imbalances after birth may leave you feeling exhausted and depressed.*

RELAXATION
• Postpartum difficulties are often linked to stress, anxiety, and fatigue. Relaxation techniques and plenty of rest will alleviate all these problems. *(See pages 158–65.)*

VISUALIZATION
• This therapy may be helpful if you have problems breast-feeding. The therapist may suggest that you imagine a calm, quiet environment with your baby feeding happily. This will give you a more positive attitude to breast-feeding and help you to relax. *(See pages 214–17.)*

PSYCHOTHERAPY
• Professional counseling can help you to come to terms with the emotional pressure and change in lifestyle that having a new baby may bring. *(See Family Therapy, pages 206–7.)*

Menopause Problems

The end of menstrual bleeding, marking the end of the ability to reproduce, is termed the menopause. Most women experience this "change of life" between the ages of 48 and 52, although some women cease to menstruate in their thirties or early forties. Hormonal changes that bring about the menopause begin four to six years before the last menstrual period. Estrogen production in the ovaries gradually decreases, causing an imbalance between progesterone and estrogen. Eventually, so little estrogen is produced that menstruation becomes erratic and finally ends completely.

For some women, the transition is uneventful. But, for many, the menopause is a difficult time accompanied by uncomfortable symptoms. The severity of the symptoms seems to depend on an individual's biochemistry and lifestyle factors, such as diet, fitness, and stress levels. Studies have shown that women suffer more severe symptoms if they are under emotional stress or consume large quantities of caffeine, sugar or alcohol.

Physical symptoms include irregular menstrual bleeding, poor circulation, breast lumpiness, aches and pains, hot flushes, night sweats, skin complaints, thinning head hair, and increased facial and body hair. The reducing estrogen levels also diminish the amount of bone in the body and can increase the risk of osteoporosis as a result. Many menopausal women experience psychological symptoms similar to those characteristic of premenstrual syndrome (PMS), including anxiety, depression, mood swings, lack of concentration, and loss of memory. These symptoms are exacerbated by the fact that women in their fifties commonly have to cope with other

LEFT *The physical and hormonal changes of the menopause often occur at a time when life is difficult in other ways, too. Children growing up and leaving home may leave a gap that you find difficult to fill.*

you may feel lonely if your child leaves home

BELOW *Ylang ylang oil can boost the libido, which is often at a low ebb at this time.*

LEFT *Excessive consumption of coffee and alcohol can make the menopause more problematic.*

DATAFILE

• Japanese women suffer fewer symptoms during the menopause, possibly due to the high level of plant estrogens, such as tofu, soya, and miso, in their diet.

• Eighty percent of women experience some menopausal symptoms.

• Twenty to twenty-five percent of menopausal women experience pain during intercourse due to thinning of the vaginal wall and lack of lubrication, both caused by estrogen deficiency.

• In general, when estrogen predominates during the menopausal process, women tend to feel anxious; when progesterone predominates, women may feel depressed and tired.

• The average age of menopause – 50 years – has remained constant since medieval times.

THERAPIES

RELAXATION
• Menopausal women suffering emotional symptoms, such as anxiety or anger, tend to store tension in their muscles. Releasing muscle tension is thought to increase energy levels and may help to release these repressed and blocked emotions. Lie on your back, arms by your sides. Inhale and exhale deeply. Clench your hand into fists and hold tightly for 25 seconds. Then relax and visualize a warm light flowing into your body, making the muscles soft. Tense and relax other parts of your body, such as the face, shoulders, back, stomach, pelvis, legs, feet, and toes. *(See pages 158–65.)*

T'AI CHI CH'UAN
• Practitioners believe this therapy promotes inner happiness and relaxation. The gentle stretching and controlled movements will help to keep the body flexible. *(See pages 46–51 and Qigong, pages 44–5.)*

AROMATHERAPY
• Essential oils are used to treat a range of menopause-related symptoms. A massage with a mood-enhancing oil, such as clary sage or rose, may help to relieve irritability and depression; chamomile may balance hormone levels and prevent night sweats and hot flushes; geranium or ylang ylang oils may increase your libido. *(See pages 104–5.)*

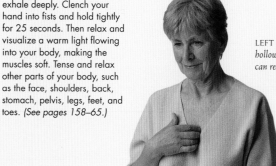

LEFT *Pressing the point in the hollow next to the breastbone can reduce hot flushes.*

stress factors, such as teenage children, children having left home ("empty nest" syndrome), or children living at home longer, aging parents, bereavement, and relationship changes, at the same time as going through the menopause.

There are many effective ways to reduce the emotional and physical impact. Physical problems caused by declining estrogen levels, such as thinning skin and hot flushes, can be treated by hormone replacement therapy (HRT) in the form of pills, patches, skin implants, and vaginal creams. This treatment is also thought to reduce the risk of heart disease and strokes. There is concern, however, that HRT may increase the risk of some cancers and research is continuing into connections between long-term use of the treatment and breast cancer. HRT will also help to lessen the risk of developing osteoporosis, but this condition can, to a large extent, be prevented by a healthy diet, vitamin D supplements and exercise.

A doctor may prescribe antidepressants, tranquilizers, sleeping tablets or mood-enhancing drugs to relieve symptoms, such as anxiety and fatigue. Some women report that symptoms are alleviated by a course of HRT. Both alternative and conventional practitioners advocate exercise, a healthy diet, an increase in calcium intake, and stress-reducing measures to minimize the effects of the menopause.

CONVENTIONAL TREATMENT

HORMONE REPLACEMENT PILLS, IMPLANTS, PATCHES, AND VAGINAL CREAMS ARE EFFECTIVE TREATMENTS BOTH FOR PHYSICAL SYMPTOMS, SUCH AS HOT FLUSHES, AND FOR PSYCHOLOGICAL SIDE-EFFECTS, SUCH AS ANXIETY. A DOCTOR MAY ALSO PRESCRIBE ANTIDEPRESSANTS, TRANQUILIZERS, OR SLEEPING PILLS TO HELP TO OVERCOME PSYCHOLOGICAL SYMPTOMS. SHE MAY ALSO RECOMMEND COUNSELING OR PSYCHOTHERAPY SESSIONS. MANY WOMEN FIND A LUBRICATING JELLY HELPS TO PREVENT PAIN DURING SEXUAL INTERCOURSE. BOTH CONVENTIONAL AND ALTERNATIVE PRACTITIONERS RECOMMEND TAKING REGULAR EXERCISE, REDUCING STRESS, AND EATING A HEALTHY DIET, ESPECIALLY CUTTING DOWN ON ALCOHOL, SUGAR, AND CAFFEINE.

LEFT *There is no need to give up exercise just because you have reached "a certain age." It may be something you and your partner can enjoy together, and it will keep you both young.*

SYMPTOMS

• *irregular periods (often heavy or light) which eventually cease completely* • *back pain* • *vaginal dryness, leading to pain during intercourse* • *skin problems*

• *hot flushes* • *night sweats* • *itching* • *incontinence* • *hair growth on face, stomach, or chest* • *poor concentration* • *memory loss* • *depression* • *insomnia* • *low sex drive*

THERAPIES

ACUPRESSURE
• Therapists recommend using acupressure points one to four times each day to balance the body and reduce hot flushes. Suggested points are at the base of the ball of the foot; in the hollow below the collarbone next to the breastbone; on the center of the breastbone three thumb widths up from the base of the bone; and between the eyebrows. *(See pages 29–31.)*

PSYCHOTHERAPY
• Professional counseling can help you combat the negative feelings you may have about the menopause by helping to promote a more positive self-image. It may also help you to come to terms with factors such as the "empty nest" syndrome. *(See pages 188–91.)*

COLOR THERAPY
• Therapists believe that the color blue has a calming, relaxing effect and use it to treat feverish conditions, including hot flushes. Blue is thought to promote serenity and help relieve tension, stress, and headaches. In addition to professional color treatment, try wearing blue nightwear and bathrobes and leave a blue light on at night to relieve menopausal symptoms. *(See pages 248–51.)*

MEDITATION
• Meditation relaxes the body, releases tension, and helps relieve anxiety by providing a respite from stressful and unpleasant thoughts. Sit comfortably and close your eyes. Breathe deeply. Focus on the breaths, noticing the rise and fall of the abdomen. Block out all other thoughts. As you inhale say the word "peace" and "calm" as you exhale. Continue until you feel deeply relaxed. *(See pages 60–63.)*

REFLEXOLOGY
• Reflexologists believe they can treat the reproductive system by working specifically on points around the ankle bones and treat the glandular system by focusing on the cushion of the big toe. A reflex point reflecting the sexual life of the patient is found just under the cushion of the fourth toe. *(See pages 66–71.)*

RIGHT *In reflexology, points round the ankle relate to the reproductive system.*

Male Reproductive Problems

The male reproductive system can be affected by various disorders. As well as ones directly affecting fertility and sexual functioning, others include problems with the prostate gland, infections and sexually transmitted diseases, and cancer. As far as the failure of a woman to conceive is concerned, the reason can be traced to the male partner in 40 percent of cases. It may be due to a low sperm count, poor sperm quality and mobility, or an abnormality in the penis. Many factors can influence sperm quality and quantity, including pollution, low hormone levels, smoking, excessive drinking of alcohol, increased temperature of the testes (caused by tight clothing, for example), stress, some prescription drugs, or insufficient vitamins and minerals in the diet. A doctor will suggest checking the sperm, take a blood test to check hormone levels, and make a physical examination. If the cause of a low sperm count is still unclear, then diet and lifestyle changes may be advised to maximize the chances of conception.

Impotence – the inability to achieve or sustain an erection – is a common problem. Doctors now believe that in 85 percent of cases the cause is physical. Conditions such as diabetes, anemia, poor circulation or liver problems, and a range of drugs, including alcohol, antihistamines, and nicotine, can all cause the condition. Psychological factors, such as anxiety, may also be part of the problem. Your doctor may give tests to check for physical causes and suggest appropriate treatment. He may also prescribe drugs that increase bloodflow to the penis, so increasing the ability to become erect, but this treatment is not suitable if you have a cardiovascular condition.

Problems with the prostate gland can also impair a man's sex life. The gland, normally the size of a walnut, is found below the bladder and surrounds the urethra, the tube connecting the bladder and the penis. An enlarged prostate, which often occurs in men over 50, causes a frequent urge to urinate and a feeling that the bladder has not emptied fully. Painful and difficult urination is also a symptom of prostate cancer, but this is often accompanied by blood in the urine or semen and frequent pain in the limbs and back. An annual digital rectal examination (DRE) to check the prostate is recommended for men over 40.

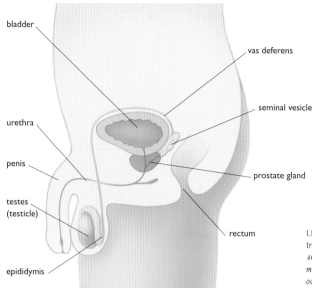

bladder

vas deferens

seminal vesicle

urethra

penis

prostate gland

testes (testicle)

rectum

epididymis

LEFT *The cause of infertility can be traced to the male partner in about 40 percent of cases, but problems in the male reproductive system may also occur as a result of infection, an enlarged prostate gland, and a number of other reasons.*

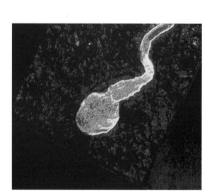

ABOVE *A low sperm count or poor quality sperm may make a man infertile. Blockages in the tubes may be cleared, but in other cases artificial insemination may be the recommended treatment.*

Though cancer of the prostate is common in men over 55, it can be treated successfully. Testicular cancer, on the other hand, attacks younger men, between the ages of 15 and 35. The symptoms include a lump in a testicle, change in the size of the testes, a dull ache in the groin, a feeling of heaviness in the scrotum, blood in the urine, a sudden collection of fluid in the scrotum, tender breasts, and pain in the testicle or scrotum. These symptoms can be caused by a number of other conditions, such as a bacterial infection, so you need to seek medical guidance quickly if they occur. Doctors recommend self-examination of the testes every month from the age of 15 to help to detect any changes as quickly as possible. If it is diognosed early enough, testicular cancer is nearly always curable.

Infections of the penis can be caused by viruses, parasites or bacteria. Poor hygiene is often a factor, which may be exacerbated by an abnormally tight foreskin. The prostate can become inflamed because of urethritis, a sexually transmitted disease, or an infection. Whether you are prescribed antibiotics or antifungals to treat such a condition depends on the type of infection. Using condoms and good hygiene will help to prevent the occurrence of most types of sexually transmitted disease and infections.

CONVENTIONAL TREATMENT

A DOCTOR WILL PRESCRIBE ANTIBIOTICS OR ANTIFUNGALS TO TREAT INFECTIONS. TREATMENT FOR AN ENLARGED PROSTATE INCLUDES TAKING DRUGS TO SHRINK THE GLAND, LASER TREATMENT OR SURGICAL REMOVAL. REGULAR SELF-EXAMINATION AND CHECKS BY A MEDICAL PRACTITIONER CAN HELP TO ENSURE EARLY DIAGNOSIS OF PROSTATE, PENILE, OR TESTICULAR CANCER. TREATMENT FOR THESE DISEASES INCLUDES HORMONE THERAPY, SURGERY, AND CHEMOTHERAPY.

CAUTION

IF YOU NOTICE BLOOD IN YOUR SEMEN OR URINE, CONSULT A DOCTOR.

SYMPTOMS

• *prostate problems: urination difficulties; swelling; aches and pains in the lower back and limbs* • *penile infections: itchy, inflamed penis and foreskin; discharge from the penis* • *testicular cancer: lumps in testes; dull ache in groin; blood in the urine*

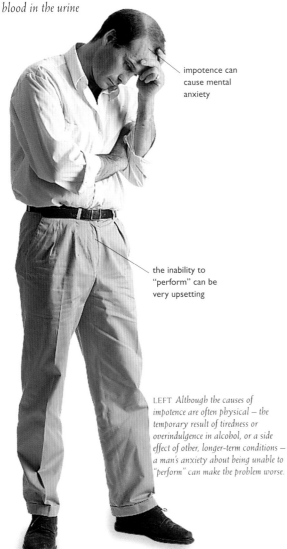

impotence can cause mental anxiety

the inability to "perform" can be very upsetting

LEFT *Although the causes of impotence are often physical – the temporary result of tiredness or overindulgence in alcohol, or a side effect of other, longer-term conditions – a man's anxiety about being unable to "perform" can make the problem worse.*

THERAPIES

ACUPUNCTURE
• Therapists believe acupuncture is an effective means of raising sperm count. They say that treatment has to be undertaken for several months to take effect since it takes 70 days to generate new sperm. *(See pages 20–28.)*

ACUPRESSURE
• Pressure on the acupoint on the lower back, two to four finger widths from the spine in line with the belly button, is thought to relieve sexual-reproductive problems. Pressure on the acupoint four finger widths below the kneecap and one finger width outside the shinbone is believed to relieve impotence. *(See pages 29–31.)*

AROMATHERAPY
• Rose oil is said to increase sperm count and quality, as well as acting as a mild aphrodisiac. A gentle massage with 2 to 3 drops of rose oil mixed with almond oil will help to relax both partners and keep anxiety and stress to a minimum during love-making. Prostate problems may be eased by a full-body massage with oestrogen-like oils, such as clary sage and geranium. *(See pages 104–5.)*

BREATHING TECHNIQUES
• Infertility has been linked to high stress levels, which have become part of everyday life for many men. Breathing techniques, meditation, and relaxation techniques will help you to unwind after a stressful day. They may also reduce levels of anxiety, which can make sexual intercourse more difficult. *(See pages 166–71; pages 60–63; and pages 158–65.)*

RIGHT *Particular acupressure points are believed to relieve sexual-reproductive problems.*

QIGONG
• Practitioners believe that Qigong helps to improve the flow of qi around the body. It is also thought to increase the flow of blood to the brain and other vital organs. The poses involved do not require great mobility or physical strength and so may be suitable for many conditions related to aging, including prostate problems. *(See pages 44–5 and T'ai Chi Ch'uan, pages 46–51.)*

PSYCHOTHERAPY AND COUNSELING
• Counseling may be helpful if no physical cause can be identified for difficulties achieving or maintaining an erection. A specialist psychosexual counselor can discuss your feelings and attitudes to sex and your body and help you to address problem areas. *(See pages 206–7.)*

YOGA
• Yoga reduces stress, tones the body, and balances energy flow, and may help overcome sexual problems, such as premature ejaculation and impotence. Prostate problems may also be eased by yoga. *(See pages 52–9.)*

HYPNOTHERAPY
• Sessions with a qualified practitioner may unlock hidden fears and doubts that may be contributing to the problem of impotence. *(See pages 218–23.)*

LEFT AND ABOVE *When sexual problems are caused or made worse by stress, yoga is an excellent way of relaxing and balancing the flow of energy in the body. Massage with rose oil may also help the libido.*

ENDOCRINE SYSTEM

Obesity

Though the terms obesity and overweight are used interchangeably, they have different meanings. Strictly speaking, overweight means an excess of body weight that includes all tissues, such as fat, bone, and muscle. Obesity refers specifically to an excess of body fat – over 25 percent fat for men and over 30 percent fat for women. This can present a major health risk. Excess fat around the abdomen, usually found on obese men, is linked to increased risk of high blood pressure, diabetes, early heart disease, and some types of cancer. Obese women increase the risk of contracting cancers of the ovaries, uterus, and breast. Carrying extra weight may also contribute to varicose veins, fertility problems, sleep apnea (irregular breathing during sleep), increased risk of osteoarthritis, and depression.

The most common causes of obesity are overeating and underexercising. When we consume more calories than we burn up, the excess calories are stored as body fat. Obesity may also be related to hormonal imbalances or prescription drugs, such as insulin. Psychological problems, such as depression, may also be contributory factors. The problem tends to run in families as well – children whose parents are obese are ten times more likely to be obese than other children – but this may be due to a combination of genetic factors and poor diet.

There is no short cut to weight loss, but a combined approach of setting reasonable weight-loss goals, changing eating habits and getting adequate exercise is recommended to tackle the problem. You should consult a doctor if you are planning to go on a weight-loss diet. He can eliminate the chance that underlying medical conditions are contributing to the weight problem, help you set a realistic weight-loss target, and advise on the level and type of exercise you should undertake. For most people, reducing daily calorie consumption by 300 to 500 calories achieves a safe weight loss of one or two pounds a week. Treatments such as ultra low-calorie diets, and stomach stapling are reserved for extreme cases of obesity.

ABOVE *Obesity can seriously damage your health, putting intolerable strain on the heart and load-bearing joints and muscles.*

CONVENTIONAL TREATMENT

A DOCTOR OR DIETICIAN CAN HELP TO DRAW UP A HEALTHY EATING PLAN, DECIDE ON A WEIGHT-LOSS GOAL, AND ADVISE ON A LEVEL OF EXERCISE THAT SUITS YOUR FITNESS LEVEL. SOME DOCTORS WILL PRESCRIBE APPETITE SUPRESSANTS, BUT THESE CAN ONLY BE TAKEN ON A SHORT-TERM BASIS. IN SEVERE CASES OF OBESITY, DOCTORS MAY ADVISE HOSPITALIZATION FOR TREATMENT, SUCH AS JAW-WIRING, OR A SUPERVISED DIET TO HELP YOU TO LOSE WEIGHT.

SYMPTOMS

- *excess body fat* • *fatigue* • *high blood pressure*
- *low self-esteem* • *depression*

THERAPIES

ACUPRESSURE
• Pressure on the acupressure point in the middle of the groove running from the nose to the top lip is thought to suppress cravings for food. *(See pages 29–31.)*

ACUPUNCTURE
• Practitioners believe that acupuncture raises the levels of endorphins in the nervous system and inhibits withdrawal symptoms from addictive substances, such as nicotine. Some acupuncturists believe that the urge to overeat is also controlled by endorphin levels. Auricular acupuncture, in which the ear is electrically stimulated or a small staple or stud is inserted, is the usual form of treatment. Patients are told to press on the acupuncture point when they feel food cravings. (See pages 20–28.)

PSYCHOTHERAPY
• Therapists can help to develop new patterns of behaviour by identifying, questioning, and changing negative or self-destructive thoughts. One approach to overeating is "reframing." The therapist asks the patient to rename hunger pangs as the screams of the inner child seeking love and attention, which only you can give. *(See Behavioral and Cognitive Therapies, pages 196–9, and Transpersonal Therapies, pages 204–5.)*

LEFT *Setting a safe and realistic weight-loss target will help the dieting program.*

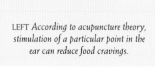

LEFT *According to acupuncture theory, stimulation of a particular point in the ear can reduce food cravings.*

LEFT *Many people who overeat also eat unhealthily, often indulging in fattening "comfort" food. But a diet that is deficient in fresh, energy-giving food such as fruit and vegetables can make you tired, moody, and more likely to crave chocolate and french fries.*

DATAFILE

• Thirty-five percent of American women and 31 percent of men aged 20 and older are considered obese, an increase from 30 and 25 percent in 1980.

• By building muscle you burn more calories at rest – one pound of muscle burns 75 calories a day compared with 2 calories burned by one pound of fat.

• Women should eat about 1,500 calories per day to lose weight. Active women can consume up to 2,000 calories. The average man should consume about 2,500 calories, and 2,000 if he aims to lose weight.

• A 1995 report from the Institute of Medicine says that Americans spend more than $33 billion every year on weight-reduction products.

• Some experts recommend drinking three quarts of water a day, each quart drunk about 30 minutes before a meal, to reduce the appetite.

BELOW *Visualizing yourself "slim" can help in the battle against weight gain.*

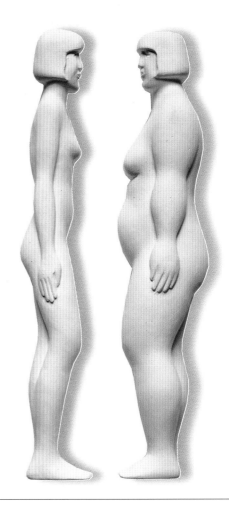

THERAPIES

HYPNOTHERAPY
• Hypnotherapy can be used to reinforce the belief that it is possible and desirable to lose weight. Therapists may discuss your attitudes to food and eating before hypnosis begins. They may then try to break the mental and emotional links between eating and reward, for example, while you are in a trance. *(See pages 218–23.)*

MEDITATION
• Many people find that stressful situations make them return to unhealthy eating habits – a bad day at work may be brightened up by eating a chocolate bar for example. Alternative practitioners recommend a variety of stress-relieving techniques, such as breathing and relaxation

techniques, to deal with this problem. *(See pages 60–63; Relaxation, pages 158–65, and Breathing, pages 166–71.)*

MASSAGE
• A full-body massage will help you to relax, boost your self-esteem, and enhance your physical and mental well-being. These are all key areas to focus on when trying to lose weight. Pampering yourself with treatments, such as massage, can also be seen as a reward for sticking to a healthy eating plan. *(See pages 96–103.)*

VISUALIZATION
• A practitioner can teach you to use visualization and self-calming techniques to change bad eating habits. During a visualization session, you can learn to repeat self-affirming

statements, such as "I can lose weight and be slim." Some therapists advise using images of the slim person you can become during visualization. *(See pages 214–17.)*

YOGA
• Practitioners believe that yoga can help you to lose weight because it strengthens both mind and body. The meditative elements of yoga help you to relax and gain control over your mind, which can help you to control your body and its food cravings. Yoga is also a suitable exercise system to follow if you are obese, since it is carefully graded. Do not practice inverted poses if you have high blood pressure. *(See pages 52–9.)*

Diabetes

Diabetes refers to an endocrine disorder that causes excessive thirst and the production of large volumes of urine. Used alone, the term generally refers to diabetes mellitus rather than the much rarer diabetes insipidus. Having diabetes means that the body is unable to control the level of sugar (glucose) in the blood as a result of the failure of the pancreas to produce the insulin required. Normally, insulin is released when the blood sugar level rises, its release being stopped or slowed down when it falls. If diabetes develops, however, there is a shortfall of insulin – or the insulin being produced by the pancreas is failing to work properly – with raised blood sugar levels as the result. If untreated, very high blood sugar levels may lead to coma and death. The exact cause of the condition is unknown, though some doctors believe that the disorder may be hereditary while others think that viral infections may be involved.

There are two basic forms of the condition – insulin-dependent diabetes, also known as Type 1 diabetes, and non-insulin-dependent diabetes (Type 2 diabetes). The former develops when there is a severe lack of insulin in the body because all, or most, of the cells that manufacture it have been destroyed. The latter arises when, though the cells can still produce some insulin, this is insufficient for the body's needs, or if the insulin that is being produced is not being utilized by the body as it should be. Both types are incurable, but both can be

medically controlled. Gestational diabetes is another form of diabetes mellitus that may arise when a woman is pregnant, but this resolves when the baby is born.

Type 1 diabetes more commonly affects people under 40, its peak incidence occurring during puberty. The condition develops fairly quickly, usually over a few weeks, and the symptoms are more often than not quite marked. They include frequent urination, and excessive thirst and tiredness. Treatment for Type 1 diabetes requires injecting replacement insulin on a daily basis to control the condition.

Type 2 diabetes is the most common form of the disease, usually affecting people over the age of 40. The overweight are at particular risk, as are people with a family history of the condition. Symptoms include thirst, a dry mouth, the passing of large amounts of urine, tiredness, itching of the genitals, weight loss, blurred vision, cuts and bruises that are slow to heal, and tingling or numbness in the hands or feet. Often, however, the condition is symptomless. Orthodox treatment for Type 2 diabetes can be through diet alone, or by a combination of insulin tablets and diet, though sometimes insulin injections may be necessary.

What is important is rapid detection of the disease because it can have life-threatening consequences if left untreated. Diagnosis involves testing the urine for abnormal glucose levels and monitoring the blood regularly. You will be shown how to do this for yourself so that you can monitor your condition. The actual treat-

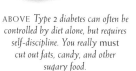

ABOVE *Type 2 diabetes can often be controlled by diet alone, but requires self-discipline. You really* must *cut out fats, candy, and other sugary food.*

BELOW *Most diabetics learn to monitor their own insulin levels, and to recognize the signals from their body that another treatment is needed.*

specific yoga exercises can concentrate energy on the main organs, so strengthening the digestive system

by increasing your sense of wellbeing, yoga makes it easier for you to be disciplined about your eating habits

RIGHT *The Backward Bend is one of the yoga positions recommended for diabetics.*

ment is aimed at achieving as near normal blood sugar levels as possible. Together with a healthy lifestyle, this will help to improve wellbeing and lessen the chances of long-term damage to the eyes, kidneys, nerves, heart, and major arteries. For this reason, it is important to take regular exercise and get your weight down to recommended levels. You should eat more high-carbohydrate, high-fiber foods, consume less sugar, cut down on fat, watch your salt intake and keep the amount of alcohol you drink to a minimum. As part of your regular health reviews, doctors will refer you to a dietician, who can advise you on how to adapt your usual meals to make them more healthy. You will also require annual check-ups to detect damage to the eyes, nerves, and blood vessels.

SYMPTOMS

• *excessive thirst* • *excessive urination* • *weight loss* • *tiredness* • *hunger* • *bad breath*

THERAPIES

YOGA
• Yoga may make controlling the diet easier and improve pancreatic function. As well as reducing stress, which, in itself, can help to destabilize blood glucose levels, it is also a relaxing form of exercise. Some Hatha yoga exercises are believed to help to balance the body's natural processes. *(See pages 52–9.)*

BIOFEEDBACK
• A practitioner can teach you how to become more aware of and so reduce stress. Guided imagery also helps you to relax by thinking of peaceful mental images and, according to practitioners, can also help diabetics by giving them positive images of controlling the disease. *(See pages 212–3.)*

AROMATHERAPY
• Back massage with a mixture of camphor, eucalyptus, geranium, juniper, lemon and rosemary oils is said to help balance pancreatic secretions, though there is no hard medical evidence to support this. *(See pages 104–105.)*

RELAXATION & BREATHING
• Any form of therapy that helps you to relax may help you to control the condition and come to terms with the disease. *(See pages 158–65 and pages 166–71.)*

BELOW *Maintaining a healthy lifestyle is vital to the control of diabetes. Regular exercise is indispensable and will also help combat any weight problems.*

DATAFILE

• Diabetes affects 15.7 million people in the U.S., of which some 5.4 million are not aware that they have the disease.

• If you suffer from undiagnosed, uncontrolled diabetes, you are at greater risk of blindness, kidney disease, nerve damage, heart disease, and stroke.

• Diabetes is one of the most expensive health problems in the U.S., with costs running at $82 billion annually.

• Approximately half of all cases of diabetes occur in people aged over 55.

• One tribe of Native Americans, the Pimas of Arizona, have the highest rate of diabetes in the world.

• It is important to eat regular meals so that the blood glucose level does not swing from one extreme to another.

• There is no need to buy special diabetic foods. They are expensive and will not help the diabetes.

• If you are diabetic, you should always carry some form of diabetes identification.

IMMUNE SYSTEM

Allergies

An allergy is when the immune system reacts to a specific substance as if it were harmful. According to the National Institute for Allergy and Infectious Disease, allergies are a major cause of disability in the U.S.: up to 50 million Americans, including two million children, suffer from some form of allergic complaint.

It is possible to be allergic to almost anything, which is why sometimes it can be difficult to pinpoint the actual cause. Whatever it may be, if you suffer from an allergy, you are the victim of a battle in the body. This is sparked off by an invading substance, medically termed an allergen, which is harmless in itself, but which your immune system mistakenly identifies as being potentially harmful. In response, the system releases antibodies to attack the antigen. The consequent conflict triggers the release of histamine and other chemicals from the surrounding cells and it is these that cause the allergic reaction that makes you ill.

The reactions among sufferers include allergic rhinitis (hay fever), allergic conjunctivitis, asthma, eczema, dermatitis, and urticaria (hives or nettle rash). Their type and severity vary from person to person. Characteristic symptoms of allergic rhinitis, triggered by airborne allergens, include sneezing, an itchy nose and throat, nasal congestion, and coughing. If these are joined by itchy, watery and red eyes, you are also suffering from allergic conjunctivitis. If both sets of symptoms occur together with wheezing and shortness of breath, the allergy may have progressed to become asthma. Some people with food allergies only exhibit what is medically termed oral allergy syndrome, the symptoms of which are an itchy nose and throat. Others develop a rash, accompanied by nausea, vomiting, or diarrhea, as the body tries to flush out the irritant. Sensitization occurs when the first encounter with an allergen causes a mild reaction but sensitizes the body so that the second contact can cause anaphylactic shock, which can be fatal. People known to be sensitized (e.g., to nuts) should carry an adrenaline syringe or an inhaler at all times.

In treatment, the priority is to determine the allergy's cause. Skin tests for the most common environmental and food allergens is normally the first thing a doctor will suggest. This may be supported by

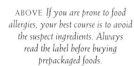

ABOVE If you are prone to food allergies, your best course is to avoid the suspect ingredients. Always read the label before buying prepackaged foods.

SYMPTOMS

• *Sneezing* • *itchy nose* • *itchy throat* • *nasal congestion* • *coughing* • *itchy, watery, reddened eyes* • *wheezing and shortness of breath* • *itchy mouth and throat* • *skin rash* • *nausea, vomiting, or diarrhea* • *hives.*

ABOVE Sneezing, weeping eyes, and a runny nose are all-too-familiar symptoms of allergies, which may be triggered by cosmetics, certain foods, animal hair and, most commonly, house-dust mite.

blood tests, if required. If a food allergy is suspected, your doctor may ask you to try elimination dieting, cutting suspected foods out of your diet one at a time and observing the effect. Once the cause has been identified, antihistamines, cortisone sprays and creams, nose drops, or bronchodilators may be prescribed.

It is important to do everything you can to reduce or eliminate exposure to the culprit allergens as much as possible. Eating sensibly, relaxing and taking care of yourself will help you to deal with and minimize an allergic response. If a food trigger is suspected, check food labels carefully and eat fresh, unprocessed foodstuffs whenever possible: if you suffer from eczema attacks, take extra care when using detergents, household cleaners, or chemicals. Vacuum daily to prevent a build-up of animal hairs and get rid of dust mites.

COSMETICS

DAIRY PRODUCTS

ANIMAL HAIR

HOUSE-DUST MITES

ABOVE The above culprits can cause an allergic reaction in some people.

THERAPIES

BIOFEEDBACK • Practitioners can train you to recognize and anticipate the body's response to an allergen. *(See pages 212–13.)*

HYPNOTHERAPY • The technique, it is claimed, has been used successfully to reduce stress and desensitize allergy victims, so alleviating the conditions from which they suffer. *(See pages 218–23.)*

KINESIOLOGY • Practitioners believe that measuring the muscular response to suspected allergy triggers enables them to pinpoint the allergen involved. *(See pages 126–33.)*

HYDROTHERAPY • Bathing the eyes and face in cold water may help to relieve symptoms, while a sitz bath may help to ease inflammation. *(See pages 172–9.)*

ACUPUNCTURE • Practitioners believe that allergic rhinitis is the result of a deficiency of Kidney, Spleen and Lung qi, combined with the retention of Wind Evil in the nose. *(See pages 20–28.)*

ACUPRESSURE • Applying pressure on the acupoint in the center of the webbing of the hand, between thumb and index finger, for two minutes, and then repeating the process with the other hand may diminish the effects of an attack. *(See pages 29–31.)*

ABOVE *Bathing tired, red eyes with cold water helps soothe away the irritation.*

AROMATHERAPY • Massaging lavender in a light carrier oil into the chest may help to reduce the severity of some allergy attacks. So, too, may massaging the sinus area under the eyes. *(See pages 104–5.)*

POLARITY THERAPY • By rebalancing or restoring the energy flows around the body, practitioners believe the therapy can treat many disorders successfully, including allergies. Bodywork, exercise, diet, and counseling are all involved. *(See pages 64–5.)*

VISUALIZATION • By making a visual picture of the problem and resolving it, you may be able to deal with the situation in real life. *(See pages 210–11.)*

ABOVE *Hypnotherapy has had considerable success in the treatment of allergies because it can stop the sufferer expecting to have an allergic reaction to a known or perceived trigger.*

ABOVE AND LEFT *There may not be much you can do about the pollution in your city, but you can help your allergies by keeping your house – and particularly your bedroom – free of dust.*

try and keep rooms free of dust

change your vacuum cleaner bag regularly

DATAFILE

• Allergies are often inherited. If one parent has an allergy, the chances of a child suffering from allergies is one in four.

• Allergies frequently occur in clusters. If you are allergic to one substance, the likelihood is that you will be allergic to others.

• Though you can be densensitized to some allergies, food allergies are life-long.

• Pollen counts are usually higher in the morning and when the weather is warm, dry, and breezy. They are at their lowest when it is chilly and wet.

• Peanuts are one of the most serious food allergens, and are often fatal because of sensitization. Other foods that are common allergy triggers include cow's milk, soy, egg whites, wheat, and shellfish.

• The three types of allergy test commonly used in orthodox medicine are the skin-prick test, the patch test, and a blood test called the Radio Allergo Sorbent Test (RAST). The RAST test is the most reliable for detecting food allergies.

CAUTION

SEVERE SYMPTOMS OR REACTIONS TO ANY ALLERGEN REQUIRE IMMEDIATE MEDICAL ATTENTION. ALWAYS CONSULT A PHARMACIST WHEN BUYING HAY FEVER TREATMENT – CERTAIN PRODUCTS CAN CAUSE SERIOUS REACTIONS IF TAKEN WITH GRAPEFRUIT JUICE OR OTHER MEDICATIONS.

HIV and AIDS

Acquired Immune Deficiency Syndrome (AIDS) is thought to be caused by the human immuno-deficiency virus (HIV), which destroys the body's infection-fighting T-cells. As the immune system weakens, "opportunistic" organisms, such as bacteria, viruses, and fungal infections, invade the body and cause diseases. Pneumonia, herpes, gastroenteritis, and meningitis are four of the more common diseases associated with the later stages of HIV and AIDS. Cancerous tumors, such as sarcoma and lymphoma, are also characteristic of the disease. In the later stages, the AIDS virus attacks the central nervous system, causing mental and neurological problems. It is estimated that up to two million people in the U.S. alone are infected with HIV, and infection is particularly prevalent in sub-Saharan Africa and parts of Asia.

HIV is spread through body fluids, such as semen, breast milk, and blood. The virus is commonly transmitted during sexual intercourse without the protection of a condom, by sharing needles when injecting drugs, or during a blood transfusion if the blood has not been screened for contamination. Mothers can pass the virus to a baby during pregnancy and delivery. It is not possible to catch AIDS by donating blood or from casual physical contact, such as holding hands. You should never share personal items that have blood on them, such as razors, and ensure that dentists and acupuncturists follow thorough sterilization procedures. Carry a sterile needle pack when traveling to developing countries in case you need to have an injection.

If you think that you have been exposed to the virus, ask your doctor or a clinic for an AIDS-screening test.

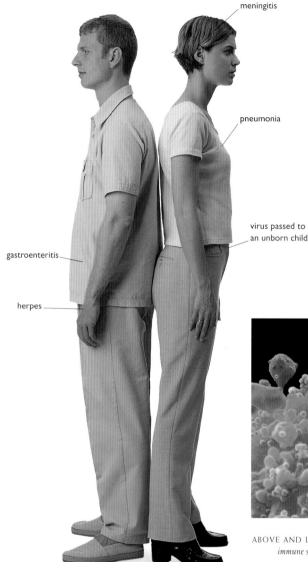

meningitis

pneumonia

virus passed to an unborn child

gastroenteritis

herpes

CONVENTIONAL TREATMENT

TWO BLOOD TESTS ARE REQUIRED TO CONFIRM THAT A PATIENT IS HIV-POSITIVE. THE SYMPTOMS OF AIDS ITSELF MAY NOT APPEAR FOR UP TO 11 YEARS AFTER THE VIRUS HAS BEEN TRANSMITTED. TREATMENT FOCUSES ON MAINTAINING A GOOD STATE OF HEALTH, AVOIDING INFECTIONS, AND COMBINED DRUG THERAPY TO SLOW THE PROGRESS OF THE DISEASE. DRUGS, SUCH AS ANTIBACTERIALS, ANTIVIRALS, AND ANTIBIOTICS, WILL BE PRESCRIBED TO TREAT INFECTIONS WHEN THEY TAKE HOLD. RADIATION THERAPY AND SURGERY IS SOMETIMES USED TO TREAT AIDS-RELATED CANCER.

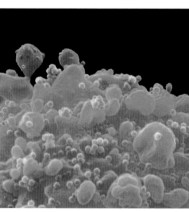

ABOVE AND LEFT *The HIV virus weakens the human immune system, making it more susceptible to infection and disease.*

THERAPIES

ACUPUNCTURE
• Stimulating various acupoints is thought to increase the functioning of the immune system and encourage the body's natural healing mechanisms. *(See pages 20–28.)*

ACUPRESSURE
• Chronic diarrhea and gastric inflammation, leading to malnutrition, is one of the most common effects of HIV. Acupressure practitioners believe that pressure on points along the Stomach and Spleen meridians can treat both these conditions. Pressure on the acupoint located near the spine next to the

shoulder blades, and on the acupoint in the center of the breast bone, are believed to strengthen resistance to infections. *(See pages 29–31.)*

AROMATHERAPY
• A lymphatic massage with antiviral oils, such as tea tree, eucalyptus, or thyme, may help to stimulate the immune system. Uplifting oils, such as bergamot, lavender, and ylang ylang, may help with the psychological effects of HIV and AIDS. *(See pages 104–5.)*

BREATHING TECHNIQUES
• Constant shallow breathing has been linked to a decline in the condition of patients. Deep breathing will aid relaxation, increase oxygen intake, and improve circulation. *(See pages 166–71 and Relaxation Techniques, pages 158–65.)*

LEFT *Ylang ylang, a very positive oil, can help combat depression and negativity.*

PSYCHOTHERAPY AND COUNSELING
• Some studies indicate that AIDS patients may be able to increase low T-cell counts by discussing and finding ways to cope with unresolved emotional issues. Crying and openly expressing emotions is also believed to strengthen the immune system. Creating positive attitudes and focusing on life goals can also be highly beneficial to AIDS patients. *(See pages 188–91.)*

BELOW *Talking through problems and maintaining positivity is essential to AIDS patients.*

You may be advised to wait up to three months before taking the test, which is the time needed for antibodies to the HIV virus to develop in the blood, and counseling is recommended because of the implications of having HIV. A second type of blood test will show whether or not you are HIV-positive. The first symptoms of AIDS may not appear until between seven and 11 years after this. These include fatigue, weight loss, chronic diarrhea, fever, swollen lymph nodes, Kaposi's sarcoma (malignant skin tumors), and night sweats. Some HIV-positive people never develop full-blown AIDS at all: researchers believe this might be connected to the strength of their immune system.

There is no cure for AIDS, but experts believe it is a manageable condition. Treatment includes medication, such as antibiotics, antivirals, and antifungals, to deal with infections. Doctors also advise boosting the body's immune system by eating a healthy diet, getting plenty of rest, lowering stress levels, and taking vitamin supplements. New combination drug therapy, using drugs such as AZT, DDI, DDC, D4T, and 3TC, have been very successful in delaying the onset and slowing down the progress of the disease, though there are side-effects.

SYMPTOMS

• *early stages of HIV: flu-like symptoms* • *later stages of HIV: fatigue, loss of appetite, chronic diarrhea, weight loss, persistent dry cough, fever, night sweats, swollen lymph nodes* • *conditions associated with AIDS: skin infections, fungal infections, tuberculosis, pneumonia, cancer, and neurological problems*

ABOVE *Never inject yourself – or allow yourself to be injected – with a needle that is not sterile. Doctors and dentists keep needles in individual sealed packets and discard them after one use.*

BELOW *A blood test can determine whether you are HIV-positive. This may be an anxious time, as it can take several months for a diagnosis to be made.*

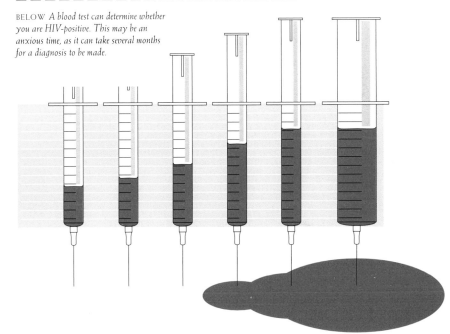

THERAPIES

HYDROTHERAPY
• Therapists believe that a healthy immune system requires the removal of toxins from the body. They recommend drinking plenty of pure water to flush out toxins, which also keeps the body hydrated, and taking regular hot baths and saunas. *(See pages 172–9.)*

MASSAGE
• Massage is thought to benefit AIDS patients in many ways. This type of touch therapy boosts self-esteem, reduces stress, and improves circulation and movement. It is also thought to encourage removal of toxins through the lymph system. *(See pages 96–103.)*

MEDITATION
• Reducing stress levels may help to slow down the progress of AIDS. Many relaxation techniques, including visualization and meditation, can be used to slow down the heartrate and relax the patient's mind and body. *(See pages 60–63 and Visualization, pages 214–17.)*

SHIATSU
• Therapy to the mid-back will help a patient to relax physically and mentally. Practitioners believe it will restore energy to the internal organs, especially the digestive system. *(See pages 32–7 and Do-in, pages 38–41.)*

QIGONG
• Practitioners believe that the immune system can be boosted by ensuring the free flow of qi through the body. This can be achieved by practicing therapies such as qigong and t'ai chi ch'uan. *(See pages 44–5 and pages 46–51.)*

OTHER THERAPIES
• Other therapies practitioners believe may help alleviate the condition include: art therapy *(see pages 238–41)*; reflexology *(see pages 66–71)*; hypnotherapy *(see pages 218–23)*; autogenic training *(see pages 210–11)*; and therapeutic touch *(see pages 90–91)*.

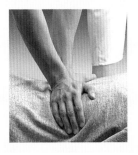

LEFT *Shiatsu massage is said to boost the body's self-healing abilities. It also has an important psychological aspect, as it involves the individual in the healing process.*

MUSCULOSKELETAL SYSTEM

Acute Frictional Tenosynovitis (AFT)

Acute frictional tenosynovitis (AFT), more commonly known as repetitive strain injury (RSI) or cumulative trauma disorder (CTD), is caused by the inflammation of the synovial sheaths of tendons, which occurs when the same movement is repeated over and over again. RSIs tend to occur in the neck, shoulders, upper back, wrist and elbow, although the lower limbs may also be affected. Most injuries affect people who work on assembly lines, use computer keyboards, or play musical instruments. Poor posture, such as sitting hunched over a computer keyboard, is thought to contribute to the occurrence of RSI. Extreme or forceful movements can cause the injury to occur more quickly.

The main symptoms of the condition are localized fatigue, swelling, numbness, and aching, most commonly in the forearm, wrist, and hand. Often the pain spreads to other areas of the body, such as the neck and back.

At first, the pain of an RSI disappears when the sufferer stops the activity. As the damage progresses, the pain and weakness become chronic.

Rapid treatment is the key to treating RSI, so consult a physician as soon as you notice any symptoms. As with many musculoskeletal injuries, the first form of treatment is RICE – rest, ice to reduce inflammation, compression by bandaging, and elevation. Anti-inflammatory painkillers and a wrist splint can also help to relieve symptoms.

Once the symptoms are under control, the next step is to minimize the chances of the injury recurring. If you use a keyboard, adjust the chair to the correct height and make sure it provides good support for the back. Use a wrist rest to keep your hands at the optimal angle as you type. Take a break from typing every 20 minutes to massage and mobilize your wrists, hands, and arms. If you need further help, consult a specialist in physical therapy, who can help you to analyze and improve your posture and work habits.

CONVENTIONAL TREATMENT

YOUR DOCTOR CAN ALLEVIATE SYMPTOMS BY PRESCRIBING PAINKILLERS AND ANTI-INFLAMMATORIES. HE WILL ALSO ADVISE REST, APPLYING ICE TO THE AREA TO REDUCE INFLAMMATION, AND WEARING A BANDAGE OR SPLINT TO IMMOBILIZE THE INJURY. IF THE CAUSE OF THE CONDITION IS USE OF A KEYBOARD, YOU MAY BE ADVISED TO WEAR A WRIST SPLINT AT WORK. YOU SHOULD ALSO HAVE YOUR WORK STATION ASSESSED BY AN EXPERT TO CHECK THAT THE CHAIR, DESK, AND KEYBOARD ARE SET AT THE CORRECT ANGLES TO MINIMIZE STRAIN, AND TAKE FREQUENT RESTS (FIVE MINUTES EVERY HALF-HOUR IS PREFERABLE).

SYMPTOMS

• *pain, stiffness, swelling, and weakness in the neck, shoulders, upper back, wrist, or forearm* • *nerve tingling in palm and fingers*

DATAFILE

• Damage to wrists and hands is one of the fastest-growing and most widespread occupational hazards in the U.S.

• The average insurance claim for RSI is $29,000, about 50 percent more than any other work-related injury or illness.

• Many large companies employ ergonomic experts to design and plan optimal work stations, from height of desks to angle of computer screens, to reduce conditions such as RSI.

• Some experts believe that the majority of RSI cases are caused by poor posture, not work station design.

• Voice recognition software can be used to minimize the amount of time you spend at the keyboard.

• Changing your working position during the day will avoid over-straining the joints and muscles.

CAUTION

CONSULT YOUR DOCTOR IF YOU FEEL PERSISTENT NUMBNESS AND TINGLING IN YOUR HAND AND FINGERS, WHICH WORSENS AT NIGHT.

BELOW *Although many orthodox doctors still deny that RSI exists, anyone who regularly repeats the same movement or sits or stands for a long time in the same position is likely to feel strain. In severe cases, abandoning the activity altogether may be the only option, but good posture can go a long way towards minimizing the effects of RSI.*

sit up straight, with your head, neck, and spine aligned

do not hunch your shoulder or poke your head forward. In addition to being uncomfortable, this may cause breathing problems

make sure your chair gives good support to your back

THERAPIES

FELDENKRAIS METHOD
• Practitioners of postural and body alignment therapies, such as the Feldenkrais method and Alexander technique, can help sufferers of RSI to correct their posture and reduce strain on the hands and arms, thus reducing the likelihood of the symptoms recurring. *(See pages 142–5 and pages 146–53.)*

MASSAGE
• Therapists advise taking regular breaks from repetitive tasks to manipulate and massage the wrist. This helps to prevent repetitive strain injury by increasing bloodflow to the area and relaxing the muscles. Back massage can also be useful for relieving tension, which may exacerbate poor posture. *(See pages 96–103.)*

MEDITATION
• Meditation can help to reduce stress levels, which is thought to be a contributory factor in repetitive strain injuries. This therapy is also useful for relieving pain. *(See pages 60–63.)*

ABOVE *and* BELOW *The acronym RICE – rest, ice, compression, and elevation – is a useful reminder of treatment for muscular injuries. If you hurt your knee playing sport, for example, apply an ice pack and a firm bandage and rest with your feet up.*

ABOVE *Acupuncture treatment is mainly holistic, promoting general wellbeing. It can also be used locally to reduce swelling and relieve pain.*

OSTEOPATHY
• Manipulative therapies, such as osteopathy and chiropractic, help to mobilize the upper back, neck, hands, and arms. Treatment can increase blood circulation in the affected area and free up the nerves that run from the back and down into the arms. Therapists can also look at correcting postural problems, which may be contributing to the condition. *(See pages 106–13 and pages 118–25.)*

YOGA
• Practitioners believe that yoga can help RSI sufferers to reduce muscle tension throughout the body, learn to become more relaxed, and help them to stretch and mobilize their bodies. Most RSI sufferers find that they feel less pain as their bodies become more flexible. *(See pages 52–9.)*

ACUPUNCTURE
• Practitioners believe that needle treatment, both localized and away from the site of the injury, may help to reduce pain, relieve muscular tension and spasm, and ease certain types of nerve pain. *(See pages 20–28.)*

ACUPRESSURE
• Pressure on the acupoint two inches above the wrist crease on the outer forearm, between the bones of the arm, is thought to relieve tennis elbow (tendinitis) and wrist pain. Massaging the acupoint in the webbing between the thumb and index finger may also reduce wrist inflammation and pain. *(See pages 29–31.)*

PSYCHOTHERAPY AND COUNSELING
•Pain clinics use cognitive-behavioral therapy to teach RSI sufferers how to cope with their pain and also how to avoid the cycle of injury through overuse and recovery through underuse. Therapists can help patients to understand their pain better and develop coping strategies to deal with it. *(See pages 196–9.)*

RELAXATION AND BREATHING
• Practitioners will teach you techniques that will help you to relax mentally and physically and to breathe more evenly and deeply. This helps to lower stress levels, which are believed to be a contributory cause of the condition. *(See pages 158–65 and pages 166–71.)*

ABOVE *A hand and wrist massage can help prevent RSI in those who do a lot of typing or similar repetitive activity with the hands. You can do this to yourself, stretching your fingers and rubbing your wrists while taking a break from work.*

OTHER THERAPIES
• Other therapies practitioners recommend to alleviate this condition include: shaolin *(see pages 42–3)*; Bowen technique *(see pages 76–7)*; craniosacral therapy *(see pages 116–17)*; kinesiology *(see pages126–33)*; Alexander technique *(see pages 146–53)*; and sound therapy *(see pages 236–7)*.

LEFT *Regular yoga practice makes the entire body, and especially the joints, more flexible. This can both relieve symptoms of RSI and make it less likely to occur.*

Back Problems

Back problems are second only to headaches as the most frequent cause of physical pain, four out of five adults experiencing a bout of back pain at some time or other during their lives. Back problems account for more lost working hours than any other ailment. The pains can occur for no apparent reason and at any point on the spine, though they are most common in the lower back, which bears the majority of your weight.

Most sources of back pain are muscle strains and spasms, usually caused by poor posture, lifting heavy objects, pregnancy, and muscle tension. The aches and pains they cause, popularly referred to as lumbago, can occur immediately, or you may develop the characteristic soreness and stiffness later. Muscle spasm occurs to immobilize you and lessen the risk of further damage.

The second most common cause of back pain is osteoarthritis, a degenerative disorder of the joints that occurs as a result of the deterioration of the spine's protective cartilage and is a natural consequence of aging. Other causes of backache include sciatica (caused by pressure on the sciatic nerve as it leaves the spinal column); osteoporosis (whereby a decrease in the amount of calcium weakens the bone structure); and a prolapsed (slipped) disc. Congenital or acquired spinal abnormalities that result in conditions such as lordosis (an excessive inward curve), kyphosis (an excessive outward curve), and scoliosis (a sideways deviation of the spine) may also cause backache. Less common causes include spinal stenosis, a complication of osteoarthritis, ankylosing spondylitis, an uncommon, though serious, form of arthritis that usually affects young men, and, rarely, infections and tumors. Sometimes, too, the brain can mistake pain signals from other parts of the body as coming from the back, which is medically termed referred back pain. It can be a sign of problems in the kidneys, uterus, or prostate gland, or an indication of cancer somewhere else in the body.

Most back problems respond well to home treatment, usually clearing up within a fortnight or so. A hot-water bottle placed on the painful area can bring temporary relief, as can crushed ice cubes, wrapped in a towel, or a pack of frozen peas, but applied for no more than 20 minutes at a time. After a few days, the application of alternating hot and cold compresses can be very effective. If backache persists for longer, your doctor may suggest X-rays and other tests to pinpoint the source of the problem and additional specialist therapy to treat it. Initially, he may advise bedrest for a day or two at most – but no more, because prolonged bedrest can actually hinder recovery – and the taking of over-the-counter pain relievers. Anti-inflammatory medications and muscle relaxants may be prescribed, or a short-term course of corticosteroid injections suggested.

Once you have recovered, you may be referred to a physical therapist, who, as well as treating the back, will advise you of a suitable exercise program to follow. Working out regularly is the surest defense against back problems recurring. You will be taught exercises that will help to correct your posture, strengthen the muscles supporting the back, and improve long-term flexibility.

SYMPTOMS

• *pain in the lower back that can range from mild to extremely severe* • *muscle spasms* • *stiffness and rigidity*

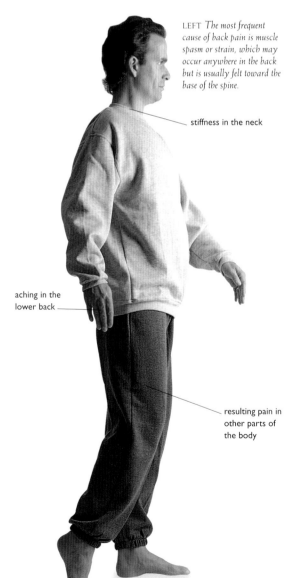

LEFT *The most frequent cause of back pain is muscle spasm or strain, which may occur anywhere in the back but is usually felt toward the base of the spine.*

stiffness in the neck

aching in the lower back

resulting pain in other parts of the body

ABOVE *Symptoms can often be relieved by applying heat or cold to the affected area.*

ABOVE *An ice pack should be used for no more than 20 minutes a day. Alternating hot and cold compresses can be effective.*

LEFT *Swimming is often recommended to strengthen the muscles of the back, but you should be careful not to strain them. Increase the amount of exercise you do gradually, rather than suddenly forcing yourself to go much farther and faster.*

CONVENTIONAL TREATMENT

YOU MAY BE REFERRED TO A PHYSICAL THERAPIST. FOR PROLONGED OR MORE SEVERE CONDITIONS, TREATMENT MAY INCLUDE ANTI-INFLAMMATORY AND MUSCLE-RELAXANT MEDICATIONS, TRACTION, PAINKILLING EPIDURALS, ANTIDEPRESSANTS, AND, IF A DISC IN THE SPINE IS PROLAPSED, SURGERY.

DATAFILE

- Back pain is a problem experienced by around 80 percent of Americans at some point in their lives.

- Losing excess weight, improving your posture when sitting or standing, and learning to lift objects correctly can eliminate much of the pain and inconvenience caused by back problems.

- It is worth considering getting a second opinion before agreeing to back surgery as the long-term outcome may often be the same with conservative treatment.

- Swimming and other water-based exercises are the safest for your back because they are non-weight-bearing.

- Tennis, racquetball, basketball and contact sports pose the greatest risk to the back because they involve twisting the body, quick stops and starts, and impact on hard surfaces.

- Wearing a corset can be counterproductive, since it may actually weaken the back muscles, especially if worn for long period.

- A slipped disc does not, in fact, slip. Rather, wear and tear or strain leads the disc to bulge or rupture (prolapse). The pain comes when a fragment of the prolapsed disc presses on an adjacent nerve.

BIOFEEDBACK
- You can be trained to become aware of habitual muscle contractions, so learning how to anticipate them and relax. *(See pages 212–13.)*

ROLFING
- Rolfing, or structural integration, as it is otherwise known, combines soft-tissue manipulation with movement education. According to its proponents, it has been succesful in reducing spinal curvature when this arises, and in easing back pain. *(See pages 134–7 and Hellerwork, pages 138–41.)*

FELDENKRAIS METHOD
- A practitioner starts by verbally guiding you through a sequence of movements designed to help you to develop better body awareness, flexibility and coordination. This is followed by one-to-one sessions, in which the movements are communicated through slow, gentle touch. *(See pages 142–5.)*

AROMATHERAPY
- Pain that results from fatigue and tension may be treated with a massage of ginger, juniper, marjoram, or rosemary. Massage with ginger or black pepper may help if the pain is acute. Bergamot and myrrh are also both useful as they have an anti-inflammatory effect. *(See pages 104–105.)*

MASSAGE
- Gentle massage may relieve the pain of muscle spasms. Although the therapy cannot resolve structural back problems, in which case it should be avoided, it works well against lumbago and chronic muscle tension. The trick is to work in firm strokes up either side of the spine, and fan out across the shoulders. *(See pages 96–103.)*

CHIROPRACTIC
- In the U.S., chiropractors claim to perform 94 percent of all back treatment involving spinal manipulation. The aim is to restore normal movement to the joints of the back and bring the spinal vertebrae and those of the neck into alignment. *(See pages 118–25.)*

OSTEOPATHY
- Treatment by an osteopath can involve gentle massage to relieve muscular tension to pressure and manipulation to stretch the spine to restore mobility. Several sessions of treatment will often prove to be necessary. *(See pages 106–13.)*

ALEXANDER TECHNIQUE
- Teachers aim at rectifying postural defects by teaching exercises to correct them. By learning how to use your body in a more natural way, you can prevent or alleviate back pain. *(See pages 146–53.)*

ACUPUNCTURE
- Stimulation of the acupoints along the Small Intestine, Bladder and Kidney meridians with needles, moxibustion or cupping may help to relieve pain. The therapy has been found to be particularly useful when the pain is too severe for other therapies – orthodox as well as complementary – to be employed. *(See pages 20–28.)*

ACUPRESSURE
- Applying pressure to the acupoints on the Bladder and Gall Bladder meridians may relieve lower back pain, according to practitioners. Like acupuncture, the pressure is thought to correct and restore the flow of qi. *(See pages 29–31.)*

QIGONG
- By combining gentle exercises with meditation techniques, practitioners argue that the therapy will relax the muscles and ease stress. *(See pages 44–5 and T'ai Chi Ch'uan, pages 46–51.)*

YOGA
- Lying flat on the back releases tension and relieves pain, rotating the back relaxes the muscles in the upper back and shoulders, and back stretches may increase flexibility in the spine. A yoga teacher will show you how to execute the appropriate poses and postures . *(See pages 52–9.)*

HYDROTHERAPY
- A practitioner may advise applying alternating hot and cold compresses to the affected area. A technique known as wrapping, whereby a sheet wrung out in cold water is wrapped around the patient , followed by a dry sheet and a blanket, is thought to be effective in treating chronic back pain. The wraps are removed when the sheet is dry. *(See pages 172–9.)*

OTHER THERAPIES
- Therapies that may help include: shiatsu/do-in *(see pages 32–41)*; polarity therapy *(see pages 64–5)*; therapeutic touch *(see pages 90–91)*; craniosacral therapy *(see pages 116–17)*; kinesiology *(see pages 126–33)*; Tragerwork *(see pages 154–5)*; Zero Balancing *(see pages 156–7)*; and sound therapy *(see pages 236–7.)*

ABOVE *The Alexander Technique teaches how to correct postural defects.*

BELOW *Yoga teachers may recommend lying flat on the floor to relieve pain.*

Arthritis

Arthritis in an inflammation of the joints characterized by swelling, pain, redness, and restriction of movement. More than 200 diseases fall under the heading of arthritis, the two most prevalent forms of the condition being osteoarthritis and rheumatoid arthritis. Osteoarthritis is a degenerative disease of the joints, which occurs when the cartilage that cushions the ends of the bones wears away, generally as a result of a loss of the synovial fluid that lubricates the joints. The consequence is pain and loss of movement as bone begins to rub against bone. The condition is made worse by the body's attempts to repair the damage by producing bony outgrowths at the margins of the affected joints.

Rheumatoid arthritis is an autoimmune disease that may be sparked off by a viral infection and linked to a disruption of the body's immune system, in which the antibodies the system produces to protect against the infection react against the joint lining. The chronic inflammation that results eventually involves the cartilage: the affected joints become swollen, painful, and stiff. Other symptoms can include fatigue, mild anemia, poor circulation, and trouble with the tendons, eyes, and thyroid gland. Stress and diet are also thought by some to be possible triggers.

Of the two conditions, osteoarthritis is by far the more common. It affects an estimated 20.7 million Americans, mostly aged over 45. Its prevalence increases with age due to natural wear and tear, though there may be a genetic component to the disease. It normally affects weight-bearing joints, such as the hip or the knees, though the fingers are frequently involved as well.

ABOVE *Acupuncture in the back can help painful joints.*

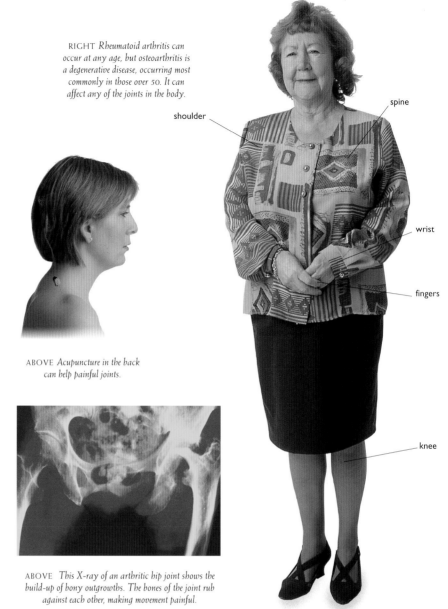

RIGHT *Rheumatoid arthritis can occur at any age, but osteoarthritis is a degenerative disease, occurring most commonly in those over 50. It can affect any of the joints in the body.*

shoulder — spine — wrist — fingers — knee

ABOVE *This X-ray of an arthritic hip joint shows the build-up of bony outgrowths. The bones of the joint rub against each other, making movement painful.*

THERAPIES

OSTEOPATHY AND CHIROPRACTIC
• For osteoarthritis, practitioners recommend manipulation to relax surrounding tissues, improve the circulation and to increase mobility in the affected joints. For rheumatoid arthritis, stretching and gentle trigger-point stimulation may be advised. Chiropractics and cranial osteopaths employ their own techniques to the same ends. *(See pages 106–13, pages 114–15 and pages 118–25.)*

AYURVEDA
• Practitioners claim that whole-body massages with

sesame or mustard oil, followed by massage of the affected joints, will help to relieve pain. Rubbing calmus oil into the affected joints, they also believe, can improve circulation and drainage. *(See pages 78–85.)*

YOGA
• Practicing yoga regularly may help to keep your muscles relaxed and your joints supple. There are specific poses for various affected joints. *(See page 52–9.)*

ACUPUNCTURE
• A series of controlled studies support claims that acupuncture can be effective in

the treatment of osteoarthritis and rheumatoid arthritis. Acupuncture may be given at points in the neck, back, abdomen, and legs, combined with moxibustion at points in the back, abdomen, legs, and arms. *(See pages 20–28.)*

MASSAGE
• Massage brings warmth to sore areas and is soothing. However, it needs to be carried out by a masseur experienced in dealing with arthritis cases, or harm may result. *(See pages 96–103.)*

REFLEXOLOGY
• Stimulation of the reflex areas related to the affected joints may help to relieve pain and inflammation, as can massage of the zone-related areas. Practitioners may also massage the reflex areas for the pituitary, adrenal and parathyroid glands, the kidneys and the solar plexus. *(See pages 66–71.)*

RELAXATION AND BREATHING
• Pain and stress can lead to tightened muscles, fast and shallow breathing, a heightened heart beat and raised blood pressure. Learning relaxation

and breathing techniques may help you to reverse these effects. *(See pages 158–65 and pages 166–71.)*

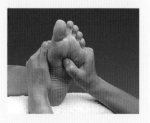

ABOVE *The stimulation of the relevant reflexology points can relieve the pain of arthritis.*

Rheumatoid arthritis generally begins between the ages of 20 and 45; three times as many women as men suffer from it. In some cases, the disease may be mild, while, in others, it can be crippling. The condition usually starts in the fingers, wrists, and toes, but the ankles, knees, and neck can also be affected.

Many things can be done to reduce the impact of arthritis, the key to successful treatment being early diagnosis. This involves physical examination, X-rays and, in the case of rheumatoid arthritis, special blood tests. While osteoarthritis cannot be cured, its symptoms can be relieved through a combination of painkillers, anti-inflammatory medication, heat treatment and physiotherapy. Eating a healthy diet, containing plenty of fruit and vegetables, can help, as will getting your weight down if you are overweight. This helps to relieve the pressure on the affected joints, while gentle exercise, such as swimming, will help to strengthen the supporting muscles. For rheumatoid arthritis, conventional treatment is basically the same, plus the use of antirheumatics and immunosuppressives.

SYMPTOMS

• *osteoarthritis: intermittent pain in affected joints, which gradually occurs more frequently, progressive limitation of movement, audible creaking in affected joint, swelling and inflammation* • *rheumatoid arthritis: morning stiffness, taking up to an hour for the joints to loosen; weakness and inflammation of ligaments, tendons and muscles; eye inflammation; bursitis; general malaise, including lethargy, muscle pain, and loss of appetite; painful, debilitating joint deformities*

LEFT *A healthy lifestyle can do a lot to inhibit the progress of arthritis. If you are seeing a physiotherapist, specific exercises may be recommended, but for self-care you should aim to keep yourself as fit and flexible as possible.*

CONVENTIONAL TREATMENT

FOR OSTEOARTHRITIS, PAINKILLERS, ANTI-INFLAMMATORY MEDICATIONS, HEAT TREATMENT, AND PHYSIOTHERAPY MAY ALL BE ADVISED. IN ADVANCED CASES, STEROID INJECTIONS AND JOINT REPLACEMENT MAY BE SUGGESTED. FOR RHEUMATOID ARTHRITIS, TREATMENT IS BASICALLY THE SAME; IMMUNO-SUPPRESSANTS MAY BE GIVEN IN SOME CASES.

CAUTION

BECAUSE EARLY DIAGNOSIS IS VITAL TO LIMIT THE EFFECTS OF ARTHRITIS, ALWAYS CONSULT A DOCTOR IF YOU BELIEVE YOU ARE SUFFERING FROM THE CONDITION. ALWAYS ASK A DOCTOR'S ADVICE BEFORE EMBARKING ON ANY COMPLEMENTARY THERAPY THAT INVOLVES MANIPULATION.

DATAFILE

• More than 20 million Americans suffer from osteoarthritis.

• Arthritis can affect people of all ages, including children.

• Nearly two-thirds of rheumatoid arthritis sufferers are women.

• Arthritis costs the U.S. economy $65 billion a year in medical care and lost wages.

• Though there can be periods of spontaneous remission, once you develop rheumatoid arthritis, it stays with you for the rest of your life.

• The condition is probably as old as humanity itself: bones of ancient Egyptian mummies, for instance, show clear signs of arthritic damage.

• In extreme cases, devices such as splints, braces, and crutches can bring relief by resting or supporting the painful joints.

• Orthopedic surgeons can correct some deformities, remove inflamed tissue, repair ligament damage, or replace a diseased joint.

THERAPIES

AROMATHERAPY
• Massage with a mixture of juniper berry, black pepper, Roman chamomile, and lavender oils, with olive or jojoba oil as the carrier, may be beneficial, as may warm compresses using a mixture of lavender, rosemary, eucalyptus, and juniper berry. Omit the juniper berry if you are pregnant. A mixture of rosemary, marigold and lavender is another alternative for massage, as are petitgrain, lemon, and cypress used individually. (See pages 104–5.)

ACUPRESSURE
• For osteoarthritis, practitioners will teach you how to stimulate helpful acupoints in the hands, hips and knees. For the best results, you should carry out treatment twice daily in the morning and in the evening, pressing the points firmly for a minute or so and massaging in a clockwise direction if required. (See pages 29–31.)

SHIATSU
• Stimulating the appropriate tsubos around the body with fingers, thumbs, elbows, knees and feet to correct the flow of ki around the body is thought to be effective in the treatment of osteoarthritis, according to its practitioners. (See pages 32–7 and Do-in, pages 38–41.)

T'AI CHI CH'UAN
Gentle t'ai chi ch'uan exercises may help to lessen stiffness and keep the joints supple. The improvements in breathing they promote may also help relieve the symptoms of both variants of arthritis. (See pages 46–51 and Qigong, pages 44–5.)

HYDROTHERAPY
•According to practitioners, water exercise is a gentle way to relax joints and lessen the stress on them, so encouraging free movement. It may also help to build muscle strength. Hot or cold compresses applied to the affected areas can also help. Epsom salts baths may relieve the discomfort of rheumatoid arthritis, though this is unsuitable for the elderly, or people with high blood pressure. Sea water (thalassotherapy) is believed to be particularly beneficial in the treatment of arthritis, as are seaweed baths. Dried seaweed can be bought for this purpose. (See pages 172–9.)

BELOW *Seaweed baths are believed to soothe and relieve pain and inflammation.*

OTHER THERAPIES
• Therapies that may help include: polarity therapy (see pages 64–5); Bowen technique (see pages 76–7); healing (see pages 86–7); therapeutic touch (see pages 90–91); kinesiology (see pages 126–33); Feldenkrais method (see pages 142–5); dance movement therapy (see pages 226–9); sound therapy (see pages 236–7); and color therapy (see pages 248–51).

Sciatica

The outward signs of sciatica are shooting pains, ranging in severity from mild to severe, that run down the back and outside of the thigh, leg, and foot. They are caused by pressure on, or irritation of, the sciatic nerve at its spinal root in the lower back, the pain being felt along the nerve's path. The onset can be sudden, with the pain worsening if you bend forward, cough, or sneeze. Common causes include a prolapsed disc, lower back strain, or muscle spasm, a sports injury, or, in pregnancy, a strained ligament or the baby lying against the spine.

Conventional treatment depends on the cause, though doctors have often advised bedrest for 24 hours (48 in severe cases) on a firm mattress. It is aimed at lessening the pain, which can last from a few days to several weeks. If a prolapsed disc is involved and the problem does not resolve itself over time, minor surgery may be necessary to remove the affected portion of the disc. Widely accepted complementary treatments include osteopathy, chiropractic, and acupuncture.

ABOVE *Back pain is often felt as a dull ache, but sciatica is a shooting pain that cannot be ignored.*

CAUTION

IF YOU SUFFER FROM A PROLONGED ATTACK OF SCIATICA, YOU SHOULD CONSULT A DOCTOR.

SYMPTOMS

• *burning sensations* • *muscle weakness* • *numbness or pins and needles in the leg, foot, or toes* • *muscle spasms in the buttock or leg* • *weakened knee and ankle reflexes*

THERAPIES

ACUPUNCTURE
• Acupoints on the meridians relating to the bladder, gall bladder, kidney, spleen,, and large and small intestines may be stimulated. Moxibustion may also be used. *(See pages 20–28.)*

ACUPRESSURE
• Practitioners advise the application of gentle pressure inward on the outside leg, a hand's width plus a thumb above the crown of the ankle bone, and between the shin and the smaller leg bone. *(See pages 29–31.)*

OSTEOPATHY
• Practitioners advise stretching the spine in the lumbar region between the lowest ribs. They will also try to release trigger points in the buttock muscle and may also suggest gentle therapy to improve the mobility of the

joints in the lower part of the back. *(See pages 106–13 and Chiropractic, pages 118–25.)*

HYDROTHERAPY
• Severe pain may be relieved by the application of an ice pack at the base of the back. If the symptoms are milder, a hot pack may prove effective. Therapists may also advise an underwater douche and teach remedial postural exercises in a hydrotherapy pool. *(See pages 72–9.)*

REFLEXOLOGY
• Pressure on the reflex points governing the spine on the top and sides of the feet as part of an overall foot massage may help in the treatment of sciatica, according to practitioners. *(See pages 66–71.)*

ALEXANDER TECHNIQUE
• A teacher can help you to correct poor posture through exercises that make you aware of what it is like to sit and stand without strain and avoid compressing the spinal joints. *(See pages 146–53.)*

AROMATHERAPY
• Lavender oil, said to be antispasmodic and anti-inflammatory, can be used in local massage, while chamomile compresses or massage may reduce the irritation and lessen the pain. *(See pages 104–5.)*

OTHER THERAPIES
• Therapies include: shiatsu/do-in *(see pages 32–41)*; healing *(see pages 86–7)*; Tragerwork *(see pages 154–5)*; craniosacral therapy *(see pages 116–17)*; and sound therapy *(see pages 236–7).*

Fibromyalgia Syndrome

Intermittent muscle aches, pains and stiffness that occur without apparent cause, accompanied by a characteristic pattern of spots on the affected muscles, are symptoms of what doctors now term fibromyalgia syndrome (FMS), myofascial pain syndrome, or myofasciitis. The lay term is fibrositis. The condition is most common among middle-aged and elderly people, and often affects the neck and back. Tension, poor posture, cold weather, emotional upsets, and lack of sleep may all be contributing factors. The condition is frequently associated with chronic fatigue syndrome, irritable bowel syndrome, and menstrual complaints.

This condition is not damaging to the body but although the pain waxes and wanes, it generally does not go away. It is frequently at its worst in the morning. It may prove resistant to painkillers and other orthodox medications, though small doses of antidepressants may help. So, too, can regular light aerobic exercise.

SYMPTOMS

• *aches and pains in muscles or tendons* • *tenderness in nine particular spots on affected muscles on the back and trunk* • *stiffness*

THERAPIES

MASSAGE
• By stimulating the circulation and relaxing trigger points and other areas of stiffness, massage may help to ease the pain. The nine points on the back and trunk that are specifically affected by this condition will be prime targets for a therapist. *(See pages 96–103.)* Aromatherapy massages may also help. *(See pages 104–5.)*

AYURVEDA
• Calamus oil can be massaged into affected joints to improve circulation and drainage, while camphor may warm affected areas, so encouraging healing. *(See pages 78–85.)*

HYDROTHERAPY
• Ice packs, alternating hot and cold compresses, and warm baths with Epsom salts (not suitable for the elderly or frail) are all advised by practitioners. *(See pages 172–9.)*

YOGA
• Gentle stretching asanas are thought to be useful in relieving the condition. Yoga relaxes the muscles and may also help to correct any postural problems that may have contributed to the development of the muscular pain. *(See pages 52–9.)*

OTHER THERAPIES
• Therapies include: Bowen technique *(see pages 76–7)*; Rolfing and Hellerwork *(see pages 134–41)*; Tragerwork *(see pages 154–5)*; Zero Balancing *(see pages 156–7)*; and sound therapy *(see pages 236–7.)*

RIGHT *FMS can be helped by gentle yoga stretches.*

Cramp

The agonizing muscular spasms that can affect the legs, feet and, in writer's cramp, the hand, are a common complaint, particularly among children, the elderly, and pregnant women. The condition can be triggered by a variety of factors, including exercise, swimming in cold water, poor circulation in the legs, and salt loss through sweating. Rubbing and stretching the affected muscle usually will bring relief. Otherwise, resting the overtaxed muscles and, in the case of persistent cramp, salt replacement is the standard prescription. Warming-up before and cooling-down after exercise is also recommended. If the cramps are being caused by poor circulation in the legs, taking small amounts of quinine may be suggested.

ABOVE *Thalassotherapy can bring relief.*

ABOVE *Repacing your salts and vitamins is essential.*

LEFT *Cramp may occur as a result of strenuous exercise, particulary if you are not used to it or you do not warm up and cool down properly. Rubbing and stretching the affected muscle should quickly ease the pain.*

rubbing the cramping muscle helps

THERAPIES

MASSAGE
• A therapist will concentrate on stretching the muscles, finishing off with chopping strokes, deep massage, or effleurage to stimulate the circulation. He can also teach you self-help techniques and show you how to knead, stroke, and stretch the affected areas. *(See pages 96–103.)*

HYDROTHERAPY
• If you are suffering from leg cramps, mustard foot baths may help. Applying hot and cold compresses is also recommended by practitioners. *(See pages 172–9.)*

AROMATHERAPY
• Regular aromatherapy massage is claimed to be good for cramp. If the condition is protracted, mixing three drops of basil, three drops of marjoram, and one drop of lemongrass with a suitable carrier oil and massaging the affected area with it twice daily should bring effective relief. (See pages 104–105.)

Bursitis

Bursitis is the term for any inflammation of the small liquid-filled sacs – or bursae – that act as cushions to reduce friction and help skin, muscles, and tendons to move smoothly over the bones. If the bursae become inflamed or are injured, excess fluid collects in the sacs, preventing the free movement of the joint and with heat, swelling, and pain as the result. The condition can also be caused by arthritis, gout, or bacterial infection.

Conventional advice is RICE (rest, ice, compression and elevation), but, once the swelling starts to go down, the affected joint must be used and exercised every day, or the bursitis may develop into a permanent condition. Otherwise, treatment is with painkillers, anti-inflammatory drugs, and sometimes draining the fluid via a fine hollow needle. Corticosteroids may be injected if there is considered to be the risk of another attack, while antibiotics may be prescribed in the event of infection.

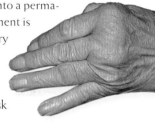

ABOVE *Bursitis can be a result of arthritis.*

SYMPTOMS

• *movement restricted in the affected joint as a result of swelling*
• *pain and tenderness in the affected area*

THERAPIES

AROMATHERAPY
• Massaging a diluted solution of essential oil of lavender into the skin may soothe the inflamed tissues. So, too, may chamomile, rosemary, juniper, black pepper, eucalyptus, marjoram, and benzoin. Massage the affected area every day until the condition clears. *(See pages 104–105.)*

ACUPUNCTURE
• Practitioners advise the stimulation of the related acupoints. This, they suggest, will reduce the pain, increase mobility, and aid the healing process generally. *(See pages 20–28.)*

HYDROTHERAPY
• Applying cold compresses to the affected area when the swelling and pain are at their worst can be beneficial, say practitioners.

Alternate or replace with hot compresses once there is an improvement. To treat acute inflammations, a bag of frozen peas can be used as an ice pack, but remember to smear the skin with olive oil first to avoid the risk of frostbite. *(See pages 172–9.)*

BELOW *Bursitis – the medical name for such conditions as housemaid's knee and tennis elbow – results in painful swollen joints with symptoms similar to arthritis.*

CHILDHOOD

Colic

Severe adbominal pain, known as colic, affects around one-third of all babies, usually starting before a baby is a month old and stopping by the time he is aged three to four months. It is characterized by protracted bouts of crying several times a day, most often in the late afternoons and evenings. Associated symptoms include the baby drawing his legs up towards his stomach, which may rumble and seem hard to the touch during attacks.

The direct cause of the condition is gas, but internal spasms may be the result of the baby swallowing air while feeding, overfeeding, food allergy, or emotional upset. Conventional medications are usually not helpful but there are steps that can be taken to relieve the symptoms. During a colic attack, try cuddling and rocking the baby, along with gentle massage of the lower abdomen, or hold the baby with its stomach on your arm and burping it. Placing a warm, wrapped hot-water bottle on the stomach may also help to soothe the baby, as may swaddling him.

Do not attempt to feed the baby every time the crying occurs because it takes around two hours for his stomach to empty after a feed. When you do, feed in an upright position and burp the baby frequently. If you are breast-feeding, your doctor may advise you to make changes in your own diet, cutting down on cow's milk, cauliflower, broccoli, cabbage, eggs, chocolate, and foods and drinks containing caffeine.

SYMPTOMS

• *restlessness* • *the baby's legs are drawn up towards his stomach* • *a sudden cry, then relaxation* • *excessive flatulence*

CONVENTIONAL TREATMENT

YOUR DOCTOR MAY PRESCRIBE AN INTESTINAL RELAXANT, WHICH IS OFTEN EFFECTIVE AND CERTAINLY SAFE, OR A SEDATIVE IN SEVERE CASES.

CAUTION

IF THERE ARE ANY SYMPTOMS ASSOCIATED WITH THE COLIC, SUCH AS VOMITING, DIARRHEA, OR BLOOD IN THE FECES, CONSULT A DOCTOR IMMEDIATELY.

LEFT *Colic can be very upsetting for both baby and parents, but cuddling and warmth relieve much of the distress.*

THERAPIES

CRANIAL OSTEOPATHY
• According to therapists, colic can arise as a result of the strains and stresses of birth and the baby's position in the uterus before and during it. Gentle manipulation of the skull is thought by practitioners to ease the resulting condition. *(See pages 114–15.)*

MASSAGE
• Gentle stomach massages may help during an attack. Baby massage is good practice in any event, since it is believed that it helps in the bonding process between mother and child. *(See pages 96–103.)*

RIGHT *When massaging your baby, make sure that he or she is warm and comfortable.*

ACUPRESSURE
• Gentle pressure on acupoints along the appropriate meridians may help soothe a baby. *(See pages 29–31.)*

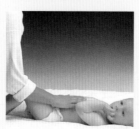

AROMATHERAPY
• Gently massaging the abdominal area with oil of chamomile, dill, lavender, rose, or a blend of all these oils, may help to ease the symptoms of colic and calm the baby. Rubbing a small amount of extremely diluted fennel oil into the abdomen before feeds may also help. *(See pages 104–5.)*

RIGHT *Even very small babies seem to respond to soothing music.*

MUSIC THERAPY
• Calming background music may help to relax and calm a distraught child. *(See pages 132–5.)*

Hyperactivity

Hyperactivity is a behavioral disorder that doctors classify as an important component of a syndrome called Attention Deficit Hyperactivity Disorder (ADHD). In the U.S., between one and five percent of school-age children are believed to suffer from the condition, whose symptoms include excessively high energy levels, restlessness, inattentiveness, prolonged and regular tantrums, disruptiveness, and general lack of control. The syndrome can appear before the age of four, but its signs are often missed until a child starts attending school on a regular basis.

No one knows exactly what causes the condition, but a number of factors may be involved. These include physical disorders in brain functioning and social problems at home, and food intolerances. Conventional treatment may include drug therapy, dietary modification, and psychological counseling.

SYMPTOMS

• *restlessness* • *inattention* • *lack of control* • *disruptiveness*
• *overactivity*

CHOCOLATE

ICE CREAM

CAKE

CONVENTIONAL TREATMENT

A DOCTOR MAY RECOMMEND DRUG THERAPY TO TREAT THE DISORDER, AND COUNSELING. DIETARY CHANGES MAY BE SUGGESTED BUT THERE IS LITTLE PROOF THAT THESE ARE EFFECTIVE.

LEFT *Food additives are believed to be one of the primary causes of hyperactivity in children. But whatever the cause, hyperactivity can make your child demanding and difficult to control at times.*

DATAFILE

• Hypersensitivities to foods, molds, pollens, chemicals, and food additives are thought by some to be underlying causes of the condition; others disagree.

• According to teachers, children suffering from the syndrome are often restless, disorganized, rarely complete their work, create mess, and are irritating to their classmates.

• As many as six percent of children in certain parts of the U.S. are taking drugs to help cope with the problem.

THERAPIES

CHIROPRACTIC
• Chiropractors argue that, by tackling what they term vertebral subluxations, and so increasing the flow of life energy, they can improve a child's attention span. *(See pages 118–25.)*

OSTEOPATHY
• Osteopaths advocate delicate cranial manipulation as a partial solution to the problem. *(See pages 106–13 and Cranial Osteopathy, pages 114–15.)*

ACUPUNCTURE
• Practitioners of a Japanese style of treatment, shoni-shim, believe that simply brushing energy in downward strokes along the arms, legs, and back with special tools like small combs, plus gentle tapping of an area in the center of the back, can be beneficial. *(See pages 20–28.)*

KINESIOLOGY
• Kinesiologists teach a series of simple exercises that cross-pattern the hemispheres of the brain. Remarkable improvements in concentration and school work are claimed as a result. *(See pages 126–33.)*

AROMATHERAPY
• Massages using a little lavender or Roman chamomile oil may be calming, as are ones with neroli, rose, and sandalwood. *(See pages 104–5.)*

PSYCHOTHERAPY AND COUNSELLING
• Cognitive and behavioral therapy, neurolinguisitic programming, child therapy, and family counseling may help children and parents to come to terms with the condition and resolve at least some of the factors that may be triggering it. *(See pages 196–9, pages 204–5, and pages 206–7.)*

DANCE THERAPY
• The therapist gives a child the opportunity to express himself, and the chance to explore new movement skills. As a result, the child learns to organize and focus energy more productively. *(See pages 226–9.)*

MUSIC THERAPY
• Therapists aim to help by using music to release tensions and deal with problems and emotions in a non-verbal way. *(See pages 232–5.)*

OTHER THERAPIES
• Other therapies that may be of benefit in alleviating this condition include: massage *(see pages 96–103)*; craniosacral therapy *(see pages 116–17)*; and color therapy *(see pages 248–51)*.

Bedwetting

There are two types of bedwetting, defined by doctors as primary and secondary nocturnal enuresis respectively. The first is used to describe children who are never dry, and the second children who are sometimes dry, but then start wetting the bed again. Children who are never dry at night may suffer from immature nerves and muscles controlling bladder function; in the second instance, the problem is usually the result of stress of some sort, such as problems at school, a new baby in the family, or family quarrels and infighting. Other possible causes include diabetes, a urinary infection, or a congenital bladder abnormality.

Medically, bedwetting is not considered to be a problem until a child has reached the age of four to five. At the age of five, only nine percent of children are bedwetters and, by the time they are 15, only two percent are. Whatever the cause, both conventional and alternative practitioners agree that it is vital not to make a child feel guilty and ashamed, and to avoid any form of punishment, or to attempt to force the child to overcome the problem. Until it is overcome, one sensible precaution is to fit the bed with a waterproof undersheet or mattress. Another is to persuade the child not to drink immediately before going to bed, and to visit the lavatory before retiring. Automatic buzzers that signal when the bed starts to become wet may also help: statistics show that three out of every four bedwetters using a buzzer become dry.

In extreme cases, some doctors may suggest the use of antidepressants. However, these may not always work and, if they do, will be effective for only as long as the drugs are being taken.

CONVENTIONAL TREATMENT

THIS MAY INVOLVE PSYCHOLOGICAL COUNSELING, PARTICULARLY IF THE BEDWETTING IS BEING TRIGGERED BY STRESS, ANXIETY, OR OTHER EMOTIONAL FACTORS. ANTIDEPRESSANTS MAY BE PRESCRIBED IN CERTAIN CASES, BUT THESE ARE BY NO MEANS UNIVERSALLY EFFECTIVE.

BELOW *Children can be very embarrassed about wetting the bed, and anxiety can make the problem worse. Remember to reassure and comfort your child rather than scolding him or her.*

THERAPIES

AROMATHERAPY
• Massaging chamomile oil into the lower back and stomach while settling a child down to sleep is thought to be helpful. *(See pages 104–5.)*

PSYCHOTHERAPY AND COUNSELING
• A therapist will focus on any underlying stress and also try to defuse any anxiety and lack of self-esteem caused by the act of bedwetting itself. The child will be given a positive role to play, perhaps by being encouraged to keep a calender or diary, in which stars are awarded for dry nights. The parents, in their turn, will be urged to offer praise and encouragement for each dry night. Cognitive-behavioral approaches and neurolinguistic programming are thought to be particularly effective therapies. *(See pages 196–9 and pages 204–5.)*

ACUPUNCTURE
• Some practitioners believe that stimulation of the appropriate acupoints can help to solve the problem. *(See pages 20–28.)*

CRANIAL OSTEOPATHY
• The therapy, which is claimed to be particularly effective for young children, aims to relieve stress by stimulating the nerve endings in the scalp and the areas between the bones of the cranium. *(See pages 114–15.)*

OSTEOPATHY
• Osteopaths believe that bedwetting can be an indication of what they term spinal dysfunction. The nerve impulses that pass between brain and bladder are disrupted as a result. Treatment is aimed at rectifying the situation. *(See pages 106–13 and Chiropractic, pages 118–25.)*

ABOVE *A cranial osteopath will gently manipulate the plates in a child's skull in order to rebalance the body's communication systems.*

Chickenpox

Known medically as varicella, chickenpox is a highly contagious viral infection spread by direct contact, or by breathing in germs from someone else's coughs and sneezes. Two weeks after exposure, a blister-like rash appears, first on the trunk and face and spreading from there to almost everywhere else on the body. The blisters appear in crops over a two- to four-day period. As they itch and break, scabs form. The contagious period for chickenpox begins about five days before the blisters first appear and lasts until they are all crusted over.

Children between the ages of five and nine account for 50 percent of all cases of the disease. Normally, it is a mild illness, but it can cause complications. After the initial attack, the virus that causes it can lie dormant in the body's nerve cells, to be reactivated later in life as shingles. The best means of prevention is vaccination: the chickenpox vaccine that became available in 1995 has been shown to prevent the illness in 70 percent to 90 percent of cases, while those who do develop chickenpox despite vaccination suffer from milder symptoms with fewer skin blisters.

Most home treatment is aimed at relieving the painful itching associated with the condition, and dealing with the accompanying fever and discomfort. Scratching can cause secondary infection and scarring. Itching may be relieved through the use of wet compresses, or by bathing the patient in cool or tepid water two to three times a day. Calamine lotion may help to relieve the itch, while, if the sores spread to the area of the genitals, anesthetic creams can be applied to dull the pain. To reduce the fever, use small doses of acetaminophen.

Most cases of chickenpox do not require special medical attention, but you should always contact a doctor if you are uncertain about the diagnosis, or if there appears to be a complication. Consult a doctor if there are signs that the skin blisters are becoming infected, the area around them is becoming swollen, red, and painful, or if the blisters are leaking pus.

SYMPTOMS

- *mild fever* • *rash of spots that turn into itchy blisters*
- *blisters burst to form scabs*

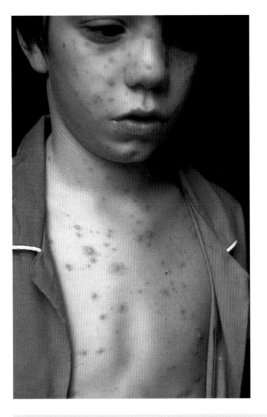

LEFT *The rash is unsightly and itchy, but do discourage your child from scratching the spots. Scratching slows down the healing process and may leave scarring.*

CONVENTIONAL TREATMENT

A MILD PAINKILLER MAY BE SUGGESTED TO RELIEVE PAIN AND LOWER THE TEMPERATURE, WHILE SOOTHING LOTIONS DABBED ON THE RASH MAY HELP TO EASE THE DISCOMFORT.

CAUTION

CALL A DOCTOR IMMEDIATELY IF A CHILD'S TEMPERATURE IS OVER 102°F (39°C), IF HE IS HARD TO AWAKEN OR CONFUSED, HAS TROUBLE WALKING, A STIFF NECK, IS VOMITING REPEATEDLY, HAS DIFFICULTY BREATHING, IS SUFFERING FROM A SEVERE COUGH, OR SEEMS VERY ILL. DO NOT GIVE CHILDREN ASPIRIN.

THERAPIES

AROMATHERAPY
• Therapists advise dabbing oil of lavender directly on to the spots to ease the itching. The dabbing may also encourage healing, as lavender has an antibacterial action that can help to prevent a secondary infection from developing. Tea tree and bergamot are possible alternatives. The oil should be well diluted in chamomile tea. Cool peppermint oil compresses may help to reduce fever. (*See pages 104–5.*)

HYDROTHERAPY
• In suspected cases of chickenpox, practitioners may advocate hot baths. The theory is that this will encourage the rash to develop and so speed up the progress of the illness. Once the condition has developed, they may suggest lukewarm baths, with natural substances like baking soda added to the bathwater. (*See pages 172–9.*)

ACUPRESSURE
• Practitioners believe that pressure on the appropriate acupoints can help to lower body temperature when there is fever present. (*See pages 20–28.*)

LEFT *Dabbing diluted lavender oil on to the spots can reduce itching and fight infection. Adding a few drops to the bathwater has the same effect. It should be well diluted in camomile tea.*

BELOW *Calamine lotion takes the heat out of spots, as does adding baking soda to the bath.*

Mumps

Mumps is a contagious disease caused by a virus that infects the parotid salivary glands, located toward the back of each cheek in the area between the ear and the jaw. The glands become increasingly swollen and painful over a period of one to three days, the pain getting worse when you swallow, talk, chew, or drink acidic juices like orange juice. A fever often accompanies the swelling, together with headache and loss of appetite. In two out of three cases, both the left and right parotid glands are affected, the second gland usually swelling about four to five days after the first.

Because the average incubation period for mumps is 18 days, during which time the condition is symptomless, it is impossible to stop the infection from spreading, and it occurs in epidemics in winter and spring. For this reason, doctors recommend that babies are immunized with MMR vaccine (the vaccine also protects against measles and rubella). If your child becomes infected, you can treat the pain and fever with acetaminophen. Soothe the swollen glands with warm or cold packs, whichever feels the better. Make sure that your child drinks plenty of fluids: water, decaffeinated soft drinks, and tea are best, as these are non-acidic and will not make the pain worse. Keep your child in isolation for 14 days from the onset of symptoms or for seven days from the subsidence of swelling.

Consult your doctor if earache or headache become severe, if the temperature goes above 101°F, and if the neck becomes stiff. Such complications are now uncommon in children. One in four young adult males who catch mumps, however, contract orchitis (painful swelling and inflammation of the testicles), which can lead to sterility. A doctor should be consulted as soon as possible.

SYMPTOMS

- *loss of appetite* • *tiredness* • *headache* • *mild fever*
- *swollen, painful glands under jaw* • *swallowing is painful*

DATAFILE

- Mumps vaccine protects between 75 to 95 percent of the people who receive it.

- In the U.S., vaccination has resulted in a decline of more than 90 percent in the incidence of mumps.

- Mumps becomes more common as children grow older, with teenagers being most at risk of contracting it.

- If you catch mumps once, you are usually protected against the condition for the rest of your life.

- The mumps virus is spread by coughing and sneezing.

CONVENTIONAL TREATMENT

BEDREST, THE APPLICATION OF COLD COMPRESSES, AND THE USE OF A MILD PAINKILLER MAY ALL BE ADVISED. MALE TEENAGERS MAY ALSO BE TREATED WITH CORTICOSTEROIDS.

CAUTION

IF ILLNESS IS ACCOMPANIED BY SEVERE HEADACHE, STIFFNESS IN THE NECK, ABNORMALLY HIGH FEVER, SENSITIVITY TO LIGHT, AND DROWSINESS, OR CONFUSION, CALL A DOCTOR. IN YOUNG ADULTS, CALL A DOCTOR IF THE TESTICLES BECOME SWOLLEN AND PAINFUL. DO NOT GIVE CHILDREN ASPIRIN.

LEFT *Swollen glands below the jawbone are the most recognizable early sign of mumps. Massaging with chamomile oil will ease the pain.*

THERAPIES

AROMATHERAPY
• A gentle neck massage with chamomile or lavender oil, diluted in grapeseed oil, may help to ease the pain. *(See pages 104–5.)*

HYDROTHERAPY
• Cool compresses may help to reduce the swelling and ease the fever. *(See pages 172–9.)*

RIGHT *Massaging the neck can help ease mumps-related pain.*

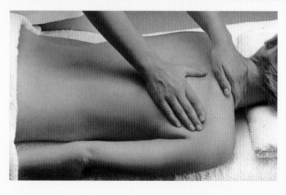

Measles

Measles is a highly contagious respiratory infection which adults can get as well as children. The initial symptoms, which usually start three or four days before the rash starts, are irritability, a runny nose, reddened eyes that are light-sensitive, a hacking cough and a high temperature. An associated symptom is red, small, irregular spots with blue-white centers inside the mouth that normally appear a day or so before the rash. Typically, the rash begins on the forehead, spreading downward over the neck, face, and body until it reaches the feet three to four days later. The condition lasts for some 10 to 14 days from the appearance of the first symptoms, and the child should be kept in isolation.

Babies are generally protected from measles for the first six to eight months of life, due to a natural immunity passed on by mothers. Otherwise, the condition can be prevented by MMR vaccination. If you suspect that your child has contracted measles, call a doctor and encourage the drinking of lots of water, fruit juice, tea, or lemonade to replace what the body is losing by sweating and also to reduce the chance of lung infections. A vaporizer may relieve coughs and soothe breathing; painkillers will help to reduce fever and ease discomfort. Watching television or using computers should be discouraged while the eyes are light-sensitive.

LEFT *Drink lots of fluids to replace what the body is losing in sweating out the fever of measles.*

SYMPTOMS

- *runny nose* • *reddened, light-sensitive eyes* • *cough*
- *fever* • *spots inside the mouth* • *a rash that starts on the forehead and consists of large, flat, red to brown blotches that often flow into each other*

CAUTION

CALL A DOCTOR IF FEVER RECURS AFTER THE RASH HAS STARTED TO HEAL, IF A CHILD COMPLAINS OF SEVERE HEADACHE, A STIFF NECK, DROWSINESS AND HAS DIFFICULTY WAKING UP, OR IF THERE ARE ANY SIGNS THAT A COMPLICATING LUNG INFECTION IS DEVELOPING.

CONVENTIONAL TREATMENT

BEDREST, DRINKING PLENTY OF FLUIDS, AND THE USE OF A MILD PAINKILLER MAY ALL BE SUGGESTED. ANTIBIOTICS MAY BE PRESCRIBED IF CHEST OR EAR INFECTIONS ARISE. DO NOT GIVE A CHILD ASPIRIN.

THERAPIES

AROMATHERAPY
- Where there is a build-up of phlegm and other cold symptoms, a gentle chest massage with a few drops of tea tree oil in a light carrier oil base may help. To relieve itching, sponge the skin with a cool lavender infusion, or a teaspoon of distilled witch hazel added to half a pint of water. *(See pages 104–5.)*

HYDROTHERAPY
- Lukewarm baths with a little baking soda dissolved in the water may help to soothe the rash. *(See pages 172–9.)*

ACUPRESSURE
- Pressure at the appropriate acupoints can help to control fever, according to practitioners. *(See pages 29–31.)*

German Measles (Rubella)

This highly contagious infection, sometimes called rubella or three-day measles, commonly starts with a day or two of mild fever and swollen glands in the neck or behind the ears. This is followed by a rash that spreads downward from the hairline to cover the rest of the body, usually clearing on the face as it spreads. The rash, which does not itch, lasts on average for three days. Other symptoms of the condition, which is a mild one in its effects, may include mild conjunctivitis, a stuffy or runny nose, swollen lymph glands, pain and swelling in the joints, especially in young women, and pain in the testicles in men.

German measles can be prevented by vaccination, but the vaccine should not be administered to anyone who is pregnant, or to someone who may become pregnant within three months of being vaccinated. If German measles occurs in a pregnant woman, serious malformations of the developing fetus can occur as a result.

SYMPTOMS

- *fever* • *swollen glands in the neck or behind the ears*
- *pinkish rash*

RIGHT *Applying a cold compress dabbed with a little peppermint oil to a German measles rash will ease pain and cool fever.*

CAUTION

IF YOU ARE THINKING ABOUT GETTING PREGNANT, MAKE SURE THAT YOU ARE IMMUNE TO RUBELLA THROUGH A BLOOD TEST. IF YOU ARE NOT SURE WHETHER OR NOT YOU HAVE BEEN VACCINATED AGAINST THE DISEASE. IF YOU ARE PREGNANT, UNPROTECTED AND EXPOSED TO RUBELLA, CONTACT A DOCTOR IMMEDIATELY.

CONVENTIONAL TREATMENT

BEDREST, THE DRINKING OF PLENTY OF FLUIDS, AND TAKING MILD PAINKILLERS MAY BE ADVISED.

THERAPIES

ACUPRESSURE
- Practitioners believe that stimulation of the appropriate acupoints can help to manage fever. *(See pages 29–31.)*

AROMATHERAPY
- Practitioners advise cool compresses, to which a few drops of peppermint oil have been added, to soothe fever. *(See pages 104–5.)*

HYDROTHERAPY
- Frequent, cool baths may relieve fever. *(See pages 172–9.)*

OLD AGE

Alzheimer's Disease

Memory loss, mood swings, confusion and mental deterioration are all signs of Alzheimer's disease, or an associated dementia. There are many theories about what causes it. Some researchers argue that a virus or some other infectious agent is responsible, while others point to brain chemical deficiencies, genetic predisposition, or environmental toxins such as aluminium and mercury as probable causes. Regardless of this, the end result is the progressive degeneration of the brain cells that control the intellect, the way the brain receives and processes information. This particular disease is irreversible.

Onset is gradual, with signs and symptoms progressing in stages. Initial indications include forgetfulness, disorientation, increasing inability to tackle routine tasks, impaired judgement, lack of initiative, depression and fear. As the condition worsens, these are joined by wandering, restless and agitation, especially at night, repetitive actions and muscle twitching, while, in the final phase, victims may be unable to recognize themselves or other people, may be unable to speak, develop a need to put everything into their mouths and to touch everything in sight, become emaciated and lose control of body functions.

Accurate medical diagnosis is important, because the symptoms of Alzheimer's disease are the same as those of a number of other conditions that, unlike Alzheimer's, can be treated and cured. If Alzheimer's disease is diagnosed, treatment concentrates on maintaining the victim's quality of life for as long as possible. Most medications currently being used are experimental.

SYMPTOMS

• *memory loss* • *mood swings* • *confusion* • *mental deterioration* • *inability to concentrate* • *behavioral changes*

DATAFILE

• Alzheimer's disease affects nearly four million Americans.

• The risk of developing the condition increases with age, though the disease itself is not thought to be age-related. The onset is usually slow and gradual.

• Brain tumors, blood clots in the brain, hypothyroidism, and depression are all problems that can be confused with Alzheimer's disease, but, unlike Alzheimer's, they can all be treated successfully.

• Problems with recent or short-term memory are common early on in the disease.

the brain loses its ability to concentrate

treatment for Alzheimer's can so far only deal with maintaining the sufferer's quality of life

ABOVE *Sufferers from Alzheimer's or senile dementia gradually become less able to cope with the ordinary demands of daily life. A familiar environment and caring support can lessen their feelings of distress and disorientation.*

CAUTION

IF MEMORY LOSS IN AN ELDERLY PERSON IS ACCOMPANIED BY SYMPTOMS OF CONFUSION, INABILITY TO CONCENTRATE, AND BEHAVIORAL CHANGES, A DOCTOR SHOULD BE CONSULTED AS SOON AS POSSIBLE, IF ONLY TO RULE OUT THE POSSIBILITY OF ALZHEIMER'S DISEASE.

ABOVE *The brain is believed to shrink or atrophy as we grow older, making us less able to think or move quickly, and eventually leading to forgetfulness and senile dementia.*

THERAPIES

QIGONG
• Breathing techniques and physical movements are combined in this Chinese therapy. Practitioners believe that it stimulates the brain and so aids concentration. *(See pages 44–5.)*

RELAXATION AND BREATHING
• Practitioners will show you how to do exercises that may help to bring about an improvement in memory by relaxing both body and mind. *(See pages 158–65 and pages 166–71.)*

T'AI CHI CH'UAN
• Practitioners believe that gentle t'ai chi ch'uan, with its meditative, relaxing movements, can help mental agility. *(See pages 46–51.)*

YOGA
• Practitioners believe that a relaxed body promotes steady breathing and a clear, untroubled mind. You can learn various asanas that are intended to help you to achieve this. *(See pages 52–9.)*

RIGHT *Practitioners believe that T'ai-chi keeps vital energy flowing through the body and the brain.*

Depression in the Elderly

Though most people experience some degree of depression from time to time, elderly people, in particular, can be affected by the condition. As they age, they can feel that they no longer matter to others, that their dependency is problematic, and that they have lost a sense of purpose or usefulness. Often, the problem is compounded by the refusal of others to allow the elderly to participate in daily chores, a reduction in opportunities for social intercourse that highlights feelings of isolation and loneliness, and lack of mental stimulation. Withdrawal and depression are common responses.

To overcome mild, hard-to-explain depression, self-help provides a number of answers. Substituting a positive thought for every negative one that comes into your head, taking some physical exercise every day, challenging yourself with a new project or task, helping others less fortunate than yourself, doing something that will help you to relax, and talking through things with others to vent your tensions and frustrations can all be helpful. You should avoid drugs and alcohol: drinking too much and the use of recreational drugs can cause or worsen depression.

If you are severely depressed, a doctor may prescribe a course of antidepressant drugs, sometimes in association with a course of psychotherapy or counseling. However, it may take some time before things begin to improve as a result of taking the drugs.

SYMPTOMS

- *irritability or aggression* • *bewilderment and disorientation*
- *fecal incontinence can be a sign of depression in the elderly*

CONVENTIONAL TREATMENT

ANTIDEPRESSANTS TO RELIEVE THE CONDITION, IF IT IS SEVERE, AND COUNSELING MAY BE RECOMMENDED. MILD DEPRESSION MAY BE TREATED WITH SHORT COURSES OF TRANQUILIZERS OR SLEEPING PILLS.

BELOW *Exercise is an easy self-help measure to combat depression. If you feel physically healthy, you are likely to feel better about yourself emotionally.*

THERAPIES

AROMATHERAPY
• Therapeutic massage with antidepressant oils may be beneficial. The oils include bergamot, chamomile, clary sage, jasmine, geranium, lavender, melissa, orange, rose, sandalwood, and ylang ylang, either blended or used singly. *(See pages 104–5.)*

HYDROTHERAPY
• Practitioners claim that sauna baths and vigorous body rubs have helped in some cases. *(See pages 172–9.)*

ACUPUNCTURE
• Practitioners class depression as a liver disorder. Accordingly, they concentrate treatment on the meridians associated with the liver, gall bladder, pericardium, spleen, and stomach. *(See pages 20–28.)*

HYPNOTHERAPY
• Therapists who practice this technique have claimed that it is successful in treating the condition. The same claims have been made for autosuggestion. *(See pages 218–23.)*

MASSAGE
• Pleasant, relaxing massages are said to help to relieve symptoms of depression by boosting feelings of wellness. *(See pages 96–103.)*

RELAXATION AND BREATHING
• Depressive tension and anxiety can be relieved by breathing exercises and exercises designed to relax the muscles. *(See pages 158–65 and pages 166–71.)*

ART THERAPY
• By encouraging the expression of feelings, therapists argue that their patients gain in confidence and self-esteem. What is produced may contain symbols that can be interpreted in much the same way that dreams are analysed in psychoanalysis. *(See pages 238–41.)*

PSYCHOTHERAPY AND COUNSELING
• Practitioners believe that counseling may help to overcome feelings of depression. *(See pages 188–91.)*

ABOVE *Aromatherapists recommend massage with a blend of uplifting and harmonising essential oils (see above).*

ABOVE *Depression often leads to – or results from – the suppression of emotions and a lack of self-worth. By encouraging you to express yourself creatively on paper, art therapy can combat these negative thoughts and feelings.*

Osteoporosis

Osteoporosis is a debilitating disorder in which the bones of the body become brittle and fragile, and so more inclined to break. Any bone of the body can be affected, but the hip, spine, and wrists are particularly at risk. Women are four times more likely to develop the condition than men, particularly after the menopause. This is because the ovaries stop producing the female hormone estrogen, which is important for maintaining bone strength.

The older you are, the greater the risk of osteoporosis developing. Calcium deficiency is thought to be a key trigger, while the chances of contracting the condition can be aggravated by various other factors, including smoking, excessive consumption of alcohol, diet, and lack of exercise. Susceptibility to fracture may also be, in part, a result of heredity, while some medical problems and some long-term drug therapies, notably the prolonged administration of steroids, can predispose you to developing the disorder. Although persistent back pain is common, the condition itself is difficult to detect in its early stages: often, the first sign may be a fracture after a minor fall. As the osteoporosis worsens, the spine gradually shortens and becomes more curved: the physical signs of this are height loss and a characteristic hunching of the shoulders (sometimes known as "dowager's hump").

There is a lot you can do for yourself to reduce the chances of developing osteporosis, or to mitigate its effects. If you smoke, give up, and also cut down on the amount of alcohol you drink. Check what you are eating – it is important to make sure that you are maintaining an

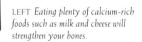

LEFT *Eating plenty of calcium-rich foods such as milk and cheese will strengthen your bones.*

adequate intake of calcium and vitamin D, as the body cannot absorb the former without the latter. Doctors recommend a daily calcium intake of 1,000 mg for most adults, though, if you are postmenopausal, this needs to go up to 1,500 mg. Milk, cheese, yogurt, bread, sardines, broccoli, and eggs are all calcium-rich, as are salmon, spinach, soy beans and peanuts. Regular exercise, particularly when you are young (when bone mass builds up) also helps to prevent bone loss – but do not push yourself too hard to start with, especially if you have not exercised for some time.

If you do not get enough calcium through your diet, your doctor can recommend an appropriate calcium substitute. If you are menopausal, your doctor may suggest estrogen replacement therapy, but, as this is not without risks, you should discuss its pros and cons first. There are alternatives that suit men as well as women.

SYMPTOMS

• *persistent back pain* • *wrist, forearm, neck, or hip fractures, resulting from minor stumbles or falls* • *loss of height as a result of shrinkage of the spine* • *hunched shoulders*

THERAPIES

YOGA
• Practitioners believe that more efficient breathing from the diaphragm can help the body deal with changes in bone structure. You will also be taught specific asanas for relaxation and to build body strength and flexibility. *(See pages 52–9.)*

T'AI CHI CH'UAN
• These slow, graceful exercises, it is believed, stimulate the flow of the life energy known as qi, so promoting the best use of mental, emotional and physical energies. They may also benefit posture and increase joint flexibility. *(See pages 46–51, and Qigong, pages 44–5.)*

REFLEXOLOGY
• Foot massage of the appropriate reflex points relaxes muscles and eases inflammation in the joints, according to practitioners. *(See pages 66–71.)*

CHIROPRACTIC
• Joint manipulation may

help to ease the persistent back pain associated with the disease. *(See pages 118–25.)*

OSTEOPATHY
• The touch and manipulation treatments on which osteopathy is based have been shown to be helpful in relieving acute back pain and other musculoskeletal problems. The therapy is particularly effective in improving mobility. *(See pages 106–13.)*

ACUPUNCTURE
• Acupuncture is generally recognized as an effective form of pain relief. Practitioners also argue that stimulating or suppressing the flow of qi to ensure that it is even is vital for good health. *(See pages 20–28.)*

LIGHT THERAPY
• Natural daylight stimulates the body to produce vitamin D. This is essential for the absorption of calcium, which strengthens bones. *(See pages 242–3.)*

ABOVE *Osteoporosis is most common in post-menopausal women, leading to the characteristic "dowager's hump." Paying attention to the diet and general health early in life can do much to prevent the onset of the disease.*

CONVENTIONAL TREATMENT

A DOCTOR MAY ARRANGE FOR X-RAYS, BLOOD TESTS, AND THE PRESCRIPTION OF PAINKILLERS, VITAMIN D AND CALCIUM TABLETS. PHYSICAL THERAPY OR REMEDIAL EXERCISES MAY ALSO BE SUGGESTED. NEW DRUGS BEING DEVELOPED MAY HELP BONES REABSORB BONE FIBER AND CALCIUM.

BELOW *Osteoporosis can be helped by chiropractic manipulation but do take care as the risk of fracture is high.*

DATAFILE

• More than 28 million Americans, mostly women, are at high risk of developing osteoporosis.

• Osteoporosis leads to 1.5 million fractures annually in the U.S., 300,000 of them affecting the hip.

• If osteoporosis is present, the risk of hip fracture for women is equal to the combined risk of developing breast cancer, cancer of the uterus, and ovarian cancer.

• Small-boned and thin women are at greater risk of contracting the disease, as are women who stop menstruating before the menopause as a result of eating disorders, such as anorexia nervosa and bulimia, or because of excessive physical exercise.

Stroke

A stroke – what doctors term a cerebrovascular accident, or CVA – is the result of an interruption of the blood supply to any part of the brain. The most common causes are blood clots, which can block an artery leading to the brain, or a hemorrhage that results in bleeding into, or around, the organ. The consequences vary, according to what caused the stroke to occur and the part of the brain affected.

Strokes are uncommon before the age of 55: after that, the risk gets greater as you get older. Smoking, diabetes, high blood pressure, and atherosclerosis are all predisposing factors. There are two main types: a complete stroke, which can lead to paralysis, takes time to recover from, and clears up only partially, and what are medically termed transient ischemic attacks (TIAs). These are milder and usually clear within minutes, but are a warning that a major stroke may occur in the future. To lessen the chances of this, you should stop smoking, keep blood pressure down, adopt a low-fat, low-salt diet, lose any extra weight, and exercise regularly.

A stroke may happen suddenly, often without warning. This is a life-threatening medical emergency. The most common signs are a sudden numbness, weakness, or paralysis of the face, arm, or leg, usually on one side of the body, loss of speech, or trouble talking or understanding, sudden blurring of vision, dizziness and loss of balance, difficulty swallowing and sudden, severe headache with no apparent cause. Conventional treatment aims at reducing the likelihood of another stroke through the prescription of anticoagulant drugs to thin the blood and so lessening the chances of new blood clots forming. Regular, small doses of aspirin are preventative. You may receive treatment to help breathing and blood circulation, while physiotherapy may be advised as part of the recovery process. Complementary therapies may aid in this as well, but a doctor should be consulted before trying any of them.

SYMPTOMS

- *you cannot feel one side of the face or body* • *vision in one eye is impaired* • *suddenly find it difficult to talk* • *cannot understand what someone is saying* • *feeling dizzy and losing your sense of balance* • *blinding, severe headache* • *loss of consciousness*

ABOVE *Smoking greatly increases the risk of suffering a stroke. All doctors and complementary practitioners advise people not to smoke.*

RIGHT *The onset of a severe headache can herald a stroke.*

CONVENTIONAL TREATMENT

ONCE THE IMMEDIATE PROBLEMS OF THE STROKE HAVE BEEN RESOLVED (THIS REQUIRES HOSPITAL TREATMENT), PHYSICAL THERAPY WILL BE PRESCRIBED TO RESTORE AS MUCH NORMALITY AS POSSIBLE.

CAUTION

A STROKE IS A MEDICAL EMERGENCY AND MUST BE TREATED AS SUCH. QUICK ACTION COULD SAVE A LIFE. ANYONE AT MEDICAL RISK OF A STROKE, OR A VICTIM OF ONE, SHOULD NOT EMBARK ON ANY COMPLEMENTARY THERAPY WITHOUT GETTING A DOCTOR'S ADVICE FIRST.

DATAFILE

- Stroke is the third largest cause of death in America today.
- The stroke mortality rate is currently increasing for the first time in four decades
- Uncontrolled high blood pressure, smoking, diabetes, and heart disease are major causes of stroke.
- Approximately 730,000 cases of stroke occur in the U.S. annually.
- The condition affects men more frequently than women.
- Some oral contraceptives increase the risk of stroke.

THERAPIES

HYDROTHERAPY
• Swimming in a heated pool may help to restore movement, body coordination and physical strength, but this must be supervised by a qualified therapist. *(See pages 172–9.)*

BIOFEEDBACK
• Learning how to use biofeedback techniques may help in rehabilitation, say the therapists. They argue that it can help in improving grip, walking, and other body functions. *(See pages 212–13.)*

MEDITATION
• The therapy may help stroke victims to cope with the depression that often follows a stroke. It may also reduce stress levels, decrease blood pressure, and relieve pain. *(See pages 60–63.)*

MASSAGE
• Massage to stimulate the blood circulation and improve the condition of affected limbs may help. It may also relieve tension and pain. *(See pages 96–103.)*

REFLEXOLOGY
• Stimulating the reflex point at the tip of the big toe is said to encourage recovery from paralysis. Reflexologists believe that this point links to the brain. *(See pages 66–71.)*

FELDENKRAIS METHOD
• Therapists aim at reprograming paralyzed limbs through gentle movement to encourage their return to normal function. *(See pages 142–5.)*

ACUPUNCTURE
• Acupuncture sessions may help in the recovery of mental and physical functions, according to therapists. *(See pages 20–28.*

T'AI CHI CH'UAN
• Practitioners believe the therapy helps by rebalancing the flow of qi and regulating the flow of body fluids. *(See pages 46–51 and Qigong, pages 44–5.)*

PSYCHOTHERAPY AND COUNSELING
• The consequences of a stroke can be devastating. Counselors can help the patient, family, and friends come to terms with the situation. *(See pages 188–91.)*

TRAGERWORK
• The practitioner senses any areas of tension in the body and then cradles, stretches, and rocks the skin, easing the pressure. *(See pages 154–5.)*

359

GLOSSARY

A

abscess
a self-contained pocket of pus that results from a bacterial infection, and causes inflammation of the local area

acupoint
the point along a meridian at which the "life force" (qi) is thought to be accessible. Acupoints are stimulated by the insertion of needles or by acupressure. They are known as *tsubos* in Japanese

acute
of sudden onset and brief duration

adenoids
lymphatic tissue at the back of the nose

adrenal glands
a pair of endocrine glands located on the top of the kidneys that secrete corticosteroid hormones, epinephrine and novepinephrine

adrenalin
a hormone secreted by the adrenal gland that defends the body against emotional and physical stresses

aggravation
the exacerbation of symptoms that can occur when taking some natural remedies, particularly in the case of chronic ailments

agni
meaning "fire," or the forces which break down substances consumed; in Indian medicine, considered to be metabolism

-algia (suffix)
meaning "pain in"; for example, arthralgia, pain in the joints

allergen
a substance that causes an allergic reaction

allergy
an abnormal response by the body to a substance that in most people causes no response. Common allergies include hay fever, eczema, asthma, and contact dermatitis, which is an inflammation of the skin caused by contact with a substance to which the person is sensitive, e.g. poison ivy

allopathy
orthodox medical treatment

alpha waves
the brain-waves associated with quiet, receptive states, produced in far higher intensity during meditation

ama
in Ayurveda, a toxic substance believed to gather in the weak parts of the body and cause disease

Ama occurs when the metabolism is impaired due to an imbalance of agni

amenorrhea
absence of menses (menstrual periods)

analgesic
pain-relieving

anaphylaxis
an extreme allergic reaction to a foreign substance. Subsequent exposure can produce a life-threatening condition called anaphylactic shock

anemia
deficiency in either quality or quantity of red corpuscles in the blood

angioplasty
surgical repair or reconstruction of obstructed arteries

anorexia nervosa
psychological problem causing extreme loss of appetite, drastic weight loss, and, sometimes, death

antacid
a remedy or medicine that reduces stomach acidity

antibacterial
checks the growth of bacteria

antibiotic
used to treat infections caused by bacteria

antibody
a protein produced by the white blood cells to neutralize foreign protein in the body

anticonvulsant
an agent that helps arrest or prevent convulsions

antidepressant
an agent that relieves depression

antidote
the term used to describe other remedies or substances that cancel or nullify the effect of a prescribed remedy

anti-emetic
an agent that reduces the incidence and severity of nausea or vomiting

antifungal
an agent that works to prevent the spread and incidence of fungal conditions

antihistamine
an agent that prevents a histamine reaction (*see Allergies, pages 338–9*)

antihypertensive
an agent to lower blood pressure

antiseptic
helps to counter infection by destroying bacteria and other microorganisms on the skin

antispasmodic
relaxes the smooth muscle of the bowel and bladder to relieve spasm

antiviral
inhibits the spread of viruses

asana
body posture adopted in yoga

astigmatism
visual defect causing a distorted view of an object

astringent
constricts the blood vessels or membranes in order to reduce irritation, inflammation, and swelling; has a binding and contracting effect, usually on the mucous membrane, to give it a protective coating against irritants or infective organisms; also one of the six tastes in Ayurveda; found in potatoes, beans, and witch hazel

atherosclerosis
thickening and hardening of the arteries due to the accumulation of fatty deposits on the artery wall

articulation
range of movement of the joints

asthma
spasm of the bronchi in the lungs, narrowing the airways

atopic
predisposition to allergies

aura
every person, animal, and plant is said to have a visible aura, or magnetic field. These are said to indicate the state of health, emotions, mind, and spirit

autoimmune disorder
a condition in which the body creates antibodies that attack healthy cells

autonomic nervous system (ANS)
the part of the nervous system responsible for the control of bodily functions that do not require conscious thought, such as breathing, heartbeat, and intestinal movements. It is divided into the sympathetic and parasympathetic nervous systems, whose actions are often antagonistic

aversion therapy
a type of behavioral therapy that discourages pleasurable but destructive habits, such as smoking or excessive drinking, by associating them with unpleasant experiences

B

bacteria
a group of microorganisms, some of which cause disease

bactericide
an agent that destroys bacteria. Substances with this property include antibiotics, antiseptics, and disinfectants

benign
of a tumor – not cancerous and will not spread through the body

beta-blocker
drug that helps regulate the rhythm of the heart

biopsy
removal of fluid or tissue from the body for examination

bitter
a tonic component that stimulates the appetite and promotes the secretion of saliva and gastric juices by exciting the taste buds; one of the six Ayurvedic tastes; found in barks, tannins, and resins

bodywork
term used to describe manual therapies such as massage and osteopathy

bronchodilator
a substance that dilates the bronchi, the air passages of the lungs

bulimia nervosa
secretive binge eating followed by purging

bursa
a small fluid-filled sac

C

calmative
a calming or sedating agent

calculus
a small crystalline mass, e.g. a kidney stone

Candida
Candida albicans, a fungus affecting the mucous membranes and skin; causes thrush

carcinogenic
an agent that can cause cancer

cardiac
pertaining to the heart

cartilage
elastic connective tissue forming parts of the skeleton and joint surfaces

catecholamines
substances such as epinephrine and novepinephrine that generally act as neurotransmitters in the functioning of the autonomic and central nervous systems

cathartic
in psychological terms, a sudden release of anxiety or tension, generally resulting from the process of uncovering repressed trauma

central nervous system (CNS)
the brain and spinal cord. It receives and analyses sensory information then decides whether or not to initiate a response

cerebral cortex
external layer of the cerebellum; is the part of the brain involved in information processing. It is divided into two hemispheres: in most people, the left is usually concerned with logic, language, and mathematics, and the right with creativity, imagination, and intuition

cerebrospinal fluid
the clear, watery fluid that surrounds, protects, and nourishes the brain and spinal cord

Cesarean section
a surgical operation whereby a baby is delivered through the abdominal wall

chakras
in Eastern medicine, circles which are thought to be found along the mid-line of the body, in line with the spinal column

channels
invisible pathways in which qi (or chi) travels; also called meridians. They occur in and on the body

cholesterol
a lipid mainly produced in the liver but a small amount absorbed from cholesterol-rich foods such as eggs. High blood levels can cause atherosclerosis, which can lead to coronary heart disease and stroke

chronic
persisting for a long time; a state showing no change or very slow change

chronic fatigue syndrome
condition of unknown cause characterized by extreme fatigue that lasts for long periods of time and is made worse by physical or mental exertion

coagulate
an agent that acts to clot or thicken the blood

cognitive restructuring
a psychotherapy whereby patients are required to question and remodel their outlook on life, removing self-defeating or denigrating thoughts and replacing them with positive ones

colonic irrigation
a form of hydrotherapy in which the lower bowel is flushed out with purified water to remove fecal matter

complementary
the term used to describe alternative forms of medical treatment – emphasizing the fact that they support rather than replace orthodox medicine

compress
a lint or pad usually soaked in hot or ice-cold water and applied to the body for relief of swelling and pain, or to produce localized pressure

compulsion
an overwhelming urge to act upon an obsession

conditioning
a term used to describe a process of learning whereby a stimulus produces a learned response

congestion
abnormal accumulation of blood, tissue fluid, or lymph

contraindication
any factor in a patient's condition that indicates that treatment would involve a greater than normal risk and is therefore not recommended

corticosteroids
(hormones) produced by the adrenal glands. Corticosteroid drugs are used in the treatment of inflammatory conditions, e.g. rheumatoid arthritis, and to suppress the immune system

cortisol
a steroid hormone produced by the adrenal glands which is important for the body's responses to stress

cradle cap
a common condition in young babies in which crusty white or yellow scales form a "cap" on the scalp

cranial rhythmic impulse
the rate at which the cerebrospinal fluid is thought to pulse (6–15 times per minute)

cryotherapy
a form of hydrotherapy that uses ice and freezing water

cupping
a practice used in Traditional Chinese Medicine whereby heated cups are applied to the skin and allowed to cool. This creates a vacuum and increases the flow of blood in the area

CVA
cerebrovascular accident: another term for stroke

cymatics
a vibrational technique used in sound therapy that aims to restore disturbed inner rhythms using sound waves transmitted by a machine

D

dantien
energy centers in the body. In Chinese medicine there are considered to be three: an upper (between the eyebrows); a middle (in the centre of the trunk); and a lower (the lower abdomen). Qi is stored here

decongestant
an agent for the relief or reduction of congestion, e.g. of the mucous membranes

degeneration
physical or chemical alterations in cells, tissues, or organs leading to reduced efficiency, e.g. the thinning and destruction of cartilage covering the surfaces of joints in the degenerative disorder osteoarthritis

depression
mental state characterized by a feeling of sadness or melancholy and a sense of reduced emotional well-being. May be a normal response to a particular event or, if it occurs for no apparent reason, deepens and persists, may be a symptom of a psychiatric illness

dermatitis
inflammatory skin reaction often in response to an allergen although may occur without apparent cause

desensitization
a method for reducing the effects of an allergen by injecting, over a period of time, gradually increasing doses of the allergen until resistance is built up. It is also a technique used in behavioral therapy to treat phobias. The thing that is feared is very gradually introduced to the patient, first in imagination and then in reality

detoxificant/detoxifier
an agent that acts to detoxify, or remove toxins from the body

dhatus
in Indian medicine, seven essential tissues which make up the body

dialogue
discussion on how habitual ideas and emotions can affect your mind, body, and spirit

diaphragm
thin, dome-shaped muscle that plays an important role in breathing

discharge
an excretion or substance evacuated from the body

diuretic
an agent that stimulates the flow of urine, reducing body fluid levels

doshas
the three basic constitutional types in Indian medicine – vatha, pitta, and kapha – which are known as the "tri-doshas"

dysfunction
abnormal or imperfect functioning of a system, organ, or joint. Osteopaths use the term to denote problems that do not seem to have any obvious cause

dysmenorrhea
severe pains accompanying the menstrual period

dyspepsia
difficulty with digestion associated with pain, flatulence, heartburn, and nausea

E

ECG
electrocardiogram: a recording of the electrical activity associated with the heartbeat

ectopic
not situated in the normal place, e.g. a pregnancy that occurs at a site other than inside the uterus, such as in the Fallopian tube, is termed an ectopic pregnancy

edema
a swelling caused by fluid retention beneath the skin's surface

educational kinesiology
a series of exercises that are thought to improve communication between the left- and right-hand sides of the brain

ego states
term used in Transactional Analysis to describe the child, parent, and adult that everyone is thought to have within them

effleurage
slow, rhythmic massage

emetic
an agent that induces vomiting

emollient
an agent that softens and soothes the skin

endocrine system
comprises a group of glands located in different parts of the body. It is responsible for the secretion of chemical transmitters called hormones

endometriosis
a common disease in women of reproductive age. It involves cells of the endometrium, which is a mucous membrane lining the uterus. During the menstrual cycle this mucous membrane is usually shed if pregnancy does not occur. Occasionally endometrial cells escape from the womb into the pelvic cavity, or other remote parts of the body, where they may attach and continue their hormone-controlled growth cycle. This condition is termed endometriosis

endorphins
a group of chemicals manufactured in the brain that influence the body's response to pain

enuresis
bed-wetting

epidural
epidural anesthesia involves injecting anesthetic into the epidural space of the spinal canal

episiotomy
an incision made in the perineum (the area between the anus and the vagina) to prevent tearing while delivering a baby

essence
the pure energy extracted from food that is transformed into qi by the body. Also the integral part of a plant, its life force, as used in flower remedies, herbalism, and aromatherapy

essential oil
a volatile and aromatic liquid (sometimes semi-solid) which generally constitutes the odorous principles of a plant. It is obtained by a process of expression or distillation from a single botanical form or species. A pure, concentrated essence taken from the plant; said to be its life force

estrogen
a hormone produced by the ovary and necessary for the development of female secondary sexual characteristics

exfoliant
an agent that flakes off the upper layers of the skin

expectorant
promotes the removal of mucus from the respiratory system

F

fascia
connective tissue that encloses muscles and supports organs

fast
abstention from all or most foods for a given period

feces
excrement, stools

fever
elevation of body temperature above normal (36.8°C/98.4°F)

fibrositis
inflammation of fibrous tissue, especially of the muscle sheath

fight or flight syndrome
automatic physiological responses to what the body perceives as a threat, making the body more efficient in either fighting or fleeing the apparent danger

five elements
the system in Chinese medicine based on observations of the natural world. Built around the elements of fire, water, wood, metal, and earth

four examinations
diagnostic techniques used in Traditional Chinese Medicine to assess a patient's condition. The examinations are: asking, observing, listening (and smelling), and touching

free association
technique used in psychoanalysis whereby the patient is encouraged to say more or less anything that comes into his or her head

friction
small circular movements used in massage; also known as frottage

ganglion
a collection of nerves; also a swelling within a tendon or joint

geopathic stress
the theory that problems in the environment, particularly electromagnetism, cause malign energy fields and have a detrimental effect on health

gunas
in Indian medicine, characteristics which can be attributed to all matter, organic and inorganic, and to thoughts and ideas

halitosis
bad breath

hallucination
a vivid and convincing perception of something that is not really there. Hallucinations may be

visual, auditory, tactile, gustatory (of taste), or olfactory (of smell)

hara diagnosis
feeling the abdomen: an important diagnostic technique in Japanese medicine widely used by shiatsuists

harmonize
to balance, or encourage something, such as the body, to work in harmony, with all systems at optimum level

healing crisis
temporary relapse of health as treatment takes effect in the body, for example, the development of a rash or headaches

heartburn
discomfort or pain, usually burning in character, felt beneath the breastbone

hemorrhage
loss of blood from a ruptured vessel

hemorrhoids
piles, anal varicose veins

hepatic
relating to the liver; an agent that tones the liver and aids its function

hernia
protrusion of an organ or tissue out of the body cavity in which it normally lies.

high-velocity thrust
an abrupt osteopathic movement that, although painless, can cause the joint to make a disconcerting "click" or "pop"

holistic
aiming to treat the individual as an entity, incorporating body, mind, and spirit, from the Greek word *holos*, meaning whole

homeostasis
the tendency of the internal environment of the body to remain constant in spite of varying external conditions

hormone
a chemical transmitter substance produced by the body that acts specifically on target cells to control their activity

hormone replacement therapy
a chemical transmitter substance produced by the body that acts specifically on target cells to control their activity

hot spots
painful, knotted areas of fascia also known as trigger points

humors
the theory of four body fluids (blood, phlegm,

choler, and melancholy), popular in the Middle Ages. In Chinese medicine the humors are still believed to determine emotional and physical disposition

hyperactivity
excessive activity. Used to describe a condition of apparently uncontrollable activity in children, strongly associated with difficulties in maintaining attention (hence the term attention deficit hyperactivity disorder, or ADHD)

hypertension
raised blood pressure

hyperton-X
a method of releasing tension in overtight muscles, used by kinesiologists mainly to treat sports injuries

hyperventilation
rapid shallow breathing that causes the level of carbon dioxide in the blood to drop, leading to dizziness and tingling limbs

hypnotic
causing sleep

hypotension
low blood pressure, or a fall in blood pressure below the normal range

hypothalamus
a small gland at the base of the brain that controls the sympathetic nervous system and the internal body systems, especially those concerned with thirst, appetite, sexual behavior, body temperature regulation, and stress

immunodeficiency
failure of the immune system's defenses to fight infection

immuno-stimulant
an agent that stimulates the immune system to produce antibodies

immunosuppressive
an agent or condition that suppresses the immune system, thereby reducing immune activity

incontinence
inability to refrain from responding to normal impulses. Usually refers to partial or complete loss of control of urination or defecation

incubation
the interval between exposure to an infection and the appearance of the first symptoms

infection
multiplication of pathogenic (disease-producing) microorganisms within the body

inferiority complex
unconscious and extreme exaggeration of feelings of inferiority indicated by defensive or overcompensatory behavior (such as aggression)

inflammation
protective tissue response to injury or destruction of body cells characterized by heat, swelling, redness, and usually pain

infusion
immersion of herbs in boiling water; also the liquid obtained from steeping a herb in hot or cold water

inhalant
a remedy or drug that is breathed in through the nose or mouth

insomnia
inability to sleep

-itis (suffix)
"inflammation of"; for example, arthritis, inflammation of the joints

joint
the point at which two or more bones are connected

kapha
the moon force, which is a basic life force or element in Ayurvedic medicine

ketones
substance chemically related to acetone produced by the breakdown of fats in the body when glucose is not available for energy. This can be due to starvation or poorly controlled diabetes mellitus and gives rise to the smell of acetone on the breath, nausea and vomiting, and can lead to confusion, loss of consciousness, and death

ki
Japanese spelling of qi

kundalini
an energy which is believed to travel upwards through the chakras, promoting spiritual knowledge

laxative
a substance that provokes evacuation of the bowels

learned response
an automatic response that occurs when an action or sequence of actions is repeated sufficiently often, also known as a conditioned reflex. Not all learned responses are useful or healthy

lesion
structural or functional change in body tissues. Can be caused by disease or injury

libido
the sexual drive. In psychoanalysis it is said to be a "life force" and one of the fundamental sources of energy for mental activity

lymph
a clear, colorless fluid containing many white blood cells. It collects in body tissue around blood vessels and is transported by the lymphatic system, playing an important role in immunity

lymphatic system
vessels and nodes throughout the body that transport and filter lymph

mahabbutas
a Sanskrit term for the elements

malaise
general feeling of being unwell

malas
in Indian medicine, waste products of the body, including feces, urine, and sweat

malignant
cancerous and possibly life-threatening

mantra
a syllable, word, or phrase which may be spoken aloud and repeated as an aid to meditation

marma puncture
in Indian medicine, the technique of inserting a needle into the marma points for certain treatments

marmas
in Indian medicine, energy points in the body where two or more important functions meet

meditation
exercising the mind in contemplation

melatonin
hormone produced by the pineal gland that helps to regulate the sleep cycle

meninges
the membranes that cover the brain and spinal cord

menopause
the normal cessation of menstruation, a life change for women

menorrhagia
an excess loss of blood occurring during menstruation

meridians
channels that run through the body, beneath the skin, in which the life force, or qi, is carried. There are 14 main meridians running to and from the hands and feet to the body and head

metabolism
the complex process that is the fundamental chemical expression of life itself, and the means by which food is converted to energy to maintain the body

microbe
a minute living organism, especially pathogenic bacteria, viruses, etc

moxa
dried mugwort, which is burned on the end of needles or rolled into a stick, and then heated in moxabustion. It is said to warm the qi in the body in order to increase its flow

mucous membranes
surface linings of the body, which secrete mucus

musculoskeletal
anything pertaining to the muscles and bones (skeletal system) of the body

myopia
short-sightedness

nadis
in yoga, these are invisible energy channels through which prana (the "life force") flows

narcotic
an agent that induces sleep

negative ions
negatively charged particles called ions thought to be beneficial for health

neuralgia
general term for severe pain originating from a nerve

noradrenaline
a hormone secreted by the adrenal gland

obsession
a recurrent thought that dominates the mind

orchitis
inflammation of the testes

orthodox
a term used to describe conventional medicine

palpation
examination with the hands

panacea
a cure-all

panchakarma
in Ayurveda, internal cleansing, which consists of five forms of therapy, including vomiting, purging, two types of enema, and nasal inhalation. It is said to prevent disease and to rebalance vitality

parasite
an organism living in or on another creature to its benefit. Some parasites destroy host tissues and release toxins, causing disease

pathogenic
referring to any disease-causing agent

peptic
a term applied to gastric secretions and areas affected by them

percussion
vigorous drumming massage that encompasses a range of brisk, rhythmic strokes, such as hacking, cupping, and pummelling, performed repeatedly with alternate hands. Also a diagnostic technique used to examine the chest and abdomen when the fingers are used to tap, producing a resonance

periodontitis
inflammation of tissues surrounding the teeth that can lead to loosening and eventual loss of teeth

personality
an individual's disposition to act and feel in characteristic ways. These patterns of behavior may be biological or arise from life experiences and are often classified into basic personality types, such as introvert (quiet and reserved) or extravert (outward-going and sociable)

petrissage
kneading massage movement

phobia
persistent and severe fear, usually irrational, of a particular event or thing

pitta
in Ayurvedic medicine, the sun force, or one of the three basic life forces of elements controlling all physical and mental processes

pituitary gland
the "master control" gland in the base of the brain. It produces many different hormones, e.g. growth hormones and those that stimulate other endocrine glands to secrete their hormones

placebo
a medicine that is chemically inert but which may help to relieve symptoms because the patient has faith in its powers

placenta
an organ that grows within the uterus during pregnancy connecting the blood supply of the mother with the fetus. Its primary function is to provide the fetus with nourishment, eliminate waste products, and exchange respiratory gases. It also secretes hormones that maintain pregnancy

plaque
dental – a soft, sticky film that forms on the teeth composed of bacteria, saliva, and food debris

plasma
the clear, yellowish fluid part of blood or lymph in which cells are suspended

post-partum
following delivery of a baby; after childbirth

poultice
the therapeutic application of a soft moist mass (such as fresh herbs) to the skin to encourage local circulation and to relieve pain

prakruti
in Indian medicine, a person's individual constitution, determined by their "dosha" type

prana
the vital energy that runs through our bodies; in Indian medicine, also known as our life force

pranayama
the breathing exercises associated with yoga

primary control
an Alexander technique theory which believes that the relationship of the head to the neck and the back governs the way the rest of the body functions

progesterone
a female sex hormone that prepares the uterus for the fertilized ovum and maintains pregnancy

prolapse
the displacement of an organ from its usual position, e.g. prolapsed uterus or intervertebral disk

proprioception
an awareness of where parts of your body are without the need to look at them

prostaglandins
hormone-like substances that occur in tissues and organs of the human body. They have many effects including protecting the stomach against ulceration and causing pain and inflammation in damaged tissue

psyche
the mind; the mental (as opposed to the physical) functioning of the individual

psychodrama
a therapy whereby patients act out troublesome emotions or situations, giving vent to feelings that are otherwise difficult to express

psychosomatic illness
the manifestation of physical symptoms resulting from a mental state

pungent
one of the six Ayurvedic tastes, found in onion, garlic, and black pepper

purgative
an agent stimulating evacuation of the bowels

purvakarma
in Ayurveda, a cleansing process involving oil and steam bath therapy

qi (chi)
the essential energy of the universe which is fundamental to all elements of life. It runs through the whole body in channels or meridians

RAST
radio allergo sorbent test: a blood test used to determine whether or not a patient is allergic to food substances

referred pain
pain that is felt in a different part of the body from the area that is actually affected

relaxant
a substance that promotes relaxation (either muscular or psychological)

remission
a period in which the symptoms of a disease abate or lessen

rhinitis
inflammation (often chronic) of the mucous membranes lining the nasal passage

RICE
acronym describing standard treatment for many musculoskeletal injuries: rest, ice (to reduce inflammation), compression by bandaging, and elevation

rishi
wise and holy men of ancient India who meditated and acquired the knowledge that was codified as Ayurveda

S

saline
one of the six Ayurvedic tastes; found in rock salt, seaweed, sea salt, and vegetables

sclerosis
hardening of tissue, e.g. atherosclerosis – hardening of the arteries

scoliosis
curvature of the spine to the side

sebum
an oily, lubricating and protective substance secreted by glands in the skin

sedative
an agent that reduces functional activity; calming

self-actualization
a psychological concept that involves the individual developing his abilities to the full and making real his potential

self-limiting
a condition that lasts a set length of time and usually clears of its own accord

septic
putrefying due to the presence of pathogenic (disease-producing) bacteria

serotonin
a substance found in many body tissues that has a number of effects including reducing blood loss and is thought to affect mood

shad rasa
the six basic food tastes identified by Ayurveda: sweet, acidic, salty, pungent, bitter, astringent

shock
sudden and disturbing mental or physical impression; also a state of collapse due to a severe reduction in blood flow characterized by pale, cold, and sweaty skin; rapid, weak pulse; faintness, dizziness, and nausea

soft tissues
tissues of the body, including muscles, tendons, ligaments, and organs

somatic education
a form of physical therapy

sour
one of the six Ayurvedic tastes; found in fats, amino acids, fermented products, fruits, and vegetables

spasm
sudden, violent, involuntary muscular contraction

steroids
fat-soluble organic compounds that occur naturally throughout the plant and animal kingdoms and play many important functional roles

stimulant
increases activity in specific organs or systems of the body; warms and increases energy

streptococci
bacteria associated with many infections

stress
the effect on a person of being subjected to conditions he is unable to terminate or avoid. Constant stress brings about changes in the balance of hormones in the body and may adversely affect a person's health and state of mind. However, a modicum of stress is an important source of motivation

stressor
something that causes stress

subconscious
mental processes including memories, motives, and intentions of which the person is not consciously aware but which could be recalled

subluxation
incomplete dislocation of any two bones where they meet at a joint. Also a term used by chiropractors to refer to defective joint movements that occur when vertebrae are misaligned

sweet
one of the six Ayurvedic tastes, found in sugar, carbohydrates, and dairy products

swish technique
a method used in visualization to replace negative images with positive ones

symptoms
perceived changes in, or impaired function of, body or mind, indicating the presence of disease or injury

synapse
the minute gap at the end of a nerve fiber across which impulses pass to another nerve fiber

syncope
medical term for fainting

syndrome
a combination of symptoms or signs that indicate a particular disorder

synovial
referring to the fluid that bathes the joints

systemic
relating to or affecting the body as a whole rather than individual parts

T

tachycardia
an unduly rapid heartbeat of over 100 beats per minute (adult)

TCM
Traditional Chinese Medicine

TENS
transcutaneous electrical nerve stimulation of body tissue with low-voltage electricity for pain relief

thalassotherapy
a form of hydrotherapy that uses seawater and sea air

TIA
transient ischemic attack: a mild form of stroke

tolerance
reduction or loss of the normal response to a drug or other substance that usually provokes a reaction in the body. Drug tolerance may develop over a period of time, requiring increased doses to achieve the desired effect

tonic
restores tone to the systems, balances, nourishes, and promotes well-being; strengthens and enlivens the whole or specific parts of the body

topical
local application of cream, ointment, tincture, or other medicine

toxin
a substance that is poisonous to the body

traction
a system of putting a part of the body under tension to realign two adjoining structures or for the treatment of spinal injury

trance
an altered state of awareness often associated with hypnosis

transference
a technique used in psychoanalysis whereby the analyst encourages the patient to transfer, or redirect, certain feelings to the practitioner, so that they can be discussed and resolved

trauma
a physical injury or wound; also an unpleasant and disturbing experience causing psychological upset

triad of health
the balance between physical, chemical, and emotional health, a term used in kinesiology

trigeminal nerve
a nerve that divides into three and supplies the mandibular (jaw), maxillary (cheek), ophthalmic (eye), and forehead areas

trigger points
tender areas in muscles that are often felt as hard nodules

trimester
any one of the three successive three-month periods into which a pregnancy is divided

ulcer
slow-healing sore occurring internally or externally

ultrasound
extremely high frequency sound waves, inaudible to the human ear. They can be used to break up kidney stones and to produce images of the interior of the human body

unconditioned response
a response or reflex action that happens automatically to a given stimulus and does not have to be learned

ureteric
referring to the ureter, the tube that carries urine from the kidney to the bladder

urethral
referring to the urethra, that canal that carries urine from the bladder out of the body

vaccination
a means of producing immunity to a disease by using a special preparation of antigenic material

to stimulate the formation of appropriate antibodies

vaginitis
inflammation or infection of the vagina

vasoconstrictor
an agent that causes narrowing of the blood vessels

vasodilator
an agent that dilates the blood vessels and so improves circulation

vasovagal attack
overactivity of the vagus nerve, causing a slowing of the heart and a fall in blood pressure, leading to fainting

vatha
the wind force in Ayurvedic medicine – one of the three basic life forces or elements that must be in balance for physical and mental processes to be balanced

Vedic
relating to the *Vedas*, the ancient, sacred literature of Hinduism

vertigo
sensation in which the affected individual feels that he or his surroundings are in a state of constant movement. It is most often a spinning sensation

vertebra
girdle-shaped bones that form the spine. There are 24 vertebrae that move (7 cervical, 12 thoracic, and 5 lumbar) plus 9 fused vertebrae that form the sacrum and coccyx

vibrational therapies
therapies such as sound therapy and therapeutic touch which treat the body on a vibrational or "energy" level. They are based on the theory that we are all dense bodies of energy, and by rebalancing the vibrational frequencies of the body's energy fields, which are thought to resonate throughout the body, we can effect a cure

virulent
extremely infective, or with a violent effect

virus
minute infectious particle that is capable of replication within living cells

vitamin
any of a small group of substances that are needed for healthy growth. They cannot be synthesized by the body and are essential constituents of the diet

Wei Qi
defensive qi, the body's energy boundary, which protects the body from invasion by external pathogenic factors. It flows just beneath the skin

white blood cells
also known as leucocytes. They are involved in protecting the body against microorganisms that cause disease and in antibody production

x-rays
electromagnetic radiation with great penetrating power. They are used in the diagnosis of disorders such as broken bones and in treating diseases such as cancer

yang
one aspect of the complementary aspects in Chinese philosophy; reflects the active, moving, and warmer aspects

yin
one aspect of the complementary aspects in Chinese philosophy; reflects the passive, still, reflective aspects

yin/yang
Chinese philosophy that explains the interdependence of all elements of nature. These contrasting aspects of the body and mind must be balanced before health and well-being can be achieved. Yin is the female force, and yang is the male

zone therapy
an integral component of reflexology. It postulates the idea that there are ten zones dividing the body from head to feet which correspond to reflex points on the hands and feet. By manipulating the reflex points, it is thought that pain can be relieved in other parts of the body in the same zone

USEFUL ADDRESSES

Acupuncture

British Acupuncture Council
63 Jeddo Road
London W12 9HQ U.K.
+44 208 735 0400
fax +44 208 735 0404

London School of Acupuncture and Traditional Chinese Medicine
60 Bunhill Row
London EC1Y 8QD
U.K.

British Medical Acupuncture Society
Newton House
Newton Lane
Lower Whitley
Warrington
Cheshire WA4 4JA U.K.
+44 1925 730727

New Zealand Register of Acupuncturists Inc.
P.O. Box 9950
Wellington 1
New Zealand
+64 4 476 8578

American Association for Acupuncture and Oriental Medicine
4101 Lake Boone Trail
Suite 102
Raleigh
North Carolina 27607 U.S.A.
+1 919 787 5181

National Acupuncture and Oriental Medicine Alliance
P.O. Box 77511
Seattle
Washington 98177-0531 U.S.A.

National Commission for the Certification of Acupuncturists (NCCA)
P.O. Box 97075
Washington DC 20090-7075 U.S.A.
+1 202 232 1404
fax +1 202 462 6157

Acupuncture Foundation of Canada
7321 Victoria Park Avenue
Unit 18
Markham
Ontario L3R 2ZB
Canada

Western Cape Su Jok Acupuncture Institute
3 Periwinkle Close
Kommetjie
7975
South Africa

Alexander Technique

British Society of Teachers of the Alexander Technique
20 London House
266 Fulham Road
London SW10 9EL U.K.
+44 207 351 0828

Australian Society of Teachers of the Alexander Technique
P.O. Box 716
Darlington
New South Wales 2010
Australia
+61 8339 571

Canadian Society of the Teachers of the Alexander Technique
P.O. Box 47025
No. 19-555
West 12th Avenue
Vancouver
British Columbia V5Z 3XO
Canada

North American Society of the Teachers of the Alexander Technique (NASTAT)
P.O. Box 517
Urbana
Illinois 61801-0517 U.S.A.
+1 217 367 6956

Art Therapy

British Association of Art Therapists
11a Richmond Road
Brighton
Sussex BN2 3RL
U.K.

Institute for Arts in Therapy and Education
2-18 Britannia Row
London N1 8QG U.K.
+44 207 704 2534
fax +44 207 354 1761

American Art Therapy Association
1202 Allanson Road
Mundelein
Illinois 60060 U.S.A.
+1 847 949 6064

National Coalition of Arts Therapy Organizations
505 11th Street
South East Washington DC 20002 U.S.A.
+1 202 543 6864

Autogenic Training

British Association for Autogenic Training and Therapy
Heath Cottage
Pitch Hill, Ewhurst
Surrey GU6 7NP U.K.
s.a.e. for info

Ayurvedic Medicine

Ayurvedic Medical Association U.K.
17 Bromham Mill
Gilford Park
Milton Keynes MK14 5KP U.K.
01908 617089

Ayurvedic Company of Great Britain
50 Penywern Road
London SW5 9XS U.K.

Ayurvedic Living
P.O. Box 188
Exeter EX4 5AB U.K.

Ayurvedic Medical Association U.K.
The Hale Clinic
7 Park Crescent
London W1N 3HE U.K.

Maharishi Ayur-Veda Health Centre
24 Linhope Street
London NW1 6HT U.K.
+44 207 724 6267

Maharishi Ayur-Veda Health Centre
The Golden Dome
Woodley Park
Skelmersdale
Lancashire WN8 6UQ U.K.
+44 1695 51008

American Association of Ayurvedic Medicine
P.O. Box 598
South Lancaster
Mass 01561 U.S.A.
+1 800 843 8332
fax +1 201 777 1197

The Ayurveda Institute
11311 Menaul N.E.
Suite A
Albuquerque
New Mexico 87112
U.S.A.

Mapi Inc.
Garden of the Gods Business Park
1115 Elkton Drive
Suite 401
Colorado Springs
Colorado 80907
U.S.A.

Canadian Association of Ayervedic Medicine
P.O. Box 541
Station B
Ottawa
Ontario K1P 5P8
Canada
+1 613 837 5737

South African Ayurvedic Medicine Association
85 Harvey Road
Morningside
Durban 4001
South Africa

Biofeedback

Association for Applied Psychophysiology and Biofeedback
10200 West 44th Avenue
Apt 304
Wheat Ridge
Colorado 80033-8436
U.S.A.

Bowen Technique

Bowen Therapy Academy of Australia
P.O. Box 733
Hamilton 3300
Victoria
Australia
+61 3 557230 00

Chiropractic

British Association for Applied Chiropractic
The Old Post Office
Cherry Street
Stratton Audley
Bicester OX6 9BA
U.K.

British Chiropractic Association
Blagrave House
Blagrave Street
Reading RG1 1QB
U.K.
+44 118 950 5950

Scottish Chiropractic Association
16 Jennymoores Road
St. Boswells TD6 0AL
U.K.
+44 1835 823 645

Anglo-European College of Chiropractic
13-15 Parkwood Road
Bournemouth BH5 2DF
U.K.
+44 1202 436275
fax +44 1202 436312

Chiropractic Association of Ireland
28 Fair Street
Drogheda
County Louth
Irish Republic
+353 41 305999
fax +353 41 51863

European Chiropractors' Union
9 Cross Deep Gardens
Twickenham
Middlesex TW1 4QZ
U.K.
+44 208 891 2546

Chiropractic Association (Singapore)
Box 23
Tanglin Post Office
Singapore
+65 293 9843/ 734 8584
fax +65 733 8380

Chiropractic Council of Japan
2621-5 Noborito Tama-ku
Kawasaki 214
Japan
+81 44 933 9547
fax +81 44 933 4449

Hong Kong Chiropractors' Association
P.O. Box 5588
Hong Kong
+852 375 5785
fax +852 537 5487

Manu R. Shah D.C.
Sheikh Ismail Building
Aquem Alto
Margao
Goa 403 601
India
+91 83 422 3707

Thailand Chiropractic Association
Medico-Chiro Center
Sukumvit 24 Road
Bangkok Thailand
+66 2 258 8694

Chiropractors' Association of Australia
P.O. Box 241
Springwood
New South Wales 2777
Australia
+61 47 515 644
fax +61 47 515 856

New Zealand Chiropractors' Association
P.O. Box 7144
Wellesley Street
Auckland
New Zealand
+64 9 373 4343
fax +64 373 5973

American Chiropractic Association
1701 Clarendon Boulevard
Arlington
Virginia 22201 U.S.A.
+1 703 276 8800
fax 1 703 243 2593

International Chiropractors' Association
Suite 1000
1110 North Glebe Road
Arlington
Virginia 22201 U.S.A.
+1 703 528 5000
fax +1 703 528 5023

World Chiropractic Alliance
2950 North Dobson Road
Suite One
Chandler
Arizona 85224-1802 U.S.A.
+1 800 347 1011

Canadian Chiropractic Association
1396 Eglinton Avenue West
Toronto
Ontario M6C 2E4 Canada
+1 416 781 5656
fax +1 416 781 7344

Cognitive Therapy

Association of Cognitive Analytic Therapists
4th Floor North Wing
Division of Academic Psychiatry
St. Thomas's Hospital
London SE1 7EH
U.K.
+44 207 928 9292 x3769

British Association for Behavioural and Cognitive Psychotherapies
Dept. of Clinical Psychology
Northwick Park Hospital
Watford Road
Harrow HA1 3UJ
U.K.
+44 208 869 2325
fax +44 208 869 2317

Colour Therapy

Colour and Reflexology
9 Wyndale Avenue
London NW9 9PT
U.K.
+44 208 204 7672

Cranio-Sacral Therapy

Cranio-Sacral Association
Monomark House
27 Old Gloucester Street
London WC1N 3XX U.K.

Dance Therapy

Laban Centre for Movement and Dance
Laurie Grove
New Cross
London SE14 6NH
U.K.
+44 208 692 4070

American Dance Therapy Association
2000 Century Plaza
Suite 108
Columbia
Maryland 21044 U.S.A.
+1 410 997 4040
fax +1 410 997 4048

International Dance Exercise Association (IDEA)
6190 Cornerstone Court East
Apt. 204
San Diego
California 92121-3773 U.S.A.
+1 619 535 8979
fax +1 619 535 8234

Dreamwork

Association for the Study of Dreams
P.O. Box 1600
Vienna
Virginia 22183
U.S.A.
+1 703 242 0062/8888

Feldenkrais

Feldenkrais Guild U.K.
P.O. Box 370
London N10 3XA U.K.

Australian Feldenkrais Guild Inc
Locked Bag Number 19
Post Office 2037
Glebe
New South Wales Australia
61 2 597 6561

New Zealand Practitioners and Students Association
P.O. Box 90091
Auckland Mail Centre
Auckland
New Zealand
+64 9 479 6529

Feldenkrais Guild
524 Ellsworth Street
P.O. Box 489
Albany
Oregon 97321-1043   U.S.A.
fax   +1 503 926 0572

Hellerwork

Hellerwork Inc (Rose-Marie Amoroso)
1 Finsbury Avenue
London EC2M 2PA
U.K.
+44 207 247 9982

Hellerwork International
406 Berry Street
Mount Shasta
California 96067 U.S.A.
+1 916 926 2500
fax +1 916 926 6839

Hydrotherapy

U.K. College of Colonic Hydrotherapy
515 Hagley Road
Birmingham B66 4AX
U.K.
+44 121 429 9191
fax +44 121 478 0871

Aquatic Exercise Association
P.O. Box 1609
Nokomis
Florida 34274 U.S.A.

Hypnotherapy

British Society of Experimental and Clinical Hypnosis
c/o Dept.. of Psychology
Grimsby General Hospital
Scartle Road
Grimsby DN33 2BA
U.K.
+44 1472 874 111

British Society of Medical and Dental Hypnosis
17 Keppel View Road
Kimberworth
Rotherham S61 2 AR
U.K.
+44 1709 554558

British Hypnotherapy Association
67 Upper Berkeley Street
London W1H 7DH
U.K.
+44 207 723 4443

National Register of Hypnotherapists and
Psychotherapists
12 Cross Street
Nelson
Lancashire BB9 7EN
U.K.
+44 1282 699378
fax +44 1282 698633

American Association of Professional
Hypnotherapists
P.O. Box 29
Boones Mill
Virginia 24065
U.S.A.
+1 703 334 3035

National Society of Hypnotherapists
2175 North West 86th
Suite 6A
Des Moines
Iowa 50325
U.S.A.
+1 515 270 2280

Massage Therapy

British Massage Therapy Council
Greenbank House
65a Adelphi Street
Preston PR1 7BH
U.K.
+44 1772 881063

Massage Therapy Institute of Great Britain
P.O. Box 27/26
London NW2 4NR
U.K.
+44 208 208 1607

London College of Massage
5 Newman Passage
London W1P 3PF
U.K.
+44 207 323 3574
fax +44 207 637 7125

Society of Clinical Masseurs
P.O. Box 483
9 Delhi Street
Mitchum 3131
Victoria
Australia
+61 3 874 6973

American Massage Therapy Association
820 Davis Street
Suite 100
Evanston
Illinois 60201-4444
U.S.A.
+1 847 864 0123
fax +1 708 864 1178

International Massage Association
92 Main Street
P.O. Drawer 421
Warrenton
Virginia 20188-0421 U.S.A.
+1 540 351 0800
fax +1 540 351 0816

National Association of Massage Therapy
P.O. Box 1400
Westminster
Colorado 80030-1400
U.S.A.
+1 800 776 6268

McTimoney Chiropractic

The McTimoney Chiropractic Association
21 High Street
Eynsham
Oxon OX8 1 HE
U.K.
s.a.e. + £1.50 for list of practitioners

Meditation

Friends of the Western Buddhist Order
London Buddhist Centre
51 Roman Road
London E2 0HU
U.K.
+44 208 981 1225

School of Meditation
158 Holland Park Avenue
London W11 4UH
U.K.
+44 207 603 6116

Transcendental Meditation
Freepost
London SW1P 4YY
U.K.

Music Therapy

British Society for Music Therapy
25 Rosslyn Avenue
East Barnet EN4 8DH
U.K.
+208 368 8879

American Association of Music Therapy
P.O. Box 80012
Valley Forge
Pennsylvania 19484
U.S.A.

National Association of Music Therapy
8455 Colesville Road
Suite 1000
Silver Springs
Maryland 20910
U.S.A.
+1 301 589 3300

Osteopathy

Osteopathic Information Service
P.O. Box 2074
Reading
Berkshire RG1 4YR
U.K.

General Register and Council of
Osteopaths
56 London Street
Reading
Berkshire RG1 4SQ
U.K.

Chiropractors and Osteopaths Registration
Board of Victoria
P.O. Box 59
Carlton South
Victoria 3053
Australia
+61 3 349 3000
fax +61 3 349 3003

N.S.W. Chiropractors and Osteopathic
Registration Board
P.O. Box K599
Haymarket
New South Wales 2000
Australia
+61 2 281 0884
fax +61 2 281 2030

American Academy of Osteopathy
3500 DePauw Boulevard
Suite 1080
Indianapolis
Indiana 46268-1136   U.S.A.
+1 317 879 1881
fax +1 317 879 0563

American Association of Colleges of Osteopathic Medicine
6110 Executive Boulevard
Apt. 405, Rockville
Maryland 20852   U.S.A.
+1 301 468 0990

American Osteopathic Association
142 East Ontario Street
Chicago
Illinois 60611
U.S.A.
+1 312 280 5800
fax +1 312 202 8200

Polarity Therapy

U.K. Polarity Therapy Association
Monomark House
27 Old Gloucester Street
London WC1N 3XX
U.K.

American Polarity Therapy Association
2888 Bluff Street
Suite 149
Boulder
Colorado 80301   U.S.A.
+1 303 545 2080
fax +1 303 545 2161

Psychotherapy

U.K. Council for Psychotherapy
167-9 Great Portland Street
London W1N 5FB
U.K.
+44 207 436 3002
fax +44 207 436 3013

European Association for Psychotherapy
Rosenbursenstrasse 8/3/7
A-1010 Vienna
Austria
+43 1 512 7090
fax +43 1 512 7091

Qigong

Tse Qigong Centre
Qi Magazine
P.O. Box 116
Manchester M20 3YN U.K.

Chi Kung School at the Body Energy Centre
James MacRitchie and Damaris Jarboux
P.O. Box 19708
Boulder, Colorado 80308
U.S.A.
+1 303 442 3131/2250
fax +1 303 442 3141

National Qigong (Chi Kung) Association of the U.S.A.
P.O. Box 20218
Boulder, Colorado 80308
U.S.A.
+1 888 218 7788

Qigong Academy
8103 Marlborough Avenue
Cleveland, Ohio 44129
U.S.A.

World Academic Society of Medical Qigong
No. 11 Heping Jie Nei Kou
Beijing 100029   China

Qigong Association of Australia
458 White Horse Road
Surrey Hills
Victoria 3127 Australia
+61 3 9836 6961
fax +61 3 830 5608

Dr Yves Requena
Institut Européen de Qi Gong
La Ferme des Vences
13122 Ventabren
France

Reflexology

British Reflexology Association
Monks Orchard
Whitbourne
Worcester WR6 5RB U.K.
+44 1886 821 207
fax   01886 822017

Association of Reflexologists
27 Old Gloucester Street
London WC1N 3XX
U.K.

Association of Vacuflex Reflexology
P.O. Box 93
Tadworth
Surrey KT20 7YB
U.K.
+44 1737 842961

British School of Reflexology and Holistic Association of Reflexologists
92 Sheering Road
Old Harlow CM17 0JW
U.K.
+44 1279 429060
fax +44 1279 445334

International Federation of Reflexologists
76-8 Edridge Road
Croydon
Surrey CR0 1EF U.K.
+44 208 667 9458
fax +44 208 649 9291

Scottish School of Reflexology
2 Wheatfield Road
Ayr KA7 2XB
U.K.
+44 1292 287142

Irish Reflexologists Institute
c/o 11 Fitzwilliam Place
Dublin 2
Irish Republic
+353 1 760137
fax +353 1 610466

China Reflexology Association
P.O. Box 2002
Beijing 100026
China
fax +86 1 5068309

Chinese Society of Reflexologists
Xuanwu Hospital
Capital Institute of Medicine
Chang Chun Street
Beijing
China

New Zealand Reflexology Association
P.O. Box 31 084
Auckland 4
New Zealand

Reflexology Association of Australia
15 Kedumba Crescent
Turramurra 2074
New South Wales
Australia
+61 4 12 190495

International Institute of Reflexology
P.O. Box 12642
St. Petersberg
Florida 33733
U.S.A.
+1 727 343 4811
fax +1 727 381 2807

Reflexology Association of America
4012 S. Rainbow Boulevard
Box K585
Las Vegas
Nevada 89103-2509
U.S.A.

Reflexology Association of Canada (RAC)
11 Glen Cameron Road
Unit 4
Thornhill
Ontario L8T 4NB
Canada
+1 905 889 5900

Reiki

Center for Reiki Training
29209 Northwestern
Highway 592
Southfield
Michigan 48034-9841
U.S.A.
+1 810 948 9534

Rolfing

Rolf Institute:Pacific Basin Branch Office
28 Davies Street
Brunswick 3056
Victoria
Australia
+61 3 383 5045

Rolf Institute: European Branch Office
Herzogstrasse 40
D-800 Munich 40
Germany
+49 8939 6802

Rolf Institute
205 Canyon Boulevard
Boulder
Colorado
80302–4920
U.S.A.
+1 303 449 5903/ 800 530 8875
fax +1 303 449 5978

Shiatsu

The Shiatsu Society of Great Britain
5 Foxcote
Wokingham
Berkshire RG11 3PG
U.K.

Shiatsu Society
31 Pullman Lane
Godalming
Surrey GU7 1XY
U.K.

Shiatsu Therapy Association of Australia
P.O. Box 1
Balaclava
Victoria 3183
Australia
+61 03 530 0067

American Shiatsu Association
P.O. Box 718
Jamaica Plain
Massachusetts 02130
U.S.A.

T'ai Chi

T'ai Chi Union for Great Britain
102 Felsham Road
London SW15 1 DQ
U.K.

Tragerwork

The Trager Institute
21 Locust Avenue
Mill Valley
California 94941–2806
U.S.A.
+1 415 388 2688
fax +1 415 388 2710

Yoga

British Wheel of Yoga
1 Hamilton Place
Boston Road
Sleaford NG34 7ES
U.K.
+44 1529 306851
fax +44 1529 303233

The Iyengar Yoga Institute
223a Randolf Avenue
London W9 1NL
U.K.
+44 207 624 3080

Sivananda Yoga Vedanta Centre
51 Felsham Road
London SW15 1AZ
U.K.

BKS Iyengar Association of Australia
1 Rickman Avenue
Mosman 2088
New South Wales
Australia

International Yoga Teachers Association
c/o 14-15 Huddart Avenue
Normanhurst
New South Wales 2076
Australia
+61 2 9484 9848

Unity in Yoga
303 2495 West 2nd Avenue
Vancouver
British Columbia VGK 1J5
Canada

Zero Balancing

Zero Balancing Association U.K.
36 Richmond Road
Cambridge CB4 3PU
U.K.
+44 1223 315480

Zero Balancing Association
P.O. Box 1727
Capitola
California 95010
U.S.A.
+1 831 476 0665

FURTHER READING

Acupressure

Acupressure Techniques • Dr. Julian Kenyon THORSONS, 1987

Acupuncture

Acupuncture for Everyone • Dr Ruth Lever PENGUIN, 1987

Acupuncture: A Comprehensive Text • J. O'Connor & D. Bensky EASTLAND PRESS, SEATTLE, 1982

Health Essentials: Acupuncture • Peter Mole ELEMENT BOOKS, 1992

Acupuncture Medicine • Dr. Y. Omara JAPAN PUBLICATIONS, 1982

Traditional Acupuncture, The Law of the Five Elements • Dianne Connelly CENTRE FOR TRADITIONAL ACUPUNCTURE, COLUMBIA, 1979

The Alexander Technique

The Alexander Technique: Natural Poise for Health • Richard Brennan ELEMENT BOOKS, 1991

Alexander Technique • C. Stevens OPTIMA, 1987

Alexander Technique: A Practical Introduction • R. Brennan ELEMENT BOOKS, 1998

Body Learning • M. Gelb AURUM PRESS, 1981

Health Essentials: The AT • Richard Brennan ELEMENT BOOKS, 1991

Aromatherapy

The Complete Illustrated Guide to Aromatherapy • Julia Lawless ELEMENT BOOKS, 1997

Aromatherapy • Christine Wildwood ELEMENT BOOKS, 1991

Aromatherapy an A–Z • Patricia Davis C. W. DANIEL, 1988

The Aromatherapy Book • Jeanne Rose NORTH ATLANTIC BOOKS, 1994

In A Nutshell: Aromatherapy • Sheila Lavery ELEMENT BOOKS, 1997

Aromatherapy for Healing the Spirit • Gabrielle Mojay GAIA BOOKS, 1996

The Complete Aromatherapy Handbook • Susanne Fischer-Rizzi STIRLING, U.S.A., 1990

The Fragrant Mind • Valerie Anne Worwood DOUBLEDAY, 1996

The Fragrant Pharmacy • Valerie Anne Worwood BANTAM BOOKS, 1995

The Complete Illustrated Guide to Aromatherapy • Julia Lawless ELEMENT BOOKS, 1997

Art Therapy

Art as Therapy • S. McNiff PIATKUS, 1994

Ayurveda

Ayurveda • Scott Gerson ELEMENT BOOKS, 1993

The Handbook of Ayurveda • Dr. Shantha Godagma KYLE CATHIE, 1997

Quantum Healing • Dr. Deepak Chopra BANTAM BOOKS, 1989

Return of the Rishi • Dr. Deepak Chopra HOUGHTON MIFFLIN CO., 1988

The Seven Pillars of Ancient Wisdom • Dr. Douglas Baker DOUGLAS BAKER PUBLISHING, 1982

A Handbook of Ayurveda • Bhagwan Dash & Acarya Manfred M. Junius CONCEPT PUBLISHING, INDIA, 1993

Ancient Indian Massage • Harish Johari MUNSHIRAM MANOHARIAL, 1994

Basic Principles of Ayurveda • Bhagwan Dash CONCEPT PUBLISHING, INDIA, 1980

Bates Method

Bates Method • P. Mansfield VERMILLION, 1995

Chiropractic

Dynamic Chiropractic Today
• M. Copland Griffiths
THORSONS, 1991

Colour Therapy

Colour Me Healing • Jack Allanach
ELEMENT BOOKS, 1997

Health Essentials: Colour Therapy
• Pauline Wills
ELEMENT BOOKS, 1993

Feldenkrais Method

Awareness Through Movement
• Moshe Feldenkrais
PENGUIN, 1990

Hydrotherapy

The Complete Book of Water Therapy
• Dian Dinsin Buchman
KEATS, 1994

Massage

Massage A Practical Introduction
• Stewart Mitchell
ELEMENT BOOKS, 1992

The Complete Book of Massage
• Clare Maxwell-Hudson
DORLING KINDERSLEY, 1988

Manipulation and Mobilisation
• Susan L. Edmund   MOSBY, 1993

Health Essentials: Massage
• Stewart Mitchell
ELEMENT BOOKS, 1992

Polarity Therapy

The Polarity Process • Franklyn Sills
ELEMENT BOOKS, 1989

Qigong

The Art of Chi Kung • J. McRitchie
ELEMENT BOOKS, 1993

Reflexology

The Complete Illustrated Guide to Reflexology • Inge Dougans
ELEMENT BOOKS, 1996

The Reflexology Partnership
• Adamson and Harris
KYLE CATHIE, 1995

Reflexology: The Definitive Practitioner's Manual • Beryl Crane
ELEMENT BOOKS, 1997

Reflexology and Color Therapy: A Practical Introduction • Pauline Wills
ELEMENT BOOKS, 1998

Shiatsu

The Art of Shiatsu
• Oliver Cowmeadow
ELEMENT BOOKS, 1992

Shiatsu: A Practical Introduction
• Oliver Cowmeadow
ELEMENT BOOKS, 1998

The Book of Shiatsu • P. Lundberg
GAIA BOOKS, 1992

Health Essentials: Shiatsu
• Elaine Liechti
ELEMENT BOOKS, 1992

Shiatsu: The Complete Guide
• C. Jarmey & G. Mojay
THORSONS, 1991

The Shiatsu Workbook • N. Dawes
PIATKUS BOOKS, 1991

T'ai Chi Ch'uan

The Complete Book of Tai Chi Chuan
• Wong Kiew Kit
ELEMENT BOOKS, 1996

The Elements of Tai Chi
• Paul Crompton
ELEMENT BOOKS, 1990

The Way of Energy
• Lam Kam Chuen
GAIA BOOKS, 1991

The Way of Harmony • H. Reid
GAIA BOOKS, 1988

Yoga

The Elements of Yoga
• Godfrey Devereux
ELEMENT BOOKS, 1994

The Complete Yoga Course
• Howard Kent
HEADLINE PRESS, 1993

The Yoga Book
• Stephen Sturgess
ELEMENT BOOKS, 1997

INDEX

376